Battleship

Also by H. P. Willmott

● Pearl Harbor (with Tohmatsu Haruo and W. Spencer Johnson)

● The Second World War in the Far East

● Empires in the Balance:
  Japanese and Allied Pacific Strategies to April 1942

● The Barrier and the Javelin:
  Japanese and Allied Pacific Strategies, February to June 1942

● Grave of a Dozen Schemes:
  British Naval Planning and the War Against Japan, 1943–1945

● June 1944

● The Great Crusade: A New Complete History of the Second World War

H. P. Willmott

Battleship

CASSELL

Cassell
Wellington House, 125 Strand
London WC2R 0BB

Copyright © H. P. Willmott 2002

First published 2002

The right of H. P. Willmott to be identified
as the author of this work has been asserted by
him in accordance with the Copyright, Designs
and Patents Act 1988

British Library Cataloguing-in-Publication Data
A catalogue record for this book is available
from the British Library

ISBN 0-304-35810-X
Distributed in the USA by
Sterling Publishing Co Inc
387 Park Avenue South, New York
NY 10016-8810

Printed and bound in Great Britain by
MPG Books Ltd
Bodmin, Cornwall

Contents

1

Philippine Waters

History does not unfold with chronological precision, but the historian, by a judicious use of fact and dates, can draw comparisons between seemingly incongruous pairings of events and impose order upon seemingly unrelated circumstances, as if to demonstrate that dishonesty, disingenuousness and selectivity are indeed the hallmark of the profession. The story of the dreadnought battleship extends across almost the whole of the twentieth century: the *Dreadnought* herself was laid down on 2 October 1905 and was launched on 10 February 1906, and the last of the line to be stricken was the *Missouri*, which tied up for the last time at Pearl Harbor on 16 June 1998. But in real terms, the story of the dreadnought was all but over by the end of the Second World War even though, somewhat improbably, two battlecruisers were laid down some four years after the instrument of Japan's surrender was signed in the *Missouri* in Tokyo Bay on 2 September 1945. Moreover, the start of the story does not reside in Portsmouth dockyard where the nameship was built because her construction, or the construction of some similar ship, had been foreshadowed for some three or four years before her keel was laid. This being so, one looks to other events that may be presented as the alpha and omega, and perhaps surprisingly one looks not to any single power or number of powers but to waters that perhaps do not readily seem synonymous with the dreadnought but in which were fought two battles that may be considered to embrace the dreadnought era.

The first of these battles was fought on 1 May 1898 in Manila Bay, and the reason why this battle may be regarded as the genesis of the dreadnought is because it was, in many ways, the last battle of the age of sail. It was an action fought on the one side by five American cruisers and two gunboats and on the other by four Spanish cruisers, three gunboats and three other vessels. The Spanish warships, inferior in gun power and of dubious seaworthiness, were anchored under the cover of guns in the fortified base of Cavite. The battle resulted in the annihilation of the Spanish force, though it was a victory that could not be exploited for two months because it was not until 30 June that US military formations arrived in the Philippines. Why this action should be considered the last battle of the age of sail is on account of its nature. It was fought with no reference to mines, torpedoes or submarines, radio, airships or aircraft, all of which were to figure so prominently in war at sea in the twentieth century. It was a battle fought in line ahead with broadsides at ranges that were reduced to 250 yards, at which distance, and with no means of aiming other than the eye, 39 rounds in every 40 still managed to miss their intended target. It was an action that should immediately invoke thoughts of Quiberon Bay (1759), the Nile (1798) and first and second Copenhagen (1801 and 1807) in terms of pedigree. Despite the fact that the warships in Manila Bay in May 1898 were steam-powered, the battle that they fought properly belonged to a previous age.

The second of these battles was fought between 23 and 28 October 1944, again in the waters of and off the Philippines, and was the greatest naval battle ever fought. The contrast between this battle, the series of actions collectively known as Leyte Gulf, and Manila Bay was profound. In 1898 the US squadron that fought at Manila Bay was at Hong Kong when the United States declared war on Spain, and its area of deployment was represented by the line-ahead formation along the 628 miles that separate Hong Kong and Manila. The area of operations was perhaps ten and certainly no more than fifteen square miles. In 1944 the area of operations covered 115,000 square miles, an area equivalent to the British Isles or Arizona, and the area of deployment was three times as large, and the battle witnessed destruction on a scale without precedence in modern naval warfare. No fewer than 32 Japanese warships of 324,891 tons and seventeen naval auxiliaries, military transports and merchantmen of 92,346 tons were sunk in the six days of this battle and in the follow-up actions in Philippine and immediately adjacent waters, and between 29 October and 30 November 1944 the Americans accounted for another 49 warships of 119,655 tons and 48 auxiliaries, transports and merchantmen of 212,476 tons.

It was in the course of two actions, on 24 October 1944 in the Visayan Sea and on the night of 24/25 October in the Surigao Strait, that the *Kaigun*, the Imperial Japanese Navy, fought and lost the decisive battle in which it continued to believe until it ceased to exist. In the first the 67,123-ton battleship *Musashi*, second only to her nominal sister ship the *Yamato* in claims upon the title of the mightiest dreadnought ever built, was sunk by a hail of torpedoes and bombs rained upon her by carrier aircraft. In the Surigao Strait some hours later the sister ships *Fuso* and *Yamashiro* were sunk, the first by torpedoes delivered by successive waves of patrol boats and destroyers and the second by the fire of five American battleships and eight cruisers in what was only the second, and last, occasion in the Pacific war when battleships on both sides did battle with one another. Eight more dreadnoughts were to be sunk before the end of the European and Japanese wars – the German battleship *Tirpitz* on 12 November 1944, and the Japanese battleship *Kongo* nine days later; the raised Italian battleship *Conte di Cavour* in February 1945 and the laid-up German battleship *Gneisenau* in late March; and the Japanese battleships *Yamato* in April and the *Hyuga*, *Haruna* and the *Ise* in July – and American and British battleships were to see more than nine months of fighting after Leyte before Japan was finally defeated, but the action in the Surigao Strait represented the battleship's denouement, when for the last time the battleship and its *raison d'être*, to do battle with its counterpart as part of the struggle for naval supremacy, came together and in so doing closed a chapter in the book of naval warfare that reached back over four centuries. This is the story of these final years, those of the dreadnought battleship.

Origins, Early Years and Arms Races

Occasionally there is a ship known even in her own time to be special: sometimes there is a ship with a place in history that is assured because of some special act, whether for good or ill, for which she is known. It may be her grace and beauty that commands acclaim. It may be that she is representative of a nation or a period in time that ensures that she is recognised to be distinctive, different. One thinks instinctively of such ships as Magellan's flagship *San Antonio* or the *Victoria*, the only ship in his flotilla to complete the first voyage around the world; the *Santa Maria*; the *Mayflower*; Grenville's *Revenge* and Nelson's *Victory*; the *Constellation*; the *Warrior*, the world's first iron warship; the *Merrimack* and *Monitor*, since they can never be separated in history; the R.M.S. *Queen Mary*; either, or both, of the *Enterprises*, but not the one with the pointed ears; and the *Mikasa*, Togo's flagship at Tsushima. One also thinks of other ships. With the liner *United States* there is a seemingly effortless beauty. The *Nautilus* will always have a place in history, not for grace or beauty but because of her submerged circumnavigation of the world and her being the first to negotiate the icecap, while the *Titanic* has her place assured for a slightly different reason. Personal choice and prejudice may extend any list of such ships, but in most would be the *Dreadnought*, not necessarily because of what she was in 1906 but because of what she came to represent in terms of all the ships that were to follow her under her name, and many of those ships would demand inclusion in their own right: the *Iowa* and *Yamato* classes, the final expression of dreadnought development and ships of elegance, power and menace; the *Hood*, a ship of grace and majesty, a majesty haunted by great sadness; the *Repulse* and *Prince of Wales*, the first capital ships to be sunk on the open sea by aircraft; and the *Warspite*, whose story is that of British naval power in the two world wars which dominated the twentieth century: mauled by her enemies, defiant in adversity, triumphant, now lost in the mists of time. Truly, as has been said, 'The great ships pass, we shall not see their like again'.[1]

The origins of the dreadnought battleship may be disputed. Obviously, its ancestry may be traced back to the age of sail's line-of-battle ship, which itself dates from the sixteenth century: the name itself, *Dreadnought*, was first used in the Royal Navy on 10 November 1573 when the 450-ton warship of that name was launched at Deptford on the Thames: the name, meaning fear not or fearless, was apparently chosen deliberately by the Queen, Elizabeth Tudor, as an encouragement, indeed an incitement, to her subjects in dealing with England's most powerful enemy, Spain. But equally, any such tracing should more properly confine itself to the nineteenth century, a period in which the symmetry of previous centuries was lost as screw replaced sail, machinery and electricity took the place of muscle, and coal displaced wind. But in seeking to establish the impact of the Industrial Revolution as it affected navies and ships there is an obvious problem. The process of movement from the line-of-battle ship to the dreadnought was, depending on perspective, either very slow or remarkably fast, incorporating as it did a single life-span. Yet it was complicated and necessarily piecemeal, and what made for evolution can be compared to a piece of rope containing many strands. Unlike those in a piece of rope, however, the various technological strands that together produced the process of evolution were neither equal in size nor regular in weave – and in providing an account of the process whereby navies moved from sail to steam and the various changes that accompanied it, the historian, in a work dedicated to the dreadnought battleship itself, can do no more than describe, and not explain, and can do so in the sure knowledge of impending criticism not simply for what is included but for what has been omitted.

The story of the dreadnought battleship can be said to begin in December 1860 with the launching of the *Warrior*, the world's first iron warship. She was to usher in a period of all but constant material change that was to continue into the twentieth century and which was stabilised, for the moment, with the appearance of the *Dreadnought*. By the time the *Warrior* was built, navies had embraced steam power, iron protection for ships and the cylindrical shell; the latter, having been developed in 1841, made its operational debut on 30 November 1853 when six Russian line-of-battle ships destroyed a Turkish force off Sinope in the Black Sea. With this development came the joining of a struggle between defensive and offensive power in which there was one immediate loser: wood could no longer support the heavier guns that came into service and in effect offered no protection; hence, after such ships as *La Gloire*, which, with its iron protection and wooden hull, represented a halfway house, the need to build in iron was recognised.

The *Warrior* ushered in change because of conflicting requirements: heavier and more powerful guns spawned the need for ever thicker and better-quality armour in order to ensure that ships had reasonable chances of survival in combat with their peers. The immediate problem here was that, with navies working to the very limits of existing scientific knowledge and with no pool of information and experience on which to draw in the finalising of designs, warships went their very separate ways: not a few of the ships that were built in the quarter century after the *Warrior* might well be considered serious contenders for the unsought title of the least seaworthy warship ever constructed. High on such a list would be the British armoured ship *Captain*, which capsized with the loss of all but seventeen of her crew on 7 September 1870. She was powered by both steam and sail, and her masts were the tallest and heaviest in the Royal Navy. She had a greater proportional length to beam (just over 6:1) of any warship built to date and indeed for the next 35 years, and with just two decks she had the lowest freeboard of any British sailing armoured ship. With two turrets each housing two 12-in/305-mm muzzle loaders, she was designed with a lower deck just 8.5-ft/2.60-m above the water line, but her freeboard was reduced during construction as extra weight was worked into her. The combination of low centre of gravity and top-heavy masts caused her to founder in a storm that she should have survived.

The loss of the *Captain* in effect spelt the end of masts and rigging in navies, but left the essential problem of balance between offence and defence within a warship unresolved. In the course of the decade after the loss of the *Captain*, there was an unprecedented increase in the size and weight of guns, but this was not matched by any increase in either the rate or accuracy of fire: in one notorious gunnery trial the British ship *Hotspur*, with a single 12-in/305-mm gun, contrived to miss a target at 200 yards/183.5 metres range, both she and the target being stationary in a flat calm. In fact, guns grew in size to the extent that their blast effect threatened to do far more damage to their user than their shells could inflict upon an enemy, and ships simply could not take the strain imposed by the prolonged firing of their own weapons. Such ships as the Italian battleship *Duilio*, which was designed with four 38-ton 12-in guns but ended with four 100-ton 17.7-in/450-mm guns but no armour, and the *Inflexible*, which had 80-ton muzzle loaders and 24-in/610-mm of compound armour of iron backed by teak and steel, may have looked very impressive, but in real terms their practical usefulness must have hovered between the minimal and the non-existent.

The next decade, the 1880s, saw two technological changes that very quickly imposed order upon the often bizarre diversity of the previous one. The development of the Bessemer process of steel-making made available for the first time cheap, mass-produced steel of good quality, with obvious consequences for ship construction and protection. The British battleships *Nile* and *Trafalgar*, laid down in 1886, were in terms of displacement the heaviest British warships built until that time, and with a third of their displacement allocated to compound armour that was 20-in/508-mm thick on their belts, they also carried a greater percentage of armour than any British battleship: with respect to the latter, the ships took this title from their immediate predecessors, the *Sans Pareil* and *Victoria*, laid down in 1885. The *Royal Sovereign* class, the first of which were laid down in 1889, were the first British battleships to have all-steel armour protection. Their armour was roughly the same proportion of displacement as that afforded the *Nile* and *Trafalgar*, but because of the qualitative improvement of steel over compound armour the ships of the new class were considerably better-protected than their predecessors. This was just as well because the *Nile* and *Trafalgar* were notable not simply because of their size and armour allocation but because they were the first British battleships to be given a secondary armament that consisted of quick-firing guns, initially 4.7-in/120-mm but later 6-in/152-mm weapons.

The combination of steel construction and the development of quick-firing guns was to transform the battleship. The immediate loss, if indeed it was loss, was the monster gun, but no less importantly its disappearance resulted in a restoration of freeboard as battleships began to assume one essential characteristic that was to become the standard feature of dreadnought battleships. The members of the *Royal Sovereign* class, the first battleships to have steel armour and displace more than 12,000 tons, carried all their armament on the weather deck and all their secondary armament in casements: perhaps more importantly, with their high freeboard they presented a balanced, symmetrical profile which contrasted very sharply with that of 'two decades of sullen and misshapen misfits'.[2]

The *Royal Sovereign* class represented two markers, two elements of constancy, at a time of very real change. The seven members of the class were laid down between July 1889 and February 1891 and were completed between May 1892 and June 1894 at an average cost of £944,140. The class thus represented the first element of constancy in a settled design which successive classes followed. The *Barfleur, Centurion* and the *Renown*, the *Majestic*-class battleships of the Spencer programme of December 1893 and the *Canopus*-class battleships of 1896–1898 represented a search for smaller, and less costly, battleships before the *Formidable* class of 1897, the *London* class of 1898 and 1900 and the *Duncan* class of 1898 and 1899 saw a return to larger dimensions at a seven-figure cost: only the *Implacable* from the *Formidable* class and the *Bulwark* from the *London* class cost less than one million pounds, while the average cost of the six units of the *Duncan* class was almost £1,100,000 and the *Prince of Wales*, from the *London* class, cost almost £1,200,000. Settled design and profile, therefore, came at a very considerable increase of cost, and with the new century the size and cost of battleships climbed even more quickly: the eight battleships of the *King Edward VII* class, laid down between March 1902 and February 1904, displaced between 15,610 and 15,885 tons and cost £1,344,804 on average while the *Lord Nelson* and *Agamemnon*, built between 1905 and 1908, displaced some 16,000 tons and cost £1,541,443 exclusive of armament. In little less than a decade, therefore, the cost of individual ships rose by four fifths (i.e., the average cost of a *Lord Nelson*-class battleship compared to the *Albion* of the *Canopus* class), and in just six years it rose by more than half (i.e., the average cost of a *Lord Nelson*-class battleship compared to the *Formidable*).

The second element of constancy that the *Royal Sovereign* class represented was Britain's determination to maintain herself as the world's foremost naval power. The *Royal Sovereign* class was the first built under the provisions of the Naval Defence Act of March 1889, which authorised the construction of 70 warships between 1889 and 1894 at a cost of £21,500,000. So expensive a programme had been foreshadowed by the report in the previous month, February 1889, which stated that Britain would be pressed to conduct a naval war against a single enemy – her navy was deemed 'altogether inadequate to take the offensive in a war with only one Great Power' – and would be out-numbered by a combination of two powers. Of course a great deal depended on the identity of these two powers, and the fact was that there were only two powers which could combine to leave the British inferior to themselves. These powers were France and Russia, and it was the combination of these two powers that resulted in the emergence of the two-power standard on which Britain based her naval construction requirements over the next dozen years. In reality, in 1889 France and Russia were not allies and there seemed no real prospect that they might be, though this was to become fact in August 1892.

From the outset the Naval Defence Act's main provision, that Britain had to measure herself against a two-power standard and that this was in effect a Franco-Russian combination, was wholly unrealistic, and for a very simple reason: the Franco-Russian alliance of 1892 was concerned not with Britain but with Germany and her alliance with Austria-Hungary. The alliance between France and Russia came about as a result of these two countries' mutual vulnerability. This vulnerability had been obvious to France ever since the war, and the defeat, of 1870–1871 but was a more recent development on the part of Russia: she had come to the realisation that Germany sought to balance between Austria-Hungary and Russia but would never support Russia in her dealings with the Hapsburg monarchy. There was, as the saying went, on the part of France and Russia the need to hang together lest they be hanged separately, and the rapid provision of military clauses to the Franco-Russian treaty of alliance secretly provided the evidence of its anti-German, not its anti-British, nature. There might have been areas of dispute beyond Europe between Britain and France and between Britain and Russia – and these were serious and major impediments to good relations between Britain and the other two powers – but in the final analysis no European country was ever going to risk a major war with Britain for the sake of naval and non-European matters: no European country was prepared to risk major complications within Europe, a compromising of position relative to a real enemy, on account of matters beyond Europe's shores.

The conclusive evidence of this was provided in the Fashoda crisis of 1898 when France quite deliberately chose not to confront Britain over claims over the Sudan. In a very real sense, this was the acid test of extra-European issues: if France was prepared to acquiesce in British primacy on this occasion, then there was never going to be an issue that could produce real crisis, at least not between Britain and France. Relations between the two countries were not good, but the simple fact was that France could never afford to challenge Britain outside Europe given her military, industrial and demographic inferiority relative to Germany. The point about Fashoda, however, was that it was one in a series of events that came together in very rapid succession, and which in very large measure re-wrote naval terms of reference. In this process, certain events – such as the Spanish-American war of 1898, the second South African war (1899–1902) and the Anglo-Japanese alliance of 1902 – are both well-known and possess an obvious significance: only little less well-known, and certainly no less significant, would be such matters as the German naval laws of 1898 and 1900 and the Anglo-French rapprochement and the Entente Cordiale of 1904. But one would suggest that all these, and other, matters have to be seen against a wider historical background.

Within Europe the period between 1890 and 1914 was one of an increasingly militant and strident nationalism which was tied to a sense of insecurity on the part of all the powers. This was a period, too, when the imperialist imperative had run its course. The 1880s had seen the scramble for Africa, and the 1890s, especially in the wake of the Spanish-American war, witnessed the redefinition of possessions throughout the western Pacific and in eastern Asia. The Spanish-American war, of course, had seen the first defeat of an European imperial power by a non-European power though, arguably, at this time the United States of America, while she physically occupied a continent, was primarily a North Atlantic rather than a North American power. More relevantly, two other matters need to be noted. The first was the publication of Alfred Thayer Mahan's *The Influence of Sea Power upon History, 1660–1783* and *The Influence of Sea Power upon the French Revolution and Empire, 1793–1812*: published in 1890 and 1892 respectively, these provided the title deeds of imperialism and navies. The books may have owed more to their author's turn of phrase than to any serious analysis – not that such a distinction would ever have concerned naval officers – yet they provided an interpretation of history that stressed the importance of financial power, trade, colonies and sea power. In a book-reading society, the impact of these books was immense, and in a sense raised the horizon for much of Europe and the for the United States. The second was that in the last decade of the nineteenth century the United States had emerged as the foremost industrial power in the world, and also that Germany stood poised to overtake Britain in terms of industrial manufacture.

The last quarter of the nineteenth century witnessed the industrialisation, and urbanisation, of Europe and, for that matter, of the United States. The American civil war and the Franco-Prussian war of 1870–1871 were not fought between industrialised societies that lived by manufacture and trade: as late as 1860, nine in ten Americans lived in settlements of less than 2,000 people. Prior to this time perhaps only two states, Britain and Belgium, were properly industrialised in the sense that they paid their way primarily through industrial production: the majority of their peoples lived by trade and manufacture. But in due course the remainder of Europe became industrialised, with the pattern of industrialisation thinning to the east. Railways, even properly metalled roads, reached out across countries, and major cities were being marked by the introduction of electricity. Production and patterns of production were in the process of change, and there was technological revolution in the making. The turn of the century witnessed the first submarine, the first trans-Atlantic wireless message being sent, and the first controlled flight by a heavier-than-air machine – and the significant fact that all three developments had an American dimension or ancestry pointed to the industrial and technological changes taking place. There were, nonetheless, the necessary elements of constancy, those matters that did not change, and two were of singular, naval, importance.

The first was that Britain remained pre-eminent in terms of finance and trade. Less than one fiftieth of all American manufacture was for export, and German industrial primacy in Europe was not general: it was marked in certain fields, most notably in the petrochemical and engineering industries and in primary, non-finished, products, but Britain retained her previous primacy in terms of overseas investments, insurance, world-wide shipping and volume of trade. The second was that in one vital respect Britain continued to lead the world, the United States and Germany included. The American steel industry was in no small measure reared on the demands of a navy deliberately raised in the last two decades of the nineteenth century as the means of strengthening and expanding national capability, while certainly by 1914 German iron and steel production was roughly three fifths greater than that of Britain. But in terms of ship-building, both capacity and speed of construction, Britain led the world, and she also led the world in terms of naval armament. Germany, not surprisingly, led the world in terms of armament manufacture, but Britain retained until the First World War primacy in naval construction precisely because her other military equipment programmes were so slender.

A certain caution needs be exercised in any examination of shipbuilding and naval armaments industries at the turn of the century, and for the simple reason that the British lead in these industries was in the process of being eroded by the end of the nineteenth century. Britain was able to sustain herself throughout the nineteenth century's last decade, after the 1889 Naval Defence Act, at more than a two-power standard because her lead in these fields still remained, but by the turn of the century the British position was increasingly strained. There was a short-term aspect of British difficulties that asserted itself around this time: a series of strikes and lock-outs and the generally appalling state of labour relations in the shipyards meant that the building and completion of the *Duncan* class of battle-ships were little short of disastrous; the shortest building time for any ship of this class was longer than the average building time of all classes save for one group of battleships between 1889 and 1907. But this should not distract from the main point, which was that Britain's advantages in ship-building and naval armaments were being eroded by the process of industrialisation which imposed itself on Europe and the United States.

The process of industrialisation meant more shipyards, and shipyards that could build more quickly than hitherto. This of course applied generally, and to Britain as well as to those states that were industrialising and had not previously warranted serious British consideration in view of the numbers of ships they laid down or the speed at which they built them. Crucial in this process was the example provided by the *Vengeance*, a *Canopus*-class battleship laid down on 23 August 1898 and completed in April 1902. She was the first major warship to be built in its entirety by one firm. She was provided with armour, guns and engines by Vickers at Barrow, and though she did not break any records in terms of speed of con-struction, how she was built was to point to the future direction of warship con-struction: there were to be very few specialist yards but each yard was to be independent in terms of available resources. This development was in itself to ensure the building of warships faster than at any time over the previous three decades, though it needs be pointed out that the general trend after 1889, at least in British yards, was for shorter periods of construction: the average time of con-struction of the seven ships of the *Royal Sovereign*-class battleships built between July 1889 and June 1894 was 42.94 months; for the eight units of the *King Edward VII*-class battleships built between March 1902 and January 1907 it was 33.69 months, although it should be noted that the building of the *Dreadnought* consid-erably delayed the completion of the last three of this class, and at a conservative estimate the average time could well have been three or four months less than was the case.

By 1900 the world was capable of building more ships more quickly than at any time over the previous century, and the implication for Britain was self-evident: the day was bound to come when her pre-eminence would be ended. In fact, by 1900 the signs were becoming very clear, but paradoxically Britain nonetheless remained in a position to out-build any potential rival or rivals in terms of both numbers and speed of construction. Within Europe, she might be able to maintain an overall margin of superiority, albeit a lesser one, over any single nation or even alliances, and this was in no small part the result of the shortcomings of Italian and Russian yards and the military distractions of Austria-Hungary and France. Outside Europe, however, the position of Britain was more difficult. Japan pre-sented no immediate problems because, at the turn of the century, she was still dependent upon foreign yards for her first-line heavy ships: it was not until May 1905, less than two weeks before the battle of Tsushima was fought, that Japan laid down a battleship. But during Theodore Roosevelt's presidency (1901–1909) the United States launched no fewer than sixteen battleships, and, perhaps more relevantly, between 2 April 1902 and 1 May 1905, in just 37 months, the United States laid down no fewer than eleven battleships. Moreover, even between the two classes – the *Virginia* and *Connecticut* classes – that together made up this total of eleven battleships there was a very significant acceleration of average building time, a cut of more than a year per ship. The five-strong *Virginia* class averaged more than 51 months between keel being laid and completion: the six-strong *Connecticut* class had an average time with the shipyards of 38.59 months, and the *Vermont* and *New Hampshire* were the first American battleships to be less than three years in their construction. What was no less significant was the fact that no fewer than seven different yards handled the construction of the last three classes of battleship to be built before the appearance of the *Dreadnought*: the days when battleship orders meant assured contracts divided between William Cramp and Sons, Ltd, of Philadelphia, Pennsylvania, and Newport News navy yard were long passed.

The changing pattern of production in terms of shipping in general but of warships in particular was one of a variety of factors which combined at the turn of the century to produce the dreadnought revolution. Within Europe, a pattern of naval construction had been established in the last two decades of the nineteenth century which stressed programmes over a period of time, not individual construction orders based on yearly parliamentary timetables. The first such programme had been signed into existence on 20 May 1882 when Russia set out a construction programme for twenty battleships, the time allowed for this programme being twenty years to the completion of the last unit. The more relevant example for the rest of Europe to follow, however, was provided by Britain with the 1889 Naval Defence Act, but real significance lay in the fact that, even in the few years which had elapsed since the Russian measure, design had largely stabilised. As a result, states could set about building classes in the sure knowledge that these, unlike their predecessors of the previous two decades, would not be more or less bordering on obsolescence when first laid down, and states could set about seeking increased capacity and increased efficiency in shipyards in order to ensure real addition to strength. Thus in November 1890 Russia devised a programme for the construction of six second-class (7,500-ton) battleships, four armoured coastal defence ships and three large armoured cruisers for the Baltic, and in 1891 France introduced a ten-year programme which was to see the construction of ten battleships, one coastal defence ship and no fewer than 45 cruisers. When France and Russia concluded their alliance, the British reaction was a revision of existing programmes and a specific programme, in December 1893, for seven battleships and 30 cruisers. The Russian response came in 1895 in the form of a programme that would result in the building of five battleships, four coastal defence ships and six armoured cruisers by 1901, and three years later Russia again implemented another building programme, this time for the construction of five battleships and sixteen cruisers within seven years.

Such measures could have pitted these various nations against one another in a full-scale naval construction race but for three things: the final Russian programme of 1898 was crafted with a view to the provision of major naval units in the Far East; the Russian 1895 programme was not geared to the British programme but to the Baltic situation; and the French programme proved to be one in which aspiration was not matched by performance. Certainly, these various endeavours produced one ship of more than passing interest: the second-class battleship *Rostislav*, of 8,800 tons, was the first major warship in the world to be fitted with oil-fired boilers and she was also the first warship to carry a secondary 6-in/152-mm armament in twin turrets: laid down in 1894, and launched on 20 August 1896, the *Rostilav* was twenty years ahead of her time on both counts. But such matters counted for little when set against one reality that slowly took shape in the 1890s. This was the fact that in real terms Germany began to emerge as a major naval power, and indeed by 1905, despite numerical inferiority to other countries, she was second only to Britain in terms of available, modern first-line units.

Germany's emergence as a major naval power was one of the most profoundly important single developments in the period between 1892 and 1914. Before this period, the Imperial German Navy, formed in 1848 and perhaps the only survivor of that disastrous year which had seen the defeat and failure of liberalism in Germany, was of no account: German concern was military and directed against France and Russia, and any naval ambitions on her part promised only to be a burden that would not be accepted. The temper of the times, however, changed such terms of reference: the naval obsessions of the new Kaiser, the influence of Mahan and the great powers' search for advantage relative to one another in securing for themselves concessions in the Far East all combined in the 1890s in preparing Germany to accept naval obligation. Under a new naval secretary, Admiral Alfred Tirpitz, who was appointed in January 1897, the German Navy found itself the recipient of a *Reichstag* vote of 10 April 1898 which set national requirements as nineteen battleships (the *Oldenburg*, the four ships of the *Sachsen* class, the four ships of the *Brandenburg* class, the five members of the *Kaiser* class then under construction and the five members of the *Wittelsbach* class then being planned), eight coastal defence ships (the members of the *Siegfried* class), six large and sixteen small cruisers, with another six large and fourteen small cruisers assigned to foreign stations.[3] This force was to be built in six years, with individual ships allocated a life-span of 25 years. With the major units already in service counted on establishment, the 1898 Act provided for the replacement of units to be carried out at the rate of two ships a year between 1906 and 1909, one ship a year over the next seven years, and two ships in 1917.

This involved a major change for an Imperial Navy that in the 1890s underwent fundamental reconstruction in terms of its small number of coastal defence ships and cruisers in commission. Many of these ships were ageing and of dubious worth, and indeed some of the older units had originally been sailing ships. The rebuilding programme provided the Imperial Navy with real additions to strength, and the 1898 navy law clearly set out the service objective of numerical respectability. Within two years, however, this had been set aside in favour of the idea that quantity had a quality all of its own. The naval bill published on 14 June 1900 set out a programme that provided for the construction of two flagships and four squadrons each with eight battleships, eight large and 24 small cruisers, a reserve of four battleships, three large and four small cruisers, and a total of three large and ten small cruisers for service on foreign stations: the destroyer allocation was fixed at 96 units. Replacements were calculated on the basis of 25 years for a battleship and twenty years for a cruiser, but perhaps the real sting in these provisions lay in the fact that it was proposed that two of the battleship squadrons were to be maintained on a war footing with the other two squadrons forming the reserve: half of the ships thus earmarked, however, were to be maintained in permanent commission. In other words, Germany aimed to build a fleet with 38 battleships, of which a minimum of 25 were to be fully operational at all times.

The German naval law of 1900 has attained such notoriety on account of its stated *raison d'être* that the provisions of the subsequent naval laws of 1906, 1908 and 1912 are seldom afforded the consideration they are due.[4] The combined effect of these laws was to add extra numbers to those already allocated, to the extent that ultimately the Imperial Navy found itself committed to programmes that totalled 41 battleships, twenty battlecruisers and 40 light cruisers: how such numbers were to be secured does not seem to have been properly addressed. The immediate point, however, was the rationale for such a force. As the naval law of 1900 stated:

> To protect Germany's sea-trade and colonies, in the existing circumstances, there is only one means: Germany must have a battle fleet so strong that, even for the adversary with the greatest sea power, a war against it would involve such dangers as to imperil his position in the world.
>
> For this purpose it is not absolutely necessary that the German battle fleet should be as strong as that of the greatest naval power, because a great naval power will not, as a rule, be in a position to concentrate all its striking force against us. But even if it should succeed in meeting us with considerable superiority of strength, the defeat of a strong German fleet would so substantially weaken the enemy that, in spite of a victory he

might have obtained, his own position in the world no longer be secured by an adequate fleet.[5]

Much, some might argue too much, has been written about the so-called 'risk theory' that this definition embodied, and these pages could not hope to add anything new. Suffice it to note three things. First, the greatest military power in the world sought by this act to secure for itself a position at sea second only to Britain's, and this could not be anything other than a direct threat to the latter's security and one that Britain could never return. Britain did not have an army that could pose a direct or even indirect threat to Germany: at the end of the day Bismarck's famous response to the question of what he would do if a British army landed in Schleswig-Holstein – that he would send a policeman to arrest it – still held good.

Second, the very wording of the risk theory was provocative, almost deliberately insulting to a Britain which at this time was beset with the revelation of a general European hostility toward herself as a result of the opening exchanges in the second South African war. This war had seen the British seizure of a number of German ships in African waters and had provoked considerable anti-British feeling within Germany, and to this there had been added other incidents that favoured the anti-British and navalist cause within Germany, most notably the British intervention between the Americans and Germans in the Samoan dispute of 1898 in which the British in effect prevented the two from coming to blows and settled their dispute in American favour.

Third, there was the risk theory's unlikely combination of offering the greatest possible offence with the least possible chance of success – not to mention the fact that Germany was sanctioning a fleet primarily for political reasons and without reference to either its geographical position or its numerical inferiority. In these respects, the whole of the risk theory was utter nonsense and for a reason that manifested itself very quickly once war came in 1914: the construction of a battle fleet in the southern North Sea, where it was wholly incapable of protecting 'Germany's sea trade and colonies', left the fleet with a desire for battle that was but the least tactical response to a lost strategic cause. On political, geographical and strategic criteria, the 1900 navy law failed its own terms of reference, although the risk theory sought to evade these because the primary objective was to force concessions from Britain, to obtain from her an undertaking either of neutrality or an alliance with Germany in the event of a general war in Europe between, on the one hand, Germany and Austria-Hungary and, on the other, France and Russia. There were within the Conservative government in Britain individuals such as Joseph Chamberlain who quite willing to seek some form of arrangement with Germany which very largely would have met these requirements, but various negotiations failed: Britain refused to involve herself in a commitment that would have stripped her of real choice. In effect, the German statement of 20 June 1900 began a search for security that was to last until the black day in British twentieth-century history, 15 May 1940 and the defeat of the French army on the Meuse: in the intervening decades, British national security in very large measure rested upon the guarantee to maintain France as a great power relative to Germany.

It was not, however, the case that Britain moved immediately to this conclusion: the closing of ranks with the French came only in the aftermath of the 1909 Bosnian and 1911 Agadir crises and, of course, was consummated in 1912 with the Cabinet and Committee of Imperial Defence decisions that in the event of war the British army would be deployed to France. What happened after 1900 was that Britain made a series of negative decisions, the most obvious being the confirmation that she would seek any political and peaceful solution to any problem that arose between herself and the United States rather than go to war with that country. The basis of this decision was to be found in the War of 1812 and the decision by both countries thereafter to solve disputes by arbitration. The American Civil War had raised more than a few problems, most notably the United States claiming the rights that she had denied Britain in 1812, but the basis of the British decision was very simple: Britain could not defeat the United States militarily and had various colonies throughout the Caribbean which would be very vulnerable to American ambitions. The United States was Britain's most important single market, and was critical in terms of overseas earnings from property, investments and carrying trade; and the cultural, historical and shared democratic practice of the two counties rendered recourse to war all but unthinkable. Indeed, in many parts of the world the United States established missions and embassies, if not under British patronage, then in certain places with a closeness between British and American representatives that was very notable.

In 1902, moreover, Britain made a second decision, to ally herself with Japan. Wars in which naval force has proved the decisive element in terms of the power of decision have been few, and alliances between naval powers even fewer. It is possible to argue that neither Britain nor Japan were primarily naval powers, and in Japan there was certainly one organisation, the *Nippon Teikoku Rikugun* or Imperial Japanese Army, which held reservations on this particular score. But the point was that Britain in this period between 1900 and 1902 made two basic calculations regarding matters Far Eastern: the first was that Russo-Japanese differences were fundamental and could only be resolved by war, and that there existed a basis for an understanding with Japan. Britain had a certain standing with Japan on account of her naval mastery, and she had not been involved in the Triple Intervention following the Sino-Japanese war whereby France, Germany and Russia made common cause and forced Japan to surrender most of the gains that she had recorded on the Asian mainland under the terms of the Treaty of Shimonoseki. Britain sought to check Russian ambitions in the Far East, and since at the turn of the century these were concentrated on Manchuria and Korea, Britain reasoned that these areas were Japan's natural areas of interest on the mainland, hence the basis of an understanding between the two countries. Japan sought to defeat Russia, and Britain could prevent any intervention on Russia's behalf, i.e., most obviously on the part of France, but perhaps by Germany. At the same time, Japan sought to ensure sympathy for her position and objectives within the United States by a deliberate orchestration of the political process and press, and with one basic objective that really makes a neat counterpoint to what was to happen in 1941. Japan calculated that she could defeat Russia in a short, limited war but that she would lose in the event of the war she intended to fight proving protracted. She therefore sought American mediation to ensure her of the gains she intended to record by force of arms, and this was to be achieved – in fact, the Japanese script was almost word-perfect – and with a bonus that was both essential to Japan and never anticipated. The waging of war against Russia all but bankrupted Japan, and she was only sustained in the final phase of the war by loans that she had been able to raise in New York, specifically among a Jewish community that took the opportunity to repay the tsarist regime for its pogroms.

The course of the Russo-Japanese war (8 February 1904–5 September 1905) is beyond the scope of this volume, but it should be noted that the year of 1904 was critical to Britain not so much because of the Russian defeats in Korea and Manchuria, and not even on account of the British military occupation of Lhasa in Tibet in August, but because of the decision whereby most extra-European disputes with France were laid to rest. The Anglo-French entente of 8 April 1904, followed by the rapprochement with Russia in 1907, marked a fundamental change in British foreign and defence policy, involving as it did an attempt to settle outstanding disputes, some many decades in the making,[6] and to ensure that they were not attended by risk of war. Even more critically, the entente with Russia was seen as a means of strengthening that country at a time of serious weakness, the defeat in the Japanese war having been compounded by revolution within Russia which had been barely contained. Less than eight years separated the last of these British decisions from the realisation that 'splendid isolation' might not be so splendid after all, and it is a small matter, of no importance in itself, yet the extent to which Britain involved herself in European affairs in the first decade of the twentieth century can perhaps best be measured by citing the fact that in her 64 years as queen Victoria undertook one state visit abroad, to Paris in 1855.

All these matters – the changing patterns of industrialisation and ship construction, long-term naval construction programmes and arms races, and Britain's redefinition of her relationship with Germany, France and Russia – came together to don their navalist hue, and as they did so they encountered three other developments. The last of these, in chronological terms, was the balance of naval power as it existed by 1905. Britain was able to sustain herself at a two-power standard in the periods 1890–1894 and 1895–1899 and in the period 1890–1904 overall and even for the whole period between 1890 and 1910. As far as the most modern ships were concerned, Britain was able to maintain her margin of superiority quite comfortably, yet Germany was emerging as the second-ranked power in terms of battleship numbers even as early as January 1905, and she displayed a consistency of performance in terms of both orders and construction.

The other two developments related to actions fought at sea during the Russo-Japanese war, primarily the battles fought in the Yellow Sea in August 1904 and off Tsushima in May 1905, and to the fact that from the turn of the century there was a naval revolution in the making. This concerned gunnery, and the fact that guns could fire to ranges far beyond the effective range of guns mounted in ships. As far as warships were concerned, the revolution was to have two dimensions. One concerned the number, size and standardisation of the size of guns, and the other the command and control systems of these weapons. Together, they were to cause the dreadnought revolution and transform the profile of the battleship.

The two dimensions of the gunnery revolution ran in tandem, though it was to be guns that made the more obvious and immediate impact upon warship design. If battleships were to engage an enemy at long range, then they could only do so by fire from a standardised armament. What this meant was that battleships could not carry mixed armament, such as the four 12-in/305-mm, four 9.2-in/234-mm and ten 6-in/152-mm guns of a *King Edward VII* class battleship. To fire accurately at extended ranges, a battleship had to spot the fall of shot and correct accordingly, but it could only do so if the shells it fired were uniform in their time of flight and were firing to a single given range. The latter point was critically important because it was the route to an entirely new system of command and control of fire that was without precedent, and which clearly marked out the battle of Manila Bay as belonging to another era: in that battle the guns were individually laid and fired, just as they had been at Trafalgar and throughout the age of sail.

The logic of the situation pointed in one direction. Range had to open, and for one very straightforward reason: the torpedo was increasing in size, size of warhead, speed and range, and battleships could no longer expect to fight the equivalent of the close-quarter battle.[7] For the greater part of the 1890s, the maximum range at which warships were expected to fight was 2,000 yards/1,830 metres, and it was not until 1898, the year of Manila Bay and Santiago Bay, that the British Mediterranean Fleet carried out the first experimental firing practice at ranges between 5,000 and 6,000 yards or 4,600 to 5,500 metres. Practice at ranges beyond 2,000 yards had become standard throughout the British Navy by 1901, but even in 1903 the official wisdom pointed to battle being fought at ranges around 3,000 yards/2,750 metres, though by 1904 this, and the standard practice range, had increased to 8,000 yards/7,350 metres.

At these extended ranges the impact of such armament as the 6-in/152-mm gun was very limited indeed, and therefore it seemed logical to standardise armament around the largest gun currently available. This point did not command widespread acceptance in navies around the turn of the century. The big guns were slow to fire. The medium guns could be fitted in greater numbers on a given displacement than their larger companions, and there was in many navies the belief that in battle range had to be closed and the enemy overwhelmed by sheer volume of fire – which in effect meant the 6-in gun. This belief was slow to die despite the fact that if the big gun did what was expected of it, then volume of fire, for secondary armament, would be of no account.

The argument over main or intermediate armament – in the British case over the 12-in/305-mm gun and either the 9.2-in/234-mm gun which was in service or the 10-in/254-mm gun which was under development in 1904–1905 – came to a head when the British Navy found itself confronted by the series of choices and decisions which resulted in the building of the *Dreadnought*. In fact, the British Navy had already found itself in such a situation after 1902 when it began to consider the possibility of deliberately building battleships with characteristics known to be superior to those of foreign contemporaries, and it was in the course of the examination of various options that the naval design committee considered a battleship equipped with sixteen 10-in guns. This option was discounted on the grounds that the greater volume of fire possible with the 10-in gun could not offset the greater destructive power of the 12-in shell, and in September 1903 the committee considered a proposal for a battleship that carried twelve 12-in guns in six twin turrets: these were arranged with single turrets fore and aft with two on each beam amidships, thus providing a broadside of eight guns – which was generally considered to be the minimum number of guns needed for long-range spotting – and six guns firing forward and aft. The committee was divided by the conflicting claims, not least because the sixteen 10-in gun option seemed so attractive, and its final recommendation represented a compromise which really did not address the problem of mixed armament and different flight times. The result was that the British 1904–1905 naval estimates had provision for two ships, the *Lord Nelson* and *Agamemnon*, that carried four 12-in guns in two twin turrets, one fore and the other aft, and ten 9.2-in guns housed in one single and two twin turrets on each beam amidships, plus two dozen 12-pdrs. The latter represented the most powerful anti-destroyer armament yet mounted in a battleship, the units of the *King Edward VII* class having been equipped with fourteen. The latter units, however, had carried ten 6-in guns, and the *Lord Nelson* and *Agamemnon* were the first British battleships in quarter of a century not to carry 6-in guns. Within a decade, however, they were to return in the *Iron Duke* class and the battlecruiser *Tiger* as a concession to the growing size and powers of resistance of destroyers.

The *Lord Nelson* and *Agamemnon* were not laid down until May 1905, and in the period between the deliberations of the design committee and their keels being laid there were three considerations which moved onto centre-stage. These were the appearance of the armoured cruiser; the initial naval actions of the Russo-Japanese war; and the person of Admiral Sir John Fisher. The armoured cruiser proved something of an unnecessary and unwelcome white elephant. The development of the new Krupp steel-making process made available a light steel capable of withstanding 6-in shells without any real increase in displacement and cost. Cruisers therefore could be, and were, armoured, and being more heavily armed than hitherto, they could be employed as a fast wing to, and reconnaissance force for, the battle force. In fact, the revived idea of the armoured cruiser was nonsense. Though the first British armoured cruisers, the *Black Prince* class, carried six 9.2-in/234-mm and ten 6-in/152-mm guns, they were most definitely not battleships in terms of gun power, and they simply lacked the defensive power to stand in the battle line. Most British armoured cruisers were despatched to distant stations where the worst of their defects would not be too obvious: unfortunately for all concerned, however, eight were retained with the Grand Fleet during the First World War, and three were destroyed by German battleship fire at Jutland.

The second consideration had in fact more to do with the receipt of reports of the initial naval actions of the Russo-Japanese war than the actions themselves.[8] As it was, the first action, which involved the presence of Japanese destroyers off Port Arthur on the morning after a night attack, was notable for the first use of electronic counter-measures in war, Russian signallers jamming the radios of the Japanese units, but reports nonetheless seemed to confirm the importance of extended range and high speed. The first major action, the battle off Port Arthur on 10 August 1904, resulted from a Russian attempt to get the battle squadron to the safety of Vladivostok[9]: the Russians were confronted by a Japanese force across their line of advance, but the Japanese, despite their superior speed, were out-manoeuvred and the Russians managed to get beyond them.

In these exchanges the Russian battleships opened fire, and only narrowly missed their Japanese targets, at a range of 18,000 yards, while the Japanese flagship, the *Mikasa*, was hit at 13,000 yards, but for the most part hits were very occasional and of no real account. The initial Russian success was set at nought, however, by two developments. The Russian force was limited by the speed of its slowest member, which meant that the faster Russian battleships had to stay with and support the last-in-line, the *Poltava*, which badly damaged the *Mikasa* as the latter closed. The *Shikishima* and *Asahi* were also damaged as the Russian battleships gave a surprisingly good account of themselves, but as the Japanese line slowly overhauled the Russian battleships – specifically first the *Peresviet* and then the *Retvizan* – these began to take hits and late in the afternoon, when for the first time escape under cover of darkness seemed to be a distinct possibility, the Russian flagship, the *Tsarevich*, was hit by two 12-in shells, one of which killed her admiral, Witgeft. The second, a shell that dropped short but ricocheted off the sea and burst at the slit of the conning tower, killed or wounded every person inside it. The roof of the tower was driven into and killed the man at the wheel, which was jammed by the various bodies strewn across it. With the helm jammed, the *Tsarevich* turned sharply to port and made a complete circle, the Russian line being reduced to chaos as a result of its at first conforming to the *Tsarevich*'s movement before it was realised that this was not deliberate. It took time for the *Tsarevich* to make the appropriate signal that ensured delegation of authority to the second-in-command, but the latter's flagship, the *Peresviet*, had lost all her signal halliards. She nonetheless was successful in leading the Russian battleships back to Port Arthur, and notably neither the Japanese line with its guns in the remaining daylight nor the Japanese light forces with their torpedoes under cover of night were able to inflict loss on the Russian formation once order had been restored to the line: in fact, despite a major advantage in numbers of torpedo-boats, the Japanese recorded only one torpedo hit on the cruiser *Pallada* just as she re-entered Port Arthur.

There were other interesting aspects to the action. In the initial period after the *Tsarevich* had been hit, the Japanese battleships had closed the range to 4,000 yards and had poured into the stricken Russian ships the volume of fire which the mixed armament thesis had deemed to be so important and vital to success, but to no overall effect. The Russian force had consisted of six battleships, four cruisers and eight destroyers, and of these the *Tsarevich* managed to beat off attacks and reach the German port of Tsingtao where she hoped to coal and make repairs but found herself – and the three destroyers that accompanied her – interned. The second-class cruiser *Askold* managed to reach Shanghai while the *Diana*, by some extraordinary process of logic, was deemed not to have enough coal to reach Vladivostok and therefore set course for Tsingtao: there she took on coal sufficient to reach Saigon, where she arrived without undue difficulty and was interned. The light cruiser *Novik* was caught in the port of Korsakov, on Sakhalin, by the Japanese cruiser *Tsushima* and the two cruisers inflicted some damage on one another before the *Chitose* appeared on the scene, the *Novik* being scuttled to prevent capture.[10] With the main part of the Russian formation forced to return to a doomed Port Arthur, the Russian defeat of 10 August was compounded three days later when the squadron of three armoured cruisers at Vladivostok, having sailed the previous day in support of a formation that had turned back to Port Arthur two days before, was caught off Ulsan: the old *Rurik* was sunk and the *Gromoboi* and *Rossiya* were damaged but able to escape back to Vladivostok.[11]

'Lessons to be Learnt' always provide hazard, especially when based on very incomplete knowledge in the middle of a war. The most obvious point about the battle of the Yellow Sea was the extent to which chance played the deciding role: the *Mikasa* was hit 22 times and the *Tsarevich* fifteen times by 12-in shells, but Togo and his staff survived the battle while Witgeft and his staff were killed.

Beyond that, the unfolding of the battle revealed that at ranges beyond 6,000 yards hits were few and most certainly not decisive in settling the outcome, and indeed the invulnerability of both sides' battleships was noteworthy: the armoured belt and turrets of the *Tsarevich*, for example, were not penetrated by the heaviest Japanese shells. But the point was, of course, that what damage was inflicted was caused by the heavy guns, not the more numerous secondary weapons, and the only damage that might prove decisive could only be done by the main armament. This, along with the demand for superior speed which enabled the Japanese to undo the effect of being out-manoeuvred and then led them to concentrate against each Russian battleship in turn, were the lessons that were heeded – and it is here that one encounters the third of our three considerations: Admiral Sir John Fisher, who became First Sea Lord in October 1904.

The story of the *Dreadnought* and Fisher are inseparable, and the latter, even at a distance of almost a hundred years since he first became First Sea Lord, remains one of the giants of the British services in the twentieth century: probably more than any other single individual, Fisher shaped and fashioned the navy that fought and ultimately prevailed in the First World War. In the time when he was First Sea Lord between 1904 and 1910 he was the subject of some of the most extravagant praise, blatant sycophancy and vituperative disparagement, and it is difficult to know which he sought and liked the most. Fisher, most definitely, was a stormy petrel, and one who on occasions could look beyond the other man's horizon. He foresaw the advantages of changing British warships over to oil as early as 1901, and he also foresaw the strategically offensive role of the submarine, as well as its role against merchant shipping. More immediately, he had grasped the implications of the changing range-gunnery-speed formula for battleships. He was utterly mendacious in argument, and from the time that he became First Sea Lord he sought to prepare the way for a dreadnought programme. In fact, Fisher was not so much sold on the dreadnought idea as the belief that speed was the equivalent of armour protection, and what he really wanted to build was what at various times he christened the *Unapproachable* and the *Uncatchable*. This was the battle-cruiser, which ultimately appeared as the *Invincible* in 1908, and which was an utterly disastrous idea. To Fisher, 'battleships have no function that first-class armoured cruisers cannot fulfil' and, even more dubiously, 'The (first-class) armoured cruiser . . . is a swift battleship in disguise. It has been asked that the difference between a battleship and armoured cruiser may be defined. It might as well be asked to define when a kitten becomes a cat'[12] – and with regard to such a fundamental error of judgement, one is left to ponder the wisdom of the saying that for every complicated human problem there is a simple solution: neat, plausible and wrong.

But this matter remained for the future, and after the disasters that overtook three such British ships at Jutland in 1916, Fisher's dictum that speed was armour was consigned to the rubbish tip. When he became First Sea Lord in October 1904, Fisher was well aware that abandoning battleship construction in favour of battle-cruisers would never be acceptable either in the navy or more generally the country, i.e., in Parliament and the press. Moreover, Fisher was also well aware that the dreadnought idea was hardly likely to command uncritical acceptance from these same audiences, and he knew that criticism of the dreadnought idea – the battleship with uniform main armament – was likely to manifest itself on two particular issues: the suppression of medium armament, i.e., the 6-in/152-mm guns, and the fact that in building a dreadnought battleship Britain, in effect, would write off her existing superiority in battleship numbers over all other nations and would create a level playing field.

Accordingly, one of Fisher's first acts was to secure authorisation of a special design committee, the deliberations of which, it was anticipated, would disarm most of the criticism that would be incurred in building dreadnought battleships. This committee, the composition of which was announced on 22 December 1904, was somewhat unusual in that it consisted of no fewer than fifteen people, naval secretary and assistant secretary excluded. There were eight naval officers, including Rear Admiral Prince Louis of Battenberg, and, representing the coming generation with a vengeance, Captains Henry Jackson, John Jellicoe, Charles Madden and Reginald Bacon, and seven civilians, who included Phillip Watts, Director of Naval Construction, and W. H. Gard, Chief Constructor, along with others preeminent in matters involving naval construction and drawn from academia and the shipbuilding industry. Both in terms of its individual members and its overall balance, the committee was heavyweight, but also heavily weighed in favour of Fisher and the dreadnought idea: the composition of the committee may have been determined on the basis of individuals whose professional opinion could not be lightly ignored, but it was also determined on the basis of individuals associated with Fisher and his ideas, and who in effect would rubber-stamp the dreadnought concept.

Fisher headed this committee, and in October 1904 set out its terms of reference with the presentation of two designs, both for battleships of about 16,000 tons displacement and 21 knots speed, one with sixteen 10-in/254-mm guns in eight twin turrets and with 10-in main belt and barbette armour, and the other with eight 12-in/305-mm guns in four twin turrets and with 12-in main belt and barbette armour: both preliminary drafts had single turrets fore and aft with the balance of turrets divided between the beams. The first design, for the battleship with 10-in guns and armour, was very quickly set aside, and in November 1904 four sketch designs were drafted that provided specifications for two 16,000–16,500-ton battleships with eight 12-in guns and for two 18,000–18,800-ton battleships with twelve 12-in guns, in each case the smaller battleships being afforded a top speed of 20 knots and the larger battleships 21 knots. The radical nature of these specifications can be understood by cross-reference to the *King Edward VII*-class battle-ships then being built, the nameship of which was but three months from comple-tion. On 16,350 tons displacement, these battleships were to have a top speed of 18.5 knots, a maximum belt of 9-in/228-mm thickness, and, of course, the mixed armament: even the most modest of the four battleships proposed – 16,000 tons, eight 12-in guns and a speed of 20 knots – represented a major increase of arma-ment, armour and speed, while the other three designs incorporated significant increases in overall size.

The various specifications did not hang together very well, but this particular problem was finessed by the suggestion that the battleships be equipped with tur-bines, which would allow for a reduction in the weight allowed for both machin-ery and hull, the weight thus saved being put 'to better effect'. In fact, it did not quite work out so neatly – the saving was relative and not absolute – because the engines and the auxiliary machinery of the *Dreadnought* weighed 1,990 tons, which was 190 tons more than the engines and machinery of the *King Edward VII*. The saving was in the size of reciprocating engines that would have been needed to achieve speeds of 20–21 knots on increased displacement to take account of arma-ment and armour: gains were to be found in the twin facts that the *Dreadnought*'s engines generated 23,000 hp for 21 knots compared to the average 18,450 hp and 18.8 knots of the eight members of the *King Edward VII* class, and that turbines were superior to reciprocating engines in terms of reliability and maintenance.[13]

But turbines were for the future, although in November 1904 the turbine alter-native was entered into later drafts so that designs were drawn up for both recipro-cating and turbine engines. On 26 November a series of designs were submitted from the constructor's office, all with eight 12-in guns, and these were followed by another series of designs, all of which armed the proposed battleship with twelve 12-in guns but for one which provided for ten 12-in guns. In the course of Decem-ber 1904 the various designs were brought together and set in order, and lettered in order to facilitate the deliberations and decision of the design committee, which met for the first time on 3 January 1905. (See Appendix 2, p.244)

At the first meeting the initial drafts (A, B and C) were discarded, as were the two radical designs that envisaged superimposed turrets mounted on centre line forward and aft (E and F). It seems that there were two considerations at work in ensuring that these last two designs were afforded summary treatment. The more important of these was the belief that blast from the superimposed guns would make the lower turrets unworkable over very considerable arcs of fire. This objec-tion was raised by Jellicoe and was based upon various experiments with superim-posed firing, none of which had been very satisfactory, but within four years it was to be reversed: the four *Orion*-class battleships, ordered in the 1909 estimates, were the first British battleships to carry all their main turrets on centre line and with superimposition fore and aft. The second objection was that superimposition risked more than one turret being knocked out by a single hit, and this appears to have been the line of reasoning that led to modification of the D1 design, its successor D2 having its paired turrets on both beams more widely separated. The basic D design, however, had relative low freeboard, which was not conducive to high-speed operations in anything like a seaway: therefore when the request was made for a recasting of this design it was asked that the new design include a raised forecastle with the centre-line turret mounted on it.

At the following day's meeting, with this modified design under examination, it was then requested that the two wing turrets facing aft be eliminated and replaced by a single centre-line turret sited between the engine and boiler rooms. This design therefore provided for four guns facing aft and, critically, eight guns available for broadside fire but at the same time allowed for a major reduction of weight in terms of the elimination of one turret and its armour. The new design, designated H, was examined at the committee meeting of 13 January and its basic layout, deemed superior to D, was approved: designs were then requested for alternative turbine and reciprocating engines, plus an appropriate model, in readiness for the next meeting, to be held on 18 January. At that meeting the turbine version, with its saving of weight and cost and under Fisher's personal patronage, was approved. The committee and various sub-committee meetings thereafter dealt primarily with detail involving such matters as internal sub-division and anti-torpedo protection, mast arrangements, boat storage and, crucially, secondary armament.

At the 23 January meeting what had been the standard secondary armament for designs prior to this date, fourteen 4-in/102-mm guns, was set aside in favour of twenty 12-pdr and 3-pdr guns. The basis of this decision is unclear, as indeed is the paternity of this particular line of reasoning. It has been suggested that Fisher had been party to the original proposal in favour of 4-in weaponry, and while the final *Dreadnought* specification was for 27 rather than twenty secondary guns, this change, the discarding of the 4-in gun, really was one of the major mistakes in the basic design: destroyers and torpedo-boats by this time had acquired a size and speed that rendered even the 4-in gun as being of marginal usefulness. The 12-pdr armament was provided for the *Dreadnought* alone – not even the three battle-cruisers of the 1905 programme were so provided – and herein, of course, was irony: the 6-in gun had been suppressed because of its limited effectiveness in battleship action at the very time when it should have been retained as the standard secondary armament against destroyers and torpedo-boats. As it was, the 6-in gun was duly restored to the inventory of British battleships in the 1911 programme and the *Iron Duke* class.[14]

Thus was the design of the battleship settled, and with three immediate riders. The first was that the *Dreadnought* was to be laid down as soon as possible and completed within a year, and her acceptance trials were to be concluded with the least possible delay. The second was that no other battleships were to be laid down until the *Dreadnought* had successfully completed her acceptance trials, and the third was the fact that the *Dreadnought*, and by implication those ships that followed her, would have their dimensions determined by the size of existing docks at Portsmouth, Devonport, Gibraltar and Malta. Both of these particular provisions to a degree threatened to undo any advantage that might be gained by the rapid construction of a novel type of battleship, but there was one other decision, against which these two matters paled into insignificance. This was the approval of the *Invincible* battlecruiser, still called an armoured cruiser at this time. There may have been a logic to not building follow-on battleships until the *Dreadnought*'s trials were completed, but it is somewhat difficult to see what possible justification there could be for the devising of a new type of unproven warship, one likely to generate even more controversy than the *Dreadnought*, and the ordering of three of these warships in the 1905 estimates.

The specifications to which the design committee worked with reference to the new 'armoured cruiser' were a 12-in main armament, armour protection on the scale afforded the planned *Minotaur* class, and a speed of 25 knots. Five designs were considered, but certainly three of these, with the forward twin turrets carried *en echelon*, raised immediate objections, even though such an arrangement had been adopted by four major European navies. Attention therefore focussed on a design that really represented a truncated version of the D1/D2 battleship designs. This design, which also bore the D designation, envisaged single twin turrets fore and aft on centre line, with one pair of twin turrets amidships, one on each beam. This would provide for six guns on either broadside, and four ahead or astern. By staggering these turrets, guns would be able to fire on the 'wrong side' of the ship within certain arcs. There were attempts to increase the distance between these turrets but on a beam of about 76 or 77 feet/23.2 or 23.5 metres this was not possible. Thus was settled the basic layout for the main armament, the new ship also having the raised forecastle and the turbines that had been afforded the *Dreadnought*.

Officially the *Dreadnought* was laid down at Portsmouth Dockyard on 2 October 1905 but work on her had begun many months before as various materials were ordered and made. Completed sections for the double bottom were on the sides of the slipway when the ship was laid down, and even before October was out the ship was well advanced. With some 3,000 men allocated to her construction, she was launched by King Edward VII on 10 February 1906 and then moved to the No. 5 Basin to be fitted out. In July Bacon was appointed her first captain, and with a nucleus crew he joined the ship on 1 September. Trials began on 17 September and on 1 October she left dock and Portsmouth for nine days of steaming trials which revealed that she needed more power to reach her designated speed than had been anticipated but no serious problems. After her return to dock to continue fitting out, she was undocked and sailed for her gunnery and torpedo trials, which passed out without undue difficulty. Acceptance trials were completed on 1 and 2 December, but on the following day she was caught by the tide and driven against the pier, damaging one of her bilges and some outer plating. Repairs were completed between 10 and 17 December, which was somewhat ironic given the fact that her official completion date, when she received her full crew and became part of the Royal Navy, was 11 December. In the new year she sailed first for Gibraltar and then to Trinidad, where she arrived on 5 February 1907. In the Caribbean she was able to work up, removed from hostile gaze whether foreign or domestic, and she returned to Portsmouth on 23 March. In April she was commissioned as flagship of the newly created Home Fleet, based at the Nore.

The first of the three 'armoured cruisers' to which the *Dreadnought* was consort was laid down on 5 February, but the *Inflexible* also proved the last of the three to be completed: the *Invincible*, the first to be completed in March 1908, was the last to be laid down in April 1906. The first three battlecruisers' time of construction was just 29 months, a very respectable rate of building but one overshadowed, obviously, by that of the *Dreadnought*, and also by the fact that the *Invincible*'s returns were more nominal than real. The battlecruisers were completed with electrical rather than hydraulic turret machinery, and this gave no end of trouble. The training gear of the turrets repeatedly broke down and, despite constant repairs, basic faults could not be remedied, while the loading gear of guns was so poorly designed and in such need of all but constant repair that the ships could not fire their guns for months at a time when first commissioned. Perhaps even more seriously, the attempt to build a capital ship on what was a cruiser hull involved beams that were so weak that the *Invincible*'s frames were distorted as a result of the time she spent in dockyard, a sign of inadequate longitudinal strength. The *Invincible* might well have been nominally completed in March 1908 but in fact it was not until March 1909 that she entered service with the Home Fleet.

The *Dreadnought*, battleship and 1905 concept, and the battlecruiser, again both ships and concept, have attracted so much attention, from the time that they were laid down, that it is very difficult either to throw fresh light upon these matters or even to summarise what knowledge is in the public domain. But one thing is clear: the speed with which the *Dreadnought* was built, irrespective of the fact that it was contrived and there was quite deliberate falsification in the claim that she was completed in either a year less one day or a year and one day, was a source of very great national pride which tended to stifle criticism of ship and concept. This being the case, with the *Dreadnought* argument having been won and lost in 1906–1907, criticism of the *Invincible* was largely forestalled. This also meant that the most serious weaknesses of the *Dreadnought*, her inadequate secondary armament and very poor underwater protection, were never seriously considered.

The criticism of the *Dreadnought* basically concentrated on two lines, both of which had been largely anticipated. The first was that the suppression of a mixed armament in favour of a single, uniform main armament was wrong, and the second concerned the adverse effect that the *Dreadnought* would have in terms of doing away with Britain's existing superiority in battleship numbers over all other nations, whether singly or in any sort of reasonable combination. On the first matter, much of the criticism of the *Dreadnought*, and of Fisher, came from Reginald Custance and Sir William White, both retired and highly respected, one an admiral and the other chief of naval design. It should also be noted that Mahan wrote many papers roundly condemning the *Dreadnought*. To these individuals have to be added the 'doves' and economists of the Liberal Party, which won the election of January 1906 after more than a decade in the political wilderness. Their main criticism was that the new warship had to usher in a period that would see increased estimates, both for ships and for capital projects such as larger and better dockyards. There was also a powerful 'peace' lobby which hoped for arms reductions as a result of The Hague conferences and which saw arms races as a destabilising factor in European affairs. To the criticisms that these individuals and groups could muster must be added the general point, namely that there was genuine unease on account of the fact that with the *Dreadnought* the British abandoned the traditional policy of waiting on events and then, should the need arise, outbuilding foreign rivals. That Germany was not markedly inferior in terms of building time and that Britain no longer necessarily had the advantage of timing was not fully appreciated, and, of course, the circumstances surrounding the *Dreadnought*'s construction tended to disguise these facts, especially the latter.

What told decisively in favour of Fisher and the *Dreadnought* was a combination of three matters. Two of these pre-date the *Dreadnought* and indeed were factors shaping the decision that led to the authorisation and design of the ship, but these have not been considered until this time and for reasons that need no elaboration. The first matter was the fact that for some five or six years there had been various ideas for new types of battleships. Fisher had been thinking in such terms when he was in command in the Mediterranean between 1899 and 1902, and his own ideas had taken shape when he was in command at Portsmouth and had access to design and construction personnel. Fisher was not unique: other individuals, in a number of different countries, could also read the signs. Perhaps the most pre-eminent of these, and certainly the best-known to historians, was the Italian navy's leading designer, Vittorio Cuniberti, who was primarily responsible for the *Vittorio Emanuele*-class battleships and who wrote the famous article, 'An Ideal Battleship for the British Navy', which appeared in the 1903 edition of *Jane's Fighting Ships*. The characteristics of this battleship were a displacement of 17,000 tons, an armament of twelve 12-in guns carried in four twin and four single turrets and a secondary armament of eighteen 3-in/76-mm guns, 12-in maximum belt armour, and a speed of 24 knots. Interestingly, the rationale for this ideal battleship, despite the obvious points of similarity with the *Dreadnought*, was to be the very opposite of that of the *Dreadnought*. In the 1904–1905 deliberations of the special committee, the requirement of salvo firing to extended range governed considerations of armament: in Cuniberti's calculations, the need for the heaviest possible fire at decisive – i.e., short – range dictated the need for the heaviest possible armament.

The fact that such individuals as Cuniberti had floated the idea of uniform main armament, good armour protection and high speed being brought together in what was certain to be a revolutionary warship design played to the advantage of Fisher after October 1905: the dreadnought concept could not be dismissed lightly as an aberration on the part of an out-of-control Admiralty headed by a lunatic. Yet there was also the second matter: as time passed, one simple fact, which critics of the *Dreadnought* tried to pass over, kept re-asserting itself: the law of 3 March 1905 passed by the US Congress. This law defined the American naval construction programme for 1905–1906 and it authorised the construction of two battleships, which in fact were dreadnoughts that predated the *Dreadnought* herself. But the two ships that had been authorised, the *Michigan* and *South Carolina*, were not laid down until December 1906 and therefore could not be of much immediate or practical assistance to Fisher's case when the anti-*Dreadnought* lobby was at its most active. The general American intention was known, however, and the fact that it had anticipated the British decision did strengthen the latter. Moreover, what would also have strengthened the dreadnought case was the fact that Japan too anticipated the *Dreadnought* with the laying down of the *Satsuma* in May 1905. Ordered under the 1903 programme, she was to have been afforded twelve 12-in guns carried in four twin and four single turrets, but lack of funds meant two things: she was not completed until 1911, and she was given four 12-in and ten 10-in/254-mm guns, which were purchased in Britain because this was cheaper than producing them in Japan. Such Japanese intent, especially given that the *Satsuma* was laid down just days before the battle of Tsushima, could have constituted useful support for Fisher and the *Dreadnought* not least because, being more than a thousand tons larger than the *Dreadnought*, the Japanese ship represented the argument in favour of scale. But whatever value she might have been afforded to Fisher was basically dissipated by the delays that attended her construction and that of her even later sister ship, the *Aki*. As it was, the construction of the *Dreadnought* left the Japanese navy flat-footed, confronted with a choice of proceeding with designs that had been overtaken by events, attempting to redesign their proposed ships with all the loss of time such a process would imply, or abandoning the attempt to build such ships altogether.[15]

The third and last matter that strengthened Fisher's case was the growing evidence of the Russo-Japanese war, though clearly both the evidence and the conclusions drawn from it were dependent on which particular argument sought justification. In fact, the one battle from this war that came to be used to justify the dreadnought concept really did lend itself to the most dishonest and manipulative of interpretation by both sides of the debate, but then the battle of Tsushima, fought on 27 and 28 May 1905, was a very unusual naval battle. It resulted in clear, overwhelming victory – in fact, annihilation – primarily because of the massive disparity that existed between the two navies in terms of ships, organisation and training. Unlike the actions of 13 April and 10 August 1904 when reasonably well-matched formations fought one another, at Tsushima there was on the one side a battle-tried fleet, a fleet which had paid for past victories with its losses, and on the other nothing more than a collection of warships.

Tsushima, given that the Russian force was limited to nine knots by the speed of its slowest auxiliary and was thus six or seven knots slower than the Japanese battle and armoured cruiser squadrons, was a battle in which the Japanese formation outmanoeuvred its enemy with contemptuous ease and was then able to concentrate its fire on the lead ships of the two leading Russian formations, the *Kniaz Suvaroff* and *Oslyabya*. Japanese fire was opened at about 7,000 yards/6,420 metres – the Russians had opened fire at greater range and seem to have shot accurately but without any luck, achieving many straddles but no hits – and then closed, the *Suvaroff* and *Oslyabya* literally being overwhelmed by sheer volume of Japanese fire, primarily from 6-in guns. In the opening phase, neither the *Suvaroff* nor the *Oslyabya* had their armour pierced, but as the range fell the *Oslyabya* lost part of her belt, presumably to heavy shells, and, thus exposed, was repeatedly holed. She very quickly capsized, the first of the Russian ships to be sunk (1450). Some twenty minutes before, the *Suvaroff* had replayed the tragedy of the *Tsarevich* at the Yellow Sea, splinters entering the conning tower and cutting down its occupants. From this time on the *Suvaroff* and her admiral ceased to have any real part in the battle, and as the Russian second-in-command had died on the eve of the battle and no notice of this had been served to Russian ships lest the death be deemed portentous and bad for morale, command within the Russian fleet, at best a somewhat delicate commodity, ceased to exist.

Contact between the opposing forces was intermittent in the patchy mists that adorned the Strait, but by dusk the *Borodino*, *Aleksandr III* and the *Suvaroff* had also been sunk and the *Oslyabya* seriously damaged. Only in one phase of the battle, when Russian battleships blundered into an action between the cruiser formations, had the Russians acquitted themselves well, both their cruisers and their battleships repeatedly hitting the Japanese cruisers and leaving four of them extensively damaged. With night, however, the Japanese battle and cruiser formations cleared the battle area, leaving the initiative with their destroyers and torpedo-boats, two elderly Russian battleships and one coastal defence ironclad being sunk during the hours of darkness, though three Japanese destroyers were sunk by Russian gunfire in the process. These were the only Japanese losses in an action that ended the following morning when the main Russian formation which remained intact, consisting of the *Oryol*, *Admiral Senyavin*, *Admiral Apraxin* and the *Izumrud*, found itself facing an enemy with more guns, greater range and higher speed, and it was surrendered by its commander. The cruiser *Izumrud* refused to capitulate, however, and broke through the Japanese formation. She would have reached Vladivostok had she not exhausted her coal supplies, and was scuttled to avoid capture. Elsewhere, individual Russian ships scuttled themselves, surrendered or sought internment in neutral ports, one even withdrawing to Madagascar. Only the old ironclad *Ushakov* fought to the end, an end that she must have foreseen but nonetheless did not attempt to avoid, and the cruiser *Almaz* survived to reach Vladivostok, bearing with her news of a disaster that spelt the end to the last, hopelessly unrealistic, hopes of St. Petersburg that somehow the 2nd Pacific Squadron would be able to reverse the defeats which had been incurred and restore Russian naval fortunes in the Far East.

At Tsushima the two sides were so mismatched in virtually every aspect of naval warfare, in terms of age and capability of ships, seaworthiness, speed, training of both individual ship's crews and formations, that drawing conclusions was a most hazardous undertaking. The Japanese more or less fought the battle as they chose, determining both the range at which it was fought and the individual ships and formations they selected as prime targets. Individual Russian ships fought bravely, and the old truism – that the men were better than the system – applied, but certainly both sides of the dreadnought dispute could latch on to this battle for material with which to support their arguments.

Two aspects of Tsushima probably received less attention at the time than they merited. The first was that the battle really conformed to the Cuniberti rather than the Fisher-dreadnought scenario, and herein lay the important second point. This was a battle that was fought without central fire control, one of the two manifestations of the gunnery revolution which was taking shape at the turn of the century. But Tsushima nonetheless demonstrated that fire from heavy guns rendered telling damage or, put another way, only fire from heavy guns rendered telling damage. Though this battle was fought at ranges that were soon to be exceeded by some margin, the key point was that medium guns could not be fired to effect and could not inflict decisive damage on the enemy at extended ranges. In this critical matter, therefore, Tsushima specifically and the Russo-Japanese war overall really underscored the dreadnought argument and concept.

Fisher and the *Dreadnought* won the arguments which surrounded them in 1906, and they did so for the very simple reason that they were in place, and their opponents had to argue an overwhelming case against the new battleship – something which was all but impossible since the evidence against the *Dreadnought* was certainly not conclusive. But before one turns to an examination of what was to happen on the international stage as other nations followed the British example, one would suggest that the construction of the *Dreadnought*, and all the acclaim that surrounds it, invites two comments. The first is somewhat esoteric and rarely commands attention, but it should be considered initially in order to concentrate on the second and, in a sense, more important point.

This first comment has to do with the fact that the construction of the *Dreadnought* marked the beginning of the end of major warship construction in southern England. Within a decade of the *Dreadnought*'s construction this building, which reached back over 600 years, had been brought to a close: the *Royal Oak* was Devonport's last battleship and the *Royal Sovereign* was the last battleship built at the dockyard at Portsmouth. Admittedly this last decade was very full: between the *Dreadnought* and *Royal Sovereign*, the Portsmouth dockyard built no fewer than seven dreadnoughts – the *Bellerophon*, *St. Vincent*, *Neptune*, *Orion*, *King George V*, *Iron Duke* and the *Queen Elizabeth* – while Devonport built the battleships *Téméraire* and *Collingwood*, the battlecruisers *Indefatigable* and *Lion*, and then the battleships *Centurion* and *Marlborough*. In addition, the Thames saw the construction of one dreadnought, the *Thunderer*.

In many ways the end of major construction on the Thames had long been foreshadowed. The Tyne had replaced London as the major shipbuilding centre in Britain as early as the 1840s, but while shipbuilding on the Thames survived until 1915 when the last firm, J. and G. Rennie, moved to Wivenhoe on the Colne, shipbuilding on the Thames was in terminal decline after a number of Thames shipyards had been made bankrupt in the wake of the Overend Gurney banking crisis in 1867. Thereafter serious building on the Thames was maintained primarily by Admiralty orders. By 1889 there were just six yards on the Thames involved in shipbuilding. Three of these firms – Green (next to the East India Docks in Blackwall), Rennie (on the eastern side of Deptford Creek where it reached the Thames) and Samuda Brothers (just above the West India Docks) – dealt mainly with small boats. The other yards – Thames Iron Works, Thorneycroft and Yarrow (between the West India Docks and Samuda Brothers) – were of some size though the latter two were particular concerned with Admiralty orders for small and fast craft. Thames Ironworks, located on the eastern side of the mouth of the Lea in Blackwall, built the *Duncan* and *Cornwallis*, while the dockyard at Chatham built the *Albemarle* and brought all the members of the *Duncan* class into commission with the exception of the *Montagu*. Chatham also built the *Africa*, a *King Edward VII* class battleship, and Pembroke built the armoured cruiser *Warrior* between 1903 and 1907.

The latter year was when R. and H. Green, which had become a limited company in 1894 and thereafter concentrated on repair rather than building, launched its last ship. In 1907, too, Thorneycroft, which had been at Chiswick, moved to Woolston, on Southampton Water, while the following year Yarrow moved to Scotstoun on the Tyne. With Samuda Brothers having gone into voluntary liquidation in 1892, Thames Iron Works was the last major shipbuilding yard on the Thames, but while she received an Admiralty order for the construction of an armoured cruiser which was laid down in June 1903, she did not receive an Admiralty order for a battleship after 1899 until 1909, and perhaps not surprisingly so. The yard had its fair share of the bad industrial relations that plagued many of the Thames yards, and indeed this was one of the reasons why so many yards left the area – to go to places such as Newcastle and Glasgow, where industrial relations, of course, were so much better. The *Cornwallis* proved a disaster, being more than 55 months under construction. The *Thunderer* was Thames Iron Works' last order, and was completed in a very reputable 26 months, but within a matter of weeks of her being completed in 1912 the yard closed. Portsmouth and Devonport continued to serve as major dockyards until the 1970s, but in terms of the construction of major units they did not long survive Thames Iron Works as the building of major warships in Britain switched exclusively to Belfast, Glasgow, Barrow, Birkenhead and the Tyne: none of the thirteen capital ships ordered and completed after 1913 were built in naval dockyards.[16]

The second comment regarding Fisher and the *Dreadnought* is more difficult to make: it poses a question which can be easily put but is extremely hard to answer because of the complexities of the issue it raises. The building of the *Dreadnought* has indeed commanded much acclaim, particularly on behalf of Fisher, and most of it has been uncritical. But the appearance of the first volume of Arthur Marder's *From the Dreadnought to Scapa Flow*, with its slavish worshipping of Fisher by an author who was hooked on the Carlyle portrayal of history as the deeds of great men, brought a withering review which made one crucial and salient point: if the construction of a dreadnought battleship was inevitable, then any claim for credit for the *Dreadnought* herself must rest either in her design or the timing of her construction.[17]

It is impossible to escape the logic of this observation, and the best that can be said is that the case for Fisher cannot be made to his advantage on either count. The design of the *Dreadnought* was much inferior to the *Michigan* class, which pre-dated the *Dreadnought*, at least in terms of when its ships were ordered, while the design of the *Invincible*-class battlecruiser ensured that any claim in Fisher's favour could not be contemplated, much less substantiated. The problem, however, is that this particular argument does not begin and end simply with 1906, because it is tied up with the question of timing after 1906: the question of credit, or otherwise, relating to the design of the *Dreadnought* and *Invincible* cannot be divorced from the design of their follow-up classes, and here the evidence against Fisher is damning. It was not until 1909 that there was any major move beyond the basic design of the *Dreadnought* and *Invincible*. Admittedly, the *Neptune*, ordered in 1908, was the first British battleship to carry a superimposed turret, but the *Indefatigable* class of that same year was nothing short of wholly and totally inadequate, especially when set against Fisher's own pronouncements about its alleged worth. The *Indefatigable* class represented no real improvement over the *Invincible* class, and most certainly never represented the improvement that, for example, the German *Goeben* represented over the *Von der Tann* or the Japanese *Kongo* class represented over the *Tsukuba* and *Ikoma*, two comparisons which more or less cover the same time span represented in the two British classes. In fact, criticism of Fisher on this particular point can be made quite simply and very bluntly: the *Indefatigable* class represented one of the worst classes, if not the worst class, of capital ship laid down before the First World War, and represented the totally irresponsible squandering of the lead that had been won by the rushing of the *Dreadnought* to completion in fourteen months.

This question, that of timing, remains especially difficult because there are two quite separate parts to any attempt to deal with the issues raised by it. The first concerns the situation which prevailed in 1905–1906, and it has been rightly noted, by many commentators, that the *Dreadnought* created a level playing field. Indeed, even at the time of the *Dreadnought*'s construction, many of Fisher's critics made the point that the effect of the ship was to demean the existing British superiority over all other nations. This was true, but it was also irrelevant. If a dreadnought-type ship was inevitable, then that British lead over the rest of the world was going to be written off in any event, yet in 1905 that British lead over the rest of the world was in the process of being written off anyway. The British margin of superiority existed primarily in terms of older ships since by 1904–1906 Britain was no longer able to out-build virtually any combination of powers as she had in the period 1889–1899. The value of these older ships was very limited indeed: the units of the *Royal Sovereign* class, laid down between July 1889 and February 1891, were by 1904–1906 fit only for guardship and reserve duties. Moreover, if the criticism is made that the *Dreadnought* effectively wrote off Britain's margin of superiority over the rest of the world, then mention must be made of the ships under construction in the years 1904 to 1906.

It was noted at the time that the battleships *Lord Nelson* and *Agamemnon*, the four armoured cruisers of the *Warrior* class and the three armoured cruisers of the *Minotaur* class which were under construction when the *Dreadnought* was rushed to completion were immediately degraded, their value overtaken, by the newcomer. This was true enough, though the inclusion of the armoured cruisers in any list of comparisons is neither helpful nor enlightening: they were not fit to lie in the line and should never have been considered in the same breath as the *Lord Nelson* and *Dreadnought*. But the *Dreadnought* also wrote down all those non-British battleships under construction in 1904–1906, and these ships, had they been completed in the normal way, would have destroyed Britain's relative position: she would not have been capable of maintaining herself at a two-power status beyond 1907. There were some 30 American, Austro-Hungarian, French,

German, Italian, Japanese and Russian battleships being built in these years, and in counting these units the value of the *Dreadnought* cannot be gainsaid. The *Dreadnought* cost Britain two battleships under construction, and also three members of the *King Edward VII* class, the completion of which had been much delayed, while in effect costing the other naval powers those 30 units: this, one would suggest, represented a clear gain for Britain

But the question of timing cannot be divorced from its second constituent part: the use to which the advantage that Britain secured with the *Dreadnought* was put. Here, of course, the evidence is damning, most obviously in the form of the 1908–1909 and the 1909–1910 naval estimates. The *Dreadnought* was followed in the 1906–1907 programme by the *Bellerophon*, *Superb* and the *Téméraire* and in the 1907–1908 programme by the *Collingwood*, *St. Vincent* and the *Vanguard*. One would suggest that, since Britain had secured a very real advantage of timing with the building of the *Dreadnought*, then certainly one, if not both, of these two programmes should have represented complete divisions and really needed to number four dreadnoughts, not three. But even if this point is not accepted, then the 1908–1909 programme, which numbered just the *Neptune* and the battlecruiser *Indefatigable*, surely represented a squandering of any advantage and for no useful purpose. The inadequacy of these three programmes between 1906 and 1908 was to be acknowledged in the 1909–1910 programme and the infamous 'We Want Eight' campaign.

One of the little-known aspects of the 1909 naval crisis in Britain was the fact that, as originally proposed, the 1909–1910 naval estimates set out a programme of four capital ships for the current year and the provision for an acceleration of another programme of four ships for the 1910–1911 programme. The purpose of this provision was to ensure that Britain could face down any numerical challenge presented by the Imperial German Navy, but, inevitably, it was overtaken by events – in the form of a crisis largely manufactured by the gutter press and Conservative Party – and in any case it would have been largely unnecessary had the 1908–1909 programme been anything more than a single dreadnought. The crisis of March 1909 arose from the mishandling of construction programmes from 1906 onwards which had very largely dissipated the hard-won lead conferred by the *Dreadnought*. As it turned out, the British government made the extra four capital ships from the 1910–1911 programme part of the 1909–1910 programme, although this programme, along with dominion additions, actually numbered ten capital ships. But the fact remained that the original 1909 programme was only for four ships, never four plus four, and most certainly never eight.

The problem with this particular aspect of the *Dreadnought*'s construction is the allocation of responsibility, and clearly this cannot be fixed solely at Fisher's door. The programmes of 1906–1907 and 1907–1908, in that they represented reductions from programmes of four battleships, reflected the coming into office of a Liberal administration committed to economy: the 1908–1909 programme reflected that same administration's need, or desire, to make some form of gesture in advance of the forthcoming disarmament conferences at The Hague. In the final analysis, the Liberal administrations of Campbell-Bannerman and Asquith must take responsibility for these programmes and their reduction from prudent levels, and the fact that three years of reduced programmes were followed by a construction programme of unprecedented size was a scathing indictment of their conduct of the nation's naval affairs between December 1905 and December 1908. Asquith's personal responsibility for this political debacle is self-evident, but Fisher nonetheless went along with these programmes without dissent and was a willing accomplice, just as he was one of the worst alarmists in 1909.

Perhaps only one thing can be said with certainty about this whole issue. The great tragedy was that Fisher was retained as First Sea Lord after 1906, when he had clearly outstayed his welcome, and thereafter contributed nothing of value but was a profoundly disruptive and negative influence. This is admittedly not a view which has attracted much interest, still less support. But it is difficult to identify any single act or policy after 1906 that was of benefit to the Royal Navy and Britain as a result of Fisher's being retained at the Admiralty, and there were many matters – most obviously his conduct of personal vendettas and his emasculation of the newly formed staff which he would never accept should wield powers he was determined to reserve for himself – in which Fisher's influence was baleful, to say the least. That point being noted, one must note its rider: many of the people with whom Fisher did battle after 1906, most obviously Beresford and Custance but others as well, were not individuals who should themselves attract much in the way of sympathy. Be that as it may, the basic conclusion would seem to hold good. Perhaps very appropriately in many ways, Fisher's time as First Sea Lord can be likened to the *Dreadnought*: major initial impact but thereafter effect not necessarily as intended.

With the *Dreadnought*, and especially with her being rushed to completion in little more than a year, Fisher hoped to paralyse foreign construction. In very large measure this hope and expectation was realised: every nation lost in terms of numbers (ships under construction) and timing (the placing of new orders). But whatever advantage Britain hoped to gain with the *Dreadnought* began to ebb away once her details were announced, once she was launched or once she was complete, although exactly when this happened is impossible to determine. The point, however, was that with the construction of the *Dreadnought*, it was inevitable that all the major European powers, and some of the lesser ones such as Greece, Spain and Turkey, would attempt to secure for themselves such ships: the dreadnought was a status symbol in a way that no other ship had been, and her appeal even extended into South America, where Argentina, Brazil and Chile vied with one another, in the form of foreign orders, for possession of warships which were seen as proof of national welfare and vitality.

Within Europe the following of the *Dreadnought*'s lead gave rise to obvious and immediate rivalries, between Austria-Hungary and Italy, Greece and Turkey, and, less obviously, France and Italy and Germany and Russia. But all these were overshadowed by the rivalry that developed between Britain and Germany, and the naval race which added its dose to the poison which affected European relationships prior to 1914. Certainly, on the British side any reading of the popular press in these years leaves a distinctly distasteful impression: the navalist lobby was closely associated with the Conservative Party, for which no matter, however mean or irrelevant, was not too small to be used for party gain, albeit cloaked in the habit of national, imperial or naval respectability: any casual consideration of the press treatment of the loss of the pre-dreadnought *Montagu* on 30 May 1906 prompts the thought that for some this incident seemed to put the very existence of nation and empire on the line. The intemperance of argument and expression in the press bordered on the hysterical throughout this period, and could not have helped the devising of national policy.

Much of the public and press agitation that made up the 'We Want Eight' mani-fested itself in the first quarter of 1909, and the reason for this, and the exact pro-cess whereby the crisis burst upon the Liberal government, is but little understood. The reason lay immediately in terms of the British and German 1908 pro-grammes, the British ordering one battleship (the *Neptune*) and one battlecruiser (the *Indefatigable*) while the Germans made financial provision for no fewer than four battleships, the largest dreadnought programme to date. At this particular time, 1908, Britain had ordered eight dreadnoughts, as had Germany. The lead which had been obtained by the rapid construction of the *Dreadnought* was on the brink of being lost, and one suspects that a second factor was at work, though one cannot prove the point: one suspects that the public, and probably many of the pundits, did not include battlecruisers in their calculations about national power. Nevertheless, as the debate within the Liberal government over the form of the 1909 estimates began, the initial intention of the administration was, of course, to authorise the construction of four capital ships in 1909 and to make provision whereby the four which would be ordered under the 1910 estimates might be laid down at the very start of the 1910–1911 financial year in order to 'gain' a year in construction time. What the Liberal government in effect chose to do was to adopt a programme over a number of years, basically four capital ships a year, and in that way maintain what should have been the numerical advantage gained by having built the *Dreadnought*.

At best this would have seemed to be a policy which worked upon very small margins, and most assuredly it did not constitute much of a response after the German 1908 programme.[18] Certainly, the Liberal proposal left its authors wide open to attack, and very unfortunately the publication of the estimates, and the first parliamentary debates on them, came at the time when the Bosnia-Hercegovina crisis broke with the German ultimatum to Russia that, unless the latter dropped her objections to Austria-Hungary's annexation of these territories, Germany would stand aside and let matters take their course. The Admiralty's calculations, which rather leave the impression of 'situating the appreciation' about German naval construction times, were discussed with Asquith over the same weekend as Britain became aware of the German move relative to Russia, and the conclusion drawn in the Admiralty calculations was basically correct: there would be a time, in 1912 or 1913, when the British margin of superiority over Germany in capital ships would be most modest.

Accordingly, the Liberal intention was changed. The idea of a programme spread over a number of years was abandoned, and the four 1910 capital ships were moved into the 1909 estimates but only on a provisional basis: the extra ships would be ordered as part of the 1909 estimates if the need for these ships was demonstrated. The catch was that the Liberal government could not afford to acknowledge what was tantamount to an admission that past programmes had been less than adequate and that its original 1909 proposals were being ditched. The Conservative opposition, in Parliament and the press, was afforded a field day, while the losers, the real losers, were the economist and peace factions within the Liberal government. The events of March-April 1909 were very much the acid test for these groups, which were largely excluded from the decision-making process: they were confronted by having to make a choice inside Parliament, and they had no place to go and certainly had no basis for any understanding with the Conservatives. As for Asquith and the ministers of his government, once they moved from the original proposal for a programme spread over a number of years, they had no position on which to try to stand against the demand that the 'extra four' be considered part of the 1909 programme. They tried to play the 'four plus four' card but were very quickly forced to acknowledge that the additional four units would be part of the current (1909) programme, and further embarrassment was heaped upon the hapless government as a result of dominion generosity, with Australia and New Zealand taking responsibility for the cost of battlecruisers that would bear their names. The British 1909 programme represented the largest peace-time capital ship programme ever put together by any country, and was exceeded only by wartime American programmes.[19]

The Anglo-German naval race in effect was decided in 1909, the rider being that Britain at this stage in effect abandoned the old two-power standard in order to make direct comparison with Germany. In this there was an irony, albeit one that is seldom appreciated: in August 1914 Britain, by adding to her own strength the battleships then being built in British yards for foreign countries, was in possession of a two-power standard. In that month, Britain had 22 dreadnoughts, nine battlecruisers and 40 pre-dreadnought battleships. The next two most powerful navies in the world were those of Germany and the United States. Germany was possessed of fifteen battleships and five battlecruisers, plus 22 pre-dreadnought battleships, while the United States had ten dreadnoughts: no other country had more than three dreadnoughts in service at this time.

Regarding the battleships and battlecruisers that were built in this period, both British and German and those of other navies, there were three aspects that should be noted. These were the general increase in size of capital ships, the increase in the number and size of guns, and the increase in the size of engines. The battleship increased in size by half in some eight years, from a design legend of 18,110 tons and a full load displacement of 21,845 tons with the *Dreadnought* to a design displacement of 31,400 tons and a full load displacement of 33,000 tons with the units of the *Pennsylvania* class. The 527-ft/161.16-m length of the *Dreadnought* had increased to the 645.75-ft/197.48-m length of the *Queen Elizabeth* class, while Japan, with her first dreadnought battleship class laid down in 1912–1913, produced in the *Fuso* and *Yamashiro* warships of 662.83 feet/202.7 metres with a full load displacements of 36,500 tons. With twelve 14-in/356-mm guns carried in six twin turrets, two amidships, these two battleships were a match for anything built in Europe or the United States, and the two classes that followed, the *Hyuga* class of 1915 and the *Nagato* class of 1917–1918, showed successive increases of length and displacement and qualitative improvement, especially in the provision of horizontal armour. For their part, the battlecruisers, given their need for high speed, were both longer and displaced more than battleships of the same year: the *Tiger*, ordered under the 1911 estimates and completed in October 1914, had a full load displacement of 35,160 tons and was over 700 feet/214-m in length, while the *Renown* and *Repulse*, laid down some three months after the *Tiger* entered service, were just shy of the 800-ft/245-m mark.

Scarcely less dramatic was the change of main armament, specifically the employment of all turrets on centre line and the widespread use of superimposition after 1909. This was to change silhouettes massively, but perhaps even more obvious was the move to triple turrets, both Italy and Russia in 1909 laying down their first dreadnoughts with twelve 12-in guns carried in four triple turrets. Both countries were content to have single turrets covering the forward and astern arcs of fire, the twelve guns being intended for broadside fire, and for both countries the great advantage of the triple turret was the concentration of firepower on modest dimensions, the *Dante Alighieri* being only 517.97 feet/158.4 metres in length, the *Gangut* 587.95 feet /179.8 metres. Inside another three years the next step had been taken, at least on the drawing boards, with the French having decided that the three members of the *Normandie* (1912) class were to carry twelve 13.4-in/340-mm guns in three quadruple turrets, each of which was subdivided in two to localise damage. By 1913 the French had gone another step with the *Lyon* class, which was to be authorised and ordered in 1915. With the 557.86

feet/170.6 metres and 24,832 (design) tons of the *Normandie* class giving way to the 621.3 feet/190 metres and 29,600 (design) tons of the new class, the *Lyon* and her three sister ships were to have carried sixteen 13.4-in guns in four quadruple turrets. The demands of fighting the First World War meant that French ambitions with both classes had to be abandoned, which perhaps was a blessing in disguise for the French navy: by 1913–1915 the 13.4-in gun was in very real danger of being left behind in terms of future building programmes, while the midships turret that both classes were to carry proved something of a liability for the Russians and Italians, though their problems were in part the result of these ships carrying not one centrally placed turret but two.

The increase in size of main armament gun, from the 12-in/305-mm 45 calibre in British service in 1905 to the 15-in/381-mm 42 calibre in 1914, via the 13.5-in/343-mm 45 calibre of the 1909–1911 classes, were matched abroad, the Japanese with the *Kongo* beating the Americans to have the 14-in/356-mm guns in service and then moving, with the *Nagato* and *Mutsu*, to the 16-in/406-mm gun for their main armament. What these changes meant in terms of weight and range was considerable. The 12-in gun of 1905, which was capable of firing a 850-lb/385-kg shell to a range of 19,000 yards/17,430 metres, was replaced by the 13.5-in/343-mm gun, which could fire a 1,400-lb/635-kg shell to ranges of 23,800 yards/21,830 metres , the change from the 12-in to the 13.5-in gun being marked by an increased elevation of guns from fifteen to twenty degrees. The British 15-in gun, introduced primarily because Japan and the United States were known to be building battleships with 14-in guns and Krupp had listed three different 14-in gun barrels in its repertoire, was capable of firing a 1,920-lb shell to a maximum range of 35,000 yards/32,100 metres, at least in trials, and in fact the gun was adopted by the British Admiralty without trials because in 1912 it was believed that Britain could not afford the loss of one whole year by making such a gun just for trials. Initially, the *Queen Elizabeth* class were considered in terms of having ten 15-in guns housed in five twin turrets, i.e., an *Iron Duke* class with larger main armament, but it was quickly realised that eight guns in four turrets still provided for a greatly increased weight of broadside compared to the 13.5-in gun yet also allowed extra space and weight to be afforded to machinery.

Thus the *Queen Elizabeth* was designed for 25 knots – for which she was considered to need 75,000 hp compared to the 30,040 hp needed to provide the *Iron Duke* class with 21.6 knots – and for use as a fast battleship, though in the event it seems that 24 knots was the best obtained by any of the five members of this class. The very considerable increase of power needed to obtain high speed can be gauged by reference to the *Tiger*, which was originally designed for 85,000 hp and 28 knots, in line with the other three members of the 'Splendid Cat' class. It took another 23,000 hp to obtain another one more knot, the *Tiger* being given Brown-Curtis as opposed to Parsons turbines. Even more significantly, she would have been given small-tube boilers if the celebrated director of naval construction Sir Eustace Tennyson D'Eyncourt had been able to force his views on subordinates and the shipyards: it has been estimated that had the *Queen Elizabeth* and *Tiger* been given small-tube boilers, then they would have been able to make 28.5 and 32 knots respectively, but such a change was too radical and the naval use of small-tube boilers for capital ships had to await the straitened circumstances of Washington and the limitation treaties. As it was, just one point may be made to conclude this section and to note the extent of change. The *Tiger* was the first warship with engines with more than 100,000 hp, and she was laid down in June 1912 and was completed in October 1914: at the time when they were built, between 1906 and 1908, the three members of the *Invincible* class, with turbines with designed to produce 41,000 hp, carried the largest and most powerful engines afloat.

Four other developments accompanied the various changes which took place between 1905 and 1913, and the *Queen Elizabeth* class was involved in one of them, namely the switch to coal to oil. As noted elsewhere, the first oil-fired battleship was the *Rostislav*, which entered service in 1899, and why the tsarist navy did not persist with such an arrangement, which clearly was years ahead of their time, is not clear: the *Barham, Malaya, Queen Elizabeth, Valiant* and the *Warspite* were thus the first class of battleships to be spared the ordeal of coaling, though many in the Royal Navy regarded the end of this necessary evil to have been profoundly unfortunate. In the 1930s, when the Royal Navy was experiencing problems of morale and discipline, the end of coaling – significantly, an operation in which both officers and men had to work physically side by side – was deemed to have been a factor in the disenchantment of the lower deck. Be that as it may, oil ended the problems of variations in quality that coal could bring and also resulted in an absence of smoke that compared most favourably with the dense clouds emitted by coal-burning ships at high speed.

The second development was the fact that after the *Dreadnought* all nations followed the British lead in adopting turbine propulsion, the British also leading the way by the adoption, with the *Neptune*, of cruise turbines, in order to reduce fuel consumption at low and medium speeds. The United States, with its second dreadnought programme, provided the *Delaware* (1906 authorisation) with two four-cylinder, triple-acting expansion engines and the *North Dakota* (1907) with two Curtis turbines, and thereafter adopted turbines for the *Florida* (1908) and *Wyoming* (1909) classes before reverting to reciprocating engines with the *New York* (1910) class. The *Nevada* class (1911) repeated the 1906–1907 division with the nameship being provided with turbines and the *Oklahoma* earning the unwanted distinction of being the last American battleship to be built with reciprocating engines. The *Oklahoma* was never converted and she retained her original engines, which made her the slowest battleship in the American navy, until the time she was sunk, at Pearl Harbor on 7 December 1941. For their part, the Japanese provided the *Satsuma* with two triple-acting expansion engines, built in Japan, and the *Aki* with Curtis turbines, courtesy of the Fore River Company of Massachusetts. Thereafter, all Japanese capital ships were equipped with turbines, the *Settsu* and *Kawachi* being afforded turbines built in Japan under licence from Brown-Curtis.

The first Austro-Hungarian, French, Italian and Russian dreadnoughts – namely the members of the *Viribus Unitis* and *Courbet* classes, the *Dante* and the members of the *Gangut* classes – were all afforded turbines: obviously these states, picking up the dreadnought bill later than others, were able to move only when the value of turbines in a major warship had been proven. The German practice, however, was somewhat less than consistent. Various German writers have suggested that the German Navy, and Tirpitz specifically, were not in the least surprised by the *Dreadnought*,[20] yet the lack of any coherent response in 1905 and 1906 and then the building of an armoured cruiser, the *Blücher*, in mistaken anticipation that the three *Invincible*-class units were similar ships would seem to indicate that the German Navy was caught just like all the others. In the matter of propulsion, the German failure to anticipate the British move would seem to be obvious. While the first German battlecruiser, the *Von der Tann*, and all which followed her were given turbines, the first two classes of battleship, comprising eight ships overall, were provided with reciprocating machinery. It was not until the *Kaiser* class that the Germans adopted turbines for their battleships, but whereas her four sister ships from this class were provided with three turbines, the *Prinzregent Luitpold* was to have been afforded only two with a central six-cylinder, two-stroke diesel engine, which was never fitted. Two members of the subsequent *König* class, the *Grosser Kurfürst* and *Markgraf*, were also to have sacrificed one turbine for a diesel producing 12,000 hp and a cruising speed of 12 knots, but this intention was abandoned and the ships were completed with three turbines. By 1913–1914 the geared and the electrical turbine were being touted as the propulsion of the future, but the outbreak of war, rather than placing such innovations on hold, may well have hastened their introduction: the geared turbine was used to power the three British hybrid cruisers *Courageous*, *Glorious* and the *Furious*, and the *California* and *Tennessee*, laid down in 1916 and 1917 respectively, were the first battleships to use electrical transmission in their engines.

The third development concerned underwater protection and torpedo armament. As far as the latter was concerned, the British moved from the 18-in/457-mm to the 21-in/533-mm torpedo with the 1909 *Colossus* class, though such an armament, in a battleship, was increasingly anachronistic. Other navies nonetheless followed the British example, with the exception of the Imperial Japanese Navy: the *Kongo* class battlecruisers, with the nameship built in Britain, carried a torpedo armament, but none of Japan's dreadnoughts were so fitted. At very best, such an armament was marginal to requirements and at worst a liability, and it is perhaps worth noting that the worst of the damage sustained by the German battlecruiser *Lützow* at Jutland in 1916 was the result of two shells hitting the torpedo compartment with such destructive effect that the whole of the forward part of the ship, forward of A turret, immediately filled with sea water.

It has, of course, been suggested that the *Hood* was lost in 1941 after being hit by a shell which detonated torpedoes with the result that the ship's back was broken, although the standard interpretation of her loss remains that the *Hood* was struck by a shell or shells which penetrated to her aft magazine. In terms of defensive arrangements, the lack of protection for battlecruiser magazines had first been raised as a major source of concern at the time the *Indefatigable* and her dominion sister ships were built, and this remained a major source of concern with respect to all British battlecruisers throughout their lifetime: the scale of protection afforded these ships was totally unbecoming such large and expensive units, the *Lion* being the first ship to cost more than £2,000,000. In fact, armour protection probably represents one of the major weaknesses of British design and construction efforts: it was almost as if the building of the *Dreadnought* released the Admiralty from any obligation of continuous development in this area. Admittedly the *Bellerophon* class, laid down in 1906–1907 and the immediate successors to the *Dreadnought*, were the first battleships in any navy to be afforded anti-torpedo bulkheads, but there are two basic points to be made about British measures.

First, it would seem that just as there was no move from the 4-in to 6-in guns for the standard secondary armament until Fisher left the Admiralty, so there seems to have been little in the way of improvements in protection and subdivision until he had retired. Indeed, there was definite regression between 1906 and 1909: in terms of protection relative to size, the *Colossus* and *Hercules* were probably less well provided defensively than had been the *Dreadnought*, while there is no doubt about this matter with the *Indefatigable* relative to the *Invincible*. Second, with the restriction on beam because of the size of existing docks, British ships most definitely were less well protected than their German opposite numbers, which had anti-torpedo bulkheads running the full length of boiler and engine rooms and magazines, and coal bunkers spread over as great an area as possible: no British battleship between the *Colossus* and *Iron Duke* classes, and no British battlecruiser, was provided with anti-torpedo bulkheads. One suspects that the reason for such neglect of defensive arrangements was a combination of the British belief in offensive action as the best protection – a belief which was very convincing until experience and reality intruded – and considerations of cost. To have provided the *King George V* and *Iron Duke* classes with 6-in as opposed to 4-in guns would, for example, have required more than 2,000 additional tons, and the cost of such provision, coming on top of average costs of £1,960,000 and £1,891,000, would have meant that these ships would comfortably have exceeded the £2,000,000 mark. Proper sub-division and protection could not have come much cheaper, and here, one suspects, was the real reason for this relative weakness in British capital ships.

The fourth and last development concerned fire control positions, though in effect this really began with another aspect of the *Dreadnought*: masts. The *Dreadnought*, all glowering menace when viewed from off the beam, possessed a single tripod mast, reversed and located behind the first funnel, an arrangement which rendered the fire control position close to untenable because of smoke and heat. With the *Bellerophon* class came major change in the form of two, not one, tripods, and aesthetically a much more pleasing, balanced, profile. More practically, the forward tripod was placed in front of the first funnel, but the second tripod, placed between the first and second funnels, was home to a control position that once again was untenable. With the *Colossus* and *Hercules*, the second tripod mast was eliminated and the mast was placed, as it had been in the *Dreadnought*, directly behind the first funnel. With the *Orion* and her sister ships, which carried a centre-line turret amidships, the same arrangement was maintained, though in these ships the two funnels were closer than they had been in the *Colossus* and *Hercules*, with the result that the four ships of this class possessed perhaps the most impressive profile of all the dreadnoughts to date. With 1912 and the building of the *King George V*-class battleships, however, the Admiralty ran into one major problem in the form of the irascible Admiral Sir Percy Scott.

The man who more than any single individual represented the gunnery revolution brought to the Admiralty's attention the simple fact that the single-pole mast which was to be fitted to the battleships of this latest class would not be strong enough to support the director control system that he was at that time trying to persuade the Admiralty to install in British capital ships. (This matter is one that raises a host of issues which should be addressed but about which much has already been written.[21]) Trials had been conducted with the Scott system in the *Neptune* in 1911. These trials had been less than successful, but the Admiralty then decided to conduct trials with a new system, largely devised by Vickers, that was fitted in the *Thunderer* in late 1911. She conducted a series of trials with the new equipment in the spring of 1912, and then she and the *Orion*, which was not fitted with director control, conducted a series of trials in October and November of that year. Whether by design or not, the trials were conducted in difficult weather conditions, but the result was that the *Thunderer* outscored the *Orion* by a minimum of five to one and, equally significantly, seemed to concentrate even those shells that missed within a much smaller grouping than had her sister ship. Interestingly, one report noted that, given the rate of improvement that the *Thunderer*'s performance represented, 'our ships should be able to hit an enemy vessel when in action with the opening salvoes' – which, of course, was precisely what they failed to do in battle.[22]

As a result of these trials, the decision was taken that the battleships of the *King George V* class would be fitted with the Vickers system, which meant that all members of the class had to be refitted with enlarged and rigid support in the form of the tripod mast. The control top itself grew massively from this time. In the place of range-finders and rudimentary calculating systems, located in small and flimsy-looking positions perched halfway up a mast, came major housings, but not until 1914. The process of retro-fitting all existing dreadnoughts and battlecruisers was necessarily a long one, not complete by the outbreak of war, and in the event it was also linked to another development, which was the reduction in the size of wireless masts as a result of new and much more powerful radios becoming available for service in 1915.

All navies were similarly engaged in such developments, and their various efforts resulted in arrangements that were distinctive and different, none more obviously than the process by which the U.S. Navy came to adopt what amounted to its battleships' signature in the form of lattice masts, which actually proved remarkably tough and resilient. The point, however, was that by July 1914 no fewer than seven countries – namely Austria-Hungary, Britain, France, Germany, Italy, Japan and the United States – had dreadnoughts in service in their navies, while another power, Russia, was to bring into service four battleships before the year was ended. Apparently ten other countries sought to secure for themselves ships that would provide them with admission to a very exclusive naval club.[23] Four countries – Argentina, Brazil, Chile and Spain – did so, as did Australia, which paid for but then took ownership of a battleship ordered in Britain for the general purpose of operating under Admiralty orders. Malaya and New Zealand ordered and paid for one capital ship each, but in both cases the ship was a gift to Britain. Turkey managed to secure one battlecruiser, but under circumstances which were rather different to those that had been envisaged, while Greece, the Netherlands and Portugal all sought to acquire dreadnoughts, but in the overworked yards of Europe and the United States in the years immediately before 1914 their efforts proved unavailing.

Nonetheless it was a comment on the time that the Anglo-German naval race should have had legacies in various parts of the world. There was the German-Russian confrontation in the Baltic, while Japan and the United States were building primarily against one another. In South America, the traditional rivalries led to naval races between Argentina and Brazil and Argentina and Chile, and the construction of some remarkable warships. The *Minas Gerais* and *São Paulo*, ordered by Brazil from British yards in 1907, were the most heavily armed dreadnoughts in the world, being equipped when these ships were completed in mid-1910 with twelve 12-in/305-mm and twenty-two 4.7-in/120-mm guns. With the Argentinians going to the United States to provide themselves with two dreadnoughts to match those of their neighbour, Brazil in 1910 then ordered a third dreadnought, again from Britain and again, with twelve 14-in/356-mm guns, the most heavily armed dreadnought in the world at the time. In the event, this latter Brazilian order fell foul of mounting financial problems encountered by the South American state, and Brazilian interest in the *Rio de Janeiro* was abandoned in 1912. Redesigned and afforded fourteen 12-in guns, she was sold to Turkey as the *Sultan Osman I* but was acquired by Britain in August 1914 and served throughout the First World War as the *Agincourt*. In 1910, however, the Brazilian move had led Chile to order two dreadnoughts from Britain. Work on the second of these ships, which after several names settled upon that of *Almirante Cochrane*, began in January 1913 but was halted with the outbreak of war in Europe: Britain purchased the hull which was ultimately completed as the aircraft carrier *Eagle*. The other, under construction as the *Almirante Latorre* in August 1914, was acquired by Britain with the outbreak of war, and she is well suited to bring this story of dreadnoughts and the pre-1914 world to a close. She was commissioned into service as the *Canada*, and after the First World War, in April 1920 to be precise, she was delivered to Chile, where she remained in service until finally stricken in October 1958. The last of the five dreadnoughts that served in South American navies, in May 1959 she was towed to Yokohama and the shameful breaker's yard, the last surviving battleship from 'the mist that mingles Jutland with the might of Scapa Flow'.[24]

CHAPTER 3

The First World War

Over the last decade, the First World War has been afforded a level of historical attention which is perhaps unprecedented since the 1920s. The reasons for this are not exactly clear, though one suspects that the First World War was in effect eclipsed by the Second World War, which followed so quickly after and was so much larger than its predecessor, both geographically and in terms of ferocity and human tragedy. One also suspects that the First World War was never able to command much in the way of such attention after 1945, in part because of the Cold War and the fact that militarily the Cold War was the 'product' of the Second World War: it was not until the Cold War ended that the First World War was able to emerge from the shadows. Nonetheless, in many recent works on the First World War, there have been revisionist themes, and one would summarise these themes under three headings. First, the revisionist argument would state that generalship was unfairly considered in many of the works that became standard reading on the subject of the First World War, most obviously because it would have been impossible in the period between November 1914 and March 1918 to have acquired tactical mobility on the battlefield. Second, that when tactical mobility was restored to the battlefield, Allied generals showed how able they were in fighting the battles which broke German capacity and will to continue the war. The sum of these two arguments, therefore, would be that much of the criticism of generalship in the First World War has been misdirected. The third, and relatively new, line of revisionist argument has been along the lines that considerations of cost point to a German conduct of war which was vastly more efficient than that of Germany's enemies.

On the first matter, the attempt to exonerate high commands of responsibility for individual operations, however stupid they may have been, on such grounds is very dubious: a plea of mitigation may be entered but responsibility cannot be evaded, and one cannot but suggest that Third Ypres really does represent proof of the difference between genius and stupidity in the sense that genius has its limits. On the second matter, one would merely observe that the argument would suggest that Allied generals were able to learn from German example: it is much to be regretted, therefore, that Allied generals were not able to learn from their own errors. On the third matter, one notes such claims with contempt: so how much did the German invasion of Belgium cost? The cost was incalculable, and the obvious question is how many states hitherto neutral joined Germany after her violation of her treaty obligations and Belgian neutrality. The answer is two, the Ottoman Empire and Bulgaria, and certainly in the case of Bulgaria her intervention was occasioned by Balkan considerations, specifically her relationship with Serbia, and other factors were of no real account: likewise, one would have to exercise a certain care about assessing the reasons for Turkish involvement in the war after October 1914. To think that the views of neutrals can be dismissed without their being weighed on the scales is facetious, and the relevance of this point as regards the United States of America is self-evident. The United States experienced very real difficulties with Britain and France but, after the German invasion and occupation of most of Belgium, there was never any question of her breaking with these countries, or undertaking any action that might result in her being associated with Germany. That was the real price of the violation of Belgian neutrality for Germany, and it is not to be costed in terms of pounds, francs or marks.

Nonetheless, there are two counts on which one has a certain sympathy with the revisionist cause. The first is one to which only passing reference can be made, since to state the full argument would need a book in its own right. It is based upon the belief that so many of the histories which have sought to explain trench deadlock, the tactical impasse on the battlefield, in terms of the imbalances between strategic movement and tactical mobility and between defensive and offensive firepower have done no more than describe the battlefield. Deadlock in the First World War was not the result of imbalances of firepower and movement, size of armies, conditions of ground or technical factors affecting the conduct of operations. Deadlock was nothing to do with either the capacity of the powers to wage total war or even possession of the means to do so. It was about their willingness to wage total war, their willingness to continue to prosecute war despite the indecisiveness of battle, their hardening determination to fight to a finish in justification of the losses that had been incurred already – it was this that explains the phenomenon of trenchlock. It was the willingness of societies to fight on, despite and because of the elusiveness of success on the battlefield – a social cohesion and a failure, and perhaps an inability, of societies to collapse under the strain of total war that by rights should have destroyed them – that explains the deadlock on the Western Front during the First World War. Trench deadlock was a military phenomenon, but primarily it was a military reflection of a political and mental phenomenon.

The second count is the one relevant to capital ships. It is specific to Jutland and there are two basic aspects of this battle that demand the most careful consideration, not least because they are contradictory. The first is the view that this battle, fought in the North Sea on 31 May and 1 June 1916, represents the greatest victory ever won by the British Navy: Germany's decision to seek the elimination of Britain from the ranks of her enemies by an unrestricted submarine campaign against Allied and neutral shipping was the one decision that cost Germany the war because it brought into the war the one country, the only country, which could guarantee Britain and France against defeat. It was a decision that cost Germany all the advantages which accrued as a result of Russia's collapse in the course of 1917, and it was a decision that cost Germany whatever advantage which she still retained as a result of trade with various neutral countries since American power and influence was used to exert undue influence upon these same neutral countries in their dealings with Britain and France on the one side and the Central Powers on the other. Germany's recourse to an unrestricted submarine campaign against shipping represented the snatching of defeat from the jaws of victory, while for Britain and France it was a recourse that ensured them against defeat. The point, however, was that the reality of Jutland's decisiveness lay in pressing Germany upon so disastrous a course of action, the aftermath of the battle being a German realisation of the narrowness of the margin by which annihilating defeat had been avoided and that the *guerre de course* offered the only possibility of ensuring Britain's defeat.

In itself, this was a measure of Britain's victory at Jutland, and the evidence of this fact came on 21 November 1918 when nine battleships, five battlecruisers, six light cruisers and 49 destroyers and torpedo boats from the High Sea Fleet surrendered to the Grand Fleet in the Firth of Forth. The surrender of a battle fleet, without battle, was unprecedented, and it was the evidence of an overwhelming British victory at Jutland which had taken almost 30 months of war to reveal itself. The route between Jutland and the Firth of Forth may have been tortuous and stormy but it was nonetheless real and direct, and the relationship between the two sets of events cannot be denied.

The second aspect of the Jutland argument is the view that it was a battle that could not be won because, very like the battle on land, forces had become so large that they could not be defeated decisively or overwhelmingly in any single battle. This fact is critically important in explaining the deadlock on land. Armies sought victory in individual battles, but the reality was that armies had become so large, and no less importantly had strength in depth which enabled them to replace their losses with relative ease for some two or three years, that victory even in a campaign had become all but impossible. Generals sought to fight, and armies fought, the wrong type of battle, the type of battle that could no longer be won against individual armies which were numbered in hundreds of thousands and national armies with millions of men under arms. The same was more or less true for battle fleets, though arguably this was less important than basic changes in the exercise of command in battle.

One of the major problems in placing naval events during the First World War in some form of historical context is the fact that historical experience pointed firmly in the direction of the decisive battle, the battle of annihilation. For Britain, obviously, the example was Trafalgar (21 October 1805), though the example of this battle was, in national terms, most pernicious: the Nelsonian legend, and the arrogance which spawned 'splendid isolation', obscured the fact that the war at sea continued for nine more years after Trafalgar, at the end of which time Britain would have faced a French Navy as powerful as the French and Spanish Navies – not fleets – had been in 1805. But thereafter Navarino (20 October 1827), Sinope (30 November 1853), the battle of Haiyang (17 September 1894), Manila Bay (1 May 1898) and Santiago (3 July 1898) and, of course, Tsushima (27–28 May 1905) all conspired to point in the direction of what was very unusual at sea: overwhelming success in battle. Such battles as Quiberon Bay (20 November 1759), the Nile (1 August 1798) and Trafalgar had entered the British historical consciousness precisely because they were unusual in that they resulted in massive victories over enemies which were ranked as serious, major powers, in a way that the British victories won outside Camperdown (11 October 1797) and Copenhagen (2 April 1801 and 2–7 September 1807) clearly were not. Battle at sea had been for the most part occasional, and victories few and partial. The experience of the hundred years prior to Jutland, when there had been very few naval battles indeed, had pointed in the direction of comprehensive victories, and what should have been self-evident – that the opposing forces in these last few battles had been hopelessly mismatched – was not.

The problem for the British was that with the outbreak of war there was a wholly unrealistic expectation of, and demand for, easy, overwhelming victory at sea, for a Trafalgar repeated. But the basic conditions of battle had changed massively, even since Tsushima, and even more massively, of course, since Trafalgar. In the 111 years between that battle and Jutland warships had grown eight- or nine-fold. Warships in 1916 had freedom of manoeuvre denied the fighting ships of 1805 which could steer through no more than 230 degrees. The speed of capital ships at Jutland was some six to eight times faster than their counterparts at Trafalgar, and there simply was no comparison between weights of broadsides and destructive power. But – and here was the but – in terms of reconnaissance and communications the fleets of 1916 were scarcely better served than those of 1805 and, in many ways, were more badly served because of a proliferation of sources – light cruisers, submarines, seaplanes, airships and land-based aircraft – where previously there had been just the frigate. Freedom of movement meant that reconnaissance was no longer needed on a linear basis but on the basis of the square. The increase of speed necessitated vastly improved reconnaissance and accurate reporting because reaction time had been correspondingly cut. But flags and lamps were of limited value, perhaps only on a one-to-one basis within a squadron or division – though Jellicoe's signal for his fleet's deployment does seem to indicate greater capability than admitted here – and radio communications were primitive and unreliable. In short, there was a disharmony of capabilities which had emerged since the passing of the age of sail that few historians have recognised as critical to an understanding of what happened at Jutland.

Herein one moves to the 'other' aspect of Jutland which is seldom considered yet raises its strategic relevance. One has already noted, and one will note again, the basic point about the raising of a German battle fleet. The High Sea Fleet, and specifically its being vested with numbers and power second only to the British fleet, was part of a political calculation belied by events: Britain did not have to allow herself to be blackmailed into the concessions that Germany sought to exact from her. This result was disastrous for Germany in the period between 1900 and 1914: it brought into the ranks of her opponents the world's greatest naval, imperial and financial power. But once war began, a second disastrous aspect of German policy manifested itself almost immediately: the creation of a German fleet without reference to its numerical and geographical inferiority to its main enemy left that fleet wholly incapable of maintaining Germany's oceanic lines of communication, and the High Sea Fleet's desire for battle, which was not as important to Germany as the maintenance of a fleet-in-being, was no more than the minimum tactical response to a lost strategic cause.

In fact, the German fleet's position was even worse than all this suggests because, even if it managed to inflict a real defeat upon its British enemy in terms of numbers, there was still little that it could do in terms of the maintenance of sea-borne lines of communication and oceanic trade. Britain's strategic position astride Germany's sea-borne lines of communication with the world beyond Europe was the equivalent of a fleet, and one that could not be fought and defeated except under the most extreme of circumstances – a situation which certainly could not be anticipated before 1914, and indeed was not anticipated even in 1939. The crucial point about these various developments was the fact that the German Navy was built to an army formula in that it was seen in terms of national need, as an army was needed, and it was seen as an end in itself: in a very odd process, the German Navy really accorded with continental (i.e., military) rather than naval terms of reference.

The First World War, given the failure to achieve a decision on land in 1914, was a siege war. It was fought not on the scale of towns or cities but countries and alliances, and it was fought between central Europe and the rest of the world. It was a total war involving the waging of war by industrial, economic and financial means, and it was a war in no small measure decided by the capacity of the Allied powers to draw upon the manpower, foodstuffs, raw materials and manufactured produce of the world beyond Europe. It was primarily an European war, and if this definition is deemed unsatisfactory, then it could be defined as a war fought primarily in Europe and the Middle East which very briefly reached into parts of Africa and China, and which found expression in the Pacific, the Indian Ocean and South Atlantic in addition, of course, to European waters and the North Atlantic. It was a war which at sea really had but five theatres of operation.

The first of these theatres was the Baltic, where Germany held decisive advantages of numbers and position over Russia but to no real effect because this was a theatre where naval matters were clearly subordinated to those on land: it was not until the decision of the war had been reached, in 1917, that naval matters assumed significance in their own right. The only exception was the Russian coup in recovering three copies of the German Navy's code-book, the *Signalbuch der Kaiserlichen Marine*, along with the current key, from the light cruiser *Magdeburg*, which was lost after running aground in fog off the entrance to the Gulf of Finland on 26 August 1914. The second theatre was the Black Sea, where Russia generally held the upper hand and successfully conducted a series of amphibious landings until revolution undid the victory she had won in this theatre. The third was the Mediterranean, which was perhaps the most confused and confusing naval theatre of war and where no fewer than eleven navies served at different times. On the one side were the navies of Austria-Hungary, Germany and Turkey, and on the other side were the obvious five, or six: the navies of France, Russia, Britain, Italy and Greece, and also the United States of America. The remaining two navies were somewhat esoteric. For the first time since the Mongol invasions of Europe in 1222 and 1237, an Asian military organisation presented itself on a European battlefield in August 1917 in the form of two destroyer formations of the Imperial Japanese Navy: perhaps even more unlikely, in the very last days of the war a Brazilian force was based on Gibraltar, and in its only action on 10 November 1918 shelled American warships by mistake.

The fourth and fifth areas of operations, which overlapped, were the North Sea, and specifically the southern North Sea, and those waters which can best be described as British home waters and the eastern North Atlantic. These were the crucial areas of the war at sea, where its decision was reached. It was in the North Sea that three of the four major actions involving capital ships on one or both sides were fought – Heligoland Bight (28 August 1914), Dogger Bank (24 January 1915) and Jutland – and it was in British waters, which included the Channel, and the eastern North Atlantic that German submarines made the final, unrestricted effort after February 1917 in what proved to be a vain attempt to bring Britain to defeat. In all five areas battleships, both dreadnoughts and pre-dreadnoughts, served, even in the eastern North Atlantic and not just while in transit: British battlecruisers were based at Queenstown in August 1914 for a brief period and the American battleships *Nevada*, *Oklahoma* and the *Utah* were stationed at Bantry Bay in south-west Ireland for part of their time in British waters.

Battleships and battlecruisers served outside these areas, and generally their operations are little-known. The battlecruiser *Australia* was involved in operations at Suva in the Pacific before, with the elimination of potential threats to troop ships,[1] she joined the British Grand Fleet in home waters. Japanese capital ships served throughout the western Pacific, but most of the Japanese forward presence, on both Australian coasts, at Singapore, Mauritius and Cape Town, took the form of cruisers because the authorities in Tokyo were never prepared to allow their major units to be deployed outside home waters. Certain reference books state that the battlecruiser *Haruna* was damaged when she hit a mine which is assumed to have been laid by the German raider *Wolf*. The date is given as 1917 and the place the 'southern' or 'south-west' Pacific, but Japanese records do not provide either the date and place of the incident or the extent of the damage and repair.

Such matters, however, represented the small change of naval warfare, at least in the period before February 1917, and the fact was that in the two main theatres of war, the southern North Sea and the Mediterranean, the Allied powers held a major advantage over their respective enemies, over Germany in the southern North Sea and over Austria-Hungary and Turkey in the Mediterranean. This major advantage was one of position, which in effect left the warships and merchantman of the Central Powers without any external source of support on the high seas and with no place to go even if they were to evade Allied, primarily British, patrols. Yet there was another British advantage which told against German raiders on the high seas. With just one exception, the Panama Canal, wherever trade routes were forced to converge and move through restricted waters, there was a British naval station and coaling facility. The victories that had been recorded in the wars of the eighteenth century, when augmented by the gains of the nineteenth century, left Britain in a position to control international shipping routes in a way that reached beyond her strength as the possessor of the world's largest merchant marine and insurance system. In the war that began in 1914, it was the Allies' ability to bring the extra-European world to the European battlefields that was so critical to their final victory, and it was their ability to confine the activities of the High Sea Fleet and to contain the *guerre de course* that ensured victory in 1917–1918.

Battle: August 1914 to January 1915

In the war's first six months, four of its five major naval actions were fought, the exception being the battle of Jutland. Of these four actions only one, that fought off Coronel in Chile on 1 November 1914, did not involve battleships or battlecruisers. The British might have had in their order of battle a pre-dreadnought battleship, but she was deemed too slow to be of any real use, though it is just possible that the presence of the *Canopus* might have served to deter the German squadron and saved half the British force from destruction. As it was, the German force, with two armoured and three light cruisers, used the superior size and range of the main armament of the *Scharnhorst* and *Gneisenau* to sink their counterparts, the armoured cruisers *Cape of Good Hope* and *Monmouth*, while the light cruiser *Glasgow* and armed merchant cruiser *Otranto* escaped.[2]

The defeat off Coronel was a very minor matter yet it was greeted with howls of national anguish and shame, the vehemence and loudness of which were inversely related to its importance. The problem with the defeat was twofold – that it was unexpected and it came at a time when German raiders had been particularly active and had embarrassed Britain: the Admiralty was in fact proposing, as a response to German cruiser operations in the North Atlantic, to send the battlecruiser *Princess Royal* to the North American station, specifically to be present off New York. But the real point about Coronel was that the defeat should have been avoided because battle should have been declined until the concentration of all available forces had become possible: indeed, battle should never have been sought. Once the defeat was a reality, however, the British moved immediately to reverse it.

From the Grand Fleet, the battlecruisers *Invincible* and *Inflexible* were ordered to proceed to Devonport for minor refits and re-coaling before sailing on 11 November for a rendezvous with light forces being congregated off Abrolhos Rocks after the 17th. With the *Canopus* deployed to Port Stanley in order to deny the Germans easy or unopposed access to the Falklands base, the British battlecruisers arrived off Caravelas nine days later, and with light forces arrived at Port Stanley on 7 December. On the following morning, some ten minutes after the *Inflexible* had begun taking on coal, the German squadron appeared off the harbour, the German hope being to surprise a British force in the process of coaling. The German expectation was that such a force would consist of the *Canopus, Cornwall, Defence, Carnarvon* and the *Glasgow*, but faced with a force that included two battlecruisers, it was as clearly outclassed as had been the British force at Coronel five weeks previously.

It took the British force some three hours from the time that the German warships were sighted approaching East Falkland to close on the rear of the German line, and it was not until 1250 that the *Inflexible* fired for the first time at a range of 16,000 yards/14,700 metres, which was some 4,000 yards farther than she had ever fired in the past. At 1320, and despite not one hit being recorded by the British, the German formation divided, the *Scharnhorst* and *Gneisenau* turning to port to close the pursuing British warships while the *Dresden, Leipzig* and *Nürnberg* turned away in an attempt to escape. The *Cornwall, Kent* and the *Glasgow* turned in pursuit of the German light cruisers, the *Carnarvon* being so far astern she sought to catch up the battlecruisers rather than her own kind: the *Bristol* and *Macedonia* sought out the colliers *Baden* and *Santa Isabel*, and in an act of very considerable stupidity ensured their surrender, transferred their crews and prisoners and then sank two ships loaded with coal and provisions. The *Dresden*, with the *Leipzig* and *Nürnberg* between herself and the British cruisers, was able to escape, but the *Leipzig* was caught and slowed by the *Glasgow*, thereby enabling the *Cornwall* to come up. Between them, the two British cruisers shot the upperworks of the *Leipzig* to pieces, the light cruiser ultimately capsizing after her seacocks had been opened: eighteen of her crew were rescued and she sank at 2123. In the meantime, the *Nürnberg*, which might have outrun the *Kent*, suffered a double boiler failure and had no option but to give battle. In so doing, she hit the *Kent* with one shell that penetrated to the hoist, and the *Kent* may well have been destroyed had it not been for the access door to the hoist being slammed and the magazine thus isolated. This one incident apart, the hour-long exchanges favoured the *Kent*, the German light cruiser's funnels, guns and masts being shot away. It took another hour for the *Nürnberg* to sink (1927), just seven men being rescued from the sea and also from the flocks of albatross which descended on and killed the Germans in the water.

The main action unfolded at the same time, with the *Invincible* matched against the *Scharnhorst* and the *Inflexible* against the *Gneisenau*. At best, the British shooting left a great deal to be desired, the intention to fight at a range beyond that of the German armoured cruisers resulting in no more than three hits being recorded on the German ships in the first hour after fire was opened. Moreover, the German ships managed to turn away and break contact on occasion, but the superior speed of the British battlecruisers ensured that range could be closed and in mid-afternoon the German flagship, the *Scharnhorst*, turned toward the British ships as the range came down to 12,500 yards/11,450 metres. In broadside action between the two pairs of ships, the *Scharnhorst* was reduced to a wreck inside 30 minutes, her fires briefly shielding the *Gneisenau* as she sought to escape. The two British battlecruisers nonetheless quickly reduced the *Gneisenau* as well to a burning wreck, and indeed reduced her to such a state that the *Carnarvon* was able to join proceedings. The *Scharnhorst* sank at 1617 with no survivors, the British warships being forced to continue their action against the *Gneisenau*. The latter sank at 1802, some 200 of her crew being saved by British ships, though many died of hypothermia as a result of exposure in the icy South Atlantic.

The German defeat at the Falklands in effect brought to an end the German threat on the high seas. The last of the auxiliary raiders voluntarily sought internment in American waters in April 1915, but with the sinking of the *Scharnhorst*, *Gneisenau*, *Leipzig* and the *Nürnberg*, the real threat to Allied trade, possessions and cruiser units beyond Europe was passed, and the recall of more than twenty British warships to home waters immediately after the battle was an acknowledgement of this fact. The victory was certainly a vindication of the battlecruiser idea, or perhaps more accurately that part of the battlecruiser *raison d'être* which lay outside the battle line: the British victory was won because of weight of shell and the fact that British armour was able to withstand the fire of lighter German guns. The *Invincible* was hit 23 times, the *Cornwall* eighteen times, the *Glasgow* six times and the *Kent* no fewer than 37 times, but, the one hit on the *Kent* excepted, no real damage was done to British warships, which suffered just six killed and nineteen wounded.

In terms of avoiding serious damage, the British policy of seeking to engage the enemy beyond the latter's effective range but at the limit of the battlecruiser's was vindicated, the real cost being that the battle lasted much of one day and the *Invincible* and *Inflexible* fired nearly 450 tons of ammunition in the process. By the end of the action, the two British battlecruiser had all but emptied their magazines, and in terms of the fighting of the battle the British had little real cause for satisfaction. The German armoured cruisers consistently and successfully manoeuvred to keep the British battlecruisers to windward, thereby ensuring that the British ships were silhouetted whereas they remained wreathed in smoke, and added to the fact that the British battlecruisers were thus tactically worsted for much of the action, there was also the evidence that the German formation had missed its two opportunities of registering a success of some strategic significance. Its advance to the Falklands was so slow that it missed its real chance to secure Port Stanley before the British battlecruisers arrived in the South Atlantic, and on the morning of 8 December it passed up the opportunity to close Port Stanley and shell the British ships as they tried to leave the harbour and when they had very little opportunity to return fire. It must be noted, however, that the German formation turned away before it realised that the enemy formation included battle-cruisers, from which there could be no escape.

In a sense, therefore, the British victory in the South Atlantic in December 1914 stemmed not so much from a better system or tactics but from the fact that battlecruisers possessed armour which rendered them invulnerable to fire from an armoured cruiser other than at very short range, and they possessed a weight of fire which armoured and light cruisers could not withstand. In these respects, the Falklands action was the second of three battles in which the same factors manifested themselves. The battlecruisers' firepower had already accounted for the light cruisers *Ariadne* and *Cöln* on 28 August 1914 in the Heligoland Bight and was to account for the armoured cruiser *Blücher* off the Dogger Bank on 24 January 1915, and in both cases secured for the British victories that other aspects of their actions – specifically, both the planning and the conduct of their offensive operations – should have denied them.

The origins of the Heligoland action lay with the patrols mounted by both sides with the outbreak of war. On the British side there was from the outset of hostilities the imposition of distant blockade, close blockade having been abandoned in 1912 as a result of the realisation that its implementation, in the face of mine and submarine threats, was impossible. In August 1914 the British did not have the cruisers needed to put distant blockade into effect. This meant that some merchantmen were able to return to Germany while a number of raiders of various descriptions were able to reach into the North Atlantic. But distant blockade, in the form of three formations, was nonetheless put in place. These were the Channel Fleet, which originally had seventeen pre-dreadnought battleships and supporting cruiser and destroyer formations, at Portland,[3] the Grand Fleet, with 21 dreadnoughts, eight pre-dreadnoughts and four battlecruisers plus cruiser and destroyer formations, at Scapa Flow,[4] and the Southern Force. The latter, based at Harwich with the 1st and 3rd Destroyer Flotillas, the 8th ('Oversea') Squadron and the 7th Cruiser Squadron under command, was nominally part of the Grand Fleet but in practice it represented an independent command.

The 'Oversea' Squadron consisted of submarines assigned the scouting role in enemy waters, and from its various reports in the first two weeks of war it became apparent that the Germans were undertaking a systematic patrol effort, involving daylight and night patrols in the southern North Sea and specifically around Heligoland which were designed to prevent British submarine and minelaying operations. Accordingly, with German light cruisers escorting their destroyers to their patrol areas at night and then meeting them in the morning, a proposal was made on 23 August for light forces from Harwich to infiltrate the German positions under cover of darkness and then attempt to catch the German light cruisers and destroyers before they had any chance of being supported by other light forces making their way to their patrol zones. In its original form, the proposed plan called for the 1st and 3rd Destroyer Flotillas to be supported by the 1st Light Cruiser Squadron, and these in turn were to be supported by two battlecruisers. These were the *Invincible*, which had been stationed at Queenstown, and the *New Zealand*, which had been with the 1st Battle Cruiser Squadron at Scapa Flow. These two units, which on the day were supported by four destroyers, had been moved to the Humber in order to better support the forces at Harwich.

When the proposal was first considered, two changes were made. The British effort was to be directed against not light forces returning from night patrols but those beginning daylight patrols, and two submarine lines, both with three submarines, were to operate at the very edge of German patrol areas in the hope that German warships could be lured forward even as British formations moved between them and their bases: two more submarines were assigned to take station off the Ems in order to intercept any German warships that might try to put to sea. No less significantly, it was suggested that all the battlecruisers, and indeed the Grand Fleet, should be at sea in support of the Harwich formations, but this was rejected only for the full battlecruiser component, with all five units gathered in a single formation, to be assigned to this operation. In the casual and very unprofessional planning phase, which lasted all of four days, this latter decision was taken very late and was not forwarded to formations already en route to the Bight.[5]

The action which was fought on 28 August 1914 was a most curious affair, not least because the 31 British destroyers with the two lead flotillas seem to have played very little part in proceedings. Admittedly, the opening did involve a pursuit of German destroyers by one British division, but seemingly to no very great purpose, while the more important exchanges were clearly between the light cruisers. The *Arethusa* fought first the *Stettin* and then the *Stettin* and *Frauenlob*, and generally came off badly: the fact that she had been in commission for just two days and had never fired her guns told massively against her. One German destroyer, the V. 187, which came upon the scene was caught by two of the light cruisers, and in an attempt to escape ran into two destroyer divisions and was overwhelmed. At this stage there were various groups of destroyers pursuing one another through and around patches of mist, even Heligoland island, with no semblance of command, still less control of proceedings, while the British light cruisers' crossing of the submarine line at one stage resulted in an attempted ramming of E. 6 that, typical of this battle, was unsuccessful.

At the time when the V. 187 sank (0910), however, the *Stettin* reappeared, and soon after she was followed into the fray by the *Strassburg*, *Stralsund* and the *Mainz*. Initially, with the *Stralsund* having been chased by British light cruisers but coming full circle to take the *Arethusa* under fire, the *Mainz* stumbled across the same ship. Because of her damage, the *Arethusa* was being escorted from the scene of battle by the *Fearless*, which somehow does not seem quite right given that the *Fearless* was leader of the other flotilla. The *Mainz* had to deal with three British destroyers, all of which she left damaged: one, the *Laertes*, was left dead in the water. At this juncture two more German light cruisers, the *Cöln* and *Ariadne*, arrived on the scene, and the British position had become rather serious. But the *Mainz* had found herself in the company of two British light cruisers and suffered damage to her rudder, and she was then torpedoed and brought to a halt. Then, with the *Cöln* and *Stettin* coming into action and the *Ariadne* on the point of entering the battle, the battlecruisers arrived on the scene. The *Mainz* was subjected to passing attention as the *Cöln* was wrecked and the *Ariadne* sunk, the British battlecruisers then doubling back to deal with the *Cöln* even as she tried to drag herself out of harm's way.

At the final count the British sank three German light cruisers and one destroyer and inflicted damage, which ranged between light and extensive, on the light cruisers *Frauenlob*, *Strassburg* and the *Stettin* while not losing one ship of their own: the *Arethusa*, which broke down, was towed home by the armoured cruiser *Hogue*. In one very important sense the battle had a salutary effect on the Germans. At this stage of proceedings the German intent was to maintain the fleet-in-being role: the war was going to be decided in the battle of the frontiers, and the German Navy's importance lay in its diplomatic role when it came to the forming of the peace that would seal Germany's victory. The sense of having been caught on one's own doorstep was severe, and thus served to reinforce the natural caution of the moment. In this respect, therefore, the British achieved very real success, but the fact was that, despite the advantages of surprise and numbers, seven German light cruisers returned safely to port and four of these, *Stralsund*, *Kolberg*, *Danzig* and the *Hela*, were quite undamaged and the issue of the day had been very much in the balance until the battlecruisers put in their appearance. Moreover, their intervention was possible in very large measure because their opposite numbers were caught behind the sand bar on the Jade and, unable to proceed to sea until just before high tide, would not have been able to reach the scene of battle until 1500. In fact, the battle was over, and British units were withdrawing, by 1335, the British battlecruisers having appeared at 1256 – which was more than five hours after the battle had opened, and during which time the British light forces had registered minimal success. The real point, however, was that the inability of German battlecruisers – the *Seydlitz*, *Moltke* and the *Von der Tann* – to get to sea had not been anticipated in any of the British planning: it was merely something that happened, and the operation had not been timed in the knowledge that German battle formations would not be able to intervene.

The battle of the Dogger Bank, however, was much more simple and clear-cut. The failure to force a favourable decision in the battle of the frontiers, along with a decline of morale as a result of inactivity, forced the German naval high command to consider offensive action. Moreover, the realisation that the British had abandoned close blockade and therefore would not pursue a policy which presented maximum risk to their major units left the German Navy with no option but to undertake raids. These raids, it was hoped, would result in either individual or isolated formations being overwhelmed or major formations being drawn across submarine traps or minefields, the operational aim being to inflict disproportionate loss on British forces which would then enable the German fleet to seek battle on the basis of equality. The first German raid on the British coast, the obvious manifestation of this forward strategy, took place on 3 November 1914, but with the Grand Fleet now fully concentrated at Scapa Flow after a period in Loch Ewe while Scapa was properly readied as a base, the British policy was to decline any opportunity to seek battle in the southern North Sea. Thus the chance of any real contact, and hence action, between the major forces of the two sides was small: neither side had any intention of giving battle except under such favourable circumstances that the enemy was certain to decline whatever opportunity presented itself.

The immediate background to the Dogger Bank action was provided on 19 January 1915, when a German aircraft sighted British light forces conducting a sweep off the Bank. With the raid on Scarborough and Hartlepool (18 December 1914) and the sinking of the pre-dreadnought battleship *Formidable* by the submarine U. 24 in the English Channel (1 January 1915) bracketing the British seaplane raid on Cuxhaven (25 December 1914), German attention turned immediately to the idea of using the battlecruiser force to scatter and destroy enemy formations employed in such sweeps. Unfortunately for the Germans, rather like the British before Heligoland, the speed with which plans were turned into intention meant that U-boats could not be employed in support of their surface forces and one battlecruiser, the *Von der Tann*, which had been damaged in the Cuxhaven raid, was not available. Even more unfortunately for the Germans, the British knew of German intentions within two hours of orders being issued to the battlecruiser force. The German use of radio, and British access to German codes and ciphers, meant that German intent was compromised immediately, and as the Germans prepared to put the battlecruiser force off the Dogger Bank, so the British planned to have their battlecruiser and Harwich-based formations meet some 30 miles/48-km north of the Dogger Bank and some 180 miles/290-km west of Heligoland. These forces would be supported by the three battle divisions, plus supporting formations, of the Grand Fleet.

The British formations effected their rendezvous at 0800 on 24 January, and some fourteen minutes later, just before dawn, the *Kolberg*, the light cruiser leading the destroyer formation to port of the German battlecruisers, sighted one of her opposite numbers, the *Aurora*. Fire was exchanged, both ships being hit, and the German battlecruiser force, with the *Seydlitz*, *Moltke*, *Derfflinger* and the armoured cruiser *Blücher*, turned toward the sound of the guns. Before this formation had an opportunity to close upon the British cruiser and her destroyers, however, thick smoke was sighted to the north-west, and this could only mean either heavy or several enemy formations. The German formation therefore turned away, the *Blücher* being engaged by British light forces as it did so, but the German formation found itself limited to the *Blücher*'s 23 knots while the British battlecruisers were coming forward at 27 knots. It was not until 0952, however, that the leading British battlecruiser, the flagship *Lion*, opened fire at a range of 20,000 yards/18,350 metres and within a matter of minutes she was joined by the *Tiger* and *Princess Royal*. The target of all three British battlecruisers was the *Blücher*, which was hit for the first time at 1009.

Thick smoke drifting from the German ships across the line of sight made firing difficult for both sides. German fire was opened, on the *Lion*, at 1011 when the range had fallen to 18,000 yards/16,500 metres but it was not until 1028 that the *Lion* was hit, at which point the British abandoned line-ahead formation and adopted quarter line in an attempt to divide German fire. The three German battlecruisers continued to concentrate their fire on the *Lion*, however, while the British battlecruisers, following an order to engage the corresponding ships in the enemy line, managed to foul their fire distribution. What was intended was that the *Lion* should engage the *Seydlitz*, the *Tiger* the *Moltke* and the *Princess Royal* the *Derfflinger* with the *New Zealand* engaging the *Blücher* – the *Indomitable*, the slowest of the British capital ships, was yet to come within range. The *Tiger*, however, engaged the *Seydlitz*, and the British cause was not improved by the fact that the *Tiger*, which was a prison ship, seemingly failed to differentiate between her fire and that of the *Lion*. This was unfortunate because she was firing to a range some 3,000 yards/2,750 metres beyond the German flagship, and her choice of target also meant that the *Moltke* was not engaged by any British battlecruiser. By contrast, all three German battlecruisers concentrated their fire on the *Lion* and seemed to have no trouble in identifying their own fall of shot.

The result was that the battle divided into two separate actions, neither of which could be protracted. The *Blücher* took the fire of each and every British battlecruiser as these drew within range, yet very significantly the British battlecruisers recorded only three hits on their opposite numbers, one on the *Derfflinger* and two on the *Seydlitz*. In contrast, the *Lion* came under sustained fire and was hit a total of sixteen times: the only other British battlecruiser to be hit was the *Tiger* and she was hit six times, though damage was minor with one of the 6-in/152-mm guns disabled and the signals bridge destroyed. What happened to the *Lion* and *Blücher*, however, was altogether very different, and crucial to the unfolding and outcome of the battle. In the erroneous belief that submarines were ahead, the *Lion* led the British force on a north-east course across the wake of the German force (1102). As she did so, she was hit and very quickly her speed fell away to fifteen knots as the other battlecruisers swept past her. These, however, were given the orders, by flags, 'Engage the enemy's rear' and, Nelsonian drama permitting, 'Keep closer to the enemy', but at the same time the signal ordering the change of course was not lowered. The result was that the battlecruisers presumed the order meant that they were to engage the enemy on a north-east course, which was the *Blücher*. Accordingly, the pursuit of the main German units was abandoned and the British battlecruisers concentrated their combined attentions on an armoured cruiser which was slowing and whose course after 1048 was increasingly erratic.

At this stage of proceedings (1250), the British commander, Beatty, shifted his flag to the destroyer *Attack*, but by the time he was able to board the *Princess Royal* at 1320, the *Blücher*, having been hit an estimated 70 times by battlecruiser and light cruiser fire, had capsized and sunk (1310) and the main German force was beyond range. The speed with which Beatty was able to board the *Princess Royal* was largely the result of the fact that the British battlecruisers, knowing the *Blücher* to be doomed and content to leave her to the attention of light cruiser *Arethusa* and her destroyers, had turned back toward the *Lion*. By 1345 perhaps twelve miles/19 kilometres separated the battlecruiser formations, and with Heligoland eight miles/13 kilometres distant, there was no realistic prospect of the British force being able to regain contact, and the chase was abandoned. Though Beatty proposed to the Grand Fleet that the *Lion* be afforded a screen while his force made for Heligoland and a night attack (1430), this was rejected, and British attention thereafter seems to have been exclusively concentrated on the very difficult task of getting the *Lion* to safety. The *Indomitable* was responsible for most of the towing which resulted in the *Lion* reaching the Forth just before dawn on 26 January.

The image of the capsized *Blücher* is one of the most famous war photographs, and it was the basis of British claims of victory. With the *Lion* and *Tiger* and the light cruiser *Aurora* and destroyer *Meteor* the only British warships damaged, the balance of losses, as at Heligoland and off the Falklands, clearly favoured the British, and in the aftermath of this battle German policy, which was attended by the dismissal of the German fleet commander and his chief of staff, was decidedly cautious. But the real significance of the Dogger Bank action was threefold. First, it was very much like the Heligoland action with respect to the incompleteness of victory. The British, with superior numbers and advantages of speed and weight of broadside, proved unable to force battle on an enemy intent on escape, and the fact was that the greater part of the German formation escaped: the only German ship not to escape was the one which was incapable of escaping in the first place. That is a conclusion which may be a little unfair, but it is not inaccurate: sinking the *Blücher* was not an adequate substitute for victory. Second, the relevance of the battle for the future lay with the flagships, and for very different reasons. The *Lion* very narrowly escaped having the whole of the main engine room flooded, and as it was she lost the use of her port engine. The *Seydlitz*, however, very narrowly escaped destruction. One shell from the *Lion* penetrated the barbette armour of the rear turret and exploded. Flash rose through the turret and into the ammunition chamber and thence into its companion chamber and through the hoist into the second turret. The entire complement of the two rear turrets, a total of 159 officers and men, were killed but the ship was saved from destruction by the flooding of the magazines, and the lesson – one that was there from the experience of the *Kent* had the British been prepared to look – was learnt: in the aftermath of the battle, the Germans set about refitting all their capital ships with anti-flash protection. The British had to await the loss of three of their battlecruisers at Jutland before they did the same.

Third, and perhaps most importantly, the Dogger Bank action in effect brought to an end a very short period of German major unit activity, but it also brought to an end an unprecedented British vulnerability which the German plan of campaign had sought to create and then exploit to full effect. In November 1914 British strength, in terms of dreadnought battleships and battlecruisers and home waters only, was not greater than that available to the High Sea Fleet. In this one month, and either for part or the whole of the month, the Grand Fleet was without no fewer than nine of its battleships and battlecruisers. In addition, three of Britain's battlecruisers, or more accurately two plus the *Australia*, had never had been with the Grand Fleet: moreover, the *Audacious* had been lost and two of the units that had joined the fleet in September, the *Agincourt* and *Erin*, were not properly worked up and could not be included in any calculation of fully operational units. In fact, the number of capital ships with the Grand Fleet throughout November 1914 was just fourteen battleships and two battlecruisers, and of the battleships ten were first-generation dreadnoughts with 12-in main armament.[6] Perhaps even more pointedly, the total of sixteen battleships and battlecruisers was one fewer than the number nominally available to the High Sea Fleet in August 1914.[7]

The Dardanelles and matters Mediterranean

The Mediterranean, and by association the Black Sea, perhaps represent the most complicated and least well understood naval theatre in the First World War.[8] It was a theatre dominated by two matters, the Dardanelles and the Otranto barrage, with the campaign against Allied and neutral shipping providing the general link between individual episodes and events, certainly from 1916 onwards, and arguably from the spring of 1915, when German submarines were deployed to the theatre. The latter, and specifically the Allied counter-measures taken in response to their arrival, provide a story of baffling complexity, but it suffices to repeat a point made earlier and to raise one which was not – that in this theatre were no fewer than eleven navies, and this was a theatre of failure, most obviously as far as battleships and battlecruisers were concerned.

This general failure was not very obvious in the opening days of the war when failure was, or at least seemed to be, very specific. The outbreak of war found the German battlecruiser *Goeben* and escort light cruiser *Breslau* in the Mediterranean, and these were responsible for the bombardments of Philippeville and Bone on 4 August, i.e., before Britain entered the war. The French had no force that could hope to match the *Goeben*, but the British had with their Mediterranean Fleet the *Inflexible*, *Indefatigable* and the *Indomitable* of the 2nd Battle Cruiser Squadron, plus the armoured cruisers *Defence*, *Black Prince*, *Duke of Edinburgh* and the *Warrior* of the 1st Cruiser Squadron, and the light cruisers *Chatham*, *Dublin*, *Gloucester* and the *Weymouth*. As a result of a number of unfortunate decisions and poor judgements, the British battlecruisers failed to bring the *Goeben* to battle, and with the *Gloucester* losing contact with the German ships on 7 August, the German squadron arrived off the Dardanelles during the afternoon of the 10th. They were allowed to enter the Straits and pass into the Sea of Marmara, with the Turkish authorities having promised the Germans that any British attempt to pursue the ships would be resisted.

The whole episode provoked much public hand-wringing in Britain, much of it distasteful and not a little of it concerned with subsequent historical inaccuracy. The *Goeben* and *Breslau* became 'warships of history', the ships that brought Turkey into the war on the side of Germany and Austria-Hungary, an entry which had with obvious implications in terms of British and French links with Russia and Russia's trading links with the outside world through her southern ports. The *Goeben* and *Breslau* were certainly welcome to Turkey, which was deeply offended by the British acquisition of two battleships that had been completed and paid for but awaited delivery to Turkish crews already in Britain. But Turkey had already aligned herself with Germany by secret treaty (2 August) and the two German warships, and their appearance at the Dardanelles, were the product rather than the cause of much wider historical events. Moreover, once the two German warships were established at Constantinople and after 16 August became nominally Turkish warships, their record belies their exaggerated status.

Certainly, their bombardment of Russian ports on 29 October 1914 was the event that set in train Turkey's involvement in war against Russia and Britain and France, but thereafter their record, and specifically their record in the Black Sea, was at best indifferent, while their one appearance in the Aegean after August 1914 – which resulted in the sinking of the British monitors *Raglan* and M. 28 off Imbros and the loss of the *Breslau* off Mudros and the mining and then grounding of the *Goeben* within the Dardanelles on 20 January 1918 – was hardly the stuff of which 'decisive events' were made. Within the Black Sea, the *Goeben* represented a real threat to any Russian naval endeavour there, at least until the second half of 1915 when the first Russian dreadnought in the Black Sea became available: before that time the Russians had sought defensive safety in numbers with a concentration of older ships. But once Russia had two dreadnoughts in this sea, as was the case in 1916, the operational effectiveness of the *Goeben* was correspondingly reduced, though this was happening anyway, albeit for reasons that were not immediately obvious. The lack of dockyard facilities and, more seriously, the limited coaling facilities available, presented serious difficulties, not least because, given Turkish collier losses by 1916, the coaling requirements of the *Goeben* were roughly equivalent to available coaling capacity. Thus came about the absurd situation whereby the *Goeben* was required to provide cover for colliers that were to secure coal for her: the colliers took such coal to Constantinople, where it was transferred, and were then required to collect more coal – again covered by the *Goeben* – in order to allow the German battlecruiser to conduct operations. The result was that as the war lengthened, so the gaps between German operational sorties lengthened, and in any case after the 20 January 1918 episode the *Goeben*, in effect, had been eliminated from proceedings.

Yet the real significance of the *Goeben*'s being mined and then grounded lay in the fact that failure had overwhelmed the Russian Black Sea fleet by this time. The story of operations in the Black Sea during the First World War was one of initial, and very short-lived, German advantage: this very quickly passed and the *Goeben*, in effect, was reduced in status from immediate threat to the only warship capable of offering serious resistance to Russian exercise of command of this particular sea. Probably the high point of Russian effectiveness in the Black Sea was the series of Russian amphibious operations in 1916 that resulted in the turning of the Turkish positions on the Arhavi on 5 February, on the Abi Vice on the 15th, and on the Buyuk-dere with the result that Rize was occupied on 7 March, and the Kara-dere line secured in mid-April. Direct amphibious assault brought the Russians control of Dorana and Polathane on 16 April, Trebizond being secured by a complementary land attack two days later. The Caucasus campaign of winter 1915–1916, which stood in sharp contrast to events on the Gallipoli peninsula, was evidence of what amphibious operations might achieve in a remote, wild area where a narrow coastal belt and long exposed coast rendered forward defence vulnerable to sea-borne landings in rear areas. With Russian military forces achieving the destruction of Turkish field armies in the Caucasus in 1915 and 1916, the Russian naval effort ensured that the initiative in the Black Sea remained firmly in Russian hands despite such disasters as the destruction of the battleship *Imperatrica Marija* as a result of a magazine explosion inside Sevastopol harbour on 20 October 1916. What Russian possession of the initiative could not survive was the impact of revolution, and it was this which ensured that the position of Russian advantage won between 1914 and 1916 unravelled in the course of 1917.

Russia's falling out the frame during 1917 brought to the fore a very real Allied fear, namely that Germany would secure control of many Russian warships and would be able to mount offensive operations in the eastern Mediterranean which would be virtually impossible to forestall. This fear was exaggerated because Russia's disintegration and German acquisition of her warships did not follow simply and quickly. The Bolshevik destroyer *Kerch* sank the battleship *Svobodnaja Rossija*, the former *Ekaterina II*, off Novorossijsk on 16 June 1918 in order to prevent her surrendering to the Germans. Other units had deteriorated in the course of 1917 and could not be brought rapidly into service even when they were surrendered in accordance with the terms of the Treaty of Brest Litovsk and its various supplementary treaties.[9] Indeed, by the time that some Russian warships were surrendered and made ready for service by the Germans, the end of the war meant that they were then surrendered to the British or French.[10] More serious, however, was the third factor working against a timely German employment of captured Russian warships, and this was something shared by all the major navies in the Mediterranean at some time or another during the First World War.

These navies had to decide the nature of their effort because, as the war reached into its fourth and fifth years, so they could not undertake simultaneous efforts with major fleet and light units. For Germany and Austria-Hungary, the seizure of Russian fleet units availed them little, if anything, of any real substance: by 1917 their commitment, and that of available manpower, was to the *guerre de course*, not fleet action, and in any case the prospects offered by fleet action confined to the Adriatic were geographically limited to the point that they were non-existent. For the Allies, the need for light units for the campaign against enemy submarines had assumed overriding importance by 1918, and herein lay their dual failure: they failed to bring enemy battle forces, whether it be the *Goeben* in the eastern Mediterranean or Austro-

Hungarian forces in the Adriatic, to battle, while their efforts in dealing with the submarine threat in the Mediterranean were somewhat unsatisfactory, even by the least exacting of standards.

Once the furore over the escape of the *Goeben* and *Breslau* to Constantinople had died down, the fate of the capital ship and the Mediterranean theatre of operations largely concentrated upon 1915 and the Dardanelles and the Adriatic. In terms of the Dardanelles, the Anglo-French bombardment of the outer forts on 3 November 1914, and the massive damage inflicted on the Sedd-el-Bahr fortress when a magazine exploded, saw the employment of the battlecruisers *Indefatigable* and *Indomitable* and two French pre-dreadnought battleships, the *Suffren* and *Vérité*. The subsequent campaign witnessed the major employment of the brand new *Queen Elizabeth*, which in effect was sent to the eastern Mediterranean and the Dardanelles to work up, and also the battlecruiser *Inflexible*. Both were in the first line of capital ships involved in the bombardment operation inside the Dardanelles on 18 March 1915 which in effect ended all Allied hopes of early victory. Three pre-dreadnoughts, the French *Bouvet* and the British *Irresistible* and *Ocean*, were lost to mines, and the *Inflexible* was one of two units – the *Gaulois* was the other – that suffered major damage. The British battlecruiser suffered damage to her bridge and forward control positions from Turkish guns and incurred extensive damage when she hit a mine. After taking on some 2,000 tons of water and down at the bows, she reached Malta only with difficulty: there she was afforded running repairs before she could sail on to Gibraltar, where she underwent the major repairs which enabled her to join the Grand Fleet on 19 June 1915.

In this account of the battleship and the First World War, any detailed analysis of the Dardanelles venture is largely out of place. Yet the episode cannot be allowed to pass without reference to certain of its aspects – most obviously that it was mounted mainly with old, largely obsolescent battleships which could only be employed on secondary or tertiary tasks – and most definitely that it was seen by the British, and specifically naval personnel at the time and many commentators thereafter, as the alternative to commitment on the Western Front. Herein, of course, one encounters the 'British way of warfare' school, complete with its claims that Britain could always stand aside from Europe and that British history represents the successful realisation of naval and maritime as opposed to continental strategic commitment.

Both the rationale for the Dardanelles venture and the whole of the 'British way of warfare' were and remain fraudulent. The thesis that an offensive against Turkey which unlocked the Dardanelles and Bosporus would conjure into existence a Balkan League that somehow would present the Central Powers with a third major front, and a commitment that might be beyond them in 1915, and would re-open the ports of southern Russia to supplies of war material, leaves itself open to two telling and conclusive counter-arguments. The Balkans states were bitterly divided among themselves and most certainly could never have presented a single endeavour on the Allied side, and indeed these states, whether singly or together, represented liabilities that needed support rather than assets that in real terms could have added to the common cause. Moreover, in 1915 Britain and France lacked the war material and shipping to supply Russia on anything like the scale that she needed to address the worst material deficits which beset her national war effort. But in any case, even if Britain and France had been better placed, the Russian problem was not simply one of supply but distribution – between ports and industrial areas, between industrial areas and battle zones, and, in terms of food distribution, between countryside and town. The Russian problem was far more complicated than this particular argument would suggest, but, of course, this was an argument that had obvious attractions after the First World War and the establishment of the Soviet Union: the implication that somehow history would have unfolded to a different end if the Allied effort at the Dardanelles had succeeded was deceptively attractive and simplistic.

The Dardanelles venture at the time represented – and the whole of the 'British way of warfare' school subsequently represented and continues to represent – an attempt to evade responsibility and obligation. The enterprise in 1915 was an attempt to undertake a limited commitment while leaving allies to shoulder the main responsibility for the waging of war and to take the burden of losses. Total war in the twentieth century allowed no such luxury, at least not to European powers which were obliged to wage war as they found it. But at the Dardanelles such matters were overtaken by others, involving the concept of operations, that defy ready understanding. In the two decades before 1915 successive British planning committees had concluded that a naval offensive, unsupported by military formations, could not force the Dardanelles, a conclusion first taken on board as a result of the 1877 deployment of a fleet in support of the Ottoman Empire against Russia, and in a sense the reason was simple enough. The basic problem in forcing the Dardanelles was that the mines could not be cleared because of the guns, and the guns could not be cleared and silenced because of the mines: the only way the conundrum could be solved was if the guns were taken from landward by military forces. This was a point specifically recognised in 1907, but after the July 1912 decision, which saw the 'roles-and-missions' argument within the British defence establishment resolved in favour of the army and thus the commitment of the British army to France and in effect the reduction of the navy to a secondary role, the latter still aspired to a major role in the Mediterranean, in no small measure because of its own institutional requirements, not least in terms of public expectations. The 'can-do' philosophy, a contempt for the Turk after the example of the Balkan wars, along with the portrayal of naval matters in terms of personality at the expense of any real consideration of the problems that attended joint operations – these were the factors at work in shaping the British Navy's espousal of the Dardanelles commitment: it was the means of showing gainful employment at the time when the army was being ground down on the Western Front; it would provide victory on the cheap. The problem was that it did not.

The failure of the 18 March offensive meant that the naval effort was abandoned in favour of a joint, in fact combined, endeavour. By this time, however, the question of how to help Turkey presented Germany and Austria-Hungary with real difficulty. The latter's naval undertakings in the previous decade had been increasingly directed to the raising of a fleet, and by the outbreak of war, she had a total of three dreadnoughts in commission, which more or less placed her on a par with France, Italy and Russia. But the *Viribus Unitis* and her two sister ships, with or without the three *Radetzky*-class pre-dreadnoughts, could not directly or indirectly help the Turks, while the navy of Austria-Hungary in 1914 had only seven submarines in service and two of these were fit only for local defence. For Germany, the question of helping Turkey came to a choice between three options: her naval personnel taking over Austria-Hungary's submarines and bringing them into service; the transportation of prefabricated submarines by rail to Pola and their being assembled and brought into service in the Adriatic; and sending sea-going U-boats from bases in Germany around the British Isles through the Straits of Gibraltar either to make for Pola or to move directly against Allied naval forces in the Aegean. Perhaps surprisingly, the German Navy preferred the second to the first option, but it had in any case to resort to the third and, of course, it was the appearance of German submarines off the Dardanelles, and the havoc which was wreaked in consequence, that was so important.

Admittedly, by the time this happened the initial Allied landing on the Gallipoli peninsula had miscarried and only by very narrow margins, but utter disaster on the day of the landings (25 April) had also only just been avoided, and overall it is hard to resist the conclusion that the various errors on both sides cancelled out one another to produce the 'inevitable' result. In terms of battleship losses at the Dardanelles, those of 18 March 1915 excluded, there were four, all pre-dreadnoughts, three British and one Turkish. The war record of the British ships involved bears recounting, if only because it illustrates the nature of the tasks which befell such ships prior to their commitment in the eastern Mediterranean. The *Goliath*, which had been involved in the Rufigi operations that resulted in the trapping of the light cruiser *Königsberg* in that east Africa river in November 1914, was hit by three torpedoes off the Dardanelles by the German-manned torpedo-boat *Muavenet-I-Miliet* on 13 May. The *Triumph*, which had begun the war in reserve, was manned by crews from river gunboats and had served with the Japanese off Tsingtao: she was sunk off Gaba Tepe by the U. 21 while she was providing fire support to Australian formations on 25 May. Two days later, also off Gaba Tepe, this same German submarine accounted for the *Majestic*, which had been involved in convoying Canadian troops to Europe. It was the *Majestic* which capsized but whose keel was held clear of the water because she came to rest on the stumps of her masts: she remained in such a state for months until a winter's gale caused the foremast to break and she disappeared. The only consolation, at least as far as battleships were concerned, exacted by the Allies was the sinking by the British submarine E. 11 of the Turkish pre-dreadnought battleship *Heireddin Barbarossa* in the Sea of Marmara on 8 August 1915: purchased by Turkey in 1910, originally she had been launched as the *Kurfürst Friedrich Wilhelm* in 1891 and as such had been a member of the first class of battleships ever built by Germany.[11]

No account of these proceedings would be complete without two acknowledgements. The first is that, with the surrender of Turkey at war's end, which took place in the pre-dreadnought battleship *Agamemnon* at Mudros, an Allied fleet led by the British dreadnoughts *Superb* and *Téméraire* passed through the Dardanelles on 12 November. British and Indian troops occupied the forts, and on the next day the Allied fleet was anchored off Constantinople: on 14 November British marines were landed, and one week later French troops were put ashore. The second, less well-known, relates to the fact that, after having secured Constantinople, Allied warships entered the Black Sea and on 26 November took possession of Black Sea Fleet units at Sevastopol: on 20 December, nine days after the city was taken by Ukrainian revolutionary forces, French troops were landed at Odessa. This was the first stage in a process that led to a deepening Anglo-French commitment to the White Russian cause against the Bolsheviks, though in 1918–1919 the immediate Allied concern was the immobilisation of Russian units. This singularly ill-judged venture, which went completely against Palmerston's famous maxim that only a fool gets involved in someone else's civil wars, ultimately provided employment for the British battleships *Ajax*, *Benbow*, *Centurion*, *Iron Duke* and the *Marlborough*, plus various pre-dreadnoughts, as well as the French battleships *France* and *Jean Bart* and, after October 1919, the *Lorraine* and *Provence*: the *Marlborough*'s main role in this episode seems to have been as chauffeur to the British high commissioner to the White Russian administration in southern Russia, the former Conservative member of Parliament and founding father of the concept of geopolitics, Sir Halford Mackinder. The Allied intervention in the Russian civil war was as unsuccessful as it was ill-judged, and ended in much the same way as Allied support for Greece in the war with Turkey ended in 1922–1923: battleships, whether dreadnoughts or not, were not a substitute for rational, reasoned and sensible policy.

In terms of the Adriatic, perhaps two points set out the basic terms of reference of the war in the central Mediterranean. The first is that when Italy entered the war, against Austria-Hungary,[12] there was both an edge to proceedings and a general certainty about how the war at sea would be waged. Italy was perhaps the only country in Europe that could provide the Hapsburg monarchy with an enemy against which every people in the Empire could identify, and, not to be forgotten, there was the small matter of the Hapsburg Navy's victory at Lissa in 1866 nestling on the historical scales. For her part Italy, given her territorial ambitions, had no liking whatsoever for the Austrians, Slovenes and various other Balkan peoples. Equally, on both sides there was a general confidence in their navies, and in the Italians' case there was the added bonus born of being allied to Britain and France.

But the reality of the situation confronting both Austria-Hungary and Italy was that there was very little to be gained, and potentially much to lose, not least in terms of standing relative to allies, by the adoption of an aggressive policy aimed at bringing about a fleet action. From their main bases the fleets of the two powers could check the other, could ensure the security of their own coastline from serious or sustained bombardments and landings, while the initial experience of war clearly pointed to the dangers inherent in the adoption of a forward strategy. On 16 August 1914 the k.u.k. *Kriegsmarine*'s light cruiser *Zenta* was caught in the southern Adriatic by a force that included the French dreadnoughts *Courbet, Jean Bart* and the *Paris,* while on 21 December, six months before Italy entered the war, the *Jean Bart* was torpedoed by U. XII in the southern Adriatic: damage was severe with the wine store destroyed and the forward magazine narrowly missed. The battleship was in dock in Malta for more than three months but, more relevantly, in French practice cruisers took over the task of sweeps and patrols while the battleships were gathered at Corfu, especially after October 1915 when Allied forces were landed at Salonika.

This particular month was somewhat unusual in that it marked not just the Salonika landings but the start of the Austro-German campaign which resulted in the conquest of Serbia: it was as part of this effort that the *Kriegsmarine* despatched the pre-dreadnought *Radetzky* in a successful attempt to ensure that French troops were denied Cattaro (present day Kotor). It is possible to argue that, had it not been for the four-strong *Monarch* class of coastal defence ships, Cattaro would have been lost long before October 1915, but in the event Cattaro proved the forward base for German and k.u.k. *Kriegsmarine* warships and submarines while the French despatch of the dreadnoughts *Bretagne, Lorraine* and the *Provence* to Corfu provided against any sortie outside the Adriatic – not that the *Lorraine* and *Provence* saw any sea-time in the whole of 1917 and very little in 1916 and again in 1918. Whatever offensive duties needed to be discharged, the various navies used not important and valuable units such as dreadnoughts or cruisers but older units of limited worth. Thus the Austro-Hungarian bombardments of Cortellazzo on 16 November 1917 and the coastal railway line near Senigallia twelve days later were undertaken in the first instance by old coastal defence battleships, the *Wien* and *Budapest*, supported by no fewer than fourteen torpedo-boats and in the second instance solely by destroyers and torpedo-boats: the earlier and abortive attack on Ancona on 4–5 April 1915 had been conducted not by warships but by a landing party put ashore, unfortunately in the wrong place, under cover of night.

The fleet-in-being role provided both Austria-Hungary and Italy with deterrents and ensured both countries against serious attack. The result was a stand-off not dissimilar to the situation in the North Sea with two obvious and related corollaries. The first was that any consideration of the operational record of the dreadnought and pre-dreadnought battleships of Austria-Hungary and Italy is striking for an almost complete absence of sweeps and any form of offensive action. The outbreak of war led to the k.u.k. *Kriegsmarine's* dreadnoughts *Viribus Unitis* and *Tegethoff* and the pre-dreadnoughts *Radetzky*, *Erzherzog Franz Ferdinand* and the *Zrinyi* bombarding Ancona (24 May 1915) but, apart from the sortie of June 1918 by all four of Austria-Hungary's dreadnoughts, which resulted in the loss of the *Szent Istvan* when she was torpedoed off Premuda, there is no record of any other offensive operation, and the reasoning behind this particular sortie is of interest.

The Allied strengthening of the barrage across the Straits of Otranto in 1918 threatened for the first time to impose real problems for submarines moving to or from the bases in the Adriatic, and this was a factor in the *Kriegsmarine's* deliberations just as it had been in May 1917, when a raid by three cruisers and two destroyers sank fourteen out of 47 drifters on the barrage and sank a destroyer and one of three transports, the other two transports being damaged: from the support forces that tried to intervene, a British light cruiser was also severely damaged and a French destroyer was sunk. The *Kriegsmarine's* intention was to mount a similar raid on the barrage but, quite deliberately, to decline any chance of battle with major enemy formations. But the factor that largely shaped the *Kriegsmarine's* decisions was the uncertainty of morale, which had been badly dented by the sinking of the *Wien* inside Trieste harbour by two Italian torpedo-boats on 10 December 1917 and then by the mutiny that affected many *Kriegsmarine* units at Cattaro in February 1918. The sortie of June 1918 was part of the process whereby the *Kriegsmarine* sought, through offensive action, to hold demoralisation and defeatism at bay.[13]

The same is true on the Italian side. The pre-dreadnoughts of the *Vittorio*

Emanuele class – the nameship, *Regina Elena*, *Napoli* and the *Roma* – may have been involved in bombardments of Tobruk and Benghazi and, interestingly, the Dardanelles during the earlier war with Turkey (1911–1912), but, as with the dreadnoughts *Conte di Cavour*, *Giulio Cesare* and the *Leonardo da Vinci*, the entries against their names note no action during the First World War. With the *Leonardo da Vinci* being destroyed by an explosion inside Taranto harbour on 2 August 1916, it was a mark of the inactivity of her sister ships that the *Cavour* notched up 40 and the *Cesare* 31 sea-hours in the course of the conflict, and these totals included the delivery times from builders to base and the sea passage to Corfu: the *Andrea Doria* gathered together some 70 sea-hours, and the *Caio Duilio* four missions, of nature and duration unknown.[14]

The only major undertaking by an Italian dreadnought during the war was in its last weeks, when Bulgaria collapsed and the demand for action that would eliminate Durazzo (present-day Durrës in Albania) as an enemy base placed the Italian naval command on the horns of a dilemma. Durazzo was within the Italian area of responsibility, and the demand for action against the base was accompanied by the request to the Allied high command that, if the Italians would not undertake some form of action, the local French force based on Corfu should be authorised appropriately. In fact neither the Italian nor the French local commands were well placed to conduct such an operation since both would have to withdraw escorts from convoys, the barrage and other duties in order to gather an attack force, but neither the Italians nor the French were prepared to leave the task to the other: for the Italians, with ambitions on Albania, the only possibility worse than the French taking Durazzo was if the place fell to the Greeks.

At the same time, the British undertook to send a dreadnought (the *Superb*) to the Aegean for the first time since the withdrawal of the *Queen Elizabeth*, but this decision was accompanied by one not to decommission the two battleships, the *Agamemnon* and *Lord Nelson*, already there: when the decision was taken to also send the *Téméraire*, the scene was set for an unseemly, unpleasant and very largely unnecessary series of incidents between the British and French, the British warships obviously being far too good to be placed under French command. Such vital matters, and their indication of the imminence of peace, placed the one operation undertaken by the first of Italy's dreadnoughts, the *Dante Alighieri*, and indeed the attack of 2 October 1918 on Durazzo, in its proper perspective, though perhaps the final, and certainly the most jaundiced, comment on the attack was Italian. No fewer than five British light cruisers, sixteen British destroyers and eleven American submarine chasers were committed to this attack alongside an Italian force that consisted of the dreadnought *Dante Alighieri*, three armoured cruisers, one light cruiser and three scouts, five flotilla leaders and two destroyers, plus assorted torpedo-

and motor-boats.[15]

Two k.u.k. *Kriegsmarine* destroyers and one torpedo-boat, along with three steamers and one hospital ship, were at Durazzo, and two submarines were off the base when the Allied attack materialised. All but one steamer escaped, one British light cruiser was torpedoed and lost her stern, while the bombardment was conducted at a range of 12,000 yards/11,000 metres and did much damage, very little of it to any military effect, and the *Dante Alighieri* never fired her guns. With Durazzo earmarked for Italian occupation, this dismal affair – the last ever fought by Hapsburg warships, which acquitted themselves honourably – was deemed by the Italians to have been staged to ensure that when their forces arrived to occupy the town, it would be partially destroyed, which would be much to the secret satisfaction of the French.

In the event, however, Durazzo was not the final episode in the Adriatic and Mediterranean. The final defeats incurred by Hapsburg armies led to the evacuation of Albania and then of Durazzo on 11 October and San Giovanni di Medua (present-day Shëngjin, about 50 miles/80-km north of Durazzo) on the 23rd, all *Kriegsmarine* involvement in the submarine campaign having ended six days earlier. In the last two weeks of October 1918 the disintegration of Austria-Hungary, 645 years after the first Hapsburg was elected Emperor, was matched by the collapse of her armed forces, and on 31 October British radio operators picked up signals indicating that the *Viribus Unitis* at Pola had been turned over to representatives of the South Slav National Council, which was at Agram (present-day Zagreb). The ship was even renamed the *Jugoslavija*, and both the events and the name could not but be an offence to Italy, which had not fought in the First World War, and suffered relative losses only exceeded by Russia on the Allied side, in order to see a Serbo-Croat state established on the Adriatic. Accordingly, the k.u.k. ensign was lowered for the last time at sunset on 31 October, a Yugoslavian flag was raised and the ship illuminated for the first time since 1914. That night two Italian teams of charioteers, with self-propelled mines known colloquially as *mignattas* or leeches, broke into an unguarded harbour and attached their charges to the *Viribus Unitis* and the liner *Wien*. The resultant explosions sank both ships in the early hours of 1 November, and thus the new Slav state lost the largest and most important warship in its possession. The French on the one side, and the Slavs on the other: what it is to have allies, and battleships that did nothing!

Jutland

Certain names go together naturally. If one thinks of the First World War and the war at sea, one's first thoughts are of Jutland. The raid on Zeebrugge naturally also recommends itself for consideration, as do the sinking of the armoured cruisers *Cressy*, *Aboukir* and *Hogue* by the German submarine U. 9 off the Dutch coast on 22 September 1914 and the attempts to maintain the Dover and Otranto barrages. Perhaps if one is American, then one's immediate thought is of the British liner *Lusitania*, sunk by the German submarine U. 20 in the south-west approaches on 7 May 1915 with the loss of 1,201 lives, of which 128 were American, an event that did much in the way of hardening American national resolve against Germany. But perhaps the one event that marks the watershed in the war at sea during the First World War was none of these but the sinking of the British steamer *Glitra*, in accordance with prize regulations, by the German submarine U. 17 off Stavanger, Norway, on 20 October 1914. This was the first sinking of a merchantman by a submarine, and it was the one act from which everything that was to follow in the form of the submarine offensive against Allied and neutral shipping flowed.

Before the war, there had been one study within the German Navy on the subject of a campaign against shipping, and despite its fairly optimistic con-clusion, the prevailing view within the service was that a number of considera-tions, some political and others technical and relating to the service in terms of numbers, manpower and other priorities, made such an offensive option impracticable. With the battle of the frontiers not unfolding as planned, and with Germany obviously committed to a war that beckoned uninvitingly into the future, the sinking of the *Glitra* was tantamount to a falling of the scales from the eyes, and over the next two years there was to be a series of disputes within the German high command on the crucial question of whether Ger-many should undertake an unrestricted submarine campaign against Allied and neutral shipping, the immediate aim of which would be to register the defeat of Britain.

Over this period the basic arguments within the German high command did not change overmuch. Those opposed to resorting to the *guerre de course* stressed the likelihood of American entry into the war and the sheer difficulty of registering losses of the order that would ensure the defeat of a nation that began hostilities with some 20,000,000 tons of shipping. In the final stages of this debate, after Jutland, another argument found employment on the part of those opposed to adopting the *guerre de course*. This was that claims to be able to inflict losses which would result in Britain's defeat made no allowance for Britain resorting to all and every expedient in order to avoid defeat – she was supposed, just like France as the Schlieffen Plan had unfolded, to sit like a hyp-notised rabbit as defeat rolled over her.

Events were to prove that these arguments were correct, but their relevance was progressively eroded by the impact of two parallel sets of events. On the one hand, the German Navy put various restricted campaigns into effect, which came preciously close to unrestricted campaigns where there was little if any American shipping, and these campaigns, unsurprisingly, seemingly proved the arguments of those wishing to commit Germany to an unrestricted *guerre de course*. On the other hand, Germany's overall position deteriorated. The prospects of victory dimmed in these two years, and increasingly the Allied blockade made inroads into German capability and genuine hunger began to stalk central Europe. The argument against Germany committing herself to an unrestricted *guerre de course* suffered from the fact that in effect it offered no real means of achieving victory and indeed did worse: the argument seemed to come close to suggesting that defeat was preferable to embracing what seemed the best, perhaps only, means of breaking the ranks of Germany's enemies by driving Britain from the war.

Ultimately, Germany embarked on an unrestricted submarine campaign against shipping on 1 February 1917: in the event, as has been noted, it amounted to a snatching of defeat from the jaws of victory because a little more than one month later there began the Russian Revolution, with the abdication of the Tsar on 16 March and the start of the process that was to result in Russian national enfeeblement, the October Revolution on 7 November and civil war. In between times, however, Germany's hesitant affair with the *guerre de course* went hand in hand with attempts to rethink the role of the fleet, and this became pressing in the first half of 1916 when, as a result of the growing crisis over the conduct of a restricted campaign against shipping, the decision to abandon the latter had to lead to the adoption of a more aggressive use of the fleet in the North Sea.

Such was the background to the battle of Jutland, the only fleet action fought in the First World War and, indeed, the only fleet action fought in European waters during the two world wars of the twentieth century. The hors d'oeuvres were provided in the form of the raid of 25 April 1916 on Lowestoft and Yarmouth, which in real terms was of little account: the battle-cruiser *Seydlitz* was mined and put out of service for a month and two of the eleven submarines that had been involved in this operation were lost, but no part of British forces were brought to battle and destroyed, something which was essential if the Germans were to seek fleet action at some stage with any chance of success. There was no weakening of the Grand Fleet as a result of the bombardment of these towns, no detachment of divisions or squadrons of dreadnoughts to southern ports that might leave them exposed to defeat in detail or weaken the main body of the British fleet and leave it vulnerable. The Germans therefore had to plan for another tip-and-run operation in the hope that this might produce those very special circumstances which would lead to a writing-down of British strength, but the plan to carry out an attack on Sunderland – as if anyone would notice if it was subjected to bombardment – had to be postponed at various times during May. This at least gave time for the Germans to put as many submarines as possible to sea for the purposes of reconnaissance, the laying of mines and the preparation of lines across which British formations would have to move. But the final postponement of the attack, which delayed the surface force moving until such a time that the submarines would be at the limit of their endurance, forced a major change.

The German intention was now to move into the Skagerrak, obviously to threaten British shipping in those waters and no less obviously to draw British formations into this area, which was much closer to German than to British bases. The German surface force would therefore have just one flank to watch and would be less dependent on Zeppelin reconnaissance than would have been the case with an attack on a British port. Thus stormy weather during much of May and the problems of co-ordination between airships and the fleet combined to result in a plan that called for a sweep by the battlecruiser force. This sweep was intended to attract British attention and, it was hoped, an intervention on the part of a British force that could be brought to action and then overwhelmed by the battleship force deployed in support of the battlecruisers.

The German plan was beset by two realities. The first was that the British were aware of German intentions, and indeed units of the Grand Fleet and the Battle Cruiser Fleet sailed even before their opposite numbers left port. This awareness stemmed from an ability to read German signals, the Germans for their part having a certain but much more limited capacity to read British signals. The intelligence advantage, at least initially, was firmly with the British, as was the second reality, the advantage of numbers. Yet the Germans could chose their moment and were able to make their move with just one of their dreadnoughts, the *König Albert*, not available for this operation: the battleship *Bayern* had not completed trials, and in May 1916 the only other units to be completed prior to the end of the war, the battleship *Baden* and battlecruiser *Hindenburg*, were several months from completion. On the British side, the British battleships *Emperor of India* and *Queen Elizabeth* and the battlecruiser *Australia*, which had been damaged in a collision with the *New Zealand* in April, were not in service, while the *Royal Sovereign* was in the same situation as the *Bayern*. Perhaps in historical terms the most notable British absentee was the *Dreadnought*, which had only just completed a refit at Rosyth and in July was to be deployed, as flagship of the 3rd Battle Squadron, to Sheerness alongside the very ships that ten years previously she had rendered obsolescent: her move was recognition of the simple fact that the decade since she had been completed had seen so many advances of design, size, armament and speed that she joined her predecessors in a double sense.[16]

Nonetheless, in overall numbers, the British held a three-to-two advantage over their opponents, but in terms of battleships and battlecruisers the British held nigh on a two-to-one advantage overall, the presence of six German predreadnoughts and eight British armoured cruisers in the respective orders of battle being discounted from (first-line) consideration.

THE NUMBER OF BRITISH AND GERMAN WARSHIPS AT JUTLAND, 31 MAY–1 JUNE 1916				
	British		German	
	Battle Fleet	Battlecruiser Forces		Battle Fleet
Dreadnought battleships	24	4	–	16
Battlecruisers	3	6	5	–
Pre-dreadnought battleships	–	–	–	6
Armoured cruisers	8	–	–	–
Light cruisers	12	14	5	6
Destroyers	51	27	30	31
Miscellaneous	1	1	–	–
TOTALS	**99**	**52**	**40**	**59**
	151		**99**	
'Capital Ship' totals:	27	10	5	16
	37		21	

Given that even if God does not favour the big battalions, then quantity does have a quality all of its own, and such a disparity of strength should have ensured a clear British victory. But part of Jutland's enduring attraction lies in the simple fact that such a victory eluded the British, and by a considerable margin. A combination of four factors largely account for this situation, and the first of them was, arguably, the most important: the British capital ships could not punch their weight.

There was between the two sides a basic equality of materiel since German capital ships possessed thicker armour but smaller main armament than their British opposite numbers. But German capital ships were better protected in one crucial respect, namely the legacy of the Dogger Bank action in the form of anti-flash protection. And British capital ships were ill served in lacking an effective armour-piercing shell. Given the weight of broadside and velocity of shell, British capital ships should have been able to penetrate the armour of their direct contemporaries, but the fact of the matter was that they could not do so, and German ships, which were short-ranged and had minimal living space compared to British warships, were able to withstand punishment that should have accounted for them. For example, at this battle the battlecruiser *Seydlitz* absorbed 21 hits by large-calibre rounds – 12-in,

13.5-in, 14-in or 15-in shells – and was struck by two torpedoes but, despite being burnt out and having some 5,300 tons of seawater in her, nonetheless managed to reach home: the flagship *Lützow* was scuttled when it was realised that she was doomed, but only after she had taken one torpedo and 24 heavy hits and had more than 7,500 tons of water inside her. British ships could not have taken such punishment without succumbing far more quickly than did the *Lützow*: in fact, the *Marlborough* was very fortunate to survive a single torpedo hit – she was undamaged by gunfire – but her surviving the battle had a great deal to do with the failure of the submarine U. 46 to press home her attack on 1 June.

British gunnery and defensive weaknesses at Jutland have attracted much comment over the years. It should be noted, however, that British warships were also hit by shells that failed to explode – the British did not have a monopoly on dud shells, despite what some commentators would have us believe – and in the third and fourth phases of the battle, when German warships were very briefly silhouetted against the sun, as British warships had been in the first and second phases, British gunnery seems to have been as good as German gunnery in the first and second phases. In terms of accuracy and hits attained, there was little to chose between the gunnery of the two sides: the real difference was in armour and defensive arrangements, which provided German warships with a degree of protection that British battle-cruisers most definitely lacked.

The second factor in the equation was the nature of scouting and reporting, which was at best somewhat haphazard and inevitably so: high-speed manoeu-vring, in largely indifferent light, made accurate scouting and reporting very difficult indeed. Yet for all the criticism of the British performance in this battle, it is worth emphasising two very obvious points. First, the German battle force twice blundered into the British battle line, and was never afforded warning by its scouting cruisers or battlecruisers of the enemy's whereabouts, and, second, that on three occasions during the daylight action British light cruisers provided reports of enemy strength and course that varied between the very good and, given the conditions, most reasonable. Undoubtedly the British reporting system left a great deal to be desired during the early evening and through the night of 31 May–1 June, though even this criticism must be tempered. The failure of reporting during the night was in no small measure the result of German electronic counter-measures, which were more than ade-quate to jam reports made by the weak and not very reliable wirelesses avail-able to destroyers. Moreover, it is arguable that the British commander and his staff should not have needed reports to tell them what was happening: the flash and sound of gunfire were the best possible indicators of the where-abouts, and by implication, the intention of the enemy.

As Homer famously observed, after the event, the fool sees it: nothing is more obvious than the matter seen with 20-20 hindsight. But any consideration of the performance of the British commander, Jellicoe, and his staff raises the whole question of command, and herein one encounters the main problem that has beset so much of the writing of naval history – the issue of personality as opposed to systemic considerations. The difficulty lies in the nature of Anglo-American historiography, specifically the Carlyle legacy that history is the biographies of great men. In the recounting of Jutland the two individuals are Beatty, an archetypal British naval officer of the twentieth century, and Jellicoe, the exception that proves the rule. Of Beatty it could be truly said that the surest way to make his eyes light up was to shine a beam of light into one of his ears. Jellicoe, on the other hand, was very different. Beatty is always credited with the observation, made on the morning of 1 June 1916 after German formations had evaded contact with the British at dawn: 'There is something wrong with our ships, and there is something wrong with our system.' It was more a comment on Beatty that he never realised this after his abysmal conduct of operations at the Dogger Bank action in January 1915, just as it was a mark of Jellicoe's professionalism that he had realised the contending strengths and weaknesses of the British naval position relative to Germany before the time he assumed command of the fleet in August 1914: battle confirmed Jellicoe's original insight and did not teach him belated lessons.

The battle of Jutland opened when the light forces of the battlecruiser formations contacted one another when both were engaged in investigating a neutral steamer, the small Danish tramp N.J. Fjord. With the major units turning toward one another as the light forces clashed, the German battlecruiser formation began 'The Run to the South' with the intention of bringing the British battlecruiser force onto the guns of the German battle fleet. Thus the German aim of overwhelming and destroying a part of British forces and thereby achieving a rough equality of numbers might have been registered, though in truth during this initial phase of the battle it did not seem that the presence of the German battle force would be required. Two of the British battlecruisers were destroyed and three were heavily hit, and for two principal reasons.

The first was that in this phase of the battle the German force had the advantage of light, British units being caught against the sunlight while German units, hull down and on the darker side, were afforded the partial cover of smoke from both the battlecruisers and from destroyer forces seeking to get into action. This was a crucial factor in ensuring that the British ships could not use what should have been one telling advantage over their German opposite numbers, the superior range of their main armament. Fire was not opened (1548) until the two battlecruiser forces were within the range of German guns, and the opening British fire was more dangerous to German destroyers a mile beyond the line than to the line itself.

The second reason was that Beatty managed to repeat the two fundamental errors of the Dogger Bank action. Basic signals failure meant that the four fast battleships of the 5th Battle Squadron – the *Barham*, *Valiant*, *Warspite* and the *Malaya* – failed to get into the battle from the outset: they were not able to engage the enemy until after one British battlecruiser had been lost. In addition, with a six-to-five initial advantage, the British battlecruisers again managed to get their fire distribution wrong. The two leading British battlecruisers, the *Lion* and the *Princess Royal*, should have concentrated their fire against the leading German battlecruiser, the *Lützow*, and thereafter the British battlecruisers should have engaged their opposite numbers, i.e., the *Queen Mary* the *Derfflinger*, and the *Tiger*, *New Zealand* and the *Indefatigable* the *Seydlitz*, *Moltke* and the *Von der Tann* respectively. But what happened was that the *Queen Mary* and *Tiger* engaged the wrong ships, namely the *Seydlitz* and *Moltke* respectively: this meant that the *Moltke* was engaged by two British battlecruisers to their mutual confusion in terms of spotting fall of shot while the *Derfflinger* was left unattended.

Thus was an initial advantage of numbers dissipated, and in the opening exchanges the *Lion* was very heavily hit (1551) while both the *Princess Royal* and *Tiger* were hit and both had two of their four turrets put out of action for most of the battle (1552). By 1600 range was below 12,900 yards/11,800 metres and the German battlecruisers had their secondary armament in action. Nonetheless the *Queen Mary* hit the *Seydlitz* twice, with one round penetrating the barbette armour of the rear superimposed turret: the resulting flash worked its way through turret and hoist but was checked by the anti-flash devices which had been installed after the Dogger Bank action. The *Lion* hit the *Lützow* with one salvo but was hit in turn, the British flagship suffering the same fate as the *Seydlitz*: only the closing of the magazine doors and flooding of the magazine, and the drowning of all crew therein, saved the ship. In fact, the *Lion* was hit by six shells in the space of some four minutes, and to the Germans appeared to stagger out the line, but even as she did so the *Indefatigable* disappeared under a massive black cloud. She had been struck, apparently fatally, near her after turret (1603), and failed to respond to a change of course: she was then hit by two shells, one of which must have penetrated to the forward turret's magazine before exploding. The result was a mass of flame and smoke hundreds of feet high which marked the end of the ship: she sank with 1,117 of her officers and men, just two survivors being recovered by a German destroyer.

Some three minutes later, at 1606, the battleships of the 5th Battle Squadron, aided by a German change of course toward the British battlecruisers, were at last able to join the fray, and three minutes later recorded their first hit on the *Von der Tann*, the German battlecruiser being very lucky to avoid a complete wrecking of her steering gear: seven minutes later, at 1616, the first 15-in shell found out the *Moltke*. The British battleships, however, were not able to sustain this initial success. A stern chase in indifferent light, and one in which only the leading British ships could fire their forward guns at a range that opened at 19,600 yards/18,000 metres, meant that the British had to range on gun flashes, and as a result their contribution really amounted to harassment rather than serious impediment, still less grievous bodily harm. Nonetheless, there is much to be said in favour of the argument that the British battlecruiser formations were only saved from even more serious loss by the belated intervention of the battleships, and perhaps the most notable feature of the latter's entry into the battle was the fact that, even at ranges some five miles/8-km greater than those at which the British battlecruisers were managing to miss their targets, the battleships registered their first hit. If nothing else, such a state of affairs reflected the relative standards of training and professionalism in the Battle Cruiser Fleet and the Grand Fleet, of which the 5th Battle Squadron was normally a part, its having been only recently detached in order to serve with Beatty's command.

The battleships' joining the battle had one immediate result. After the *Indefatigable* had been sunk, the range between the battlecruiser forces opened as neither side could hope to sustain itself at a range that had closed to 10,400 yards/9,500 metres: fire slackened as range opened. With the battleships engaged, however, the British battlecruisers turned back (1612), the *Lion* immediately being hit heavily and enveloped in smoke which meant that she could not be seen by the German battlecruisers. As a result, the *Derfflinger* shifted her fire from the *Princess Royal* to the *Queen Mary*, which was still engaged with the *Seydlitz* (1616). At 1620 and again at 1623 the *Von der Tann* took very damaging hits, her after turret being jammed and rendered inoperable during what remained of the battle: more seriously she, like the *Lion*, was wrapped in smoke after the second hit, with the result that the *New Zealand* shifted her fire to the *Moltke*. At 1625, however, the *Queen Mary*, was hit first by three shells from a salvo of four and then by two shells. Her back was broken and with her masts and funnels falling inward, the ship was destroyed by a massive explosion with flame and smoke reaching a height of 2,000 feet/600 metres. A total of 1,266 officers and men died in the *Queen Mary*, eight being rescued by British and German destroyers.

No commensurate compensation for the British was exacted from the *Moltke*, and no redress was secured by the destroyer attacks, by both sides, which were mounted just after the *Queen Mary* was destroyed. The British did score one torpedo hit on the *Seydlitz* in one of the subsequent skirmishes (1657), but for the most part both battlecruiser forces countered the enemy move by turning away, and thus opening the range, while most of the destroyers' efforts tended to be concentrated against one another. Two German destroyers, the V. 29 and then the V. 27, were sunk while the *Nomad* was disabled (1633), to sink later. Nonetheless by this time, and just as the battleships of the 5th Battle Squadron seemed ready to punch their weight, the leading ships from the two opposing battlecruiser forces sighted the German battle force to the south (1633).

The light cruiser *Southampton* signalled her sighting report at 1638, and its contents came as a shock to both Beatty and Jellicoe because the Admiralty had informed the two commanders that the German fleet had not left its base in the Jade. In fact, within the Admiralty it was known that the German battle force was at sea, but the Director of Operations had asked members of the deciphering branch (Room 40) where the call-sign DK – the flagship of the German battle force – was located. He was informed that it was in Wilhelmshaven, and a signal was sent at 1100 to Jellicoe and Beatty informing them that the German battle force was in harbour. But the call-sign DK was transferred to a wireless station ashore whenever the flagship went to sea. This was known to personnel from Room 40, and these individuals were also aware that on this day, 31 May, the German battle force was at sea. But they were not informed of the purpose of the Director of Operations' question, hence the Admiralty's error in its 1100 signal. There were two problems here. The first was institutional. Room 40 was not properly part of Admiralty Intelligence – an oxymoron if ever there was one – and therefore was not able to contribute properly to the decision-making process: indeed, it was not until July 1917 that Room 40 became a section of the Intelligence Division in the first of a series of administrative changes which placed the sections dealing with signals intelligence and German movements under a single officer with direct and immediate access to Operations. The second problem related to personalities, and specifically to the ingrained prejudices of such individuals as the Director of Operations, who, typical of British naval officers, was never more certain of the correctness of his views than when he knew absolutely nothing about the subject under consideration.

As it was, the presence of the German battle force immediately turned on its head whatever advantage the British battlecruisers stood to gain as a result of the *Barham*, *Valiant*, *Warspite* and the *Malaya* coming fully into action, and it was now the turn of the British battlecruiser force to lead the enemy onto the guns of the Grand Fleet. It is a mark of those accounts which hold to German superiority in so many aspects of this battle that they never really answer the question of how this phase, 'The Run to the North', was so successfully achieved, though two caveats need to be noted. The first is that this phase of the battle began very unfortunately for the British. The sighting of the enemy battle force led to a turn away, but a turn away in succession with the British units following the *Lion*. This meant that the last British ships to turn – the last of the battlecruisers and the 5th Battle Squadron – were forced to negotiate the fire of the leading German battleships, the *Kronprinz* and *Kaiserin*. The *New Zealand* was bracketed but only the *Barham* was hit, twice and not seriously, yet the British battleships were placed in a situation which could have become extremely perilous. Once again, there had been a potentially disastrous failure of communications: the *Barham* had not received the initial sighting report from the *Southampton* and had failed to see flag signals from the *Lion*.

The second caveat is that this phase – and the delivery of the German battle-cruiser and battle forces onto the guns of the Grand Fleet – are illustrative of the maxim that no plan ever survives the first contact of battle. Discrepancies of navigation regarding relative positions and courses on the British side meant that, while the German formations were indeed following the British forces to the north, they did so in a manner which afforded Jellicoe little warning time for they were approaching from a direction he had not anticipated. Moreover, during this phase of the action the British lost the destroyer *Nestor*, and the *Nomad* was despatched in the course of an abortive attack on the German line, while the British battlecruisers, hitherto only under fire from the *König*, *Markgraf* and the *Prinzregent Luitpold*, were engaged by the German battlecruisers as the range closed.

The *Lion* was hit twice and this caused many fires which were only extinguished with difficulty, but the speed differential between the British battlecruisers and their pursuers meant that the British warships pulled clear (*c*. 1700), leaving the *Barham*, *Valiant*, *Warspite* and the *Malaya* to take the brunt of the action. At this point the German ships were all but invisible while the British ships were silhouetted clearly against the setting sun: the *Malaya* was hit by four shells, one of which set off cordite fires throughout the starboard secondary armament, and in the last moments before contact with the Grand Fleet a near-miss jammed the steering gear of the *Warspite*. Both ships were very fortunate to escape so relatively lightly from German attention, but in return between 1709 and 1719 the British battleships hit the *Grosser Kurfürst* and *Markgraf*, and the battlecruisers *Lützow*, *Derfflinger* and the *Seydlitz*, though thereafter some relief was gained as range opened. The German battlecruisers, however, were ordered to close with their opposite numbers even as the British battlecruisers sought to come across the German line of advance (1733) in order to mask the approach of the Grand Fleet. The result was that fire was resumed with the British battlecruisers and the *Barham* and *Valiant* directing their attentions to the German battlecruisers, the *Warspite* and *Malaya* to the *König* and *Grosser Kurfürst*, and at this stage of the battle the initiative was firmly in British hands.

The immediate British advantage lay in the fact that the setting sun now blinded German observation, and between 1742 and 1816 the *Derfflinger* was unable to fire. The result was that the toll of accumulating damage began to favour the British by some margin, and this despite the fact that overall there was still, even in this phase, a rough balance of hits: the difference, however, was that three-quarters of the hits recorded by German guns – thirteen of eighteen – were sustained by the British ships best able to absorb damage, i.e., the *Barham*, *Warspite* and the *Malaya*, while the exact reverse was the case with the German warships: fourteen of nineteen hits were taken by the *Lützow*, *Derfflinger* and the *Seydlitz*, and it was now that the damage which ultimately was to account for the *Lützow* and almost the *Seydlitz* began to be registered.

What was even more significant about these exchanges was that only one of the hits on German ships was registered by the British battlecruisers, yet for the British real advantage seemed to beckon after 1730 because, as the Grand and Battle Cruiser Fleets converged, British formations, including the 3rd Battle Cruiser Squadron, with the *Invincible*, *Inflexible* and the *Indomitable* and the light cruisers *Chester* and *Canterbury*, held the advantage of position, across the line of the German advance and sweeping around the head of the German line. At this point, German command arrangements were as poor as German scouting provisions. The fleet commander, Scheer, in the *Friedrich der Grosse*, was in the middle of the German line, quite unable to see the enemy and reduced to ordering his force to follow in the wake of the leading ship, the battleship *König*, while Hipper, the commander of the battlecruiser force, was in a flagship that had lost her wireless while certainly three, if not four, of his ships should by now have been heading for home, such was the extent of their damage. What compounded the German problem was that as the leading units from the two battle formations converged, the initial exchanges favoured the British. The Germans' scouting forces were failing to report the presence of the enemy and the light cruiser *Wiesbaden* was crippled by a shell from the *Invincible* that exploded in her engine room (1800), although losses among the light forces began to even out as more formations entered the battle.[17]

Jellicoe, however, found himself obliged to order the deployment of the British battle force on the basis of incomplete information and with only a matter of minutes to avert disaster: he had expected to encounter the German formations at or about 1830 and to the south, whereas the battle formation encountered Beatty's battlecruisers to the south-west and nearly 30 minutes before the expected time of contact. His decision was to form a line of battle by deploying on the 1st Battle Division, which was the eastern column of the fleet in its cruise formation. This order was hoisted in the *Iron Duke* at 1814, the divisional flagship, the *King George V*, leading the British battle formation on a course of south-east by south, i.e., around the head of the German line and potentially toward a position which would place the British battleships between the enemy and his ports. The deployment was not without its problems, most notably that Beatty's battlecruisers were between the British battleships and German battlecruisers and thus obscured the view of the former, and that the battleships at the end of the line – the rear ships from the starboard column, namely the *Hercules* and *Agincourt* – were left rather like the *Warspite* and *Malaya* had been when 'The Run to the South' turned into 'The Run to the North'. Nonetheless, in something like two minutes the British battle formation was transformed from six columns each with four battleships into a single column some six miles/10-km in length, and within another minute, at 1817, the *Marlborough* opened fire on the four *Kaiser*-class battleships at the head of the German line.

Jellicoe's order was much criticised in the immediate post-war period when certain of his personal and professional enemies sought to denigrate both the man and this decision but, these attacks apart, there has never been any serious questioning of a decision which in a sense represented the whole career of an individual, the whole ethos of the service, and was the final comment on national policy over the decade which had elapsed since the launch of the *Dreadnought*. It was a decision that placed the British battle force across the German line of advance and in a position from which it could inflict maximum damage on the enemy line, and it was one that placed Jellicoe beyond reasoned criticism.

It was not, however, a decision that guaranteed immediate success: indeed, the initial contact between the two battle forces most definitely favoured the Germans on two separate scores. As the Grand Fleet deployed into action, the *Warspite*'s helm jammed and the battleship completed two circles to starboard at full speed. This involuntary manoeuvre had the effect of drawing German attention from the crippled armoured cruiser *Defence* but took the British battleship twice to within 10,000 yards/9,100 metres of German battleships. For some four minutes, between 1820 and 1824, the *Warspite* was the target of five German battleships – the *König*, *Friedrich der Grosse*, *Ostfriesland*, *Thüringen* and the *Helgoland* – as they came north: thereafter the *Oldenburg* and *Nassau* engaged her. Somehow the *Ostfriesland* apparently continued to fire on the *Warspite* until 1845, though how she did so is not readily understandable. The British battleship suffered a number of hits that, according to source, vary between six and eleven, but it was a near-miss, which freed her helm, that proved crucial: heavily damaged and with obviously unreliable steering, she was ordered home to Rosyth, which she reached during the afternoon of 1 June after surviving two attacks by German submarines.

In the period between the *Warspite*'s helm jamming and just after 1830, when three German destroyers carried out a torpedo attack on the head of the

British line, the German battlecruisers came under sustained and accurate fire from the 3rd Battle Cruiser Squadron. The *Lützow* was hit an estimated eight times by the *Invincible* while the latter was herself subjected to fire from both the *Lützow* and *Derfflinger*. Then, at or about 1832, the *Invincible* was caught in sunlight, and at a range below 8,000 yards/7,300 metres one of the salvoes from the German battlecruisers hit her between the midships turrets and penetrated to the magazine. The British battlecruiser was consumed in a massive explosion similar to those which had engulfed the *Indefatigable*, *Queen Mary* and the *Defence*. Six survivors, from a crew of 1,026, were rescued by the destroyer *Badger*.

Thus at both the head and the rear of the line events unfolded in ways that most definitely were not to British advantage, but along the line things were very different, and this despite Beatty's continuing efforts to keep his battlecruisers in a position that obstructed the view and fire of the British battleships. As the German van came north, it found itself under concentrated fire from the north-east as the British battleships began to work their way around the head of the German line, while along the length of the British line various British battleships opened fire as individual German battleships came briefly into view. In the initial contact four ships from four different divisions, the *Benbow*, *Iron Duke*, *Hercules* and the *Colossus*, fired on enemy units, and at around 1831 the *Centurion*, *Orion* and the *Monarch* also joined the action. Then, with more British battleships entering the battle and the British flagship *Iron Duke* hammering the *König* at a range of 12,000 yards/11,000 metres, at 1833 the German commander, Scheer, gave his famous *Gefechtskehrtwendung* order.

This order, which had never been executed under fire, permitted a fleet to reverse course by all units turning together through sixteen points, each ship beginning its turn only when it saw the next astern begin to turn out of line. Given the fragmentation of the German line, there was no formal waiting and the German ships turned together: within six minutes the turn-away had been conducted without mishap and within another ten minutes the German ships were set on a course to the south-west and clear of the British line. The only immediate problems presented to the Germans by this manoeuvre were that the rear was brought up by the *König*, *Grosser Kurfürst*, *Kronprinz* and the *Markgraf* of the 5th Battle Division, the most heavily damaged of the German battleships and the ones least able to fend for themselves, while the situation which had imposed itself on the battlecruiser force was dire. The *Derfflinger* and *Seydlitz* had been massively damaged while, more seriously, the flagship *Lützow* could not maintain station and limped away to the south-west while Hipper was transferred by one destroyer and others tried to hide the stricken battlecruiser behind smokescreens (1850).

At first, the loss of contact with the enemy was believed in British ships, and by Jellicoe, to be the result of worsening visibility rather than an enemy manoeuvre. Only one British warship, the light cruiser *Falmouth* at the head of the line, had seen the German turn-away, but it had not reported the manoeuvre because it assumed that it had also been seen from the British battleships and battlecruisers. It was not until 1640, when Jellicoe made an enquiry about the enemy's bearing of Beatty, that a report was made. It was at this stage that the *Lion* unfortunately suffered a failure of steering, which cost her valuable minutes before she was able to come south in an attempt to regain contact with the German formations, but there were now more important considerations at work. Dusk was approaching, and Jellicoe had long been determined to avoid what he regarded as the lottery of a night action: from the time that he took command of the Grand Fleet, he had made clear his intention not to pursue an enemy that retired, convinced as he was that such a manoeuvre had to be intended to draw British warships either into minefields or across U-boat patrol lines. However sensible this general intention was, in these particular circumstances the German retirement could hardly have been deemed to be intended to draw British forces unwittingly into minefields or torpedoes. Nonetheless, Jellicoe's basic caution – a caution born in large measure from the knowledge that Britain's geographical position and superiority of numbers provided control of German naval movements and severed Germany's oceanic trade, all of which meant that Britain was winning the war at sea without battle – was justified. As the British formations came around to the south, they were clearly ready to resume battle and, more importantly, they stood between the German formations and their bases.

Jellicoe ordered British forces to come around to the south at 1855, at exactly the time that Scheer ordered a second *Gefechtskehrtwendung*. If the first such order was to become famous, this one was to become infamous, for Scheer's conduct of this battle made Beatty's look percipient in comparison. No proper explanation has ever been given for this second change of course, while the comment in the official German history –

> Whereas at (1830) the German leader had been taken by surprise when the enemy, owing to various particularly favourable circumstances, had been able to encircle and hold the van of the German line, Scheer now advanced with the consciously and freely determined intention of inflicting another forcible blow at the centre of the hostile line, although he knew that this movement would very soon expose him to a second 'crossing of the T'

– would seem to be at best a description rather than an explanation of events, and a dishonest description into the bargain. There could never have been any question of Scheer deliberately risking a second 'crossing of the T', and lest the point be missed, there could not have been another forcible blow at the centre of the hostile line because there had not been one in the first place. One suspects very strongly that his decision to reverse course was shaped by simple miscalculation. Scheer may have hoped to be able to pass astern of Jellicoe's formations and thereby regain the crucial advantage of position between the enemy and the High Sea Fleet's home bases, but it was his misfortune that the British were not as far to the south as he had anticipated and, instead of reversing course and coming behind the British, the German van came into the centre of the British line, with the battleships now at the head of the German line clashing with British light cruisers moving from the north against the crippled *Wiesbaden*. This action, in which ranges were down to less than 10,000 yards/9,200 metres, took place around 1905, which was when Jellicoe began to turn his forces onto a course of south-west by south in order to close with an enemy reported to be in sight to the west. Unfortunately for the British, the order was very quickly countermanded because of reports of contact with U-boats and it also seemed that German destroyers were in the process of mounting torpedo attacks on the British line. The reports concerning U-boats were erroneous – there apparently being no submarines of either side within 50 miles/80-km of the battle area – and the destroyer attacks were a trick of the light, but the result was that, rather than closing with the enemy, the British divisions were forced to turn away, although inevitably there was some confusion both between and within individual divisions.

At this point, both the German battlecruisers and leading battleships became visible and were immediately taken under fire, the initial British fire beginning with the divisions at the rear and then working its way along the centre and van. Then a real attack by German destroyers did materialise against the rear British divisions. These divisions were the ones with the best view of the German battlecruisers and leading battleships, and their being forced to turn away to avoid torpedoes meant they were hard pressed to retain contact with the enemy or to maintain their volume and accuracy of fire: this element of mischance was compounded by the fact that the onus of responsibility in this final part of the battleship action fell upon those battleships with the least punch. Of the Grand Fleet's battleships, two possessed 15-in/380-mm main armament, one had 14-in/356-mm and eleven 13.5-in/343-mm main armament, and the remainder, ten, were equipped with 12-in/305-mm guns. More than half (57 per cent) of the main armament shells fired by these battleships were from 12-in guns: less than one in ten rounds were from the 15-in guns of the *Revenge* and *Royal Oak*. In both the first and second battleship actions, it was the battleships at the rear of the British line that were most heavily involved, and nine of the ten 12-in main armament battleships were in the last three divisions.

Within a matter of minutes of his issuing the order, Scheer's second reversal of course threatened to engulf the whole of the German battlecruiser and battleship formations in disaster. The battlecruisers found themselves in the van but literally wilted as the volume of fire from the British line increased: the German battleships bunched up, and with other battleships coming up from astern, collisions and total confusion must have seemed unavoidable for a fleet on the brink of a debacle. As it was, Scheer was able to extricate his forces by a combination of three actions: a third *Gefechtskehrtwendung* (1918); an order to the destroyer flotillas to launch torpedo attacks on the British line and to lay smokescreens to cover the retirement of the battle formations (1915); and the order to the battlecruisers to close the enemy in what was clearly intended by Scheer to be the sacrifice to be paid for the extrication of the main force (1913). The combination, when taken alongside Jellicoe's refusal to be drawn, meant that the German formations successfully broke contact with the enemy: even the battlecruisers, by virtue of the destroyers' exertions, were able to escape. But without anyone realising it at the time, this combination of measures, the German turn-away and destroyer attacks and the British refusal to close, spelt the end of the battle, at least for the main formations. Admittedly, even after this third *Gefechtskehrtwendung*, two German battleships – the *Kaiser* and *Markgraf* – were hit, the former by a number of shells and the latter once, while the *Kronprinz* was shaken by a number of near misses, and even in the last minutes of light, around 2019, there was an exchange between British light forces and German battleships and also a more serious exchanges between first the battlecruiser formations, the *Derfflinger* and *Seydlitz* being hit and, very surprisingly, the *Lion* and *Princess Royal* being hit in return, and then between the British battlecruisers and German pre-dreadnoughts.

Be that as it may, in terms of battleships and battlecruisers the story of the battle of Jutland, and also in a wider context the First World War, in effect ended at this stage. Jellicoe sought to maintain his force between enemy formations and the German bases, but faced with a choice of which channel to cover and once more very badly served by Admiralty Operations on the matter,[18] he chose the wrong one: dawn, and a whole day in which to complete the business begun on the previous day, brought only an empty sea, with no sign of the enemy. In the night certain of the British battleships had sighted their opposite numbers but had not challenged or engaged the enemy, and did not report their contact: thus the *Seydlitz* was seen by the *Agincourt*, *Marlborough* and the *Revenge*, none of which challenged or fired upon her and none of which reported her presence to Jellicoe in the *Iron Duke*. There were exchanges between British light forces and German formations as the latter crossed the British track, astern of the main British formations, and notwithstanding the sinking of the pre-dreadnought battleship *Pommern* with all hands, these night-time exchanges favoured the Germans, probably in part because the Germans had secured part of the British night challenge: Beatty and the *Lion* had lost the challenge and had sought challenge and reply from the *Princess Royal*, but the exchange between the two British battlecruisers was witnessed by German warships. Certainly during the night actions German fire, even as challenges were being flashed, was overwhelming, while conversely such units as the German light cruiser *Rostock* and destroyer S. 54 managed to escape destruction by returning the answer to challenges flashed by British warships.

In the course of the night, a number of ships on both sides were lost as German formations crossed the wake of their British counterparts, the failure on the part of Jellicoe and the staff in the *Iron Duke* to realise what was happening astern being one of the real mysteries of Jutland. Once they had concluded that the Germans would not use Horn's Reef but would come farther to the south, subsequent events conformed to this interpretation of them: Jellicoe and the staff saw the flashes and heard the sound of the guns astern yet drew the conclusion that both forces were on the same course, rather than that German battle formations were fighting their way through British light forces. Why at some stage someone did not work out what was in retrospect so obvious is hard to discern: the lack of reporting of contacts was vital, but one suspects that sheer exhaustion played its part. Jellicoe's original deployment order, at 1814, represented at the personal level not a decision made in a matter of minutes but a career of 42 years, and one suspects that it was a decision that drained its author. Perhaps.

In terms of battleships and battlecruisers, the night of 31 May–1 June saw only the destruction of the *Pommern* and the scuttling, with the dawn, of the *Lützow*, the *coup de grâce* of two torpedoes being administered by the destroyer G. 38 after the battlecruiser's crew had been removed. Two German units, the *König* and the *Seydlitz*, were very fortunate to survive. The *König*, drawing 34.5 feet/10.6-m of water, and the *Seydlitz*, drawing 41 feet/12.5-m, were both unable to proceed to base, having to wait for high water to get them over different bars: caught off Horn's Reef before dawn, they would have been lost had even modest British forces been gathered there. During the night other units such as the *Elbing*, *Rostock* and the *Wiesbaden* sank or were sunk by escorts, while on the British side, apart from the *Warspite* and *Warrior*, only the *Marlborough* was in real need of care and attention, and only with difficulty did she reach the Tyne and a three-month sojourn in dockyard. But the real point was that after the British battlecruisers had briefly engaged their counterparts around 2015, the battle was over and the arguments about the conduct of operations and conflicting claims on victory could begin.

The historical argument, especially in the 1920s, has largely concentrated on two issues, namely the claim on victory and the gunnery of the two sides.

With respect to the latter, the preserve of those cognoscenti with unrivalled knowledge of the thickness of armour to one hundredth of an inch or the number of rivets in individual ships, one can be suitably brief. A great deal of effort and ink has been expended on this subject, and to no very great purpose. Probably the best single summary of hits and rounds fired was provided in the official German history, but there has never been any serious disputing the observation of Arthur J. Marder to the effect that the figures are selective, that like with like are not necessarily compared and there was no allowance for hits on the *Wiesbaden*: the conclusion was that German percentage of hits should be lowered and the British raised, but by how much was impossible to determine.

In terms just of main armament (i.e., with shells of 12-in or greater) the German battleships and battlecruisers recorded an estimated 120 hits with 3,597 rounds, a hit rate of 3.34 per cent, whereas the British battleships and battlecruisers, with an estimated 100 hits and 4,598 rounds fired, achieved a hit rate of 2.17 per cent. Overall, one would suggest that perhaps one round in 40 found its mark, and that there was not a great deal to chose between the gunnery of the two sides. The returns reflect the fact that for the greater part of the exchanges German warships held the advantage of position, the element that made for equality being the fact that when the British held the advantage of position, they also held the advantage of numbers. What undoubtedly depressed British returns was the sorry fact that more than a third of British rounds – 1,609 or 34.99 per cent of the total – were fired by Beatty's six battlecruisers, and they most certainly never registered 40 hits on their enemy: the four battleships of the 5th Battle Squadron fired between them 1,099 rounds (23.90 per cent of the British total) and if it seems very unlikely that they recorded 27 hits, unlike the battlecruisers they did have the mitigating circumstance of extremely long range for much of proceedings.

In terms of victory, German claims were immediate and in the end prolonged, lasting for much of the inter-war period. The basis of these claims was very obvious, and it was provided by the photographic evidence of the destruction of the *Indefatigable*, *Queen Mary* and the *Invincible*. The British made no attempt to disguise the loss of three of their armoured cruisers, while the Germans suppressed details of their light cruiser losses. But the outcome of battles are seldom determined by losses unless these are so great as to have strategic repercussions in their own right, and this was most definitely not the case at Jutland. Because Britain possessed such superiority of numbers, her losses in this battle came within the margin of tolerance in that they could be absorbed without adverse strategic consequence. Just what this meant in terms of numbers is sometimes difficult to comprehend, but the British losses at Jutland – specifically three battlecruisers, three armoured cruisers and seven destroyers and one leader – should be set against the twenty dreadnoughts, nine battlecruisers, 62 light and 46 other cruisers, and 216 leaders and destroyers with which Britain went to war on 4 August 1914. In November 1918 Britain had 33 dreadnoughts, nine battlecruisers, 82 light and 27 other cruisers, and 433 leaders and destroyers – and these figures conceal the fact that in the course of hostilities Britain lost two dreadnoughts, three battlecruisers, a dozen light and thirteen other cruisers, and 67 leaders and destroyers.[19] The battlecruiser totals apart, these figures clearly show that the losses sustained off Jutland were, for Britain, no more than small change.

The question of which side prevailed at Jutland goes back to the question of why the battle was fought, and as has been noted, Jutland came about largely because the desire for battle was the minimum possible tactical response of the High Sea Fleet to its lost strategic position. No victory that a German fleet won in the southern, central, even northern North Sea was ever going to materially affect its strategic situation. No victory that it won was ever going to affect Britain's ability to trade on a world-wide scale, and no victory won by a German fleet was ever going to lift the Allied blockade. A fleet built primarily for political reasons could never win a victory of any real, still less major, strategic significance.

Such a reality manifested itself in two ways. The first, and immediate, was the reaction of the German naval high command to Jutland – that never again could the fleet be exposed to dangers of the kind it had so narrowly evaded in this battle. This, of course, became translated, in British argument, to the charge that the German fleet never came out again in order to give battle, and, in some cases, that the German fleet never came out again. Neither allegation was true, but nor was it true that the German fleet had come out in May 1916 in order to give battle – or at least the battle that was fought. It wanted a battle, a battle in which it set its terms of reference, but wars, campaigns and battles seldom have terms of reference determined by one side and one side alone. The German Navy most definitely read the lesson of Jutland correctly, that it had been very fortunate to have avoided overwhelming defeat. It came out again in August 1916 and again in November 1916, on both occasions not to give battle with the British fleet but again to seek to overwhelm part of the British fleet in order to achieve an equalisation of forces and thereby win the opportunity to give battle with genuine hope of success. In fact, in August 1916 it was very fortunate indeed not to be caught. Jellicoe and the British did everything right, but success, indeed even contact, nonetheless eluded them: no amount of German bombast after this sortie could disguise the fact that the High Sea Fleet had been very lucky to have avoided contact with the Grand Fleet.[20]

These efforts were part of the continuing German strategy of attrition, but begged the real question and consequence of Jutland: whether Germany should risk resorting to the *guerre de course* in order to eliminate Britain from the ranks of her enemies. In this respect, the result of Jutland was both very simple and profound. In the second half of 1916 Germany could countenance failure at Verdun, the loss of the initiative on the Western Front with the Anglo-French offensive astride the Somme, the elusiveness of decisive victory on the Eastern Front despite the victories of 1915, and the serious weakening of Austria-Hungary as a result of the Brusilov offensive, and failure at sea. As the Allied blockade bit ever deeper, so the reasoning that sought to justify adoption of the *guerre de course* became ever more strident, and herein was the evidence of victory at Jutland. The British and French were capable, whether separately or together, of stupidity of horrendous proportions, but they were never so stupid as to embark upon the one course of action that could only result in the United States of America joining the ranks of their enemies.

Along with the various German sorties in the North Sea after June 1916, there was to be the employment of German battleships and battlecruisers in the Baltic, most obviously as Russian resistance crumpled under the impact of revolution. The most important of these Baltic activities was the sequence of operations after 19 September 1917 which culminated with the move against Riga in October, and the action between the *König* and *Kronprinz* and the Russian pre-dreadnoughts *Tsarevich* and *Slava* off Moonsund on 17 October. After a most spirited resistance, evidence of the fact that she was one of the very few Russian ships not eaten away by revolutionary defeatism, the *Slava* was hit by several shells and disabled. As a result of flooding, she drew too much water to negotiate the dredged channel, and she was scuttled by the destroyer *Turkmenets-Stavropolsky*. This was the only example from the Russo-German war of major units fighting one another to the destruction of one of the parties, but lost and damaged warships afflicted themselves on both sides alike.

The Germans deployed five battleships and one battlecruiser from mid-September 1917 and four battleships specifically for the Riga endeavour in October: one of the original group of warships, the *Bayern*, and one of the second group, the *Grosser Kurfürst*, were mined and put out of service for some weeks. The main German effort in the Baltic, however, came in February 1918 when three of the older dreadnoughts were committed to the Gulf of Finland in an attempt to underwrite Finnish independence from Russia in advance of the signing of the Treaty of Brest Litovsk, the piece of paper that cast Germany as an insatiable conqueror and caused her irreparable moral injury. The effort with regard to Finland was successful: Germany concluded her alliance with the Finnish White Guards on 7 March and Bolshevik Russia recognised Finnish independence by treaty three days later, but the price the German Navy paid was the *Rheinland* running aground in fog off Lagskar Island in the Aland Sea on 11 April 1918 and then quite deliberately refusing to be pulled clear. The *Rheinland* defied salvage until 9 July, by which time she had lost all her guns, part of her armour and overall some 6,000 tons weight. She was then towed to Kiel, but given her state and as she was one of the first class of Germany's dreadnoughts, it was decided not to repair her and she was decommissioned, ending the war as an accommodation ship.

In terms of the Baltic and the battleship, the period after mid-1918 saw a number of actions but all were of small account: the Russian civil war and the wars of secession were not settled by sea power, though arguably what was the most famous single act in these wars, the British attack on the Kronstadt naval base, did involve battleships, and very much so. This attack, which took place in the early hours of 18 August 1919 and coincided with an air attack that was staged as a diversionary effort, is generally portrayed as having resulted in the sinking of two battleships, the dreadnought *Petropavlovsk* and the pre-dreadnought *Andrei Pervozvanni*, though some sources name the *Poltava* as the dreadnought and other sources have cited the *Impetator Aleksandr II* as the pre-dreadnought: the various sources do not seem to agree whether neither, one or both of the battleships were sunk. Russian sources, published since the end of the Soviet system, indicate that the dreadnought *Petropavlovsk* and the pre-dreadnought *Andrei Pervozvanni* were the only battleships at Kronstadt on 18 August 1919, and that the *Andrei Pervozvanni* was torpedoed and damaged but not sunk. She was subjected to major repairs, apparently just to keep her going for the moment, but was stripped of her secondary armament, which was issued to military, lake and riverine forces. She was laid up in 1920 and sold for scrap in 1923. The *Petropavlovsk* was not torpedoed in this attack, and the Soviet and western accounts that represent her as having been missed by torpedoes that exploded against the quayside appear to be correct.

The only other Baltic matter of passing interest from this period is the fact that the Russian dreadnought *Poltava*, which was laid up in the Petrograd naval harbour after October 1918, was wrecked by a major fire in her forward boiler room on 25 November 1919. She was then laid up and cannibalised but was the subject of plans for rebuilding in the period 1926–1932. She was to be rebuilt as a battleship, but when this intention was abandoned it was proposed that she be rebuilt as an aircraft carrier. This intention was abandoned, and the ship was stricken on 1 December 1940: she was then handed over for scrapping and laid up in the Leningrad canal, where, inevitably, she was involved in the defence of the city during the Great Patriotic War. She was sunk, but raised in May 1944, and after what seems an unconscionable delay was handed over for scrapping in 1949. Western sources have her being scrapped in 1923 or 1939 or 'during the mid-'50s', and given the extraordinary long lead times in such matters it may very well be that 'during the mid-'50s' is correct.

To return to more immediate matters, however, the North Sea in 1918 saw

German sorties, most notably the operation off Stavanger in April which involved more dreadnoughts and battlecruisers than had been present on the German side at Jutland. Armed with the element of surprise and choice in terms of when, where and in what strength to make their moves, the Germans were able to irritate, to wound, but never to inflict serious injury. Individual merchantmen and warships represented unfortunate losses for Britain, losses that perhaps should have been avoided, but no number of such raids could redeem a German situation which by this time was clearly a failing one. The submarine offensive could not drive Britain from the war and it could neither prevent nor seriously delay the arrival in Europe of American troops who were vital to the maintenance of Anglo-French will to win in the midst of the disasters of the spring of 1918. And herein was perhaps a final comment on the dreadnought battleships and the battlecruisers of the First World War, though the event itself took place more than two years before the armistice and indeed before the initiation of the unrestricted campaign against shipping.

The First World War at sea, in so many ways, represented a negation of all that had gone before in terms of the nature and conduct of war. War ceased to be one-dimensional. It was fought below the surface and on the surface, and it was fought in the air. It saw the mightiest of warships face any number of enemies that could sink it, something which had never happened in the age of sail. It was a war that saw smoke screens employed operationally for the first time in the Dogger Bank action in January 1915, and at Jutland there was an attempt to conduct reconnaissance with seaplanes from a carrier. Warships engaged targets beyond the horizon. Japanese, American and Brazilian warships made their way to European waters, and Japanese- and American-built merchantmen helped safeguard the Allies from defeat. These, and many other matters such as wireless, engines and fuel, represented aspects of war that were new, that were different, but in November 1916 there took place an incident, small in itself, but heavy in terms of symbolism and of change.

On 3 November, having broken down just to the west of Bergen the previous day, the German submarine U. 30 was returning to base in the company of U. 20, which eighteen months earlier had been responsible for the sinking of the *Lusitania*. In thick fog both submarines ran aground off Bövbjerg, northern Jutland. The next day salvage ships managed to refloat the U. 30, which could not submerge but nonetheless was able to make port, but the U.20 had broken her back and was blown up. In support of these salvage ships, the High Sea Fleet employed four battleships, one battlecruiser and a half-flotilla of destroyers, but German efforts attracted such attention that a number of British submarines were directed to the area, one of which, the J. 1, on 5 November torpedoed both the *Grosser Kurfürst* and *Kronprinz* with a single salvo of four torpedoes.[21] It was the only occasion in history when two capital ships were thus struck, and for the British perhaps unfortunately so, since nei-ther German battleship was seriously damaged, still less sunk: the *Kronprinz* was ready for operations on 6 December 1916, the *Grosser Kurfürst* on 10 February 1917. The point of significance, however, was obvious. Some three months before the start of the German unrestricted submarine campaign against Allied and neutral shipping, the dreadnought had been employed to support the submarine: a complete battle formation, with supporting ships, had been hazarded in an attempt to recover two stranded submarines. It was a remarkable development in terms of a weapons system less than two decades old, and it was an indicator of the massive change that had affected the nature and conduct of war in the industrial age. Here was a state, Germany, seeking the defeat of another not by ensuring its military defeat – the defeat of its armed forces – but by ensuring its economic, industrial and financial defeat through a course of action chosen in very large measure because the dread-nought fleet had to avoid battle: submarines would achieve what battleships could not, and indeed the battle fleet, in which so much political, moral and financial investment had been placed, was assigned merely the largely passive, 'fleet-in-being', role. In the end, of course, the German submarine offensive against shipping failed, though the German effort was not defeated, merely contained, but clearly war at sea, at least as far as Europe in general and Britain in particular were concerned, had undergone profound change. The nature and extent of this change, however, was most hard to discern at the time, and in any case had to await redefinition in the inter-war period.

The Inter-War Period:
Limitation, Reconstruction and the New

The end of the First World War saw the United States re-affirm her 1916 'second-to-none' intention, one inevitably directed against her wartime associates and which, by 1921 and in the straitened financial circumstances of the time, threatened to bankrupt all involved in a 'beggar-my-neighbour' race. Accordingly, the major powers met at Washington to limit naval armaments and to craft arrangements to ensure order and security in the western Pacific and eastern Asia. In the process the U.S. Navy attained parity with the British Navy, but if the Great Depression and empty treasuries ensured that limitation and reduction continued into the 1930s, the attempt to attain security through arms control miscarried: arms races were the symptom, not the cause, of national rivalries, which re-asserted themselves with unprecedented virulence in the Thirties.

The story of the inter-war period, in naval terms, is the story of limitation and its immediate aftermath, a process which was begun at Washington in 1921–1922 and was subsequently continued and then brought to an end at London. But without in any way demeaning such terms of reference, the story of the dreadnought battleship in the inter-war period can be told primarily by reference to the one nation afforded but little consideration in this book's earlier chapters. Japan has figured but briefly in previous pages, and then primarily concerning the Russo-Japanese war and the battle of Tsushima, and for obvious reasons: she was only marginal to the story of the dreadnought battleship prior to the First World War, and during that conflict, she, her dreadnoughts and indeed the *Nippon Teikoku Kaigun* (Imperial Japanese Navy) itself, were again but marginally involved.

It is one of those unfortunate facts that Japanese naval participation in the First World War is so little-known in Europe and North America, but apart from operations in 1914 against German possessions in the western Pacific and in China, the *Kaigun* sent three destroyer formations to the eastern Mediterranean in 1917,[1] and at different times had cruisers based on Singapore, Mauritius, Cape Town and on both the west and east coasts of Australia. Even less well-known is the fact that at various times during the First World War both Britain and the United States separately asked Japan to send capital ships to various theatres. On 2 September 1914, and in the immediate aftermath of the *Goeben* debacle, the British Foreign Secretary, Sir Edward Grey, asked ambassador Inoue Katsunosuke that Japan send battlecruisers to the Mediterranean, and two months later, on 4 November, ambassador Sir Conyngham Greene asked the Japanese government to send battlecruisers to European waters: at the same time Winston Churchill, as First Lord of the Admiralty and using the informal naval network between the British and Japanese Navies, seconded this request with a 'Most Secret Message' to Navy Minister Yashiro Rokuro. Perhaps more surprisingly, but in a manner reminiscent of the first British request that had come a month after Britain entered the war, on 11 May 1917 U.S. Secretary of State Robert Lansing asked the Japanese to send two battlecruisers to the American east coast, a request repeated on 5 August by U.S. Navy Secretary Josephus Daniels. On 21 October 1917, possibly at a Trafalgar meeting, and again the following month, the British Foreign Secretary, Arthur Balfour, asked ambassador Chinda Sutemi to send two battlecruisers to Europe, specifically to join the Grand Fleet.

In light of later events, it may well be that Japan was singularly ill-advised not to have complied with these various requests, most obviously those American requests which would have resulted in Japanese battlecruisers, however temporarily, finding themselves based at New York or Norfolk: if nothing else, such an eventuality might well have defused some of the more virulent American antagonism toward Japan in the inter-war period. Be that as it may, these episodes share two facts of life. The first, quite simply, is that the Japanese refused to do the bidding of their allies, and both in 1914 and 1917 justified their refusal in terms of fear of German naval activity in the Pacific. While a certain sympathy can be extended to the Japanese with reference to 1914, at least until the Falklands battle finally eliminated von Spee's squadron as a possible threat against which provision had to be made, Japanese hesitations in 1917, in the face of the occasional armed merchant raider, hardly justified the retention in home waters of the fourth largest dreadnought force in the world. What was at work here was a Japanese unwillingness to shoulder more of a war than was strictly necessary: as it was, and as has been noted, the despatch of a destroyer force to the eastern Mediterranean represented the first Asian military involvement in European matters since the thirteenth century (the operations of the Indian Army on the Western Front after October 1914 and at Gallipoli and Salonika excepted).

The second fact of life was perhaps somewhat surprising. This related to the quality of Japanese dreadnoughts and battlecruisers, which were probably the best in the world whether in 1914 or 1917, and it provides an element of continuity throughout the inter-war period that went alongside limitation and reduction. This state of affairs, namely the high quality of Japanese warships, was very deliberate. It had originated in the 1896 programme, when Japan had committed herself to build a force of six battleships and four armoured cruisers as the minimum force needed to deal with any naval formation, from one or more nation, that might be sent from Europe to the Far East. The four battleships ordered under this programme were more powerfully armed and possessed of thicker armour than any other battleship in existence – something that sat somewhat strangely alongside the fact that the first two ships to be ordered, the *Asahi* and *Mikasa*, were built in Britain and British battleships were not excluded from Japanese calculations. The same formula, the demand for qualitatively superiority relative to more numerous enemies, was repeated with the *Kongo*-class battlecruisers. These were Japan's response to the *Dreadnought* and were ordered under the 1910–1911 budget: the *Kongo* herself was the last major Japanese warship built overseas, in the same Vickers yard at Barrow which had built the *Kashima* and *Mikasa*.

The *Kongo*-class battlecruisers were improvements on the *Lion* class of 1909 and 1910. Though there were variations between the *Kongo* and her home-built sisters, the basic point of difference between these and their contemporary British equivalents was a heavier armament, specifically the secondary armament, which included sixteen 6-in/152-mm guns, and a considerably greater radius of action: in most other details there really was not a great deal to chose between the two sets of ships. With the *Nagato*-class battleships of the 1916–1917 programme, however, the *Kaigun* aimed to secure for itself two units that combined the offensive and defensive capabilities of a battleship with a battlecruiser's speed, the *Nagato* and *Mutsu* having a full load displacement of 38,500 tons compared to the 32,200 tons of the *Kongo* and her three sisters. The qualitative advantage that the *Kaigun* sought over potential enemies lay in the provision of a main armament of eight 16-in/406-mm guns and a speed of 26–27 knots, which compared to the twelve 14-in/356-mm guns and 21 knots of the contemporary *New Mexico* and *Tennessee* classes. The offensive advantage that Japan sought by adopting a heavier guns than those used in the British and American navies was obvious from the start: the advantage that the *Kaigun* sought to obtain from the high speed of the *Nagato* and *Mutsu* was long kept secret. The link between the 1896 programme, which within a year was modified in favour of a programme of six battleships and six armoured cruisers, and the two *Yamato*-class battleships of the 1937 Third Replenishment Programme is direct, as is the link with the Washington and London limitation treaties.

The problem, however, is that nothing about the *Kaigun* is either simple or straightforward, not least the definition of the starting point for an examination of its dreadnoughts and battlecruisers. In one sense, the logical starting point is the series of calculations made in the aftermath of the war with China (July 1894–April 1895) and the Triple Intervention, on the part of France, Germany and Russia, which deprived Japan of most of the gains that she had registered in that war. These calculations governed Japanese naval policy, most clearly in terms of construction programmes, until 1904 and the start of the war with Russia, but they do not represent a realistic point of departure for a reason that is not immediately clear.

Japan initiated hostilities with Russia in February 1904 at a time when the main strength of her fleet consisted of six battleships and eight armoured cruisers: in addition, Japan had six protected cruisers and sixteen other cruisers of various descriptions, including 'armoured cruisers' of an age which suggested they belied their title. None of the battleships or armoured cruisers and just one of the protected cruisers had been built in Japan, and she, the *Niitaka*, which had been built in the Kure navy yard, was only completed on 27 January 1904, less than two weeks before the start of war. Most of the main units of the fleet – all the battleships and four of the armoured cruisers – were built in the country with which Japan after 1902 was formally allied, Britain. This alliance was critical in four respects: first, alliance with the greatest naval power in the world conferred on Japan respectability, a basic recognition of equality which few powers were really prepared to formally acknowledge; second, the alliance checked any other European country coming to Russia's support during the war of 1904–1905; third, the alliance provided the basis of Japanese intervention on the Allied side in 1914; and fourth, the alliance, and the success registered in the war with Russia, encouraged Japan and the *Kaigun* to think outside their previous naval terms of reference. This latter point was crucially important because after the Russian war the *Kaigun* faced its real enemy – the *Nippon Teikoku Rikugun* (Imperial Japanese Army).

In the confrontation between the *Kaigun* and the *Rikugun* after 1905 three interrelated matters were at stake. The first was institutional, and was in many ways a throwback to the days before 1893 when, in effect, the navy was part of the army and afforded only a local defence role. The second was budgetary because what was at stake, in the straitened circumstances of the immediate post-war period, was spending priorities, specifically whether naval spending should take pride of place ahead of military spending. The third was the definition of national priorities, what today would be called 'national security strategy'. The three were linked in the immediate aftermath of the Russian war by the fact that the *Kaigun* saw the lessons of the war in naval terms. Bringing together various arguments that had been circulated before the war, the navy affirmed that whereas a *Rikugun* defeat on the mainland would have been most unfortunate, a naval defeat would have been tantamount to a national disaster. There was no real basis of argument on this particular point, but it was one that left two matters unresolved. The fact was that as a result of the victories which had been won by the army during this war, Japan had a presence on the Asian mainland, in Korea and southern Manchuria, and it was to the continent, as a source of raw materials and investment as well as its potential as an export market, that so much Japanese attention was directed in the aftermath of the 1904–1905 war. Moreover, the combination of the British alliance and elimination of Russia from consideration as a potential enemy left the *Kaigun* with no real opponent, and in any case with all the Pacific islands under American or European control and China in the process of being divided into spheres of influence, there was no real *raison d'être* for the navy after 1905: Japan's oceanic trade was modest and whatever the *Kaigun's* arguments, in reality there was no place to go, unless it was to Korea, Manchuria and northern China.

What was really at stake in the confrontation between the two Japanese services was the right to be considered the senior service, with all that this implied in terms of social standing and prestige, access to state funding and definition of national priorities, and perhaps the result of this clash between the services was inevitable: there was a compromise that denied both services priority. This was disastrous: inter-service rivalry became institutionalised with the basic issue, the definition of national priorities, never resolved. In a more immediate sense, however, the result was most unfortunate for the *Kaigun* because in the articulation of its argument it had to make comparisons and define potential enemies. After 1905 there was no European enemy against which provision had to be made, and that left just the United States of America. But in this period, between 1905 and 1907, there was no clash of fundamental interests between Japan and the United States, and there was no evidence that Washington harboured aggressive intent toward Japan. Nonetheless, the Imperial Defence Policy statement of April 1907, which defined Russia as Japan's most likely military opponent in eastern Asia, underwrote two sets of *Kaigun* demands. In effect it sanctioned the *taikan kyohoshugi* doctrine, which stressed the importance of acquiring big ships with big guns in the form of a construction programme for eight 20,000-ton dreadnoughts and eight 18,000-ton battlecruisers. The justification for such a programme – and it bears recall that it was not until 1901 that armour plate was produced in Japan and that the first battleship to be built in Japan was not laid down in Yokosuka navy yard until 15 May 1905 – was identified as the United States and the U.S. Navy. In reality the latter had been selected if not as the only possible enemy, then the only potential enemy that could justify programmes of the size which the *Kaigun* sought.

This 1907 definition of priorities, or perhaps more accurately this 1907 failure to define priorities, represented the first stage in what was to take shape as the eight-eight programme that acquired status close to holy writ by the time of the Washington limitation conference. There were, however, two more pressing matters. The first, simply, was that the whole programme made no sense whatsoever: at this time there was little, if any, point in identifying the United States as the power against which Japan had to measure herself in terms of naval security. The second was that the eight-eight formula came to be linked with certain rather esoteric calculations that likewise entered into naval usage before the First World War.

Foremost among these calculations was the idea that a fleet needed a 50 per cent margin of superiority in order to have any chance of recording decisive victory in a fleet action. This was a rough rule of thumb which was being taken on board by various navies, but in the case of the *Kaigun* the definition was very precise because it provided the basis of the subsequent argument that the *Kaigun* had to maintain itself at a strength of 70 per cent of that of the U.S. Navy. The argument seems specious because the *Kaigun*'s attempt to resist the 60 per cent standard at Washington would appear to be based on a 5 per cent calculation, i.e., that Japan was afforded a measure of security on a 70 per cent standard because the Americans could not have half as much again, and such security could never be secured on a 60 per cent standard. Nonetheless, this set of calculations entered the *Kaigun* lexicon, as indeed did two more over the years.

The second of these calculations, which really did belong to the inter-war period rather than before 1914, was that a fleet lost one-tenth of its fighting effectiveness with every thousand miles/1,600-km it advanced from its base. The first was the formula that suggested that the basis of fleet comparison lay in the difference between relative squares. Sometimes known as the N^2 Law and given algebraic form in 1914, this held that the cumulative advantage of superior numbers would result in a fleet of ten battleships annihilating an enemy force of seven battleships at the cost of three of its own number – the square root of the difference between the square of ten and the square of seven, i.e., the square root of 100 less 49 or the square root of 51, being, in real terms, seven. More relevantly, the Japanese calculation on the 70 per cent standard was that American obligations outside the Pacific would ensure that the United States would always be forced to divide her fleet and that perhaps no more than five battleships might be available for battle. On this basis, the Japanese would hold the advantage of numbers and could expect to lose just two of seven battleships in annihilating a five-strong American battle force, and thereafter would be left to fight any American battle formation sent to the Pacific on the basis of equality.

The best that can be said about these calculations and the use to which they were to be put by the Imperial Navy is that they were thoroughly mendacious in the correct sense of that word: they were used to support arguments that had already been decided. The two obvious points of concern had to be the selection of the United States as the country against which naval strength would be compared and the simple fact that, if she so decided, the United States could build on a scale and at a pace that would quickly render *Kaigun* hopes of maintaining itself at seven-tenth's strength a mere illusion. Nonetheless, the Imperial Defence Policy statement of April 1907, the eight-eight formula and these other mathematical calculations provide the essential background to the process whereby Japan started building dreadnoughts and battlecruisers and found herself by the end of the First World War in a construction race with the United States which was ended only by the Washington naval limitation treaty of February 1922.

The building of the *Dreadnought* caught the Japanese with four battleships either under construction or about to be laid down, and immediately presented the problem of whether these were to be scrapped, re-armed or built as originally intended. The ships concerned were the *Kashima* and *Katori* and the *Satsuma* and *Aki*, the latter being laid down after the *Dreadnought* was launched. The *Satsuma* and *Aki* were all but sister ships and both were larger than the *Dreadnought*, but given the financial limitations of the day the decision was taken not to re-arm these two ships along the lines of the *Dreadnought* and their construction was deliberately slowed in an attempt to save money. These two ships nonetheless were the first battleships to be built in Japan, though the greater part of the material that went into the *Satsuma* had been made abroad. Also wrong-footed at this time were the sister ships *Ibuki* and *Kurama*. These two ships were armoured cruisers and, like their predecessors the *Tsukuba* and *Ikoma*, which had been laid down during the Russian war, they were overtaken by events in the form of the *Invincible* class of battlecruiser. The combination of continuing budgetary difficulties and the realisation that these particular ships had been relegated from the first rank meant that their construction and completion proved somewhat leisurely affairs: the *Ibuki* was not completed until November 1909 and the *Kurama* evaded completion for another two years.[2]

When completed, the four armoured cruisers were rated as battlecruisers, which, manifestly, they were not. In terms of firepower and armour, they were at least the equal of the *Invincible*, but in the crucial matter of speed they were really no better provided than battleships, whether Japanese or British. By the time all of these warships were in service, however, the *Kaigun* was a little more than a year from taking delivery of its first dreadnoughts, though very oddly these first two ships, the *Kawachi* and *Settsu*, are often not afforded the appropriate dignity of such status. This has been on account of their twelve 12-in/305-mm guns being of different calibre, which would seem to be not a very good reason to thus insult them. The two battleships had 50-calibre guns in the two main-line turrets, but in the four echelon turrets they carried 45-calibre guns. The point of difference was important in that different calibrations necessitated different elevations to a given range, but in other respects these two warships really did belong to the dreadnought *specie* and represented a significant advance over the *Dreadnought* herself in terms of secondary armament. In terms of armour, they were as well provided as the contemporaneous *Ostfriesland* class, or slightly better provided than the *Neptune* or the *Colossus* class. The *Kaigun* chose to install turbines, secured from Britain, and was thus only the third navy in the world to adopt such propulsion for its battle force. The most obvious weaknesses of the *Kawachi* and *Settsu* were that they had four turrets *en echelon*, which meant that two would not be in action at any one time, and that even for this class, the first class of battleship designed wholly in Japan, the *Kaigun* remained dependent upon Britain, and specifically Armstrong Whitworth, for the provision of guns and mountings.

The *Kawachi* and *Settsu* were good ships, as indeed were the *Satsuma*, *Aki* and, at a different level, the *Tsukuba* and *Ikoma*, the latter being very favourably received when they visited Britain soon after completion. The obvious Japanese problem was the pace of development generated by the Anglo-German naval race by 1908–1909 and the fact that, just as Russia after 1900 had been forced into major construction programmes by German aspirations, so the United States from this time, in the second half of the first decade of the twentieth century, was beginning to build at a pace which would assure her of at least third place in the naval pecking order. It was one of the odd features of a European arms race that the United States and Japan should have embarked on programmes that very quickly both publicly identified in terms of need against the other.

In 1910, however, the Imperial Navy found itself caught by the financial legacy of the Russian war. The *Kaigun* staff formally requested the Navy Ministry to secure approval for the eight-eight formula, and with it a construction programme that would authorise the construction of eight battleships and eight battlecruisers. The Ministry reduced this request to seven battleships and three battlecruisers, but the Cabinet, with very little compunction, cut these totals to one battleship and four battlecruisers: the Diet authorised this programme. The lengthy process whereby *Kaigun* hopes were curbed nonetheless had one unanticipated bonus. In 1909 the battlecruiser programme had been geared to the British *Invincible* class, but in the course of the year it became clear that the British were planning major increases in battlecruiser displacement, armament, armour and speed. The 555-ft/169.72-m length and 18,800 tons of the *Indefatigable*, which had carried eight 12-in/305-mm guns and some six to seven inches of armour in her belt and turrets, was to be followed by the 26,270 tons of the *Lion* class, which were to carry eight 13.5-in/343-mm guns in four centre-line turrets: class members were to have 27 knots compared to the 23 knots of the *Indefatigable*. Confronted by the reality that the British were planning as a response to the *Moltke* class a new class which was very considerably superior to the *Invincibles*, the *Kaigun* hesitated before placing the order for the first of its four battlecruisers with Vickers in Barrow-in-Furness. With this move the *Kaigun* anticipated its being able to gain access to the very latest of British thinking and also design and manufacture, and while the first battlecruiser was being built it planned to import the more sophisticated items, such as guns, mounting and turrets, for the second of its four battlecruisers: the third and fourth would be built in Japan, at Kobe and Nagasaki, using Japanese materials copied from the newly acquired imports.

By such means the Japanese avoided building an initial class of battlecruisers grossly inferior to the best that was abroad, the critical point being that they instead they were able to match both the increase of size of ships and the increase in armament. As originally conceived, this new class was to have been equipped with 12-in/305-mm guns, but during the planning process an awareness that the British planned to adopt the 13.5-in/343-mm gun with their new classes of battleships and battlecruisers prompted the Japanese, aware that the Americans were likely to follow the British lead, to adopt the untried 14-in/356-mm gun. The overall result of these various developments was that the *Kongo*, when finally completed and despatched to Japan in November 1913, was perhaps the best battlecruiser in the world. In terms of armour and speed, she was a match for any battlecruiser in the British and German navies, while she carried a strong secondary armament and a powerful main armament on centre line with the two forward turrets superimposed: the turret amidship was also afforded good arcs of fire. Overall, the *Kongo* class served notice of Japan's earnestness in matters naval, that she had to be considered one of the leading naval powers, though there was irony here: the *Kongo* class was one of the most successful class of capital ship ever built by any nation, but was never repeated.

The *Fuso*, authorised at the same time as the four battlecruisers, was laid down at the same time as the *Haruna* and *Kirishima*, and was complemented in the 1913 programme by a sister ship, the *Yamashiro*. These eight units – the *Kawachi* and *Settsu*, the four *Kongo*-class battlecruisers and two *Fuso*-class battleships – represented the sum of Japanese dreadnoughts and battlecruisers ordered prior to the outbreak of war in Europe in 1914: with the battlecruiser *Hiei* being completed on the day that Britain declared war on Germany, the outbreak of war itself found the *Kaigun* in possession of two dreadnought battleships and two battlecruisers. On such numbers, Japan belonged to the second group of would-be naval powers, alongside France, Italy and Russia, and in the wake of Britain, Germany and the United States, but this situation was to be transformed by the First World War and for two reasons. The first was that the European continental powers in effect ceased to count as major naval powers either because of the demands of continental war, as was the case for France and Italy, or because of the combination of the demands of continental warfare and defeat, as was the case for Germany and Russia. By 1919 just three powers remained in the naval frame: Britain, Japan and the United States.

The second matter related to the fact that the First World War brought massive change to the international order. The immediate point of relevance, noted in the opening to this chapter, was that Japan was largely spared the burden of war: she was in that very fortunate position of being free to take as much or as little of the war as she chose. But Japan was far more fortunate than this bare statement would suggest. Allied shipping all but disappeared from the Pacific and Indian Oceans during the war, and Japanese shipping and, at least until late 1917, Japanese freight charges, took their place: the critical gain this represented for Japan was that earnings from shipping made good the national deficit on visible trade. Markets that had been in receipt of European, and particularly British, exports had to look elsewhere to meet their needs, and in the case of Japan this proved to be a massive boost to the general process of the industrialisation of the country because it provided assured profitability. Japan took on the role of major supplier to her various allies, most notably Russia, and perhaps surprisingly this latter task produced one little-known development. Japanese shipping earmarked to carry exports to Europe was detailed to return home not the way it had come, either through the Mediterranean or around the Cape, but across the North Atlantic, where it was to collect war material made in the United States, and paid for by Britain in cash or credit, and then moved via the Panama Canal and Vancouver and thence by the great circle route either to Japanese home ports or direct to Vladivostok. Such a development, when tied to the other matters that worked to Japan's advantage, gave rise to the saying that was common in the Japanese business community in these years: the war brought 'an opportunity that comes along once in a thousand years'.

Many examples could be cited in order to spell out the various changes and what these meant to Japan, and in order to keep these in perspective, it suffices to note two matters, namely the Japanese shipping and steel industries, both of which received massive boosts as a result of the demands of war. Prior to 1914, Japan was heavily dependent on British and German steel imports. Forced to meet growing demands by an expansion of indigenous resources, Japanese steel output increased by half during the war years, while the Japanese coal industry's output rose by some 37 per cent in the same period. In terms of usage, Japanese shipyards used some 55,000 tons of steel in 1913 but Allied demands for shipping meant that this figure had risen to 646,000 tons in 1919: the number of private yards capable of building steel ships of more than 1,000 tons rose from five in 1913 to 41 by 1918, while no less than 292,754 tons of ships were exported during the war years, almost half to Britain.

In effect, the war 'granted' Japan a shipbuilding industry and a sizeable merchant marine with shipping companies assured of major returns: before 1914, the biggest of these companies, Nippon Yusen Kaisha, never had an annual profit of more than six million yen, but in 1918 alone it made 86 million yen. What was equally significant about this development was the relative lightness of Japanese merchantmen losses during the war: these amounted to about 7 per cent of oceanic tonnage compared to 37.3 per cent for Britain or, more interestingly, a staggering 60.3 per cent for neutral Norway. Nonetheless, two codicils need to be noted. Industrial output and the number of workers in industry declined after 1921, and Japanese industry was not able to recover to its wartime output in coal, iron and cotton production until the late 1920s. Moreover, the major wartime expansion of industry was directed to light engineering and not heavy industry. Metal and machine engineering industries accounted for just 4.3 per cent of all Japanese output in 1900 but by 1920 for 21.5 per cent, while the number of employees in light industry rose from 267,000 in 1914 to 1,288,000 in 1919, almost a five-fold increase primarily as a result of war and the change that it wrought to trade patterns.[3]

What all this meant was that by 1914–1915 Japan was better placed to build warships on any significant scale than at any time over the previous decade, and in two respects such a situation constituted not luxury but necessity. The advantage that the Japanese gained with the *Kongo*-class battlecruisers, specifically their 14-in/356-mm gun main armament, was all but overtaken even as the *Kongo* and her sisters were ordered and laid down. The American decision to adopt a battleship design with ten 14-in/356-mm guns with the *Texas* (ordered on 17 December 1910) and *New York* (ordered on 1 May 1911) naturally invited an immediate counter: the *Fuso* and *Yamashiro*, and their successors, the *Hyuga* and *Ise*, carried twelve 14-in/356-mm guns in six turrets, all on centre line. With the American decision that the *Pennsylvania* (ordered on 22 August 1912) and the *Arizona* (ordered on 4 March 1913) would also carry twelve 14-in/356-mm guns, albeit in four triple turrets, the Japanese moved to the decision that the two battleships which would be ordered under the 1916–1917 programme, the *Nagato* and *Mutsu*, would be the first in the world to be armed with 16-in/406-mm guns: the two warships were to carry eight such guns, in four twin turrets. With the exception of the subsequent *Mary-*

land-class battleships, no other battleships or battlecruisers ever carried this combination of gun size and numbers.

There were three points of significance about these developments. The first was the fact that Japan's financial well-being allowed her to embark on a programme which by 1915 was termed 'eight-four' and represented a halfway house to the eight-eight programme. The second was that the *Hyuga* and *Ise* had been planned as advanced versions of the *Fuso* and *Yamashiro*, but during the planning and early construction phases so many changes were incorporated that they emerged from their yards as belonging to a new class. In their turn, the *Nagato* and *Mutsu* clearly, and not simply on account of their 16-in/406-mm guns, also belonged to a very different class. There was major qualitative improvement in these three successive classes, and the obvious point of difference between these and their American and British contemporaries was their much greater length. In these days, before small tube boilers, the demand for high speed meant boiler and engine rooms in numbers that added some 100 feet/30.6 metres on overall lengths. The *Fuso* and *Yamashiro*, at 673 feet/205.81 metres overall length, were exactly 100 feet longer than the *New York* and *Texas*, while the *Hyuga* and *Ise*, at 683 feet/208.87 metres overall length, again were exactly 100 feet longer than the *Nevada* and *Oklahoma*. The battleships of the *New Mexico*, *Tennessee* and *Maryland* classes were all of 624 feet/190.83 metres overall length: the *Nagato* and *Mutsu*, at 708 feet/216.51 metres overall length, were second only to the *Renown*, *Repulse* and the *Hood* in terms of length, the *Courageous* class and the *Furious* thankfully being excluded from serious consideration. Increased size, and with it increased cost, were the prize exacted by the search for qualitative advantage.

The third point of significance was that the *Kaigun* request – for four battleships and in effect an eight-four formula – was rejected in 1916 by a Diet which refused to authorise more than one battleship and two battlecruisers. Most unfortunately, this restraint came at the very time when the United States was vociferously claiming the right to build for herself a fleet 'second to none'. To realise such an ambition, the U.S. Congress authorised the construction of no fewer than 162 warships, including ten battleships and six battlecruisers,[4] which were to be built between 1916 and 1919. With six of the battleships and five of the battlecruisers named,[5] this programme came on the heels of the 1915 programme, which had authorised the construction of the *California* and *Tennessee*, and the *Colorado*, *Maryland*, *West Virginia* and the *Washington*. The two programmes were to be part of a general effort that was to result in the creation of a fleet with no fewer than 60 battleships and battlecruisers by 1925. With the *Indiana* battleships assigned an armament of twelve 16-in/406-mm guns on a 43,200-ton displacement and the *Saratoga* or *Constellation* battlecruisers an armament of eight 16-in/406-mm guns on a

43,000-ton displacement, the implications of these programmes for Japan need no elaboration – suffice it to note that had these two programmes been fully implemented, the *Kaigun* would have been reduced to impotent irrelevance.

As it was, in 1917 the *Kaigun* secured authorisation for a programme of 63 warships, three battleships included, and in 1918 two more battlecruisers were authorised. In other words, on the back of the unprecedented prosperity that the First World War brought to Japan, the Imperial Navy in 1917 secured the endorsement of what was an eight-six programme and in the following year its full eight-eight programme. The catch, however, was obvious. In 1915 and 1916 the United States authorised the construction of sixteen battleships and six battlecruisers, and these numbers were on top of the seventeen battleships that had been ordered and laid down before or in 1915.[6] Of this latter total, only the three members of the *New Mexico* class, which were ordered in January 1914, had not been completed prior to November 1916. The days of American paper programmes, those days in the last decades of the nineteenth century when American building programmes seemed to take forever and a day, were passed: it could be assumed that American declared intent would be translated into timely reality – or so it must have seemed.

The interesting point about the situation that had developed by 1916 was that in framing its programme the U.S. Navy, quite deliberately, had set aside the situation created by general war in Europe in favour of what it considered the 'worst-case' possibility that might emerge after this war. What it stated was the need to guard against either a German-Japanese or Anglo-Japanese alliance that would be capable of threatening the United States in two oceans and also capable of preventing any expansion of American overseas trade. The least that could be said about such logic was that it seemed only to grasp at the exceedingly unlikely in order to justify the manifestly unnecessary.

For Japan, however, the development was little short of disastrous. Perhaps the most pre-eminent study of the Imperial Navy in this period suggests that between 1911 and 1923 the *Kaigun* more or less matched the U.S. Navy in terms of commissioning battle units: the figures given cite fourteen Japanese warships compared to seventeen American.[7] But these totals are somewhat misleading, in part because of a convenient exclusion of 1910 returns and with them four American dreadnoughts which entered service, and in part because the figures include armoured cruisers which cannot be considered battle units after 1911. Eliminating armoured cruisers from consideration, the overall balance of commissioning between 1910 and 1918 was fifteen American battleships compared to six Japanese dreadnoughts and four battlecruisers entering service in these years, the Japanese battleship total having to be adjusted downward to take account of the loss of the *Kawachi* in 1916. What made the

situation even worse for Japan was that even if the early American dreadnoughts were discounted from consideration, her position really did not
change much because in 1918 the United States had another five dreadnoughts
under construction compared to just two being built in Japanese yards.

Thus the situation in which Japan found herself was potentially disastrous.
She had been out-built 3:2 – the crucial 50 per cent margin of superiority – by
the United States, and in fact at the end of 1916 she had just six dreadnoughts
and battlecruisers compared to fourteen American battleships. Even allowing
for the quality of her last three classes of battleship, plus the battlecruisers,
there was no escaping the fact that she simply could not match either the
immediate 1916 programme or the general American building intention with
its 1925 perspective. For the moment at least, Japan had been spared a more
obvious display of American industrial and financial might. Notwithstanding
the American intention to build a fleet 'second to none', after 1916 the United
States had found herself unable to act upon her intention. Her entry into the
war, and specifically her need to support her allies with escorts, shipping and
steel, meant that the decision to build a battle fleet had to be set aside. By the
time the First World War came to an end, however, the situation in which the
United States found herself had changed in two crucial respects. Working in
Japan's favour was the very simple fact that the costs involved in the American
programme, coming on top of a war which had seen the American national
debt rise from about a billion dollars in 1914 to nearly 27 billion dollars in
1919, made even the United States hesitate: with almost seven dollars in ten of
all state spending in 1918 financed by borrowing, the simple fact was that the
United States was ill-placed to pick up the bill that would be presented for the
'second to none' programme.

The situation in which the United States found itself was matched, in very
different ways, by those of Britain and Japan. For Britain, the American declaration of intent was nothing short of potentially disastrous. She ended 1918
the possessor of no fewer than 33 dreadnoughts and nine battlecruisers, plus
three hybrid cruisers, and with the *Hood* under construction. But of this total
of 42 capital ships in commission, no fewer than ten dreadnoughts and four
battlecruisers, one third of overall numbers, were equipped with 12-in/305-
mm guns: 1919 found each and every one of these either relegated to reserve
status awaiting disposal or allocated to secondary or tertiary duties which
indicated that they could no longer be regarded as fit for the battle line.[8]
Herein, of course, was the long-term legacy of having initiated the original
dreadnought race: with the destruction of the German battle fleet in 1919,
Britain alone possessed the long tail of first-generation dreadnoughts and battlecruisers, the value of which had been disproportionately reduced as a result
of the successive qualitative improvements of their successors. Both the United

States and Japan possessed first-generation dreadnoughts – the Americans eight and the Japanese just the battleship *Settsu* – but would never have to replace ageing units on the scale that confronted the British simply in order to maintain existing numbers.

As regards Japan, however, both the situation in which she found herself in 1918 and her reaction to it were all but wilfully perverse. What had happened over the previous decade pointed clearly, unambiguously, to one conclusion: not to get involved in an arms race with the United States of America. It was to be a conclusion grasped by certain leading naval officers at this time, and the point was so evident it scarcely needed recounting, still less explaining. By 1918, and despite Japan having somehow taken on board the eight-eight formula, she risked being overwhelmed numerically by a United States that had comfortably outstripped her in terms of numbers of capital ships without really trying. But that, of course, was not how all Japanese naval officers saw things.

In June 1918, the Japanese government undertook the first revision of its Imperial Defence Policy since 1907. Not altogether surprisingly, this revision belied its name: Russia, then in the grip of revolution, remained the enemy on the mainland, and in effect the United States retained her position as the country against which naval provision had to be made. To deal with the American naval challenge, the Imperial Navy proposed that it should accept the eight-eight formula over an eight-year period with Japan committed to the building of three capital ships every year. By this time it had come to the conclusion that massed battle fleets and extended battle lines were not viable, that in effect no battle formation should consist of more than a couple of divisions numbering more than eight dreadnoughts or battlecruisers. Therefore the *Kaigun* was feeling its way to the idea whereby in eight years it would come into possession of three fleets, each with eight capital ships. Of course, on the basis of such numbers the American programme of 60 capital ships to face an Anglo-Japanese combination seemed to come within the realms of the necessary, but there was the added dimension to Japanese calculations: qualitative superiority. The *Nagato* and *Mutsu* were ordered under the 1916 and 1917 programmes respectively, but in 1917 two more units were planned. These were the battleships *Tosa* and *Kaga*, and though these still had to be laid down in November 1918, work was already in hand on two other capital ships, the battlecruisers *Akagi* and *Amagi*, which had also been authorised under the 1917 programme. These latter ships seem to have anticipated the Imperial Defence Policy statement of 1918.

The *Tosa* and *Kaga* were designed as high-speed battleships capable of 26.5 knots and armed with ten 16-in/406-mm guns in five twin turrets. A notable feature of these two ships was to have been improved quality and sloped armour, though this remained more modest than in contemporary American battleships and the Japanese units revealed their ancestry by their retention of a secondary armament which remained housed in casements, partly on the main deck. The two ships were laid down in 1920 and both were to be launched at the end of 1921. The *Akagi* and *Amagi* represented one more step beyond the *Tosa* and *Kaga*. On a full load displacement of 47,000 tons, these were to have the same ten 16-in/406-mm guns, slightly thinner armour and, with an almost 50 per cent increase in power, a speed of 30 knots. These two ships were authorised in 1919 and laid down in 1920, while their sister ships *Atago* and *Takao* were authorised in 1920 and laid down in 1921. They were deliberately conceived as direct counters to the British *Hood*, then nearing completion, and the American *Saratoga*-class battlecruisers.

These six ships, however, were not the sum of *Kaigun* aspirations and planning at the end of the First World War. At the same time as the various designs were being cast and recast and initial appropriations voted, there were two more classes for which plans and designs were being prepared. The first, planned for the 1921 programme, was a four-strong class of slightly improved *Tosa*s, the second, planned for the 1922 programme, was a four-strong class of battleships nearly 100 feet/30.58 metres longer than the members of the *Tosa* class and afforded thicker armour, the same speed and eight 18-in/457-mm guns. The first of these two four-strong classes were numbered between nine and twelve with the first two named *Kii* and *Owari* respectively, the second between thirteen and sixteen, and all had been assigned their respective shipyards, with the Kure and Yokosuka navy yards and Kawasaki at Kobe and Mitsubishi at Nagasaki each assigned one unit from each class.

Overall the Japanese situation is cause for a certain wonderment: the fact that Japan was out-built by a potentially decisive margin between 1906 and 1916 seems only to have deepened a commitment to a failed eight-eight formula which, despite and because of its inadequacies, was thereafter expanded. For Britain, however, there could be no hiding because, whatever her various calculations, everything came back to the declared intention that she maintain a one-power standard, i.e., that she maintain her navy at parity with that of the United States. There were two problems herein. The first was that Britain's traditional shipbuilding superiority over the rest of the world ended in the course of the First World War: by 1918 American shipyards were building twice as much shipping as their British counterparts. The second was cash.

The context of the problem presented to Britain by declared American intent was that in 1918–1919 British state expenditure, at £3,146,475,568, was some sixteen times greater than it had been in 1913–1914: interest on debt was greater than the whole of state expenditure in the last full financial year before the outbreak of the First World War. In 1918–1919 the state was having to try to deal with the fact that the National Debt, the army, the navy, loans to allies and dominions and the Ministry of Munitions, Ministry of Shipping and civil service votes were all, each and every one, greater than total state expenditure before the war. The Royal Air Force budget, the least of the three services, alone was the equivalent of all service expenditure in 1913–1914, while it needs be remembered that war pensions, loans to allies, payments to the railway companies, miscellaneous war expenditures, and various ministry payments simply had not existed in 1913. In 1918–1919 these latter budgets totalled £1,227,877,945 or, together, more than six times total state expenditure in 1913–1914.

The point of relevance in terms of naval construction programmes in general and battleship costs in particular, however, was that in 1918–1919 the British government was committed to reducing state expenditure in 1919–1920 to £1,231,076,000, or about one third of its 1918–1919 level, and this despite the fact that debt payments were expected to rise from £269,964,650 to £345,000,000. When set against such totals, the cost of an individual battleship, around £7,000,000 or $32,000,000,[9] would not seem excessive, but, of course, the point was not the cost of an individual capital ship: naval construction programmes necessarily had to involve many capital ships and their attendant cruisers, destroyers and auxiliary support shipping. The fact was that by 1921 Britain, Japan and the United States were committed to programmes which would have involved costs of £252,000,000 for just the required number of capital ships. Nonetheless, given the American reach for the ownership of the trident, in 1921 the British naval estimates made provision for four 48,000-ton battlecruisers with nine 16-in/406-mm. guns in three triple turrets, a 14-in/356-mm armour belt and a speed of 32 knots. This class was to be followed by another of four 48,500-ton battleships which were to be armed with nine 18-in/457-mm guns. In some ways the similarity between British and Japanese programmes was rather odd, but in the light of the fact that both were having to deal with a situation largely created by the United States, this coincidence of programmes was perhaps inevitable.

Thus both Britain and Japan thus found themselves in a situation bordering on crisis as a result of American aspirations, but redemption was at hand. Reference has been made to two crucial changes in the American national position with the end of the First World War, but only one was cited: herein was the second, and it was that by 1919–1920 the aspiration on the part of the United States to acquire a fleet 'second to none' was no longer national. Such a fleet was, in many ways, a reflection of President Woodrow Wilson's vision of American right, specifically the defence of democracy worldwide. Wilson's proclamation of the universal applicability of the rights of democracy and of law naturally travelled hand in hand with the acquisition of the means of physically enforcing those rights, though Wilson had expressed the view that it would be quite proper for the United States to believe that she was 'too proud to fight'. Be that as it may, Wilson's internationalism did not survive the First World War, and as the United States turned away from international obligations and responsibilities, so ebbed the naval tide.

This whole process was, in one way, a very unusual development. In a century which witnessed armament and nationalism march too often hand in hand, the American naval experience was the reverse: the case for a navy second to none was based upon international dimensions, and the repudiation of the international in favour of a much narrower national dimension was attended by the ditching of the naval armaments programme. The precise sequence of events embraced the Congressional elections of November 1918, which amounted to a repudiation of Wilson's vision of the future by returning Republican Party majorities in both houses, and then the Senate vote of 19 March 1920, which failed to ratify the Treaty of Versailles (signed on 28 June 1919) and denied the United States membership of the League of Nations, which had been formed on 20 April 1919.[10] This American turning of its collective back on the rest of the world, and the refusal to undertake the Wilsonian expansion of the navy, were based upon a reaction against involvement in the First World War *per se* (and this made American opinion hostile to any form of overseas commitment or undertaking), and upon a growing awareness within the United States that the Wilsonian undertaking could easily lead to war in the Pacific, which was something that American opinion was not prepared to casually accept. The final repudiation of Wilson and his works came in the form of the presidential election of November 1920. Somehow very appropriately, the Democrats selected their presidential candidate on the 44th ballot, and he was defeated by the Republican Senator Warren G. Harding, from Ohio, who won with a record share of the popular vote.

The move to limit naval armament was led by Secretary of State Charles Hughes, who on 12 November 1921 opened a nine-power conference in Washington devoted to the settlement of naval and related Far East questions. These discussions, and the seven accords which were concluded, were for east Asia, the western Pacific and naval matters what the Locarno process was for Europe. In terms of naval matters, four of the treaties were specifically relevant, and these were the four-power treaty of 13 December 1921, the nine-power and Sino-Japanese treaties of 4 February 1922 and the naval limitation treaty of 6 February 1922. The last of these dealt primarily with battle forces, and set down the size of forces for the five major navies. Britain was afforded capital ships totalling 580,450 tons, the United States 500,450 tons, Japan 301,320 tons, France 221,170 tons and Italy 182,800 tons. When all scrapping and replacement programmes were complete, the celebrated 5:5:3 ratio was to be established, with Britain and the United States afforded 500,000 tons of capital ships, Japan 300,000 tons and France and Italy 175,000 tons. After considerable debate, capital ships were limited to 35,000 tons standard displacement, which was defined as that of a ship being fully ready to proceed to sea but without fuel and reserve feed water on board, and were not permitted to carry guns greater than the 16-in/406-mm gun.

There was to be no construction of capital ships over the next ten years, and capital ships could not be replaced within twenty years of completion: reconstruction of existing ships was permitted but limited to improvement of protection against air and underwater attack, with maximum increased displacement of 3,000 tons. Because France and Italy had not been able to undertake various building and reconstruction of warships during the First World War, they were allowed greater latitude in these matters. In addition, aircraft carriers were assigned on the basis of 135,000 tons for Britain and the United States, 81,000 tons for Japan and 60,000 tons for France and Italy, with a maximum size of 27,000 tons per carrier and with all powers entitled to build two carriers of 33,000 tons subject to their aggregate totals remaining within overall quota allowances. Because aircraft carriers were deemed experimental ships, they could be replaced at any time.

There was no agreement over limitation of the aggregate total of numbers and tonnage of cruisers, destroyers and submarines for the various powers, though Britain agreed with the American view that cruisers should be limited to a maximum of 10,000 tons and 8-in/203-mm armament but not the view that cruisers should be afforded a seventeen-year life expectancy: after a hardworking war, Britain needed to replace cruisers on a shorter time scale. In terms of destroyers, there was a general agreement that the maximum size should be 1,500 tons, with destroyer leaders afforded an additional 500 tons. The British attempt to limit if not dispense with submarine forces foundered on a French refusal to comply: the submarine was expected to comply with prize regulations, but no restrictions were placed on either individual size or aggregate tonnage of submarines.

Britain was allowed to retain eighteen battleships and four battlecruisers, namely the five *Revenge* class, the five *Queen Elizabeth* class, and four *Iron Duke* and three *King George V* class battleships, the battlecruisers *Hood*, *Renown* and *Repulse*, plus the *Tiger*, and the battleship *Thunderer* as a training ship. This meant that a total of 21 completed dreadnoughts and battlecruisers were scrapped over a number of years, and the 1921 programme, with four battlecruisers which had been ordered on 21 October, was abandoned.[11] This represented the scrapping of 382,070 tons of completed dreadnoughts and battlecruisers, and 5,522 tons of battlecruisers then built. The loss of so many ships, and what amounted to a disproportionate British shedding of existing warships relative to the United States and Japan, was a source of great bitterness within the British navy and the navalist press. But, as noted earlier, of the 21 capital ships scrapped no fewer than fourteen – the *Dreadnought*, the *Bellerophon, Superb* and the *Téméraire*, the *Collingwood* and *St. Vincent*, the *Neptune*, the *Colossus* and *Hercules*, and the *Agincourt* and the battlecruisers *Indomitable* and *Inflexible*, and the *Australia* and *New Zealand* – predated 1910 and were equipped with 12-in/305-mm guns, and so their loss did not amount to very much. In fact, a number had been sold in readiness for scrapping even before the Washington conference, and these ships, the two dominion ships excluded, had been earmarked for early disposal. Two of the other ships, the *Canada* and *Erin*, having been requisitioned while building in Britain in 1914, did not have sister ships and were likewise of limited value. In real terms, the British were forced to scrap only five ships that they would not have scrapped at or about this time: these were the dreadnoughts *Conqueror, Monarch* and the *Orion* and the battlecruisers *Lion* and *Princess Royal* (i.e., all the 13.5-in/343-mm capital ships of the 1909–1910 programme less the *Thunderer*).[12]

The United States was obliged to scrap all her pre-dreadnoughts plus four dreadnoughts, the *South Carolina* and *Michigan* immediately and the *Delaware* and *North Dakota* when the *Colorado* and *West Virginia* entered service: in the event, however, the *North Dakota*, which was decommissioned on 22 November 1923, became a target ship. In addition, the *Washington*, then under construction and three-quarters complete, was expended as a target ship. The Americans also abandoned their post-1916 programmes, a total of fifteen battleships and battlecruisers. The Japanese had to discard just one dreadnought, the *Settsu*, which was disarmed at Kure in 1921 but converted to serve as a target ship. The major signatories also scrapped all pre-dreadnought battleships, though in Britain's case very few such units remained after 1920: when these, however, are added to the total of capital ships, the total list, as proposed by Hughes, numbered 30 American, 23 British and seventeen Japanese warships. In the Japanese case, the newer ships were either scrapped (three) or sunk as target ships (four), while no fewer than six were reduced to hulks, training ships and various other guises: the *Mikasa* was preserved as a memorial at Yokosuka, where, after restoration in 1960, she still remains.[13]

Because Japan and the United States had adopted the 16-in/406-mm main armament for their capital ships, with the *Mutsu* being completed during the time of the Washington conference, Britain was permitted to build two new battleships, which were to be the *Nelson* and *Rodney*. As regards capital ships under construction, both Japan and the United States were permitted to converted two such units to aircraft carriers. Accordingly, the American battlecruisers *Lexington* and *Saratoga* were converted while in their yards, while the Japanese earmarked the battleships *Akagi* and *Amagi* for conversion: Britain, with no units being built but the *Furious* already in dockyard hands, was allowed to convert the *Courageous* (June 1924 to March 1928) and *Glorious* (February 1924 to January 1930). The *Amagi*, which was being built at the Yokosuka navy yard, was some two-fifths complete when all new capital ship construction in Japan was halted on 5 February 1922. It was not until the summer of 1923 that work was resumed, but the *Amagi*'s hull was badly damaged in the Tokyo earthquake of 1 September 1923 with the result that she was scrapped in April 1924 along with her original sister ships *Atago* and *Takao*. Her place was taken by the battlecruiser *Kaga*, which had been laid down at Kobe on 19 July 1920 and launched 17 November 1921: her conversion was completed on 31 March 1926. Conversion work on the *Akagi*, which had been laid down on 6 December 1920 at the Kure navy yard, began on 19 November 1923: she was launched 22 April 1925 and completed on 25 March 1927.

The three other treaties complemented the naval limitation treaty. The most important was the four-power treaty that prohibited the construction of fortifications and naval bases by Britain east of Singapore, by the Americans west of the Hawaiian and Aleutian Islands, and by the Japanese outside the home islands.[14] Along with France, these three countries undertook to respect one another's rights and possessions in the western Pacific and eastern Asia and to consult in the event of future dispute. As part of these arrangements, the Anglo-Japanese treaty was allowed to lapse. The nine-power and Sino-Japanese treaties both re-affirmed the principle of China's sovereignty and territorial integrity. The first also re-affirmed the principle of equal access to China's markets (i.e., the 'Open Door' policy sponsored by the United States) and gave future undertakings to China regarding her recovery of customs and revenue rights and various other concessions. The Sino-Japanese treaty saw Japan agree to her evacuation of Shantung and her acceptance of various other Chinese claims regarding the return of concessions that had been made to Germany but which Japan had won for herself as a result of the First World War: in return Japan received guarantees of her very substantial economic interests in Shantung.

These measures, when combined with the fact that from this time the United States did involve herself in various League of Nations endeavours, represented something very new. It was an attempt to ensure, by political means and the control of armaments, that disputes might be resolved without recourse to war. In retrospect, it can be seen that the effort was flawed, but the obvious weaknesses, which are easily identified, were not necessary the cause of this situation. Those weaknesses were lack of verification and, much more seriously, the fact that these arrangements, so carefully crafted and so deliberately arranged in order to prevent the various powers threatening one another, left Japan in a position of overwhelming advantage in the western Pacific and in effect left the Philippines, and to a lesser extent Hong Kong, dependent for their security on Japanese goodwill. It was this position of Japanese advantage, in fact a positional advantage which ensured that Japan was not immediately accountable, that provided the military security for Japanese expansionist policies in the 1930s and ensured that there was little that the western powers could do to restrain her. But the real weakness of these arrangements, and one that might have prevented the subsequent unfolding of events, was the failure of the western powers, and particularly of the United States, to adopt a free trade policy with respect to Japan. Most Japanese imports to the United States were subjected to discriminatory taxes, and while this issue did not seem so important at this particular time, it was to become so in the 1930s when economic issues moved to centre stage and Japan, subjected to tariffs that limited her export capacity, sought to secure in eastern Asia an exclusive economic zone for colonisation, investment, raw materials and markets. What Japan sought to establish for herself was a Monroe Doctrine with reference to eastern and south-east Asia – not that the United States saw things in such terms, not least because she had assigned for herself a very special place with respect to China, and expected American institutions and ideology to provide the example to be followed by the infant Chinese republic.

The Washington naval treaty proved to be the major international agreement in the inter-war period affecting capital ship limitation. There were to be three other conferences, at Geneva in July and August 1927, at London between February and April 1930 and again at London between December 1935 and March 1936. The Geneva conference primarily concerned itself with questions of cruiser numbers, size and aggregate tonnages, and, with little political direction from either the American or British governments, very quickly became a somewhat esoteric and arcane dispute between two sets of naval staffs. The first London conference was very different because here, as had been the case in Washington, there was the political will to 'take risks for peace' on the part of American and British governments which saw security in terms of the elimination of confrontation and competition. The first London conference provided what was to be the last major limitation agreement of the inter-war period, and it was only partial in that the agreement which was concluded involved just Britain, Japan and the United States: France and Italy attended but were not parties to the final agreement.[15] The last of these conferences, the second London conference, in effect marked the end of the whole limitation endeavour, and naval limitation formally ended on 31 December 1936.[16]

The most important aspects of the first London agreement concerned the numbers, size and aggregate tonnages of heavy cruisers, light cruisers, destroyers and submarines for the British, Japanese and U.S. Navies. In one sense, the conference's deliberations on the subject of capital ships really did not amount to very much: a general agreement permitted Britain and the United States to retain fifteen capital ships, while Japan was allowed to retain nine: the moratorium on building replacements was extended for another five years. What this meant was that Britain, with the *Nelson* and *Rodney*, the five *Revenge*-class and five *Queen Elizabeth*-class battleships and the battlecruisers *Hood, Renown* and *the Repulse*, had to divest herself of three *Iron Duke*-class battleships and the battlecruiser *Tiger*: the other battleships that she had retained after 1922 had already been scrapped. She was also allowed to retain two suitably converted battleships, the *Iron Duke* as a gunnery training ship and the *Centurion* as a radio-controlled target ship.

For her part, the United States discarded the *Florida*, which had undergone a major modernisation programme between July 1924 and June 1926, and also the target ship *North Dakota*, which had always been a problem ship on account of her poor turbines and had been consigned to the reserve as early as July 1915. She had been re-engined but played no active role during the First World War and was decommissioned in November 1923. The *Florida* and *North Dakota* were scrapped in the two years after the London treaty. The *Utah*, having been subjected to a major modernisation programme between August 1926 and October 1928, was decommissioned and after conversion returned to service in July 1931 as a target ship for gunnery and bombing trials, while the *Wyoming* was reduced to the status of training ship.

For the Japanese, the London arrangements meant merely that at the end of the 1920s only one capital ship, the battlecruiser *Hiei*, had to be degraded to serve as a gunnery training ship: with an allocation of nine capital ships, the *Kaigun* was left with three pairs of battleships and three *Kongo*-class battlecruisers. But its situation was much more complicated than this statement would suggest, largely because of the precise nature of its allocations for other types of warship and the place that these assumed in its concept of battle. At London the overall tonnage for all Japanese warships other than capital ships was 368,340 tons, or 69.75 per cent of that allowed the British and the United States navies. This should have been a very considerable source of reassurance for the Japanese, involving as it did a very substantial change from the 60 per cent margin of Washington. But the Japanese were obliged to accept 108,400 tons as the upper limit on their heavy cruisers, a 60.23 per cent limit in the type of warship which the *Kaigun* had convinced itself, given the limits on capital ships, now represented the key element in war at sea. In addition, Japan would be allowed to build up to a 70 per cent limit in light cruisers, of which the *Kaigun* was very dismissive, and it was allowed to attain the same 70 per cent limit for destroyers (at 105,500 tons) and submarines (at 52,700 tons).

While all this seemed very liberal, and the Americans were prepared to accept these higher limits and to delay in the building of their own allocation of heavy cruisers in deference to Japanese wishes, the fact was that Japanese destroyer and submarine strengths were already in excess of these aggregates and therefore these represented very substantial reductions, from 132,495 tons in destroyers and from 77,842 tons in submarines. At London, therefore, Japan had been afforded an overall seven-tenths' standard, and even in the matter of heavy cruisers her position was better than the bare statement of allowances would suggest: relative strengths were set at eighteen to twelve, a two-thirds standard, while the promised delays that would attend American building actually presented the *Kaigun* with an 80 per cent standard in heavy cruisers. Moreover, there was an irony about the Japanese situation which was no doubt missed by all concerned at the time. The 15:9 ratio established at London was exactly the situation that had existed in terms of capital ships in 1918, i.e., before the Americans stood to receive deliveries of battleships and battlecruisers that would have reduced the *Kaigun* to coast guard status. The London terms really did confirm that in reality the Japanese Navy had lost nothing in the limitation process, and had only gained.

The terms of the London treaty did not enjoy widespread support within either Japan in general or the *Kaigun* in particular: this had also been true of the terms of the Washington treaty. At work was a racial resentment at the treatment Japan was afforded, which of course was a spin-off of the treatment Japanese immigrants had received in the western states of the United States and of the denial of the principle of racial equality by the western powers at Versailles in 1919 with respect to the founding of the League of Nations. But with Japan not being in the same industrial and financial leagues as the United States and Britain, domestic expectations that she might be afforded equality of treatment in terms of naval forces were not high, though the allocation of the 60 per cent standard at Washington left the Imperial Navy with all the difficulties inherent in trying to solve an insoluble question. The problem, of course, was simply defined: how could the *Kaigun* mount a successful defence of the home islands and Japanese interests in the western Pacific and eastern Asia on the basis of a strength that its doctrine held was insufficient to conduct a successful defensive campaign?

Clearly, Japan's acceptance of the three-fifths standard at Washington in 1921–1922 was the result of one calculation on the part of those responsible for her navy. This was the calculation, embodied in the person of Admiral Kato Tomosaburo, the Navy Minister, that the only eventuality that could be worse for Japan than an unrestricted naval construction race with the United States would be war against that country. As Kato saw it, an unrestricted naval race could only result in the remorseless and irreversible erosion of Japan's position relative to the United States, and Japan had to seek security through peaceful co-operation and diplomatic arrangements rather than through international rivalry and conquest. In terms of the navy itself, individuals such as Kato Tomosaburo saw its role as a deterrent and, in the event of war, defensive, but they also saw Japan's best interest served not by confrontation and conflict with the United States but by arrangements which limited American construction relative to Japan's and which provided the basis of future American recognition and acceptance of Japan's regional naval position.

The essential reasonableness of this position was belied most obviously by the disparity of strengths between Japan and the United States, but also by attitudes within the Imperial Navy. Within the latter, what emerged as the anti-treaty faction was powerful enough to frustrate a redefinition of the Imperial Defence Policy along the lines laid down by Kato and to insist upon the United States being defined as the most likely enemy for both services. As far as this faction was concerned, racist agitation against Japanese immigrants in the western United States, along with American commercial activities in China, pointed to the inevitability of war at some point in the not too distant future, and the death of Kato in 1923 opened the way for the anti-treaty faction to establish its primacy within the *Kaigun* by the end of the 1920s. Its problem, however, was that it had to abide by the treaty which Japan had signed, and it had to relate the reality of strategic imbalance to Japanese naval doctrine. Herein lay the hidden implication of the Washington and London arrangements in terms of Japanese capital ships. The issue was not one of numbers but qualitative matters as the Imperial Navy sought to ensure for itself advantages that would offset its numerical inferiority.

Kaigun thinking for a war against the United States was predicated on an advance by American naval forces into the western Pacific which would result in 'the decisive battle'. In one sense, the Japanese could anticipate American intention because, in effect, the Americans had to decide between alternative routes, one directly from the Hawaiian Islands to the Bonin and Mariana Islands and thence to the home islands, and the other to the south via the Gilbert and Marshall Islands and thence to Guam, and thereafter via the Bonins and Marianas again to the Japanese home islands. Of the two routes, orthodox *Kaigun* thinking held that the Americans were likely to move deliberately and hence on the second of the two alternative courses. The basic response that the Imperial Navy considered appropriate was to stand on the defence but to undertake offensive operations intended to secure the Philippines and the destruction of the U.S. Asiatic Fleet at the earliest possible opportunity and certainly before the arrival of an American battle force in the western Pacific. To achieve this aim, the *Kaigun* anticipated committing cruiser, destroyer, submarine and aircraft formations to these offensive operations, but not the battle force.

In the period before, during and immediately after the First World War, one which would include the Washington conference and its immediate aftermath, the *Kaigun* thought in terms of battle being given in the general area of the Ryukyu Islands. As the years of the inter-war period slipped by, however, the scene of battle shifted eastward. In this period's middle years, until the mid-'30s, the *Kaigun* thought in terms of battle being given west of the Bonins and Marianas, but thereafter battle was to be fought to the east of these islands, and by the time this idea had taken hold, the whole concept had undergone major change. The original idea, on which the *Kaigun* based all its planning, was the concept of *yogeki sakusen*, or interceptive operations, which had originally governed its operations prior to and then during the battle of Tsushima in May 1905: in its inter-war form, Japanese ideas were codified in what was called The Strategy of Interceptive Operations. In its final form, the strategy and the battle were to find expression with the opening of the defensive battle off Hawaii by submarines, and three types were built in order to fight an attritional battle as the U.S. Pacific Fleet advanced into the western Pacific. Scouting submarines, equipped with seaplanes, would find the American fleet, which would then be subjected to night surface attacks by cruiser-submarines brought to the point of contact by command-submarines. These cruiser-submarines were endowed with a very high surface speed of 24 knots, the Japanese calculations being that such a speed would allow them to outpace an American fleet advancing at economical cruising speed and thereby to mount successive attacks to the limit of their torpedo capacity during the approach-to-contact phase.

These operations would be supported, as the American fleet arrived in the western Pacific, by shore-based aircraft. To this end the Japanese developed in the form of the Betty medium bomber an aircraft that in its own time possessed a speed and range superior to any other medium bomber in service in the world. Thereafter the carriers, operating in independent divisions separately and forward from the battle line, would locate the advancing American fleet and immobilise its carriers through dive-bombing attacks that were to smash enemy flight-decks. With the American fleet thus blinded, it would be engaged by midget submarines laid across its line of advance, and at the same time it would be engaged by light forces. With the fast battleship and heavy cruiser squadrons sweeping aside enemy screening forces, massed light cruiser and destroyer flotillas, built around massive torpedo armaments, would attack the head of the American line in a series of night attacks. These would be delivered by formations advancing to contact line abreast with perhaps as many as 120 torpedoes launched in single, scissor-formation attacks.

The Japanese hoped and expected that each of these three phases of operations would cost the American fleet perhaps 10 per cent of its strength, the overall loss being in the order of 30 per cent of its strength and, more importantly, its cohesion. At this point action would be joined by the battle force, and herein all the elements of limitation, capital ship construction and qualitative improvement came together. Between the wars the *Kaigun* undertook the most comprehensive reconstruction of its capital ships of any navy, stressing the importance of the possession of superior speed and armour, weight of broadside and gunnery range over potential enemies: the counter to American numerical superiority was qualitative superiority of both ships and men. The *Kaigun* anticipated that the battle line would engage its counterpart in a conventional line of battle engagement with such advantages that the Japanese fleet would inflict a crushing defeat upon the American enemy, and this was to be achieved by battleships with extended range and size: the Japanese planned to build successive battleship classes with 18.1-in/460-mm and 19.7-in/500-mm guns. The weight of shell fired by these guns – over 3,200 lbs or a third bigger than the 16-in/406-mm shell – was certain to possess irresistible smashing power, while the Japanese aimed to bring the very special battleships that were home to such guns into battle at ranges of and beyond 40,000 yards/36,700-m, i.e., beyond the range at which American battleships could answer.

Such was the basic *Kaigun* intent, known as the *zengen sakusen* or The Great All-Out Battle strategy, and it invites a series of comments. The first is that in the period after 1939 the forward defence area was extended eastward to include the Marshalls. The second, and related to this, was the fact that by the time that Japan went to war in December 1941, planning indicated the intention to secure islands and groups in the central and south-west Pacific on which would be hung a perimeter defence, and on which the Americans would be fought to exhaustion. *Kaigun* planning sought to provide for mutually supporting land-based air formations and intact fleet formations. With the Japanese aware that any attacking American force would possess numerical superiority over either a land-based or a naval force, compensation was sought in securing the means whereby land-based air and naval formations would support one another. The third fact was that in the inter-war period the Japanese were unable to complete their various airfields in the various island chains, hence it was very unlikely they would be able to complete new airfields in the newly acquired islands and groups of the central and south-west Pacific given the lack of shipping for such a task.

More seriously, and all but unbelievably, the basic Japanese plan was never subjected to a fleet exercise before the outbreak of war. Moreover, and this is the fourth point, certain parts of the plan – specifically the submarines' role – were subjected to exercise in 1939 and 1940 and found not to work, but the Japanese went to war with their doctrine unchanged, though in a sense this was perhaps unavoidable: there was very little that the *Kaigun* could have done about such a situation at this stage. Nonetheless, and fifth, the *zengen sakusen* concept dictated both ship design and, more critically, *Kaigun* thinking throughout the inter-war period. The design of Japanese warships was geared specifically for battle in the western Pacific, most notably in terms of individual ships being possessed of moderate endurance and the navy itself of very limited capability to refuel at sea: because battle would be joined in the western Pacific, i.e., close to bases in the home islands, ships and formations needed speed, extra guns, better and more torpedoes rather than extra range.

The sixth and the last point is simple. It is so obvious, so important and therefore so elusive, yet it is evident in the English translation of the phrase, The Great All-Out Battle Strategy. What the *Kaigun* had here was nothing more than a tactical plan for the conduct of battle, but by some mysterious process, something akin to transubstantiation, it became a plan of campaign and then the basis of a national security strategy. Herein was evidence that the Imperial Navy never understood the difference between war and a war, between a war and a campaign, between a campaign and a battle, and by some process which defies understanding identified them as one and the same. Be that as it may, the point was that the Imperial Navy had the better part of two decades to devise these ideas and ensure that doctrine and procurement were harmonised – but perhaps not as the Imperial Navy intended. The whole of the idea can only be described as the Japanese naval equivalent of a de Dondi creation, a majestic clockwork of wheels-within-wheels that represented the mediaeval view of the universe: ingenious, lovingly created, beautifully crafted, hopelessly wrong.

If one had to select just one warship to illustrate what the *yogeki sakusen*, at one level, and the *zengen sakusen*, at another, meant, one would be hard pressed to resist the claims of the light cruiser *Oi*. Laid down on 24 November 1919 under the provisions of the 1918 programme, the *Oi* was launched on 15 July 1920 and completed, as a 532-ft/162.7-m long, 5,832-ton light cruiser armed with seven single 5.5-in/140-mm guns, two of which were sited *en echelon* slightly behind her bridge. With a belt of 2.5-in/63-mm armour and a top speed of 36 knots, the *Oi* and her sisters carried eight 21-in/533-mm torpedo tubes. In 1927 she was refitted with a catapult and was afforded a seaplane, but neither this warship nor her sisters were given any major refit, still less rebuilt, until the very eve of the Pacific war. Then, with their seaplanes and catapults removed and the brand new Type 13 radar set installed, the *Oi* and the *Kitakami* were rebuilt as torpedo ships. They carried four 5.5-in/140-mm guns and eight 25-mm anti-aircraft guns, and 40 24-in/533-mm torpedo tubes in ten quadruple mountings, five on each side of the ship. This was what was meant by the night attack by massed light formations.

Nonetheless it was in many ways the capital ship that carried the most obvious hallmarks of the *zengen sakusen*. The battlecruisers of the *Kongo* class were the first to be taken in hand, and the *Kongo*, *Haruna* and the *Kirishima* were to be rebuilt twice in the inter-war period, on the second occasion so extensively that they emerged reclassified as fast battleships and indeed possessed of a top speed which was greater than that registered when they first appeared as battlecruisers. The major change in the first reconstruction – between March 1927 and March 1930 for the *Kirishima*, between July 1927 and July 1928 for the *Haruna*, and between September 1929 and March 1931 for the *Kongo* – was the provision of much greater armour, specifically for turrets, the decks over magazines and machinery, and anti-torpedo bulges. The amount of armour carried by these three capital ships increased by nearly 4,000 tons but most of this was carried without major economies in other respects: improved boilers meant that power was maintained despite the new machinery being some 800 tons lighter than the original, the overall cost being no more than one or two knots at top speed. In terms of fighting capability, this reconstruction was notable for the fact that the original four torpedo tubes were removed and the elevation of the main armament was increased to 43 degrees, thereby conferring on it the ability, at least theoretically, to engage an enemy at some 38,000 yards, or about 22 miles or 35 kilometres.

The second reconstruction, which began in August 1933 for the *Haruna* and ended in January 1940 for the rehabilitated *Hiei*, saw only minor additions to armour but the reconstruction of their power plants. The first reconstruction had seen the Japanese persist with a dual coal and oil arrangement, but in this second reconstruction the three capital ships were fitted just for oil-burning. The *Haruna* and *Hiei* were equipped with eleven boilers while the *Kirishima* and *Kongo* were equipped with eight, and overall machinery weight was reduced to 2,929 tons while power available to the ships was more than doubled. With trials showing speeds of upward of 30.3 knots being recorded, the battlecruisers were reclassified as fast battleships. The only other major feature was that whereas as a result of their first reconstruction the *Haruna*, *Kirishima* and *Kongo* were equipped with either two or three seaplanes but no catapult or catapults, after this reconstruction the three capital ships each carried three seaplanes and had one catapult. The fourth ship of the class, the *Hiei*, was afforded somewhat different treatment. Because of treaty requirements she was rebuilt as a gunnery training ship at the Kure navy yard between September 1929 and December 1932. In this role she was robbed of her belt, one turret and four fifths of her power. These, and more, were returned to her when she was rebuilt after treaty limitations expired, and her second reconstruction saw her returned to more or less parity with her sister ships. With a range of 10,000 nautical miles/18,400-km at eighteen knots, and a top speed of 30 knots, the importance of the four ships lay in the support they were expected to provide light forces in breaking through the enemy's screening formations in order that these light forces could then conduct massed torpedo attacks on the enemy battle line in the hours of darkness during the approach-to-contact phase. These capital ships were also expected to support the battleships as they closed upon a dishevelled and worse for wear enemy in the line action on the following day.

All six of Japan's battleships were subjected to one major rebuilding programme during the inter-war period. These were very similar, and along with various refits the overall result was much the same as that registered with the *Kongo*-class capital ships. As might be reasonably expected, these rebuilding programmes concentrated mainly on three sets of changes. The first was their being stripped of their original mixed-firing (coal and oil) boilers in favour of oil-firing Kanpon boilers – from 24 to six in the *Fuso* and *Yamashiro*, from 24 to eight in the *Hyuga* and *Ise* and from 21 to four, with six small reserve, boilers for the *Nagato* and *Mutsu* – and all the battleships were given new turbines. The result was more mixed than the rough standardisation of equipment and numbers might suggest. The power made available to the first two classes more or less doubled, while that available to the *Nagato* and *Mutsu* was only very slightly increased. The result was that all three classes were able to make a top speed of about 25 knots, a loss of almost two knots for the *Nagato* and her sister ship, but it was the *Fuso* and *Yamashiro* that emerged as the real losers. Though less than a knot slower than the other battleships, they were assigned training and secondary duties during the Pacific war and their planned conversion to serve as battleship-carriers was scheduled to follow, not precede, that of the *Hyuga* and *Ise*: in the event, the losses suffered by air groups at the Philippine Sea in June 1944 meant that this planned conversion was never effected.

The second of the changes was the adding of armour, which in the *Fuso* class rose from 8,588 tons to 12,199 tons with protection over machinery and magazines doubled to over 4-in/102-mm. The *Hyuga* and *Ise* were given slightly more armour over their vitals as their armour allocation rose from 9,374 to 12,444 tons, and the *Nagato* and *Mutsu* saw only relatively minor changes as their armour rose from 10,231 to 12,824 tons: in fact, refits in 1941 saw more significant armour changes than those of this rebuilding with the armour afforded the barbettes increased from 11.9-in/302-mm to 19.7-in/500-mm. All six ships had their beams increased by some 20 feet/ 6.12 metres as a result of anti-torpedo bulges being added, and all were lengthened by some 25 feet/7.65 metres as part of the effort to maintain the silhouette which afforded best speeds.

The third of the changes affected the battleships' armament. The *Fuso* and *Yamashiro* had the elevation of their 14-in/356-mm guns increased from 30 to 43 degrees and the elevation of their 6-in/152-mm guns increased from fifteen to 30 degrees. They received 5-in/127-mm and 25-mm anti-aircraft guns in place of their original 3-in guns, and their torpedo tubes were removed. The same changes applied to the *Hyuga* and *Ise* and the *Nagato* and *Mutsu* but for the fact that the 5.5-in/140-mm gun was their standard secondary weapon. All six battleships were afforded single catapults and three seaplanes.

These various modifications, and their being listed here, nonetheless fail to disclose the real changes that were entailed, and on these counts two matters, plus a third matter relating to the timing of these rebuilding undertakings, need to be considered. The first point relates to the major improvement in terms of fighting capacity that these changes represented. The changes represent the relentless search for qualitative advantage – the superiority of three or four knots over an American battle formation, the extra range and the enhanced survivability conferred by additional armour protection – that would enable the six units, when supported by the *Kongo*-class fast units, to join battle, to fight the *zengen sakusan*. The second point relates to the massive change of appearance that went hand in hand with the reconstruction of these ships. The huge reduction of the number of boilers permitted a reduction of funnels. Whereas the *Kongo*-class battlecruisers had carried three funnels but in their fast battleship guise carried two, so all the battleships were reduced from two funnels to one and all of them lost their fore funnel close to the bridge and the control tops. This left all the Japanese battleships with a rather isolated funnel amidships and a somewhat unusual appearance, but what was even more striking was that, beginning with the *Fuso*, the pagoda mast appeared. This was the gathering of command centres together in a built-up bridge area and which, in the case of the *Fuso*, earned her the title of the ugliest ship in the Imperial Navy. The other battleships were not quite so badly affected as was the *Fuso* in this respect, but this seemingly top-heavy arrangement, which from certain angles could look most impressive, is something that immediately identifies these ships in terms of time.

And it is time, or perhaps more accurately the timing, that makes the rebuilding of the Japanese capital ships so very interesting. The first of the battleships to undergo extensive modernisation was the *Fuso*, at the Kure navy yard between April 1930 and May 1933, while her sister ship, the *Yamashiro*, underwent reconstruction in the Yokosuka navy yard between December 1930 and March 1935, by which time the *Hyuga*, *Nagato* and the *Mutsu* were all in dockyard hands. The *Hyuga* was reconstructed in the Sasebo navy yard between October 1934 and September 1936. The *Ise* followed, and her reconstruction was completed in the Kure navy yard between August 1935 and March 1937. The *Nagato* was rebuilt, again in the Kure navy yard, between April 1934 and January 1936, while the *Mutsu* was in the Yokosuka navy yard being rebuilt from September 1934 to September 1936. In other words, the whole process of rebuilding the Japanese capital ships, with the exception of the *Hiei*, was completed by March 1937, some eight months before the *Yamato* was laid down, again in the Kure navy yard.

But what is perhaps most interesting about the Japanese programme is that the 1930s opened with no fewer than six of the nine available capital ships undergoing some form of major refit in 1930, a total that fell to five in 1931, to three in 1932 and to just two – the *Fuso* and *Yamashiro* – in 1933. In 1934, however, no fewer than six of Japan's nine capital ships spent at least part of the year in the shipyards, and one, the *Yamashiro*, spent her fourth consecutive and full year being rebuilt – or, to put it another way, she spent twice as long being rebuilt as it took to build her in the first place. In 1935 four of Japan's capital ships spent the entire year being rebuilt while another four spent different parts of the year in the shipyards: as a basic rule of thumb, and with just a couple of months' error, there were normally six capital ships in shipyard hands at any time in this year, and for most of the next year, 1936, five ships were being rebuilt.

What is also interesting is that in 1934 and 1936, but not in 1935, the Japanese appear to have had the carriers *Kaga* and *Ryujo* and the *Akagi* and *Ryujo* in dockyard hands for most of these respective years, while of the twelve heavy cruisers that had entered service by 1933 five, the four members of the *Ashigara* class plus the *Kako*, underwent major refit in 1935 or 1936, and the *Kako* only entered the Sasebo navy yard when three of the *Ashigara* class heavy cruisers had already returned to service and the last, the *Nachi*, was on the point of leaving the shipyard. The major refitting of heavy cruisers awaited the last quarter of 1937, with six in dockyard hands for all or part of 1938: eight were so placed in 1939 but only four spent any part of 1940 undergoing modernisation. Any marrying of the record of modernisation programmes for the capital ships and heavy cruisers reveals that the battleship reconstruction programmes were mainly completed between 1934 and 1936 while the heavy cruiser programmes were undertaken between 1937 and 1939, i.e., when all the capital ships (less the *Hiei*) had returned to service. Clearly these various programmes and timetables were dictated by the end of treaty limitation and the certainty of major construction programmes being put in hand in and after 1937, but the dove-tailing of the various undertakings does indicate a degree of co-ordination of effort that was not matched elsewhere at this particular time as well as the manner in which the *zengen sakusen* dictated design and ship characteristics in a way that was not equalled in the British and American navies. As it was, the *Kaigun* could not put a balanced fleet to sea either in the period 1934–1936 because it had so few capital ships or in the period 1937–1939 because it had so few cruisers, but with the new carriers becoming available after late 1939, it had a balanced fleet from 1940.

The Japanese battleship reconstruction programmes, involving as they did all ten of Japan's capital ships, were clearly of a different scale and intent than anything put in hand in Britain and the United States in the aftermath of first the Washington and then the London treaties. Under the terms of the Washington naval treaty, Britain was afforded two exemptions. The first was that she was allowed to retain the fast battleship *Hood*. She had been laid down in 1916 and had been one of a class of four, but the construction of the other three had been suspended in March 1918 when it was learnt that German capital ship construction had been halted: their orders were cancelled in March 1919 with the ending of the First World War. The *Hood*, however, had been launched in August 1918 and she was completed, at 42,670 tons standard displacement, in March 1920.

As American and Japanese intentions took shape, and the naval race that was to lead to Washington beckoned, the British were obliged to consider their future capital ship programme, and thus emerged, in planning terms, two classes of capital ship. The first class are generally known as the 1921 battlecruisers. Their building yards had been assigned and it was generally known that they were to be given the names of the first four battlecruisers, though which was to be built where was never defined. The design of these ships was far advanced by the time of Washington, and indeed orders were placed for the four ships on 21 October 1921 but suspended on 18 November. Though classified as battlecruisers, they were to be fast battleships: on a standard displacement of 48,000 tons they were to have had battleship armour, with a 14-in/356-mm sloped belt, nine 16-in/406-mm guns, and, on 160,000 shp, a top speed of 31–32 knots. Also being prepared, but less well advanced, was a design for a 'proper' battleship, which would have been roughly the same displacement as the 'super-*Hoods*' but slower, possessed of thicker armour and armed with nine 18-in/457-mm guns. Design work on this class was suspended on 17 November 1921 and abandoned on 9 February 1922, three days after the Washington naval treaty was signed and designs were approved for the construction of the *Nelson* and *Rodney*. These battleships formed the second of Britain's exemptions, and as noted earlier were allowed to her because Japan and the United States had already moved to secure for themselves capital ships armed with 16-in/406-mm main armament.

The *Nelson* and *Rodney* were the only two ships allowed the three major naval powers at Washington, and obviously their main characteristics were determined by the treaty's provisions. They were allocated the 35,000-ton limitation, secured by Britain only after considerable difficulty, and were armed with nine 16-in/406-mm guns. They remained the only British battleships to be given such guns and they were the first British warships to be afforded triple turrets: in an attempt to save weight, all three turrets were sited forward of the bridge, and protection, thus concentrated, was afforded on the all-or-nothing principle. The use of small-tube boilers provided the two ships with 46,000 shp and a top speed around 23.6 knots while helping to ensure that treaty limits were scrupulously maintained.

The overall result was two battleships that were held at the time to be, with the *Hood*, perhaps the most powerful capital ships in the world, but whereas the *Hood* had grace and majesty with lines that had come down to her through the years, the *Nelson* and *Rodney* exuded a certain rugged steadfastness. There was perhaps an element of calm stateliness about these two ships, but the fact was that the British did encounter major problems with them. Experience taught that firing the main armament abaft the beam was to be avoided at all costs because of the damage to bridges, while firing ahead was likewise to be avoided because of the damage incurred between decks. An enemy that conveniently took station well abeam was needed for these ships, while their handling characteristics were also difficult. One of the captains of the *Nelson* noted in a report that when proceeding at twelve knots with a wind of Force Six on the port beam, twelve degrees of starboard rudder was required to maintain course, and it was generally conceded that they handled badly in shallow water or wind: they were described as 'exhibiting a majestic dilatoriness in answering the helm and propellers', but perhaps their most unfortunate feature was that it took five years after they were commissioned in 1927 before they could maintain salvo firing, such were the various problems that afflicted the guns, mounts and turrets.[17] Nonetheless the guns were given 40-degree elevation, and had a maximum range of 35,000 yards, or about 20 miles or 32 kilometres.

Four of Britain's remaining thirteen capital ships were rebuilt in the inter-war period. These were, in order, the *Warspite*, *Renown*, *Valiant* and the *Queen Elizabeth*, and, if anything, their rebuilding was even more comprehensive than that afforded Japanese capital ships in the 1930s. The British ships, which had been subject to major refits in the 1920s that had seen them given anti-torpedo bulges, trunked funnels, modified bridges and new tertiary armament, were opened to the keel and then rebuilt. In the case of the *Warspite* (and her two sister ships) the 24 Yarrow boilers were removed and replaced by six Admiralty boilers capable of generating the same power. The two original funnels were removed, and boiler intakes merged into one single funnel, an arrangement that enabled the battleship to be afforded extra anti-aircraft guns and a hangar and catapult for the two Swordfish spotter-reconnaissance aircraft. Perhaps most importantly, deck armour was increased to thicknesses of 5.5-in/140-mm over vitals, while the entire bridge structure was altered in a manner that transformed the ships' appearance. In terms of armament, the major changes were the increased elevation of the main 15-in/380-mm guns from twenty to 30 degrees and an increase in range from around 23,500 yards/13 miles or 22 kilometres to 32,000 yards/18 miles or 29 kilometres, while the 6-in/152-mm secondary armament was reduced in favour of 4-in/ 102-mm guns and pom-poms.

Of the fifteen American battleships allowed under the Washington and London treaties, ten were afforded major refits in the period between 1926 and 1934: the *Wyoming*, which was retained as a gunnery training ship, underwent conversion in 1931–1932 and served throughout the Second World War in that capacity. For the battleships that remained, their refits generally conformed to a basic pattern of increased secondary armament, reduced number of boilers while retaining the previous level of power, the provision of anti-torpedo bulges and increased horizontal armour over vital spaces. In addition, all the American battleships were afforded greater fuel and hence increased range, augmented tertiary armament, and seaplanes and catapults. The one exception to the general pattern of increased capability was the *Oklahoma*, which was not given new boilers during her 1927–1929 refit: as a result she was only able to make a top speed of 19.7 knots thereafter, which must have made her one of the slowest battleships of the inter-war period.

After the Second World War the British took an inordinate pride in what the *Warspite*'s reconstruction achieved, and in one sense this was natural given her record in that war. She was in service in September 1939 and engaged an enemy for the last time in November 1944: between those two dates she wore out three sets of barrels for her main armament and won the equivalent of six-teen battle honours. The *Renown* likewise served throughout the war, and in 1945 was still the fastest capital ship in British service, while the *Queen Elizabeth* and *Valiant* had commendable records limited only by the lateness of their re-entering service. In the case of the *Queen Elizabeth*, there was irony in that she had been built to meet the challenge presented by the navy of Imperial Germany, but the only enemies that she ever engaged were Turkish and Japanese: in the case of the *Valiant*, her service was curtailed when she was badly damaged by the collapse of the floating dock in which she lay at Trinco-malee in August 1944. The British programme drew from the official naval his-torian, Captain S. W. Roskill, the observation that

> the reconstruction of the four ships actually completed was an outstand-ing success, and they all proved invaluable in the 1939–1945 war. Rarely can new wine have been more successfully poured into old bottles, or money have been spent by the Navy to better purpose than in rejuvenat-ing the *Warspite* and her sisters. It cost, in the case of the *Warspite*, £2,362,000 – less than a third of the cost of the *Nelson*, and far less than the later-built *King George V* class; and it gave the Navy what was virtually a new ship.[18]

Some of this may well be contentious, and for reasons which are not immediately obvious. The four British capital ships really represented little, if any, improvement over contemporary American battleships subjected to major overhaul or rebuilding between August 1925 and October 1934. The *Warspite* was rebuilt between March 1934 to June 1937, and though at best the equal of her American counterparts, in one respect she was definitely inferior. The tertiary, anti-aircraft, systems employed in British warships were much inferior to those used in American warships, the result of a wrong Admiralty decision which, ironically, Roskill was called upon to overcome when he was in the Admiralty staff in the war's early years. But there would seem to be two major criticisms of the British programme that need be considered at this juncture.

The first criticism is the obvious one – that only four ships were rebuilt and only two before the outbreak of war in Europe in 1939. The whole British programme, irrespective of its detail for individual ships, was wretchedly inadequate, and the point must be made. At the time of the outbreak of war in September 1939, the British had the *Warspite* and *Renown* in service, the *Queen Elizabeth* and *Valiant* undergoing reconstruction, and two more *Queen Elizabeth*s awaiting their time in dockyards. The five *Royal Sovereign* class battleships were not scheduled for any major refitting programme, and there were the two other battlecruisers, which were earmarked for major refitting but which operational necessity kept at bay until both ships were lost. The major responsibility for so inadequate a programme clearly rested with a British government that throughout the 1930s consistently refused to respond to the emerging threats from Japan, Italy and, finally, Germany. The second criticism, however, is more obtuse, and it is to note that Roskill's summary is contradictory. The reconstruction of the four British ships, like that of the American battleships, was an outstanding success, but what the reconstructions did not do was to provide Britain and the United States with virtually new ships. What the programmes did was to provide Britain and the United States with new versions of ships that pre-dated the Washington naval treaty, not new ships in the sense of ships that came on line as a result of the lapsing of limitation arrangements.

What is so striking about the *Warspite*, *Renown*, *Valiant* and the *Queen Elizabeth* and the American battleships from the *Arkansas* to the *West Virginia* is the extent to which, even with their major refitting and modernisation programmes prior to 1941, they all remain of First World War vintage. Despite all the effort that was made in terms of individual reconstruction programmes, each and every one of these ships carry the hallmarks of that period, and this is something that they share, to a very large extent, with their Japanese counterparts. The *Hood* and, more obviously, the *Nelson* and *Rodney* are different, but even these three ships belong to this period, if only because they are clearly very different indeed from the ships that were to come after 31 December 1936.

Herein lies the oddity of the situation that existed after the end of limitation relative to the situation that prevailed before it. The capital ships which were built after 1936, even the French and Italian ships which were built in the first part of the 1930s, are so clearly very different and so superior to those which were built before 1922 that there is no real comparison, as even the most cursory of comparisons would reveal:

	Warspite 1915	*Warspite* 1937	*Iowa* 1943
Displacement			
standard	27,500 tons	31,315 tons	48,110 tons
full load	33,000 tons	36,450 tons	57,540 tons
Length	645.75 feet/197.25 metres	646 feet/197.55 metres	860 feet/262.13 metres
Beam	90.50 feet/27.68 metres	104 feet	108.25 feet/32.99 metres
Maximum Draft	30.67 feet/9.38 metres	31.75 feet	36 feet/10.96 metres
Armament			
guns	Eight 15-in/380-mm	Eight 15-in/380-mm	Nine 16-in/406-mm
guns	Fourteen 6-in/152-mm	Eight 6-in/152-mm	Twenty 5-in/127-mm
guns	Two 3-in/76-mm AA	Eight 4-in/102-mm	Eighty 40-mm
guns		32 2-pdr AA	49 x 20-mm
	Four torpedo tubes	One seaplane	Four seaplanes
Protection			
belt	13-in/330-mm	13-in/330-mm	12.2-in/310-mm
turrets	13-in/330-mm	13-in/330-mm	17-in/430-mm
barbettes	10-in/255-mm	10-in/255-mm	17.3-in/439-mm
CT	11-in/280-mm	11-in/280-mm	17.3-in/439-mm
deck	3-in/76-mm	5-in/127-mm	5.6-in/142-mm
Propulsion	77,510 shp	80,000 shp	212,000 shp
Maximum speed	24 knots	23.6 knots	32.5 knots
Range	5,000 nm/12 knots	7,400 nm/12 knots	15,000 nm/12 knots

The ultimate irony is provided by the fact that the *Warspite*'s original capabilities were those of a battleship which was built to win and exercise command of the sea and which belonged to the most powerful type of ship afloat. Her reconstruction was an attempt to ensure that she continued to win and exercise that command, but she was hopelessly outclassed in every respect by new classes of battleship which, when complete, were themselves basically no longer capable of discharging the battleship's function. Thus the ending of the limitation treaties in effect initiated a search into the realms of obsolescence.

This was the final phase of battleship development, and it was one dominated by the classes built, by the classes proposed and abandoned by the major powers, and by war. Inevitably, perhaps the most interesting capital ships from this time were those that were never built – the super-*Yamato* class, the five-strong *Montana* class, and the four fast battleships of the *Lion* class which would have represented their builders' final comment on capital ship endeavour. There were, however, four other countries involved in battleship construction at this time. Two of these countries, France and Italy, were bound by the Washington treaty while the other two countries, Germany and the Soviet Union, were outside the limitations arrangement, though Germany was bound by the naval clauses of the Treaty of Versailles.

The only one of these four countries not to complete capital ships in the inter-war period was the Soviet Union, and in the light of the various trials and tribulations that inflicted themselves upon her this was not altogether surprising. The Soviet Union which emerged in 1924 from civil war and foreign intervention faced three major problems even before she could consider capital ship construction. Her various shipyards needed massive investment in terms of equipment and enlargement, and new yards at Molotovsk and Komsomolsk had to be created. Many of the older yards had to be cleared, and various commands properly reconstituted: it was not until 1932 that Soviet formations in the Arctic and Far East were formed. Thereafter the Soviet Navy was the victim of Stalin's terror even as the dictator, who created a Ministry of Naval Construction in December 1937, set down various programmes that together would have committed the Soviet Union to the construction of fifteen dreadnoughts, fifteen battlecruisers, 28 cruisers, 164 destroyers and 336 submarines. Of the 30 capital ships cited, six were laid down, the *Sovetskij Soyuz* and *Sovetskaja Ukraina* in July and October 1938 respectively, the *Sevastopol* and *Kronstadt* both in November 1939, the *Sovetskaya Rossia* in December 1939 and the *Sovetskaya Belorossia* in July 1940. None had been launched by the start of the Great Patriotic War in June 1941 – in fact, none of these ships was scheduled to be launched before September 1942 – with the result that the only capital ships available to the Soviet Union during the inter-war period were four tsarist survivors, the *Poltava*, *Petropavlovsk* and the *Gangut*, and the *Sevastopol*. Of these, the first, under the name *Frunze*, was not in service after 1923, though it was not until 1939 that she was finally broken up at Leningrad. The *Petropavlovsk*, renamed the *Marat*, the *Gangut*, renamed the *Oktjabrskaja Revolucija*, and the *Sevastopol*, renamed the *Parishskaja Kommuna*, were in turn rebuilt between 1928 and 1938, but these programmes were not comprehensive and the three battleships in the latter part of the 1930s looked what they were: reconditioned pre-1914 ships, fit only for limited and local operations.

The other three states, naturally enough, shared one basic characteristic, namely distrust of the other two. In terms of naval construction, what bound the three together was the provision whereby Germany, under the Treaty of Versailles, retained eight pre-dreadnoughts of the *Deutschland* and *Braunschweig* classes but was allowed to replace each battleship twenty years after launch with one 10,000-ton warship: contrary to common belief, there was no limit on the size of the main armament with which the new ships could be equipped, but on a 10,000-ton limit, and in the aftermath of the Washington Treaty, it was clear that the maximum size which might be embarked was the 11-in/280-mm gun. Though one design prepared in the 1920s settled for a ship with four 15-in/380-mm guns, the limitation on size presented Germany in the first half of the decade with the utmost difficulty of choice. Coastal monitors could be constructed on such a displacement, but the seagoing choice, between battleship and cruiser, was an impossible one. A cruiser might have speed but no real armour and armament, while the standard orthodoxy of the day held that a battleship had to have six 12-in/305-mm guns in three turrets, and this left very little tonnage for engines and protection.

It was not until 1925 that this construction conundrum began to unravel with the proposal to equip the planned ships with diesel engines, which would be most economical in terms of weight. At the same time, German thoughts turned to the example of the *Nelson* and *Rodney* in terms of the layout of main armament, but the third turret provided problems regarding what might be afforded in the way of secondary armament and protection. The triple turret, one forward and one aft, thus presented itself as the means whereby the various competing claims might be resolved with a ship provided with 4-in/102-mm armour protection and a speed of 26 or 27 knots but also a radius of action of 10,000 miles/18,400-km at twenty knots. Overall, the final design provided for a ship that, with six 11-in/280-mm guns in triple turrets, could outshoot a cruiser and outrun a battleship. In fact, only the British battlecruisers *Hood*, *Renown* and *Repulse* and the Japanese *Kongo*-class battlecruisers, were superior in gun size and numbers, armour and speed to what were referred, somewhat quaintly, as 'armour-clads' or, more popularly, as 'pocket battleships'. The first such ship, the *Deutschland*, considerably exceeded permitted displacement, being 11,700 tons standard and 15,200 tons full load: her successors, the *Admiral Scheer* and *Admiral Graf Spee*, were larger at 15,900 tons full load displacement.

With the *Deutschland* the Germans had produced a formidable warship, one as formidable on her own terms of reference as the *Dreadnought* in 1906. She was not a battleship and she was not a substitute for a battleship, but she presented an obvious difficulty for the French Navy as it entered the 1930s. France was entitled, under the Washington Treaty, to build three battleships.[19] For the French Navy, however, the *Deutschland* was one of two problems, the other being Italy and Italian naval ambitions in the Mediterranean. At the London conference in 1930 formal agreement with Italy proved elusive, but informally the French and Italians promised one another to observe a 70,000-ton aggregate tonnage for new battleship construction and the 35,000-ton limit on individual battleships. On these figures, the French Navy could build for itself four warships each superior to the *Deutschland* – in May 1925 parliament had been asked for but refused funds to build two 17,200-ton warships with eight 12-in/305-mm guns and capable of 35 knots – but the difficulty was obvious: such warships would be hopelessly outclassed if the Italians chose to build just two battleships on their 70,000 ton allowance.

The initial French response was the programme of 18 June 1931 which committed France to the construction of three 23,700-ton battleships armed with eight 12-in guns, but while such ships would have been more than a match for the *Deutschland* and her sisters, two considerations seem to have combined to close down this particular programme. The more important of these considerations was the fact that such battleships would have been more than a match for the pocket battleships, but nothing else, while the Italian heavy cruiser programme clearly presented the French with the need for a qualitative superiority which simply could not be matched on 23,700-ton hulls. Therefore the French Navy settled for the *Dunkerque*, which came with eight 13-in/330-mm guns. On a standard displacement of 27,900 tons and full load displacement of 35,000 tons, she had 8.85-in/225-mm main belt, 5.5-in/140-mm deck and 13-in/330-mm turret armour, her total of 10,665 tons of armour being complemented by a speed of 29.5 knots and the adoption of two quadruple turrets, which weighed 4,520 tons compared to the 6,240 tons of four twin turrets. The turrets were carried forward, and were spaced 88 feet/27 metres apart in order to prevent the possibility of a single hit disabling both. The *Dunkerque*, which logged 31 knots on trials, was followed by the very slightly different *Strasbourg*, but even before the latter was laid down, Italy's announcement of her intention to build two 35,000-ton battleships (26 May 1934) presented France with the problem of formulating an immediate and effective response.

The Italian move and the French response resulted in the construction of two classes of battleship that were among the most handsome dreadnoughts ever built. On the French side, the *Richelieu* class battleship was really an enlarged *Dunkerque*, the French using the Abyssinian crisis to justify their recourse to treaty provisions that allowed the construction of capital ships over the 35,000-ton limit. On a standard displacement of 35,000 tons and a full load displacement of 47,548 tons, this class was to have housed eight 15-in/380-mm guns in two quadruple turrets forward and to have been provided with 13-in/330-mm belt and 16.93-in/430-mm turret armour. With six boilers and four turbines, these battleships were capable of 32 knots, and for France the tragedy of this class was that only one, the nameship of the class, was completed before 1940: discounting the *Dunkerque* and *Strasbourg* from consideration, she was indeed the only battleship completed in France between 1917 and 1 May 1955, when the *Richelieu*'s much delayed sister ship, the *Jean Bart*, was finally completed.

On the Italian side, with the same tonnage and the same dates of replacement as the French, initial interest in the mid-1920s had concentrated on the possibility of building three 23,000-ton warships carrying either six 13.5-in/343-mm guns or six 15-in/380-mm guns in three twin turrets, but as in the French case, and for much the same reasons, this intention had been set aside in favour of building battleships with a starting point of 35,000 tons displacement. The *Littorio* comfortably exceeded treaty limitations, being of 40,724 tons standard displacement and 45,236 tons deep load displacement. Given that Italian industry had never produced a 16-in/406-mm gun, the *Littorio* and her sisters were afforded nine 15-in/380-mm guns in three triple turrets, the 50-calibre weapon at an elevation of 35 degrees giving a theoretical maximum range of 46,800 yards, or 27 miles or 43 kilometres – which were the elevation and, within a few hundred metres, the range of the main armament in the *Strasbourg* and *Richelieu* classes. With eight boilers and four geared turbines, plus diesel generators, the *Littorio* was afforded 128,000 shp and a top speed of 30 knots, but on trials her propulsion plant, which weighed only 2,366 tons, provided 137,649 shp and a top speed of 31.3 knots.

These formidable characteristics were not obtained at the expense of protection, which was one of the main features of novelty of this ship and her sister, the *Vittorio Veneto*. The two ships were afforded a waterline armoured belt of a 2.75-in/70-mm strake, which was backed by 0.40-in/10-mm plate, which in turn was backed, at a distance of some 10 inches/250 millimetres, by the main 11-in/280-mm armour, which was supported by 2 inches/50 millimetres of wood and 0.6 inches/15 millimetres of plate. The whole was inclined at fourteen degrees outward from bottom to top, the general idea of this arrangement being that of spaced armour and the decapitation of armour-piercing shells. With a series of watertight bulkheads and (inward) sloped and spaced armour, the *Littorio* was afforded a maximum deck armour that was 6.4-in/162-mm thick: her turrets and barbettes were afforded maximum thicknesses of 13.8 inches/350 millimetres of armour, and her conning tower was given 10.2 inches/260 millimetres.

With two of the class ordered in 1934 and completed in 1940 and another two ordered in 1938, Italy sought to secure for herself a class of perhaps the most powerful battleships in Europe: what Italy most certainly did in the completion of three of these ships was to build perhaps the most aesthetically pleasing of all European dreadnoughts: with their two capped funnels and graceful balance, they were elegant and formidable, their only possible weaknesses being that their armour protection was perhaps not all that it was hoped. They were limited in range (some 4,580 miles/7,300-km at sixteen knots) and carried relatively little ammunition, just 55 armour-piercing and nineteen high-explosive rounds for each of the main guns, but presumably Italy's central position in the Mediterranean accounted for such limitations being worked into the ships of this class.

Matters Mediterranean in the second half of the 1930s, however, were overshadowed by events to the north, though these were not primarily naval: indeed, matters naval were, in Hitler's reckoning, *minor inter pares*, but not so *minor* as not to be worthy of a treaty along the way. The Anglo-German naval treaty of 18 June 1935 was the first international endorsement of German re-armament, and it permitted Germany a 35 per cent ratio to British tonnage in all categories of warship other than submarines, in which she was permitted a 45 per cent ratio. Germany expressed a willingness either to abolish submarines or limit their size, but in the absence of any international agreement on either score, she claimed the right of parity with Britain. It has been argued that the one redeeming feature of this supine British compliance with German demands was that it perhaps delayed German construction, but in fact Germany had laid down submarines, and two battleships, even before the treaty was concluded. The assertion that the German Navy's problems in the Second World War stemmed largely from its fundamental mistake in believing Hitler's assessment that war would not come until 1943 or 1944, and its preparation of the famous Plan Z of March 1937, is really neither here nor there. The coming of war in 1939 found the German Navy at least two years off readiness to fight a war, but it could only have avoided such a situation if it had known war was to come in 1939 and had been afforded priority ahead of the other services in the 1930s, something which Hitler would never had initiated.

The original German intention had been to build six *Deutschland*-class 'pocket battleships' and to have begun their fourth and fifth ships, replacements for the *Elsass* and *Hessen*, some two years before their scheduled starting dates in 1936 and 1937. But even as early as 1932, before Hitler's coming to power, knowledge of the intention represented by the *Dunkerque* class pointed the German Navy in the direction of the counter, specifically an improved *Deutschland* class. The design parameters for the new ships were a displacement of 26,000 tons, armour protection of some 320 millimetres and proof against 13-in/330-mm shells, and an armament of either 11-in/280-mm or 13-in/330-mm guns in twin, triple or quadruple turrets. In the event, it was to take one false start, when two ships – the *Hannover* and *Schleswig-Holstein* – were laid down and then halted, before a number of different considerations imposed themselves upon the decision-making process.

Hitler's overwhelming concern not to initiate a naval race which would alienate Britain went alongside two naval calculations, that an improved *Deutschland* of some 19,000 tons would use virtually the whole of the balance of tonnage for armour protection but that the next qualitative increase necessarily had to involve three turrets, which meant a displacement of 26,000 tons and steam, not diesel, propulsion. Ultimately, the decision was taken to equip the new ships with the same armament as the *Deutschland*s, Hitler's belated wish that they be armed with 15-in/380-mm guns being withdrawn when it was realised that two years would be lost in waiting for such guns: provision was made, however, whereby they could be re-armed with either 13-in/330-mm or 15-in/380-mm guns. Such provision went alongside 13.8-in/350-mm belt, 14.2-in/360-mm turret and 1.97-in/50-mm deck armour, and boilers and turbines that could generate 165,000 shp and a top speed of 32 knots. The first of two ships, the *Gneisenau*, was laid down at Kiel on 6 May 1935 and ten days later was followed by the *Scharnhorst*, which was laid down at Wilhelmshaven. At this time, one month before the British treaty, it was announced that the displacement of these ships was 26,000 tons: in reality the two ships had a standard displacement of 31,850 tons and a full load displacement of 38,900 tons. Within five months of their being laid down, preliminary work began at Hamburg for another battleship, which was laid down the following July.

This ship was the *Bismarck*, and she and her sister ship the *Tirpitz* were to be the last capital ships built by Germany. Plan Z, which Hitler approved in January 1939, was to have resulted in the German Navy acquiring six battleships by 1944 and three battlecruisers by 1943: in addition, four aircraft carriers, four heavy and seventeen light cruisers, plus destroyers and no fewer than 221 submarines were to be completed between 1941 and 1948. The battleships and battlecruisers in this programme were in addition to those already laid down and in various stages of completion. The battleships, generally known as the H-class, were to have a standard displacement of 52,607 tons and a full load displacement of 62,497 tons, which would have made them about half as big again as the *Hood*, which was the largest capital ship in the world. The first two members of this class, the *Friedrich der Grosse* and *Gross Deutschland*, were laid down in summer 1939 at Hamburg and Bremen respectively. The battlecruisers, generally known as the P-class, were to be afforded 30,500 tons standard displacement, but none was ever laid down.

The battleships were to have carried eight 16-in/406-mm guns and been given a top speed of 30 knots: the battlecruisers were to have carried six 15-in/380-mm guns and been given a top speed of 33.5 knots. The gestation period for the *Bismarck* and *Tirpitz* had seen such performance figures worked into various specifications and designs, but always in association with such considerations as size of shipyards and locks on the Kiel canal, plus draughts on the approaches to Germany's ports. These, plus alternating expansion and contraction of armour as other specifications were changed, meant that the entire planning phase was one of great confusion, though the cause of clarity was helped by Hitler's abrogation of the Treaty of Versailles and the tacit decision to ignore the 35,000-ton limitation on capital ships. The basic German problem was that if the 15-in/380-mm main armament was accepted, then a balanced design necessitated a standard displacement of some 42,500 tons, which was too big to use the largest lock at Wilhelmshaven. In April 1935, therefore, the German Navy set displacement at 41,000 tons and adopted a main armament of eight 13.7-in/350-mm guns, but within a month this latter decision had been reversed in favour of a main armament of eight 15-in/380-mm guns. It was not until July 1936, after the *Bismarck* had been laid down, that a decision was made between turbo-electric and steam engine systems, in favour of the latter.

The *Bismarck* was commissioned in service in August 1940 and the *Tirpitz* in February 1941, and they were so formidable the comment that they were 'exceptionally resistant and they were among the best ever built. No similar foreign type could be compared with them' is not untypical of the praise they have attracted.[20] There is no doubt that they were indeed formidable fighting ships, though the obvious points need to be made: both were destroyed, the *Bismarck* on her maiden voyage, and they certainly should have been formidable, given that the standard and full load displacement of the *Bismarck*, which was the smaller of the two, were respectively 45,172 tons and 50,900 tons, and this on declared limit of 35,000 tons. Had the British deliberately lied and evaded the terms of treaties to which they had voluntarily subscribed, there would have been no end to denunciation.

The critical point would seem to be that if the *Bismarck* is considered in such terms as have been cited here, the point of superiority of these German ships lay in the fact that the British did observe treaty terms, and one is left to question the fact that the *Kriegsmarine* entered the Second World War committed to a doctrine of tonnage warfare aimed at the defeat of Britain through the destruction of her sea-borne trade: whether such ships as the *Bismarck* and *Tirpitz* were relevant to the needs of such a war is very doubtful indeed, and it is difficult to believe that in terms of national requirement they were more useful than perhaps four or six 19,000-ton or 26,000-ton *panzerschiffe* might have been in 1941. As it was, the *Bismarck*, despite her sinking of the *Hood* in the Denmark Strait on Empire Day 1941, was caught and sank, on the anniversary of Tsushima, after she had attempted to enter an ocean covered by enemy aircraft and warships, while the *Tirpitz* led a lonely, furtive and harassed existence until finally sunk by land-based aircraft in November 1944 after a singularly ineffective career. In comparison, the four surviving British battleships of the *King George V* class, so obviously inferior to these two German ships, served in the European theatre before making their way to the Far East where the *Duke of York*, in conducting the bombardment of the Hamamatsu aircraft factory on the night of 29/30 July 1945, was the last British battleship ever to fire her guns in anger, two months after Germany and tonnage warfare were no more.

The immediate point of contrast between British and German battleships of the Second World War, in effect the *King George V* class and the *Bismarck* and *Tirpitz*, was the former's 14-in/356-mm main armament, which was frankly out of its depth in a conflict in which even the 15-in/380-mm gun and its shell were really admitted to the gun club only on past performance. The arming of this class with the 14-in/356-mm gun arose from a combination of two reasons. The 1936 London treaty set down the limitation of the 14-in/356-mm gun for a capital ship of 35,000 tons, and the Admiralty was firmly of the view that on such a displacement this gun represented the best available armament. In fact, in the early 1930s designs had been drawn up for such guns and mounts, but the problem was that this particular section of the 1936 treaty was valid only if Japan agreed to abide by its terms: if she did not, then the original Washington limitation, the 16-in/408-mm gun, was deemed to represent the maximum size of armament that could be installed in capital ships.

With two battleships ordered in 1936 and another three scheduled to be ordered in 1938, the problem for the British was that the first to be completed could be expected to enter service in 1940 but would be delayed for at least a year if a decision was made in favour of a larger main armament. The Japanese did not have to show their hand until 1937, but with both Germany and Italy having laid down capital ships, Britain could not delay a decision and chose the 14-in/356-mm gun. What this meant was that, relative to those of Japan and the United States, and also, albeit to a lesser degree, those of Germany and Italy, the most modern of British capital ships could not really punch their weight, but this situation had as much to do with the greater size of other nations' capital ships of the late 1930s and not simply their armament, and in many ways the real point of comparison should have been between these various foreign ships and the *Lion* class of fast battleship, two of which were laid down in 1939.

The construction of this class was suspended in October 1939 and finally stopped in March 1941 when the rather perverse decision was taken to halt construction on the grounds that the battleships could not be completed in two years: this decision was accompanied by an order for one battleship that was to be completed by 1943 by using the 15-in/380-mm guns from the *Courageous* and *Glorious* which had been in storage since 1925. This ship, the *Vanguard*, was not completed until after the end of the Second World War, but she, and the members of the *Lion* class, would have stood comparison with the best that could have been produced by Germany – everything after the projected German battleship H. 42 being dismissed from serious consideration. As it was, there were only six actions in the Second World War between capital ships which involved loss and three of these actions involved a *King George V*-class battleship: none were lost and two enemy warships, the *Bismarck* and *Scharnhorst*, were destroyed. Nevertheless, it needs be said that in facing the most powerful ships of the enemy, members of this class really did need to go around in pairs: the *Duke of York*'s sinking of the *Scharnhorst* off North Cape in December 1943, like the *Washington*'s sinking of the *Kirishima* off Guadalcanal in November 1942, was very much the exception – which, very conveniently, leads us back to where this chapter started: Japan, the United States and the Pacific.

The story of the dreadnought battleship and the battlecruiser has to come back to the Pacific. It is right and proper that this should be so because here, in the actions of Japan and the United States, was written the last chapter in this story, and on three separate counts. First, the ending of the limitation process was a defining moment in the 1930s. Other matters were more readily obvious or of greater immediate significance, but the end of limitation arrangements marked the end of what had been at best a process which had brought mixed results but which nonetheless had not been attended by war between the great powers. The end of limitation marked the start of a journey which within a year was to see Japan committed to full-scale war in China and within five years was to result in Japan and the United States being at war after a process in which naval calculations, indeed a naval race, proved critically important. This, indeed, is the second point, noted herein separately because it was so unusual. Even the most casual acquaintance with history reveals that wars are seldom caused by naval power, and very seldom have wars been primarily concerned with naval matters. The Second World War in the Pacific, not the Far East, is unusual in this respect because it was a war in which naval power was central to the process by which war began and by which its outcome was decided. To compound the point, and as one has argued elsewhere, this war was also unusual in the sense that nations as mismatched as Japan and the United States very seldom fight one another, and even less frequently do they fight wars initiated by the weaker side: normally they arrange their common concerns without recourse to arms.

The third matter, however, is reason enough in itself for a return to matters Pacific, and it can be simply stated: the final phase of the dreadnought era does properly belong to the Pacific on account of both the ships Japan and the United States built – and then deployed in the Pacific war – and the ships Japan and the United States would have wished to have built. Without any doubt, the ships which were built after 1937 represented the most powerful classes of dreadnoughts ever constructed, while the ships which were not built would have been to these ships what they had been to their predecessors. The list is, or perhaps more accurately both lists are, impressive, and by any standard.

Simply to list the ships built and projected brought this writer to a realisation that was, at best, perhaps 30 years belated. The story of the end of limitation has been told so often, and always to one refrain: that the *Kaigun* quite deliberately refused to countenance limitation because it wished to complete its various planned building programmes in accordance with the *zengen sakusen*. There is no doubting the essential correctness of this interpretation, but it is rather interesting to note that the Americans laid down their first battleship after the end of limitation, the *North Carolina*, a little more than a week before the Japanese laid down their equivalent, the *Yamato*. In fact, the Japanese were the last of the three major naval powers to turn intention into the laying of keels, but in reality the Japanese had been preparing for the laying down of the *Yamato*, which was to be the first in a class of five, for some time. As indicative of these efforts, two matters may be noted, namely that there were 23 separate designs prepared between 10 March 1935 and March 1937,[21] and that in order to build the *Musashi* at Mitsubishi at Nagasaki and the *Shinano* at Yokosuka navy yard the Japanese had to build a very unusual ship, the 10,360-ton *Kashino*, capable of carrying turrets (which weighed 2,730 tons or more than a destroyer) and guns from the Naval Ordnance Factory at Kure. Laid down on 1 July 1939 and launched on 26 January 1940, the *Kashino* was completed in the following July and delivered the first turret and gun to the *Musashi* on 6 October 1941.

All the major naval powers experienced difficulty with their programmes during the Second World War, and all suffered from having major units unconscionably delayed or cancelled altogether: as the lists indicate, even the United States, with shipyards that were without equal in terms of speed and volume of output, was obliged to postpone the laying down of major classes because of other priorities, in the case of the *Montana*-class battleships those afforded to six *Midway* fleet carriers, three of which were in their turn cancelled. The Japanese, however, experienced a related but very different difficulty: her yards could not undertake the building of new naval vessels and merchantmen, and at the same time undertake major refitting and modernisation programmes both to warships and merchant vessels. The Japanese navy was able to begin hostilities in December 1941 with just one destroyer in dockyard hands: every other capital ship, carrier, cruiser, destroyer and submarine was in service. But even as crucially important warships as fleet carriers were being delayed by more than a year in construction in 1938–1939, and by late 1941 about one eighth of the mercantile tonnage under the Japanese flag was laid up for want of maintenance. Japanese shipyard and completion problems began long before the start of the Pacific war, and worsened dramatically in the course of hostilities. It suffices to note just one matter. The *Yamato*, *Musashi* and the *Shinano* were intended as the first of the new battleships deliberately built to a size that could not be exceeded by any American warship which sought to use the Panama Canal, but the *Shinano* was not completed as a battleship and two other units, which were supposed to be sister ships, were abandoned, indeed one was not even laid down. Moreover, as has been noted, the *Yamato* class battleships were intended as an interim class, and pencilled in for inclusion in the initial 1942 programme were two battleships that, depending on source, were to have embarked six 19.7-

in/500-mm or 20-in/508-mm guns: these never progressed past the preliminary design stage, though they were included in the provisional 1942 programme which was cancelled. In any event, the battle of Midway accounted for these ships with as much finality as it did for four of Japan's carriers.

The *Yamato* and *Musashi* therefore remained the largest battleships ever built by Japan, and, given the abandonment of the *Montana* programme by the United States, the largest battleships ever built by any nation. Certainly they were among the most beautiful of battleships: the photograph of the *Yamato* on her trials in October 1941, complete with her clean lines, depressed forward turret and spray, can so easily be regarded as the moment where perfection passed into obsolescence, and indeed one of the *Kaigun*'s wartime jokes – that the three most useless things in the world were the Pyramids, the Great Wall of China and the battleship *Yamato* – made the point. The *Yamato* was built for one purpose, to withstand punishment while being able to inflict the same upon American battleships in the course of 'the decisive battle' in which the Imperial Navy con-tinued to believe until it ceased to exist. In this sense, the *Kaigun* and the *Yamato* were worthy of one another, and their stories were complementary. The tragedy of both, other than the *Kaigun*'s responsibility for taking Japan into a disastrous war, was that, for all the effort and resources spent upon the *Yamato* and *Musashi*, the ships were clearly inferior to the members of the *Iowa* class and would have been inferior to the *Montana*-class battleships had these been built. The 18.1-in/460-mm gun was not worth the effort which went into its acquisi-tion, and the Japanese would have been much better advised to have built new battleships around the proven 16-in/406-mm gun which had armed the *Nagato* and *Mutsu*.

For their part, the Americans built battleships that certainly matched the *Yamato* and *Musashi* in terms of quality, and the Japanese total of two battleships completed after 1937 formed a sad comment upon Japanese intentions given the fact that American yards completed no fewer than ten battleships, and also two battlecruisers, after the end of limitation – which was more than the rest of the world combined. In so doing, they built warships which, though they never fought a line action, complemented and helped protect the fleet carriers, and with the *Iowa* class the United States built a class of battleships with a place in history that was secured on several counts, and not simply because Japan's sur-render on 2 September 1945 was signed in the *Missouri*. This may be unfair to the *North Carolina* and *South Dakota* classes, and is definitely unfair to the *Washington*, but the claims of the *Iowa* class lie in their combination of qualities, not least the fact that these four battleships made the building of the *Alaska* and *Guam* utterly irrelevant: at $74,000,000 apiece, these two battlecruisers were not faster than the *Iowa* class, which thereby destroyed their rationale, and the speed of the *Iowa* class was indeed both unprecedented and one never seriously considered by any other navy. The development of the small-tube boiler from the time of the First World War over the next twenty years made possible speeds and, crucially, speed-to- weight ratios that previously had been the stuff of imaginations. The top speed of 33 knots of the *Iowa* class – and it beggars the imagination to try to think what the crew of the destroyer *Nowaki* must have felt when they found their ship in danger of being overhauled by battleships off Truk in February 1944 – was obtained on engines that weighed 2,500 tons, which was less than two-thirds of the weight of the engines of the *Queen Elizabeth*-class battleships of 1912 and not much larger than the engines of the *New Mexico* class of 1914: in fact, the engines of the *Iowa*-class battleships weighed about one tenth less than those of the *Bismarck*.

Such, then, were the battleships and battlecruisers, and their projected programmes, of all the major powers after 1937 and as the world lurched toward the greatest, most destructive war in history. What is most notable is the yawning disparity of quality between the various capital ships. The seven leading naval powers between them mustered some 57 battleships and battlecruisers in 1939–1940, and these varied from obsolete First World War museum pieces to state-of-the-art warships, with new and still more formidable units in dockyards or on the order books. But there were two developments that had arrived on the scene by the time of the outbreak of war, and a third which always tried not to be seen to arrive on the scene, that were to affect the battleship immensely. The first was radar, which first went to sea in 1938 in the *Admiral Graf Spee* and, in December, the training ship *New York*: British capital ships first embarked radar in 1939. Obviously, and notwithstanding the censor's activities, the new equipment wrought change to the silhouette of warships, but none so massive as the technical change it set in train. The second was the aircraft, which after 1937, in land-based form, took on monoplane configuration: biplane carrier aircraft were more slowly ousted, and indeed even in 1941 the American carrier *Yorktown* still retained biplanes. The point, however, was that by 1937 aircraft had acquired the range, speed and payload that for the first time really presented a serious threat to warships. It is possible to argue that until 1937 or 1938 the British plan for a war against Germany, the mining of the southern North Sea and distant blockade of First World War vintage, would have worked, but very abruptly, and without there being any means of effective response, this situation changed, with obvious implications for navies and with very different results in the European and Pacific theatres. In the Pacific, navies could only hope to prevail if they moved in strength with their own naval aircraft and, wherever possible, in association with land-based aircraft: against enemies dispersed and inferior in numbers, they could overwhelm individual bases or even bases within single island groups. In the European theatre, where navies were faced by a contiguous land mass, the balance of advantage lay with land-based air power, and to the detriment of navies in general and fleets and capital ships in particular. For evidence to this effect, one need look no farther than the Mediterranean, which in terms of British losses in the Second World War proved more costly than both the North Atlantic and home waters.

The third development was the submarine, which perhaps surprisingly failed to account for a single dreadnought or battlecruiser during the First World War, albeit not for wanting of trying. It was not until November 1941 that a submarine accounted for an operational capital ship at sea, and just sixteen days later aircraft accounted for their first capital ships which were at sea and had full power of manoeuvre. In many ways the juncture of these events – the loss in the eastern Mediterranean of the British battleship *Barham* as a result of her being torpedoed by the German submarine U.331 and the loss in the South China Sea of the British battlecruiser *Repulse* and battleship *Prince of Wales* to Japanese land-based aircraft – provide the point of balance in the story of the capital ship in the Second World War.[22] Before these events the battleship had played an important role in the war at sea, but thereafter its role was ever more restricted as ownership of the trident passed to new hands and a new type of warship.

5

The Second World War, 1939–1945

In the course of the Second World War, and perhaps for the only time in history, ownership of the trident changed hands without predecessor and successor fighting one another for its possession. Before the entry of the United States into the war, the Royal Navy, by virtue of tradition and prestige, was still the pre-eminent of navies, but in partnership with it, and in the course of a two-ocean struggle, the U.S. Navy was to emerge during this war as the world's greatest navy possessed of a strength that, at war's end, rendered it unchallengeable. It did so in the course of what was really not one war but three separate naval wars, one against Germany, the second against Italy and the third against Japan, the last of which was remarkable in two respects. The example of history teaches that the naval dimension of wars invariably is slow in manifestation and result, and naval power is limited in terms of application and effect. Yet in this war the United States defeated what was the fifth most powerful state in the world in the remarkably short time of just 44 months, and she did so across the width of the Pacific. Very seldom have states been overwhelmed from the sea, and the only previous examples of such a phenomenon, and their distance in time from the present, make them both dubious comparisons.[1] The U.S. Navy, with only minor assistance from its various allies, carried war across the Pacific, overwhelming the Imperial Japanese Navy and destroying her merchant marine in the process, until it cast ashore a man-made *tsunami* of high-explosive hatred that completed the comprehensive defeat of Japan even without the necessity of an invasion and conquest of the home islands. In terms of scale, distance and time, the American defeat of Japan in the Second World War was an unprecedented achievement but, it must be noted, it was one in which the capital ship played only a secondary and supporting role: in this particular conflict there were but two occasions when capital ships did battle with one another.

The other two wars were very different from one another though linked by the fact that the U.S. Navy was but little involved in these conflicts: the main American contributions to both the German and the Italian naval wars was provided by the United States Army Air Force, and the main agencies of common defeat for the *Kriegsmarine* and the Royal Italian Navy were the Royal Navy and Royal Air Force. Be that as it may, there are two statistical matters which, drawn from the three conflicts, provide the terms of reference for this account of proceedings. Both have a somewhat surprising dimension because seldom have historians troubled themselves to count the number of capital ships that served in the Second World War, yet the seven major combat powers between them mustered no fewer than 80 capital ships,[2] and of this total no fewer than 35 were sunk. Perhaps surprisingly, one of these ships was sunk twice and another two were sunk on three occasions: another six were sunk after the war, two in 1946, three in 1948 and one in 1955. Of the capital ships that were sunk in the course of hostilities, 24, more than half the total number sunk during the Second World War, were sunk in ports or shallow water and it is arguable that twenty-two of these losses came after the decision of war had been reached. The capital ships that were sunk or destroyed after 27 November 1942 were the victims of triumphant sea power. These ships were lost after the battle for command of the seas had been decided, and not in the course of the struggle for that command.[3]

In an account of the Second World War and the capital ship, the story is to be told not in terms of victorious sea power but failing sea power and its contraction. Most obviously, if one considers German sea power, the point which is too easily missed is the fact that, in the period between 1939 and 1941, the war against Allied and neutral shipping was prosecuted by capital ships and the pocket battleships in the Indian Ocean and South Atlantic, though by 1941 the range of raider operations had been restricted to the North Atlantic: thereafter the operational responsibility of major German warships was Norwegian waters and the Arctic, but after mid-1944 this was reduced to the Baltic and coastal waters, where virtually every surviving major surface unit was sunk or rendered *hors de combat* by Allied air power by war's end.

Mutatis mutandis, the same phenomenon repeated itself in the Japanese war, though in this case there was but one ocean that presented itself as the theatre of war. In 1941–1942 Japanese battleships appeared in areas as widely separated as the South China Sea and the Hawaiian Islands, the Japanese home islands and the lower Solomons. Yet the *Kaigun*, perhaps surprisingly, had lost only three battleships – the *Hiei*, *Kirishima* and the *Mutsu*, the latter to a magazine explosion in the Inland Sea – by October 1944 when the battle that completed Japan's defeat at sea was fought: after this battle the Imperial Navy was no more than an ineffective coastal defence force reduced to a furtive, unavailing existence in home waters, and its last three battleship losses in the last week of July 1945 at or off Kure in the Inland Sea was a recognition of this fact.

In the Mediterranean, the Royal Italian Navy's fate was very similar to that of the Imperial Japanese Navy, though events unfolded on a much smaller scale in terms of distance and there were different numbers and types of ship at Italy's disposal. She had, for example, no aircraft carriers, and the relative smallness of the theatre meant that there was a very different relationship between land-based air power and warships than generally applied in the Pacific, or at least until the last weeks of the war. The important point of similarity between the Mediterranean and the Pacific wars was that the Italian and Japanese battle fleets had been reduced to irrelevance months before the respective national surrenders in 1943 and 1945. Ironically the only Italian capital ship lost at sea was sunk on the day of the Italian surrender by Italy's erstwhile ally. In the loss of this ship, the *Roma*, there was an additional fact worth noting *en passant*: 35 capital ships were sunk in the course of the Second World War but of this total only ten – one British, two French, four German, one Italian and two Japanese battleships – post-dated the Washington treaty:[4] put the other way, two thirds of the capital ships sunk in the course of the Second World War had been built before 1921.

The European Conflict, 1939–1945: 1. The German War

The European war at sea was dominated by two facts of life. The first, very simply, was that there was no German surface fleet, and what few German capital ships there were could not hope to challenge British command of the sea. The second, no less simply, was that in the Mediterranean theatre of operations the preservation intact of her fleet, not least for reasons relating to a post-war settlement, was more important to Italy than any detail in terms of the conduct of operations. The combination of the two served to ensure that action involving capital ships was largely limited to secondary matters – the protection of convoys, the provision of escort to carriers, and the support of amphibious landings – rather than matters relating to winning and exercising command of the sea *per se*.

In 1939, with the outbreak of war in Europe, Britain and France possessed command of the sea and massive advantage over Germany in terms of numbers and position. In September 1939 Germany had available for operations the *Gneisenau* and *Scharnhorst*, the three pocket battleships *Deutschland*, *Admiral Scheer* and the *Admiral Graf Spee*, the four pre-dreadnought survivors from Versailles, the heavy cruiser *Admiral Hipper*, six light cruisers and just 21 operational destroyers.[5] In virtually every respect the German Navy in 1939 was no better placed to wage war than it had been in the previous conflict, and for much the same reason: what amounted to its second creation, after 1935, without reference to its numerical and geographical inferiority to its enemies, left it lacking any real *raison d'être*. The concept of tonnage warfare with which it had waged the last two years of the First World War with such disastrous results had survived this failure and by a process in the inter-war period that defies ready understanding had brought the German Navy back more or less to its original, 1917, starting point. In this inter-war period the German Navy had come to recognise that its search for battle in the southern North Sea was but the failing tactical response to a lost strategic cause, and it came to see its role as not simply related to the avoidance of battle but the conduct of economic warfare and the improvement of Germany's strategic position in terms of the waging of economic warfare by the occupation of Denmark and southern Norway.

In reality, this 'solution' to German naval problems was no solution at all: the occupation of Denmark and southern Norway would not break the British distant blockade and it would not really give Germany direct access to the North Atlantic. Moreover, this 'solution' begged the real issue because a fleet off southern Norway would scarcely be in a better position to ensure the protection of German oceanic trade than a fleet in home ports. But the very argument, by forcing attention on the strategic purposes of sea power (the maintenance of seaborne lines of communication), by pointing to just one aspect of Germany's strategic situation (her geographical position) to overcome wider strategic disadvantages, and by moving away from the primary importance of battle, opened up a wholly insidious line of reasoning that had assumed the status of holy writ for the inter-war German Navy. To the German Navy, war at sea was about lines of communication, whereas in reality it was about command of the sea, and it was about both control of enemy movement as a means of breaking his sea-borne communications and the reality that the control of enemy movement was in large part determined by the outcome of battle. What happened in the inter-war period was that the German Navy came to embrace the idea that command of the sea was something that was wholly identifiable with control of lines of communication, that war at sea was essentially an economic rather than a military contest, that battle should be avoided and that the command of the sea could be divided and localised, and, even more dangerous, that the denial of sea control to an enemy was really the equivalent of possession of sea control for oneself. By such a process of deduction the German Navy argued itself around a full circle. In 1917 it had committed Germany to the waging of tonnage warfare on the basis that sinkings in the order of 600,000 tons of merchantmen over a six-month period would deprive Britain of the trade of neutrals and force her from the war. By 1939 the figure was 750,000 tons a month and the period was a year, and the navy was much weaker – both relatively and in absolute terms – than it had been 25 years previously.

Such developments, combined with the imbalance of resources, largely explain the nature and conduct of the war at sea in the European context during the Second World War, the conflicts in the Mediterranean, Baltic and Black Seas excluded. They also explain the outcome of this conflict in terms of German commitment to a *guerre de course* – a stern chase in an attempt to destroy 9,000,000 tons of shipping in a year – against a Britain that was able to reduce her national requirements from some 60,000,000 tons of imports, plus oil, in 1938 to 27,000,000 tons by 1944 while she was protected against the impact of the worst ravages of the German submarine offensive against shipping by two sets of circumstances. First, the German invasion and conquest of Norway and the Netherlands in 1940 had the effect of driving into British ports the shipping of those two states, and moreover, the German naval concentration for the Norwegian campaign meant that the prosecution of tonnage war in the North Atlantic had to be suspended for some five months or more. Some 8,000,000 tons of Dutch and Norwegian shipping found their way into British service, and this, along with the break in the prosecution of tonnage war at this time, meant that Britain was in effect given a respite of perhaps eighteen months at a time of maximum weakness and vulnerability. Second, American shipyards were able to provide proof against defeat. This aspect of Allied success is sufficiently well known to allow relatively little treatment, but it suffices to note two facts – that by the third quarter of 1943 American shipyards, after 21 months of war, had made good all losses incurred by Allied and neutral shipping since the start of the European war, and that in March 1943 these same yards, which between 1922 and 1937 had produced just two merchantmen other than oilers, witnessed the launch of 140 Liberty ships.

This was the bottom line in the German campaign against shipping, and the fact was that by the beginning of 1943, when the return of merchantmen sunk in a given month against the number of operational U-boats shrank to just 0.17, the latter needed to have quintupled their rate of sinkings in order to offset new construction and still be able to reduce shipping by the 750,000 tons target figure. The defeat of the German attack on shipping was the result of the coming together of many factors, amongst the more important of which were the strengthening of convoy defences in terms of numbers of escorts allocated to individual formations, the qualitative improvement of individual escorts, the increasing Allied ability to use set formations rather than collections of individual escorts, increasing air support and an Allied operational superiority that exerted itself to ever greater effect during and after spring 1943. New and much improved escorts, radar, radio locating equipment, radio, sonar and integrated weapons systems were the natural complement to these factors, as indeed was the fact that after 1942 there was a massive reduction of the number of independent sailings, and hence of losses among ships sailing independently, as world-wide convoy was finally put into place. Ashore, after 1942 the defeat of the German attack on shipping was tied to growing Allied advantages in intelligence, routing, diversion and tracking, operational research and, critically, the growing imbalance of experience. Dilution and heavy losses, the latter concentrated among the more aggressive and successful units, meant that from 1942 the U-boat arm was having to send boats to sea with officers with perhaps only two or three missions to their credit. With escorts taking relatively few losses, the Allies held advantages of experience and technique that became ever more pronounced with the passing of time. The latter was important given that the German submarine arm was obliged to prosecute the war against shipping virtually without support: there was no naval air force, and after 1941 the other branches of the naval service were fully occupied elsewhere. In short, the submarine service found itself committed to a stern chase of an enemy endowed with massive strength in depth, and was always eighteen months, perhaps as much as two years, behind operational requirements.

These matters apart, the story of the capital ship and the European war is best told from the perspective of first the German war and then the Italian conflict. As normally told, the story of the German failure at sea is straightforward enough: it is that of the failure of the attack on shipping, primarily in the North Atlantic. But in fact Germany also failed to maintain both her oceanic and coastal shipping and to ensure her conquests against invasion from the sea. The record of German capital ship and *panzerschiffe* operations shows declining areas of responsibility and interest with the passing of time. Between September 1939 and March 1941 German warships ranged through the North and South Atlantic and entered the Indian Ocean, but after the summer of 1941 German operations were ended even in the North Atlantic and capital ships were thereafter restricted to home waters, the Baltic and Norway and the Arctic. In effect, however, the Arctic was closed to German heavy units after December 1943, and the major units of the *Kriegsmarine* were reduced to training duties and then defensive operations in the Baltic before being overwhelmed in the last weeks of the war.

The German dimension of the war at sea was largely resolved without reference to capital ships, but the outbreak of war in Europe saw but two German warships, the *Admiral Graf Spee* and *Deutschland*, committed to operations on the high seas. Both sailed from Germany before the war began, the *Admiral Graf Spee* on 21 August 1939 and the *Deutschland* three days later. The latter, operating in the North Atlantic, sank just two merchantmen before returning to Germany and a refit in readiness for the Norwegian campaign: she was renamed the *Lützow* and re-rated as a heavy cruiser at this time. The *Scharnhorst* and *Gneisenau* sought to enter the North Atlantic in November 1939 but though they sank the armed merchant cruiser *Rawalpindi* in 63° 40' North 11° 31' West on the 23rd, the action cost the German warships the element of surprise and they, like the *Deutschland*, returned to Germany in order to prepare for the Norwegian campaign. The *Admiral Graf Spee* was committed to operations in the South Atlantic and Indian Oceans, and by October 1939 had the distinction of her enemies having formed no fewer than eight task groups to ensure her destruction. Of these groups one, based on Ceylon, employed the fleet carrier *Eagle* and two heavy cruisers, a second, based on Brest, consisted of the battlecruiser *Dunkerque*, the carrier *Béarn*, and three light cruisers, and there were two groups in the West Indies and off the South American coast: one of these had the fleet carrier *Ark Royal* and battlecruiser *Renown* and the other the French battlecruiser *Strasbourg*, British light carrier *Hermes* and one British light cruiser under command. Perhaps both perversely and wholly predictably, none of these major units were involved in the action fought off the estuary of the Rio Plata on 13 December that marked the *Admiral Graf Spee*'s end after a career in which she sank just nine merchantmen of 50,089 tons. Though she worsted two of the three British cruisers ranged against her, the *Admiral Graf Spee* put into Montevideo after this action and scuttled herself four days later as various British formations from the Cape, Freetown and the South American and Falklands stations made their way at best speed to the La Plata estuary.[6]

For a class of ship of which so much had been expected, the outcome of this action, which was not well fought on the German side, came as a grave disappointment, and the waters where the *Admiral Graf Spee* had operated saw just one other warship raider, the sister ship *Admiral Scheer*, ply her trade. After leaving German waters she sailed from Stavanger on 28 October 1940 and passed through the Denmark Strait on 31 October–1 November. On 5 November 1940 she encountered Convoy HX 84 with 37 merchantmen, of which she sank five ships of 33,331 tons and damaged another three of 27,853 tons after having sunk the 14,164-ton armed merchant cruiser *Jervis Bay* in 52° 41' North 32° 17' West in the middle of the North Atlantic. The battleships *Nelson* and *Rodney* were moved to the Faeroes and Britain's three battlecruisers were temporarily deployed across the direct line to Brest in an attempt to bring the *Admiral Scheer* to battle, but while convoy sailings were not resumed until 17 November, the German raider sailed for the South Atlantic before moving into the Indian Ocean and a rendezvous with the armed merchant raider *Atlantis*, and various prizes, about a thousand miles east of Madagascar in mid-February 1941. After capturing a number of merchantmen, one of which was sailed to the Gironde as a prize, the *Admiral Scheer* was sighted by a seaplane from the British light cruiser *Glasgow* on 22 February and thereafter left the Indian Ocean. She re-entered the South Atlantic on 3 March and on 26–27 March passed through the Denmark Strait to emerge off Bergen on 30 March. After an

The *Dreadnought* (above, photographed in 1909) and the *South Carolina*. Designed and ordered before but not laid down until after the *Dreadnought* was completed, the *South Carolina* class was superior in armament and armour protection to the British ship but, with two shafts and reciprocating engines, inferior in machinery, speed and range.
(*Imperial War Museum; Naval Historical Center, Washington*)

A member of the 1909 class of 'super-dreadnoughts,' the *Thunderer* was the second battleship to have
a full director control firing system, located high on the tripod mast. In trials in 1912 she outscored her sister ship
Orion, which used the system of firing individual guns independently.

One of the first class of German battlecruisers with the turrets of the main armament all centre line, the *Derfflinger* accounted, at least in part, for the *Queen Mary* and *Invincible* at Jutland, which she survived, with the *Seydlitz*, as the most heavily damaged of German capital ships. (*Imperial War Museum*)

ABOVE The *Canada*. Prior to the second *King George V* class, the *Canada* was the only British battleship with a main armament of 14-in. guns. Requisitioned by Britain in August 1914, she was re-sold to Chile in 1920 and remained in service until 1958. She was the last surviving capital ship from Jutland. (*Imperial War Museum*)

OPPOSITE The *Maryland* (above) and the *Rodney*. One of the last American pre-limitation class of battleship, the *Maryland* was the first American battleship to be fitted with a catapult for seaplanes. The *Rodney*, built to limitation specifications, was long considered, with the *Nelson*, to be the most powerful battleship in the world. (USN; *Imperial War Museum*)

ABOVE The only occasion when they were in company: the *Jean Bart* leading the *Richelieu*, 30 January 1956.(*USN*)

BELOW The *Vittorio Veneto* on her way to internment in the Suez Canal, September 1943.
In the background are the Italian light cruiser *Duca d'Aosta* and the destroyer *Velite*. (*Imperial War Museum*)

Prince of Wales (above) and the *Gneisenau*: two counterparts in terms of displacement. The *Gneisenau* was mined during the Channel
...h and then incurred severe damage in an air raid at Kiel, both in February 1942; she was taken from service for a refit that was to have
...ipped her with six 15-in guns. She never returned to service and was scuttled in March 1945. The *Prince of Wales*, seen arriving at
...gapore on 2 December 1941, was sunk eight days later in the South China Sea. (*Imperial War Museum*)

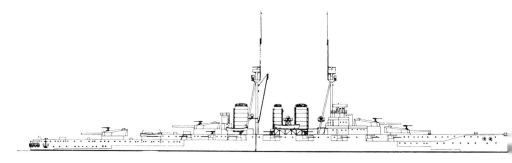

1 Kongo (1913)

The *Kongo*. The transformation of the ship over her lifetime. The *Kongo* in her original 1913 state (1), and (2), in 1923 after her first modification involving the construction of positions and platforms around the forward tripod and bridge.

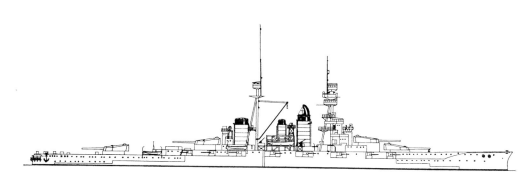

2 Kongo (1923)

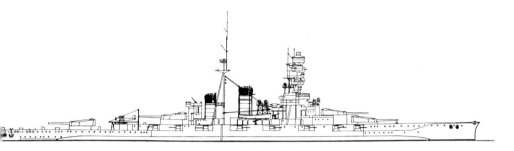

3 Kongo (1931)

After a reconstruction that ended in 1931 and which added 8 m. to her length (3), the *Kongo* emerged as a fast battleship complete with a 30-knot speed and new tertiary armament. The second reconstruction to which all four ships of the class were subjected saw the *Hiei*, for most of the Thirties a gunnery training ship, with a bridge arrangement (4) similar to that given the other three ships. (*Macdonald & Co*)

4 Hiei (1940)

One of the most famous pictures of the day 'that will live in infamy':
the *West Virginia*, torn apart by bombs and torpedoes, settling with her
rear turrets just above water, and beyond her, next to Ford Island, the
Tennessee. It took a month to free the battleships from their moorings
inside their less fortunate sisters. The *West Virginia*, despite being hit by
six or seven torpedoes, was raised in May 1942 and, in effect, was rebuilt
at Puget Sound navy yard between June 1942 and July 1944. (*Corbis*)

The *Wisconsin* alongside the *Oklahoma*, Pearl Harbor, October 1944.
Few photographs better illustrate the difference between battleships of
different generations. The *Oklahoma* was laid down in October 1916,
the *Wisconsin*, half as long again and more than twice the full load
displacement, almost 25 years later. The disparity between the two
was adequate comment on the Japanese attack on an obsolescent
battle line on 7 December 1941. (*USN*)

The *Tennessee* survived Pearl Harbor with only minor damage, inflicted by two bombs. Repairs were completed by March 1942. After convoy duties at Pearl Harbor, she was subjected to a modernisation programme between September 1942 and May 1943 and emerged from Puget Sound navy yard with a profile very similar to that of the *South Dakota* class. She was assigned secondary duties but was in the Surigao Strait during the battle of Leyte Gulf. (*USN; CPL*)

Yamato (above) and the *South Dakota*: near-contemporaries. The end of limitation arrangements was regarded as essential in Japan [gene]rally and the Imperial Navy in particular, but while the *Yamato* and her sister ship the *Musashi* were superior in size and armament to any [othe]r battleship, the American advantage in numbers and overall quality was no less real. However, these ships, the members of the *Yamato* [clas]s and the *North Carolina*, *South Dakota* and *Iowa* classes never did battle with one another.(*Imperial War Museum; USNI*)

ABOVE The *New Jersey* class. The *New Jersey* in New York Harbour, September 1943, with the French *Richelieu* in the background. (*USN*)

BELOW The *Iowa*, in the foreground, with the *Wisconsin*, *Missouri* and the *New Jersey* beyond her, on the only occasion, 7 June 1954, when the four ships of the class exercised together. (*USNI*)

The Breaker's Yard. Thomas W. Ward and Co, Inverkeithing, Firth of Forth, 24 May 1949 – Empire Day
(Queen Victoria's birthday) and the eighth anniversary of the loss of the *Hood*. The *Rodney* is in the finishing berth,
with the *Revenge* outboard of the *Nelson*. 1949 saw the scrapping of 500,000 tons of ships in Britain,
the equivalent of all the battleships allowed Britain under the terms of the Washington treaty, or more
than 300 destroyers. (*Aerofilms*)

The observing of courtesies. The *New Jersey* passing the *Arizona* Memorial on 24 May 1986.
The last battleship, the sister ship *Missouri*, tied up for the last time at Pearl Harbor twelve years later. (*USNI*)

operation in which she accounted for sixteen merchantmen of 99,059 tons, she arrived on 1 April at Kiel and was immediately subjected to refit.

The *Admiral Scheer*'s operations in the southern oceans were the last conducted by a German warship in the Second World War, but they coincided with what proved to be the main German warship effort against commerce. The *Scharnhorst* and *Gneisenau* sailed on 28 December 1940 for operations in the North Atlantic but were compromised and forced to abandon their mission on 2 January 1941. They sailed a second time on 22 January and arrived, undiscovered, off southern Greenland on 5 February. With the heavy cruiser *Admiral Hipper* entering Brest eight days later after a thirteen-day cruise in which she accounted for eight ships of 34,000 tons, the *Scharnhorst* and *Gneisenau* in a six-week period sank or captured 22 merchantmen of 115,622 tons before arriving at Brest on 22 March: the two German ships would have gathered greater success had it not been for the presence of the *Ramillies* with Convoy HX 106, which the two German capital ships encountered on 8 February off Newfoundland, of the *Malaya* with Convoy SL 67, which was encountered on 7 March some 300 miles north-east of the Cape Verde Islands, and of the *Rodney* with Convoy HX 114, which was encountered on 16 March in mid-ocean. By this stage of proceedings, of course, the *Bismarck* had all but completed her various trials while the *Tirpitz*'s entry into service was but a matter of a few months away. But any thoughts that the German naval staff may have entertained concerning a gathering of forces in Brest for operations in strength in the North Atlantic were destroyed in the course of the spring of 1941. On 6 April the *Gneisenau* was torpedoed by a land-based aircraft and in the heavy bomber raid of 10/11 April was hit by four bombs with the result that she was under repair until Christmas 1941. The *Scharnhorst* was similarly afflicted. She completed refit in Brest and then moved to La Pallice on 21 July where, three days later, she was hit by five bombs, and forced to return to Brest: like the *Gneisenau*, she was under repair until end of the year. Far more seriously, May saw the destruction of the *Bismarck*, and it was her loss that in effect spelt the end of the employment of major German warships on commerce warfare.

The *Bismarck*, in the company of the heavy cruiser *Prinz Eugen*, sailed from Gotenhafen on 18 May 1941, their departure being known to the British. In the Denmark Strait they encountered two heavy cruisers, which reported their presence to the Home Fleet commander in the *King George V* some 600 miles to the south-east. Moving to intercept the German force were the *Hood* and *Prince of Wales*, six destroyers being in company, but when this force encountered the *Bismarck* and *Prinz Eugen* on 24 May, British intent unravelled to a disastrous end. Because the *Hood* was old and had not been modernised, she needed to close the range down to 12,000 yards/10,970 metres, but the *Prince of Wales*, which had only just been commissioned and was not fully operational, was possessed of an invulnerability that was lost at that range. With neither British warship able to match the German ships for speed, the British force needed to approach the German ships more or less head on and in open order, an arrangement which would have conferred full freedom of manoeuvre to the *Prince of Wales* and enabled the advantage of numbers and firepower to be employed to the full. In the event, however, a loss of contact with the German ships by the shadowing cruisers led the British formation, in close order, to alter course to the north. With the use of radar forbidden lest the presence of the British formation was betrayed, the *Hood* and *Prince of Wales*, which sighted the German ships at 0535, in effect voluntarily accepted positional inferiority: the British ships, slightly before the beam, were exposed to full broadsides of eight 15-in/380-mm and eight 8-in/203-mm guns while they were able to employ only their forward turrets with four 15-in and five 14-in/356-mm guns (one of the *Prince of Wales*'s guns was defective). Fire was opened by all four ships at about 0553 at a range of 26,500 yards/24,300 metres, the *Hood* signalling the order for a twenty degree turn to port, the prerequisite for a full broadside action, at 0555. Before the manoeuvre could be completed, however, the *Hood*, having sustained a hit by the *Prinz Eugen* in ammunition storage areas which caused a large fire on the upper deck, was hit, probably in the torpedo compartment. The result was an enormous explosion and the ship's bow and stern rose almost vertically as she broke amidships and sank with just three survivors from a crew of 1,421 officers and men.

Coming as it did on Empire Day, the loss of the *Hood*, throughout the interwar period more than any other single ship the embodiment of British naval power and certainly one of the most graceful of dreadnoughts, was nothing short of a national disaster, but the remainder of the day scarcely represented any improvement of fortunes for British arms. With the *Hood* destroyed, German fire was concentrated on the *Prince of Wales* which, hit by a minimum of four 15-in and three 8-in shells and badly damaged, was forced to break off the action. The *Bismarck* was hit three times and the damage she sustained to her fuel tanks was reason enough to cause her to abandon her mission and set a course for Brest, but on this day she was able to part company with the *Prinz Eugen* without trailing British ships being aware of the fact and around 2300 she was able to shrug off being hit on her main armoured belt by a torpedo from a Swordfish biplane from the fleet carrier *Victorious*. Very soon afterward the British cruisers trailing the *Bismarck* lost contact, and this was not to be regained until she was spotted by a shore-based Catalina patrol aircraft 31.5 hours later, by which time the German battleship was clear of all the formations that were searching for her but for two. One of these formations included the carrier *Ark Royal*, a ship that, like her air group, was of somewhat dubious reputation, and the other, less than 100 miles astern of the *Ark Royal*, the carrier *Eagle*.

The initial attack by Swordfish from the *Ark Royal* was misdirected against the cruiser *Sheffield* which, at a range of twenty miles, had re-established contact with the *Bismarck*. A second attack, which began at 2047 on 26 May, recorded certainly two, possibly three, torpedo hits on the *Bismarck*, one of which wrecked her steering. It is one of the dubious features of historical recording that when the *Hood* was sunk, it was because the German ships shot well, but when the *Bismarck* was crippled, it was because the British were lucky: in fact, both sides aimed at the enemy and fortune proved even-handed. The real event of significance would seem to have taken place next morning after the *Bismarck* had been subjected throughout the night of 26/27 May to destroyer torpedo attacks, none of which hit the German battleship but which undoubtedly were wearing and brought home to the *Bismarck*'s crew the hopelessness of their position. As it was, on the following morning, when the British battle force that was to account for the *Bismarck* came into contact, the British commander's report noted that the announcement 'Enemy in sight' was greeted by wild cheering throughout the *King George V*: after the loss of the *Hood*, the certainty that vengeance was at hand, the sureness of victory that obviously permitted no thought of defeat, is most notable, and contrasted with the silence aboard the *Bismarck* as battle was joined.

The action began at 0847 on 27 May 1941 and ended at 1015, by which time the *King George V* and *Rodney* had shot the *Bismarck* to pieces but had to break off the action because of fuel shortage. They left the heavy cruiser *Dorsetshire* and the destroyer *Maori* to administer the *coup de grâce*, and those commentators who seemingly take comfort or pride in the fact that the *Bismarck* finally succumbed to her own scuttling charges are free to do so: their view does not alter the fact that the British accounted for a ship that, along with her near sister ship the *Tirpitz*, were the most powerful battleships ever built in Europe. Her loss convinced the *Kriegsmarine* that warship raiders could not hope to operate effectively in a North Atlantic that was patrolled to ever-increasing effect by a growing number of long-range land-based aircraft and in which a numerically superior enemy was able to deploy naval strength in depth. As it was, the *Bismarck* chase involved virtually every type of naval aircraft and warship: even British submarines were ordered to patrol lines west of Finistere. And regarding the episode as a whole, two matters may be noted. The first was that during the night of 26/27 May the *Bismarck* employed radar to control her gunfire in fighting off destroyer attacks, the first occasion when radar was used in a night action. The second was perhaps less obvious, but of greater real importance. The ideal British formations always included battleship and carrier, but it is noticeable that three of the worst disasters which overwhelmed British formations took place when this balance was lacking – the loss of the *Glorious* in June 1940, the loss of the *Hood* in May 1941 and the loss of the

Prince of Wales and *Repulse* in December 1941. In the North Atlantic theatre the balance was essential, not least because weather could so easily close down flying operations, but if the achievement of the *Ark Royal*'s air group was so impressive in the second strike of 26 May, then two points need to be made. The first is that the *Eagle* could probably have mounted a strike mission late on 26 May if the one conducted by the *Ark Royal*'s group had miscarried, and one wonders what might have been achieved if the *Hood* and *Prince of Wales* had been accompanied by a carrier, such as the *Victorious*, with an air group that would have been able to attack the *Bismarck* and *Prinz Eugen* in the Denmark Strait when, given the ice, their freedom of manoeuvre would have been limited. Certainly one cannot assume that an attack would have been successful, but given that three carriers were involved in the search for the *Bismarck*, their employment, particularly together in northern waters, might have enabled the British to avoid the one type of battle they really did not have to fight – the battle which turned out to be an unmitigated disaster.[7]

As has already been noted, the sinking of the *Bismarck* marked the end of German capital ship commitment to the Battle of the Atlantic, and after May 1941 the story of the *Kriegsmarine*'s surface force can be readily summarised. On 11–13 February 1942 there took place the Channel Dash by which the *Scharnhorst, Gneisenau* and *Prinz Eugen* returned to German waters from Brest. It was an episode that has attracted much criticism of Britain in general and the Royal Navy in particular, but given the fact that Britain moved coastal shipping through the Dover Straits throughout the war, it is not exactly clear why the Germans should not have been able to get their major warships through coastal waters covered by concentrated air power at a time of their own choice. Moreover, if the German withdrawal of their units to German home waters was tactically successful, it was quite obviously a strategic failure in that the menace to shipping in the North Atlantic was ended, while the price exacted in the process was considerable: the *Scharnhorst* was mined twice and the *Gneisenau* once. The former was out of service for the remainder of 1942 and was not able to proceed to northern waters until March 1943, and on 25 February the *Gneisenau* was hit by a bomb near her foremost turret which killed about a hundred of her crew and set off fires that burned for three days. She was moved to Gotenhafen and decommissioned on 1 July 1942, the intention being that she would be overhauled and fitted with 15-in guns, but in the event her repairs and refit were never completed and she remained at Gotenhafen until scuttled in an attempt to block the harbour on 27 March 1945.

Then there was the series of operations in northern waters between February 1942 and December 1943, during which time German units played the fleet-in-being role, most obviously in helping to bring about the PQ 17 debacle in June–July 1942. It was a phase that opened with and for most of its duration was characterised by chronic German weakness. Initially the *Kriegsmarine* was able to deploy no more than just the *Tirpitz*, *Admiral Scheer* and the *Lützow* in northern waters, and while this combination, in the company of the *Admiral Hipper* and assorted destroyers, submarines and land-based aircraft, accounted for 24 merchantmen of 142,695 tons from convoy PQ 17, its other endeavours met with little success. Admittedly, in August 1942 the *Admiral Scheer* was involved in one of the most esoteric operations of the Second World War, clearly so critical to the outcome of this conflict, in the form of the raid on Dikson, in 73° 32' North 80° 39' East,[8] at the end of which she returned to Germany and refitted at Wilhelmshaven until March 1943: thereafter she was reduced to training duties. The latter development was the product of Hitler's decision to run down the surface force in the aftermath of the German failure in the battle of the Barents Sea (30–31 December 1942) when a German formation, which included the *panzerschiffe Lützow* and heavy cruiser *Admiral Hipper* was out-fought by convoy escorts and a light cruiser force. In fact, Hitler's decision was partially reversed when the advantage it would have conferred to the Allies was finally appreciated, but the units that remained in northern waters were not unlike men in the condemned cell for much of 1943. The bombardment of Spitzbergen (6–9 September 1943) by the *Tirpitz* and *Scharnhorst* was mean compensation for a failing strategic mission, and confirmation of this brutal reality was provided when the *Scharnhorst*, tasked to attack Convoy JW 55B which had sailed from Loch Ewe on 19 December for the Kola Inlet, was caught off the North Cape on 26 December 1943 by British covering forces which numbered the battleship *Duke of York*, the heavy cruiser *Norfolk* and light cruisers *Belfast*, *Jamaica* and the *Sheffield*, and the destroyers *Musketeer*, *Matchless*, *Opportune* and the *Virago*.

The sinking of the *Scharnhorst* marked the end of an oceanic role for German heavy units, of which only one, the *Tirpitz*, remained. She, however, was less of a threat than a target, not least because by the end of 1943, with the elimination of Italy from the ranks of the enemy and Anglo-American forces established on the continental mainland, British attention was shifting away from the European theatre. British priorities as 1943 passed into 1944 were to maintain sufficient naval forces in the Mediterranean and home waters to effect whatever amphibious operations were to be carried out, but in terms of capital ships and aircraft carriers the British priority was to carry out major refitting programmes in order to get the most modern units into the Indian Ocean in readiness for the raising of a British fleet in the Pacific. As regards the *Tirpitz*, she was useful for working up the fleet carriers to full operational effectiveness, and after having been damaged by midget submarine attack in Altafjord on 22 September 1943, which put her out of action for six months, she was subjected to three sets of attacks by carrier aircraft. On the first occasion, at Altafjord on 3 April 1944, she was the subject of attention of aircraft from the fleet carriers *Furious* and *Victorious*, which were covered by the escort carriers *Emperor*, *Fencer*, *Pursuer* and the *Searcher* and by the battleship *Anson*, three cruisers and five destroyers. On the second occasion, at Kaafjord on 17 July, she was successfully shielded by smoke from the attention of aircraft from the *Formidable*, *Furious* and *Indefatigable*, which were covered by the *Duke of York*, two heavy and two light cruisers, and assorted destroyers, and in the following month she was subjected to a series of attacks by aircraft from the same fleet carriers, covered again by the *Duke of York* and various cruisers and destroyers but also by the escort carriers *Nabob* and *Trumpeter*. Only the raids of 3 April and 24 August inflicted appreciable damage on the *Tirpitz*, but the German battleship sustained severe damage in the raid of 15 September by RAF Lancaster heavy bombers using 12,000-lb 'Tallboy' bombs: one near-miss just off the forecastle caused massive shock damage, twisting the hull and lifting her propulsion machinery off its foundations. No longer seaworthy, she was able to steam slowly to a berth near Tromsö where, after surviving a raid on 29 October, she was hit by three more six-ton bombs, and smothered by near-misses, which caused her to blow up and capsize with the loss of 1,204 of her officers and men.

The loss of the *Tirpitz* marked the end of the German surface force outside the Baltic, and there the *Lützow*, after June 1944, and the *Admiral Scheer,* after November 1944, operated in support of military forces during the final, disastrous, stages of the war against the Soviet Union. The *Admiral Scheer* was employed initially off the Sworbe peninsula and then off Courland in February 1945. She was finally employed off Wollin in March 1945, after which she returned to Kiel, where she capsized and sank in the course of the RAF strategic bombing raid of 9–10 April 1945. The *Lützow* was employed off the Aland Islands in June and September 1944 and then in the defence of Memel in October and in the evacuation of the Sworbe peninsula in October and November. She was involved in bombardments in February 1945 and in March and April in the Gotenhafen-Danzig areas, after which she was sent to Swinemünde, where she was sunk in the course of the RAF strategic bombing raid of 16 April: she settled on the bottom and was scuttled on 4 May 1945.

Such was the record of major German warships in terms of tonnage warfare and ill-assorted endeavours in the Second World War's final stages, and what is most notable about the *Kriegsmarine*'s record with these ships is their operations, not a campaign. Only on one occasion did the German surface units put together a campaign, between April and June 1940 with reference to Norway, and, of course, it has been argued that this particular effort cost the German Navy so much in terms of light force numbers and, critically, balance. With only two capital ships, the *Gneisenau* and *Scharnhorst* along with the *panzerschiffe*

Admiral Scheer and *Lützow,* the heavy cruisers *Admiral Hipper* and *Blücher,* the light cruisers *Emden, Karlsruhe, Köln* and the *Königsberg* plus assorted destroyers, torpedo boats, minesweepers and auxiliaries, the Germans conducted simultaneous landings from Narvik to the Belt, and in the process stole a critical advantage of timing that the British and French could not reverse. With German land-based air power established throughout southern Norway, the lengthening hours of daylight placed Allied naval units at a massive disadvantage despite initial contacts generally being resolved in their favour. The *Gneisenau* and *Scharnhorst* chose to use their speed to avoid action with the *Renown* off the Lofoten Islands on 9 April. The *Gneisenau* was hit twice, heavily, and the *Scharnhorst* incurred weather damage, and both were forced to return to Wilhelmshaven for repairs. When they returned to the fray in June, they caught and sank the fleet carrier *Glorious* and the destroyers *Ardent* and *Acasta* some 350 miles west of Narvik in 68° 45' North 4° 30' East, the *Scharnhorst* being torpedoed by the *Acasta* in the process and forced to retire to Trondheim: twelve days later, on 20 June, the *Gneisenau* was torpedoed by the submarine *Clyde.* With the *Blücher, Karlsruhe* and the *Königsberg* sunk,[9] the *Lützow* torpedoed by the British submarine *Spearfish* on 11 April and the *Admiral Hipper* badly damaged after being rammed three days earlier by a sinking British destroyer, German casualties in terms of lost and damaged were serious even without the losses incurred in the two battles of Narvik. In the first battle, on 10 April, two German and two British destroyers were sunk, but three days later there took place one of the very few naval actions in the Second World War that, very literally, was fought to a finish. Few capital ship actions compare in dramatic quality and awesome background to the second battle of Narvik of 13 April 1940 when, in the company of her escorts, the British battleship *Warspite* entered a snow-surrounded Norwegian fjord and hounded no fewer than eight German destroyers, and one U-boat, to destruction.[10] Almost one year later the *Warspite* was to be involved in another such battle fought to the finish, this time in the Mediterranean.

The European Conflict, 1939–1945: 2. The Italian War

The Italian war possessed a certain coherence, continuity and comprehensiveness that the German war lacked, and for an obvious reason: the Mediterranean war in very large measure was determined by two battles of supply – that of the Italians to supply Axis formations in North Africa, and that of the British to sustain Malta. There were elements of inter-dependence between land and naval operations, most obviously for the British in terms of the possession of Cyrenaica since control of its airfields provided any attempt to fight convoys through to Malta with protection for much of its passage, and there were aspects of operation that were not wholly determined by supply by sea. For example, the Italian problem in supplying their forces in North Africa was threefold. The Italians had to secure shipping, fuel and escorts for the voyage to North Africa, and they were faced by the problem that all their ports in North Africa had very limited handling capacity. Even more seriously, the Italians then had to move supplies forward to the areas of battle, and with Tripoli in effect the only port with major handling and storage capacity but no railway to move supplies forward into Cyrenaica, the Italian logistical problem in fighting a campaign in North Africa was really beyond solution. Despite all the many claims made over the years to the effect that British naval operations against Italian sea-borne lines of communication played a very large part in the Axis defeat in North Africa, the fact of the matter was that this defeat came at a time when Axis forces in Egypt were as well, if not better, supplied than at any time over the previous two years: quite contrary to the claims, the naval contribution to the Axis defeat in North Africa was very minor.

The naval battlefield consisted of the Malta crossroads, where the Italian routes to Tripoli crossed the British routes to Malta from Gibraltar and, more importantly, from Alexandria. In this concentrated area rival surface formations, often complete with battleships and, on the British side, aircraft carriers, submarine forces and minefields sought their various victims, and in this same area shore-based air power, specifically German shore-based air power based primarily in Sicily, held the upper hand for much of the Mediterranean war. This commodity, German shore-based air power, manifested itself in two ways. First, it very largely did away with the need for the Royal Italian Navy to commit its battle units in defence of convoys to North Africa. The period when the Italian battleships were most active, and most important as regards the balance of power in the Mediterranean, was before the arrival of *Luftwaffe* formations in Sicily and southern Italy, and in any event there were two additional matters affecting the Italian Navy and its battleships. Liaison between the Italian Navy and Air Force was always a somewhat hazardous, delicate affair, and Italian Air Force bombing efforts always seemed to draw the observation that they were very accurate but always seemed to miss the target. In terms of Italian battleships and, most relevantly, Italian battleship numbers, the presence of German Air Force formations in the Mediterranean theatre eased a seldom-acknowledged Italian problem.

When war came to the Mediterranean theatre, the Italian Navy had a total of six battleships, but only two, the two oldest, were properly operational: by 1942 the Italian Navy was having to decommission its older battleships on account of age but also because of growing difficulties relating to refits and modernisation programmes, manpower shortages and fuel problems. The point was that the German air presence made good a real Italian numerical inferiority that was not immediately apparent on the basis of apparent numbers, and certainly this numerical inferiority, when combined with the weakness of Italy's central position and the lack of effective co-ordination with the Italian Air Force, largely explains Italian naval caution for much of the war: the Italians may have had seven battleships between 1940 and 1943 but in real terms probably never had more than three at any one time. The German air presence thus finessed many Italian problems, but at an obvious price. On the Axis side Germany, not Italy, held the power of decision in this theatre, and as long as Germany was never prepared to enter into any more than the minimum possible commitment in this theatre, the Mediterranean was a defeat waiting to happen, and herein was the second, paradoxical manifestation of German shore-based air power.

The Mediterranean was for the British Navy the most costly single theatre of operations of the Second World War, one which claimed more British warships than even home waters or the North Atlantic: two of the five carriers that she lost, seventeen of the 33 heavy and light cruisers, 63 of the 154 destroyers, 52 of the 90 submarines and fourteen of the 39 minesweepers, were sunk in the Mediterranean theatre, and in all 169 of the total of 431 British warships and submarines that were lost during the Second World War were sunk in this theatre. German land-based air power was the most important single factor in British losses and in prolonging the struggle here into 1943, but at the end of the campaign in North Africa, British sea power registered a victory second only to the surrender of the German fleet in November 1918 when the Italian battle fleet surrendered at Malta on 9 September 1943, and it was British sea power that took the war to the continental mainland four years to the day that Britain and France had declared war on Germany.

The war in the Mediterranean theatre lasted from June 1940 to May 1945, and only one country, Britain, fought throughout that time: Italy served as an unwilling battlefield after September 1943. In the 39 months when Italy was a belligerent there were a host of actions significant in terms of theatres and outcome of the struggle in hand and also in terms of the nature and conduct of war. As regards the latter, the one great event was the attack by British carrier aircraft on the Italian battle force at Taranto on the night of 11–12 November 1940 when Swordfish torpedo-bombers from the carrier *Illustrious* crippled the *Conte di Cavour*, which was never returned to service, put the *Caio Duilio* out of action for a year, and damaged the brand-new *Littorio* with the result that she was not returned to service until August 1941. The mauling of three Italian battleships was long held by British commentators to have been the example to which the Japanese looked when planning their attack on Pearl Harbor, but what is perhaps little appreciated is that two operations in July 1940 foreshadowed the attack on Taranto while the Imperial Japanese Navy, which at this stage was considering offensive carrier operations in terms of two or three hundred aircraft, certainly did not need British tutelage in such matters. The two operations were the attack on 5 July by Swordfish torpedo-bombers from the *Eagle* which resulted in the sinking of the destroyer *Zeffiro* and one freighter and caused the destroyer *Euro* and two more freighters to be run aground inside Tobruk harbour, and the attack the next day when Swordfish torpedo-bombers from the *Ark Royal* sank first the collier *Esterel* and then the auxiliary *Terre Neuve* inside Mers-el-Kebir harbour, the latter setting off a series of depth-charge explosions which ripped open the battleship *Dunkerque* lying alongside.

It took the French three months to restore the *Dunkerque's* watertight integrity, and thereafter a series of accidents and the tide of operations in the western Mediterranean ensured that she did not make her way to Toulon until February 1942 and did not begin major refit until the following June. Sadly, she was far from completing her refit when she was scuttled to prevent her falling into German hands when the Germans occupied Vichy France, and herein two matters came together: the harassed story of the *Dunkerque* really began with the shameful British attack on the French fleet gathered inside Mers-el-Kebir harbour on 3 July 1940 and ended with the decision to undertake the futile scuttling of the French fleet in 1942 rather than to seek safety in flight to Allied ports in the aftermath of the Anglo-American landings in French north-west Africa on 8 November (Operation Torch).

The British attack on the French fleet in July 1940 saw the employment of the *Hood, Resolution* and the *Valiant*, plus the aircraft carrier *Ark Royal*. The battleship *Bretagne* was destroyed with heavy loss of life, the *Provence* settled and the *Dunkerque* was badly damaged: the *Strasbourg* escaped, despite the fact that she was inside the harbour when the British attacked.[11] The Allied landings of November 1942 saw the employment of the American battleships *Massachusetts* and *Texas*, along with the carrier *Ranger*, four escort carriers, three heavy and four light cruisers and 38 destroyers off Casablanca, while the covering force within the Mediterranean consisted of the battleships *Duke of York, Nelson* and the *Rodney*, the battlecruiser *Renown*, and the fleet carriers *Formidable, Furious* and *Victorious*, plus three light cruisers and seventeen destroyers. The differences in numbers and nationalities between the two operations are self-evident, but the element of continuity is easy to miss. In the first case the British action was prompted by the fear of French warships falling into German and Italian hands and in the second case by the hope that French forces would willingly come over to the Allied side. It is very difficult, if not impossible, to consider any circumstances in 1940 in which the French Navy would have placed itself in a position whereby it would have been obliged to relinquish control of its ships to Germans and Italians, and in 1942, as in 1940, it resisted attack, most notably at Casablanca where the incomplete battleship *Jean Bart* attracted the attention of carrier aircraft, the *Massachusetts* and the heavy cruiser *Augusta* on 9 and 10 November. The fire from the *Massachusetts* jammed the *Jean Bart*'s only operational main turret, while the combination of shells and bombs left the French battleship settling on the bottom by the stern with some 4,500 tons of water inside the ship. It was not until September 1943 that she was salved and provided with immediate repairs, but unlike her sister ship, the *Richelieu*, she was not to be afforded the care and attention of an American shipyard with the result that, while the *Richelieu* served with British fleets in home waters and the Indian Ocean, the *Jean Bart* remained at Casablanca as an accommodation and training ship.

The month of July 1940 thus provided three actions heavy with future significance, but it also produced another not without interest and relevance. The action off Calabria, alternatively known as Punto Stilo, on 9 July was, with the possible exception of Navarino (1827), the first fleet action in the Mediterranean since 1798, and it possessed a complexity that contrasted sharply with the losses and damage sustained by the two sides. Covering various convoys from Malta to Alexandria were three British forces, one with four light cruisers and one destroyer, the second with the fleet flagship *Warspite* (newly arrived from Norway) and five destroyers, and the third with the fleet carrier *Eagle*, the unmodernised and slow *Malaya* and *Royal Sovereign*, and destroyers that at various times numbered between ten and seventeen. The Italians, with convoys en route between Naples and Benghazi, had at sea various formations defensively deployed as well as submarines and a battle force, consisting of the *Cavour* and *Giulio Cesare*, four light cruisers and sixteen destroyers.[12] Quite late in the afternoon, after skirmishing which included the easy Italian evasion of torpedoes launched by aircraft from the *Eagle*, the *Cavour* and *Cesare* encountered an unsupported *Warspite* which, at a range of fifteen miles or 24 kilometres, recorded on the *Cesare* what is believed to have been the longest-range hit ever registered at sea without the assistance of radar. This caused fires in the ammunition store of one of the 37-mm mountings which in turn ignited charges among secondary ammunition, smoke from which was then drawn into the boiler rooms, putting half of the *Cesare*'s boiler out of action and reducing her speed to eighteen knots.

Perhaps not surprisingly, the Italians broke off the action at this point, the destroyers covering the battleships' withdrawal with smoke, but with the British declining to pursue the Italian formation for fear of submarines and the Calabrian coast coming into view, the pattern of indecisive action, which so frequently repeated itself over the next two years, was apparent. The Italians made concerted air attacks on the British formation that came from the west, from Gibraltar, and which consisted of the *Hood*, *Resolution* and the *Valiant* and had the carrier *Ark Royal* in company, but despite many near-misses no damage of any significance was inflicted though the Italian submarine *Guglielmo Marconi* torpedoed and sank the destroyer *Escort* in 36° 11' North 3° 36' West, one hundred miles east of Gibraltar. It was a success that cancelled out the sinking of the Italian destroyer *Leone Pancaldo* in the roads at Augusta, in Sicily, the previous day by torpedo bombers from the *Eagle* before British forces withdrew to Alexandria: salvaged, the *Leone Pancaldo* was to be sunk a second time by aircraft in April 1943.

Amid the number of indecisive engagements, of which the second battle of Sirte is the best known, there were three main episodes involving major loss. The first of these was the battle of Matapan which, fought on 28 March 1941, arose from an Italian attempt to attack British convoys to Greece. The attempt was made with four separate forces that together numbered the battleship *Vittorio Veneto*, six heavy and two light cruisers and thirteen destroyers. Contrary to intention, the Italian formation was unsupported and singularly ill-served by German aircraft, and its attempt to reach the Aegean was compromised while it was left unaware that British formations, including one aircraft carrier and three battleships, were at sea. On the morning of the 28th a running fight developed between British cruisers and Italian destroyers before the *Vittorio Veneto*, in attempting to join the fray, was forced to turn away under attack by carrier aircraft. Around midday the decision was made to abandon the mission and return to Taranto, but in the afternoon British carrier aircraft torpedoed the *Vittorio Veneto*. She was hit aft and her screws were damaged, but though flooded with some 4,000 tons of seawater and brought to a halt, she was able to get under way again in some ten minutes and, at twenty knots on just her starboard machinery, was able to make her way to the safety of Taranto. At sunset a second strike, mounted in the face of intense anti-aircraft fire, recorded one torpedo hit on the heavy cruiser *Pola*, which fell out of formation and was brought to a stop. The Italian admiral initially did not realise what had happened to the *Pola* and continued to withdraw, but when appraised of the absence of the heavy cruiser, and totally unaware that a British battle force was at sea, he ordered the *Pola*'s sister ships *Fiume* and *Zara*, and their escort of four *Oriana*-class destroyers, to return and stand by the stricken cruiser. The British battle formation, with the *Warspite*, *Valiant* and the *Barham* in line, encountered the stationary *Pola*, the vital first contact being obtained by the *Valiant*, which alone of the battleships had radar. At the very time that the British battleships cleared for action, however, the returning Italian ships were sighted from the *Warspite*'s bridge. The Italian ships, none of which sighted the British force, were engaged at ranges as low as 2,900 yards/2,700-m, the two heavy cruisers and two of the destroyers (the *Vittorio Alfieri* and *Giosue Carducci*) being sunk immediately and one of the remaining destroyers being damaged as it made its escape: the *Pola* was then sunk at leisure before the British formation moved clear of the area.[13]

Commentaries that have afforded this action somewhat dismissive treatment on account of the disparity between the British and Italian performance miss the point of this battle: the disparity of performance, the result of the British having invested in years of battle practice at night, was the reason for the outcome of this engagement – or at least was one reason to set alongside such matters as the inadequacy of the German and Italian performance in the air and the fact that the British had forewarning of Italian intention as a result of their intelligence advantage. But this success, which undoubtedly provided the British with added confidence in facing Italian formations, was short-lived: April 1941 saw the German conquest of Yugoslavia and Greece and May the disastrous campaign for Crete.

The Crete campaign is illustrative of the maxim that the gravest danger posed to any fleet is when it is obliged to operate in conjunction with land forces, and clearly the most dangerous threat is presented when armies are stationary or are in defeat. The examples of Guadalcanal and Okinawa in the Pacific war are evidence of the risks run by navies when operating in support of forces ashore, and Greece and Crete are their counterparts in the European war. The relevance of British losses during these two campaigns in the Mediterranean theatre is threefold. First, they were sustained in the withdrawal phase, and along with the withdrawal from the Greek mainland this was the third British defeat and withdrawal from the European mainland in less than a year: as far as British military performance was concerned, ineptitude had become habitual. Second, the losses were therefore concentrated in a very short period of time. In this campaign the British lost one heavy cruiser, three light cruisers and six destroyers, which stood comparison with the fleet carrier, two light cruisers and six destroyers lost during the Norwegian campaign.[14] Yet third, and most significantly, the losses off Crete were sustained in a twelve-day period compared to the nine weeks of the Norwegian campaign, and in any case were accompanied by the fact that the battleships *Warspite* and *Barham*, the fleet carrier *Formidable*, the light cruisers *Ajax, Carlisle, Dido, Naiad, Orion* and the *Perth*, and the destroyers *Nubian, Decoy, Kelvin* and the *Napier* all sustained varying degrees of damage, and this was little short of disastrous on a station so ill-served in terms of repair facilities as Alexandria. The gravity of the British situation can be gauged by reference to the fact that it was not until March 1943 that the British Navy was able to reconstitute its destroyer formations on a proper basis for the first time since spring 1940. But what was undoubtedly seen as the seriousness of the defeat in Greece and Crete and the naval losses sustained in the course of these campaigns undoubtedly owed much to their timing: the defeat on Crete unfolded at the same time as the *Hood* was lost.

The defeat at Crete, however, did not represent the nadir of British fortunes in the Mediterranean: the eclipse of British naval power in this theatre came, of

Italian making, on 18 December 1941 with the loss of one cruiser and one destroyer, with another cruiser badly damaged, from the formation (Force K) based at Malta in a minefield outside Tripoli, and, on the next day, the sinking of the battleships *Queen Elizabeth* and *Valiant* and the Norwegian tanker *Sagona* inside Alexandria harbour by three Italian charioteer teams from the submarine *Scire*. The battleships settled and were salvable. The *Valiant*, with a hole 60 by 30 feet/18.3 by 9.2 metres abreast her 'A' turret and her forward magazines flooded, was afforded running repairs sufficient to ensure that she reached Durban in May 1942. Proper repairs were completed by July but in effect she was relegated to junior division with a posting to South Atlantic command, and she remained at Freetown until February 1943, when she returned to Britain for full refit. The *Queen Elizabeth*, with 11,000 square feet/1,029 square metres of her bottom destroyed and three boiler rooms flooded, was likewise afforded running repairs which took until late June 1942, after which time she sailed to Norfolk navy yard for full repair and refit.

The events of mid-December 1941 marked a watershed in terms of capital ship operations, indeed the capital ship's *raison d'être*, and the Second World War. Until this time capital ships had been employed upon a variety of tasks which seldom really accorded with their status. British and French battleships had provided heavy protection for both routine and special status convoys, especially those involving the movement of troops, and they had been employed in 1939 and 1940 on such specialist tasks as the moving of national gold and foreign currency reserves to Canada; fast battleships and battlecruisers had, of course, been prominent in the groups formed to hunt down German raiders. Throughout the first eighteen months of war in the Mediterranean, they had been involved in covering various movements with a view to offering battle if circumstances allowed, but in the event the Italian refusal to give battle unless endowed with overwhelming advantage, and certainly to decline battle on the basis of numerical equality, meant that such battles as Matapan were fought in large part because of miscalculation and were not repeated. In addition, there were a number of bombardments of various ports. Bardia was bombarded (20–21 June 1940) by the French battleship *Lorraine* and British cruisers and destroyers in what was the last combined Allied operation before the French armistice took effect, and Bardia was bombarded again on 3 January 1941 by three British battleships and then by light forces preparatory to the Australian attack that took the port two days later. Genoa was subjected to bombardment, or at least its electrical works, main power station, dry docks, oil tanks and railway installations were supposedly subjected to attack by the *Malaya* and *Renown*, supported by the light cruiser *Sheffield*, on 9 February 1941, while just under two months before, in an operation that conjured up images of the Eastern Empire, Venice and the operations of 1083, the *Valiant* and *Warspite*, in an attempt to help the Greeks by striking at the enemy port of entry into the Balkans, bombarded Valona.

But these operations were very much the small change: only briefly in this period did the capital ship have an opportunity to discharge its main duties. The miserable affair of 3 July 1940 at Mers-el-Kebir was one of those occasions when one wishes it had not had the opportunity to discharge its *raison d'être*, and the only other real time it had discharged its major role, or attempted to discharge it, it had been unsuccessful. Between September 1939 and May 1940 the British and French had been forced to call upon their formations in the Mediterranean for duties elsewhere, but they had always tried to maintain forces in this theatre in order to demonstrate to Italy their intentions and capabilities. They sought to check Italian ambition by displays of strength, to indicate their own resolve and power, but in the end naval power could not check or prevent Italy's entry into the war: the Allied defeat in north-west Europe, and the likelihood of the war being brought to a close in a matter of weeks, counted for more than Allied naval power in the Mediterranean.

Throughout the period between September 1939 and December 1941, the capital ship and the aircraft carrier were complementary rather than in competition with one another. Note has been made of their respective losses when not in the other type of ship's company, and the significance of November 1941, when both types of ship suffered serious losses, has also been noted. The loss of the *Ark Royal*, torpedoed by the submarine U. 81 in 36° 03' North 4° 45' West, some 40 miles east of Gibraltar, and of the battleship *Barham*, torpedoed by the submarine U. 331 in 32° 34' North 26° 24' East, off Bardia, represented change of profound significance, when fully operational warships became the first members of their respective types to be sunk in the open sea,[15] but by the time of these losses in the Mediterranean theatre, the focus of attention had switched elsewhere, specifically for Britain first to the South China Sea and the line of the Malay Barrier and then to India and the Indian Ocean. By the time that attention refocused upon the Mediterranean theatre, profound changes had occurred, and in terms of the naval conduct of operations they can be simply defined with reference to Operation Pedestal in August 1942: the formation gathered to provide cover for the convoy bound for Malta from Gibraltar mustered two battleships, the *Nelson* and *Rodney*, three light cruisers and thirteen destroyers, and no fewer than four aircraft carriers, and these from a total British front-line strength of six fleet carriers.[16] Notwithstanding the fact that in this operation one of the carriers was sunk and another rendered *hors de combat*, from this time the carrier emerged as the most important single type of warship in the European theatre of operations, and it is this fact that adds a special poignancy to the sinking of the *Scharnhorst* in December 1943. This was the last occasion when a British battleship fought an enemy opposite number, the last time in a history that reached back over four centuries, and it happened because there was not the slightest possibility of relying primarily upon aircraft carriers in a covering force committed to the waters off the North Cape in the middle of winter. In those very special Arctic conditions the battleship might have found a last home, but in effect Pedestal marks the point in the European theatre when the initiative, disputed throughout the inter-war period, finally passed to the aircraft carrier.

For the remainder of the European war, therefore, the main tasks of the capital ship were twofold. They were the most powerfully armed of the escorts detailed to the protection of the carriers, and they were to provide close support in amphibious operations. In fact, in the European theatre the discharge of these functions was demeaned by the fact that no amphibious landings could be undertaken without the assault having first secured at least some measure of superiority in the air, and the winning of such superiority could not be registered by carrier forces. In the Pacific, the Americans used massed carrier formations to fight and win the battle for air superiority. In July 1945 in one operation they put over 1,700 carrier aircraft into the skies over the Inland Sea, Shokaku and Honshu, and flew combat air patrols over Japanese airfields and systematically employed ECM aircraft at night solely for disruptive purposes. In the European theatre of operations, however, the more modest numbers of fleet carriers available and their smaller air groups, plus the fact that they were opposed by an enemy air force that could draw upon continental-wide resources, meant that the basic task of fighting for and winning air superiority had to be undertaken by land-based aircraft. This had to be done on a scale that left naval air groups very much *minor inter pares*.

At Normandy, land-based air forces employed 3,467 heavy bombers, 1,645 medium, light and other bombers, 5,409 fighters and 2,319 transports on 6 June 1944 alone, and this came after months in which the 8th U.S. Air Force had systematically used its new P-51 Mustang fighters to fight for and win superiority in the skies over Germany. In the invasion of Sicily, in July 1943, the number of land-based aircraft available to support the landing operations – some 3,630 aircraft – was much smaller and carriers, with battleships, had operated in support of the landing forces, but herein was the thread that links the major naval and amphibious undertakings in the last two years of the European war. Between July 1943 and November 1944, Allied forces undertook five major and a number of minor landing operations of which only the first major effort, in July 1943, differed from the other major undertakings in that these landings did not take place on the continental mainland. This was Operation Husky, the landings in Sicily, and the others were Operation Avalanche, the landings in southern Italy, most notably at Salerno, in September 1943; Operation Shingle, the landings at Anzio in January 1944; Operation Neptune, the landings in Normandy in June 1944; and Operation Dragoon, the landings in southern France in August 1944. In addition to these landings there was Operation Infatuate, the landings on Walcheren in November 1944 and which alone of the second-string landing operations involved an opposed landing in a major theatre of war. The British landings in Greece in September and October 1944 involved seven escort carriers and seven light cruisers, plus destroyers, but encountered no major or sustained opposition, as was the case with, *inter alia*, the French landings on Elba in mid-June 1944 and the British landings on Hvar in the Adriatic one month later.

Two matters linked the major amphibious undertakings in the European theatres after July 1943 and the first was the mounting effectiveness of land-based air power during the landing phase and initial period ashore, i.e., the times of maximum vulnerability. In July 1943 the co-ordination between air power and the other services barely merited the term, but at Salerno, and even more obviously at Anzio, air power was crucially important in contributing to German failure to eliminate Allied beachheads. These landings, however, were not registered in the main theatre of operations, and in the case of Sicily and Salerno the Germans had very few formations with which to oppose Allied landings. The point, however, was that by January 1944 the Allied air forces had acquired the technique and numbers which enabled them to play a full part in defeating German counter-attacks, and the proven effectiveness of Allied air power was the prerequisite for the Normandy invasion. The invasion of north-west Europe could never have been attempted without the Allies first having won command of the air, and it was the ability to strike from the air *en masse* that ensured that German armour could never be concentrated in sufficient strength to attempt any major counter-offensive with any real prospect of success. The second matter was that in this process whereby air power established itself as the main guarantor of forces put ashore, which really had been unthinkable even in 1940, the declining role of the capital ship manifested itself in a division of labour between old and new capital ships, and in the increased importance of the cruiser in providing fire support.

At Sicily, the Allies deployed three monitors and twelve light cruisers with the various landing formations: in the covering role were held four old battleships, two fleet carriers and four light cruisers, while the reserve consisted of two modern battleships and two light cruisers, all formations having attendant destroyers and escorts.[17] For the landings in southern Italy, the cover and reserve formations remained basically unaltered, but what was most notable was the addition to the orders of battle of the light fleet carrier *Unicorn* and four escort carriers.[18] Scarcely less notable was the fact that the Italian surrender and Operation Avalanche saw, respectively, the sinking of the battleship *Roma*, and the near-fatal damaging of the American cruiser *Savannah* and the

British battleship *Warspite* by FX 1400 radio-controlled and Hs 293 glider bombs. In the case of the *Warspite*, she was hit by one bomb that penetrated six decks before exploding against her double bottom and was near-missed by another bomb that slashed her open along her starboard bulge compartments. One boiler room was totally destroyed and four of the remaining five quickly flooded, and she was totally without power. With some 5,000 tons of sea water inside her, she was towed to Malta and thence to Gibraltar, where she was afforded repairs sufficient to enable her to return to home waters and to be one of the seven battleships allocated to Operation Neptune.[19] Of these seven, four – the *Nelson*, *Ramillies*, *Rodney* and the *Warspite* – were British, and with the exception of the *Nelson* this operation in effect marked their last entry onto centre stage, though admittedly the *Ramillies* did take part in Operation Dragoon before being reduced to the reserve at the end of January 1945. For the three American battleships involved in the Normandy landings, the *Arkansas*, *Nevada* and the *Texas*, the situation was slightly different. All three took part in Operation Dragoon before being transferred to the Pacific where all were involved in the Iwo Jima and Okinawa campaigns and where they remained on station until the end of the Japanese war.

The different fates of the British and American battleships reflected the disparity of industrial strength which enabled the United States to hold solely for bombardment duties more battleships than Britain retained in service. Britain, financially and morally exhausted by six years of war, in effect could concentrate resources only on the four surviving *King George V*-class battleships while reducing the older units to secondary and tertiary duties: the *Malaya*, for example, was reduced to the status of target ship at Greenock for RAF training for an attack on Japanese warships gathered at Singapore, though such were the needs of Operation Overlord that she did conduct one bombardment after June 1944. Of greater immediate relevance, however, were two facts. The first was that in early 1944, when the question of the British reinforcement of the Eastern Fleet suddenly became very urgent, Britain simply did not have available a single *King George V*-class battleship to send to the Indian Ocean, and her representatives in Washington were obliged to ask their American opposite numbers for their agreement to send the French battleship *Richelieu* to the Far East until she could be relieved in the second half of the year. The *Richelieu* at this time was serving with the Home Fleet and had attracted much favourable comment on her sea-keeping and steaming qualities, her heavy tertiary armament and good operational performances, but to have been obliged to ask the Americans to allow a French battleship to be used as reinforcement for the Eastern fleet would have been cause for national mortification had this episode been made public. As it was, the *Richelieu* was sent to the Indian Ocean and served with the Eastern and East Indies Fleets where her performance was very credible indeed, and in terms of speed and fuel economy better than that of the *King George V*-class battleships.

The second fact was one of those little-known details concerning British capital ships and the Second World War, namely that at its end the *Renown*, which had been completed in 1916 and then reconstructed between September 1936 and September 1939, remained the fastest and, in terms of tertiary anti-aircraft armament, the most heavily armed capital ship in British service: relative lightness of armour precluded her from being assigned to the British Pacific Fleet, and she was recalled home from South African waters in March 1945. Indeed, at war's end Britain had just the *Queen Elizabeth*, *Nelson* and *Renown*, along with the four surviving *King George V*-class battleships, in service. At this time the latter were with the British Pacific Fleet, but one, the *Howe*, was at Durban, South Africa, while for all practical purposes the presence of three battleships on station in the Pacific allowed just one to be maintained operationally at any one time. Such were the administrative margins of the navy second only to the United States Navy in September 1945, but which, on the day that Japan's surrender was announced, possessed a Home Fleet the operational strength of which comprised the battleship *Rodney*, which was at Rosyth and in effect had been decommissioned, four light cruisers, one of which had served throughout the war and for the moment remained with her Polish crew, and twelve destroyers, two of which again were manned by their Polish crews and one of which retained her Dutch crew. Virtually everything else that had fought the European war had been decommissioned into the reserve and laid up, had been assigned for scrapping, was awaiting transfer to other navies, was in dockyard hands, or was in the Indian and Pacific Oceans for the final phase of the Japanese war. Lest the extent of British weakness be doubted, the Mediterranean Fleet on 15 August 1945 had the same operational strength as the Home Fleet less one battleship, but its destroyer numbers were maintained at a dozen only by the expedient of having escort destroyers in one destroyer flotilla.[20] In terms of fleet units and thus excluding minesweepers, convoy escorts and submarines from consideration, in the last year of the European war the British Mediterranean Fleet was the fourth largest fleet in the Mediterranean, behind the American, Italian and French Navies, and marginally ahead of the Greek Navy. By August 1945 Matapan and Salerno must have seemed an age passed. *O quam cito transit gloria mundi.*

The War in The Far East and Pacific, 1941–1945

The coming of war to the Pacific is noteworthy on a number of counts, but it suffices here to observe that it began with an attack on the U.S. Pacific Fleet at its base at Pearl Harbor in the Hawaiian Islands and that, in the absence of the

American carriers, this attack fell primarily upon the battleships. In fact, the American battleships were afforded priority ahead of the carriers in the Japanese plan of attack, and the critical calculation was that the elimination of four American battleships would buy the time needed for the securing of certain islands and the construction of a defensive perimeter around their conquests on which the Japanese air and naval forces would fight their American enemy to a standstill. The Japanese achieved their various objectives – they sank the *Arizona*, *California*, *Oklahoma* and the *West Virginia* and secured their various island targets with no difficulty other than temporarily at Wake – yet still suffered decisive, comprehensive defeat in less than four years. This would seem to indicate not that there was a failure in their conduct of the initial operations on which so much seemed to depend, but that something was fundamentally wrong with their basic calculations.

Of course, both the plan for, and the conduct of, the attack on Pearl Harbor were flawed, disastrously so. It was not, as has been so often alleged, that the flaw lay in the fact that the Japanese left intact the base facilities, specifically the power station, graving docks and oil depot, at Pearl Harbor: any careful consideration of the events of 7 December 1941 will reveal that by the time that the last aircraft had returned from the morning's double strike, there were insufficient hours of daylight remaining for Japanese aircraft to be made ready and launched, conduct another strike against the base installations and then return to their carriers without running the lottery of a night landing. No responsible commander, irrespective of navy, at the very start of a war would have accepted responsibility for such an undertaking, especially after the morning's strikes had registered apparent success. But if the Japanese did not mount a follow-up third strike on the afternoon of 7 December 1941, it is very difficult to see when such an operation might have been conducted.[21]

The Japanese attack on the U.S. Pacific Fleet invites two sets of very different comments. The first set has two parts, one of which one can be defined very simply by referring to a single photograph, that of the salvaged *Oklahoma* alongside the *Wisconsin* in 1944. Even allowing for the fact that none of the *Iowa*-class battleships were in service in 1941, the disparity of size and capability between the battleships of the 1911 and 1940 programmes is so obvious and so great that one wonders how the *Kaigun* could have persuaded itself that sinking four potential museum exhibits really would constitute massive strategic success. The second part of this matter, however, is the answer to the question, and it is that the Japanese success in the strike of 7 December 1941 provides evidence of the fundamental Japanese failing in war, which can be defined more easily than it can be explained: as has been noted earlier, the Japanese never understood the distinction between war and a war, between a war and a campaign, between a campaign and a battle, and they produced, with the *zengen sakusen*, a national security strategy that was in fact not even a campaign but a plan of battle. The various elements, the stepping stones that form the essential component parts of war, were one and the same to an Imperial Navy that certainly never understood that a war in the Pacific necessarily had to have separate naval and maritime dimensions – the *Kaigun* simply dismissed the war against Japanese shipping with the assertion that Japanese shipbuilding would make good these losses – just as it never understood the relationship between power and military force and it never understood the limitations of Japanese national power within the community of nations. In initiating the Pacific war, the *Kaigun* never understood that the terms of reference of the war which it started were not its to determine, and it never understood that the alternative to Japan's victory in a limited war ended by a negotiated settlement was not Japan's defeat in a limited war but Japan's defeat in a total war in which there would be no mitigating circumstances.

The second set of comments would seem to be at direct variance with the first, since the effort with which Japan initiated hostilities was awesome in terms of imagination and power. Here was a related series of offensives conducted across 100 degrees of longitude, and it was this ability to develop synchronised attacks across the whole width of an ocean, unique at the time, which conferred upon Japan's intention an element of security arising from the fact that her future enemies simply could not contemplate simultaneous offensives across thousands of miles of ocean and at distances of thousands of miles from the Japanese home islands. Of course, the Japanese success was overtaken by events, and the only comparison with the Japanese opening moves of December 1941 is the American effort of June 1944, this latter month seeing operations in Italy that resulted in the capture of Rome; the landings in Normandy; the strategic air offensive in the European theatre of operations; the American landings in the Marianas; the overwhelming American victory in the battle of the Philippine Sea; and the start of the strategic bombing of the Japanese home islands from bases in China.

Yet there is a neat juxtaposition between the two separate efforts. In December 1941, the Imperial Japanese Navy used just four of its ten capital ships in its opening moves, the most important of which was an operation that incorporated the use of carrier aircraft against American battleships in an attempt to secure the strategic initiative and command of the sea: the remaining Japanese battleships made virtually no move whatsoever, neither at this point nor indeed in the first six months of this war. In June 1944, the U.S. Navy possessed no fewer than 21 capital ships – the thirteen surviving pre-Washington battleships and eight of the ten battleships ordered between 1936 and 1940 – and the operations conducted in June 1944 saw no fewer than seventeen of this total do battle with America's various enemies,[22] and this at a time when the carrier's pride of place as arbiter of sea power was beyond dispute and when there were just eight fleet and seven light fleet carriers in the American order of battle.

The story of the first year of the Pacific war with respect to the capital ship is somewhat odd. The conflict opened with the Japanese using nothing other than their four fast battleships as support units, the *Hiei* and *Kirishima* with the carrier force that attacked Pearl Harbor and the *Haruna* and *Kongo* supporting operations in the south: the other six battleships and the *Yamato*, which entered service in December 1941, basically played a passive 'distant support' role in the war's opening months. These other units were involved in gesture operations, a sortie in December 1941 to support the carrier force which was nearer Hawaii than the Japanese home islands and another sortie by certain units in April 1942 in response to the Doolittle Raid. Prior to May 1942, there were only two major operations involving Japanese capital ships, and both involved all four fast battleships: indeed the second operation, the attack on Ceylon, represented the only occasion when these units were together in one formation. The first was the sweep south of Java in February–March 1942 as the Japanese sought to destroy Allied units seeking to flee the defeat that was unfolding throughout the Dutch East Indies, and the second was the sortie into the Indian Ocean in April 1942. In both endeavours, Japanese battleships operated either directly or in association with the carriers. In the first case, in the first six days of March 1942, Japanese warships picked off Allied warships and merchantmen at will, with the main carrier effort being made against Tjilatjap on the 5th, while two days later the *Hiei* and *Kirishima*, supported by four destroyers, shelled Christmas Island. Very fortunately for the British, the Japanese did not stumble across the transports and troop convoys which were then in the eastern Indian Ocean taking Australian troops home: for example, one troop convoy, with twelve transports and over 10,000 troops embarked, was escorted by three destroyers, one corvette, one auxiliary and the British battleship *Royal Sovereign* and heavy cruiser *Cornwall*, and all these units, transports and warships, would have been overwhelmed without the Japanese breaking sweat had there been contact with the enemy formations.

The second endeavour, the Ceylon operation, represented a grave humiliation for Britain, and indeed in Whitehall when this operation began to unfold there were genuine fears that it might herald the beginning of the end for Britain: however exaggerated this reaction may appear with the advantage of hindsight, the danger confronting British India in the aftermath of the abject surrender in Malaya, along with the fact that the British simply did not have the necessary military, air and naval forces to contest any Japanese move into the western Indian Ocean and against either the Persian Gulf or Aden and the Red Sea, suggests that there may indeed have been some reason for such fears. As it was, Japanese forces sank the light carrier *Hermes*, two heavy cruisers and two destroyers, one escort and one armed merchant cruiser off Ceylon or in her ports, and a second carrier force ravaged shipping along India's coast on the Bay of Bengal, the Japanese foray into the Indian Ocean in April 1942 accounting for 23 merchantmen of 112,312 tons.

But just as the Japanese unknowingly missed the opportunity to inflict potentially disastrous losses on the troop ships and convoys of March, in April they missed contacts with British formations south-west of Ceylon, though they did sink six detached warships in the course of their operations. The British Eastern Fleet had been organised into two formations, one with the *Warspite*, the fleet carriers *Formidable* and *Indomitable*, two heavy and two light cruisers and six destroyers, and the other with the battleships *Ramillies*, *Resolution*, *Revenge* and the *Royal Sovereign*, the *Hermes*, three light cruisers and eight destroyers. The best that can be said about these formations is that, whether separate or together, they were no match for the Japanese carrier formation concentrated off Ceylon, but despite orders that, uniquely in British naval history, set out a fleet-in-being role for the Eastern Fleet, these formations were deployed at ranges from Ceylon which, *prima facie*, it would seem impossible for the Japanese to have missed. At one stage of proceedings, on the afternoon of 5 April, the distance between the first British formation and the Japanese force was less than 200 miles/320 kilometres but the British formations were never found and withdrew to East Africa having been very fortunate indeed to have evaded detection. Had they been detected, their destruction would certainly have followed: as it was, six detached units were destroyed. The excuse that the formations were taken so close to the enemy during daylight as part of an attempt to fight a night action reveals the extent to which the British Navy was wholly ignorant of Japanese night fighting capacity, a defect that it shared with the U.S. Navy: moreover, these antics were totally out of place given the fact that part of the reason for the concentration of heavy units in the western Indian Ocean in April 1942 was that the British and Americans were determined upon the occupation of Vichy French Madagascar, in order to prevent the Japanese occupation of the island. This, of course, was also the time when the British made provision for a Canadian force to be sent to the Falklands, in order to forestall a possible Japanese landing in those islands.

The months of May and June 1942 saw two major amphibious endeavours by the Japanese. Perversely, the attempt that invites the description dire was the one that succeeded while the other, which by any standard had to result in the Japanese occupation of Kure and Midway in the Hawaiian Islands and various islands in the Aleutians, was the one that failed, and so badly that perhaps the best yardstick of its failure is seldom realised: the Imperial Navy committed 109 warships, a total that included eight carriers and 439 aircraft, plus 24 submarines, to the offensives in the central and northern Pacific, and with this number of warships, aircraft and submarines it managed to attack just one American aircraft carrier – and it sank two American warships, the carrier *Yorktown* and the destroyer *Hammann*, the latter by a torpedo aimed at the *Yorktown*. Be that as it may, for the Japanese capital ships the related Aleutians and Midway operations represented their first real undertaking, and every one of the battleships in commission were committed to them. The *Hyuga* and *Ise* and the *Fuso* and *Yamashiro* provided the basis of the support force allocated to the inhospitable Aleutians, while allocated to the various formations bound for Midway were the *Hiei* and *Kongo* with the main force, the *Yamato* (with the fleet commander), *Mutsu* and *Nagato* with the main support formation, and the *Haruna* and *Kirishima* with the main carrier force which had the four front-line fleet carriers assigned to these operations. Very interestingly, and just like the British Eastern Fleet in April, after the Japanese carrier force encountered disaster on 4 June the fleet commander pressed forward with his battle force and other cruiser formations in the hope that a night action would result in a balancing of losses, but the American carriers, having won an overwhelming victory that day, stayed on a course that took them well clear of the battle area, and ultimately the only sinking that the Japanese registered, the *Yorktown* by the submarine I. 168, was of a carrier that had been crippled on 4 June and which, despite all the American efforts, could not be towed clear of the battle area.

The British amphibious operations at Madagascar, which went under the collective name of Ironclad, resulted in the battleship *Ramillies* being torpedoed inside Diego Suarez on 30 May by a midget submarine launched by the submarine I. 16: within four days she had been repaired sufficiently to make the voyage to Durban. Thereafter she returned to Britain for full repairs and refit before sailing for duty with the Eastern Fleet in September 1943 and returning to home waters in January 1944 – in which month the carrier *Illustrious*, battleships *Queen Elizabeth* and *Valiant* and battlecruiser *Renown* arrived at Ceylon and thereby marked the point when the Eastern Fleet began to employ a more forward and aggressive strategy in the Indian Ocean. For her part, the *Ramillies* was the only member of the *Royal Sovereign* class in gainful employment after January 1944, and in many ways her story very closely resembled that of the older dreadnoughts in American service.

When war came to the United States, she had eight battleships at Pearl Harbor, four of which were sunk and one more, the *Nevada*, was extensively damaged: three other battleships, the *Maryland*, *Pennsylvania* and the *Tennessee*, suffered minor damage. One battleship, the *Colorado*, was undergoing a major overhaul at Puget Sound navy yard, on the west coast, from which she did not emerge until March 1942. In the North Atlantic, as part of an ever-encroaching presence throughout 1941, were the *Arkansas*, *New York* and the *Texas*, the *Idaho*, *Mississippi* and the *New Mexico*, and the *North Carolina* and *Washington*, the latter two units being the first of the new, post-limitation dreadnoughts but ships that brought with them a number of problems, most notably severe vibration, which meant that they were to spend almost a year after nominal completion before becoming properly operational. As a result of the Japanese attack on the battle line at Pearl Harbor, the *Maryland*, *Pennsylvania* and the *Tennessee* were returned to the west coast and, at varying times, separate repair and modernisation programmes that alternated with training and secondary duties such as the escort of convoys to the Hawaiian Islands. As part of these tasks, the three battleships returned to Pearl Harbor between June and October 1942, and they were joined not just by the *Colorado* but also the *Idaho*, *Mississippi* and the *New Mexico* which arrived in San Francisco in January 1942 having been transferred from the North Atlantic. They were also based on Pearl Harbor after June 1942, but the *New Mexico* was employed on escorting convoys to the Fiji Islands after August, the *Mississippi* on the same task after December 1942, in which month the *Nevada*, having been raised in February, completed a major refit and overhaul at Puget Sound. By this time the *California* and *West Virginia* had also been raised and were undergoing major repair and reconstruction, again in the Puget Sound navy yard, but their priority was low and they were not completed until January and July 1944. They then began trials preparatory to being fully commissioned, and their first operations were Saipan (June 1944) and Leyte (October 1944) respectively.

The other pre-Washington battleships, however, began to find gainful employment at the end of 1943, specifically in providing gunfire support in operations that resulted in the recovery of islands in the Aleutians which had been lost to the Japanese in June 1942. Operation Landcrab, the assault on Attu that began on 11 May 1943, was supported by the *Idaho*, *Nevada* and the *Pennsylvania*, which very narrowly escaped being torpedoed on two occasions during this operation; Operation Cottage, the landings on Kiska, which had been abandoned by the Japanese, on 15 August 1943, was supported by the *Idaho*, *Pennsylvania* and *Tennessee*, the *Mississippi* and *New Mexico* having also been involved at different times in preliminary bombardments over the previous three weeks. But if these six pre-Washington battleships found employment at this time in this inhospitable part of the Pacific, their activities were very much small change when set alongside the fact that two of their number, the *Colorado* and *Maryland*, were involved at the end of June 1943 in the landings on Rendova, the first of the American amphibious moves into the central Solomons. What was significant about this operation, and the employment of the two old battleships in it, was that in the formations in company were the *Indiana*, *Massachusetts* and the *North Carolina*, three new battleships drawn from two distinct classes, and the operation, or more accurately the series of operations, to which all five were committed had been made possible by the fact that by this stage of proceedings the United States had fought for and won the initiative – and the victory won by the battleship *Washington* in the second naval battle of Guadalcanal in November 1942 had been crucially important in the process whereby that initiative was won. It also was a marker. That American victory was the point when, for the first time, the Japanese were brought to the realisation that they could not win the campaign in the lower Solomons to which they were committed.

The second naval battle of Guadalcanal, inevitably, was just one of the factors that together decided Japanese defeat in the lower Solomons, and the action, in which the *Washington* accounted for the *Kirishima* in some seven minutes, possessed obvious significance precisely because the rival carrier forces had neutralised each other and the Japanese could not overcome American air power based at Henderson Field on Guadalcanal. Between the American landings on the island on 7 August 1942 and the final evacuation of Japanese forces from Guadalcanal in February 1943, there were more than 50 actions involving warships or aircraft from the two sides, yet in a very elusive sense what was fought in this time was Japanese intention in reverse. The perimeter defence which the Japanese intended to create around their conquests and on which they planned to fight the Americans to exhaustion in reality consisted mostly of gaps: there were the occasional islands and garrisons, but these were wholly unable to sustain themselves in the face of an enemy with choice in the place, scale and timing of offensive operations. The *Kaigun* planned to have base and fleet complement one another, the fleet being held to support garrisons and bases, which in any event would be reinforced by land-based aircraft fed through the advance bases to the threatened sector of the front. Such an intention begged a number of questions, not least how the Imperial Navy would be able to maintain a fleet at permanent readiness to meet any American offensive, but the immediate point after August 1942 was that the Americans seized Guadalcanal and its airfield, and then, by getting into this base enough land-based aircraft to dominate the waters that washed the lower Solomons, they were able to secure local control of these waters in the hours of daylight. Thus the Americans in effect were able to fight the battle that the *Kaigun* had intended to fight and win, but ironically the Imperial Navy never seemed to realise that initial American success thus condemned it to fight the type of battle that throughout the inter-war period the *Kaigun* expected the Americans to lose.

Defeat, however, was slow to manifest itself, and certainly the initial encounters resulted in easy Japanese success: indeed, the defeat incurred off Savo Island was as comprehensive as any suffered by the U.S. Navy in its history. But in the two carrier battles fought during this campaign, Eastern Solomons in August and Santa Cruz in October, neither side could secure the upper hand, and losses, both of carriers and aircraft, were more or less evenly balanced. With their forces on Guadalcanal unable to overrun Henderson Field, the Japanese were forced to commit bombardment formations and, with them, battleships to the waters off Guadalcanal in an attempt to inflict such overnight damage to Henderson Field and its aircraft that the Americans would not be able to take a toll of the Japanese warships and shipping left within striking distance of Guadalcanal at daylight. It was in trying to mount this particular endeavour that the *Kaigun*'s problems really began to start.

In mid-July 1942 the Imperial Navy had set about a re-organisation of its major formations and units as a result of the losses that had been sustained off Midway and, in effect, it gathered its offensive capability into three fleets. The main strike force was the 3rd Fleet, which deployed the 1st Carrier Squadron with the fleet carriers *Shokaku* and *Zuikaku* and the light carrier *Zuiho*, the 2nd Carrier Squadron with the fleet carriers *Hiyo* and *Junyo* and the light fleet carrier *Ryujo*, the 11th Battleship Division with the *Hiei* and *Kirishima*, the 7th Cruiser Division with the heavy cruisers *Kumano* and *Suzuya*, the 8th Cruiser Division with the scout-cruisers *Chikuma* and *Tone* and the 10th Destroyer Flotilla with the light cruiser *Nagara*, four *Kagero*-class destroyers in each of the 4th, 16th and 17th Destroyer Divisions, and four *Yugumo*-class destroyers of the 10th Destroyer Division. The 2nd Fleet was the main support formation, and it deployed the 4th Cruiser Squadron with the heavy cruisers *Atago*, *Maya* and the *Takao*, the 5th Cruiser Squadron with the heavy cruisers *Haguro* and *Myoko*, and the 3rd Battleship Division with the battleships *Haruna* and *Kongo*. It also had under command the 2nd Destroyer Flotilla with the light cruiser *Jintsu* and four *Kagero*-class destroyers of the 15th Destroyer Division and three *Shiratsuyu*-class destroyers of the 24th Destroyer Division, and the 4th Destroyer Flotilla with the light cruiser *Yura*, complete with four *Shiratsuyu*-class destroyers of the 2nd Destroyer Division, three *Asashio*-class destroyers of the 9th Destroyer Division, and four destroyers of the *Hatsuhara*- and *Shiratsuyu*-classes of the 27th Destroyer Division. In addition, the 2nd Fleet had under command the grandiloquently named 11th Carrier Squadron, which consisted of the seaplane carrier *Chitose*, the 6,853-ton seaplane tender (AV) *Kamikawa Maru* and the 4,918-ton (APV) *Kamikaze Maru*. The final force, held under the fleet commander, was the 1st Fleet, which had under command the 2nd Battleship Squadron, with the battleships *Nagato*, *Mutsu*, *Fuso* and the *Yamashiro*, after 5 August the 1st Battleship Squadron with the battleships *Yamato* and *Musashi*, and the 9th Cruiser Squadron, with the light cruisers *Kitakami* and *Oi*. It also had under command the 1st Destroyer Flotilla with the light cruiser *Abukuma*, and three *Akatsuki*-class and three *Hatsuhara*-class destroyers of the 6th and 21st Destroyer Divisions, and the 3rd Destroyer Flotilla with the light cruiser *Sendai*, which was accompanied by four ageing *Fubuki*-class destroyers from each of the 11th, 19th and 20th Destroyer Divisions.

What is easy to miss in this re-arrangement of formations was the division of the capital ships between three separate fleets, and that nominal front-line strength had been reduced by the fact that two battleships, the *Hyuga* and *Ise*, had been relegated to training duties in the Inland Sea. Even allowing for the importance of having units available for training, the *Kaigun* at this stage of proceedings was hardly in a position to afford itself the luxury of detaching such units and ensuring that they were not to be involved in the campaign that was to unfold, but the fact was that the *Fuso* and *Yamashiro* were also left in the Inland Sea, apparently because of oil shortages which precluded their being sent forward into the battle areas. Moreover, the *Musashi* and *Nagato* were also left in home waters when the *Mutsu* and *Yamato* sailed separately for Truk on 11 August. And to these measures, which together reduced what in effect was the strategic reserve from eight to just two battleships, one must add the fact that the Imperial Navy chose to divide its fast battleships between two separate fleets. Moreover, the concentration of battleships, and specifically the battleships with 16-in/406-mm guns and better, with the 1st Fleet meant that the battleships which were best equipped in terms of ability to hand out and take punishment in the type of battle the *Kaigun* was called upon to now fight were not with the two front-line formations on which, in terms of fleet actions, the brunt of the campaign for Guadalcanal would inevitably fall.

The extent of unemployment among the Japanese capital ships during the Guadalcanal campaign can be gauged by reference to the *Kongo*. It was not until 11 July that she returned to Japan after service in the central and northern Pacific, and she returned to Yokosuka and thence to the Inland Sea. On 10 August, three days after the American landings in the lower Solomons, she was assigned to a stand-by force. On 6 September she sailed, along with the *Haruna*, from Kure for Truk, arriving on the 10th. On the following day, and again in the company of the *Haruna*, she sailed for Guadalcanal and was attacked by seven heavy bombers on the 14th. She and the *Haruna* returned to Truk on 23 September. On 5 October the two battleships were assigned to a bombardment group and sailed on 11 October to bombard Henderson Field on the night of 13–14 October. This operation having been completed, and the *Kongo* having fired 430 rounds of 14-in ammunition in the process, the bombardment force was disbanded the next day but the *Kongo* remained at sea and supported the carrier force in the battle of Santa Cruz. She and the *Haruna* returned to Truk on 30 October, only to be attached to the depleted carrier force on 8 November. This formation, which had just the *Hiyo* and *Junyo* whereas at the Battle of Santa Cruz it had had the *Shokaku*, *Zuikaku* and the *Zuiho* under command, sailed next day to operate north-east of Guadalcanal and cover various formations that were to bombard Henderson Field on successive nights.

The Japanese plan was for the *Hiei* and *Kirishima*, escorted by one light cruiser and fourteen destroyers, to bombard Henderson Field on the night of 12–13 November: the next night the heavy cruisers *Maya* and *Suzuya*, screened by one light cruiser and four destroyers, were to conduct a bombardment. These two efforts were designed to neutralise Henderson Field even as eleven large transports brought the bulk of the 38th Infantry Division, with its heavy equipment, to Cape Esperance as part of the process of concentrating on Guadalcanal a force sufficient to overrun Henderson Field. Given that by this stage of proceedings it had become clear that cruiser fire could not neutralise the airfield and air group on Guadalcanal, the force assigned to the bombardment of 13–14 November would seem to be dubiously relevant at best. On the night of 12–13 November, however, the Japanese battle formation was met by an American force consisting of two heavy and two light cruisers and nine destroyers. Perhaps the only action during the Second World War that compares to the subsequent battle in terms of sheer ferocity was the exchange on 1 November 1943 between the *Borie* and the German submarine *U. 405* which included rammings and attempts to board by both sides and resulted in the destruction of destroyer and submarine alike. In this action, the light cruiser *Atlanta* and three destroyers were sunk outright, the heavy cruisers *Portland* and *San Francisco*, the light cruiser *Juneau* and two destroyers were badly damaged: undoubtedly American losses would have been more severe had the action not been fought at such short ranges that the Japanese battleships' armament could not be depressed sufficiently to engage the enemy. At these ranges, torpedoes would not arm, but the *Hiei* was wrecked by upwards of 50 hits, mainly 8-in/203-mm. With her superstructure wrecked and largely unmanoeuvrable, she was subjected to a series of attacks throughout 13 November by aircraft from Henderson Field and from the carrier *Enterprise*, and was finally scuttled late in the evening by the destroyers that had stood by her throughout the day but had so lamentably failed her the previous night.

The *Hiei*'s loss was very largely to do with lack of armour: her battlecruiser pedigree had much to do with her failure to withstand fire that a proper battleship should have been able to shrug off, though the sheer number of hits she sustained does raise the question of whether she could have survived, however well-armoured. During the next night Henderson Field was again shelled as planned by the *Maya* and *Suzuya*, but to such little effect that the next day aircraft from the base and from the *Enterprise* sank the heavy cruiser *Kinugasa* and rendered the heavy cruisers *Chokai* and *Maya*, the light cruiser *Isuzu* and one destroyer *hors de combat* and then set about the transports, six being sunk in successive attacks: the cover that was supposed to be provided by aircraft from the *Hiyo* and *Junyo* was singularly ineffective. With the onset of darkness, the Japanese again committed a formation to the bombardment of Henderson Field, on this occasion the battleship *Kirishima*, the heavy cruisers *Atago* and *Takao*, the light cruiser *Sendai* and eight destroyers. To meet this threat the Americans committed a force of two battleships, the *South Dakota* and *Washington*, plus four destroyers, to the defence of their positions on Guadalcanal. In the first encounter, three of the American destroyers were sunk by torpedoes and gunfire while the *South Dakota*, her radar not in service, was caught by the *Kirishima* and the two Japanese heavy cruisers and sustained an estimated 42 hits. Unseen by the main Japanese ships and their destroyers, however, the *Washington* was able to take the *Kirishima* under fire at ranges between 8,400 and 12,650 yards/7,700 and 11,600 metres, and with 75 rounds from her main armament and another 105 rounds from her 5-in/127-mm guns, she in the space of seven minutes inflicted massive damage on the Japanese battleship, achieving a minimum of nine hits with 16-in/406-mm shells. The *Washington* recorded that her radar tracked the *Kirishima* make a turn through 500 degrees. Reduced to a burning wreck, the *Kirishima* sank that same day, 15 November 1942, with her surviving crew members being rescued by the destroyers *Asagumo*, *Terusuki* and the *Samidare*. And lest the point be forgotten or missed, these episodes were taking place as the *Kongo* returned to Truk, which she reached on 18 November and from where she conducted just one more sortie in the Guadalcanal campaign, between 31 January and 9 February 1943, when she was involved in covering the Japanese evacuation of the troops from the island.

The best that could be said about the Japanese conduct of operations in the course of the Guadalcanal campaign is that its various parts do not hang together very well. Note has been taken of the process of shedding numbers which reduced the reserve force at Truk to just two battleships, the *Yamato* and the *Mutsu*, but the fact was that these two units did next to nothing once they arrived in the Carolines. The *Mutsu*, admittedly, did take part in the Eastern Solomons battle in August before returning to Truk on 2 September, where she remained until 7 January when she sailed for Yokosuka. The *Yamato* arrived at Truk on 28 August, and remained there, without sailing on a single mission, until she sailed for Kure on 8 May 1943: the reasons for such apparent indolence were a lack of oil and of suitable rounds to enable the *Yamato* to carry out bombardment duties. This raises the question of why she should have been despatched to Truk in the first place, and prompts the suggestion that institutional and personal reasons underpinned the decision: the Imperial Navy's commitment to the campaign in the south-west Pacific could not be doubted with the *Yamato* at Truk, and no doubt the fleet commander wanted to be away from the home islands and navy staff after the Midway debacle.

But the real point is that next to nothing was done to reinforce the naval units in the south-west Pacific in the month following the American landings on Guadalcanal, and that in effect the subsequent campaign was lost in that month: nothing that the Japanese were able to do thereafter could ever reverse the advantage that the Americans had secured for themselves on 20 August when they put aircraft ashore at Henderson Field. Thereafter the Japanese commitment of forces to the theatre was at no stage adequate to the task in hand: the two battleships at Truk did nothing at any stage of proceedings, while the two with the carriers seem to have ensured that there were never enough available for bombardment duties. If two battleships had been insufficient to conduct the bombardment on the night of 12–13 November, then what two heavy cruisers were supposed to achieve on the following night, and the one surviving battleship on the night after that, is wholly impossible to discern.

The loss of two battleships in three nights brought the Imperial Navy to the realisation that it could not win the campaign in the lower Solomons, and in this respect these two engagements, and the loss of the *Hiei* and *Kirishima*, were critical. It must be noted, however, that these defeats and losses were only part of the equation, and that by mid-November 1942 there were three other aspects of defeat that came together. The Japanese had been trying to conduct an air offensive from Rabaul against Guadalcanal, and this was falling to pieces because of losses and the inadequacy of reinforcements. The Japanese light formations based in the south-west Pacific were beginning to lose their organisation for much the same reason. The loss of ten of the eleven transports bringing the 38th Infantry Division to Guadalcanal – four transports reached the island on the night of 14–15 November and, knowing that they would be caught next morning by aircraft from Henderson Field, were run ashore and their loss accepted – represented losses that the Imperial Navy, indeed Japan herself, simply could not afford.

The Imperial Navy had gone to war calculating that shipping losses to an American *guerre de course* would run at or about 75,000 tons a month, and, very conveniently, its assessment of shipbuilding capacity was 900,000 tons in a year, and this despite the fact that over the previous decade Japanese shipyards had never produced more than half this amount of shipping in any single year. The *Kaigun* was guilty of blatant mendacity on this issue, as on others, but during the Guadalcanal campaign it had lost more than 75,000 tons of shipping on a single mission over three days and by this stage of proceedings had something like 750,000 tons of shipping committed to the south-west Pacific theatre, which was one of the more distant parts of the defensive perimeter. Japan could not afford either the scale of such commitments or losses of this order, and she could not conduct two major campaigns in the south-west Pacific theatre at the same time. Since June 1942 her forces had been involved in a campaign in eastern New Guinea, and while it cannot be argued that the campaign in the lower Solomons was lost because Japanese attention and forces were distracted, after the defeats of mid-November 1942 off Guadalcanal the Japanese nonetheless had to cut their losses in both areas in order to prepare for the next phase of operations.

For the Americans, of course, the victories won in the exchanges of 12–13 and 14–15 November paid for past defeats. Yet these defeats had purchased the experience which, along with the critical advantage of radar, had brought about a rough equivalence between American and Japanese night-fighting capabilities – one that in turn translated itself into the overwhelming victory of the *Washington* over the *Kirishima*. This action was only one of two in the whole of the Pacific war when capital ships did battle with one another, and it was the only battle in which possession of the initiative, command of the sea, was there, like a gun lying in the street, waiting for one side or the other to pick it up and use. The critical importance of this battle lay in the fact that carrier forces had previously cancelled out one another and light forces could not force a decision one way or another, but for all this the capital ship actions were only one part of mutually dependent efforts, and on the Japanese side these efforts, both separately and collectively, had unravelled by mid-November 1942. On the American side, however, the scale of national resources was beginning to manifest itself – and it is worth noting that the *Washington* fought the *Kirishima* one week after the *Massachusetts* fought the *Jean Bart* at Casablanca – and there was one other point that marked out a critical difference between Japan and the United States, between the *Kaigun* and U.S. Navy, and between the capital ships of the two nations and navies. At the battle of Santa Cruz in October 1942, the *South Dakota* was credited with the destruction of 26 Japanese aircraft, and this on account of the fact that the Americans had developed proximity fuses for anti-aircraft ammunition. For the first time, therefore, the battleship was provided with the means whereby it would be able to afford real cover to a carrier against air attack. Certainly at this time battleships were inadequately equipped in terms of numbers of secondary and tertiary weapons, and, of course, for most of the first year of the Pacific war the main escort to the carrier was the cruiser because none of the pre-Washington battleships had the speed to keep pace with the carrier. But with this type of fuse, and the capability of destroying enemy aircraft by blast rather than direct hits, the Americans came into possession of an advantage that, alongside the massive advantage which possession of superior radar conferred, placed their carrier formations in a position to carry the war to the Japanese with a degree of unprecedented defensive security.

However, in November 1942 the United States did not have any carrier formations on hand with which to take the war to the Japanese, and indeed did not have such formations for the first half of 1943. Here one must return to Rendova and the events of June 1943 and the acknowledgement of one fact: covering this amphibious endeavour were the carrier *Saratoga* and the British carrier *Victorious*, which the Americans had requested be sent to the south-west Pacific to make good the precariousness of their carrier position. To date the U.S. Navy had lost the *Lexington* in the Coral Sea in May 1942, the *Yorktown* off Midway in June, the *Wasp* off the lower Solomons in September and the *Hornet* at Santa Cruz in October. But in mid-1943 the U.S. Navy was some six to twelve months off the arrival in service of carriers in such numbers as to provide a strength in depth which was unchallengeable and would enable it to move against Japanese island bases in such strength that it would be able to isolate them from all outside sources of support and ensure their prompt destruction. Yet there was a rather perverse aspect to the Rendova operation: the U.S. Navy was not able to deploy its full number of modern battleships in the covering force because the *South Dakota* and *Alabama* had been sent to Scapa Flow in order to guard against the possibility of a sortie by the *Tirpitz*, while virtually the whole of the British Home Fleet was sent into the Mediterranean in order to be on hand for the landings on Sicily. Few such incidents better illustrate the flexibility of naval power than the fact that the *Victorious* was in the south-west Pacific and the *South Dakota* and *Alabama* were in British home waters at the same time: when the proper order of things re-imposed itself, in November 1943, the Americans were in a position to move against the Gilbert and Ellice Islands in what was the first of the assaults in the offensive across the central Pacific.

The Pacific war ended in November 1943, but no one realised it at the time. It ended in November 1943 in the sense that its overall outcome was now predictable: in this month the Americans moved against Japanese positions in the central Pacific with such overwhelming force that the outcome of this particular effort, and indeed those of all that were to follow, were assured before the first shots were fired. With such superiority of force available to the Americans and the issue of victory and defeat resolved, all that remained to be decided was the timing and exact nature of the final victory and the cost that would be exacted in the process.

The capital ship, on the Allied side, was now divided between two primary functions: the fast battleships provided escort to carriers and the slow battleships provided the backbone of bombardment forces involved in amphibious landings. There were, of course, exceptions to this basic division, and one was obvious. The fast battleships were concentrated on occasions in order to carry out bombardments. In December 1943 all six of the American new battleships then available – the *North Carolina* and *Washington* and the *Alabama*, *Indiana*, *Massachusetts* and the *South Dakota* – took part in the bombardment of Nauru, which was not subjected to a landing but to an attempt to neutralise it as a staging base. This was the first occasion when the fast battleships were thus employed, and in the following month the first two of the next class, the *Iowa* and *New Jersey*, joined the others in the bombardment of Kwajalein prior to the 'proper' bombardment by the old battleships – the *Idaho*, *Mississippi*, *New Mexico* and the *Pennsylvania* (T.G. 52.8) and the *Colorado*, *Maryland* and the *Tennessee* (T.G. 53.5) – and their cruiser and destroyer associates. The same pattern of operations repeated itself during the June 1944 landings on Saipan, the *Massachusetts* being absent on this occasion, while at Iwo Jima the *North Carolina* and *Washington*, with three cruisers and screening destroyers, were involved in the bombardment on the morning of the assault. In most of the operations by which the U.S. Navy took the war to the Japanese home islands, however, there was a clear distinction between the fast battleships and bombardment duties: in the overall balance of responsibilities these commitments, never more than a matter of hours in duration, were relatively minor, and wholly secondary when set against the provision of support for the carriers.

Nonetheless such duties did present themselves anew once the war reached the Japanese home islands, and in the last month of the war there were a number of night bombardments conducted against targets in the home islands and five of these involved battleships. The *Indiana*, *Massachusetts* and the *South Dakota* were involved in the bombardment of Kamaishi, on Honshu, on 14 July 1945 and next night the *Iowa*, *Missouri* and the *Wisconsin* bombarded Muroran on Hokkaido. On 18 July the *Alabama*, *Iowa*, *Missouri*, *North Carolina* and the *Wisconsin* bombarded Hitachi on Honshu and on 29–30 July the *Indiana*, *Massachusetts* and the *South Dakota* were involved in the bombardment of the aircraft factories at Hamamatsu in southern Honshu: on 9 August the same three battleships were involved in a second attack on Kamaishi. In terms of bringing the war to the Japanese home islands and particularly to Japanese society, these bombardments, and the patent demonstration of the failure of the Japanese naval and air forces, could hardly have been bettered, but there was an additional and poignant rider. The bombardments of 18 and 29–30 July also were witness to a British involvement in the shape of the *King George V*:[23] one of the ironies of this war was that for the British it began with the loss of the *Prince of Wales* and *Repulse* in the South China Sea and ended with one of their battleships being involved in bombardments of Honshu. The bombardment on the night of 29–30 July 1945, however, was not the last bombardment of Japanese targets involving British warships, but it was the last occasion when a British battleship fired her guns in anger.

Most obviously, the journey from Malaya to Hamamatsu indicates that the march of events had come full circle, and so they had at least in terms of surrenders: the instrument of Japan's surrender was signed in the battleship *Missouri* in Tokyo Bay on 2 September 1945, and this completed the sequence of the German naval surrender in 1918 in the *Queen Elizabeth* and the Italian surrender in 1943 in the *Nelson*, which also took the surrender of Japanese forces on Penang. But inevitably, of course, there was the one event that broke the pattern of battleship employment, and this occurred in the course of the greatest naval battle in modern times and was the action fought in the Surigao Strait on the night of 24–25 October 1944 when battleships from both sides fought a night action. The battleships on the American side were old and slow but happened to be in the right place: the American fast battleships could have fought a similar action off Samar the next morning but happened to be in the wrong place. Nevertheless, this latter development, or perhaps non-development, did not prevent the Americans recording an overwhelming victory in the series of actions known as the battle of Leyte Gulf: as noted earlier, between 23 and 28 October 1944 American warships, aircraft and submarines accounted for 32 warships of 324,891 tons and seventeen service transports and civilian merchantmen of 92,346 tons. But, a fact seldom fully appreciated, with Japanese fleet strength in effect destroyed and shore-based air power for the moment eclipsed, between 29 October and 30 November 1944 the Americans accounted for 49 warships of 119,655 tons and 48 navy and army transports and civilian merchantmen of 212,476 tons, and these were just the Japanese losses in Philippine waters.

Leyte Gulf represents a decisive battle in terms of Japanese losses and the comprehensive nature of the *Kaigun*'s defeat, but perhaps its real significance lies in the way the carrier transformed battle: Leyte, more than any other action, is illustrative of the massive change in the conduct of operations wrought by naval aircraft. Reference was made to this in Chapter 1 but the point nonetheless bears repetition. In the battle of Leyte the area of operations covered 115,000 square miles, an area equivalent to the British Isles or Iowa and Missouri, and the area of deployment was three times as large, an area roughly equivalent to France and Germany or Colorado, Arizona and New Mexico. And, of course, there is the one linking fact that only the thoroughly awkward and mendacious historian could identify. A mere 28 years and four months and 25 days separated the battles of Jutland – the last fleet action fought broadside to broadside – and Leyte, and somehow it does seem very appropriate that only one of the American battleships in the Surigao Strait on the night of 24–25 October had been launched at the time Jutland was fought, indeed was just twelve days from completion, and that she, the *Pennsylvania*, was the one American battleship in the action which was not able to open fire.

For the Japanese, of course, the situation was very different, but even within the *Kaigun* the twin realities of defeat and its own helplessness was never properly grasped until the aftermath of the battle of the Philippine Sea in June 1944. Until the end of 1943, the Japanese could delude themselves with the belief that the year had seen verý little territory change hands, that at the present rate of American advance it would take decades for the United States to take the war to Japanese home waters. Then, on both sides of the turn of the year the Japanese position in the central Pacific crumbled and, after the shattering defeat at Truk in February and the rampage of American carrier formations throughout the western Pacific in March and April, there was the collapse of the Japanese position in the south-west Pacific. In one month, and this is not much of an exaggeration, the Americans moved from one end of northern New Guinea to the other: by the end of May 1944, the Americans were in a position to move directly against either or both the southern resources area and the Philippines. But until spring 1944 the *Kaigun* could and did take comfort from the fact that at no stage after November 1942 had the Americans been able to force it to give battle, and while there had been a number of small actions in the Solomons that had resulted in reverses, none were of any real account. Indeed, one of the more remarkable diaries of the Second World War, kept by the admiral who commanded the battle force, noted that as the Japanese warships gathered to give battle in the Philippine Sea, there could be no question of failure given the battleship and cruiser strength available.

At the ensuing battle the *Kaigun* deployed three formations with five fleet and four light fleet carriers, five battleships, eleven heavy and two light cruisers and 27 destroyers; the Americans had seven fleet and eight light fleet carriers, seven battleships, eight heavy and thirteen light cruisers and 67 destroyers, and these American totals do not include submarines, which accounted for two of the three Japanese fleet carriers sunk in this battle, and they do not include the units allocated to bombardment, escort and replenishment duties. What is very notable about the Japanese formations is that there were almost as many major units – carriers, battleships and heavy cruisers – as there were destroyers in the screens, but the total of just 27 destroyers with the three carrier forces was wretchedly inadequate. The Japanese had lost so many destroyers by mid-1944 that they no longer had the means to screen the fleet properly when it was at sea, and what exacerbated this crucial vulnerability was the fact that the concentration of seaplanes with the lead formation for scouting duties could only be achieved by robbing the two main formations, with the bulk of Japanese aircraft, of seaplanes for anti-submarine patrols.

These matters, however important, were nonetheless secondary when set alongside how both sides planned to fight this battle, and for all their many and very real differences there was a curious parallel between the American and Japanese orders of battle and plans of campaign. On the Japanese side, the vanguard formation consisted of the three light carriers, the battleships *Yamato* and *Musashi* and the *Haruna* and *Kongo*, six heavy cruisers, the seaplane-cruisers *Tone* and *Chikuma*, one light cruiser and eight destroyers. This task group was divided into three with the carriers spaced at intervals of six miles across the line of advance. Each carrier had its own screen. The *Chitose* was afforded close escort by the *Musashi*, *Atago* and the *Takao*, the *Zuiho* by the *Yamato*, *Kumano* and the *Suzuya*, with the *Chikuma* and *Tone* also in company, and the *Chiyoda* by the *Haruna* and *Kongo* and the *Chokai* and *Maya*: the screen was divided between the three separate formations. The purpose behind these arrangements was to produce a sizeable concentration of reconnaissance seaplanes whose task was to find and track the enemy, thereby delivering him up to the two main strike forces coming up 100 miles in the rear. But this task group's heavy concentration of battleships and cruisers left it well suited to act as a decoy in the event of any American attack. It was hoped that the heavily armoured capital ships and cruisers would be able to soak up any punishment that the American forces might hand out, thereby sparing the fleet carriers to the rear which, given the number of battleships and heavy cruisers allocated to their protection, most definitely were poorly supported.

For their part, the Americans stripped the seven fast battleships, along with four heavy cruisers and fourteen destroyers, from their four carrier task groups and concentrated them in a single formation astern of the three main carrier formations as the American formations steamed to the east. This new formation, with the weakest of the carrier formations being assigned an escorting role, was thus placed between the Japanese formations known to be to westward and the main American carrier strength, which was to be deployed defensively with fighters massed over the various American formations. Simply in terms of numbers, such an arrangement left the Americans with little more than immediate equality, but the Americans had more fighters than the Japanese had aircraft, and with unrivalled radar and command facilities, qualitative superiority of aircraft and air personnel, and formidable firepower available to each of the individual task groups, the Americans possessed potentially overwhelming advantage, though probably not even the most optimistic of American commanders could have anticipated the extent of the victory won on 19 June. In the course of this one day, the Japanese air strength of five fleet and four light fleet carriers was reduced from 450 to about 100 aircraft, and by nightfall on 20 June to not much more than the equivalent of the air group of one light fleet carrier. This was a disaster from which the *Kaigun* never recovered: it was never able to reconstitute its air groups for its remaining carriers in the fourteen months that were left of the war.

The only hits recorded by Japanese aircraft on American warships in the Philippine Sea were a single hit on the *South Dakota*, which did little damage but killed and wounded some 50 men, and another on the *Indiana*, in the form of a stricken Jill dive-bomber that was deliberated crashed into the battleship.[24] It is very doubtful if any senior Japanese commander was aware of this latter development, but in the aftermath of the battle the Imperial Navy deliberately chose to use the one advantage that the Japanese armed forces held over all their enemies: a willingness to die in order to fight.[25]

The recourse to *kamikaze* attack went hand-in-hand with a determination to fight 'the decisive battle' in defence of the Philippines, and for an obvious reason. The Philippines represented the *ne plus ultra* line for the Japanese empire: the loss of the archipelago would leave the Americans astride Japan's lines of communication with the southern resources area. As it was, Japan by the summer of 1944 was all but defeated as a state: industrially, financially and with respect to mainland Asia, the national defeat had already assumed reality, and with Japanese industry entering end-run production in the first quarter of 1945, the fact of the matter was that Japan, as a state, society and military entity, could not continue to wage war into 1946 – to do so was physically beyond her means. In every way the most sensible thing for the warring parties to have done after the battle of the Philippine Sea was to have sat down, examined strengths, building programmes and present strategic realities and concluded that Japan's defeat was assured and then acted accordingly. But, of course, human beings and states are not so rational, and in any case the inevitability of the outcome is only apparent with hindsight. Be that as it may, the Japanese armed services determined upon the defence of the Philippines in depth, and with the archipelago the Japanese possessed a strategic advantage that they had lacked in every other campaign to date. In strategic terms, the Philippines was a contiguous land mass with a plethora of air bases and strips that provided dispersal, camouflage and strategic depth for their air power, all of which had been lacking in the previous campaigns fought on individual islands that the Americans had been able to isolate from outside support. The new situation brought problems in terms of co-ordination of various different organisations, but the sheer scale of the Philippines and the spread of air facilities there afforded the Japanese with proof against being overwhelmed in one single, opening, air assault – and to this basic point had to be added both the recourse to *kamikaze* attack and the use of the *Kaigun*'s capital ships and heavy cruisers in an attempt not to do battle with their opposite numbers but to fall upon American amphibious shipping.

Such was the basis of the battle of Leyte Gulf, which was a series of actions fought over perhaps five days, between 23 and 27 October 1944. It was certainly the greatest, and the most complicated, naval battle in modern history, and its very complexity prevents a full recounting of its various episodes. There were six separate parts, or phases, to the battle, excluding the American landings on Leyte on 20 October 1944 which precipitated the battle. The first was the initial exchanges which saw the American carrier groups strike at bases throughout the Philippines and the Japanese Navy begin its deployment of forces: it was in this phase that the main Japanese strike force lost two heavy cruisers (the *Atago* and *Maya*) sunk and a third badly damaged even before it was able to enter the Visayan Sea and the central Philippines (22–23 October). The second phase (24 October) concerned this same formation when it was in the Visayan Sea and under attack by American carrier aircraft, attacks which led to the loss of the battleship *Musashi* and damage to the heavy cruiser *Myoko* which forced her to turn back, and to the Japanese force temporarily withdrawing before resuming its advance toward Samar under cover of dark. At the same time as this development, the American light carrier *Princeton* was hit by a lone Judy bomber, its bomb setting off fuel in the hangar and torpedoes on her Avengers: she had to be abandoned and sunk, the first American fleet or light fleet carrier to be sunk since October 1942 and the last to be sunk during the Pacific war. The third phase, which overlaps with the second, was the movement of two more Japanese formations into the southern Philippines in an attempt to move against American shipping via the Surigao Strait, and these efforts culminated in the rout of the lead Japanese formation and the withdrawal of the second without serious contact (24–25 October): the battleships *Fuso* and *Yamashiro* were lost in the Surigao Strait, as were the heavy cruiser *Mogami* and three of the four screening destroyers.

The fourth phase of the battle, which overlaps with both the second and third, was the series of operations conducted by a token Japanese carrier force to the east of Cape Engano (24–25 October). This formation, with one fleet and three light fleet carriers, had but 116 aircraft – the Americans at this action had more destroyers than the Japanese had carrier aircraft – and its role was to lure the main American strength from defensive positions off the Philippines. Its role was sacrificial, to draw attention and attacks upon itself and thus allow the main Japanese strike force to get through the central Philippines and among the American amphibious shipping and covering forces gathered off Samar and Leyte. It was a role that was played to perfection, and with the result that was expected: on 25 October the Japanese lost their four carriers, one light cruiser and two destroyers. But the American carrier and battle formations, lured north to do battle with this force, left the San Bernardino Strait uncovered.

The fifth phase represented the action fought off Samar on the morning of 25 October, an action in which the Japanese held such advantage that they should have registered overwhelming victory but which ended in their losing three heavy cruisers in return for sinking one escort carrier, two destroyers and one destroyer escort. The sixth and last phase represented two quite separate efforts. On the American side there were the 'mopping-up' operations as various damaged Japanese units were hunted down over the next couple of days, but on the Japanese side the battle continued with the *kamikazes* making their first appearance on the morning of 25 October with strikes against American escort carrier formations and, often forgotten, with normal operations, such as the sinking three days later of the American destroyer escort *Eversole* by the Japanese submarine I. 45 which, however, was probably sunk in the process.

Such definition of phases is infinitely less difficult than providing an account of this battle: more difficult still is the provision of an American order of battle which changed frequently during the course of the battle. In terms of capital ships, however, there were three major episodes: the actions that led to the loss of the *Musashi*; the actions in the Surigao Strait; and the action off Samar. To these could be added two other matters. The first was the American attempt to get a battle force to the San Bernardino Strait on 25 October when the consequences of the removal of the covering force from the area were realised. The result of this belated attempt to reverse the uncovering of the San Bernardino Strait was that the battle force missed engaging the enemy off both Cape Engano and the Strait.

The second was the fate of Japanese capital ships after the battle, as a direct consequence of the defeat in Philippine waters. This, in fact, can be defined fairly easily, not least because of the six battleships left to the *Kaigun*, five sailed immediately for home waters after the battle: the exception was the *Kongo*, which apparently stayed in Philippine waters. The Japanese defeat in this battle exposed the whole of the Philippines to American carrier air power, and indeed areas beyond the Philippines as the American rampage through the South China Sea in January 1945 demonstrated. This reality forced the Japanese to try to withdraw their warships and shipping from the south back to home waters while the opportunity to do so still remained, though in the event the opportunity lasted longer than might have been expected: it was not until March 1945, when the Americans placed their various task groups around Okinawa, that the route between the home islands and the southern resources area was finally closed.

As it was, after the defeat at Leyte the Imperial Navy despatched the *Hyuga* and *Ise* to the southern resources area, specifically to reinforce the few remaining formations in southern waters: in reality the lack of fuel in the Japanese home islands lay behind this decision, which in any case was reversed in February 1945. The *Hyuga* and *Ise* sailed from Singapore loaded with stores and fuel on 11 February and arrived at Moji, at the entrance to the Shimonoseki Straits, on the 19th, and they were among the very last warships to reach home waters from the south. The only capital ship loss incurred by the Japanese during this protracted phase of withdrawal from southern waters was that of the *Kongo* which, along with the destroyer *Urakaze*, was torpedoed in 26° 09' North 121° 23' East off north-west Formosa in the East China Sea on 21 November 1944. The Imperial Navy may have lost no other battleship or fleet carrier in these waters as units were withdrawn from the southern resources area, but Japanese ships remained very vulnerable. In November 1944 alone, the *Kaigun* lost the heavy cruisers *Kumano* and *Nachi*, the light cruisers *Kiso* and *Yasoshima*, and the destroyers *Akebono*, *Akikaze*, *Akishimo*, *Hatsuharu* and the *Okinami* either in or off Manila Bay, and mostly to American carrier aircraft, while the destroyers *Hamanami*, *Naganami*, *Shimakaze* and the *Wakatsuki* were sunk by carrier aircraft off Cebu in the course of one day, 11 November. These and the *Kongo* and *Urakaze*, of course, represented only the fleet units, and the bulk of Japanese losses were sustained by escorts, mine and patrol craft, and amphibious units.

Of the three episodes in the battle of Leyte Gulf in which there was direct capital ship involvement perhaps the most significant was the first, which culminated with the sinking of the *Musashi*. The significance, obviously, lies in the fact that the *Musashi* and her sister ship were supposedly unsinkable, but on this day the formation of which she was a member was subjected to attack by five separate formations which together numbered 259 aircraft. The *Musashi* was hit in each of the first four attacks, initially by a single torpedo on the starboard beam, then by three torpedoes and two bombs along her port side, then by two torpedoes to port and one to starboard and, in the fourth attack, apparently first by single torpedo hits on each side and then by three torpedoes to starboard. In human terms, the losses incurred in these first four attacks were considerable. The *Musashi* had aboard crew members from the *Maya* who had been rescued after their ship had been sunk, and these were topside: in addition, of course, there were the battleship's many machine-gun positions, none of which could be afforded protection. With American fighters joining in the attacks with strafing runs, casualties in the *Musashi* were very heavy, Japanese accounts noting that the third attack registered three torpedo hits, and that 'torrential waves from the explosions crashed over the main decks, sweeping a tide of blood and dismembered bodies before them'. With the battleship's first aid and operating posts by now full, a bomb hit near the bow during the fourth attack killed scores of doctors and wounded crewmen in the forward infirmary, but it was this attack that accounted for the *Musashi* and for reasons which are not immediately obvious.

The *Musashi* was able to maintain 24 knots even after the third attack, by which time she had been hit by seven torpedoes – five to port and two to starboard – which probably would have been more than enough to have accounted for any other battleship in existence, the *Yamato* excluded. Even after the fourth attack, the *Musashi* initially reported that she was able to make 22 knots, but the ship was down at the bows and this could not be corrected, while at least one of the hits incurred in this attack sliced into the innards of the ship through a hole made by an earlier torpedo hit. The damage caused by this latest hit could be neither corrected nor contained, and very quickly the *Musashi*'s speed fell away to sixteen knots and she fell out of formation. Without effective support and with her speed continuing to fall away – the engine rooms, sealed by advancing water, smothered their men as the oxygen within these spaces was exhausted – the *Musashi* was very literally all but taken to pieces by the fifth and final attack, apparently delivered by aircraft from the carriers *Enterprise* and *Franklin* and the light carriers *Belleau Wood* and *San Jacinto* (T.G. 38.4), which registered eleven torpedo and ten bomb hits, with six more bombs noted as near misses.

Even if these numbers were exaggerated, the result of this attack was not. Part of the anti-aircraft control room collapsed into the ship's bridge, killing or injuring many senior officers. Many control rooms throughout the ship were destroyed with mains electricity all but extinguished and most of the back-up systems simply overwhelmed. Much more seriously, the bow, which normally drew 13 feet/4 metres of water, was drawing 26 feet, which meant that water rushing into the ship was bypassing the ship's defences and reaching immediately into the main deck area. With her speed having fallen to six knots, the *Musashi* was afforded the dignity of an escort of two destroyers, detached from her sister ship's formation, which were to attempt to get the stricken monolith into San Jose in north-east Mindoro: in the event, even the attempt to run the ship into a local reef in order to get stores and men ashore the more easily failed with the loss of power. The darkness inside the ship was matched by the ebbing of the day, and just before sunset the rituals were played out: the national anthem, the removal of the Emperor's portrait and the lowering of the battle ensign on the rear mast. Then, as the ship rose, she was abandoned amid the usual gruesome scenes of men caught in propellers and wake, others swept into the holes made in the hull by the torpedo hits, and still others caught in the propellers of rescuing destroyers or so covered with oil, and so exhausted, that they could not grip ropes and be saved.

In all, the amazingly high total of 1,376 of her crew of 2,399 were rescued by the destroyers *Kiyoshimo* and *Shimakaze*, but the *Kaigun*, indeed both the *Kaigun* and its sister service, the *Rikugun*, seem to have shared a curious attitude towards the survivors. Apparently, the survivors of the battleship *Mutsu*, which was destroyed by an accidental explosion in her magazines off Hashirajima in Hiroshima Bay in June 1943, were cut down as they staggered ashore by army personnel wielding samurai swords as punishment for having lost their ship. With the loss of a ship, the *Kaigun* seems to have abandoned any sense of responsibility for her men. About half of those who survived the loss of the *Musashi* were kept in the Philippines, many incommunicado, with, it is claimed, just 29 surviving the war, while the other half were sent to Japan, and if they survived the sinking of their merchantman en route, they were lucky: those that returned to Japan in what seems to have been the carrier *Junyo* were more fortunate in that she survived being torpedoed off Nagasaki. Once in Japan, the survivors were either confined to one of the islands in the Inland Sea or in isolated barracks at Kure. As for all military personnel of whatever nationality and whichever war, the cause may have been just but the old lie, as always, was too much.

Elsewhere, the actions in the Surigao Strait must represent one of the most one-sided episodes of the entire naval war. The Americans, forewarned about Japanese movements around noon on 24 October, had the better part of twelve hours in which to clear various command and supply ships from the general area and to form their three main commands into battle formation. These comprised three heavy and two light cruisers, with nine destroyers in attendance; six old battleships with six destroyers assigned; and one heavy and two light cruisers, with thirteen destroyers as escort: in the latter force the heavy cruiser and one destroyer were Australian, the only non-American ships in company. These task groups were organised into two patrol lines between Hingatungan Point on Leyte and Hibuson Island, the battleships in the rear line and the cruisers in front of them, with destroyers patrolling across the Strait or placed to move against any Japanese formation attempting to pass through it. In addition, the Americans had no fewer than 39 PT boats which were in position in the eastern Mindanao Sea and the southern reaches of the Surigao Strait between Panaoni and Mindanao and Leyte and Dinagat. The only real problem that the Americans faced in making such arrangements was that their battleships had been provisioned primarily with bombardment ammunition, and less than a quarter of their rounds were armour-piercing. As a result, the Americans planned to fire their first five salvoes with armour-piercing ammunition before switching to bombardment rounds, and they were to engage the enemy at ranges between 17,000 and 20,000 yards/15,600 and 18,350 metres, which would be the ideal range at which to do so given the ability of the battleships to track and predict enemy movements on the basis of radar readings.

The initial exchange, between the leading Japanese formation – the battleships *Fuso* and *Yamashiro*, the heavy cruiser *Mogami* and the destroyers *Asagumo*, *Michishio*, *Shigure* and the *Yamagumo* – and the various PT formations resulted in no Japanese ship being torpedoed and ten PT boats being hit though only one was ultimately lost. As the Japanese force approached Hibuson Island, however, the American destroyers mounted a scissors attack. The *Yamagumo* was hit and blew up (0319), the *Michishio* was badly damaged and left in a sinking condition, and the *Asagumo* lost her bow but was able to retire: the *Yamashiro* took one torpedo hit which caused no real damage while the *Fuso* was hit by at least one torpedo and fell out of line. As the *Shigure*, *Yamashiro* and the *Mogami* pressed forward, a second destroyer attack materialised, the battleship being temporarily slowed by a second torpedo hit. By the time that this attack was over, the three remaining Japanese ships had become separated, and the *Michishio* had been hit again with the result that she was lost (0358). A third destroyer attack was then delivered, and it is believed that the *Yamashiro* was hit by two torpedoes, possibly from the destroyer *Newcomb*: it was in this attack that the destroyer *Albert W. Grant* was hit by Japanese gunfire, the only Allied ship (other than the PT boats) to be thus afflicted.

These various exchanges opened either side of midnight, 24–25 October 1944, and with the first contact report made by an American destroyer noted at 0026, the various destroyer attacks were conducted between 0240 and 0350. It was not until 0323 that radars in the battleships and cruisers registered the presence of the enemy at a range of nearly nineteen miles, and fire was opened by the cruisers at 0351 and by the battleships at 0353 at ranges of 15,600 yards and 22,800 yards/14,300 metres and 20,900 metres respectively. On the Japanese side, the range was so great that star shells fell short and thus failed to illuminate the Allied warships, and not one of the battleships, cruisers and their escorts was remotely threatened by Japanese fire. On the American side, the main responsibility for engaging the *Yamashiro* fell to the *West Virginia*, *Tennessee* and the *California*, which were the first, fourth and fifth in line and were equipped with the Mark VIII fire-control radar. These battleships fired 93, 69 and 63 rounds, the first two initially firing only in six-gun salvoes in order to conserve their limited number of armour-piercing shells.[26] The other battleships, equipped with the Mark III radar, were not so fortunate. The *Maryland* managed 48 rounds in six salvoes but the *Pennsylvania* did not fire at all because she could not find a single target, though in truth there really was only one target to be found: at 0408 the *Mississippi* was able to fire but one full, twelve-gun, salvo, at 19,700 yards, just after the battle force had completed a reversal of course.[27] This proved to be the last salvo fired by the American battleships in this battle, and the last rounds ever fired by a battleship in battle with an enemy counterpart.[28] It was also one of the classic examples of the famous 'crossing the T' tactic, though in truth this was almost a case where the cross was all but drawn by the victim.

By the time that ceasefire orders were given and received in the Allied warships (*c.* 0409), the *Yamashiro* appeared to be on fire along the whole of her length, the *Mogami* had already turned back and the *Shigure*, hit but once by a shell that did not explode, had also retired. As Allied fire was checked, so the *Yamashiro* turned back but capsized and sank in 10° 23' North 125° 21' East at 0419, the American destroyer *McDermut* generally being credited for a final torpedo hit that brought about her end.[29] It was at this time when, with American destroyers cleared from the immediate area, that the Allied battleships and cruisers were again given permission to fire, but by this time the *Mogami* and

Shigure had been able to escape from immediate danger, in the *Mogami*'s case despite having been hit extensively by gunfire and even being briefly halted at 0402. By the time that the *Yamashiro* sank, however, the second Japanese formation[30] detailed to proceed to Leyte Gulf via the Surigao Strait had almost reached what remained of the first formation. It must have been possessed of a well-developed sense of realism – one perhaps installed by its passing what were thought to be the *Fuso* and *Yamashiro* burning furiously but which in fact was the *Fuso*, which had broken in two[31] – because it turned back without making any serious attempt to give battle. As it did so, the *Nachi* and the *Mogami* collided, but if the *Nachi* was badly damaged, the *Mogami*, which had been involved in a collision with another cruiser under not dissimilar circumstances off Midway in June 1942, seemed revived by the experience, and she and the *Shigure* joined the second formation as it withdrew. With dawn, however, the crippled *Asagumo* was found and despatched; the *Mogami*, after having withstood attack by PT boats, surface units and aircraft, was abandoned and scuttled; and the *Abukuma*, after having been slowed as a result of her being the only Japanese warship to have been torpedoed by the PT boats, was caught by American land-based bombers, operating from bases off New Guinea, and sunk off Negros. From the American perspective this particular battle was over, but the victory that had been won threatened to be immediately overtaken by events to the north where the Japanese main force, having made it way through the Visayan Sea and San Bernardino Strait, found itself in action with the American escort carriers, and their consorts, off Samar.

The action off Samar is probably the most celebrated single episode of the battle of Leyte Gulf, and at least on the American side for good reason: in a battle in which the Americans held an overwhelming, decisive superiority of numbers both overall and in all but one of its constituent parts, this was the one action where everything went wrong, even though, against all the odds, it was at worst drawn, at best won. But in the story of the capital ship this action was not really the important part of the battle off Samar on 25 October. This action must be recounted and its salient features noted, but the significant development, the one that was to have most bearing on the capital ship in the remaining ten months of the war, was the appearance of *kamikaze* aircraft and their assault on TU 77.4.3 after it emerged from its ordeal at the hands of the Japanese main force.

The story of the action between the Japanese main force and the American escort carrier formation can be related under three headings. The first, quite simply, has to do with the definition of responsibility on the American side for the situation which left the escort carrier formations off Samar without cover. The problem here was that such responsibility rested with one person, the commander of the 3rd U.S. Fleet, Admiral William F. Halsey Jr., but then Halsey had already entered the pantheon of American heroes, one which permitted neither questioning of him nor reproach, and even in the post-war accounts of the battle his culpability was side-stepped by the portrayal of these events as an issue of command: it was suggested that there were two fleets in action on the American side, the 3rd and 7th Fleets, and that the understandable confusion arose because the real responsibility for matters specific to operations in and over the Philippines at this stage lay with the latter. This was, by any standard, somewhat disingenuous. The issue was not one of command but of function, and in this regard TF 38 had the task of ensuring TF 77 against the very attack that materialised on 25 October. Its failure to do so was all the more surprising given the fact that Halsey, in his first major battle, had access to all the relevant information on Japanese plans and procedures, most obviously the use of decoys. Nonetheless, at the first opportunity Halsey took his force in pursuit of the decoy, away from the position in which he could cover and support TF 77. Then, when the reality of the Japanese move through the San Bernardino Strait was belatedly recognised, a battle force was detached and thus prevented from taking part in the destruction of the decoy force off Cape Engano. It was also too late either to support the escort carriers off Samar or prevent the Japanese main force withdrawing by the route it had come: just one Japanese destroyer, the *Nowaki*, was caught and destroyed before it had chance to enter the Strait soon after midnight 25–26 October. The whole episode was an abysmal performance, particularly at a staff level within the 3rd Fleet but also at a personal level by Halsey, who, it must be admitted, was never noted for his cerebral capacity and indeed was well-known for his lack of it. It is very hard to resist the conclusion that this battle was fought on a scale that defeated Halsey, and, in fairness to him, it was fought on a scale that would have defeated most admirals and especially those that sought to command afloat rather than ashore.

The second heading concerns the events and balance of losses in this action off Samar. As regards the latter, the American losses can be stated simply: the escort carrier *Gambier Bay*, the destroyers *Hoel* and *Johnston* and the destroyer escort *Samuel B. Roberts*. The Americans lost only one escort carrier at this stage of proceedings partly because the carrier formations made skilful use of rain squalls and smoke screens in order to hide from Japanese sight, and they were also spared additional losses by the deliberate sacrifice of escorts which mounted counter-attacks in order to buy protection for their charges. In addition, the carriers under attack, and also the carriers in its neighbouring formation, flew off as many aircraft as possible, and if there was a certain lack of order to the manner in which these aircraft were despatched and carried out their attacks, their numbers and sheer ferocity in all probability more than compensated for any lack of deliberate organisation. Flying in small groups, these aircraft mounted successive attacks and in the process torpedoed the heavy cruisers *Chikuma*, *Chokai* and the *Suzuya*, which had to be scuttled by the *Nowaki*, *Fujinami* and the *Okinami* respectively.

Important though the writing down of Japanese numbers undoubtedly was at this stage, the real importance of these attacks lay under the third heading concerning the action off Samar, which concerned the question of who was in command of the Japanese force. The answer, of course, was nobody. Nominally in command was Vice Admiral Kurita Takeo, but in reality his conduct of operations prompts the previous answer on a number of counts. Once the Japanese were in contact with the American carrier force, there appears to have been no plan and very little in the way of issued orders, and by the time that the Japanese force had somehow managed to work itself into a position where the annihilation of the American carriers could be predicted in terms of minutes, Kurita broke off the action. After the war this decision was justified by resort to the belief that the Japanese force was involved in an action with American fleet carriers, but if that was true, then surely Kurita should have pressed the issue to a conclusion rather than attempt to retire and play a fleet-in-being role. While it is quite possible that Kurita's less than adequate direction of the Japanese effort may have been the result of three disasters on three days – the loss of his flagship, the loss of the *Musashi*, and then the fury of the American response and the crippling of three heavy cruisers from his much depleted force – the fact of the matter was that with four battleships and seven heavy cruisers, plus a full screen of destroyers, only two of which had been detached, the number of American ships sunk in these exchanges was decidedly modest, not least because the *Kongo* seems to have been responsible for the sinking of the *Hoel* and *Johnston* and to have contributed to the destruction of the *Gambier Bay* – and if this was indeed the case, such a record poses obvious questions about what the other ships in formation were doing.

But, and this is the important but, as far as American capital ship employment in the last ten months of the war was concerned, what happened in this action was less important than the *kamikaze* attacks that followed. As the action off Samar was joined, Japanese land-based aircraft attacked TU 77.4.1, which was some 130 miles to the south. Two escort carriers were hit and another two near-missed but the operational efficiency of this formation was not really affected by the time that the main Japanese *kamikaze* effort fell upon TU 77.4.3 just as it was recovering aircraft following the disappearance of Japanese warships over the horizon. One of the escort carriers, the *St. Lo*, was hit by a Zeke which exploded on the hangar deck, setting off a chain of explosions from bombs and torpedoes that doomed the ship. Three other carriers were damaged, one badly, just one escort carrier from this formation being left undamaged and intact.

In themselves, these attacks, and their relatively minor success, might not have amounted to very much in real strategic terms, but the significance of the day's events lay in the shock value of the *kamikaze*s and the fact that this was just for openers: on 30 October the fleet carrier *Franklin* and the light carrier *Belleau Wood* were severely damaged by *kamikaze* attack, and within a matter of days the fleet carrier *Lexington* was forced from the battle for the Philippines with extensive damage courtesy of *kamikaze* attack. This was the start of a Japanese effort that was to continue through the Lingayen Gulf landings and Luzon campaign, and then the struggle for Okinawa, to the end of the war but which reached its climax during the campaign for Okinawa. Between 24 March and 21 June 1945 the 5th US Fleet lost 36 ships sunk and had another 371 damaged by all forms of enemy attack and accidental and natural causes, and of these totals 27 of the ships that were sunk and 168 of those damaged were the victim of *kamikaze* attack: conventional air attack accounted for just one destroyer and damaged another 63 vessels of all descriptions. Amid these ships lost and damaged, there were fourteen incidents involving twelve battleships and damage, the latter being inflicted by *kamikaze* aircraft in eight instances: only five of these cases involved damage that was officially recorded as major, but in one case the battleship was hit a second time by a *kamikaze* one month later, which would seem to suggest that the damage inflicted on the first occasion really was not too serious.[32]

For the capital ship, this new form of attack presented obvious problems. Depending on one's perspective, one can argue that the Americans had mastered the *kamikaze* threat by the end of the war; or that the real American mastery of this particular threat would have come in 1946 with the replacement of massed 40-mm anti-aircraft tertiary weapons with a new 3-in/76-mm gun which had both sufficient volume of fire and stopping power to deal with a *kamikaze* aircraft. In any event the *kamikaze* threat would have ended in 1946, because by that time Japan would not have possessed fuel for her aircraft and what air forces remained to her would have been all but wrecked by training programmes geared to the single mission. The difficulty with these contending interpretations of events is that each and every one has much to recommend it. The crucial point was not that the threat could be eliminated or Allied warships rendered invulnerable to attack: neither of these eventualities were practicable and both went unrealised. It was that losses, or ship losses at least, could be reduced to acceptable levels, and the Americans were able to reduce losses to manageable proportions as a result of three major changes.

The first of these changes was the establishment of picket lines that existed to draw attacks upon themselves, away from carrier formations. The second was a major recasting of carrier air groups with larger groups and an ever higher number of fighters within air groups, which in any case was a trend in American air group establishment as the war progressed: as the American carriers moved into the western Pacific and Japanese home waters, so the fighter element in groups increased as the American formations wedded strategically offensive and tactically defensive roles. The Americans were forced to have to hand sufficient numbers of fighters with their carriers to be able to fight and win air superiority over Japanese airfields. Such was the defensive trend exaggerated by the *kamikaze*s that before the war came to an end, the Americans had brought into service one all-fighter carrier air group. The third change was increased numbers of warships in screens and numbers of guns in ships. The American calculation in 1945 was that a single 3-in/76-mm 50 calibre gun, which could fire a 13-lb/5.91-kg shell to a range of 14,600 yards/13,400 metres and a maximum ceiling of 29,800 feet/9,100 metres, was as effective as two quadruple 40-mm mounts against ordinary *kamikaze* aircraft, and five such mounts in dealing with the *Baka* bomb. It was intended that the 40-mm and 20-mm batteries of the *Iowa*-class battleships would be replaced with fifteen twin 3-in/76-mm mounts, but the end of the war did away with the need for this change. Nonetheless, in the last year of the Pacific war there was a general but small increase in the number of guns carried in ships, the battleships' limit being about 80 40-mm Bofors and 50 20-mm Oerlikons: effective fire control was not possible with greater numbers, and with the numbers that were embarked the American battleships were in a different league from those of their Japanese enemy and, for that matter, their British ally.

In terms of the balance within a task group, there were self-evident difficulties, most obviously the disputes within the U.S. Navy concerning the maximum size of an individual task group and related matters dealing with night-fighting capability and whether specialist carriers and air groups should be made responsible for this aspect of operations. In large part the latter question was answered by the damage sustained during daylight operations by the two carriers, the *Enterprise* and *Saratoga*, detailed for such specialist duties, but the question of the optimum number of carriers in a group, and with it the number and type of warship detailed as escort, was never resolved. Be that as it may, the difference between the task group of 1944–1945 from the task groups that fought the four carrier battles of 1942 is massive:

The Battle in the Coral Sea (7/8 May 1942)

Task Force 11
The fleet carrier *Lexington*, the heavy cruisers *Minneapolis* and *New Orleans*, and the destroyers *Aylwyn*, *Dewey*, *Farragut*, *Monaghan* and the *Phelps*.

Task Force 17
The fleet carrier *Yorktown*, the heavy cruisers *Astoria*, *Chester* and the *Portland*, and the destroyers *Anderson*, *Hammann*, *Morris* and the *Russell*.

The Battle off Midway Islands (4/6 June 1942)

Task Force 16

The fleet carrier *Enterprise* and *Hornet*, the heavy cruisers *Minneapolis*, *New Orleans*, *Northampton*, *Pensacola* and the *Vincennes*, the light cruiser *Atlanta*, and the destroyers *Aylwyn*, *Balch*, *Benham*, *Conyngham*, *Ellet*, *Maury*, *Monaghan*, *Phelps* and the *Worden*.

Task Force 17

The fleet carrier *Yorktown*, the heavy cruisers *Astoria* and *Portland*, and the destroyers *Anderson*, *Gwin*, *Hammann*, *Hughes*, *Morris* and the *Russell*.

Task Force 58: The overture to Iwo Jima: February 1945

Task Group 58.1

The fleet carriers *Bennington*, *Hornet* and the *Wasp*, the light carrier *Belleau Wood*, the battleships *Massachusetts* and *Indiana*, the light cruisers *Miami*, *San Juan*, *Vicksburg* and the *Vincennes* and the destroyers *Blue*, *Brush*, *Collett*, *Dashiell*, *De Haven*, *Harrison*, *John Rodgers*, *Lyman K. Swenson*, *Mansfield*, *McKee*, *Murray*, *Ringgold*, *Samuel N. Moore*, *Schroeder*, *Sigsbee*, *Stevens* and the *Taussig*.

Task Group 58.2

The fleet carriers *Hancock* and *Lexington*, the light carrier *San Jacinto*, the battleships *Missouri* and *Wisconsin*, the heavy cruisers *Boston*, *Pittsburgh* and the *San Francisco*, and the destroyers *Benham*, *Colahan*, *Cushing*, *Halsey Powell*, *Hickox*, *Hunt*, *Lewis Hancock*, *Marshall*, *Miller*, *Owen*, *Stephen Potter*, *Stockham*, *The Sullivans*, *Tingey*, *Twining*, *Uhlmann*, *Wedderburn* and the *Yarnall*.

Task Group 58.3

The fleet carriers *Essex* and *Bunker Hill*, the light carrier *Cowpens*, the battleships *New Jersey* and *South Dakota*, the heavy cruiser *Indianapolis*, the light cruisers *Astoria*, *Pasadena*, *Springfield* and the *Wilkes-Barre*, and the destroyers *Ault*, *Borie*, *Callaghan*, *Cassin Young*, *Charles S. Sperry*, *English*, *Hank*, *Haynsworth*, *Irwin*, *John W. Weeks*, *Porterfield*, *Preston*, *Waldron* and the *Wallace L. Lind*.

Task Group 58.4

The fleet carriers *Randolph* and *Yorktown*, the light carriers *Cabot* and *Langley*, the battleships *North Carolina* and *Washington*, the light cruisers *Biloxi*, *San Diego* and the *Santa Fe*, and the destroyers *Barton*, *Clarence K. Bronson*, *Cotten*, *Dortch*, *Franks*, *Gatling*, *Haggard*, *Hazelwood*, *Healy*, *Heermann*, *Ingraham*, *Laffey*, *Lowry*, *McCord*, *Moale* and the *Trathen*.

Task Group 58.5

The fleet carriers *Enterprise* and *Saratoga*, the battlecruiser *Alaska*, the heavy cruiser *Baltimore*, the light cruiser *Flint*, and the destroyers *Laws*, *Longshaw*, *McDermut*, *McGowan*, *McNair*, *Melvin*, *Mertz*, *Monssen*, *Morrison*, *Norman Scott*, *Prichett* and the *Remey*.

	Fleet Carriers	Light Carriers	Capital Ships	Heavy Cruisers	Light Cruisers	Destroyers	Total
CORAL SEA	2	–	–	5	–	9	16
MIDWAY	3	–	–	7	1	15	26
TASK FORCE 58							
TG 58.1	3	1	2	–	4	17	27
TG 58.2	2	1	2	2	–	18	25
TG 58.3	2	1	2	5	–	15	25
TG 58.4	2	2	2	–	3	16	25
TG 58.5	2	–	1	1	1	12	17
TOTAL	11	5	9	8	8	78	119

Three aspects of the 1945 order of battle are notable. First, just one, any one, of the four task groups at Leyte was as large as the U.S. fleet at Midway. Second, of the 119 warships in Task Force 58 in 1945 just the *Enterprise* and *Saratoga*, *North Carolina* and *Washington*, and the *Indianapolis* and *San Francisco* were in commission before the Japanese attack on Pearl Harbor, and only another four (the *Massachusetts* and *South Dakota* and the *San Diego* and *San Juan*) had been launched: the remaining 109 warships awaited being acquainted with the sea. And third, what is equally noteworthy is the fact that no fewer than nine of the eleven new battleships and battlecruisers were with the fleet: with the *Guam* awaiting her first operational deployment, the only absentees, undergoing short refits at Puget Sound and San Francisco, were the *Alabama* and the *Iowa* respectively, and three of the five task groups had battleships that were sister ships. It was all a very long time since the *Maine*, Dewey and Manila Bay, Santiago, Theodore Roosevelt and the Great White Fleet, but no time at all since Wilson and the fleet second to none.

Where does one end the story of the Second World War and the capital ship? It would seem that, at first sight, there are two obvious alternatives, and the first would be some 130 miles, nearly 210 kilometres, west by south-west of Kagoshima, in Kyushu, where on 7 April 1945 the battleship *Yamato* was sunk by aircraft from Task Force 58. Ostensibly she had been sent to support the garrison on Okinawa, but without adequate fuel reserves in the home islands she was not expected to survive her sortie, though in fact for the *Kaigun* her primary mission was to be sunk: the battleship that bore the ancient name of Japan could not survive national defeat. The second alternative would be in the Inland Sea, specifically off Kure, where on 24 July 1945 American carrier aircraft sank the battleship *Hyuga* and, four days later, her sister ship the *Ise* and also the *Haruna*. The sinking of these three battleships, in their base, represents the final comment on the Japanese attack that had opened proceedings, the attack on the Pacific Fleet at Pearl Harbor on 7 December 1941. Moreover, it bears recounting that during the attacks mounted on 24 July 1945 American carrier aircraft sank the heavy cruiser *Tone*, and she was the last surviving member of the carrier force which had executed the attack which began the Pacific war. Of the twenty warships in this formation, the six oilers that sustained it, and the 30 submarines that provided general support, just one oiler, the *Kyokuto Maru*, and one submarine, the I. 21, survived the war.

There is, however, only one place where the story can be brought to a conclusion, and that was in Tokyo Bay and the date was 2 September 1945. But the ship that would be the object of attention would not be the *Missouri*, though what happened in her on that morning possessed an importance which surpassed all and everything else that this day witnessed. The surrender of a nation brought to defeat by sea power, and the instrument of that surrender being signed in a warship, have no parallel in history, and there can be no belittling of an achievement primarily registered by the United States and her armed forces. But rather, attention should be directed to an event small in itself but full of imagery and significance. One has used the example elsewhere, but one tires not of it, not least because the account of the proceedings at dusk in the *Duke of York* was written by an American admiral who, one suspects from what he wrote, had glimpsed reality. On that evening all the Allied delegations which had been party to the surrender ceremony that day were invited to the Beating the Retreat by the massed bands of the British Pacific Fleet. As was the tradition, proceedings were brought to a close with the Sunset Hymn, and during the singing of its last verse,

> So be it, Lord, Thy throne shall never
> Like Earth's proud empires pass away
> Thy kingdom stands, and grows for ever
> Till all thy creatures own Thy sway

the flags of all delegations were lowered in unison. Symbolism – the end of one of the greatest and worst wars in history, the end of Allied unity and the end of the supremacy of the capital ship as arbiter of sea power – was complete.

The Last Goodbye

Western history is written on the basis of moving noughts: a decade is an era, a century an age. It has been written that the twentieth century was the American century, and most certainly by the end of the Second World War anyone outside the Soviet Union and eastern Europe, and perhaps China, who expressed such a view would not have encountered much in the way of serious academic or intellectual dispute. The American achievement in the Second World War was awesome, and hence it is important to note what tended to be disregarded both at the time and in later years. The defeat of the Axis powers in the Second World War required an effort on the part of an alliance that ultimately became the United Nations, and necessarily single nations could only handle part of that effort. The United States could not have won the Second World War by her own efforts. She could have achieved the defeat of Japan, as indeed she did and with only minor military contributions on the part of other nations, but the defeat of Germany and Italy, and their various allies, was something that she could not have achieved had it not been for her allies, namely Britain and the Soviet Union. Without Britain it is very hard to see how the United States could have landed forces anywhere on a hostile continental shore, and there can be no dodging the point that Germany's military defeat was registered primarily by the Soviet Union. The American contribution to Germany's defeat was very considerable, principally in the air and in the political and economic dimensions of total war, but, say it *sotto voce*, the military contributions of the United States and Britain to the defeat of the European Axis powers were of secondary importance.

In terms of naval power, the United States ended the Second World War unchallenged and unchallengeable, possessed of such margins of superiority over all and any other nation and navy as to render future rivalry all but unthinkable. Industrial and financial power were the basis of American national strength, but in terms of power the U.S. Navy was the basis of the *Pax Americana*, while the pertinence of the old joke – that the Monroe Doctrine had established that no one could have a war in the western hemisphere except the U.S. Marine Corps – could be said to have been extended across the Pacific and, in the course of 1946, into the western Indian Ocean and Persian Gulf. It was this national strength and power that provided the United States with the means whereby she underwrote the countries of western Europe as the post-war confrontation with the Soviet Union took shape, and perhaps somewhat oddly, her guarantees covered four states which were the major naval powers in the world after the U.S. Navy.

For her part, Britain ended the Second World War as second only to the United States in naval power but, critically, the war had exhausted her and if she nonetheless retained global presence, she no longer retained global power. In fact, this point had been painfully demonstrated in 1942–1944 when she was shown to be incapable of mounting a serious, independent contribution to Japan's defeat before the end of the European war: ironically, by the time she was able to put together a serious effort in the Far East, the Pacific war was drawing to its close, its end hastened by an overwhelming American power which had taken two years off the anticipated length of the Japanese war even as the German war had staggered into 1945. But at the end of the European war, which nation came after Britain in the naval pecking order is difficult to determine. In terms of numbers of battleships, probably Italy was third, but she was a defeated power on parole and it was recognised that the price she would pay for fascist misdemeanours would be primarily at imperial and naval expense. France, by virtue of her small but very fine fleet and, of course, her historical naval role, could be regarded as third, but ranking third after Britain in the naval hierarchy in the immediate aftermath of the war was probably Canada. In terms of destroyers and escorts, the Canadian contribution to the Allied victory in the North Atlantic is not to be underestimated. The Royal Canadian Navy was not without its wartime problems, and its contribution to the defeat of the German *guerre de course* was somewhat fitful, but it was nonetheless very real by 1943–1945, by which time Canada was considering her future naval contribution with reference to aircraft carriers and cruisers. By the same yardsticks, the Royal Australian Navy could probably be marked off as fourth in the naval list and, perhaps more contentiously, the fifth could be the Royal Indian Navy: the latter's main strength, however, was local and limited to inshore and landing operations and, more relevantly, in 1945–1946 it probably could not be included in any table of comparative strengths because of the uncertainties governing its future – or, to be more accurate, the certainty that very soon it was to be no more.

Perhaps rather oddly, nine states had dreadnoughts in 1946. It is odd in the sense that the yardstick of naval power by 1945 was the aircraft carrier, not the battleship, and such was the disparity between the U.S. Navy and the rest of the world, even the disparity between the Royal Navy and the rest of the world, that the individual tends not to think of 1945 and the post-war world in terms of battleship numbers, and certainly most people would not think that more than four or five countries possessed capital ships in 1945. Just two countries which had possessed battleships in 1939 no longer retained them, and for those countries, Japan and Germany, there had been no choice in the matter: their changed status was the product of national defeat. The other nine countries that had had one or more capital ships in 1939 still retained them, despite the loss of 35 of their number during the war. The nine countries were the United States, Britain, France, Italy and the Soviet Union, all of which had been involved in the war, plus Turkey and Argentina, Brazil and Chile. Conversely, at the end of the war just the United States and Britain possessed fleet and light fleet carriers though, an indication of the battleship's eclipse, four countries were immediately concerned with the acquisition of carrier capability. These were France and the Netherlands, Australia and Canada.

Navies and nations after 1945 did not look immediately to the battleship: to borrow the apt comment, battleships fell into the 'nice-to-have, not need-to-have' category. The battleship was most certainly a symbol of status, and those that survived the war most certainly possessed lines and profiles that were distinctly impressive in a way that a fleet carrier, unless viewed from off the port beam, could never be: the carrier silhouette told against beauty. The battleship, if it was there and if it belonged to the post-limitation period, would be retained, but in many ways the crucial decisions that shaped all matters involving the capital ship were made in the summer of 1943. The American decisions not to proceed with the *Montana* class, specifically the 21 July 1943 cancellation of orders,[1] and, perhaps even more telling, the halting of the construction of the *Iowa*-class battleship *Kentucky* between June 1942 and December 1944 in order to free resources for building landing craft, really served notice that the battleship's equivalent of three score years and ten were drawing to a close. The *Montana* class, which was to have numbered five battleships, was authorised under the 1940 Two-Ocean Naval Expansion Act and work on their design began when that of the *Iowa* class was completed.[2] Had these ships been built, they would have represented the most powerful and best protected battleships ever built by any navy. In armament, their twelve 16-in/406-mm guns, mounted in four triple turrets, would have been at least the equal of the nine 18.1-in/460-mm guns of the *Yamato* class, while there simply was no comparison between American and Japanese radar and fire control equipment. Only in speed would any battleship or battlecruiser ever have been their superior, but with these 70,965-ton warships detailed to make 28 knots, this was not too serious a deficiency.[3]

If the United States, at her peak in terms of capacity to build and the U.S. Navy's ability to order, turned her back on such ships, then the rest of the world was not going to make any move in this particular direction. There was clearly little, if any, point in other countries building warships that were inferior, if not to the *Montana* specifications, then at least to the *Iowa*-class battleships that were already in existence, and besides, no other nation had the industrial capacity to build such ships. At the end of the war perhaps Britain and France could justify the completion of dreadnoughts then under construction, in Britain's case the *Vanguard* and in France's the *Jean Bart*, but the latter's completion was beset by problems caused by the shortage of funds, and it was not until May 1955 that she was completed. Indeed, it seems that the French ship's construction was not abandoned precisely because her completion had become a matter that touched on national honour. Nearly 50 years after the event this may seem somewhat unlikely, but apparently it was the case.

There was, inevitably, the unfortunate rider to all this, and it was a very simple one: if the battleships that belonged to the post-limitation period would be retained, then those of an earlier period were to depart, those belonging to the Turkish and South American navies excepted. For Britain, this involved eight surviving pre-1914 battleships of the *Queen Elizabeth* and *Royal Sovereign* classes, plus the *Renown* and the *Nelson* and *Rodney*. It was a sign of the recognition of this basic fact of life that the process of taking these ships from front-line service into the reserve and detailing them for various tertiary activities pending disposal was well advanced even in January 1945. In fact, it had begun even as early as 1943 with respect to most of the *Royal Sovereign* class battleships, and for an obvious reason: denied the extensive reconstruction or modernisation programmes that enabled such ships as the *Queen Elizabeth* to remain in service until the spring of 1945, they were marginal to requirements by the end of 1943, and the *Resolution*, *Revenge* and the *Royal Sovereign* had been reduced to reserve status between September and November 1943, though the last of the three was refitted as part of her transfer in 1944 to the Soviet Union as the *Archangelsk*. By the spring of 1945, apart from the four surviving members of the *King George V* class, only the *Queen Elizabeth* and *Renown* were actively employed with the East Indies Fleet in the Indian Ocean, and both were recalled to home waters and relegated to the reserve. The *Nelson*, after extensive refit at Philadelphia navy yard, was the only British battleship with the East Indies Fleet: with the end of the Japanese war, she proceeded to Penang where the local Japanese surrender was signed on the same table as that of Italy two years before.

The *Nelson*'s sister ship, the *Rodney*, remained nominally in service in home waters but in reality without adequate refit her assignment to the reserve depended only on the time of the arrival back in British waters of members of the *King George V* class, all of which were in the Indian and Pacific Oceans when Japan surrendered. Thus the end of the Japanese war found the *Ramillies* as part of the shore training establishment at Portsmouth, and the *Resolution* and *Revenge* employed similarly at Devonport. The latter two were joined after June 1946 by the *Valiant*, which had been very badly damaged in August 1944 when the floating dock at Trincomalee in which she was being tended collapsed. This left just the *Malaya* and *Warspite* in reserve, and the *Warspite* was in such a state that she was the first British capital ship stricken and sold for scrap. Like the *Oklahoma* in May 1947 and the *São Paulo* in November 1951, however, she decided against ending in the breaker's yard and broke her tow, but unlike the other two ships she could not contrive to sink in an unknown position: the *Warspite* ran herself ashore on 23 April 1947 and was scrapped in situ over the next eight years. After the *Warspite*'s demise, the remaining ten British capital ships built before the end of limitation were stricken and scrapped, the *Malaya*, *Queen Elizabeth* and the *Valiant*, the *Ramillies* and *Resolution*, the *Renown* and the *Rodney*, and also the old carrier *Furious*, which had begun life as one of Fisher's cruisers, in 1948, and the *Revenge* and returned *Royal Sovereign*, plus the *Nelson*, in 1949.[4]

France found herself in much the same situation as Britain though it was complicated by the fact that certain of her older ships, and a couple of newer ones, had been scuttled or sunk in harbour and, with the return of peace, these had to be raised in order to clear bases and ports. Recounting the fate of two of France's oldest battleships is problematic. The pre-dreadnought *Condorcet* had been stricken in 1931 but had remained in service as an accommodation ship at Toulon. The dreadnought *Océan* had been in service after 1931 as a training ship and after 1937 as a stationary training ship and then as a hulk at Toulon; she had been scuttled in November 1942 but raised by the Germans, who used her as a target ship. Both the *Condorcet* and *Océan* were sunk in the course of 1944, the former possibly on 18 August when American medium bombers struck at shipping inside Toulon harbour. The two ships were salvaged, the *Océan* in the course of 1944, with the result that her scrapping was completed in December 1945, and the *Condorcet* in the course of 1945, but by some extraordinary process, while she was stricken in 1947, it was not until 1959 that she was finally scrapped. The dreadnought *Courbet*, used as a breakwater at Normandy, was broken up in situ, while her sister ship *Paris* returned to France and to Brest in 1945 after wartime service at Plymouth as an accommodation ship: she slowly deteriorated as a result of lack of use and was finally stricken on 21 December 1955 and scrapped in 1956.

The three *Bretagne*-class battleships had very different wars. The nameship, sunk by British warships at Mers-el-Kebir on 3 July 1940, was salvaged in 1952 and broken up. The *Provence* was scuttled at Toulon on 27 November 1942 but was raised and stripped by the Germans, who scuttled her as a blockship in August 1944: she was salvaged in April 1949 and broken up. The *Lorraine*, interned by the British at Alexandria in 1940 but taken over by Free French forces in 1943, was used as a target ship between 1945 and February 1953, when she was finally listed for disposal: she was scrapped after January 1954. The *Strasbourg* seemed intent on combining the record of the *Provence*, *Lorraine* and the *Condorcet*. She was scuttled at Toulon in November 1942 but raised by the Italians in 1943, only to be sunk in the bombing raid of 18 August 1944 and salvaged for a second time in 1945. Thereafter she was used as a trials ship, actually an experimental hulk, until sold for scrapping in May 1955. Her sister ship, the *Dunkerque*, was scuttled in dry dock in November 1942 at Toulon, and her wreckage was removed in 1945 and was eventually sold for scrap in 1958. The last French ship in this sorry tale was the incomplete *Clemenceau*, which the Germans had intended to use as a blockship at Toulon but which was sunk in the American air raid of 27 August 1944. Salvage work on her did not begin until February 1948 and she was raised by the following September: her scrapping was completed by August 1951.[5] Thus the French were left with just the *Richelieu* in service in 1945 when, with the end of the Japanese war, she was involved in the French attempt to re-occupy the former colony of Indo-China. Her sister ship, the *Jean Bart*, was completed in time to serve as a fire support ship at Suez in 1956 though she never fired her main armament.

The fate of Italian battleships was inversely related to their value, and the details of their fate have become somewhat obscure with the passing of time. The *Vittorio Veneto* and the *Italia* (ex-*Littorio*), having surrendered in September 1943, were interned in the Suez canal, the *Vittorio Veneto* until October 1946 and the *Italia* until February 1947, whereupon they were allowed to return to Augusta. Under the terms of the treaty ending the war, the *Italia* was allocated to the United States and the *Vittorio Veneto* to Britain. These two countries returned the ships to Italy on condition they were scrapped. Both ships were decommissioned and stricken in the course of 1948 and thereafter broken up at La Spezia. Their would-be sister ship, the incomplete *Impero*, had been at Trieste and used by the Germans as a target after September 1943, and she was then sunk in the American air raid of 20 February 1945. She was raised and then beached outside Venice where she was broken up. The *Andrea Doria* and *Caio Duilio* were returned to the Italian Navy, which retained them as training ships after 1947: in fact the two ships alternated with one another as flagship of the service until 1953, when they were placed in reserve. The *Caio Duilio* was stricken on 15 September 1956, the *Andrea Doria* on 1 November, and both ships were scrapped thereafter at La Spezia. With the *Guilio Cesare* assigned to the Soviet Union, the only other battleship on Italian strength was the *Cavour*, which had been sunk twice, the second time at Trieste. She was raised in 1947 and then scrapped between 1950 and 1952. In effect, therefore, Italy ceased to deploy operational battleships from the middle part of the 1950s.[6]

In the South American navies, the dreadnoughts that had been secured before or immediately after the First World War continued in service until the 1950s, when all were sold and scrapped. In the case of all five warships, as advancing years found them out, their service was more nominal than real. Brazil's two battleships, the *Minas Gerais* and *São Paulo*, were the first to depart. The *São Paulo* served after November 1942 as guardship at Recife, but was decommissioned in the course of 1946 and then stricken on 2 August 1947. She was not listed for disposal until July 1951 but was sold in the following month to a British ship-breaking firm, and on 20 September was taken under tow for British waters. On the night of 4–5 November 1951 when she was 150 miles north of the Azores, her tow parted and the ship, along with the eight men aboard her, was never seen again. The *Minas Gerais* served during the Second World War as guardship at Salvador and continued in service until 16 May 1952, when she was decommissioned, though perversely, and no doubt because she was the only remaining battleship in the navy, she remained the commander's flagship until December. Stricken on the last day of 1952, she was sold to Azienda, the breaking firm at Genoa, during 1953 and on 1 March 1954 she sailed under tow for Genoa, arriving on 22 April: thereafter she was broken up.[7] Argentina's *Moreno* remained in active service until 1949, from which time she, too, was left at Puerto Belgrano (below Bahia Blanca) but as an accommodation and administrative base ship. After 1955 she was used temporarily as a prison ship, and was stricken on 1 October 1956. She was sold for scrap on 11 January 1957, and on 12 May 1957 was taken from Puerto Belgrano under tow on what was at the time, via the Panama Canal and the Hawaiian Islands to Yawata, the longest tow ever undertaken. The story of her sister ship, the *Rivadavia*, was similar. She was in effect abandoned at Puerto Belgrano after 1948, though it was not until 1952 that she had lost her armament: between 1952 and 1956 she was stripped of most of her remaining equipment and was stricken on 1 February 1957. She was sold to Azienda, at Genoa, on 30 May 1957, and on 3 April 1959 was taken from Puerto Belgrano under tow, arriving at Savona on 23 May.[8] Chile's *Almirante Latorre* was the last of the South American battleships to be scrapped. Perhaps in the best condition of all these battleships in 1941, she, along with several destroyers, is supposed to have been the target of an American attempt to purchase in the aftermath of the Japanese attack on Pearl Harbor, but this effort came to nothing and the battleship continued in service until a nasty engine room accident in 1951, the result of progressive corrosion which itself was the result of age, provided an intimation of mortality. By the 1950s she had been in effect abandoned, having been reduced to the status of oil storage tank in the port of Talcahuano, but on 1 August 1958 she was accorded full honours when she was paid off. She was sold for scrap to Mitsubishi Heavy Industries on 25 August and sailed under tow from Talcahuano on 29 May 1959. After calling at Callao, in Peru, and the Hawaiian Islands, she arrived at Yokohama on 30 August 1959, and thereafter was scrapped.[9]

As far as the lesser navies were concerned, the passing of these five dreadnoughts left just the Turkish navy's *Yavuz* in existence, and she was destined to be the last dreadnought in existence outside the United States. Spain had possessed three dreadnoughts at the end of the First World War, but one, the *España*, was wrecked in a storm on 20 August 1923 off the Moroccan coast during service in the Riff war: her guns were salvaged and thereafter she was broken up where she lay. Spain's remaining two battleships divided between government and rebel forces during the Spanish civil war (1936–1939). The new *España*, formerly the *Alfonso XIII*, fought for the nationalist forces but was mined and sunk off Santander on 30 April 1937: the *Jaime I*, which fought for the republican forces, was badly damaged by aircraft before being massively damaged by an internal explosion at Cartagena on 17 June 1937. Thereafter laid up, she was scrapped in 1939 with the end of the civil war. The declared intention of the victorious nationalists to build 35,000-ton battleships with 15-in/380-mm guns, given the wrecked state of the Spanish ship-building industry, was quite incapable of realisation.[10] The old German battlecruiser *Goeben*, therefore, was the only battleship held by any state that was not caught up in the second European war. At the end of the first, on 1 November 1918 to be exact and after Turkey had signed the armistice that ended her involvement in that war, she had been formally handed over to Turkey by her German crew. She remained at Izmit and in reserve for much of the 1920s, the Allied powers foregoing their opportunity to demand her surrender and the state of Turkish national finances precluding proper maintenance and repair before 1926. In a German-supplied floating dock, with French help and at Gölcük on the bay opposite Izmit, the *Yavuz Sultan Selim* was subjected to comprehensive refit between 1927 and 1930. She remained in service, being renamed *Yavuz* in 1936, until 1938, when she was afforded another refit, and she remained in service until 1948, when she was laid up at Gölcük. She was decommissioned on 20 December 1950 and was stricken, almost four years later, on 14 November 1954. With nothing done to ensure her disposal and scrapping, she was the subject of a West German offer to repurchase in 1963 but this endeavour was allowed to quietly die. She was finally sold in 1971 but remained at her berth until 7 June 1973 when, with full honours which were not her due because she was no longer in service but which were nonetheless thoroughly appropriate, she was towed from her berth for scrapping, a process which was completed in 1976.[11]

There thus remain, from the list of states with capital ships at the end of the Second World War, only the two great powers that measured themselves against one another as the Cold War ushered in conflict by other means. In 1945 these two powers, the Soviet Union and the United States, were in terms of naval strength as mismatched as they were in terms of national power, though two points, both obvious, need be acknowledged at the outset of any examination of their naval relationship. The first, on the Soviet side, is that the Soviet and Russian states had always aspired to a measure of sea power and, indeed, Russia historically had been a major naval power since the time of Peter the Great. The Soviet move after 1945 to acquire a measure of sea power, therefore, formed part of an established historical pattern, though its emphasis, on submarines, was perhaps somewhat different from what might have been expected. There was absolutely no point in seeking some measure of sea power in terms of capital ships and aircraft carriers: given the over-whelming American superiority of numbers in these types of warship, at the end of the Second World War there was not the slightest possibility of the Soviet Union acquiring any genuine blue-water capability in the foreseeable future. The second, on the American side, is the exact reverse of this situation, namely inevitable and massive reduction from the levels of strength that were available in 1945. In mid-1945, the U.S. Navy numbered some 3,400,000 personnel, and had a total of some 5,200 warships, submarines, amphibious ships and craft, and auxiliaries, and of this total about 1,200 units were major fleet units. It had some 40,000 aircraft on establishment and, of course, it had a Marine Corps of about 475,000 officers and men. On 30 June 1950, the U.S. Navy had on establishment 381,538 officers and men. The fleet strength was 237 warships, with some 4,300 aircraft: the U.S. 7th Fleet, in the western Pacific, consisted of just one carrier, one heavy cruiser, eight destroyers and four submarines, plus a number of auxiliaries, and the full measure of reductions had yet to work their course: in August 1949, the U.S. Navy, which had just eight aircraft carriers in service, was ordered to reduce this total to four.[12]

Against such backgrounds, which in a sense converged since they spelt a reduction of American naval defence capability at a time when deterrence not defence came to the forefront of national policy, the Soviet attempt to build two battlecruisers makes some sort of sense, though in the wider context any attempt to build capital ships after 1945 really made little or no sense at all. As it was, the laying down of the *Stalingrad* in 1951 and *Moskva* in October 1952 seems to have been more the product of Stalin's lack of realism than any serious consideration, the construction of these two ships being abandoned at some time in the 1950s. Apparently the two ships, which supposedly were derivations of the *Kronstadt*-class large cruisers which had been laid down in 1939, were to have had a 40,000-ton full load displacement, machinery with 212,000 hp and 33 knots, and an armament of six 12-in/305-mm guns and, interestingly, one or two missile launchers, the two ships having been earmarked to carry surface-to-surface missiles.

On the American side, the end of a global war meant that the battleships were very quickly divided between five categories and their fates assigned accordingly. The first category was the collection of the ill-assorted. The *Oklahoma*, which had been sunk at Pearl Harbor on 7 December 1941 and been salvaged, was assigned for scrapping but, as noted earlier, broke her tow en route to the breakers and sank on 15 May 1947. The *Arizona*, sunk at the same time as the *Oklahoma*, was left where she had come to rest. Certain parts, most obviously turrets and guns, were recovered, but she was dedicated as a memorial at Pearl Harbor on 30 June 1962: she was never decommissioned or stricken, and thus is afforded the full courtesies that her service demands. The *Texas* found herself involved in trooping in the Pacific until 26 February 1946, when she was decommissioned and passed into the reserve at Baltimore. In 1948 she given to the state of Texas, and towed to San Jacinto state park, where she was formally decommissioned on 21 April 1948 and stricken nine days later. The gunnery training ship *Wyoming*, which during the Second World War probably fired as many shells as most of the other battleships put together, was stricken in September 1947 and then scrapped in New Jersey in 1948.

The second group of American battleships were the *Arkansas*, *New York*, *Nevada* and the *Pennsylvania*. These four battleships were assigned as target ships in the atomic bomb tests that were held in July 1946. The *Arkansas* sank on 25 July 1946 after the second test, but the *New York* and *Nevada* both survived the full programme and were towed back to Pearl Harbor, where they were decommissioned but found to be too radioactive to be scrapped. Both were used as target ships and were sunk off Oahu in July 1948. The *Pennsylvania*, much younger than the other three, was included in this group because she had been torpedoed and had incurred serious damage off Okinawa on 12 August 1945. She had three shafts damaged and only with difficulty was she saved from sinking, but she was towed to Guam for temporary repairs and on 4 October she sailed for Puget Sound navy yard on one shaft. She survived the Bikini tests, and thereafter was towed to Kwajalein and decommissioned on 29 August 1946. There she was used as target ship and was sunk on 10 February 1948.

The third group consisted of the *Mississippi, Idaho* and the *New Mexico,* the *California* and *Tennessee,* and the *Colorado, Maryland* and the *West Virginia.* The battleships of these three classes had very similar fates. The first three were all in Tokyo Bay on 2 September 1945 and four days later sailed for the Norfolk navy yard. The *Idaho* and *New Mexico* arrived on 16 and 17 October 1945 respectively, and were decommissioned in July 1946. The *Idaho* was stricken on 16 September 1946, the *New Mexico* on 25 February 1947. The *New Mexico* was sold for scrap on 13 October 1947 and arrived at Newark on 24 November: her sister ship was sold for scrap on 24 November and arrived at Newark on 12 December 1947. The *Mississippi* arrived at Norfolk navy yard on 27 November 1945 and was immediately taken in hand for conversion to gunnery tender and test ship. She returned to service in these capacities in July 1947 and remained in service until decommissioned on 17 September 1956: she was sold for scrap on 28 November and was towed out for scrapping on 7 December. The *California* and *Tennessee* were involved with occupation duties in Japan until October 1945 when both sailed for Philadelphia navy yard, arriving on 7 December. Both were decommissioned and then on 7 August 1946 placed in reserve. They were finally paid off on 14 February 1947 and stricken on 1 March 1959. They were both sold for scrap to Bethlehem Steel on 10 July 1959 and were broken up at Baltimore. The *Colorado, Maryland* and the *West Virginia,* though the end of hostilities found them very differently engaged, were all committed to trooping in the Pacific, after which they were passed into the reserve at Bremerton navy yard. The *Colorado* and *West Virginia* were paid off in January 1947, the *Maryland* in April 1947. All three were stricken on 1 March 1959 and were then sold for scrap in the summer of 1959. The *Colorado* was broken up at the Todd Shipyard at Seattle after July 1959, the *West Virginia* after January 1961: the *Maryland* was scrapped at the Todd Shipyard at San Pedro after August 1959.

The two members of the *North Carolina* class and four members of the *South Dakota* class formed the fourth group of battleships, all of which remained in service into 1947. After fifteen years in reserve, the latter were stricken on 1 June 1962. The *South Dakota* was scrapped after October 1962, certain of her parts being kept by the state of South Dakota as a war memorial at Sioux Falls, and the *Indiana* was scrapped at Richmond, California, after December 1963, her mast being kept at Bloomington and certain of her other parts being held at museums and schools throughout the state. The *Alabama* was sold to the state of Alabama and left Bremerton under tow on 2 July 1964 for Mobile: the *Massachusetts* was formally transferred in June 1965 to the state of Massachusetts in order to become a war memorial in the Fall River.

Somewhat strangely, the *Alabama*'s engines were removed and her guns were plugged with concrete when she left the federal service: presumably the U.S. Navy was fearful that she might be used to try to reverse the verdict of the battle fought on the only previous occasion when Mobile had played an important part in national affairs. The *North Carolina* and *Washington* were used to return troops from Europe before being decommissioned and put in the reserve at Bayonne, New Jersey, from 27 June 1947. Both were stricken on 1 June 1960, the *Washington* being sold for scrap on 24 May 1961 and the *North Carolina* being purchased by the state of North Carolina and formally dedicated as a war memorial at Wilmington on 3 October 1961.

Both classes were the subject of a design study ordered in July 1954, the basic idea being that the top speed of the members of these classes should be about 31 knots in order that they might better work with carriers. Given that the main armament was considered to be considerably in excess of operational requirements, it was proposed that the after turret be suppressed, the hull and the whole of the after section thus being provided with the volume needed for extra machinery. The problem, however, was that the 115,000 shp power plants in the *North Carolina* and *South Dakota* classes would have to be increased to 240,000 shp, or to 215,000 shp if the main belt armour was removed. The difficulty here was that the extra power would necessitate larger propellers, which in turn would necessitate various changes to shafts, rudders and hull, *et al*. The sum of these changes rendered the proposed change more or less impractical, and with the cost of the various modifications estimated at $40,000,000 per ship, the design study was abandoned in September 1954.

That left just the fifth group, the four members of the *Iowa* class. These four battleships were to be different from the other American battleships in that all of them remained in service after 1945. They were reduced to training ship status and three were to be paid off into the reserve in 1948 or 1949, these therefore becoming the only American battleships ever to be recommissioned. One battleship, the *Missouri*, which was sent to Turkish waters in the spring of 1946 to demonstrate American interest in the eastern Mediterranean at a time of mounting Soviet pressure on Turkey, was not reduced to the reserve in this period between 1945 and 1949, and indeed in 1949–1950 was the only battleship in American service. Naturally, therefore, in September 1950 she was to be the first battleship to serve in Korean waters (September 1950 to March 1951 and October 1952 to April 1953). Her three sister ships were recommissioned and served in this conflict, the *New Jersey* (May to November 1951 and April to October 1953) completed two tours and the *Wisconsin* (November 1951 to March 1952) and *Iowa* (April to October 1952) single tours.

The Korean conflict gave the battleships of the *Iowa* class a new lease of life: the battleship could provide a weight of firepower in support of ground forces that aircraft from carriers could not very easily match. The problem for the battleship, however, was that with the end of the Korean war it was immediately involved in a renewed competition for manpower and financial resources even at a time when new carriers were being built at the rate of one a year, new supersonic aircraft were being ordered, and new missiles were being acquired. Nuclear propulsion made its appearance in 1952 when the keel of the submarine *Nautilus* was laid down. The result was that after the *Iowa*-class battleships returned to American waters after the Korean war and were afforded refits and overhauls before being assigned to training duties, all were paid off into the reserve between 1955 and 1958. The *Missouri*, perhaps fittingly, was the first to go. She was decommissioned and placed in the Pacific Fleet reserve at Puget Sound navy yard, Bremerton, Washington, on 26 February 1955. The *New Jersey*, which had been placed in reserve at Bayonne, New Jersey, after June 1948, found herself back there, with similar status, after 21 August 1957 though she was subsequently towed to the Philadelphia navy yard. The *Iowa* began the process of reduction to the reserve at the Philadelphia navy yard in October 1957 and was decommissioned on 24 February 1958, while the *Wisconsin*, like the *New Jersey*, was decommissioned and berthed at Bayonne, New Jersey, on 8 March 1958, and was subsequently towed to the Philadelphia navy yard, where she was laid up.[13]

Thus, for the first time since 1895, the U.S. Navy thereafter had no battleship in service, and the passing of the four *Iowa*-class battleships from service more or less coincided with the British and French navies ridding themselves of a type of warship which, with limited manpower resources, had become a prohibitively expensive luxury, and which, in the austerity of the post-war years, simply could not be afforded. For the British, the four surviving members of the *King George V* class shared a common fate, more or less the same in terms of timing and employment. All returned from duty in the Far East, whether in the Indian or the Pacific Ocean, in the course of 1946 and, after refit, found employment in the training squadron until 1949 when, after refitting, they passed into the reserve and then were laid up in the Clyde. None were ever recommissioned, and on 30 April 1957 all were listed for disposal. The *Anson* arrived at Faslane for breaking up in December 1957, and in 1958 the *King George V* at Dalmuir and Troon, the *Duke of York* at Faslane and the *Howe* at Inverkeithing were scrapped. Why one of these four was not retained as a memorial or a naval museum is not clear: if there were pressing reasons for scrapping the earlier battleships one decade earlier, there seems to have been no good political, financial or any other reason why one could not have been retained: the only battleship that survived these, the *Vanguard*, had never served in the Second World War and thus had no good reason to be retained. As it was, she was retained as flagship of the Home Fleet until 1954 when she was refitted: she was placed in reserve in March 1956 at Plymouth, where she remained until listed for disposal in June 1960. Following the *Anson* and *Duke of York*, she was scrapped at Faslane after August 1960.[14]

In the French Navy, after five years as a gunnery training ship, the *Richelieu* was reclassified in 1956 as an accommodation ship, and was placed in reserve at Brest on 1 August 1958. She was not stricken until December 1967 and was sold for scrap, leaving Brest under tow for the breaker's yard at Genoa in August 1968. The *Jean Bart* briefly took on the role of gunnery training ship – the two ships were in company for the only time for a matter of hours on 31 January 1956 – before she was placed in reserve on 1 August 1957: she nonetheless continued to operate as the gunnery school tender until 1961 and was used as an accommodation ship until 1969. Despite there having been talk of her being retained as a museum, funds for such an enterprise were not forthcoming and she was stricken on 15 June 1970: she left Toulon on 24 June 1970 to be scrapped in Japan.[15]

The story of the dreadnought battleship might well have ended here, in the second half of the 1950s, because, logically, here was the combination of decisions and facts that together spelt *finis*. Perversely, however, American involvement in another Asian war meant that the *New Jersey* was recalled to service because she could provide the heavy fire support to forces ashore that was deemed so important in 1967. All four *Iowa*-class battleships were considered for re-activation, but in the event the *Iowa* herself was deemed less suitable than the *New Jersey* because of her dated electronics systems, which would have to be replaced; the *Missouri* had the most hours under way of all the four battleships and there were fears that she might be found out by defects that were the result of an accidental grounding in 1950; and the *Wisconsin* had been damaged by a small fire during the period when she was being laid up. The best that can be said about some of these reasons relating to the *Missouri* and *Wisconsin* is that they are less than convincing: whatever damage the *Missouri* had sustained in 1950 had not manifested itself during her tours of duty in the Korean war, while the *Wisconsin*'s fire was so minor that repairs were not effected at the time, and presumably they could have been carried out with little real difficulty.

Nonetheless, the *New Jersey* did have two marked advantages over her sister ships: her general condition was better than theirs and, unlike the other three ships of the class, she had been re-gunned prior to being laid up in 1957. The decision to proceed with just the one battleship had one very great advantage in that the *Iowa* and *Wisconsin* were thus made available for cannibalisation, the proviso being that whatever they made available to the *New Jersey* to speed her on her way had to be replaced. Given the changes of industrial production over the previous twenty years, this was no mean task, but while these and various new electronic systems were worked into the *New Jersey* there was one provision that the United States could not fill. One of the little-known facts about the *New Jersey*'s return to service was that there was no one in the U.S. Navy of the appropriate rank who knew how the fire control systems worked, and her gunnery officer, both for the time when she was being recommissioned and then in the four-month period in 1968–1969 when she served in south-east Asia, was loaned from the Royal Navy. Equally little-known is the fact that while she was in south-east Asia her targets were seldom to be found in Vietnam. The standard reference books indicate that she fired some 10,000 shells, and that this total included 3,229 16-in/406-mm shells. In fact, she used 14-in/356-mm sub-calibre rocket-assisted projectiles, and given these had a range of more than 90 miles/150 kilometres, her targets were to be found, as often as not, in Laos, chasing North Vietnamese units and formations down the Ho Chi Minh Trail with fire directed by aircraft.

The *New Jersey* left south-east Asia in April 1969 for overhaul, it being the intention that she would return for a second tour of duty. In the event, however, in the wake of the Tet offensive the Nixon administration chose not to commit her a second time to this fray and she was once more retired, on this occasion at the Puget Sound navy yard on 17 December 1969. Again, however, this was not to be the end of the story because, less than ten years later, steps were taken that resulted in all four members of the class, which could not be readied for something as urgent as the Vietnam war, being returned to service.

The immediate context for so unlikely a development was the difficult years of the Carter administration (1977–1981). This was the period when, in the aftermath of SALT I and American concession of the principle of superpower status to the Soviet Union, American power was in retreat: in the 1970s the Soviet Union was seen to possess a genuine global reach, most obviously in supporting client states in Angola and on the Horn of Africa, and the Soviet Navy seemed to acquire a real blue-water capability. This was a time which, in the aftermath of the collapse of South Vietnam and the fall of Saigon (April 1975), also saw the collapse of the imperial regime in Iran (January 1979), the seizure of the American embassy in Tehran (November 1979) and then the Soviet invasion of Afghanistan (December 1979). It was a period of American disarray, not least because of the aftermath of the resignation of Nixon and the apparent enfeeblement of government in the United States. It was also one of block obsolescence for the U.S. Navy, when a host of warships ranging from carriers to destroyers that had first seen service in the Second World War either had to be assigned the status of target ships or directed to the ship-breakers.

The Carter administration seemed wholly incapable of responding to the challenges it faced, and so the U.S. Congress took it upon itself to add to programmes the provision for the return of the *Iowa*-class battleships to service in an Aegis capacity, as if the return to service of warships that were the very symbols of American national greatness would somehow halt the current march of events. The Carter administration blocked this particular provision but, somewhat unfortunately, Jimmy Carter's opponent in the 1980 presidential election, Ronald Reagan, seemed to believe at least some of this hyperbole. He, however, had no problems in winning the 1980 election: the margin of victory in the electoral college was one of the greatest ever recorded, though in terms of popular vote Reagan barely polled a majority, being less than two points ahead of all the other presidential candidates combined.

In the eight years of the Reagan presidency the United States found itself committed to a 600-ship navy and a return of all four *Iowa*-class battleships to service: the doubling of the national debt in these same years was afforded less coverage and public attention. Scarcely better heeded were the ostensible reasons for returning these ships to service, there being two. The first was the alleged vulnerability of carriers during operations, and the protection that the battleship would be able to afford them, but since no carrier had been sunk, or even imperilled, by enemy action since 1945, the logic of this particular argument is somewhat hard to discern, not least because it is very difficult to see what protection a battleship would be able to afford a carrier that the carrier could not provide for itself in the event of serious attack: what remains ironic about this whole question is that during the 1991 Gulf campaign a British destroyer shot down a Silkworm aimed at the *Missouri*, when by rights she should never have been in need of such care and attention. The second reason was the value of the battleship as a platform for concentrated missile systems, specifically the BGM-109 Tomahawk cruise missile and the RGM-84 Harpoon anti-ship missiles. Whatever the merits of this particular argument – and it is worth noting that *Arleigh Burke*-class destroyers could embark more missiles than a battleship and that American cruisers could carry twice as many missiles as a destroyer – the necessary approval from Congress was immediately forthcoming and so the U.S. Navy then had two problems, namely the order in which the four battleships were to be brought back into service and providing the necessary manpower for the ships. There was also the additional problem of persuading Bremerton to part with the *Missouri*, which had become one of the city's main tourist attractions.

The condition of the *Missouri* and *New Jersey* was remarkably good, that of the *Iowa* and *Wisconsin* less so but still within very reasonable limits: in any event, their advancing years, and their increasing obsolescence, paradoxically had saved them from the cannibalisation which might have rendered them past recall. There were different problems with different ships but rewiring and the presence of asbestos were common to all, as was the provision of electronic systems at various levels clear of blast from guns and missiles. In final form, and with due allowance for minor individual variations, the old and the new Iowa-class battleships were characterised thus:

THE *IOWA*-CLASS BATTLESHIPS 1945

Standard Displacement:	45,000 tons.	
Full Load Displacement:	*Iowa* and *New Jersey*	*Missouri* and *Wisconsin*
	57,450 tons.	57,216 tons.
Armament:	Nine 16-in/406-mm 50 calibre,	
	twenty 5-in/127-mm 38 calibre,	
	twenty quadruple and forty-nine other 20-mm AA guns.	
Aircraft:	Three or four aircraft, two catapults.	

THE *IOWA*-CLASS BATTLESHIPS 1985

Standard Displacement:	45,280 tons.
Full Load Displacement:	*Iowa*
	57,256 tons.
Armament:	Nine 16-in/406-mm 50 calibre,
	twelve 5-in/127-mm 38 calibre,
	Thirty-two (8 x 4) BGM-109 Tomahawk cruise missiles,
	Sixteen (4 x 4) RGM-84 Harpoon anti-ship missiles,
	Four six-barrelled 20-mm 76 calibre Phalanx CIWS.
Helicopters:	Facility to land and refuel but not re-arm.

In their revised state, the four battleships each carried two sets of radars for the main 16-in/406-mm armament and two sets of radars for the 5-in/127-mm guns. There was also one weapons-control system for the Tomahawks and there were two for the Harpoons, as well as an automated signal processing and active jammer, an IFF (Identification Friend or Foe) system plus an air search radar and two surface search radars. The battleships also had two Combat Information Centers though the one located in the superstructure had been renamed the Combat Engagement Center: there was a deliberate redundancy built into the battleships that enabled the original CIC to continue to function, if only in being able to direct gunfire, in the event of the new centre being destroyed.

The first of the battleships to return to service were the *New Jersey* and *Iowa*. Fitted out at the Long Beach navy yard, the *New Jersey* was recommissioned on 28 December 1982: with unconscious irony, the *Iowa* was towed from the Philadelphia navy yard to Avondale Shipyards, in Louisiana, for reactivation, and after her modernisation programme was recommissioned on 28 April 1984. The

Missouri did not begin her refitting programmes at Long Beach navy yard until October 1984 and she was not commissioned until 10 May 1986. The *Wisconsin* only just managed to return to service during the Reagan years, and her return was marked with all sorts of difficulties with her decks, which had rotted badly during her period in reserve. It was not until 22 October 1988 that she was recommissioned, and then she needed the best part of a year to iron out various other problems with air conditioning and feed pumps. By the time that she was readied for operations, the *Iowa*, which on 19 April 1989 had suffered an accidental explosion in her second turret which killed 47 of her crew, was a year from being returned to the reserve.

Despite what was claimed at the time, the experience of the refurbished *Iowa*-class battleships was not particularly auspicious. Many of the problems centred upon their employment in the Middle East, most notably in the bombardment of Syrian artillery positions near Beirut by the *New Jersey* in 1982. The propellant was old and of very variable quality, the result being that no one could tell whether a salvo, despite its being fed correct range, would fall short, be massively over or, by chance, hit the target. Basically it took newly manufactured propellant to stabilise fire, but throughout their period in service, and for all their impressiveness in terms of appearance, the battleships were beset by two increasingly serious, and indeed insoluble, problems.

The first problem, simply, was that American industry was no longer capable of providing the spare parts and equipment essential to the health and well-being of these ships. Just as in 1990 the U.S. Navy had to deal with nine foreign states in order to ready itself for a war with Iraq, a situation that would have been unthinkable even twenty or 30 years before, the changing patterns of industrial production meant that maintaining these ships, which were then approaching the fiftieth anniversary of their having laid down, would be increasingly difficult. The second, no less simply, was that the U.S. Navy was increasingly pressed to find 1,653 officers and men for one of these battleships. Such numbers seem slight when compared to the crew of some 6,000 officers and men needed for one of the carriers, but very roughly the battleship's complement was equivalent to the number needed to man eight destroyers. Moreover, by the early 1990s the U.S. Navy was gripped by a growing manpower problem that was itself the product of an increasingly intense operational cycle for ships and manpower. As seagoing time increased, with less time ashore and with families, re-enlistment, on which the U.S. Navy was heavily dependent, declined. In addition, as numbers of ships in service declined, so the need to keep those ships that remained at sea for longer periods increased: the extent of the problem can be understood by the fact that in the second half of the 1990s, as the U.S. Navy noted the lack of building of replacement warships, the problems inherent in trying to keep warships over ten years old in service and the lack of manpower numbers, it could be foreseen that by 2010 the U.S. Navy was certain to shrink below the 200-ship mark, and perhaps have no more than 150 warships and submarines in service. On such numbers, it would only be able to maintain nine carrier groups, and when overhauls and refits, training and time spent moving onto and from station were taken into account, this meant that its real strength, on station, would probably be reduced to no more than two carriers and their groups.

In such circumstances, the retention of the *Iowa*, *Missouri*, *New Jersey* and the *Wisconsin* in service made very little sense, and indeed the process of re-evaluation of these ships had progressed so far even by the end of the Reagan presidency that two of the battleships that had been recommissioned at very considerable cost did not see service in the 1991 Gulf campaign. The *Iowa* was decommissioned on 26 October 1990 at the Norfolk navy yard, and the *New Jersey* was paid off on 8 February 1991 even as the *Wisconsin* and *Missouri* contributed in full to proceedings in the Middle East. The *Wisconsin* fired 24 of her Tomahawk cruise missiles in the first two days of hostilities, the *Missouri* 28 of hers. With some targets between 700 and 800 miles distant, these two battleships, in the last actions ever fought by their kind, demonstrated a reach inland that was unprecedented in terms of direct firepower for a warship, and historically such distances were beyond carriers and their aircraft. It was a remarkable demonstration of unprecedented capability, and it was followed by a series of bombardments after 2 February.[16] After Kuwait City had been liberated, the *Missouri* and *Wisconsin* alternated in the close support role, the *Wisconsin* firing her guns for the last time on 28 February. One month later to the day, she was at Norfolk navy yard, and on 30 September she was paid off at the Philadelphia navy yard. The *Missouri* was to have been paid off at the same time, but she was retained in service in order to be present at the ceremonies that marked the fiftieth anniversary of the Japanese attack on the U.S. Pacific Fleet at Pearl Harbor. It was not until the last day of March 1992 that she was decommissioned at Long Beach navy yard, and was later towed to Puget Sound. All four members of the *Iowa* class were stricken on 12 January 1995, just ten months short of 100 years after the first American battleship, the *Indiana*, entered service. The torch, finally, had been passed from failing hands to those that would keep the faith.[17]

Jutland and the first encounter between the battle fleets

Jellicoe's decision was to form a line of battle by deploying on the eastern column of the fleet in its cruise formation. This order was hoisted in the *Iron Duke*, and given over the radio, at 1814, the divisional flagship, the *King George V*, leading the British battle formation on a course of southeast by east, i.e. around the head of the German line and toward a position between the enemy and his ports. In something like two minutes the British battle formation was transformed from six columns each with four battleships into a single column some six miles in length, and within another minute, at 1817, the *Marlborough* opened fire on the four *Kaiser*-class battleships at the head of the German line. Lest the point be missed, Jellicoe's decision was taken, and the deployment completed, without the enemy having been seen. The British battle force was thus placed across the German line of advance and in a position from which it could inflict maximum damage on the enemy line, but the advantages were set at nought by the High Sea Fleet's *Gefechtskehrtwendung*.

THE HIGH SEA FLEET
3rd Battle Squadron: 5th Battle Division.
The *König, Grosser Kurfürst, Kronprinz* and the *Markgraf.*
3rd Battle Squadron: 6th Battle Division
The *Kaiser, Kaiserin* and the *Prinzregent Luitpold.*
The fleet flagship *Freidrich der Grosse.*
1st Battle Squadron: 1st Battle Division
The *Ostfriesland, Thüringen, Helgoland* and the *Oldenburg.*
1st Battle Squadron: 2nd Battle Division
The *Posen, Rheinland, Nassau* and the *Wesfalen.*
3rd Battle Squadron: 5th Battle Division
The *Deutschland, Hessen* and the *Pommern.*
3rd Battle Squadron: 5th Battle Division.
The *Hannover, Schlesien* and the *Schleswig-Holstein.*

THE BATTLECRUISER FORCE
The *Lützow, Derfflinger, Seydlitz, Moltke* and the *Von der Tann.*

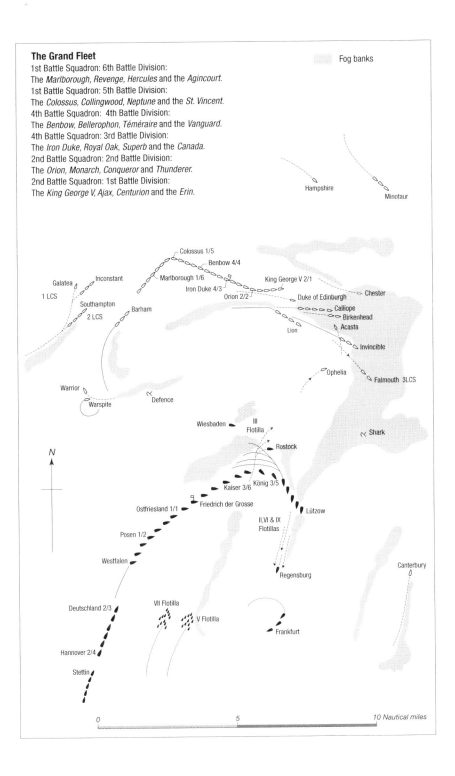

The Grand Fleet
1st Battle Squadron: 6th Battle Division:
The *Marlborough, Revenge, Hercules* and the *Agincourt*.
1st Battle Squadron: 5th Battle Division:
The *Colossus, Collingwood, Neptune* and the *St. Vincent*.
4th Battle Squadron: 4th Battle Division:
The *Benbow, Bellerophon, Téméraire* and the *Vanguard*.
4th Battle Squadron: 3rd Battle Division:
The *Iron Duke, Royal Oak, Superb* and the *Canada*.
2nd Battle Squadron: 2nd Battle Division:
The *Orion, Monarch, Conqueror* and *Thunderer*.
2nd Battle Squadron: 1st Battle Division:
The *King George V, Ajax, Centurion* and the *Erin*.

Fog banks

Hampshire

Minotaur

Colossus 1/5
Benbow 4/4
Galatea
Inconstant
Marlborough 1/6
King George V 2/1
1 LCS
Iron Duke 4/3
Chester
Southampton
Orion 2/2
Duke of Edinburgh
2 LCS
Barham
Calliope
Birkenhead
Lion
Acasta
Invincible

Ophelia
Falmouth 3LCS

Warrior
Defence
Warspite

Wiesbaden
III
Flotilla

Shark

Rostock

N

Kaiser 3/6
König 3/5

Ostfriesland 1/1
Friedrich der Grosse
Lützow

II, VI & IX
Flotillas

Posen 1/2

Canterbury

Westfalen
Regensburg

Deutschland 2/3
VII Flotilla

V Flotilla

Hannover 2/4
Frankfurt

Stettin

0   5   10 Nautical miles

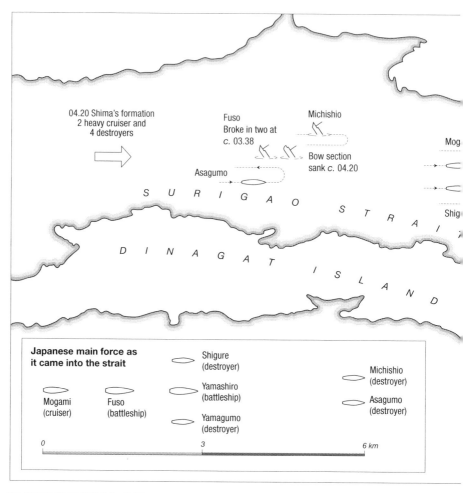

04.20 Shima's formation
2 heavy cruiser and
4 destroyers

Fuso
Broke in two at
c. 03.38

Michishio

Bow section
sank c. 04.20

Mog

Asagumo

S U R I G A O

S T R A I

Shig

D I N A G A T

I S L A N D

**Japanese main force as
it came into the strait**

Shigure
(destroyer)

Yamashiro
(battleship)

Yamagumo
(destroyer)

Mogami
(cruiser)

Fuso
(battleship)

Michishio
(destroyer)

Asagumo
(destroyer)

0   3   6 km

The Surigao Strait, 25 October 1944

The battle of Leyte Gulf was the greatest naval battle in modern history. With the Americans having landed on Leyte on 20 October and their carrier formations in position covering the various assault and support formations, the battle divided into six parts: the preliminary phase that saw Japanese formations approach the Philippines and take losses en route; on 24 October the battle of the Visayan Sea, when the main Japanese battle force lost the *Musashi* as it sought to reach the San Bernardino Strait; on 25 October the Surigao Strait action; the action off Samar between the main Japanese battle force and the escort carrier formations of T.G. 77.4; the action off Cape Engano, which saw the Japanese carrier formation lose every one of its four carriers; and the follow-up actions after 25 October as American air groups, submarines and warships sought to deal with damaged Japanese warships and inflict fresh casualties on the back of comprehensive victory. Between 23 and 28 October 1944 American forces accounted for 32 Japanese warships of 324,891 tons, five naval support ships of 33,883 tons, four military transports of 12,586 tons and eight merchantmen of 45,877 tons in Philippine and immediately adjacent waters.

See pp. 195–201 and Appendix 15.

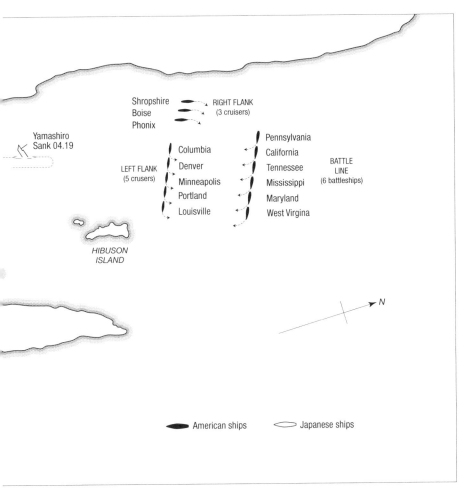

Shropshire — RIGHT FLANK
Boise — (3 cruisers)
Phonix —

Yamashiro
Sank 04.19

Pennsylvania

Columbia   California
LEFT FLANK   Denver   Tennessee   BATTLE
(5 crusers)   Minneapolis   Mississippi   LINE
              Portland   Maryland   (6 battleships)
              Louisville   West Virgina

HIBUSON
ISLAND

N

━━ American ships   ⬭ Japanese ships

THE ACTION

Given notice by aircraft of the Japanese approach, the Americans deployed a battle and two cruiser forces across the mouth, and PT boat and destroyer formations along the sides, of the Surigao Strait.

The PT boats' attacks were easily repulsed but the Allied destroyers registered immediate success. The *Yamagumo* was torpedoed and sank immediately: the *Michishio* was wrecked, but remained afloat, and the *Asagumo*, less her bow, attempted to withdraw (0320). The *Fuso* was hit and withdrawing when she exploded and broke in two (0338).

The *Yamashiro* took a torpedo hit, but continued to come forward in the company of the *Mogami* and *Shigure* and was initially engaged by the cruisers at 0351. The first to fire was the *Louisville* at a range of 15,600 yards: the *Boise* also opened fire at 0351. The battleships joined at 0353: as they did so destroyers moved against the *Asagumo* and *Michishio*. The latter, again hit, sank at 0358.

The main action was over by 0402 when the battleships turned, their manoeuvre complete at 0406: only the *Mississippi* fired after this time, at 0408. The *Yamashiro* staggered from the line under the hammering she took, and capsized and sank at 0419. Astern, the bow of the *Fuso* sank at about 0420.

As the *Mogami* and *Shigure* turned away they ran into the second Japanese formation, the *Mogami*, and heavy cruiser *Nachi*, at 0430. After they were disentangled, the ships withdrew though the *Mogami* and *Asagumo* were sunk the following morning.

NOTE Dates shown against ships represent the year of completion, other than for British destroyers, which is the year of launch.

Appendices

Appendix 1
The battleships and battlecruisers of the dreadnought era

	Britain	Germany	United States	Japan
1905	Dreadnought		South Carolina	
	CC Indomitable		Michigan	
	CC Inflexible			
	CC Invincible			
1906	Bellerophon	Nassau	Delaware	
	Superb	Westfalen		
	Téméraire			
1907	Collingwood	Posen	North Dakota	
	St. Vincent	Rheinland		
	Vanguard	CC Von der Tann		
1908	Neptune	Helgoland	Florida	
	CC Indefatigable	Ostfriesland	Utah	
		Thüringen		
		CC Moltke		
1909	Colossus	Oldenburg	Arkansas	
	Hercules	Friedrich der Grosse	Wyoming	
	Conqueror	Kaiser		
	Monarch	CC Goeben		
	Orion			
	Thunderer			
	CC Lion			
	CC Princess Royal			
	CC Australia*			
	CC New Zealand*			
1910	Ajax	Kaiserin	New York	CC Haruna
	Audacious	König Albert	Texas	CC Hiei
	Centurion	Prinzregent Luitpold		CC Kirishima
	King George V	CC Seydlitz		CC Kongo
	CB Queen Mary			
1911	Benbow	König	Nevada	Fuso
	Emperor of India	Markgraf	Oklahoma	
	Iron Duke	Grosser Kurfürst		
	Marlborough	CC Derfflinger		
	CC Tiger			
	Agincourt**			
	Erin**			
	Canada**			
1912	Barham	Kronprinz	Pennsylvania	
	Malaya*	CC Lützow		
	Queen Elizabeth			
	Valiant			
	Warspite			
1913	Ramillies	Baden	Arizona	Yamashiro
	Resolution	Bayern		
	Revenge	CC Hindenburg*		
	Royal Oak			
	Royal Sovereign			

	France	Italy	Russia/Soviet Union	Austria-Hungary
1905				
1906				
1907				
1908				
1909		Dante Alighieri	Gangut	
			Petropavlovsk	
			Poltava	
			Sevastopol	
1910	Courbet	Conte di Cavour		
	France	Guilo Cesare		
	Jean Bart	Leonardo da Vinci		
	Paris			
1911			Imperator Aleksandr III	Prinz Eugen
			Imperatritsa Ekaterina Velikaya	Szent Istvan
			Imperatritsa Mariya	Tegetthoff
				Viribus Unitis
1912	Bretagne	Andrea Doria	Borodino***	
	Lorraine	Caio Duilo	Izmail***	
	Provence		Kinburn***	
			Navarin***	
1913	Béarn***			
	Flandre***			
	Gascogne***			
	Languedoc***			
	Normandie***			

	Britain	Germany	United States	Japan
1914	Repulse***	Sachsen***	Idaho	Hyuga
	Renown***	Württemburg	Mississippi	Ise
	Resistance	CB Mackensen	New Mexico	
	CC Repulse			
	CC Renown			
	CC Courageous			
	CC Glorious			
1915	CC Furious	Prinz Eitel Friedrich***	California	
		Graf Spee***	Tennessee	
		Fürst Bismarck***	Colorado	
		Yorck***	Maryland	
		Gneisenau***	West Virginia	
		Scharnhorst***	Washington***	
1916	CC Hood		Indiana***	Mutsu
	CC Anson***		Montana***	Nagato
	CC Howe***		South Dakota***	
	CC Rodney***		Iowa***	
			Massachusetts***	
			North Carolina***	
			CC Constellation***	
			CC Constitution***	
			CC Lexington***	
			CC Ranger***	
			CC Saratoga***	
			CC Unnamed unit***	

1917 No shipbuilding

1918				Kaga****
				Tosa***
				CB Akagi****
				CB Amagi***
				CB Atago***
				CB Takao***

1919 – 1920 No shipbuilding

1921				K.2***
				Owari plus
				two more units***
1922	Nelson			Four units planned***
	Rodney			

1923 – 1930 No shipbuilding

1931

1932 – 1933 No shipbuilding

1934		Scharnhorst		
		Gneisenau		
1935				
1936	Anson	Bismarck	North Carolina	
	Duke of York	Tirpitz	Washington	
	Howe		Indiana	
	King George V		South Dakota	
	Prince of Wales			
1937				Yamato
1938	Lion***			Musashi
	Téméraire***			

	France	Italy	Russia/Soviet Union	Austria-Hungary
1914	Lille***	Francesco Caracciolo***	Imperator Nikolai I	Budapest***
	Lyon***	Cristofor Colombo***		Hapsburg***
		Marcantonio Colonna***		Monarch***
		Francesco Morosimi***		Wien***
1915	Dunkerque***			
	Tourville***			
1916				
1918				
1921				
1922				
1931	Dunkerque			
1934	Strasbourg	Littorio		
		Vittorio Veneto		
1935	Richelieu			
1936	Jean Bart			
1937				
1938		Impero***	Sovetskii Soyuz***	
		Roma	Sovetskaya Ukraina***	
			CB Kronstadt***	

	Britain	Germany	United States	Japan
1939	*Conqueror****	*Friedrich der Grosse****	*Alabama*	
	Thunderer***	*Gross Deutschland****	*Massachusetts*	
		CC Unit Q***		
1940	*Vanguard*		*Iowa*	*Shinano*
			Missouri	Unit 111
			New Jersey	
			Wisconsin	
			Illinois***	
			Kentucky***	
			Louisiana***	
			Maine***	
			Montana***	
			New Hampshire***	
			Ohio***	
			CB *Alaska*	
			CB *Guam*	
			CB *Hawaii****	
			CB *Philippines****	
			CB *Puerto Rico****	
			CB *Samoa****	
1941 – 1948 No shipbuilding				
1949				

IN ADDITION TO THE SHIPS LAID DOWN BY THE MAJOR NAVAL POWERS, THE FOLLOWING UNITS WERE ORDERED BY OTHER NAVIES

	Greece	Spain	Turkey	Argentina
1906				
1907 – 1908 No shipbuilding				
1909		*Alfonso Trice*		
		España		
		Jaime Primero		
1910				*Moreno*
				Rivadavia
1911			*Reshadieh***	
			Sultan Osman I**	
1912	*Salamis****			
1913 No shipbuilding				
1914				

*   Denotes ships built by Britain for service under British operational control but funded by the Dominion and colony after which the ship was named.

**   On the outbreak of war in 1914 Britain requisitioned three battleships then nearing completion in British yards:
the *Reshadieh, Sultan Osman I* and *Almirante Latorre* entered British service as the *Erin, Agincourt* and *Canada* respectively.

***   Ships planned but never completed.

**** Ships completed as aircraft carriers.

CB = Large cruiser

CC = Battlecruiser

All other ships are battleships.

	France	Italy	Russia/Soviet Union	Austria-Hungary
1939	*Clemenceau****		CB *Sevastopol****	
	Gascoigne***			
1940			*Sovetskaya Rossiya****	
			Sovetskaya Belorossiya***	
1949			CB *Moskva****	
			CB *Stalingrad****	

	Brazil	Chile
1906	*Minas Gerais*	
	São Paulo	
1909		
1910	*Rio de Janeiro****	
1911		*Almirante Latorre***
		Almirante Cochrane
1912		
1914	*Riachuelo****	

Appendix 2
The dreadnought designs, 1904–1905

	Design A	Design B	Design C	Design D	Design D1/ Design D2	Design E	Design F	Design G	Design H	
Length	460-ft	425-ft	410-ft	520-ft	500-ft	550-ft	530-ft	550-ft	490-ft	500-ft
Beam	81.5-ft	82.6-ft	83-ft	84-ft	84-ft	85-ft	82-ft	85-ft	83-ft	84-ft
Draught	25.5-ft			27.25-ft	27.25-ft	26.75-ft	26-ft	27-ft	26.5-ft	
Displacement:										
turbines	16,500	15,350	14,700		18,500				17,850	
reciprocating	16,000	15,750	15,000	19,000		21,000	19,000(?)	21,000		18,670
Weights in tons:										
Hull	5,800			6,450	6,250	6,540	6,100		6,150	6,350
armour	4,275			4,875	4,700	6,400	5,620		5,000	5,200
machinery	2,150			2,200	1,700	2,500	2,300		1,700	2,400
armament	2,615			3,775	3,775	3,860	3,280		3,300	3,300
various	560			600	575	600	600		600	600
coal	900			900		900	900		900	900
margin	200			200	100	200	200		100	100
Engine type				RCPTG	Turbines	RCPTG	RCPTG (?)	RCPTG	Turbines	RCPTG
Horse power	23,000			23,500	23,000	27,500	25,000		23,000	23,500
Maximum speed	21 knots	20 knots	19 knots	21 knots	21 knots	21 knots	21 knots	21 knots	21 knots	
Armament: guns	Eight 12-in 35 x 12- and 3-pdr guns	Eight 12-in	Eight 12-in	12 x 12-in 35 x 12- and 3-pdr guns	12 x 12-in 35 x 12- and 3-pdr guns	12 x 12-in 16 x 4-in guns	10 x 12-in 16 x 4-in guns	12 x 12-in	10 x 12-in 14 x 4-in guns	
Torpedo tubes	None			Five	Five	Six	Six		?	

Designs A, B and C catered for three different layouts, one with two turrets fore and two turrets aft superimposed and on centre line, one with single turrets forward and aft on centre line and two turrets paired amidship on either beam and one as the second but with the paired turrets staggered *en echelon*. Which design went with which letter is not known.

Designs D1 and D2 envisaged single turrets forward and aft on centre line and the remaining four turrets in two pairs on the beam. The difference between the designs was that in D2 these paired turrets were farther apart than in D1. In layout, D and D2 were more or less the same.

Designs E and F envisaged superimposed turrets on centre line, E three forward and three aft and F two forward and three aft. Design G envisaged single turrets forward and aft raised on centre line, each with two turrets *en echelon* forward of the forward turret and aft of the aft turret.

RCPTG = reciprocating engine

Appendix 3

Principle characteristics of the *Dreadnought* and *Invincible*

		Battleship *Dreadnought*: 1905 programme	Battlecruiser *Invincible*: 1905 programme
Ordered:		8 July 1905	
Laid down:		2 October 1905	2 April 1906
Launched:		2 February 1906	13 April 1907
Completed:		3 December 1906	20 March 1908
Builder:		Portsmouth naval yard	Armstrong-Whitworth, Elswick
Dimensions:	Length	527-ft/161.16-m	567-ft/173.39-m
	Beam	82-ft/25.08-m	78.5-ft/24.01-m
	Draught	26.5-ft/8.10-m	27-ft/8.26-m
Displacement:	Standard	17,900 tons	17,420 tons
	Full load	21,845 tons	20,135 tons
Armament:	Guns	Ten 12-in/305-mm 45 calibre,	Eight 12-in/45 calibre,
		27 x 12-pdrs	sixteen 4-in/45 calibre, one 3-in/76-mm
	Torpedoes	five 18-in/457-mm torpedo tubes,	five 18-in/457-mm torpedo tubes,
		four beam and one stern:	four beam and one stern:
		stern tube removed in 1916	
		23 18-in torpedoes	23 18-in/457-mm torpedoes
		Six 14-in torpedoes	Six 14-in/356-mm torpedoes
Armour:	Belt	11- to 4-in/280- to 102-mm	6- to 4-in/152- to 102-mm
	Turret	11-in/280-mm	7-in/178-mm
	Barbette	11- to 4-in/280- to 102-mm	7- to 2-in/178- to 50.8-mm
	Conning Tower	11- to 8-in/280- to 203-mm	10-in/254-mm
	Decks, main	0.75-in/19-mm	1- to 0.75-in/25.4- to 19-mm
	middle	3- to 1.75-in/76- to 44-mm	
	lower	4- to 1.5-in/102- to 38-mm	2.5- to 1.5-in/64- to 38-mm
	Weight of armour:	5,000 tons (including backings)	3,460 tons
Machinery:		Eighteen Babcock and Wilcox boilers,	Thirty one Yarrow boilers,
		four Parsons turbines,	four Parsons turbines,
		four shafts	four shafts
		23,000 hp	41,000 hp
Machinery weight:		1,990 tons	3,300 tons
Maximum Speed:		21 knots	25 knots
Trials performance:			44,875 hp and 26.2 knots
Fuel		2,400 tons coal, 1,120 tons oil	3,084 tons coal, c.725 tons oil
Radius of action:		6,620 nm at 10 knots,	6,210 nm at 10 knots,
		4,910 nm at 18.4 knots	3,050 nm at 22.3 knots
Complement:		695 to 773	784

Appendix 4

The major powers at sea: 1 August 1914

Type of Warship	Britain	France	Russia	Germany	Austria-Hungary	Italy	Greece	Turkey	Japan	United States
Dreadnoughts	22	2	–	15	3	3	–	–	2	10
Pre-dreadnoughts	40	20	10	22	9	8	2	2	10	23
Battlecruisers	9	–	–	5	–	–	–	–	1	–
Coast-defence ships	–	1	1	–	3	–	3	1	4	–
Armoured cruisers	34	19	6	7	2	7	1	–	12	12
Protected cruisers	52	9	6	17	3	11	1	2	15	22
Scouting cruisers	15	–	–	–	–	–	–	–	–	–
Light cruisers	20	–	–	16	2	3	6	–	6	–
Destroyers	221	81	25	90	18	33	14	8	50	50
Torpedo boats	109	187	72	115	70	85	17	9	–	23
Submarines	73	75	22	31	5	22	2	–	12	18

The destroyer and torpedo boat totals must be regarded with caution since they include all such warships thus classified though many were old and of very limited utility (e.g. many torpedo boats were suitable only for defensive, coastal duties).

Appendix 5
Heligoland: 28 August 1914

The British order of battle

For this operation the British employed eight submarines. Six were employed in two lines on the limit of German patrol areas. These were the (1913) E. 4, (1913) E. 5 and the (1914) E. 9. with another three, (1913) E. 6, (1914) E. 7 and the (1914) E. 8, some 40 miles distant in a second line. Two other submarines, one of which was the (1911) D. 2 and the other unknown, were deployed to the mouth of the Ems.

The leading British formation was the 3rd Destroyer Flotilla with the light cruiser (1914) *Arethusa* and the destroyers (1913) *Laurel*, (1913) *Liberty*, (1913) *Lysander* and the (1913) *Laertes* from the 4th Destroyer Division; the (1913) *Laforey*, (1913) *Lawford*, (1913) *Louis* and the (1914) *Lydiard* from the 3rd Destroyer Division; the (1913) *Lark*, (1914) *Lance*, (1913) *Linnet* and the (1914) *Landrail* from the 2nd Destroyer Division; and the (1914) *Lookout*, (1913) *Leonidas*, (1914) *Legion* and the (1914) *Lennox* from the 1st Destroyer Division. The divisions were in line ahead and five cables apart. The formation was followed, at a distance of two miles, by the 1st Destroyer Flotilla, with the light cruiser (1913) *Fearless* and the destroyers (1911) *Goshawk*, (1911) *Lizard*, (1911) *Lapwing* and the (1911) *Phoenix* from the 5th Destroyer Division; the (1911) *Druid*, (1911) *Defender*, (1911) *Ferret* and the (1911) *Forester* from the 3rd Destroyer Division; the (1911) *Ariel*, (1913) *Llewellyn* and the (1913) *Lucifer* from the 2nd Destroyer Division; and the (1911) *Acheron*, (1911) *Archer*, (1911) *Attack* and the (1911) *Hind* from the 1st Destroyer Division. The 1st Destroyer Flotilla was deployed in the same manner as the 3rd Destroyer Flotilla.

These were supported, at a distance of eight miles, by 1st Light Cruiser Squadron, which was divided into three divisions which were two miles apart: these were the (1914) *Nottingham* and (1914) *Lowestoft* (the 2nd Light Cruiser Division), the (1913) *Southampton* and (1914) *Birmingham* (the 1st Light Cruiser Division), and (1911) *Falmouth* and (1910) *Liverpool* (3rd Light Cruiser Division).

This formation in its turn was supported by the (1912) *New Zealand* and the (1908) *Invincible*, which had the destroyers (1911) *Badger*, (1911) *Beaver*, (1911) *Jackal* and the (1911) *Sandfly* in company. On the day this formation was backed by the 1st Battle Cruiser Squadron in the shape of the (1912) *Lion*, (1912) *Princess Royal* and the (1913) *Queen Mary*.

The balance of British battlecruisers – the (1908) *Inflexible* (flagship), (1911) *Indefatigable* and the (1908) *Indomitable* – were in the Mediterranean, and at this time were supposedly in the process of being withdrawn from that theatre in order to take up station in the North Sea. In fact, with the drift of Turkey into the war the *Indefatigable* and the *Indomitable* were to remain in the Mediterranean into 1915: the *Inflexible* was withdrawn but in November, in the aftermath of the British defeat at Coronel, was sent with the *Invincible* to the South Atlantic.

The German warships present

The light cruisers (1901) *Ariadne*, (1907) *Danzig* (1904) *Frauenlob*, (1895) *Hela*, (1910) *Cöln*, (1910) *Kolberg*, (1910) *Mainz*, (1907) *Stettin*, (1912) *Stralsund* and the (1912) *Strassburg*, and the destroyer (1911) V. 187.

Appendix 6
The Falklands: 8 December 1914

On the British side the armoured cruisers (1909) *Defence*, (1905) Carnarvon and the (1904) *Cornwall* and the armed merchant cruisers *Otranto* and *Orama* (both with the Orient line and converted in 1914) arrived at the Abrolhos Rocks on 17 November: the armoured cruiser (1903) *Kent* and the armed merchant cruiser *Edinburgh Castle* were already there. The (1910) *Bristol* and *Macedonia* (P.&.O, line, converted 1914), and then the (1910) *Glasgow*, arrived thereafter, the *Bristol* and *Macedonia* after searching for the (1914) *Karlsruhe* and the *Glasgow* after having been in dock in Rio de Janeiro for five days having the damage she had sustained at Coronel made good. The *Invincible* and *Inflexible* arrived at the Rocks on 26 November, at which time the *Defence* was detached to St. Helena and the Cape squadron and the *Otranto* was detached to Sierra Leone with boiler problems. The force thus concentrated consisted of two battlecruisers (the *Invincible* and *Inflexible*), three cruisers (the *Carnarvon*, *Cornwall* and the *Kent*) two light cruisers (the *Bristol* and *Glasgow*) and one armed merchant cruiser (the *Macedonia*), the *Orama* being tasked with escorting some of the colliers to Port Stanley: presumably the armed merchant cruiser *Edinburgh Castle* was either left at Abrolhos Rocks or ordered into the Caribbean. The (1899) *Canopus* had arrived at Port Stanley on 9 November.

The German East Asiatic Squadron was based at Tsingtao, the German concession in northern China. At this time Germany owned the Carolines and Palaus, the Marianas, the Marshalls, Bougainville, what are now New Britain and New Ireland, and German Samoa, and the Squadron in effect was the only means of defence of these various colonies as well as being the means of "showing the flag" throughout the Pacific. With the deterioration of the European situation, the (1908) *Scharnhorst* and (1908) *Gneisenau* made for Ponape in the Carolines where on 6 August they were joined by the (1908) *Nürnberg*, which had been at San Francisco. The three German ships then made their way to Pagan Island, in the Marianas, where they were joined by the light cruiser (1909) *Emden* on 12 August. With the Squadron committed to making for the west coast of South America, where supplies of coal were expected to be plentiful, the *Emden* parted company on 14 August and made for the Indian Ocean. The *Scharnhorst*, *Gneisenau* and the *Nürnberg* were met by the light cruisers (1908) *Dresden* and (1906) *Leipzig* on 12 October at Easter Island, the formation leaving six days later for Chile. The *Dresden* had come from the Caribbean, the *Leipzig* from Mazatlan on Mexico's Pacific coast.

With the German squadron off the Falklands on 8 December were the colliers *Baden* and *Santa Isabel*: also in company was the supply ship *Seydlitz* which escaped but surrendered herself for internment at San Antonio, Argentina, on 18 December. The *Dresden* escaped, and was ultimately trapped by the *Cornwall* and *Glasgow* (with the *Orama* in company) in Cumberland Bay, Robinson Crusoe Island, in the Juan Fernandez Group, Chile, where she was scuttled after a brief action on 14 March 1915.

Various auxiliary cruisers and supply ships, plus the occasional prize, appeared at different times, e.g. the *Prinz Eitel Friedrich* and *Markomannia* which arrived with the *Emden* at Pagan on 12 August. In addition, as the German formation crossed the Pacific there were various colliers in company at different times: the *Luxor*, *Memphis* and the *Ramses* were just three of the colliers in German employment in South American waters. These have not been included in this account.

Appendix 7
Dogger Bank: 24 January 1915

British deployment: at Scapa Flow the Grand Fleet held the three dreadnought formations plus the 1st and 6th Cruiser Squadrons and the 2nd Light Cruiser Squadron. The 2nd Cruiser Squadron was at Cromarty. The battlecruisers and the 3rd Battle Squadron were at Rosyth, as were the 3rd Cruiser Squadron and the 1st Light Cruiser Squadron. The 1st and 3rd Destroyer Flotillas, and one submarine formation, were at Harwich.

The southern formations

The light cruiser (1914) *Arethusa* in the company of six destroyers, (1914) *Meteor*, (1914) *Milne*, (1914) *Minos*, (1915) *Mentor*, (1914) *Mastiff* and the (1914) *Morris*.

The 1st Destroyer Flotilla with the light cruiser (1914) *Aurora* and the destroyers (1911) *Acheron*, (1911) *Ariel*, (1911) *Attack* and the (1912) *Hydra* from the 1st Destroyer Division; the destroyers (1911) *Ferret*, (1911) *Forester*, (1911) *Defender* and the (1911) *Druid* from the 3rd Destroyer Division; the destroyers (1911) *Hornet*, (1911) *Jackal*, (1911) *Sandfly* and the (1911) *Tigress* from the 4th Destroyer Division; and the destroyers (1911) *Goshawk*, (1911) *Lapwing* and the (1911) *Phoenix* from the 5th Destroyer Division.

The 3rd Destroyer Flotilla with the light cruiser (1914) *Undaunted* and the destroyers (1914) *Lookout*, (1913) *Lysander* and the (1914) *Landrail* from the 1st Destroyer Division; the destroyers (1913) *Laurel*, (1913) *Liberty*, (1913) *Laertes* and the (1913) *Lucifer* from the 2nd Destroyer Division; the destroyers (1913) *Laforey*, (1913) *Lawford*, (1914) *Lydiard* and the (1913) *Louis* from the 3rd Destroyer Division; the destroyers (1914) *Legion* and (1913) *Lark* from the 4th Destroyer Division; and the destroyer (1914) *Miranda*, which should have been with the *Arethusa* but which did not arrive from Sheerness in time to leave with the others. The Oversea Squadron put two destroyers, the (1912) *Firedrake* and (1912) *Lurcher*, and four submarines to sea.

The battlecruiser force

The Battle Cruiser Force with the 1st Battle Cruiser Squadron and the battlecruisers *Lion*, *Tiger* and the *Princess Royal*, and the 2nd Battle Cruiser Squadron and the battlecruisers *New Zealand* and *Indomitable*. (Note: The *Queen Mary* had sailed for Portsmouth and dockyard.)

The 1st Light Cruiser Squadron with the (1913) *Southampton*, (1914) *Birmingham*, (1914) *Nottingham* and the (1914) *Lowestoft*.

The Grand Fleet

In support of the battlecruiser force the Grand Fleet put to sea. It had under command the (1914) *Iron Duke*, with the light cruiser (1893?) *Sappho* and destroyer (1912) *Oak* attached, the 1st Battle Squadron with the (1914) *Marlborough*, (1910) *St. Vincent*, (1910) *Collingwood*, (1911) *Colossus*, (1911) *Hercules*, (1911) *Neptune* and the (1910) *Vanguard* and the light cruiser (1910) *Bellona*; the 2nd Battle Squadron with the (1912) *King George V*, (1912) *Orion*, (1913) *Ajax*, (1913) *Centurion*, (1912) *Monarch* and the (1912) *Thunderer* and the light cruiser (1909) *Boadicea*; the 4th Battle Squadron with the (1914) *Benbow*, (1914) *Emperor of India*,

(1914) *Agincourt*, (1909) *Bellerophon*, (1906) *Dreadnought*, (1914) *Erin* and the (1909) *Téméraire* and the light cruiser (1911) *Blonde*; the 1st Cruiser Squadron with the armoured cruisers (1906) *Duke of Edinburgh*, (1906) *Black Prince* and the (1907) *Warrior*; the 2nd Cruiser Squadron with the armoured cruisers (1908) *Shannon*, (1907) *Achilles* and the (1907) *Natal*; the 6th Cruiser Squadron with the armoured cruisers (1902) *Drake*, (1903) *Donegal* and the (1903) *Leviathan*; and the 2nd Light Cruiser Squadron with the (1911) *Falmouth*, (1910) *Gloucester* and the (1912) *Yarmouth*, plus the 2nd Destroyer Flotilla with the light cruiser (1914) *Galatea* and destroyer leader (1914) *Broke* and either twenty or twenty-eight destroyers.

The German side

The battlecruisers *Seydlitz*, *Derfflinger* and the *Moltke* and the armoured cruiser (1910) *Blücher*. The light cruisers (1914) *Graudenz* and (1912) *Stralsund*, both with half flotillas, formed the van: the (1914) *Rostock* and (1910) *Kolberg* led the half-flotillas on the port and starboard wings respectively. In all there were nineteen destroyers.

Balance of losses

On the British side the *Lion* was heavily damaged but the damaged inflicted on the *Tiger*, the light cruiser *Aurora* and destroyer *Meteor* was minor. On the German side the *Blücher* was lost and the *Seydlitz* was seriously damaged. The damage inflicted on the *Derfflinger* and light cruiser *Kolberg* was minor.

Appendix 8

The Battle of Jutland: 31 May–1 June 1916 – Orders of Battle

Both the British and Germans fought this battle with two formations. On the British side these were the Grand Fleet and the Battlecruiser Fleet. On the German side there were the battle and scouting formations.

The Grand Fleet (commander Admiral Sir John Jellicoe) consisted of:

The 2nd Battle Squadron with the (1912) *King George V*, (1913) *Ajax*, (1913) *Centurion* and the (1914) *Erin* of the 1st Battle Division, and the (1912) *Orion*, (1912) *Monarch*, (1912) *Conqueror* and the (1912) *Thunderer* of the 2nd Battle Division, and the light cruiser (1909) *Boadicea*.

The 4th Battle Squadron with the (1912) *Iron Duke*, (1916) *Royal Oak*, (1909) *Superb* and the (1915) *Canada* of the 3rd Battle Division, and the light cruisers (1911) *Active* and (1910) *Blanche*, and the minelayer (1916) *Abdiel*, plus the destroyer (1912) *Oak*, which was attached to fleet flagship *Iron Duke*, and the (1913) *Benbow*, (1909) *Bellerophon*, (1909) *Téméraire* and the (1910) *Vanguard* of the 4th Battle Division.

The 1st Battle Squadron with the (1912) *Marlborough*, (1915) *Revenge*, (1911) *Hercules* and the (1914) *Agincourt*, of the 6th Battle Division, and the (1911) *Colossus*, (1910) *Collingwood*, (1911) *Neptune* and the (1910) *St. Vincent* of the 5th Battle Division, and the light cruiser (1910) *Bellona*.

The 3rd Battlecruiser Squadron with the (1908) *Invincible*, (1908) *Inflexible* and the (1908) *Indomitable*, and the light cruisers (1916) *Chester* and (1916) *Canterbury*.

The 1st Cruiser Squadron with the armoured cruisers (1909) *Defence*, (1907) *Warrior*, (1906) *Duke of Edinburgh* and the (1906) *Black Prince*.

The 2nd Cruiser Squadron with the armoured cruisers (1908) *Minotaur*, (1905) *Hampshire*, (1907) *Cochrane* and the (1908) *Shannon*.

The 4th Light Cruiser Squadron with the (1915) *Calliope*, (1915) *Constance*, (1914) *Caroline*, (1915) *Royalist* and the (1915) *Comus*.

The 4th Destroyer Flotilla with the flotilla leader (1914) *Tipperary*, the destroyers (1912) *Acasta*, (1912) *Achates*, (1913) *Ambuscade*, (1913) *Ardent*, the flotilla leader (1914) *Broke*, the destroyers (1912) *Christopher*, (1913) *Contest*, (1913) *Fortune*, (1913) *Garland*, (1912) *Hardy*, (1913) *Midge*, (1916) *Ophelia*, (1913) *Owl*, (1913) *Porpoise*, (1912) *Shark*, (1912) *Sparrowhawk*, (1912) *Spitfire* and the (1913) *Unity*.

The 11th Destroyer Flotilla with the light cruiser (1915) *Castor*, the flotilla leader (1915) *Kempenfelt*, the destroyers (1916) *Magic*, (1915) *Mandate*, (1915) *Manners*, (1915) *Marne*, (1915) *Martial*, (1915) *Michael*, (1915) *Milbrook*, (1915) *Minion*, (1915) *Mons*, (1915) *Moon*, (1915) *Morning Star*, (1915) *Mounsey*, (1916) *Mystic* and the (1915) *Ossory*.

The 12th Destroyer Flotilla with the flotilla leader (1914) *Faulknor*, the destroyer (1915) *Maenad*, the flotilla leader (1915) *Marksman*, the destroyers (1915) *Marvel*, (1916) *Mary Rose*, (1916) *Menace*, (1915) *Mindful*, (1915) *Mischief*, (1916) *Munster*, (1916) *Narwhal*, (1915) *Nessus*, (1916) *Noble*, (1916) *Nonsuch*, (1916) *Obedient*, (1916) *Onslaught* and the (1916) *Opal*.

The Battlecruiser Fleet (commander Vice Admiral Sir David Beatty) consisted of:

The (1912) *Lion* (fleet flagship and not assigned to any formation):

The 1st Battlecruiser Squadron with the (1912) *Princess Royal*, (1913) *Queen Mary* and the (1914) *Tiger*.

The 2nd Battlecruiser Squadron with the (1912) *New Zealand* and the (1911) *Indefatigable*.

The 5th Battle Squadron with the (1915) *Barham*, (1916) *Valiant*, (1915) *Warspite* and the (1916) *Malaya*:

The 1st Light Cruiser Squadron with the (1914) *Galatea*, (1915) *Phaeton*, (1915) *Inconstant* and the (1915) *Cordelia*;

The 2nd Light Cruiser Squadron with the (1913) *Southampton*, (1914) *Birmingham*, (1914) *Nottingham* and the (1913) *Dublin*.

The 3rd Light Cruiser Squadron with the (1911) *Falmouth*, (1912) *Yarmouth*, (1915) *Birkenhead* and the (1910) *Gloucester*.

The 1st Destroyer Flotilla with the light cruiser (1913) *Fearless*, the destroyers (1911) *Acheron*, (1911) *Ariel*, (1911) *Attack*, (1911) *Badger*, (1911) *Defender*, (1911) *Goshawk*, (1912) *Hydra*, (1911) *Lapwing* and the (1911) *Lizard*.

The 13th Destroyer Flotilla with the light cruiser (1915) *Champion*, the destroyers (1916) *Moresby*, (1916) *Narborough*, (1916) *Nerissa*, (1916) *Nestor*, (1916) *Nicator*, (1916) *Nomad*, (1916) *Obdurate*, (1916) *Onslow*, (1916) *Pelican* and the (1916) *Petard*.

The 9th and 10th Destroyer Flotillas, which were combined, with the destroyers (1914) *Lydiard*, (1914) *Landrail*, (1913) *Laurel* and the (1913) *Liberty* from the 9th Destroyer Flotilla and the destroyers (1915) *Moorsom*, (1914) *Morris*, (1916) *Termagent* and the (1916) *Turbulent* from the 10th Destroyer Flotilla.

Also in company was the seaplane carrier (1914) *Engadine*. The seaplane carrier (1915) *Campania* was not able to raise steam and leave Scapa Flow with the rest of the fleet: she sailed soon after midnight 30/31 May but was ordered to return at 0430. The kite balloon ship (n/d) *Menelaus* remained in harbour.

On the German side were the battle and scouting forces

The battle force (commander Vizeadmiral Reinhard Sheer) consisted of:

The 3rd Battle Squadron with the (1914) *König*, (1914) *Grosser Kurfürst*, (1914) *Kronprinz* and the (1914) *Markgraf* of the 5th Battle Division, and the (1912) *Kaiser*, (1913) *Kaiserin* and the (1913) *Prinzregent Luitpold* of the 6th Battle Division.

The fleet flagship (1912) *Friedrich der Grosse* (which was not assigned to any formation).

The 1st Battle Squadron with the (1911) *Ostfriesland*, (1911) *Thüringen*, (1911) *Helgoland* and the (1912) *Oldenburg* of the 1st Battle Division, and the (1910) *Posen*, (1910) *Rheinland*, (1909) *Nassau* and the (1909) *Westfalen* of the 2nd Battle Division.

The 2nd Battle Squadron with the pre-dreadnoughts (1906) *Deutschland*, (1905) *Hessen* and the (1907) *Pommern* of the 3rd Battle Division, and the (1907) *Hannover*, (1908) *Schlesien* and the (1908) *Schleswig-Holstein* of the 4th Battle Division.

The 4th Scouting Group with the light cruisers (1907) *Stettin*, (1905) *München*, (1904) *Hamburg*, (1904) *Frauenlob* and the (1908) *Stuttgart*.

The light cruiser (1914) *Rostock* with from the 1st Destroyer Flotilla, the destroyers (1915) G. 39 (leader), (1915) G.40, (1915) G. 38 and the (1914) S. 32 from the 1st Half-Flotilla: from the 3rd Destroyer Flotilla, the destroyer (1915) S. 53 (leader) and from the 5th Half-Flotilla the destroyers (1916) V. 71, (1916) V. 73 and the (1916) G. 88 and from the 6th Half-Flotilla the destroyers (1916) S. 54, (1915) V. 48 and the (1915) G. 42: from the 5th Destroyer Flotilla, the destroyer leader (1912) G. 11 and from the 9th Half-Flotilla the destroyers (1912) V. 2, (1912) V. 4, (1913) V. 6, (1912) V. 1 and the (1912) V. 3 and from the 10th Half-Flotilla the destroyers (1912) G. 8, (1912) G. 7, (1913) V. 5, (1912) G. 9 and the (1912) G. 10: and from the 7th Destroyer Flotilla, the destroyer (1913) S. 24 (leader) and from the 13th Half-Flotilla the destroyers (1912) S. 15, (1912) S. 17, (1913) S. 20, (1912) S. 16 and the (1913) S. 18 and from the 14th Half-Flotilla the destroyers (1913) S. 19, (1913) S. 23 and the (1911) V. 189.

The scouting force (commander Vizeadmiral Franz von Hipper) consisted of:

The 1st Scouting Group with the battlecruisers (1915) *Lützow*, (1914) *Derfflinger*, (1913) *Seydlitz*, (1911) *Moltke* and the (1910) *Von der Tann*.

The 2nd Scouting Group with the light cruisers (1915) *Frankfurt*, (1915) *Wiesbaden*, (1915) *Pillau* and the (1915) *Elbing*.

The light cruiser (1914) *Regensburg* with from the 2nd Destroyer Flotilla, the destroyer (1915) B. 98 (leader) and from the 3rd Half-Flotilla the destroyers (1915) G. 101, (1915) G. 102, (1915) B. 112 and the (1916) B. 97, and from the 4th Half-Flotilla the destroyers (1915) B. 109, (1915) B. 110, (1915) B. 111, (1915) G. 103 and the (1915) G. 104: from the 6th Destroyer Flotilla, the destroyer (1915) G. 41 (leader) and from the 11th Half-Flotilla the destroyers (1915) V. 44, (1916) G. 87 and the (1916) G. 86, and from the 12th Half-Flotilla the destroyers (1916) V. 69, (1915) V. 45, (1915) V. 46, (1915) S. 50 and the (1915) G. 37: and from the 9th Destroyer Flotilla, the destroyer (1915) V. 28 (leader) and from the 17th Half-Flotilla the destroyers (1914) V. 27, (1915) V. 26, (1915) S. 36, (1915) S. 51 and the (1915) S. 52, and from the 18th Half-Flotilla the destroyers (1916) V. 30, (1914) S. 34, (1914) S. 33, (1914) V. 29 and the (1914) S. 35.

NOTE: In the German system of nomenclature B represented destroyers built at the Blohm & Voss yard in Hamburg, G at Krupp's Germania yard at Kiel, H at the Howaldt yard at Kiel, S by Schichau at Danzig and V at the Vulkan yard at Stettin.

British units absent

The battleships (1906) *Dreadnought*, (1913) *Emperor of India*, (1915) *Queen Elizabeth*, and the (1916) *Royal Sovereign*, and the battlecruiser (1913) *Australia*, and the armoured cruisers (1907) *Achilles* and (1903) *Donegal* from the 2nd Cruiser Squadron, and the destroyer leader (1914) *Botha* and the destroyers (1911) *Archer*, (1911) *Jackal*, (1911) *Phoenix* and the (1911) *Tigress* from the 1st Destroyer Flotilla, the (1912) *Cockatrice*, (1913) *Paragon* and the (1913) *Victor* from the 4th Destroyer Flotilla, the (1915) *Marmion* and (1915) *Musketeer* from the 11th Destroyer Flotilla, the (1915) *Mameluke* and (1916) *Napier* from the 12th Destroyer Flotilla and the (1916) *Negro*, (1916) *Nepeans*, (1916) *Nereus*, (1916) *Paladin*, (1916) *Penn* and the (1916) *Pigeon* from the 13th Destroyer Flotilla.

German battle units absent

The battleship (1913) *König Albert* and the battlecruiser (1912) *Goeben*.

British and German warship losses at the Battle of Jutland

The British lost the battlecruisers *Indefatigable*, *Invincible* and *Queen Mary*, the armoured cruisers *Black Prince*, *Defence* and *Warrior*, the destroyer leader *Tipperary* and the destroyers *Ardent*, *Fortune*, *Nestor*, *Nomad*, *Shark*, *Sparrowhawk* and *Turbulent*.

The Germans lost the battlecruiser *Lützow*, the pre-dreadnought *Pommern*, the light cruisers *Elbing*, *Frauenlob*, *Rostock* and *Wiesbaden*, and the destroyers S.35, V.4, V.27, V.29 and V.48.

Appendix 9
The Allied arrival at Constantinopolis: November 1918

The precise number and identity of the ships in the Allied formation that presented itself at Constantine's city in November 1918 is never given in British histories, perhaps because the official naval history dealing with the eastern Mediterranean was never written. One would readily admit liability to correction, but it seems, from the distribution list of orders issued by the British admiral concerning such matters as the course to be followed through the Dardanelles and Sea of Marmara and moorings outside Constantinople that were to be used, that the Allied fleet consisted of four sections, British, French, Italian and Greek, and in that order and with 30 minutes' sailing time between each section.

The British part consisted of the battleships *Superb* and *Téméraire* and the pre-dreadnoughts *Lord Nelson* and *Agamemnon*, with the seaplane carrier (1907) *Empress*. In attendance were two light cruiser formations, the one with the (1916) *Canterbury*, (1905) *Skirmisher* and the (1905) *Forward* and the other with the (1910) *Liverpool*, (1905) *Sentinel* and the (1905) *Foresight*. With these were the flotilla leader (1918) *Tribune*; the destroyers (1911) *Acheron*, (1910) *Cameleon*, (1911) *Jackal* and the (1912) *Hydra*; the (1916) *Parthian*, (1918) *Tilbury*, (1916) *Northesk* and the (1918) *Shark*; the three Australian destroyers (1910) *Yarra*, (1915) *Torrens*, (1910) *Parramatta* and the British destroyer (1911) *Beaver*; the destroyers (1910) *Rifleman* and (1911) *Hind* and the destroyer-minesweepers (1911) *Forester*, (1911) *Hornet*, (1910) *Redpole* and the (1911) *Archer*. The French part consisted of the pre-dreadnoughts (1907) *Justice* and (1907) *Démocratie*, and one destroyer. The Italian part consisted of the pre-dreadnought (1908) *Roma* and the cruiser (1900) *Agordet*: the latter, however, at about 1,300 tons, appears to have been built as a torpedo-cruiser, but by 1918 it seems she had been assigned a minelaying role. The Greek section consisted of two destroyers, neither of which was named in the British orders. Certain sources indicate that either the Greek contribution, or one of the Greek ships, was an armoured cruiser. If either was indeed the case, it would seem that such a ship could only have been the (1911) *Giorgios Averoff.*

In addition to these units, however, there were a number of other British ships that were to form part of this particular operation. The monitor (1915) *Abercrombie* was tasked to station herself at Chanak, the monitor (1914) *Mersey* at Cape Helles. The latter's sister ship, the (1914) *Severn*, was to serve as guard ship at the Izmit naval base until the pre-dreadnought (1898) *Caesar*, which probably was serving as a depot ship at this late stage in her career, arrived on station. The last member of this rather odd class of monitors, which had been building for Brazil at the outbreak of war and had been intended for service on the Amazon, was the (1914) *Humber*: she along with the monitors (1915) M. 16, (1915) M. 17 and the (1915) M. 18, were to stand off the Ismid/Ismit naval base until such time that the main force was opposite Constantinople, at which point they were to move into the Bosporus.

Completing the British contingent were an assortment of ships, which appear to be a number of logistical or support ships with the occasional warship. These were the seaplane carrier (1916) *Manxman*, which was cited in orders along with the (1915) *Queen Victoria* and (1915) *Prince Edward*, which are given in reference books as either paddle minesweepers or stores ships. The destroyer depot ship (1907) *Blenheim* was listed alongside four unnamed destroyers, which whether individually or together could have been drawn from any number of bases in the eastern Mediterranean. The stores carrier (1915) *Bacchus* was in the company of two colliers and one oiler, again unnamed. Also listed were the old light cruiser (1900) *Pyramus*, the gunboat (1915) *Aphis*, the survey ship (1912) *Endeavour*, the water carrier (n/d) *Shamrock* and the submarine depot ship (1911) *Adamant*, the latter being named along with the submarine (1915) E. 21. (Source: Adm. 116.1823.)

Appendix 10

The internment of German warships in the Firth of Forth: 21 November 1918

Under the terms of Article 23 of the armistice, the Germans were supposed to sail ten battle-ships, six battlecruisers, eight cruisers and 50 destroyers and torpedo-boats to a port of internment. A neutral port could have played host but no neutral country would accept such a responsibility. Accordingly, after a series of meetings between representatives of the British and German fleets on 15 and 16 November in the *Queen Elizabeth* in the Firth of Forth, it was arranged that nine German battleships, five battlecruisers, seven light cruisers and 50 destroyers would present themselves in the Firth of Forth on 21 November 1918. Among the various administrative details that were settled at these meetings was the amount of fuel, whether coal or oil, that the various German warships would be allowed to embark: the Allied insistence was sufficient for the ships to steam 1,500 miles at twelve knots, this being deemed adequate for crossing the North Sea and then proceeding to Scapa Flow and for immediate "domestic" requirements thereafter, but not sufficient to allow the German units to attempt to make their way to Spanish waters.

The Allied terms were very exact, and named every battleship, battlecruiser and light cruiser that was to be interned. One of the battleships, however, either had never been completed or was unfit to make the sea crossing at the time set down: the battleship *König* is not listed as having been present in the Firth of Forth on 21 November but is given as interned at Scapa Flow on 6 December, and obviously would represent the tenth dreadnought, though whether this was in her own right or as a substitute for another is not clear. The battlecruiser *Mackensen* and light cruiser *Wiesbaden*, both among the named warships to be interned, had never been completed. Without sufficient time to ready their replacements, however, it was agreed that the designated number of warships would be interned and that replacements for the "missing" units would make their way to British waters as and when appropriate. The *Mackensen*'s place was filled by the battleship *Baden*, which arrived in British waters on 14 December 1918, and was interned at Scapa Flow on 9 January 1919: the *Wiesbaden* was replaced by the *Dresden*, date of arrival in British waters unknown to this author.

The warships named and which sailed from their bases after 1330 on 20 November were the battleships (1912) *Friedrich der Grosse*, (1913) *König Albert*, (1913) *Kaiserin*, (1913) *Prinzregent Luitpold*, (1912) *Kaiser*, (1916) *Bayern*, (1914) *Grosser Kurfürst*, (1914) *Kronprinz Wilhelm* and the (1914) *Markgraf*; the battlecruisers (1913) *Seydlitz*, (1911) *Moltke*, (1917) *Hindenburg*, (1914) *Derfflinger* and the (1910) *Von der Tann*; and the light cruisers (1914) *Karlsruhe*, (1915) *Frankfurt*, (1915) *Emden*, (1916) *Nürnberg*, (1914) *Brummer*, (1918) *Cöln* and the (1914) *Bremse*. The *Brummer* and *Bremse* were minelaying cruisers.

The destroyers were not identified individually but the Allied specification was that they were to be members of the 1st, 2nd, 3rd, 6th and 7th Destroyer Flotillas. With regard to this speci-fication, there would seem to be some discrepancy between Allied requirement and German organisation at this stage of proceedings. According to a German return made to the Grand Fleet with reference to supply requirements, the destroyers that made their way to the Firth of Forth were the (1916) G. 86, (1915) G. 38, (1915) G. 39, (1915) G. 40 and the (1914) *S. 32* from the 1st Half-Flotilla, the (1915) G. 101, (1915) G. 102, (1915) G. 103, (1915) G. 104 and the (1915) V. 100 from the 3rd Half-Flotilla, and the (1915) B. 109 (1915) B. 110, (1915) B. 111 and the (1915) B. 112 from the 4th Half-Flotilla; from the 3rd Destroyer Flotilla the (1915) S. 53, (1916) S. 54, (1916) S. 55, (1916) V. 70, (1916) V. 73, (1916) V. 81, (1916) V. 82 and the (1916) G. 91; from the 6th Destroyer Flotilla the (1917) V. 128, (1917) V. 125, (1917) V. 126, (1917) V. 127, (1917) S. 131 and the (1917) S. 132 from the 11th Half-Flotilla and the (1915)

V. 43, (1915) V. 44, (1915) V. 45, (1915) V. 46, (1915) V. 49 and the (1915) S. 50 from the 12th Half-Flotilla; from the 7th Destroyer Flotilla the (1918) S. 138, (1916) S. 56, (1917) S. 65, (1916) V. 78, (1916) V. 83 and the (1916) G. 92 from the 13th Half-Flotilla, the (1918) S. 136, (1918) S. 137, (1918) H. 145 and the (1916) G. 89 from the 14th Half-Flotilla, and the (1916) V. 80, (1916) S. 60, (1915) S. 36, (1915) S. 51 and the (1915) S. 52 from the 17th Half-Flotilla. The return does not indicate the existence of the 1st and 2nd Destroyer Flotillas, and would suggest that the 7th Destroyer Flotilla had three half-flotillas under command. The return states that the senior officer of the destroyer formations was in the S. 138. Standard reference books suggest that the V. 43 was in fact the G. 43, and V. 125 is given in the return as V. 124, which did not exist.

Of the light cruisers one, the *Cöln*, broke down and had to return to base for repair: she then proceeded to British waters and internment at a date that is not recorded. The destroyers individually identified in the return number not 50 but 49: one, the V. 30, was sunk by a mine on 20 November. It is not readily apparent from the 29 November return from which half-flotilla the V. 30 came, though it seems that she was from the 1st Half-Flotilla: she was replaced in the German lists by the V. 129.

According to British plans, twenty German destroyers were to proceed from the Firth of Forth on Friday 22 November to Scapa Flow, with another twenty to follow on the following day. The remaining ten, along with the five battlecruisers that presented themselves in the Firth of Forth on 21 November 1918, were to be interned at Scapa Flow on 24 November: which of these three days was one destroyer light is not known. Five German battleships and four light cruisers were to be interned at Scapa Flow on 25 November, and the remaining four battleships and three light cruisers on the following day, 26 November. In the event it seems that battleship numbers were reversed. On 25 November four German battleships, namely the *Friedrich der Grosse*, *Kaiser*, *Kaiserin* and the *Prinzregent Luitpold*, made their way to Scapa Flow with the remaining five bringing up the rear on the following day. Which cruisers, whether by numbers or identity, made their way to Scapa Flow on these two days is not clear from the available record, or at least the record that was consulted. The German major units were escorted during their move to Scapa Flow by an equal number of British warships, the battlecruisers by the *Lion* and units of the 1st Battle Cruiser Squadron and the battleships by units from the 1st Battle Squadron. (Source: Adm. 116.2074.)

On 19 November 1918 the first twenty German submarines to be surrendered presented themselves at Harwich, on the 21st another 39 were surrendered: 28 were surrendered on 24 November and 27 on that date. Thus by 1 December a total of 114 had been surrendered, at which time another 62 remained in German ports. Ultimately 176 U-boats were surrendered and another seven sank en route to Britain. Another eight that were in neutral ports were surrendered to the Allied powers, while one scuttled herself in order to avoid transfer and surrender.

Appendix 11
Battleships and battlecruisers lost during and after the First World War

27 Oct 1914	British battleship (1913) **Audacious** sunk by mine and internal explosion off Loch Swilly.
31 May 1916	British battlecruiser (1913) **Queen Mary**, by explosion of magazine, in action with German warships.
	British battlecruiser (1911) **Indefatigable**, by explosion of magazine, in action with German warships.
	British battlecruiser (1908) **Invincible**, by explosion of magazine, in action with German warships.
1 Jun 1916	German battlecruiser (1915) **Lützow**, scuttled by the German destroyer G. 38, as a result of severe damage, sustained in action with British warships.
2 Aug 1916	Italian battleship (1915) **Leonardo da Vinci** by internal explosion at Taranto.
20 Oct 1916	Russian battleship (1915) **Imperatrica Marija** by internal explosion at Sevastopol.
9 Jul 1917	British battleship (1910) **Vanguard** by internal explosion at Scapa Flow.
12 Jul 1918	Japanese battleship (1912) **Kawachi** by internal explosion in Tokuyama Bay.
11 Jun 1918	Austro-Hungarian battleship (1914) **Szent Istvan**, off Premuda Island torpedoed by an Italian MTB.
30 Jun 1918	Bolshevik battleship **Svobodnaja Rossija**, formerly the Tsarist battleship (1914) [*Imperatritsa*] **Ekaterina II**, off Novorossijsk: scuttled in order to avoid surrender.
1 Nov 1918	Austro-Hungarian battleship (1912) **Viribus Unitis**, after having been surrendered to a Slav council at Pola and renamed the **Jugoslavija**, as a result of being mined by Italian saboteurs.

21 Jun 1919	German battleship (1916) *Bayern*, interned at Scapa Flow: scuttled in order to avoid surrender.
	German battleship (1912) *Friedrich der Grosse*, interned at Scapa Flow: scuttled in order to avoid surrender.
	German battleship (1914) *Grosser Kurfürst*, interned at Scapa Flow: scuttled in order to avoid surrender.
	German battleship (1912) *Kaiser*, interned at Scapa Flow: scuttled in order to avoid surrender.
	German battleship (1913) *Kaiserin*, interned at Scapa Flow: scuttled in order to avoid surrender.
	German battleship (1913) *König Albert*, interned at Scapa Flow: scuttled in order to avoid surrender.
	German battleship (1914) *Kronprinz Wilhelm*, formerly the *Kronprinz*, interned at Scapa Flow: scuttled in order to avoid surrender.
	German battleship (1913) *Markgraf*, interned at Scapa Flow: scuttled in order to avoid surrender.
	German battleship (1913) *Prinzregent Luitpold*, interned at Scapa Flow: scuttled in order to avoid surrender.
	German battlecruiser (1914) *Derfflinger*, interned at Scapa Flow: scuttled in order to avoid surrender.
	German battlecruiser (1917) *Hindenburg*, interned at Scapa Flow: scuttled in order to avoid surrender.
	German battlecruiser (1911) *Moltke*, interned at Scapa Flow: scuttled in order to avoid surrender.
	German battlecruiser (1913) *Seydlitz*, interned at Scapa Flow: scuttled in order to avoid surrender.
	German battlecruiser (1910) *Von der Tann*, interned at Scapa Flow: scuttled in order to avoid surrender.
26 Aug 1922	French battleship (1912) *France* foundered after running aground in Quiberon Bay
24 Nov 1922	The Bolshevik battleship *Mikhail Frunze*, formerly the Tsarist battleship (1911) *Poltava* was deemed to be beyond economical repair as a result of a major fire in her forward boiler room. It was not until 1925, however, that the decision was taken that she should be treated as a constructive total loss (i.e. the subject of cannibalisation), and this process continued until 1941. After the German invasion it was decided that she should be towed to Kronstadt and used as a decoy but either was sunk en route by German aircraft or sunk as a blockship, date unknown.

Appendix 12
The last generation: Europe's unbuilt

German Designs 1939–1944					
	Friedrich der Grosse	German 1941 design	German H 42	German H 43	German H 44
Displacement					
standard	55,453 tons	68,000 tons	90,000 tons	111,000 tons	131,000 tons
full load	62,497 tons	76,000 tons	98,000 tons	120,000 tons	141,500 tons
Length	908.4-ft/277.8-m	899.25-ft/275.0-m	998.00-ft/305.20-m	1,079.10-ft/330.00-m	1,128.48-ft/345.10-m
Beam	121.64-ft/37.2-m	127.53-ft/39.0-m	139.96-ft/42.80-m	156.96-ft/48.00-m	168.41-ft/51.50-m
Maximum Draft	33.35-ft/10.2-m	39.57-ft/12.1-m	41.53-ft/12.70-m	41.86-ft/12.80-m	44.15-ft/13.50-m
Armament					
guns	Eight 16-in/406-mm	Eight 16-in/406-mm	Eight 16-in/406-mm	Eight 20-in/508-mm	Eight 20-in/508-mm
guns	Twelve 5.9-in/150-mm	Twelve 5.9-in/150-mm	Twelve 5.9-in/150-mm	Twelve 5.9-in/150-mm	Twelve 5.9-in/150-mm
guns	Sixteen 105-mm	Sixteen 105-mm	Sixteen 105-mm	Sixteen 105-mm	Sixteen 105-mm
guns	Twelve 37-mm	Sixteen 37-mm	Twenty-eight 37-mm	Twenty-eight 37-mm	Twenty-eight 37-mm
guns	Twenty-four 20-mm	Twenty-four 20-mm	Forty 20-mm	Forty 20-mm	Forty 20-mm
torpedo tubes	Six 21-in/533-mm	Six 21-in/533-mm	Six 21-in/533-mm	Six 21-in/533-mm	Six 21-in/533-mm
seaplanes			Four	Six	Nine
Protection					
belt	8.66-in/220-mm	11.81-in/300-mm	11.81-in/300-mm	14.96-in/380-mm	14.96-in/380-mm
turrets	15.16-in/385-mm				
barbettes	14.37-in/365-mm				
CT	15.16-in/385-mm				
deck	3.15-in/80-mm	5.91-in/150-mm	13.78-in/350-mm	13.78-in/350-mm	18.50-in/470-mm
Propulsion	165,000 shp	165,000 shp	280,000 shp	240,000 shp	240,000 shp
Maximum speed	30 knots	30 knots	32 knots	31 knots	30 knots
Range	19,000 nm/16 knots	20,000 nm/19 knots	20,000 nm/19 knots or	20,000 nm/19 knots or	20,000 nm/19 knots or
			25,000 nm/19 knots	25,000 nm/19 knots	25,000 nm/19 knots

Soviet Designs in the Late Thirties

	Soviet UP41 class	Soviet Design A	Soviet Design B	Soviet Design C	Soviet Design D
Displacement					
standard	42,000 tons	66,074 tons	71,850 tons	44,200 tons	45,000 tons
full load	50,000 tons	72,000 tons	74,000 tons	55,200 tons	53,680 tons
Length	816.6-ft/248.9-m	1,000.0-ft/304.8-m	1,005.0-ft/306.3-m	844.83-ft/257.50-m	903.83-ft/275.5-m
Beam	116.5-ft/35.5-m	126.0-ft/38.4-m	128.0-ft/39-m	129.50-ft/39.50-m	113.50-ft/34.6-m
Maximum Draft	29.5-ft/9-m	34.5-ft/10.5-m	34.5-ft/10.5-m	33.50-ft/10.20-m	33.50-ft/10.2-m
Armament					
guns	Nine 16-in/406-mm	Eight 18-in/457-mm	Twelve 16-in/406-mm	Ten 16-in/406-mm	Ten 16-in/406-mm
guns	Twelve 7.1-in/180-mm	28 5-in/127-mm	28 5-in/127-mm	Twenty 5-in/127-mm	Twenty 5-in/127-mm
guns	24 3.9-in/100-mm	24 1.1-in/28-mm	32 1.1-in/28-mm		Sixteen 1.1-in/28-mm
guns	Forty-eight 45-mm				
guns	Twenty-four 13.2-mm				
seaplanes	Four	None	None	None	
aircraft	None	36 and two catapults	36 and two catapults	24 and two catapults	None
flight deck	None				None
Protection					
belt	13.20-in/335-mm				
turrets	15.75-in/400-mm				
barbettes	13.80-in/350-mm				
CT	13.20-in/335-mm				
main deck	2.56-in/65-mm				
Propulsion	177,500 shp,				
Maximum speed	32 knots	34 knots	31.9 knots	31.9 knots	31 knots
Range					

The French *Provence* class 1940: possible options

Displacement				
standard	35,000 tons	40,000 tons	42,500 tons	45,000 tons
full load				
Length				
Beam				
Maximum draft				
Main armament	Eight 15-in/380-mm	Nine 15-in/380-mm	Nine 16-in/406-mm	Twelve 15-in/380-mm
	Two quadruple turrets, one forward, one aft	Three triple turrets, two forward, one aft	Three triple turrets, two forward, one aft	Three quadruple turrets, two forward, one aft

Appendix 13
Japanese and American capital ship construction after 1937

Imperial Japan:

	Laid down	Launched	Completed	
BB *Yamato*	4.11.1937	8. 8.1940	16.12.1941	72,809 tons, nine 18.1-in/460-mm guns,
BB *Musashi*	29. 3.1938	11.11.1941	5. 8.1942	25.59-in/650-mm turret, 27.46 knots.
BB *Shinano*	4. 5.1940	11.11.1944 as an aircraft carrier.		
BB No. 111	7.11.1940	Work halted in November 1941: order cancelled September 1942.		
BB No. 797	Projected for 1942 programme but never ordered.			
BB No. 798	Projected for 1942 programme but never ordered.			c. 70,000 tons, six 20-in/508-mm guns,
BB No. 799	Projected for 1942 programme but never ordered.			27 knots.
CB No. 795	Projected for 1942 programme but never ordered.			34,800 tons, nine 12.2-in/310-mm guns,
CB No. 796	Projected for 1942 programme but never ordered.			7.5-in/190-mm belt, 33 knots.

United States:

	Laid down	Launched	Completed	
BB 55 *North Carolina*	27.10.1937	13. 6.1940	9. 4.1941	45,370 tons, nine 16-in/406-mm guns,
BB 56 *Washington*	14. 6.1938	1. 6.1940	15. 5.1941	17.99-in/457-mm turret, 28 knots.
BB 57 *South Dakota*	5. 7.1939	7. 6.1941	20. 3.1942	45,216 tons,
BB 58 *Indiana*	20.11.1939	21.11.1941	30. 4.1942	nine 16-in/406-mm guns,
BB 59 *Massachusetts*	20. 7.1939	23. 9.1941	15. 5.1942	17.99-in/457-mm turret,
BB 60 *Alabama*	1. 2.1940	16. 2.1942	16. 8.1942	28 knots.
BB 61 *Iowa*	27. 6.1940	27. 8.1942	22. 2.1943	57,600 tons,
BB 62 *New Jersey*	16. 9.1940	7.12.1942	23. 5.1943	nine 16-in/406-mm guns,
BB 63 *Missouri*	6. 1.1941	29. 1.1944	11. 6.1944	19.69-in/500-mm turret,
BB 64 *Wisconsin*	25. 1.1941	7.12.1943	16. 4.1944	33 knots.
BB 65 *Illinois*	15. 1.1945	Work halted 12. 8.1945 and scrapped.		
BB 66 *Kentucky*	6.12.1944	20. 1.1950	Never completed: scrapped 1959.	
BB 67 *Montana*	Ordered 9. 9.1940: cancelled 21. 7.1943 before laid down.			70,500 tons,
BB 68 *Ohio*	Ordered 9. 9.1940: cancelled 21. 7.1943 before laid down.			Twelve 16-in/406-mm guns,
BB 69 *Maine*	Ordered 9. 9.1940: cancelled 21. 7.1943 before laid down.			22.50-in/572-mm turret,
BB 70 *New Hampshire*	Ordered 9. 9.1940: cancelled 21. 7.1943 before laid down.			28 knots.
BB 71 *Louisiana*	Ordered 9. 9.1940: cancelled 21. 7.1943 before laid down.			
CB 1 *Alaska*	17.12.1941	15. 8.1943	17. 6.1944	34,253 tons,
CB 2 *Guam*	2. 2.1942	21.11.1943	17. 9.1944	Nine 12-in/305-mm guns.
CB 3 *Hawaii*	20.12.1943	11. 3.1945	Construction halted 16. 4.1947.	12.80-in/325-in turret,
CB 4 *Philippines*	Ordered 9.10.1940: cancelled 24. 6.1943 before laid down.			33 knots.
CB 5 *Puerto Rico*	Ordered 9.10.1940: cancelled 24. 6.1943 before laid down.			
CB 6 *Samoa*	Ordered 9.10.1940: cancelled 24. 6.1943 before laid down.			

Appendix 14

Battles, capital ships and orders of battle:
Eastern Solomons to the Philippine Sea (August 1942–June 1944)

1. At THE BATTLE OF THE EASTERN SOLOMONS (24 August 1942)

The Americans deployed three carrier groups. These had under command:

The carrier (1927) *Saratoga*, the heavy cruisers (1928)(RAN) *Australia*, (1934) *Minneapolis* and the (1934) *New Orleans*, the light cruiser (1936)(RAN) *Hobart*, and the destroyers (1935) *Dale*, (1934) *Farragut*, (1935) *MacDonough*, (1936) *Phelps* and the (1935) *Worden*;
The carrier (1938) *Enterprise*, the battleship (1941) *North Carolina*, the heavy cruiser (1933) *Portland*, the light cruiser (1942) *Atlanta*, and the destroyers (1936) *Balch*, (1939) *Benham*, (1939) *Ellet*, (1941) *Grayson*, (1938) *Maury* and the (1941) *Monssen*; and
The carrier (1940) *Wasp*, the heavy cruisers (1929) *Salt Lake City* and (1934) *San Francisco*, the light cruiser (1942) *San Juan*, and the destroyers (1942) *Aaron Ward*, (1942) *Buchanan*, (1942) *Farenholt*, (1939) *Lang*, (1936) *Selfridge*, (1939) *Stack* and the (1939) *Sterett*.

The Japanese order of battle contained seven formations with the following units:

The heavy cruisers (1932) *Atago*, (1929) *Haguro*, (1932) *Maya*, (1929) *Myoko* and the (1932) *Takao*, the light cruiser (1923) *Yura*, and the destroyers (1938) *Asagumo*, (1940) *Hayashio*, (1940) *Kuroshio*, (1940) *Oyashio* and the (1938) *Yamagumo*;
The battleship (1921) *Mutsu*, the seaplane carrier (1938) *Chitose*, and the destroyers (1937) *Harusame*, (1937) *Murasame*, (1938) *Natsugumo* and the (1937) *Samidare*;
The carriers (1941) *Shokaku* and (1941) *Zuikaku*, and the destroyers (1941) *Akigumo*, (1942) *Kazegumo*, (1942) *Makikumo*, (1929) *Shikinami*, (1929) *Uranami* and the (1941) *Yugumo*;
The battleships (1914) *Hiei* and (1915) *Kirishima*, the heavy cruisers (1939) *Chikuma*, (1937) *Kumano* and the (1937) *Suzuya*, the light cruiser (1922) *Nagara*, and the destroyers (1942) *Akizuki*, (1940) *Hatsukaze*, (1941) *Maikaze*, (1941) *Nowaki*, (1941) *Tanikaze* and the (1940) *Yukikaze*;
The light carrier (1933) *Ryujo*, the heavy cruiser (1938) *Tone*, and the destroyers (1940) *Amatsukaze* and (1940) *Tokitsukaze*;
The light cruiser (1925) *Jintsu*, and the destroyers (1937) *Suzukaze*, (1937) *Umikaze* and the (1926) *Uzuki*; and
The destroyers (1940) *Isokaze*, (1939) *Kagero*, (1937) *Kawakaze*, (1926) *Mutsuki* and the (1926) *Yayoi*.

The Americans and their allies lost no ships, the Japanese the light carrier *Ryujo* and the destroyer *Mutsuki*.

2. At THE BATTLE OF SANTA CRUZ (26 October 1942)

The Americans deployed three formations. These had under command:

The carrier (1938) *Enterprise*, the battleship (1942) *South Dakota*, the heavy cruiser (1933) *Portland*, the light cruiser (1942) *San Juan*, and the destroyers (1936) *Conyngham*, (1936) *Cushing*, (1936) *Mahan*, (1938) *Maury*, (1936) *Porter*, (1936) *Preston* and the (1936) *Smith*;
The carrier (1941) *Hornet*, the heavy cruisers (1930) *Northampton* and (1930) *Pensacola*, the light cruisers (1942) *Juneau* and (1942) *San Diego*, and the destroyers (1939) *Anderson*, (1942) *Barton*, (1939) *Hughes*, (1940) *Morris*, (1939) *Mustin* and the (1939) *Russell*; and

The battleship (1941) *Washington*, the heavy cruiser (1934) *San Francisco*, the light cruisers (1942) *Atlanta* and (1939) *Helena*, and the destroyers (1942) *Aaron Ward*, (1939) *Benham*, (1942) *Fletcher*, (1942) *Lansdowne*, (1942) *Lardner* and the (1942) *McCalla*.

The Japanese order of battle contained five formations with the following units:

The battleships (1915) *Haruna* and (1913) *Kongo*, the heavy cruisers (1932) *Atago*, (1932) *Maya*, (1929) *Myoko* and the (1932) *Takao*, the light cruiser (1923) *Isuzu*, and the destroyers (1939) *Kagero*, (1937) *Kawakaze*, (1942) *Makinami*, (1942) *Naganami*, (1940) *Oyashio*, (1937) *Suzukaze*, (1942) *Takanami* and the (1937) *Umikaze*;

The carrier (1942) *Junyo*, and the destroyers (1940) *Hayashio* and (1940) *Kuroshio*, the carrier (1942) *Hiyo* having been forced to return to Truk in the company of the destroyers (1932) *Inazuma* and (1928) *Isonami*;

The carriers (1941) *Shokaku* and (1941) *Zuikaku*, the light carrier (1940) *Zuiho*, the heavy cruiser (1937) *Kumano*, and the destroyers (1940) *Amatsukaze*, (1941) *Arashi*, (1941) *Hamakaze*, (1940) *Hatsukaze*, (1941) *Maikaze*, (1942) *Teruzuki*, (1940) *Tokitsukaze* and the (1940) *Yukikaze*;

The battleships (1914) *Hiei* and (1915) *Kirishima*, the heavy cruisers (1939) *Chikuma*, (1937) *Suzuya* and the (1938) *Tone*, the light cruiser (1922) *Nagara*, and the destroyers (1941) *Akigumo*, (1940) *Isokaze*, (1942) *Kazegumo*, (1942) *Makikumo*, (1941) *Tanikaze*, (1940) *Urakaze* and the (1941) *Yugumo*; and

The light cruiser (1923) *Yura*, and the destroyers (1942) *Akizuki*, (1937) *Harusame*, (1937) *Murasame*, (1937) *Samidare*, (1937) *Yudachi*, (1932) *Akatsuki*, (1932) *Ikazuchi* and the (1936) *Shiratsuyu*.

The Americans lost the carrier *Hornet* and the destroyer *Porter*, the Japanese the light cruiser *Yura*.

3. At THE FIRST NAVAL BATTLE OF GUADALCANAL (12–13 November 1942)

The Americans deployed:

The heavy cruisers (1933) *Portland* and (1934) *San Francisco*, the light cruisers (1942) *Atlanta*, (1939) *Helena* and the (1942) *Juneau*, and the destroyers (1942) *Aaron Ward*, (1942) *Barton*, (1936) *Cushing*, (1942) *Fletcher*, (1942) *Laffey*, (1941) *Monssen*, (1942) *O'Bannon* and the (1939) *Sterett*.

The Japanese deployed the battleships (1914) *Hiei* and (1915) *Kirishima*, the light cruiser (1922) *Nagara*, and the destroyers (1932) *Akatsuki*, (1940) *Amatsukaze*, (1938) *Asagumo*, (1937) *Harusame*, (1932) *Ikazuchi*, (1932) *Inazuma*, (1937) *Murasame*, (1937) *Samidare*, (1936) *Shigure*, (1936) *Shiratsuyu*, (1942) *Teruzuki*, (1937) *Yudachi*, (1935) *Yugure* and the (1940) *Yukikaze*.

The Americans lost the light cruiser *Atlanta* and destroyers *Laffey*, *Barton*, *Cushing* and the *Monssen*: the light cruiser *Juneau* was sunk the next day, 13 November 1942, after being torpedoed by the Japanese submarine I. 26. The Japanese lost the battleship *Hiei* and the destroyers *Akatsuki* and *Yudachi*.

4. At THE SECOND NAVAL BATTLE OF GUADALCANAL (14–15 November 1942)

The Americans deployed:

The battleships (1942) *South Dakota* and (1941) *Washington*, and the destroyers (1939) *Benham*, (1936) *Preston*, (1941) *Gwin* and the (1940) *Walke*.

The Japanese deployed the battleship (1915) *Kirishima*, the heavy cruisers (1932) *Atago* and (1932) *Takao*, the light cruisers (1922) *Nagara* and (1924) *Sendai*, and the destroyers (1938) *Asagumo*, (1930) *Ayanami*, (1929) *Hatsuyuki*, (1937) *Samidare*, (1929) *Shikinami*, (1928) *Shirayuki*, (1942) *Terazuki* and the (1929) *Uranami*.

The Americans lost the destroyers *Benham*, *Preston* and the *Walke*, the Japanese the battleship *Kirishima* and destroyer *Ayanami*.

5. THE BATTLE OF THE PHILIPPINE SEA 19/20 June 1944

U.S. Navy's order of battle:

TG 58.1: The fleet carriers (1943) *Hornet* and (1943) *Yorktown*, the light carriers (1943) *Bataan* and (1943) *Belleau Wood*, the heavy cruisers (1943) *Baltimore*, (1943) *Boston* and the (1943) *Canberra*, the light cruiser (1942) *Oakland*, and the destroyers (1943) *Bell*, (1943) *Boyd*, (1943) *Bradford*, (1943) *Brown*, (1943) *Burns*, (1943) *Charette*, (1943) *Conner*, (1943) *Cowell* and the (1943) *Izard*.

TG 58.2: The fleet carriers (1943) *Bunker Hill* and (1943) *Wasp*, the light carriers (1943) *Cabot* and (1943) *Monterey*, the light cruisers (1943) *Biloxi*, (1943) *Mobile*, (1942) *San Juan* and the (1942) *Santa Fe*, and the destroyers (1943) *Hickox*, (1943) *Hunt*, (1943) *Lewis Hancock*, (1943) *Marshall*, (1943) *Miller*, (1943) *Owen*, (1943) *Stephen Potter*, (1943) *The Sullivans* and the (1943) *Tingey*.

TG 58.3: The fleet carriers (1938) *Enterprise* and (1943) *Lexington*, the light carriers (1943) *Princeton* and (1943) *San Jacinto*, the heavy cruiser (1932) *Indianapolis*, the light cruisers (1943) *Birmingham*, (1942) *Cleveland*, (1942) *Montpelier* and the (1943) *Reno*, and the destroyers (1943) *Anthony*, (1943) *Braine*, (1943) *Caperton*, (1943) *Clarence K. Bronson*, (1943) *Cogswell*, (1943) *Cotten*, (1943) *Dortch*, (1943) *Gatling*, (1943) *Healy*, (1943) *Ingersoll*, (1943) *Knapp*, (1943) *Terry* and the (1943) *Wadsworth*.

TG 58.4: The fleet carrier (1942) *Essex*, the light carriers (1943) *Cowpens* and (1943) *Langley*, the light cruisers (1943) *Houston*, (1943) *Miami*, (1942) *San Diego* and the (1944) *Vincennes*, and the destroyers (1936) *Case*, (1942) *Charles Ausburne*, (1942) *Converse*, (1942) *Dyson*, (1939) *Ellet*, (1939) *Lang*, (1942) *Lansdowne*, (1942) *Lardner*, (1942) *McCalla*, (1943) *Spence*, (1942) *Stanly*, (1939) *Sterett*, (1943) *Thatcher* and the (1939) *Wilson*.

Total: 904 aircraft all types.

TG 58.7 was initially dispersed between the four carrier groups. It consisted of: The battleships (1942) *Alabama*, (1942) *Indiana*, (1943) *Iowa*, (1943) *New Jersey*, (1941) *North Carolina*, (1942) *South Dakota* and the (1941) *Washington*, the heavy cruisers (1934) *Minneapolis*, (1934) *New Orleans*, (1934) *San Francisco* and the (1939) *Wichita*, and the destroyers (1937) *Bagley*, (1943) *Bennett*, (1936) *Conyngham*, (1943) *Fullam*, (1942) *Guest*, (1943) *Halford*, (1943) *Hudson*, (1941) *Monssen*, (1937) *Mugford*, (1937) *Patterson*, (1936) *Selfridge*, (1944) *Stockham*, (1943) *Twining* and the (1943) *Yarnell*.

Support formations included:

The battleships (1921) *California*, (1923) *Colorado*, (1921) *Maryland* and the (1920) *Tennessee*, the heavy cruiser (1931) *Louisville*, the light cruisers (1943) *Birmingham*, (1942) *Cleveland* and the (1942) *Montpelier* all of which doubled in other groups, and the destroyers (1943) *Albert W. Grant*, (1937) *Bagley*, (1942) *Coghlan*, (1943) *Halsey Powell*, (1943) *McDermut*, (1943) *McGowan*, (1943) *McNair*, (1943) *Melvin*, (1943) *Mertz*, (1941) *Monssen*, (1943) *Norman Scott*, (1943) *Remey*, (1943) *Robinson*, (1943) *Stockham*, (1941) *Twining*, (1943) *Wadleigh* and the (1943) *Yarnell*: of these seventeen destroyers, five doubled in other groups.

The battleships (1919) *Idaho*, (1918) *New Mexico* and the (1916) *Pennsylvania*, the heavy cruisers (1934) *Minneapolis*, (1934) *New Orleans*, (1934) *San Francisco* and the (1939) *Wichita*, the light cruisers (1938) *Honolulu* and (1939) *St. Louis*, and the destroyers (1943) *Anthony*, (1943) *Bennett*, (1943) *Braine*, (1943) *Fullam*, (1942) *Guest*, (1943) *Halford*, (1943) *Hudson*, (1943) *Terry* and the (1943) *Wadsworth*: three of the heavy cruisers and all of these nine destroyers doubled in other groups.

The escort carriers (1943) *Fanshaw Bay*, (1943) *Kalinin Bay*, (1943) *Midway* and the (1943) *White Plains*, and the destroyers (1943) *Callaghan*, (1936) *Cassin*, (1943) *Irwin*, (1943) *Longshaw*, (1943) *Porterfield*, (1944) *Ross* and the (1943) *Young*.

The escort carriers (1943) *Coral Sea*, (1943) *Corregidor*, (1943) *Gambier Bay* and the (1943) *Kitkun Bay*, and the destroyers (1943) *Benham*, (1943) *Bullard*, (1943) *Chauncey*, (1943) *Kidd*, (1943) *Laws* and the (1943) *Morrison*.

In addition, fifteen destroyers were held in a screening formation, while four escort carriers, ten destroyers and a variety of other units constituted the reserve.

[NOTE: Other figures indicate first formation had fourteen and second formation twelve destroyers.]

The Japanese had under command three formations thus constituted:

The light carriers (1944) *Chitose*, (1943) *Chiyoda* and the (1940) *Zuiho* (with eighteen Zeke fighter, 45 Zeke dive-bombers and 27 Jill torpedo-bombers), the battleships (1915) *Haruna* and (1913) *Kongo*, (1942) *Musashi* and the (1941) *Yamato*, the heavy cruisers (1932) *Atago*, (1932) *Chokai*, (1937) *Kumano*, (1932) *Maya*, (1937) *Suzuya* and the (1932) *Takao*, and the (1939) *Chikuma* and (1938) *Tone*, the light cruiser (1943) *Noshiro*, and the destroyers (1943) *Asashimo*, (1943) *Fujinami*, (1941) *Hamakaze*, (1943) *Kishinami*, (1942) *Naganami*, (1943) *Okinami*, (1943) *Shimakaze* and the (1943) *Tamanami*;

The fleet carriers (1941) *Shokaku*, (1944) *Taiho* and the (1941) *Zuikaku* (with 81 Zeke fighter, ninety Zeke dive-bombers and 54 Jill torpedo-bombers), the heavy cruisers (1929) *Haguro* and (1929) *Myoko*, the light cruiser (1943) *Yahagi*, and the destroyers (1942) *Akitsuki*, (1938) *Asagumo*, (1942) *Hatsutsuki*, (1940) *Isokaze*, (1944) *Shimotsuki* and the (1943) *Wakatsuki*;

The fleet carriers (1942) *Hiyo* and (1942) *Junyo*, the light carrier (1935) *Ryuho* (with 54 Zeke fighter, 63 Zeke dive-bombers and eighteen Jill torpedo-bombers), the battleship (194.) *Nagato*, the heavy cruisers (1935) *Mogami*, and the destroyers (1944) *Akishimo*, (1944) *Hayashimo*, (1937) *Michishio*, (1941) *Nowaki*, (1937) *Samidare*, (1936) *Shigure* and the (1938) *Yamagumo*.

Total number of aircraft: 153 Zeke fighters, 198 Zeke dive-bombers and 99 Jill torpedo-bombers, and 450 aircraft all types.

In addition, there were two other formations:

The destroyers (1934) *Hatsushimo*, (1933) *Hibiki*, (1920) *Tsuga* and the (1925) *Yunagi* and four oilers and the destroyers (1926) *Uzuki* and (1940) *Yukikaze* and two oilers.

The Americans lost no ships, but 130 carrier-based aircraft; the Japanese the fleet carriers *Hiyo*, *Shokaku* and the *Taiho*, the oilers *Genyo Maru* and *Seiyo Maru*, and 415 carrier- and more than 100 land-based aircraft.

Appendix 15
The Battle of Leyte Gulf 22–28 October 1944

The American order of battle (21 October) was as follows:

The carrier formations
TG 38.1: The fleet carriers (1943) *Hornet* and (1943) *Wasp*, the light fleet carriers (1943) *Cowpens* and (1943) *Monterey*, the heavy cruisers (1943) *Boston* and (1943) *Canberra*, the light cruisers (1943) *Houston* and (1942) *San Diego*, and the destroyers (1943) *Bell*, (1943) *Boyd*, (1943) *Brown*, (1943) *Burns*, (1943) *Caperton*, (1943) *Charrette*, (1943) *Cogswell*, (1943) *Conner*, (1943) *Cowell*, (1941) *Grayson*, (1943) *Ingersoll*, (1943) *Izard*, (1943) *Knapp*, (1942) *McCalla* and the (1942) *Woodworth*.

TG 38.2: The fleet carriers (1943) *Bunker Hill*, (1944) *Hancock* and the (1943) *Intrepid*, the light fleet carriers (1943) *Cabot* and (1943) *Independence*, the battleships (1943) *Iowa* and (1943) *New Jersey*, the light cruisers (1943) *Biloxi*, (1943) *Miami*, (1942) *Oakland* and the (1944) *Vincennes*, and the destroyers (1943) *Benham*, (1943) *Colahan*, (1943) *Cushing*, (1943) *Halsey Powell*, (1943) *Hickox*, (1943) *Hunt*, (1943) *Lewis Hancock*, (1943) *Marshall*, (1943) *Miller*, (1943) *Owen*, (1943) *Stephen Potter*, (1944) *Stockham*, (1943) *The Sullivans*, (1943) *Tingey*, (1943) *Twining*, (1943) *Uhlmann*, (1944) *Wedderburn* and the (1943) *Yarnall*.

TG 38.3: The fleet carriers (1942) *Essex* and (1943) *Lexington*, the light fleet carriers (1943) *Langley* and (1943) *Princeton*, the battleships (1942) *Indiana* and (1942) *Massachusetts*, the light cruisers (1943) *Birmingham*, (1943) *Mobile*, (1943) *Reno* and the (1942) *Santa Fe*, and the destroyers (1943) *Callaghan*, (1943) *Cassin Young*, (1943) *Clarence K. Bronson*, (1943) *Cotten*, (1943) *Dortch*, (1943) *Gatling*, (1943) *Healy*, (1943) *Irwin*, (1943) *Laws*, (1943) *Longshaw*, (1943) *Morrison*, (1943) *Porterfield*, (1944) *Preston* and the (1944) *Prichett*.

TG 38.4: The fleet carriers (1938) *Enterprise* and (1944) *Franklin*, the light fleet carriers (1943) *Belleau Wood* and (1943) *San Jacinto*, the battleships (1942) *Alabama* and (1941) *Washington*, the heavy cruisers (1934) *New Orleans* and (1939) *Wichita*, and the destroyers (1937) *Bagley*, (1937) *Gridley*, (1937) *Helm*, (1938) *Maury*, (1938) *McCall*, (1937) *Mugford*, (1941) *Nicholson*, (1937) *Patterson*, (1937) *Ralph Talbot*, (1941) *Swanson* and the (1941) *Wilkes*.

Other formations
TF 77: AGC (1944) *Wasatch*.
TG 77.1: The light cruisers (1938) *Nashville*, and the destroyers (1943) *Abner Read*, (1943) *Ammen*, (1943) *Bush* and the (1943) *Mullany*.

TG 77.3: The heavy cruisers (1928) (RAN) *Australia* and (1929) (RAN) *Shropshire*, the light cruisers (1939) *Boise* and (1939) *Phoenix*, and the destroyers (1942) (RAN) *Arunta*, (1942) *Bache*, (1942) *Beale*, (1943) *Daly*, (1942) *Hutchins*, (1944) *Killen* and the (1942) (RAN) *Warramunga*.

TU 77.4.1: The escort carriers (1942) *Chenango*, (1944) *Petrof Bay*, (1944) *Saginaw Bay*, (1942) *Sangamon*, (1942) *Santee* and the (1942) *Suwanee*, the destroyers (1944) *Hazelwood*, (1943) *McCord* and the (1943) *Trathen*, and the destroyer escorts (1943) *Coolbaugh*, (1944) *Edmonds*, (1944) *Eversole*, (1944) *Richard M. Rowell* and the (1944) *Richard S. Bull*.

TU 77.4.2: The escort carriers (1944) *Kadashaw Bay*, (1943) *Manila Bay*, (1944) *Marcus Island*, (1943) *Natoma Bay*, (1944) *Ommaney Bay*, (1944) *Savo Island*, and the destroyers (1943) *Franks*, (1943) *Haggard* and the (1943) *Hailey* and the destroyer escorts (1944) *Abercrombie*, (1944) *LeRay Wilson*, (1944) *Oberrender*, (1944) *Richard W. Suesens* and the (1944) *Walter C. Wann*.

TU 77.4.3: The escort carriers (1943) *Fanshaw Bay*, (1943) *Gambier Bay*, (1943) *Kalinin Bay*, (1943) *Kitkun Bay*, (1943) *St. Lo* and the (1943) *White Plains*, and the destroyers (1943) *Heerman*, (1943) *Hoel* and the (1943) *Johnston*, and the destroyer escorts (1944) Dennis, (1943) *John C. Butler*, (1944) *Raymond* and the (1944) *Samuel B. Roberts*.

TF 78: AGC (1943) *Blue Ridge*.
The battleships (1921) *Maryland*, (1917) *Mississippi* and the (1923) *West Virginia*, and the destroyers (1942) *Aulick*, (1942) *Cony* and the (1943) *Sigourney*.

TG 78.1: The destroyers (1943) *Harrison*, (1943) *John Rodgers*, (1943) *McKee* and the (1943) *Murray*.

TG 78.2: The destroyers (1939) *Anderson*, (1942) *Fletcher*, (1942) *Jenkins* and the (1942) *La Vallette*.

TG 78.3: The destroyers (1943) *Dashiell*, (1939) *Hughes*, (1942) *Ringgold*, (1943) *Schroeder* and the (1943) *Sigsbee*.

TG 78.4: The destroyers (1939) *Lang*, (1939) *Stack*, and the frigates (1944) *Bisbee* and the (1944) *Gallup*.

TG 78.6: The destroyers (1944) *Howorth*, (1940) *Morris*, (1939) *Mustin* and the (1943) *Stevens*, and the frigates (1944) *Burlington* and (1944) *Carson City*.

TG 78.7: The destroyers (1943) *Hopewell*, (1942) *Nicholas*, (1942) *O'Bannon* and the (1942) *Taylor*, and the frigates (1944) *Muskogee* and (1943) *San Pedro*.

TG 78.8. The destroyers (1936) *Drayton*, (1936) *Flusser*, (1936) *Lamson*, (1936) *Mahan* and the (1936) *Smith*, and the frigates (1943) *El Paso*, (1944) *Eugene*, (1944) *Orange* and the (1943) *Van Buren*.

TF 79: AGC (1944) *Mount Olympus*.
The battleships (1921) *California*, (1916) *Pennsylvania* and the (1920) *Tennessee*, the heavy cruisers (1931) *Louisville*, (1934) *Minneapolis*, and the (1933) *Portland*, the light cruisers (1942) *Columbia*, (1942) *Denver* and the (1938) *Honolulu*, and the destroyers (1943) *Albert W. Grant*, (1942) (RAN) *Arunta*, (1942) *Bache*, (1942) *Beale*, (1943) *Bennion*, (1943) *Bryant*, (1943) *Daly*, (1942) *Edwards*, (1943) *Halford*, (1942) *Hutchins*, (1944) *Killen*, (1944) *Leutze*, (1943) *McDermut*, (1943) *McGowan*, (1943) *Melvin*, (1941) *Monssen*, (1943) *Newcomb*, (1943) *Remey*, (1944) *Richard P. Leary* and the (1944) *Robinson*.

TG 79.3: The destroyers (1943) *Abbot*, (1943) *Black*, (1943) *Braine*, (1943) *Chauncey*, (1943) *Erben*, (1942) *Gansevoort*, (1943) *Hale* and the (1943) *Walker*.

TG 79.4: The destroyers (1943) *Charles J. Badger*, (1943) *Halligan*, (1943) *Haraden*, (1943) *Isherwood*, (1943) *Luce*, (1935) *MacDonough*, (1943) *Picking*, (1943) *Sproston*, (1943) *Twiggs* and the (1943) *Wickes*.

TG 79.11. The destroyers (1943) *McDermut*, (1943) *McGowan*, (1943) *McNair*, (1943) *Melvin*, (1943) *Mertz*, (1941) *Monssen* and the (1943) *Remey*.

TG 30.2: The heavy cruisers (1930) *Chester*, (1930) *Pensacola* and (1929) *Salt Lake City*, and the destroyers (1936) *Case*, (1936) *Cassin*, (1936) *Cummings*, (1937) *Downes*, (1937) *Dunlap* and the (1937) *Fanning*.

TG 30.8: The escort carriers (1942) *Altamaha*, (1943) *Barnes*, (1944) *Cape Esperance*, (1944) *Kwajalein*, (1942) *Nassau*, (1944) *Nehenta Bay*, (1944) *Rudyerd Bay*, (1944) *Sargent Bay*, (1943) *Shipley Bay*, (1944) *Sitkoh Bay* and the (1944) *Steamer Bay*, and the destroyers (1935) *Aylwin*, (1943) *Capps*, (1935) *Dale*, (1943) *David W. Taylor*, (1934) *Dewey*, (1942) *Dyson*, (1943) *Evans*, (1934) *Farragut*, (1943) *Hailey*, (1943) *Hall*, (1942) *Hobby*, (1935) *Hull*, (1944) *John D. Henley*, (1935) *Monaghan*, (1943) *Paul Hamilton*, (1943) *Thatcher*, (1943) *Thorn* and the (1943) *Welles*, and the destroyer escorts (1943) *Acree*, (1943) *Bangust*, (1944) *Crowley*, (1943) *Donaldson*, (1943) *Elden*, (1944) *Halloran*, (1944) *Hilbert*, (1944) *Kyne*, (1944) *Lake*,

(1944) *Lamons*, (1943) *Levy*, (1944) *Lyman*, (1943) *McConnell*, (1943) *Mitchell*, (1943) *O'Neill*, (1943) *Osterhaus*, (1943) *Parks*, (1944) *Rall*, (1943) *Reynolds*, (1943) *Riddle*, (1943) *Samuel S. Miles*, (1943) *Stern*, (1943) *Swearer*, (1943) *Waterman*, (1943) *Weaver* and the (1943) *Wesson*.

Lost
The light fleet carrier *Princeton*, the escort carriers *Gambier Bay* and *St. Lo*, the destroyers *Hoel* and *Johnston*, and the destroyer escorts *Eversole* and *Samuel B. Roberts*.

The Japanese order of battle was as follows:

The Main Body or Northern Force
The fleet carrier (1941) *Zuikaku*, the light fleet carriers (1944) *Chitose*, (1943) *Chiyoda* and the (1940) *Zuiho*, the battleships (1918) *Hyuga* and (1917) *Ise*, the light cruisers (1923) *Isuzu*, (1943) *Oyodo* and the (1921) *Tama*, and the destroyers (1942) *Akitsuki*, (1942) *Hatsutsuki*, (1944) *Shimotsuki* and the (1943) *Wakatsuki*, and the escorts (1944) *Kiri*, (1944) *Kuwa*, (1944) *Maki* and the (1944) *Sugi*: also two oilers with the destroyer (1921) *Akikaze* and six corvettes.

The Centre Force
The battleships (1915) *Haruna*, (1913) *Kongo*, (1942) *Musashi*, (1920) *Nagato* and the (1941) *Yamato*, the heavy cruisers (1932) *Atago*, (1939) *Chikuma*, (1932) *Chokai*, (1929) *Haguro*, (1937) *Kumano*, (1932) *Maya*, (1929) *Myoko*, (1937) *Suzuya*, (1932) *Takao* and the (1938) *Tone*, the light cruisers (1943) *Noshiro* and the (1943) *Yahagi*, and the destroyers (1944) *Akishimo*, (1937) *Asashio*, (1943) *Fujinami*, (1941) *Hamakaze*, (1943) *Hamanami*, (1944) *Hayashimo*, (1940) *Isokaze*, (1943) *Kishinami*, (1944) *Kiyoshima*, (1942) *Naganami*, (1941) *Nowaki*, (1943) *Okinami*, (1943) *Shimakaze*, (1940) *Urakaze* and the (1940) *Yukikaze*.

Southern Force
The battleships (1915) *Fuso* and (1917) *Yamashiro*, the heavy cruiser (1935) *Mogami*, and the destroyers (1938) *Asagumo*, (1937) *Michishio*, (1936) *Shigure* and the (1938) *Yamagumo*.

The Second Striking Force
The heavy cruisers (1929) *Ashigara* and (1928) *Nachi*,the light cruiser (1925) *Abukuma*, and the destroyers (1931) *Akebono*, (1933) *Hatsuhara*, (1934) *Hatsushimo*, (1939) *Kasumi*, (1939) *Shiranuhi*, (1931) *Ushio* and the (1934) *Wakaba*.

The heavy cruiser (1927) *Aoba*, the light cruiser (1922) *Kinu*, and the destroyer (1929) *Uranami* plus four transports.

Lost
The fleet carrier *Zuikaku*, the light fleet carriers *Chitose*, *Chiyoda* and the *Zuiho*, the battleships *Fuso*, *Musashi* and the *Yamashiro*, the heavy cruisers *Atago*, *Chikuma*, *Chokai*, *Maya*, *Mogami* and the *Suzuya*, the light cruisers *Abukuma*, *Kinu*, *Noshiro* and the *Tama*, and the destroyers *Akizuki*, *Asagumo*, *Fujinami*, *Hatsutsuki*, *Hayashimo*, *Michishio*, *Nowaki*, *Shiranui*, *Uranami*, *Wakaba* and the *Yamagumo*.

Appendix 16
Capital ship losses during the Second World War

Capital ship losses, in chronological order of loss, during the Second World War were as follows:

14 Oct 1939 British battleship (1916) *Royal Oak*, inside the Scapa Flow anchorage,
by the German submarine U. 47

 3 Jul 1940 French battleship (1913) *Bretagne*, at Mers-el-Kebir,
in surface action with British warships

11 Nov 1940 Italian battleship (1915) *Conte di Cavour*, in Taranto harbour, by carrier aircraft

24 May 1941 British battlecruiser (1920) *Hood*, in the Denmark Strait,
in surface action with German warships

27 May 1941 German battleship (1940) *Bismarck*, in the North Atlantic,
in surface action with British warships

23 Sep 1941 Soviet battleship (1914) *Marat*, at Kronstadt, by German land-based aircraft*

25 Nov 1941 British battleship (1915) *Barham*, in the eastern Mediterranean,
by the German submarine U. 331

 7 Dec 1941 US battleship (1916) *Arizona*, at Pearl Harbor, by Japanese carrier aircraft

US battleship (1921) *California*, at Pearl Harbor, by Japanese carrier aircraft*

US battleship (1916) *Oklahoma*, at Pearl Harbor, by Japanese carrier aircraft

US battleship (1923) *West Virginia*, at Pearl Harbor, by Japanese
carrier aircraft*

10 Dec 1941 British battlecruiser (1916) *Repulse*, in the South China Sea,
to Japanese land-based aircraft

British battleship (1941) *Prince of Wales*, in the South China Sea,
to Japanese land-based aircraft

18 Dec 1941 British battleship (1915) *Queen Elizabeth*, in Alexandria harbour,
to Italian charioteer attack*

British battleship (1916) *Valiant*, in Alexandria harbour,
to Italian charioteer attack*

13 Nov 1942 Japanese battleship (1914) *Hiei*, off Guadalcanal, in action involving
US light forces and land- and carrier-based aircraft

14 Nov 1942 Japanese battleship (1915) *Kirishima*, off Guadalcanal,
in surface action with US battleship Washington

27 Nov 1942 French battleship (1916) *Provence* scuttled in Toulon harbour, to avoid capture

French battleship (1937) *Dunkerque* scuttled in Toulon harbour, to avoid capture

French battleship (1938) *Strasbourg* scuttled in Toulon harbour, to avoid capture

 8 Jun 1943 Japanese battleship (1921) *Mutsu*, in Hiroshima Bay, by explosion of magazine

 9 Sep 1943 Italian battleship (1942) *Roma*, west of Bonifacio Strait,
by German land-based aircraft

26 Dec 1943 German battleship (1939) *Scharnhorst* in the Arctic,
in surface action with British warships

24 Oct 1944 Japanese battleship (1942) *Musashi*, in the Visayan Sea, by US carrier aircraft

25 Oct 1944 Japanese battleship (1915) *Fuso*, in the Surigao Strait,
in surface action with US light forces

Japanese battleship (1917) *Yamashiro*, in the Surigao Strait,
in surface action with allied warships

12 Nov 1944 German battleship (1941) *Tirpitz*, at Tromsø, by British land-based aircraft

21 Nov 1944 Japanese battleship (1913) *Kongo*, northwest of Formosa,
by the US submarine *Sealion*

15 Feb 1945 Italian battleship (1915) *Conte di Cavour*, in German ownership,
at Trieste, by US land-based aircraft

27 Mar 1945 German battleship (1938) *Gneisenau* scuttled as blockship at Gotenhafen

 7 Apr 1945 Japanese battleship (1941) *Yamato*, southwest of Kyushu,
by US carrier aircraft

24 Jul 1945 Japanese battleship (1918) *Hyuga*, in Kure harbour, by US carrier aircraft

28 Jul 1945 Japanese battleship (1915) *Haruna*, off Kure by US carrier aircraft and
Japanese battleship (1917) *Ise*, in Kure harbour, by US carrier aircraft

Capital ships that sank or were sunk, after September 1945 were as follows:

25 Jul 1946 US battleship (1912) *Arkansas*, at Bikini atoll

29 Jul 1946 The surrendered Japanese battleship (1920) *Nagato*,
in American ownership, at Bikini atoll

10 Feb 1948 US battleship *Pennsylvania*, expended as a target off Kwajalein
after having survived the Bikini tests

 8 Jul 1948 US battleship (1914) *New York*, expended as target
off Pearl Harbor after having survived the Bikini tests

31 Jul 1948 US battleship (1916) *Nevada*, expended as target
off Pearl Harbor after having survived the Bikini tests, and

29 Oct 1955 Soviet battleship *Novorossisk*, formerly the Italian battleship (1914)
Cesare, mined in Sevastopol harbour

* indicates battleships that were returned to service, the definition being loosely applied to the *Marat*.

Certain of the losses – such as those of 7 and 18 December 1941 – may be disputed, as indeed may be the inclusion of the *Gneisenau* in the list on the grounds that she was no longer in commission and hence could not be considered for inclusion in this list. The author is aware of such caveats and that a number of entries may not wholly accord with definitions of sinking, but the list has been devised on the basis of what might be reasonably defined as capital ships that settled on the bottom with no place to go, if only for the moment. Whether by such a definition the *Nevada* should have been included in this list poses an obvious problem: a number of sources cite her being raised in February 1942, but none suggest her being sunk, rather her being run aground but not in a sinking condition. Note should be made of the fact that this list, being one primarily concerned with the Second World War, makes no reference to the loss of Spanish nationalist battleship *Alfonso XIII*, which sank after being mined off Santander on 30 April 1937. It appears that she was the only battleship to be lost in action in the inter-war period, the *Ekaterina II-Svobodnaja Rossija* and the definition of "inter-war period" being the obvious problem confronting such a statement.

Appendix 17
The world's battleships and battlecruisers, 1905–1998

ARGENTINA

BATTLESHIP **RIVADAVIA**
1909 authorisation. Fore River, Quincy, Massachusetts. Laid down: 25 May 1910. Launched: 28 June 1911. Official completion and hand over: 27 August 1914. Sailed for Argentina: 23 December 1914.

BATTLESHIP **MORENO**
1909 authorisation. New York Shipbuilding, Camden, New Jersey. Laid down: 9 July 1910. Launched: 23 September 1911. Completed: 15 February 1915. Hand over: 20 February 1915. Arrived at Puerto Belgrano: 26 May 1915.

Dimensions
583-ft/178.3-m x 96.5-ft/29.5-m x 27.80-ft/8.5-m. Displacement: 27,940 tons (normal), 30,600 tons (full load). Armament: Twelve 12-in/305-mm 50 calibre guns in six twin turrets, four centre line with two forward and two aft superimposed, and two turrets diagonally offset: twelve 6-in/152-mm 50 calibre, initially sixteen and then eight single 4-in/102-mm guns. Two 21-in/533-mm torpedo tubes. Armour: 11-in/279-mm belt, 12-in/305-mm turrets, barbettes and conning tower, 3-in/76-mm deck. Weight of armour: 7,600 tons. Machinery: Eighteen Babcock mixed boilers, three Curtis turbines, three shafts. 39,500 shp. Speed: 22.5 knots. Fuel: 4,000 tons coal or 1,600 tons coal and 660 tons oil. Range: 7,000 n.m. at 15 knots, 11,000 n.m. at 11 knots.

Fate
Rivadavia: stricken on 1 February 1957. Sold on 30 May 1957, and on 3 April 1959 was taken from Puerto Belgrano under tow, arriving at Savona, Italy, on 23 May and scrapped thereafter. **Moreno**: stricken 1 October 1956. Sold for scrap on 11 January 1957. Tow to Yawata, Japan, began in May 1957: scrapped on arrival.

AUSTRIA-HUNGARY

BATTLESHIP **VIRIBUS UNITIS**
1911 programme. Stabilmento Tecnico Triestino. Laid down: 24 July 1910. Launched: 20 June 1911. Completed: 6 October 1912.

BATTLESHIP **TEGETTHOFF**
1911 programme. Stabilmento Tecnico Triestino. Laid down: 24 September 1910. Launched: 21 March 1912. Completed: 14 July 1913.

BATTLESHIP **PRINZ EUGEN**
1911 programme. Stabilmento Tecnico Triestino. Laid down: 16 January 1912. Launched: 30 November 1912. Completed: 8 July 1914.

BATTLESHIP **SZENT ISTVÁN**
1911 programme. Danubius Vereingte Schiffbau- under Maschinenfrabrik, Fiume. Laid down: 29 January 1912. Launched: 17 January 1914. Completed: 17 November 1915.

Dimensions
495-ft/151.4-m x 89.27-ft/27.3-m x 28.12-ft/8.6-m. Displacement: 21,730 tons (as designed), 22,500 tons (full load). Armament: Twelve 12-in/305-mm 45 calibre guns in four three-gun turrets, centre line and superimposed fore and aft, twelve single 5.9-in/150-mm 50 calibre

guns. **Prinz Eugen** and **Szent István** four, **Viribus Unitis** and **Tegetthoff** two 21-in/533-mm torpedo tubes. Armour: 11-in/280-mm belt, turrets, barbettes and CT, 1.9-in/48-mm deck. Machinery: **Szent István** twelve Babcock boilers, two AEG turbines and two shafts. Others twelve Yarrow coal-burning boilers, two Parsons turbines and four shafts. 25,000 shp. Speed: 20 knots. Fuel: 2,000 tons coal. Range: 4,200 n.m. at 10 knots.

Fate
Viribus Unitis handed over to representatives of the south Slav national council at Pola on 1 November 1918 and mined and sunk the same night by Italian frogmen. **Tegetthoff** allocated to Italy at the end of the First World War and transferred 25 March 1919. Remained at Venice until 1923. Scrapped at La Spezia 1924–1925. **Prinz Eugen** allocated to France at the end of the First World War and transferred 20 August 1920. Used as target ship and sunk 28 June 1922 by the **France** and **Bretagne** off Toulon. **Szent István** sunk 11 June 1918 by Italian MAS boat off Premuda Island in the Adriatic.

BRAZIL

BATTLESHIP **MINAS GERAIS**
October 1904 authorisation: contracted 20 February 1907. Armstrong, Elswick, Britain.
Laid down: 17 April 1907. Launched: 10 September 1908. Completed: 6 January 1910.
Arrived at Rio de Janeiro: 17 April 1910.

BATTLESHIP **SÃO PAULO**
October 1904 authorisation: contracted 20 February 1907. Vickers, Barrow-in-Furness, Britain. Laid down: 30 April 1907. Launched: 19 April 1909. Completed: July 1910. Sailed 16 September 1910 from Greenock, and arrived at Rio de Janeiro 25 October.

Dimensions
543-ft/166.05-m x 83-ft/25.38-m x 28-ft/8.56-m. Displacement: 19,281 tons (normal), 21,200 tons (full load). Armament: Twelve 12-in/305-mm 45 calibre guns in six twin turrets, superimposed fore and aft and two turrets diagonally offset on the side decks, the foremost to starboard: 22 single secondary guns cited as 5-in/152-mm or 4.7-in/120-mm 50 calibre. Armour: 9-in/229-mm belt, turrets and barbettes, 12-in/305-mm CT, 3-in/76-mm deck. Machinery: Eighteen Babcock coal-burning boilers, two triple-acting reciprocating engines, two shafts. 23,500 shp. Speed: 21 knots. (**Minas Gerais** 22 knots on 30,000 shp). Fuel: 2,360 tons coal. Range: 8,000 n.m. at 10 knots.

Fate
Minas Gerais: Paid off 16 May 1952. Stricken 31 December 1952 and sold 1953. Between 1 March and 22 April 1954 towed to Genoa and broken up thereafter. **São Paulo**: Paid off 1946. Stricken 2 August 1947. Sold August 1951 to British breakers. Towed from Rio de Janeiro 20 September 1951: lost north of Azores in a storm 4 November.

CHILE

BATTLESHIP **ALMIRANTE LATORRE**
Ordered under the 1911 programme, the **Almirante Latorre** was being built in Britain at the outbreak of war in 1914 and was requisitioned accordingly and saw service as the **Canada**. Re-purchased by Chile in April 1920 and transferred as the **Almirante Latorre** on 20 August 1920: formal transfer completed 27 November at Devonport. Arrived at Valpariso on 20 February 1921. Subjected to a major modernisation programme at Devonport navy yard between 24 June 1929 and 5 March 1931. In 1950 she was subjected to major overhaul of her machinery, and was fitted for radar.

Fate

Paid off 1 August 1958 and sold on 25 August 1958. Tow began in May and arrived on 30 August 1959 at Yokohama for scrapping. See **UNITED KINGDOM**: Battleship **Canada**.

FRANCE

BATTLESHIP **COURBET**

1910 programme. Brest navy yard. Laid down: 1 September 1910. Launched: 23 September 1911. Completed: 19 November 1913.

BATTLESHIP **JEAN BART**

1910 programme. Brest navy yard. Laid down: 15 November 1910. Launched: 22 September 1911. Completed: 5 June 1913.

BATTLESHIP **FRANCE**

1911 programme. Brest navy yard. Laid down: 30 November 1911. Launched: 7 September 1912. Completed: August 1914.

BATTLESHIP **PARIS**

1911 programme. Forges & Chantiers de la Mediterranée, La Seyne. 10 November 1911. 28 September 1912. 1 August 1914.

Dimensions

544.6-ft/166.54-m x 88.6-ft/27.09-m x 29-ft/8.87-m. Displacement: 22,189 tons (standard), 25,597 tons (full load). Armament: Twelve (six twin turrets) 12-in/305-mm 45 calibre, 22 5.5-in/ 138.6-mm 55 calibre, four 47-mm guns. Four 17.7-in/450-mm submerged torpedo tubes (removed 1927–1929). Originally up to thirty mines were carried in these battleships. Armour: 10.6-in/270-mm belt, 12.6-in/320-mm turrets, 10.6-in/270-mm barbettes and conning tower. Weight of armour 6,672 tons. Machinery: Twenty-four mixed coal- and oil-burning boilers. Four turbines. Four shafts and 28,000 shp. Speed: maximum trials speed was 22.6 knots by the **Jean Bart**. Fuel: 2,700 tons coal, 300 tons oil. Range: 4,200 n.m. at 10 knots.

Fate

Courbet: Scuttled as part of harbour breakwater at Normandy in June 1944. Torpedoed twice thereafter. Scrapped *in situ*. **Jean Bart**: Renamed **Océan** in 1936. Disarmed in 1938 for service as training ship. Thereafter hulk at Toulon and scuttled 27 November 1942. Badly damaged in Allied air raid in March 1944 and expended in explosives trials by Germans. Salvaged and scrapped at Toulon in 1945. **France**: Foundered after running aground in heavy gale in Quiberon Bay on 26 August 1922. **Paris**: Crossed Channel to Britain in June 1940: served as depot and accommodation. Returned to Brest in 1945. Depot ship until stricken December 1955. Scrapped in 1956.

BATTLESHIP **BRETAGNE**

1912 programme. Brest navy yard. Laid down: 22 July 1912. Launched: 21 April 1913. Completed: 10 February 1916.

BATTLESHIP **LORRAINE**

1912 programme. St. Nazaire. Laid down: 7 November 1912. Launched: 30 September 1913. Completed: 10 March 1916.

BATTLESHIP **PROVENCE**

1912 programme. Lorient navy yard. Laid down: 21 May 1912. Launched: 20 April 1913. Completed: 1 March 1916.

Dimensions

544.5-ft/166.5-m x 88.75-ft/27.14-m x 29.75-ft/9.10-m. Displacement: 22,189 tons (standard),

26,600 tons (full load). Armament: Ten (five twin turrets) 13.4-in/340-mm 45 calibre, fourteen 5.5-in/138.6-mm 55 calibre, four 47-mm guns. Armour: 10.63-in/270-mm belt, 15.75-in/ 400-mm turret, 10.63-in/270-mm barbette, 1.57-in/40-mm main deck. 12.20-in/ 314-mm CT. Weight of armour 7,683 tons. Machinery: **Provence** eighteen, others twenty-four boilers, two turbines, four shafts and 29,000 shp. Speed: 20.0 knots. Fuel: 2,700 tons coal, 300 tons oil. Range: 2,800 n.m. at 18.75 knots.

Fate
Bretagne: Sunk at Mers-el-Kebir on 3 July 1940 by British warships. Salvaged in 1952 and scrapped. **Lorraine**: Stricken 17 February 1953 and sold 18 December: scrapped at Pergaillon after January 1954. **Provence**: Settled after bombardment by British warships at Mers-el-Kebir on 3 July 1940 and salved. Scuttled at Toulon 27 November 1942. Raised by Italians in July 1943, taken over by Germans in September 1943 and scuttled in August 1944 as blockship. Raised April 1949 and scrapped.

BATTLESHIP **DUNKERQUE**
Brest navy yard. Laid down: 24 December 1932. Launched: 2 October 1935. Completed: 1 May 1937. Commissioned: 9 June 1938.

BATTLESHIP **STRASBOURG**
St. Nazaire. Laid down: 25 November 1934. Launched: 12 December 1936. Completed: December 1938. Commissioned: 6 April 1939.

Dimensions
Dunkerque 703.75-ft/215.2-m, **Strasbourg** 707-ft/216.2-m x 102.25-ft/31.27-m x 28.75-ft/ 8.79-m. Displacement: **Dunkerque** 26,500 tons (standard), 35,500 tons (deep load). **Strasbourg** 27,300 tons, 36,380 tons (deep load). Armament: Eight (two four-gun turrets) 13-in/ 330-mm 50 calibre, sixteen 5.1-in/130-mm 50 calibre DP, **Dunkerque** ten, **Strasbourg** eight 37-mm 50 calibre, eight quadrupled 13.2-mm Hotchkiss machine guns. Four seaplanes, one catapult. Armour: **Dunkerque**: 8.85-in/225-mm main belt, 13-in/330-mm turret, 12.2-in/ 310-mm barbette, 5.5-in/140-mm deck. **Strasbourg**: 11.14-in/283-mm main belt, 14.17-in/ 360-mm turret, 13.39-in/340-mm barbette, 5.5-in/140-mm deck. Weight of armour in the **Dunkerque**: 11,200 tons. Machinery: Six boilers. Four turbines. Four shafts and 112,500 shp. Speed: 29.5 knots (designed): 135,585 shp and 31.06 knots (on trials). Fuel: 6,500 tons oil. Range: 7,500 n.m. at 15 knots.

Fate
Dunkerque: In dock at Toulon and massive self-inflicted damage on 27 November 1942. Undocked August 1945 and left in bay until 1958 when sold and scrapped. **Strasbourg**: Scuttled 27 November 1942 at Toulon. Salved by Italians and taken over by Germans in September 1943. Sunk by American medium bombers on 18 August 1944 at Lazaret Bay. Raised in October 1944 but used for explosives trials. Scrapped May 1955.

BATTLESHIP **RICHELIEU**
1935 programme. Brest navy yard. Laid down: 22 October 1935. Launched: 17 January 1939. Commissioned: 15 June 1940.

BATTLESHIP **JEAN BART**
1935 programme. Ateliers et Chantiers de la Loire, St. Nazaire. Laid down: 12 December 1936. Launched: 6 March 1940. Commissioned: 1 May 1955.

Dimensions
813.25-ft/247.85-m x 108.25-ft/33-m x 31.75-ft/9.63-m. Displacement: 37,960 tons (standard), 47,548 tons (full load). Armament: Eight (two four-gun turrets) 15-in/380-mm 45 calibre, nine (3 x 3) 6-in/152-mm 55 calibre, **Richelieu** twelve 3.9-in/100-mm 45 calibre, eight 37-mm 50 calibre guns, thirty-six 13-mm machine guns. ? seaplanes, two catapults. Armour:

13-in/330-mm main belt, 16.93-in/430-mm turret, 3.93-in/100-mm barbette, 6.69-in/170-mm deck. Weight of armour 16,400 tons. Machinery: Six boilers, four turbines. Four shafts and 150,000 shp. Speed: 30.0 knots designed. **Richelieu** 179,000 shp and 32.63 knots: **Jean Bart** 176,030 shp and 32.13 knots. Fuel: **Richelieu**: 6,796 tons oil. **Jean Bart**: 6,476 tons oil. Range: **Richelieu**: 5,500 n.m. at 18 knots.

Fate
Richelieu: Placed in reserve 25 May 1956. Paid off 1 August 1958. Hulk used as accommodation ship at Brest: sold after 1965 and scrapped at La Spezia August 1968. **Jean Bart**: Placed in reserve 1 August 1957. Stricken January 1961: thereafter accommodation ship for gunnery school. Sold 1969. Scrapped in Japan after 1970.

GERMANY

BATTLESHIP **NASSAU**
1906 programme. Wilhelmshaven navy yard. Laid down: 22 July 1907. Launched: 7 March 1908. Completed: 1 October 1909. In service: 3 May 1910.

BATTLESHIP **WESTFALEN**
1906 programme. A.G. Weser, Bremen. Laid down: 22 July 1907. Launched: 1 July 1908. Completed: 16 November 1909. In service: 3 May 1910.

BATTLESHIP **RHEINLAND**
1907 programme. A.G. Vulcan, Stettin. Laid down: 1 June 1907. Launched: 26 September 1908. Completed: 30 April 1910. In service: 21 September 1910.

BATTLESHIP **POSEN**
1907 programme. Friedrich Krupp Germaniawerft, Kiel. Laid down: 11 June 1907. Launched: 12 December 1908. Completed: 31 May 1910. In service: 21 September 1910.

Dimensions
479.33-ft/146.59-m x 88.42-ft/27.04-m x 29.25-ft/8.94-m. Displacement: 18,570 tons (normal), 21,210 tons (full load). Armament: Twelve 11-in/280-mm 45 calibre, twelve 5.9-in/150-mm 45 calibre guns. Armament weight: 2,655 tons. Armour: 11.81-in/300-mm belt, 11-in/280-mm turret, barbette, 15.75-in/400-mm CT., 3.15-in/80-mm deck. Armour weight: 6,537 tons. Machinery: Twelve coal-burning Schulz-Thorneycroft boilers, three three-cylinder triple expansion engines, three shafts. 22,000 ihp. Machinery weight: 1,355 tons. Speed: 19.5 knots. Fuel: 2,952 tons coal. Range: 9,400 n.m. at 10 knots.

Fate
Nassau: Stricken 5 November 1919. Surrendered on 7 April 1920 to Japan as war reparations. Sold to British company in June 1920 and scrapped at Dordrecht in the Netherlands in 1920. **Westfalen**: Stricken 5 November 1919. Surrendered on 5 August 1920 to Britain as war reparations. Scrapped at Birkenhead in 1924. **Rheinland**: Surrendered to allies as war reparation and sold. Towed to Dordrecht in the Netherlands 29 July 1920 and scrapped in 1921. **Posen**: Stricken 5 November 1919. Surrendered on 13 May 1920 to Britain as war reparations. Scrapped at Dordrecht in 1922.

BATTLECRUISER **VON DER TANN**
1907 programme. Blohm and Voss, Hamburg. Laid down: 25 March 1908. Launched: 20 March 1909. Completed: 1 September 1910. In service: 19 February 1911.

Dimensions
563.33-ft/172.27-m x 87.25-ft/26.68-m x 29.67-ft/9.07-m. Displacement: 19,064 tons (normal), 21,700 tons (full load). Armament: Eight 11-in/280-mm 45 calibre, ten 5.9-in/150-mm 45 calibre guns. Armament weight: 2,096 tons. Armour: 9.84-in/250-mm belt, 9.06-in/230-mm

turret, barbette, 9.84-in/250-mm CT., 1.97-in/50-mm deck. Armour weight: 6,201 tons. Machinery: Eighteen coal-burning Schulz-Thorneycroft boilers, two Parsons turbines, four shafts. 42,000 shp. Machinery weight: 2,805 tons. Speed: 24.8 knots. Fuel: 2,756 tons coal. Range: 4,400 n.m. at 14 knots.

Fate
Surrendered 21 November 1918 and interned at Scapa Flow after 24 November 1918. Scuttled 21 June 1919. Raised 7 December 1930 and thereafter scrapped in 1934.

BATTLESHIP **HELGOLAND**
1908 programme. Howaldtswerke, Kiel. Laid down: 24 November 1908. Launched: 30 September 1909. Completed: 23 August 1911. In service: 20 December 1911.

BATTLESHIP **OSTFRIESLAND**
1908 programme. Wilhelmshaven navy yard. Laid down: 19 October 1908. Launched: 30 September 1909. Completed: 1 August 1911. In service: 15 September 1911.

BATTLESHIP **THÜRINGEN**
1908 programme. A.G. Weser, Bremen. Laid down: 2 November 1908. Launched: 27 November 1909. Completed: 1 July 1911. In service: 10 September 1911.

BATTLESHIP **OLDENBURG**
1909 programme. Ferdinand Schichau, Danzig. Laid down: 1 March 1909. Launched: 30 June 1910. Completed: 1 May 1912. In service: 1 July 1912.

Dimensions
548.58-ft/167.76-m x 93.5-ft/28.59-m x 29.24-ft/8.90-m. Displacement: 22,437 tons (normal), 24,312 tons (full load). Armament: Twelve 12-in/30.5-mm 50 calibre, fourteen 5.9-in/150-mm 45 calibre guns. Six 19.7-in/500-mm torpedo tubes. Armament weight: 3,388 tons. Armour: 11.81-in/300-mm belt, turret, 10.63-in/270-mm barbette, 15.75-in/400-mm CT., 3.15-in/80-mm deck. Armour weight: 8,212 tons. Machinery: Fifteen coal-burning Schulz-Thorneycroft boilers, three four-cylinder triple expansion engines, three shafts. 28,000 ihp. Machinery weight: 1,773 tons. Speed: 21 knots. Fuel: 3,150 tons. Range: 3,600 n.m. at 18 knots.

Fate
Helgoland: Stricken 5 November 1919. Surrendered on 5 August 1920 to Britain as war reparations. Used for testing explosives and scrapped at Morecombe in 1924. **Ostfriesland**: Stricken 5 November 1919. Surrendered on 7 April 1920 to the United States as war reparations, and recommissioned that day: decommissioned at New York 20 September 1920. Used as a target ship off Cape Henry, Virginia, and sunk on 21 July 1921. **Thüringen**: Stricken 5 November 1919. Surrendered 29 April 1920 to France. Transferred to Cherbourg where she was used as target ship until being scrapped at Gavres-Lorient in 1933. **Oldenburg**: Stricken 5 November 1919. Surrendered on 13 May 1920 to Japan. Sold to British company and scrapped at Dordrecht in the Netherlands in 1921.

BATTLECRUISER **MOLTKE**
1908 programme. Blohm and Voss, Hamburg. Laid down: 7 December 1908. Launched: 7 April 1910. Completed: 30 September 1911. In service: 31 March 1912.

BATTLECRUISER **GOEBEN**
1909 programme. Blohm and Voss, Hamburg. Laid down: 7 December 1909. Launched: 28 March 1911. Completed: 2 July 1912. In service: 28 August 1912.

Dimensions
611.92-ft/187.13-m x 96.83-ft/29.61-m x 29.46-ft/9.01-m. Displacement: 22,616 tons (normal), 25,300 tons (full load). Armament: Ten 11-in/280-mm 50 calibre, **Moltke** twelve, **Goeben** ten 5.9-in/150-mm 45 calibre, twelve 3.9-in,/88-mm 45 calibre guns. Armour:

10.63-in/270-mm belt, 9.06-in/230-mm turret, 9.84-in/250-mm barbette, 13.78-in/350-mm CT., 1.97-in/50-mm deck. Machinery: Twenty-four coal-burning Schulz-Thorneycroft boilers, two Parsons turbines, four shafts. 52,000 shp. Speed: 25.5 knots (designed). **Moltke** 85,782 shp and 28.4 knots, **Goeben** 85,661 shp and 28 knots on trials. Fuel: 2,952 tons coal. Range: 4,120 n.m. at 14 knots.

Goeben. 1926–1930 refit. Displacement: 22,734 tons (normal). Armament: Ten 11-in/280-mm, ten 5.9-in/150-mm, four 3.7-in/88-mm AA, four machine guns. Two 19.7-in torpedo tubes. Machinery: new boilers. Speed: 27.1 knots. 1941 refit: Four 3/7-in/88-mm, ten 40-mm and four 20-mm AA guns added. Final tertiary armament reported as twenty-two 40-mm and twenty-four 20-mm AA guns, but unclear when additional numbers were added. The main mast was removed to provide for AA fire control position.

Fate
Moltke: Involved in the surrender of 21 November 1918. Interned at Scapa Flow on 24 November 1918. Scuttled 21 June 1919. Raised 10 June 1927 and scrapped at Rosyth in 1929. **Goeben**: 2 November 1918 formally handed over to Turkey. See **TURKEY**.

BATTLESHIP **KAISER**
1909 programme. Kiel navy yard. Laid down: October 1909. Launched: 22 March 1911. Completed: 1 August 1912. In service: 7 December 1912.

BATTLESHIP **FRIEDRICH DER GROSSE**
1909 programme. A.G. Vulcan, Hamburg. Laid down: 26 January 1910. Launched: 10 June 1911. Completed: 15 October 1912. In service: 8 December 1912.

BATTLESHIP **KAISERIN**
1910 programme. Howaldtswerke, Kiel. Laid down: July 1910. Launched: 11 November 1911. Completed: 14 May 1913. In service: 13 December 1913.

BATTLESHIP **KÖNIG ALBERT**
1910 programme. Schichau, Danzig. Laid down: 17 July 1910. Launched: 27 April 1912. Completed: 31 July 1913. In service: 8 November 1913.

BATTLESHIP **PRINZREGENT LUITPOLD**
1910 programme. Friedrich Krupp Germaniawerft, Kiel. Laid down: October 1910. Launched: 17 February 1912. Completed: 19 August 1913. In service: 6 December 1913.

Dimensions
565.58-ft/172.95-m x 95.17-ft/29.10-m x 30-ft/9.17-m. Displacement: 24,330 tons (normal), 27,400 tons (full load). Armament: Ten 12-in/305-mm 50 calibre, fourteen 5.9-in/150-mm 45 calibre, eight 3.5-in/88-mm 45 calibre, four 3.5-in/88-mm 45 calibre AA guns. Five 19.7-in/500-mm torpedo tubes. Armour: 13.78-in/350-mm belt, 11.81-in/300-mm turret, barbette, 15.75-in/400-mm CT., 4.72-in/120-mm deck. Machinery: Sixteen coal-burning Schulz-Thorneycroft boilers, three turbines, three shafts. 31,000 shp. Speed: 21 knots. Fuel: 2,952 tons coal. Range: 7,900 n.m. at 12 knots.

Fate
All involved in the 21 November 1918 surrender, interned 25 November 1918 (**König Albert** the next day) at Scapa Flow and scuttled 21 June 1919. **Kaiser**: Raised 20 March 1929, scrapped at Rosyth. **Friedrich der Grosse**: Raised 29 April 1937, scrapped at Scapa. **Kaiserin**: Raised 14 May 1936, scrapped at Rosyth. **König Albert**: Raised 31 July 1935, scrapped at Rosyth. **Prinzregent Luitpold**: Raised 9 July 1931, scrapped at Rosyth in 1933.

BATTLECRUISER **SEYDLITZ**
1910 programme. Blohm and Voss, Hamburg. Laid down: 4 December 1911. Launched: 30 March 1912. Completed: 22 May 1913. In service: 17 August 1913.

Dimensions
657.92-ft/201.19-m x 93.50-ft/28.59-m x 30.25-ft/9.25-m. Displacement: 24,594 tons (normal), 28,100 tons (full load). Armament: Ten 11-in/280-mm 50 calibre, twelve 5.9-in/150-mm 25 calibre, twelve 3.5-in/88-mm 45 calibre guns. Four 19.7-in/500-mm torpedo tubes. Armour: 11.81-in/300-mm belt, 9.84-in/250-mm turret, barbette, 11.81-in/300-mm CT., 3.15-in/80-mm deck. Machinery: Twenty-seven Schulz-Thorneycroft boilers, four turbines, four shafts. 67,000 shp. Speed: 26.5 knots. Fuel: 3,543 tons coal. Range: 4,200 n.m. at 14 knots.

Fate
Involved in surrender of 21 November 1918. Interned at Scapa Flow 24 November 1918. Scuttled 21 July 1919. Raised 2 November 1928. Scrapped between 1928 and 1930 at Rosyth.

BATTLESHIP **KÖNIG**
1911 programme. Wilhelmshaven navy yard. Laid down: 3 October 1911. Launched: 1 March 1913. Completed: 9 August 1914. In service: 23 November 1914.

BATTLESHIP **GROSSER KURFÜRST**
1911 programme. A.G. Vulcan, Hamburg. Laid down: 3 October 1911. Launched: 5 May 1913. Completed: 30 July 1914. In service: 25 October 1914.

BATTLESHIP **MARKGRAF**
1911 programme. A.G. Weser, Bremen. Laid down: November 1911. Launched: 4 June 1913. Completed: 1 October 1914. In service: 10 January 1915.

BATTLESHIP **KRONPRINZ**
1912 programme. Friedrich Krupp Germaniawerft, Kiel. Laid down: July 1912. Launched: 21 February 1914. Completed: 8 November 1914. In service: 2 January 1915.

Dimensions
575.50-ft/175.98-m x 96.95-ft/29.65-m x 30.54-ft/9.34-m. Displacement: 25,391 tons (normal), 28,148 tons (full load). Armament: Ten 12-in/305-mm 50 calibre, fourteen 5.9-in/150-mm 45 calibre, six 3.5-in/88-mm guns. Five 19.7-in/500-mm torpedo tubes. Armament weight: 3,073 tons. Armour: 13.78-in/350-mm belt, 11.81-in/300-mm turret, barbette, CT., 3.94-in/100-mm deck. Armour weight: 10,283 tons. Machinery: Three oil-burning and twelve coal-burning Schulz-Thorneycroft boilers, three turbines, three shafts. 31,000 shp. Initially proposed that all ships, then only the **Grosser Kurfürst** and **Markgraf**, should be fitted with one MAN six-cylinder two-stroke diesel engine with a cruise capacity of 12 knots on 12,000 shp. This intention was abandoned. Machinery weight: 2,133 tons. Speed: 21 knots. Fuel: 3,543 tons oil. Range: 8,000 n.m. at 12 knots.

Fate
König: On 6 December 1918 interned at Scapa Flow. Scuttled 21 June 1919. Not salved. **Grosser Kurfürst**: Involved in the surrender of 21 November 1918. Interned 26 November 1918 at Scapa Flow. Scuttled 21 June 1919. Raised 29 April 1936 and scrapped thereafter at Rosyth. **Markgraf** and **Kronprinz**: Involved in the surrender of 21 November 1918. Interned 26 November 1918 at Scapa Flow. Scuttled 21 June 1919. Not salved.

BATTLECRUISER **DERFFLINGER**
1911 programme. Blohm and Voss, Hamburg. Laid down: January 1912. Launched: 12 July 1913. Completed: 1 September 1914. In service: 6 November 1914. (The launch was to have been 14 June but she jammed on the slip for four weeks before taking to water.)

BATTLECRUISER **LÜTZOW**
1912 programme. Ferdinand Schichau, Danzig. Laid down: July 1912. Launched: 29 November 1913. Completed: 8 August 1915. In service: 20 March 1916.

Dimensions
690.25-ft/211.07-m x 95.17-ft/29.10-m x 31-ft/9.48-m. Displacement: 26,180 tons (normal), 30,707 tons (full load). Armament: Eight 12-in/305-mm 50 calibre, fourteen (**Lützow** twelve) 5.9-in/150-mm 45 calibre, eight 3.5-mm/88-mm 45 calibre guns. Four **Derfflinger** 19.7-in/500-mm **Lützow** 23.6-in/600-mm torpedo tubes. Armour: 11.81-in/300-mm belt, 10.63-in/270-mm turret, 10.23-in/260-mm barbette, 13.78-in/350-mm CT., 3.15-in/80-mm deck. Machinery: Fourteen twin coal-burning Shulz-Thorneycroft boilers, two turbines, four shafts. 63,000 shp. Speed: 26.5 knots. Fuel: 3,842 tons coal, 984 oil. Range: 5,300 n.m. at 14 knots.

Fate
Derfflinger: Surrender of 21 November 1918: interned 26 November 1918 at Scapa Flow. Scuttled 21 June 1919. Raised in 1939, and left floating inverted inside Scapa Flow throughout the Second World War: scrapped between 1945 and 1948 at Faslane. **Lützow**: scuttled at the battle of Jutland 1 June 1916: partially scrapped 1959–1962.

BATTLESHIP **BAYERN**
1913 programme. Howaldtswerke, Kiel. Laid down: 20 September 1913. Launched: 18 February 1915. Completed: 18 March 1916.

BATTLESHIP **BADEN**
1913 programme. Ferdinand Schichau, Danzig. Laid down: 29 September 1913. Launched: 30 October 1915. Completed: 19 October 1916.

Dimensions
589.83-ft/180.37-m x 98.42-ft/30.09-m x 30.75-ft/9.40-m. Displacement: 28,061 tons (normal), 31,691 tons (full load). Armament: Eight 15-in/380-mm 45 calibre, sixteen 5.9-in/150-mm 45 calibre, eight (as originally planned, but none at time of commissioning and then four) 3.5-in/88-mm AA guns. Five 23.6-in/600-mm torpedo tubes. Armour: 13.78-in/350-mm belt, turret, barbette, CT., 3.94-in/100-mm deck. Machinery: Eleven coal-burning and three oil-burning Schulz-Thorneycroft boilers: **Bayern** three Parsons, **Baden** three Schichau, turbines, three shafts. 48,000 shp. Speed: 22 knots (as designed). **Baden** 21 knots. Fuel: 3,346 tons coal, 610 tons oil. Range: 5,016 n.m. at 12 knots.

Fate
Bayern: Involved in surrender of 21 November 1918. Interned 26 November 1918 at Scapa Flow. Scuttled 21 June 1919. Raised on 1 September 1934 and scrapped in 1935 at Rosyth. **Baden**: Surrendered and interned at Scapa Flow in January 1919. On 21 June 1919 prevented from sinking by tugs which pushed her ashore. Raised July 1919. Used as target ship and sunk off Portsmouth 16 August 1921.

BATTLECRUISER **HINDENBURG**
1913 programme. Wilhelmshaven navy yard. Laid down: 30 June 1913. Launched: 1 August 1915. Completed: 10 May 1917. In service: 25 October 1917.

Dimensions
698.17-ft/213.49-m x 95.17-ft/29.10-m x 31-ft/9.48-m. Displacement: 26,513 tons (normal), 31,002 tons (full load). Armament: Eight 12-in/305-mm 50 calibre, fourteen 5.9-in/150-mm 45 calibre, eight 3.5-mm/88-mm 45 calibre guns. Four 23.6-in/600-mm torpedo tubes. Armament weight: 2,730 tons. Armour: 11.81-in/300-mm belt, 10.63-in/270-mm turret, 10.23-in/260-mm barbette, 13.78-in/350-mm CT., 3.15-in/80-mm deck. Armour weight: 9,809 tons. Machinery: Fourteen twin coal-burning Shulz-Thorneycroft boilers, two turbines, four shafts. 72,000 shp. Machinery weight: 2,916 tons. Speed: 27 knots. Fuel: 3,842 tons coal, 984 oil. Range: 5,300 n.m. at 14 knots.

Fate
Involved in the surrender of 21 November 1918. Interned 24 November 1918 at Scapa Flow. Scuttled 21 June 1919. Raised 22 July 1930 and scrapped at Rosyth.

BATTLESHIP **GNEISENAU**
Deutsche Werke, Kiel. Laid down: 6 May 1935. Launched: 8 December 1936. Completed: 21 May 1938.

BATTLESHIP **SCHARNHORST**
Wilhelmshaven navy yard. Laid down: 16 May 1935. Launched: 3 October 1936. Completed: 7 January 1939.

Dimensions
741.42-ft/226.72-m x 98.42-ft/30.09-m x 32.50-ft/9.94-m. Displacement: 26,000 tons (standard declared), 31,850 tons (standard in reality), 38,900 tons (full load). Armament: Nine 11-in/280-mm 54.5 calibre with 45 degree elevation, twelve 5.9-in/150-mm 55 calibre, fourteen 4.1-in/105-mm 65 calibre, sixteen 37-mm 69 calibre, eight 20-mm 65 calibre AA guns. Three or four aircraft. Armament weight: 5,121 tons. Armour: 13.8-in/350-mm belt, 14.17-in/360-mm turret, 13.8-in/350-mm barbette, CT., 4.1-in/105-mm deck. Armour weight: 14,006 tons. Machinery: Twelve Wagner extra high-pressure boilers, three **Gneisenau** Germania **Scharnhorst** Brown-Boveri geared turbines, three shafts. 165,000 shp. Machinery weight: 2,578 tons. Speed: 32 knots. Fuel: 6,200 tons oil. Range: 8,800 n.m. at 19 knots, 10,000 n.m. at 17 knots.

Fate
Gneisenau: decommissioned at Gotenhafen 1 July 1942 in readiness for reconstruction that was intended to fit her with 15-in/380-mm guns. Work halted in January 1943. 23 March 1945 towed into the harbour and scuttled: raised and scrapped after 1947. Completed 12 September 1951. **Scharnhorst**: Sunk 26 December 1943 off the North Cape, in the Arctic Ocean, in action with British force, which included the battleship **Duke of York**.

BATTLESHIP **BISMARCK**
Blohm and Voss, Hamburg. Laid down: 1 July 1936. Launched: 14 February 1939. Completed: 24 August 1940. In service: 19 May 1942.

BATTLESHIP **TIRPITZ**
Wilhelmshaven navy yard. Laid down: 26 October 1936. Launched: 1 April 1939. Completed: 25 February 1941.

Dimensions
813.67-ft/248.81-m x 118.08-ft/36.11-m x 34.75-ft/10.63-m. Displacement: 35,000 tons (standard declared), **Bismarck** 41,700 tons, **Tirpitz** 42,900 tons (standard in reality), **Bismarck** 50,900 tons, **Tirpitz** 52,600 tons (full load). (Design displacement 45,172 tons). Weight of hull: 11,474 tons. Armament: Eight 15-in/380-mm 47 calibre, twelve 5.9-in/ 150-mm 55 calibre, sixteen 4.1-in/105-mm 65 calibre, sixteen 37-mm 69 calibre, twelve 20-mm 65 calibre AA guns: **Tirpitz** final tertiary armament was ten 20-mm and ten quadruple 20-mm guns. Eight (two groups of four) 21-in/533-mm torpedo tubes (no fire control systems). Between four and six seaplanes, one double catapult. Armament weight: 7,453 tons. Armour: 12.60-in/320-mm belt, 14.17-in/360-mm turret, 13.39-in/340-mm barbette, 13.80-in/ 350-mm CT., 4.72-in/120-mm deck. Armour weight: 17,256 tons. Machinery: Twelve Wagner extra high-pressure boilers, Three **Bismarck** Blohm and Voss **Tirpitz** Brown-Boveri geared turbines, three shafts. 138,000 shp. Machinery weight: 2,756 tons. Speed: 29 knots (as designed): on trials **Tirpitz** 30.8 knots on 163,000 shp. Fuel: **Bismarck** 7,775 tons, **Tirpitz** 8,641 tons oil. Range: **Bismarck** 9,280 n.m., **Tirpitz** 10,200 n.m. at 16 knots.

Fate
Bismarck: Sunk, west of Brest, on 27 May 1941, by British forces which included the **King George V** and **Rodney**. **Tirpitz**: Sunk at Tromsø on 12 November by three hits and three near-misses by 12,000-lb. bombs, which caused her to capsize and blow up. Scrapped *in situ* between 1948 and 1957.

ITALY

BATTLESHIP **DANTE ALIGHIERI**

1907 programme. Cantieri di Castellamare di Stabia (navy yard). Laid down: 6 June 1909. Launched: 20 August 1910. Completed: 15 January 1911 but for main armament which, from Armstrong, was not delivered until 1913.

Dimensions
551.5-ft/168.1-m x 87.25-ft/26.6-m x 31.7-ft/9.7-m. Displacement: 19,500 tons (as designed), 21,800 tons (full load). Armament: Twelve (four three-gun turrets) 12-in/305-mm 46 calibre, twenty (four twin and twelve single) 4.7-in/120-mm 50 calibre, initially sixteen but reduced to twelve 76-mm 40 calibre guns. Two beam and one stern 17.7-in/450-mm torpedo tubes (submerged). She carried one seaplane from 1913. Armour: 10-in/254-mm belt, 10-in/254-mm turret, 11-in/280-mm CT, 1.18-in/30-mm deck. Machinery: Sixteen mixed and seven oil-fired boilers. Three turbines. Three shafts and 32,200 shp. Speed: 23 knots (as designed). On trails 35,000 shp and 24.2 knots (and very briefly the fastest battleship in the world). Fuel: 2,400 tons coal, 600 tons oil. Range: 5,000 n.m. at 10 knots.

Fate
Obsolete by 1918 and incapable of major reconstruction. Partially modernised in 1923 but stricken 1 July 1928 and scrapped thereafter.

BATTLESHIP **CONTE DI CAVOUR**

Authorised/ordered in 1908 but 1910 programme. Arsenale do La Spezia (navy yard). Laid down: 10 August 1910. Launched: 10 August 1911. Completed: 1 April 1915.

BATTLESHIP **GIULIO CESARE**

1910 programme. Cantieri Ansaldo, Genoa. Laid down: 24 June 1910. Launched: 15 October 1911. Completed: 14 May 1914.

BATTLESHIP **LEONARDO DA VINCI**

1910 programme. Cantieri Odero, Genoa. Laid down: 18 July 1910. Launched: 14 October 1911. Completed: 17 May 1914.

Dimensions
575.85-ft/176.1-m x 91.83-ft/28-m x 30.83-ft/9.4-m. Displacement: 23,088 tons (as designed), 25,086 tons (full load). Armament: Thirteen 12-in/305-mm 46 calibre guns carried in three triple and two twin turrets: the twin turrets were superimposed fore and aft, with the third triple turret carried amidships between the two funnels. Eighteen 4.7-in/120-mm 50 calibre, thirteen 76-mm 40 calibre guns. Two beam and one stern 17.7-in/450-mm torpedo tubes (submerged). Armour: 10-in/250-mm belt, 11-in/280-mm turret, 9.45-in/240-mm barbette, 11-in/280-mm CT, 1.69-in/43-mm deck. Weight of armour 6,220 tons. Machinery: Twelve coal- and eight oil-burning boilers (except **Giulio Cesare** with twelve coal- and twelve oil-burning boilers). Three turbines. Four shafts. 31,000 shp. Speed: 21.5 knots as designed: **Conte di Cavour** 22.2 knots on trials. Fuel: Initially 570 tons coal, 350 tons oil: later 1,450 tons coal, 850 tons oil. Range: 4,800 n.m. at 10 knots.

Fate
Leonardo da Vinci: Destroyed by a magazine explosion in Taranto on 2 August 1916. Raised 17 September 1919 and docked in November 1919. Stricken 23 January 1921. Sold 26 March 1923 and scrapped at Taranto. **Conte di Cavour**: Sunk by single torpedo hit at Taranto by carrier aircraft on night 11/12 November 1940. Raised in July 1941 and towed to Trieste for repairs. Work halted early 1943. Scuttled 10 September 1943 at time of national surrender. Raised by Germans and sunk in U.S. strategic bombing raid on 15 February 1945. Raised and scrapped between 1950 and 1952. **Giulio Cesare**: Surrendered at Malta in September 1943 and served at Taranto. Surrendered to Soviet Union 3 February 1949 as part of

peace treaty: served as the **Novorossijsk** in the Black Sea Fleet. Lost 28–29 October 1955 in Sevastopol harbour after being mined.

BATTLESHIP **ANDREA DORIA**
1911 programme. Arsenale do La Spezia, completed at Genoa. Laid down: 24 March 1912. Launched: 30 March 1913. Completed: 13 March 1916.

BATTLESHIP **CAIO DUILIO**
1911 programme. Cantieri di Castellamare di Stabia (navy yard). Laid down: 24 February 1912. Launched: 24 April 1913. Completed: 10 May 1915.

Dimensions
575.85-ft/176.1-m x 91.56-ft/28-m x 31.08-ft/9.5-m. Displacement: 22,694 tons (standard), 25,200 tons (full load). Armament: Thirteen 12-in/305-mm 46 calibre, sixteen 6-in/152-mm 45 calibre, eighteen 3.1-in/76-mm guns, two 17.7-in/450-mm torpedo tubes. After 1926 one seaplane, one catapult. Armour: 9.84-in/250-mm belt, 9.49-in/240-mm turret, barbette, 12.60-in/320-mm CT., 1.73-in/44-mm deck. Machinery: Twenty (twelve coal, eight oil) Yarrow boilers, three Parsons geared turbines, four shafts. 32,000 shp. Speed: 21.5 knots. Fuel: 1,450 tons coal, 850 tons oil. Range: 4,800 n.m. at 10 knots.

Fate
Andrea Doria: In reserve after June 1953. Stricken 1 November 1956 and scrapped at La Spezia between 1959 and 1962. **Caio Duilio**: In reserve after May 1953. Stricken 15 September 1956 and scrapped at La Spezia between 1959 and 1962.

BATTLESHIP **LITTORIO**
1934 programme. Cantieri Ansaldo, Genoa. Laid down: 28 October 1934. Launched: 22 August 1937. Completed: 6 May 1940.

BATTLESHIP **VITTORIO VENETO**
1934 programme. Cantieri Rinunti dell'Adriatico, Trieste. Laid down: 28 October 1934. Launched: 22 July 1937. Completed: 28 April 1940.

BATTLESHIP **ROMA**
1938 programme. Cantieri Rinunti dell'Adriatico, Trieste. Laid down: 18 September 1938. Launched: 9 June 1940. Completed: 14 June 1942.

Dimensions
780-ft/238.5-m (**Roma** 789.5-ft/241.43-m) x 107.4-ft/32.72-m x 31.4-ft/9.60-m. Displacement: 40,714 tons (standard), 45,236 tons (full load). Weight of hull: 10,440 tons. Armament: Nine (three triple turrets) 15-in/380-mm 50 calibre, twelve 6-in/152-mm 52 calibre, four 4.7-in, twelve 3.5-in/88.9-mm, twenty 37-mm 54 calibre, sixteen 20-mm 65 calibre guns. One catapult, three seaplanes. Armament weight: 6,465 tons. Armour: 13.78-in/350-mm main belt, 11.42-in/290-mm turret, 13.78-in/350-mm barbette, 8.15-in/207-mm deck. Weight of armour: **Littorio** 13,453 tons. Machinery: Eight boilers, four geared turbines, four shafts. 128,000 shp = 30 knots (designed). Machinery weight: **Vittorio Veneto**, 2,366 tons. Trials speeds: **Littorio** 31.29 knots. **Vittorio Veneto**, 31.43 knots. Fuel: 4,140 tons oil. Range: 4,580 n.m. at 16 knots.

Fate
Littorio: On 30 July 1943 renamed **Italia**. Peace treaty of 1947 allocated her to the United States, which ordered her scrapping. Paid off 1 June 1948 and scrapped at La Spezia between 1948 and 1950. **Vittorio Veneto**: Peace treaty of 1947 allocated her to Britain, which ordered her scrapping. Paid off 3 January 1948 and stricken 1 February and scrapped at La Spezia between 1948 and 1950. **Roma**: Sunk on 9 September 1943 while en route to surrender at Malta. Hit by two armour-piercing glider bombs launched by German aircraft. The first passed through and exploded under her: the second penetrated and exploded in the forward magazine.

JAPAN

BATTLESHIP **SETTSU**
1907 programme. Yokosuka navy yard. Laid down: 18 January 1909. Launched: 30 March 1911. Completed: 1 July 1912.

BATTLESHIP **KAWACHI**
1907 programme. Kure navy yard. Laid down: 1 April 1909. Launched: 15 October 1910. Completed: 31 March 1912.

Dimensions
526-ft/160.86-m x 84.25-ft/25.76-m x 27-ft/8.26-m. Displacement: 20,823 tons (as designed), 21,443 tons (standard). Armament: Four 12-in/305-mm 50 calibre, eight 12-in/305-mm 45 calibre, ten 6-in/152-mm 50 calibre, eight 4.7-in/120-mm 50 calibre, twelve 3-in/76-mm guns. Three (including one stern) 18-in/457-mm torpedo tubes. Armament weight: 4,458 tons. Armour: 12-in/305-mm belt, 11-in/279-mm turret, barbette, 10-in/254-mm CT, 1.2-in/30-mm deck. Armour weight: 4,960 tons. Machinery: Sixteen Miyabara (coal) boilers, two (**Settsu** Parsons, **Kawachi** Curtis) turbines, two shafts. 25,000 shp. Speed: 20 knots. Fuel: 2,300 tons coal, 400 tons oil. Range: 2,700 n.m. at 18 knots.

Fate
Kawachi: Destroyed on 12 July 1916 in Tokuyama Bay by magazine explosion. **Settsu**: Disarmed and decommissioned 7 September 1921 at Kure navy yard. Converted to serve as target ship. Run aground when sinking off Tsukumo, near Kure, during 24 July 1945 raid by U.S. carrier aircraft. Salvaged and scrapped at Kure by July 1947.

BATTLECRUISER **KONGO**
1910 programme. Vickers Armstrong, Barrow-in-Furness, Britain. Laid down: 17 January 1911. Launched: 18 May 1912. Completed: 16 August 1913.

BATTLECRUISER **HIEI**
1910 programme. Yokosuka naval yard. Laid down: 4 November 1911. Launched: 21 November 1912. Completed: 4 August 1914.

BATTLECRUISER **HARUNA**
1911 programme. Kawasaki at Kobe. Laid down: 16 March 1912. Launched: 14 December 1913. Completed: 19 April 1915.

BATTLECRUISER **KIRISHIMA**
1911 programme. Mitsubishi at Nagasaki. Laid down: 17 March 1912. Launched: 1 December 1913. Completed: 19 April 1915.

Dimensions
704-ft/214.6-m x 92-ft/28.0-m x 27.58-ft/8.4-m. (**Haruna** 28.3-ft/8.65-m). Displacement: 26,230 tons (standard), 27,500 tons (normal), 32,200 tons (full). Armament: Eight 14-in/356-mm 45 calibre at 33 degrees, sixteen 6-in/152-mm 50 calibre, eight 12-pdr, 8 x 21-in/533-mm torpedo tubes with sixteen torpedoes. Armour: 8-in/203-mm belt, 9-in/229-mm turret, 10-in/254-mm barbette, 10-in/254-mm CT., 2.75-in/60-mm deck. Armour weight: 6,502 tons. Machinery: Thirty-six coal-burning Yarrow (**Haruna** Brown-Curtis) boilers, four Parsons turbines, four shafts. 64,000 shp. Machinery weight: 4,750 tons. Speed: 27.5 knots. Fuel: 4,200 tons coal, 1,000 tons oil. Range: 8,000 n.m. at 14 knots.

First reconstruction
Hiei at Kure naval yard as gunnery training ship between 15 October 1929 and 31 December 1932. Dimensions: 704-ft/214.6-m x 92-ft/28.0-m x 20.75-ft/6.35-m. Displacement: 19,500 tons (standard). Armament: Six 14-in/356-mm 45 calibre, eight 5-in/127-mm, four 3-in/76-mm AA guns. Armour: 9-in/229-mm turret, 2.75-in/60-mm deck. Machinery: Eleven boilers, four turbines. Four shafts. 13,800 shp. Speed: 18 knots. **Haruna** at Yokosuka naval yard between

March 1924 and 31 July 1928. **Kirishima** at Kure naval yard between March 1927 and 31 March 1930. **Kongo** at Yokosuka naval yard between either .. September 1929 and 31 March 1931 or 20 October 1928 and 20 September 1931. Dimensions: 704-ft/214.6-m x 95.25-ft/ 29.13-m x 31-ft/9.48-m. Displacement: 29,330 tons (standard). Armament: Eight 14-in/ 356-mm 45 calibre at 43 degrees, sixteen 6-in/152-mm 50 calibre, four 3-in/76-mm AA guns. Four 21-in/533-mm torpedo tubes. Three seaplanes. Armour: 8-in/203-mm belt, 11-in/ 280-mm turret, 10-in/254-mm barbette, 10-in/254-mm CT., 4.75-in/120-mm deck. Armour weight: 10,313 tons. Machinery: Sixteen boilers (six coal, ten oil), four turbines, four shafts. 64,000 shp. Machinery weight: 3,943 tons. Speed: 25.9 knots. Fuel: 2,661 tons coal, 3,292 tons oil. Range: 9,500 n.m. at 14 knots.

Second reconstruction
Haruna at Kure naval yard between August 1933 and 30 September 1934. **Hiei** rebuilt at Kure navy yard as fast battleship between 26 November 1936 and 31 January 1940. **Kirishima** at Sasebo naval yard between June 1934 and 8 June 1936. **Kongo** at Kure navy yard between either .. November 1936 and 31 January 1940 or 1 June 1935 and 8 January 1940. Dimensions: 728-ft/222.63-m x 101-ft/30.89-m x 31-ft/9.79-m. Displacement: 32,156 tons (standard), 36,601 tons (full). Hull weight: 13,439 tons. Eight 14-in/356-mm 45 calibre at 43 degrees, fourteen 6-in/152-mm 50 calibre, eight 5-in/127-mm AA. Tertiary armament: **Haruna** four 40-mm AA, eight 13-mm AA until 1936/thereafter twenty 25-mm AA, **Kirishima** and **Kongo** twenty 25-mm AA guns. Three seaplanes. Armament weight: 5,133 tons. Armour: 8-in/203-mm belt, 11-in/280-mm turret, 10-in/254-mm barbette, 4.75-in/120-mm deck, 10-in/254-mm CT. Armour weight: 10,732 tons. Machinery: Eight Kampon boilers, four Kampon turbines, four shafts. 136,000 shp. Machinery weight: 2,929 tons. Speed: 30.5 knots, **Hiei** 29.9 knots. Fuel: 6,330 tons oil. Range: 10,000 n.m. at 18 knots.

Fate
Haruna capsized 28 July 1945 in 34°15'N 132°29'E off Kure, in the Inland Sea, as a result of damage inflicted by carrier aircraft: raised and scrapped at Kure, 1946. **Hiei** sunk 13 November 1942 in 9°00' 159°00' off Guadalcanal by U.S. light forces and carrier- and land-based aircraft. **Kirishima** sunk 14 November 1942 in 9°5'S 159°42'E in the second naval battle of Guadalcanal. **Kongo** sunk 21 November 1944 in 26°9'N 121°23'E off northwest Formosa by the U.S. submarine **Sealion**.

BATTLESHIP **FUSO**
1911 programme. Kure naval yard. Laid down: 11 March 1912. Launched: 28 March 1914. Completed: 8 November 1915.

BATTLESHIP **YAMASHIRO**
1913 programme. Kure naval yard. Laid down: 20 November 1913. Launched: 3 November 1915. Completed: 31 March 1917.

Dimensions
673-ft/205.81-m x 94-ft/28.75-m x 28.25-ft/8.64-m. Displacement: 29,326 tons (standard), 30,600 tons (normal), 35,900 tons (full). Armament: 12 x 14-in/356-mm 45 calibre at 30 degrees, sixteen 6-in/152-mm, four 3-in/76-mm AA guns. Six 21-in/533-mm torpedo tubes. Armament weight: 5,539 tons. Armour: 12-in/305-mm belt, 12-in/305-mm turret, 8.07-in/205-mm barbette, 13.82-in/351-mm CT., 2-in/50.8-mm deck. Armour weight: 8,588 tons. Machinery: Twenty-four Miyabara boilers, four Brown turbines, four shafts. 40,000 shp. Machinery weight: 3,554 tons. Speed: 23 knots. Fuel: 5,022 tons coal, 1,026 tons oil. Range: 8,000 n.m. at 14 knots.

Reconstruction
Fuso at Kure navy yard between April 1930 and 10 May 1933. **Yamashiro** at Yokosuka navy yard between December 1930 and 30 March 1935. Dimensions: 698-ft/213.46-m x 108.5-ft/ 33.18-m x 31.75-ft/9.7-m. Displacement: 34,700 tons (normal), 39,154 tons (full). Armament:

Twelve 14-in/356-mm 45 calibre at 43 degrees, fourteen 6-in/152-mm, eight 5-in/127-mm AA, sixteen 25-mm AA guns. Three seaplanes. Armament weight: 6,248 tons. Armour: 12-in/305-mm belt, turret, 8-in/203-mm barbette, 13.8-in/350-mm CT., 3.85-in/98-mm deck. Armour weight: 12,199 tons. Machinery: Six Kampon boilers, four Kampon geared turbines, four shafts. 75,000 shp. Machinery weight: 2,284 tons. Speed: 24.7 knots. Fuel: 5,100 tons oil. Range: 11,800 n.m. at 16 knots.

Fate
Fuso: Sunk 25 October 1944 in the approaches to the Surigao Strait. **Yamashiro**: Sunk 25 October 1944 in 10°22'N 125°21'E in action in the Surigao Strait.

BATTLESHIP **HYUGA**
1914 programme. Mitsubishi at Nagasaki. Laid down: 6 May 1915. Launched: 27 January 1917. Completed: 30 April 1918.

BATTLESHIP **ISE**
1914 programme. Kawasaki at Kobe. Laid down: 10 May 1915. Launched: 12 November 1916. Completed: 15 December 1917.

Dimensions
683-ft/208.87-m x 94-ft/28.75-m x 29-ft/8.87-m. Displacement: 29,980 tons (standard), 31,260 tons (normal), 36,500 tons (full). Armament: Twelve 14-in/356-mm 45 calibre, twenty 5.5-in/140-mm 50 calibre, twelve 3.1-in/80-mm 40 calibre and four 3.1-in/80-mm 28 calibre guns, six 21-in/533-mm torpedo tubes. Armour: 12-in/305-mm belt, turret, barbette, CT., 2.25-in/57-mm deck. Armour weight: 9,525 tons. Machinery: Twenty-four Kampon boilers, four (**Hyuga** Parsons, **Ise** Curtis) turbines, four shafts. 45,000 shp. Speed: 23.5 knots. Fuel: 4,607 tons coal, 1,411 tons oil. Range: 9,680 n.m. at 14 knots.

First reconstruction
Hyuga at Kure navy yard between 23 November 1934 and 7 September 1936. **Ise** at Kure navy yard between 1 August 1935 23 March 1937. Dimensions: 708-ft/216.51-m x 111-ft/33.94-m x 30-ft/9.17-m. Displacement: **Hyuga** 36,000 tons, **Ise** 35,800 tons (standard), **Hyuga** 39,657 tons, **Ise** 40,169 tons (full load). Armament: Twelve 14-in/356-mm 45 calibre, sixteen 5.5-in/140-mm 50 calibre, eight 5-in/127-mm, **Hyuga** twenty 40-mm and 13-mm **Ise** twenty 25-mm AA guns. Three aircraft. Armour: 12-in/305-mm belt, turret, barbette, CT, 6.75-in/171.45-mm deck. Armour weight: 12,644 tons. Machinery: Eight Kampon boilers, four Kampon turbines, four shafts. 80,825 shp. Speed: 25.3 knots. Fuel: 5,113 tons oil. Range: 7,870 n.m. at 16 knots.

Second reconstruction
Hyuga at Sasebo naval yard between 1 July 1943 and 30 November 1943. **Ise** at Kure navy yard between 15 March 1943 and 8 October 1943. Dimensions: 720-ft/220.18-m x 111-ft/ 33.94-m x 30.17-ft/9.23-m. Displacement: 35,350 tons (standard), 38,657 tons (full load). Armament: Eight 14-in/356-mm 45 calibre, sixteen 5.5-in/140-mm 50 calibre, 57 (post-June 1944 108) 25-mm AA (post-September 1944) 180 5-in/127-mm rocket launchers. 22 aircraft, one elevator. Armour: 12-in/305-mm belt, barbette, CT, 6.75-in/171.45-mm deck. Armour weight: 12,101 tons. Machinery: Eight Kampon boilers, four Kampon turbines, four shafts. 80,825 shp. Machinery weight: 2,715 tons. Speed: 25.3 knots. Fuel: 4,249 tons oil. Range: 9,450 n.m. at 16 knots.

Fate
Hyuga: Sunk 24 July 1945 in 34°10'N 132°33'E in Kure harbour by carrier aircraft. Raised and scrapped at Kure in 1946. **Ise**: Settled 28 July 1945 in 34°12'N 132°31'E in Kure harbour after attack by carrier aircraft. Raised and scrapped at Kure in 1946.

BATTLESHIP **NAGATO**
1916 programme. Yokosuka naval yard. Laid down: 28 August 1917. Launched: 9 November 1919. Completed: 25 November 1920.

BATTLESHIP **MUTSU**

1917 programme. Kure naval yard. Laid down: 1 June 1918. Launched: 31 May 1920. Completed: 24 October 1921.

Dimensions

708-ft/216.51-ft x 95-ft/29.05-m x 30-ft/9.17-m. Displacement: 32,720 tons (standard), 33,800 tons (normal), 38,500 tons (full). Armament: 8 x 16-in/406-mm 45 calibre at 20/25 degrees, twenty 5.5-in/140-mm, 4 x 3.1-in/80-mm AA guns. Eight 21-in/533-mm torpedo tubes. Armour: 11.81-in/300-mm belt, 14-in/356-mm turret, 11.81-in/300-mm barbette, 14.61-in/371-mm CT., 3.5-in/89-mm deck.

Armour weight: 10,395 tons. Machinery: Twenty-one boilers, four Gihon turbines, four shafts. 80,000 shp. Machinery weight: 3,687 tons. Speed: 26.7 knots. Fuel: 1,600 tons coal, 3,400 tons oil. Range: 5,500 n.m. at 16 knots.

Reconstruction

Nagato at Yokosuka naval yard between April 1934 and January 1936. **Mutsu** at Kure naval yard between September 1934 and September 1936. Dimensions: 738-ft/225.69-m x 113.5-ft/34.71-m x 31-ft/9.48-m. Displacement: 39,130 tons (normal), 42,850 tons (full). Hull weight: 11,883 tons. Armament: Eight 16-in/406-mm 45 calibre at 35 degrees, eighteen 5.5-in/140-mm, eight 5-in/127-mm, twenty 25-mm AA guns. Three aircraft. Armament weight: 7,357 tons. Armour: 11.81-in/300-mm belt, 14-in/356-mm turret, 11.81-in/300-mm barbette, 14.61-in/371-mm CT., 7-in/188-mm deck: after refitting in 1940 barbette armour was 19.69-mm/500-mm Armour weight: 13,678 tons. Machinery: Ten Kampon boilers, four Kampon turbines, four shafts. 82,000 shp. Machinery weight: 3,179 tons. Speed: 25 knots. Fuel: 5,650 tons oil. Range: 8,650 n.m. at 16 knots.

Nagato. After refit in first half of 1944: Armament: Eight 16-in/406-mm 45 calibre at 35 degrees, eighteen 5.5-in/140-mm, eight 5-in/127-mm, sixty-eight 25-mm AA guns. Three aircraft. After refit in summer 1944: Displacement: 43,581 tons (full). Armament: Eight 16-in/406-mm 45 calibre at 35 degrees, eighteen 5.5-in/140-mm, eight 5-in/127-mm, ninety-eight 25-mm AA guns. Speed: 24.98 knots.

Fate

Nagato: Surrendered at the end of the war: badly damaged in the Baker test at Bikini atoll on 24 July 1946 and sank on 29 July 1946. **Mutsu**: Sunk 8 June 1943 in 34°5'N 132°20'E in Hiroshima Bay, Honshu, as result of magazine explosion.

BATTLESHIP **YAMATO**

1937 programme. Kure navy yard.
Laid down: 4 November 1937. Launched: 8 August 1940. Completed: 16 December 1941.

BATTLESHIP **MUSASHI**

1937 programme. Mitsubishi at Nagasaki.
Laid down: 29 March 1938. Launched: 1 November 1940. Completed: 19 May 1942. In service: 5 August 1942.

Dimensions

862.83-ft/263.86-m x 127.75-ft/39.07-m x 34.5-ft/10.55-m. Displacement: 64,000 tons (standard), 67,123 tons (normal), 71,659 tons (full). Hull weight: 23,846 tons. Armament: Nine 18.1-in/460-mm 45 calibre, twelve 6.1-in/155-mm 55 calibre, twelve 5-in/127-mm, twenty-four 25-mm AA, four 13-mm AA guns. Seven aircraft, two catapults. Armament weight: 11,660 tons. Armour: 16-in/406-mm belt, 25.6-in/650-mm turret, 22-in/558-mm barbette, 19.7-in/500-mm CT., 9-in/229-mm deck. Armour weight: 22,534 tons. Machinery: Twelve boilers, four geared turbines. Four shafts. 158,000 shp. Machinery weight: 5,218 tons. Speed: 27.7 knots. Fuel: 6,300 tons oil. Range: 8,600 n.m. at 19 knots, 4,100 n.m. at 27 knots.

First refit. **Yamato**: in 1943. **Musashi**: at Yokosuka navy yard in June 1943 or June/July 1943.

Armament change: Thirty-six 25-mm AA guns. Second refit. **Yamato**: in 1943. **Musashi**: at Kure navy yard between April and May 1944. Armament change: Six 6.1-in/155-mm 55 calibre, fifty-four 25-mm AA guns. Third refit. **Yamato**: at Kure navy yard between 16 January and 21 April 1944. Armament change: Between 98 and 116 25-mm AA guns. **Musashi**: at Kure navy yard between June 1944 and 7 July 1944. 116 x 25-mm AA guns. Four additional radars fitted. Final tertiary armament: 35 triple and 25 single 25-mm AA guns. Fourth refit. **Yamato**: completed in July 1944. Between 130 and 152 25-mm AA (finally 29 triple and 63 single 25-mm) guns.

Fate
Yamato: Sunk 7 April 1945 in 30°22'N 128°4'E southwest of Kyushu by carrier aircraft. Estimates of hits vary between ten torpedoes and five bombs and thirteen torpedoes and eight bombs. **Musashi**: Sunk 24 October 1944 in 12°50'N 122°35'E in the Visayan Sea, central Philippines, by carrier aircraft: she was hit by perhaps as many as twenty torpedoes and seventeen bombs in four and a half hours before capsizing.

OTTOMAN EMPIRE/TURKEY

Prior to 1914 Turkey sought to secure four battleships ostensibly in order to maintain her position relative to Greece. She purchased the Brazilian battleship **Rio de Janeiro**, being built in Britain in 1913, and refused an Italian attempt to secure this ship, renamed the **Sultan Osman I**, by an offer of two **Pisa** class cruisers: the offer was declined on the grounds of Turkey's need to possess a ship at least the equal of the **Giorgios Averoff**. In addition, Turkey ordered two battleships in June 1911. These were the first of a class of three **Reshadieh** class battleships, the **Reshadieh** herself being laid down by Vickers on 1 August 1911 and the **Reshad-in-Hamiss** by Armstrong on 6 December 1911: the third and last, the **Faith**, was laid down by Vickers on 11 June 1914 after the Armstrong order was cancelled in 1912 in the wake of the Italian and Balkan wars. The **Sultan Osman I** and the **Reshadieh** were requisitioned by Britain in August 1914. The former served throughout the First World War as the **Agincourt**, the latter as the **Erin**. The characteristics of this second ship would have applied to the other members of her class had they been completed. The **Faith** was dismantled on the slipway after August 1914.

The German battlecruiser **Goeben** formally handed over to Turkey on 2 November 1918. 1919–1926 not in service. 1926–1930 refitted and overhauled at Izmir by French company. Returned to service as the **Jawus Selim**: renamed the **Yavuz** in 1936. After 1948 at Ismit. Decommissioned on 20 December 1960 and stricken 14 November 1964. Sold in 1971 and scrapped between June 1973 and February 1976.

RUSSIA/SOVIET UNION

BATTLESHIP **GANGUT** (renamed **OKTYABRSKAYA REVOLUTSIA** 27 June 1925)
1908 programme. St. Petersburg navy yard. Laid down: 15 June 1909. Launched: 7 October 1911. Completed: December 1914.

BATTLESHIP **SEVASTOPOL** (renamed **PARISHKAYA KOMMUNA** after 1926)
1908 programme. Baltic Shipyard, St. Petersburg. Laid down: 15 June 1909. Launched: 29 June 1911. Completed: November 1914.

BATTLESHIP **PETROPAVLOVSK** (renamed the **MARAT** between 31 March 1921 and 31 May 1943, original name until renamed the **VOLKOV** 28 November 1950)
1908 programme. Baltic Shipyard, St. Petersburg. Laid down: 15 June 1909. Launched: 9 September 1911. Completed: December 1914.

BATTLESHIP **POLTAVA** (renamed **MIKHAIL FRUNZE** in 1920)
1908 programme. St. Petersburg navy yard. Laid down: 15 June 1909. Launched: 10 July 1911. Completed: December 1914.

Dimensions
590.5-ft/180.58-m x 88-ft/26.9-m x 27.5-ft/8.41-m. Displacement: 23,260 tons (normal), 25,850 tons (full load). Armament: Twelve 12-in/305-mm 52 calibre guns in four triple turrets all centre-line and without superimposition, sixteen single 4.7-in/120-mm 50 calibre guns, two 75-mm AA guns. Four 18-in/457-mm torpedo tubes. Armour: 8.86-in/225-mm belt, 8-in/203-mm turrets and barbettes, 10-in/254-mm CT, 1.5-in/38-mm deck. Machinery: 24 Yarrow coal-burning boilers, four Parsons turbines, four shafts. 42,000 shp. Speed: 23 knots. Fuel: 3,000 tons coal plus 1,170 tons oil maximum. Range: 900 n.m. at 23 knots or 4,000 n.m. at 16 knots.

Fate
Gangut: 12 March 1918 moved from Helsinki to Kronstadt, and until 1925 laid up at the Petrograd naval base. Major refit 18 April 1925 to 20 July 1926 and rebuilt 12 October 1931 to 4 August 1934. Served during Winter and Great Patriotic Wars. Reduced to training ship 24 July 1954. Stricken 17 February 1956 and broken up at Leningrad in 1956–1957. **Sevastopol**: Reduced to training ship 24 July 1954. Stricken 17 February 1956 and broken up at Sevastopol in 1956–1957. **Petropavlovsk**: Severely damaged, and lost bow, as a result of air attack 23 September 1941 at Leningrad. Laid up but used as floating battery in 1944. Reduced to (static) training ship 25 September 1951. Stricken 4 September 1953 and broken up at Leningrad thereafter. **Poltava**: At Petrograd naval harbour after October 1918. Wrecked by a major fire 25 November 1919. Laid up and cannibalised. Stricken on 1 December 1940: handed over for scrapping and laid up in the Leningrad canal. Involved in the defence of city during the Great Patriotic War. She was sunk, but raised in May 1944, and after what seems an unconscionable delay handed over for scrapping in 1949 which was completed "during the mid-Fifties."

BATTLESHIP **IMPERATRICA MARIJA (Imperatritsa Mariya)**
1911 programme. Russian Shipbuilding, Nikolaev. Laid down: 30 November 1911. Launched: 1 November 1913. Completed: 6 July 1915.

BATTLESHIP **EKATERINA II** (25 April 1917 renamed the **Svobodnaja Rossija**)
1911 programme. Nikolaev Factories. Laid down: 30 November 1911. Launched: 6 June 1914. Completed: 5 October 1915.

BATTLESHIP **IMPERATOR ALEKSANDR III** (29 April 1917 renamed the **Volya**)
1911 programme. Russian Shipbuilding, Nikolaev. Laid down: 30 November 1911. Launched: 15 April 1914. Completed: June 1917.

Dimensions
550.5-ft/168.35-m x 89.25/27.3-m x 27.5-ft/8.41-m. (**Ekaterina II** 557-ft/170.33-m x 91.25-ft/27.9-m x 27.5-ft/8.41-m.) Displacement: 22,600 tons (normal), 24,000 tons (full load). Armament: Twelve 12-in/305-mm 52 calibre guns in four triple turrets all centre-line and without superimposition, twenty single 5.1-in/130-mm 55 calibre guns, eight 75-mm AA and four 47-mm guns. Four 18-in/457-mm torpedo tubes. Armour: 10.35-in/263-mm belt, 12-in/305-mm turrets, 8-in/203-mm barbettes, 12-in/305-mm CT, 3-in/76-mm deck. Weight of armour: 7,036 tons. Machinery: Twenty Yarrow coal-burning boilers, four Parsons (**Imperator Aleksandr III** Brown-Curtis) turbines, four shafts. 26,500 shp. Speed: 21 knots. Fuel: 1,200 tons coal plus 720 tons oil normal. Range: 1,000 n.m. at 21 knots

Fate
Imperatrica Marija: Capsized as a result of magazine explosion in Sevastopol on 20 October 1916. Salvage and docked 1919. Approved for scrapping June 1925. Formally stricken 21 November 1925. **Ekaterina II**: Sunk off Novorossijsk on 18 June 1918 by the Bolshevik

destroyer *Kerch* in order to avoid having to surrender her to the Germans. **Imperator Aleksandr III**. Arrived Sevastopol 19 June 1918 and surrendered to, or seized by, German forces: in German order of battle 1 October 1918. Surrendered to Anglo-French forces 24 November 1918 and sent to Izmit. Allocated to White Russian forces in October 1920 as the **GENERAL ALEKSEEV.** Involved in evacuation of Crimea, arriving 14 November at Constantinople. Interned at Bizerta 29 December 1920. Remained Russian warship until 29 October 1924. Scrapping began "at the end of the Twenties:" completed at Brest in 1936.

SPAIN

BATTLESHIP **ESPAÑA**
1908 programme. Ferrol navy yard. Laid down: 5 February 1909. Launched: 5 February 1912. Completed: 23 October 1913.

BATTLESHIP **ALFONSO XIII**
1908 programme. Ferrol navy yard. Laid down: 23 February 1910. Launched: 7 May 1913. Completed: 16 August 1915.

BATTLESHIP **JAIME I**
1908 programme. Ferrol navy yard. Laid down: 5 February 1912. Launched: 21 September 1914. Completed: 20 December 1921.

Dimensions
459.16-ft/140.04-m x /78.75-ft/24.08-m x 25.5-ft/7.82-m. Displacement: 15,452 tons (normal), 15,840 tons (full load). Armament: Eight 12-in/305-mm 50 calibre guns in four twin turrets, all centre line, twenty single 4-in/102-mm guns, four 3-pdr and two machine guns. Weight of armament: 2,250 tons. Armour: 9-in/229-mm belt, 8-in/203-mm turrets, 10-in/254-mm barbettes and CT, 1.5-in/38-mm deck. Weight of armour: 4,750 tons. Machinery: Twelve Yarrow coal-burning boilers, four Parsons turbines, four shafts. 15,500 shp. Weight of machinery: 1,320 tons. Speed: 19.5 knots as designed, 20.3 knots recorded on trials. Fuel: 1,900 tons coal. Range: 6,000 n.m. at 10 knots.

Fate
España: Ran aground 26 August 1923 off Cap des Trois Fourches in Morocco and after salvage broke up in storm. **Alfonso XIII**: renamed the **España** in 1931. In civil war fought on Nationalist side. Mined and sunk off Santander 30 April 1937. **Jaime I**: In civil war fought on Republican side. Severely damaged at Malaga by bomb 13 August 1936 and by internal explosion at Cartagena 17 June 1937. Laid up at Cartagena and scrapped 1939.

UNITED KINGDOM

BATTLESHIP **DREADNOUGHT**
1905 programme. Portsmouth naval yard. Ordered: 8 July 1905. Laid down: 2 October 1905. Launched: 2 February 1906. Completed: 3 December 1906.

Dimensions
527-ft/161.16-m x 82-ft/25.08-m x 26.5-ft/8.10-m. Displacement: 17,900 tons (standard), 21,845 tons (full load). Armament: Ten 12-in/305-mm 45 calibre, 27 x 12-pdr guns, five 18-in/457-mm torpedo tubes, four beam and one stern: stern tube removed in 1916. Carried 23 torpedoes. Armour: 11- to 4-in/280- to 102-mm belt, 11-in/280-mm turret, 11- to 4-in/280- to 102-mm barbette, 11- to 8-in/280- to 203-mm CT., 4-in/102-mm deck. Armour weight: 5,000 tons (including backings). Machinery: Eighteen Babcock and Wilcox boilers, four Parsons turbines, four shafts. 23,000 hp. Machinery weight: 2,000 tons. Speed: 21 knots. Fuel: 2,400 tons coal, 1,120 tons oil. Range: 6,620 n.m. at 10 knots, 4,910 n.m. at 18.4 knots.

Fate
Stricken 31 March 1920. Sold May 1921. Scrapped Inverkeithing after January 1923.

BATTLECRUISER **INDOMITABLE**
1905 programme. Fairfield, Glasgow. Laid down: 1 March 1906. Launched: 16 March 1907. Completed: 25 June 1908.

BATTLECRUISER **INFLEXIBLE**
1905 programme. John Brown, Clydebank. Laid down: 5 February 1906. Launched: 26 June 1906. Completed: 20 October 1908.

BATTLECRUISER **INVINCIBLE**
1905 programme. Armstrong-Whitworth, Elswick. Laid down: 2 April 1906. Launched: 13 April 1907. Completed: 20 March 1908.

Dimensions
567-ft/173.39-ft x 78.5-ft/24.01-m x 27-ft/8.26-m. Displacement: **Indomitable**: 17,410 tons (standard), 20,125 tons (full load). **Inflexible**: 17,290 tons (standard), 19,975 tons (full load). **Invincible**: 17,420 tons (standard). 20,135 tons (full load). Armament: Eight 12-in/45 calibre, sixteen 4-in/45 calibre, one 3-in/76-mm guns. Twenty-three 18-in/457-mm torpedoes with five tubes. Six 14-in/356-mm torpedoes. Armour: 6- to 4-in/152- to 102-mm belt, 7-in/ 178-mm turret, 7- to 2-in/178- to 50.8-mm barbette, 10-in/254-mm CT., 2.5-in/63.50-mm deck. Armour weight: 3,460 tons. Machinery: Thirty one Yarrow boilers (**Indomitable** Babcock), four Parsons turbines, four shafts. 41,000 hp. Machinery weight: 3,300 tons. Speed: 25 knots. Fuel: 3,084 tons coal, c. 725 tons oil. Range: 6,210 n.m. at 10 knots, 3,050 n.m. at 22.3 knots.

Fate
Indomitable: March 1920 paid off. December 1921 sold. August 1922 towed to Dover and scrapped after April 1923. **Inflexible**: March 1920 paid off. December 1921 sold. April 1922 towed to Dover but resold and towed to Germany and scrapped. **Invincible**: Sunk on 31 May 1916 at Jutland at the start of the first main fleet action.

BATTLESHIP **BELLEROPHON**
1906 programme. Portsmouth naval yard. Ordered: 30 October 1906. Laid down: 3 December 1906. Launched: 27 July 1907. Completed: 20 February 1909.

BATTLESHIP **SUPERB**
1906 programme. Armstrong-Whitworth, Elswick. Ordered: 30 October 1906. Laid down: 1 January 1907. Launched: 24 August 1907. Completed: 15 May 1909.

BATTLESHIP **TÉMÉRAIRE**
1906 programme. Devonport naval yard. Ordered: 26 December 1906. Laid down: 6 February 1907. Launched: 7 November 1907. Completed: 9 June 1909.

Dimensions
526-ft/160.86-m x 82.5-ft/25.23-m x 27-ft/8.26-m. Displacement: 18,800 tons (standard). 22,102 tons (full load). Armament: Ten 12-in/305-mm 45 calibre, sixteen 4-in/102-mm 50 calibre, four 3-pdr guns. Fourteen 18-in/457-mm, six 14-in/356-mm torpedoes and three tubes. Armour: 10-in/254-mm belt, 11-in/280-mm turret, 9-in/229-mm barbette, 11-in/280-mm CT, 4-in/102-mm deck. Machinery: Eighteen Babcock boilers (**Téméraire** Yarrow), four Parsons turbines, four shafts. 23,000 hp. Speed: 20.75 knots. Fuel: 2,648 tons coal, 842 tons oil. Range: 4,250 n.m. at 18.3 knots.

Fate
Bellerophon: March 1921 placed on disposal list. 8 November sold to Slough Trading Company. 14 September left Plymouth under tow for scrapping in Germany. **Superb**: March 1920 placed on disposal list. December 1920 detailed for gunnery experiments at Portsmouth. December 1922 sold. April 1923 left Portsmouth under tow for scrapping at Dover.

Téméraire: April 1921 left Portsmouth for Rosyth and placed on disposal list. Sold and in February 1922 towed to Dover and scrapped.

BATTLESHIP **COLLINGWOOD**

1907 programme. Devonport naval yard. Ordered: 26 October 1907. Laid down: 3 February 1908. Launched: 7 November 1908. Completed: 19 April 1910.

BATTLESHIP **ST. VINCENT**

1907 programme. Portsmouth naval yard. Ordered: 26 October 1907. Laid down: 30 December 1907. Launched: 10 September 1908. Completed: 3 May 1910.

BATTLESHIP **VANGUARD**

1907 programme. Vickers, Barrow. Ordered: 6 February 1908. Laid down: 2 April 1908. Launched: 22 February 1909. Completed: 1 March 1910.

Dimensions

536-ft/163.91-m x 84-ft/25.69-m x 28.5-ft/8.72-m. Displacement: 19,250 tons (standard). 23,030 tons (full load). Armament: Twelve 12-in/305-mm 50 calibre, twenty 4-in/102-mm, four 3-pdr guns. Fourteen 18-in/457-mm, six 14-in/356-mm torpedoes and three tubes. Armour: 10-in/254-mm belt, 11-in/280-mm turret, 9-in/229-mm barbette, 11-in/280-mm CT., 3-in/76.2-mm deck. Machinery: Eighteen Babcock boilers (**Collingwood** Yarrow), four Parsons turbines, four shafts. 24,500 hp. Speed: 21 knots. Fuel: 2,800 tons coal, 940 tons oil. Range: 6,900 n.m. at 10 knots, 4,250 n.m. at 18.7 knots.

Fate

Collingwood: July 1921 placed on disposal list. March 1922 paid off. December 1922 sold. March 1923 towed from Portsmouth to Newport and scrapped. **St. Vincent**: March 1921 placed on disposal list. December 1921 sold. March 1922 towed to Dover and scrapped. **Vanguard**: Destroyed by internal explosion at Scapa Flow on 9 July 1917.

BATTLESHIP **NEPTUNE**

1908 programme. Portsmouth naval yard. Laid down: 19 January 1909. Launched: 30 September 1909. Completed: January 1911.

Dimensions

546-ft/166.97-m x 85-ft/25.99-m x 28.5-ft/8.72-m. Displacement: 19,900 tons (standard). 22,720 tons (full load). Armament: Ten 12-in/305-mm 50 calibre, sixteen 4-in/102-mm 50 calibre, four 3- pdr guns. Eighteen 18-in/457-mm and six 14-in/356-mm torpedoes, with three tubes. Armour: 10-in/254-mm belt, 11-in/280-mm turret, 9-in/229-mm barbette, 11-in/280-mm CT., 3-in/76.2-mm deck. Machinery: Eighteen Yarrow boilers, four Parsons turbines, four shafts. 25,000 hp. Speed: 21 knots. Fuel: 2,710 tons coal, 790 tons oil. Range: 6,300 n.m. at 10 knots, 3,820 n.m. at 18.5 knots.

Fate

March 1921 on disposal list. Sold September 1922 and towed to Blyth for scrapping.

BATTLECRUISER **INDEFATIGABLE**

1908 programme. Devonport naval yard. Laid down: 23 February 1909. Launched: 28 October 1909. Completed: 24 February 1911.

BATTLECRUISER **AUSTRALIA**

J. Brown, Clydebank. Laid down: 23 June 1910. Launched: 25 October 1911. Completed: 21 June 1913.

BATTLECRUISER **NEW ZEALAND**

Fairfield, Glasgow. Laid down: 20 June 1910. Launched: 1 July 1911. Completed: 9 November 1912. Sister ships of the **Indefatigable**, 1908, the two battlecruisers were ordered by the two Dominions as supplementaries to the 1909 programme.

Dimensions
590-ft/180.43-m x 80-ft/24.46-m x 27-ft/8.26-m. Displacement: 18,800 tons (standard). 22,080 tons (full load). Armament: Eight 12-in/305-mm 50 calibre, sixteen 4-in/102-mm 50 calibre, four 3-pdr guns. Twelve 18-in/457-mm and six 14-in/356-mm torpedoes, two torpedo tubes. Armour: 6-in/152-mm belt, 7-in/213-mm turret, barbette, 10-in/254-mm CT., 2.5-in/63.50-mm deck. Machinery: Thirty-one Babcock and Wilcox boilers, four Parsons turbines, four shafts. 44,000 shp. Speed: 25 knots. Fuel: 3,170 tons coal, 840 tons oil. Range: 6,330 n.m. at 10 knots, 2,290 n.m. at 23.5 knots.

Fate
Indefatigable: Sunk on 31 May 1916 at Jutland. **Australia**: December 1921 paid off into reserve at Sydney. October 1923 stripped in readiness for disposal. 12 April 1924 scuttled off Sydney. **New Zealand**: April 1922 paid off under terms of Washington naval treaty. December 1922 sold and scrapped at Rosyth after August 1923.

BATTLESHIP **COLOSSUS**
1909 programme. Scotts, Greenock. Laid down: 8 July 1909. Launched: 9 April 1910. Completed: 8 August 1911.

BATTLESHIP **HERCULES**
1909 programme. Palmer, Newcastle. Laid down: 30 July 1909. Launched: 10 May 1910. Completed: 31 July 1911.

Dimensions
546-ft/166.97-m x 85-ft/25.99-m x 29-ft/8.87-m. Displacement: 20,225 tons (standard). 23,050 tons (full load). Armament: Ten 12-in/305-mm 50 calibre, sixteen 4-in/102-mm 50 calibre, four 3- pdr guns. Eighteen 18-in/457-mm and six 14-in/356-mm torpedoes, with three tubes. Armour: 11- in./280-mm belt, turret, barbette, CT., 4-in/102-mm deck. Machinery: Eighteen (**Colossus** Babcock, **Hercules** Yarrow) boilers, four Parsons turbines, four shafts. 25,000 hp. Speed: 21 knots. Fuel: 2,900 tons coal, 800 tons oil. Range: 6,680 n.m. at 10 knots, 4,050 n.m. at 18.5 knots.

Fate
Colossus: February 1928 paid off. August 1928 sold. Towed to Charlestown and scrapped after September 1928. **Hercules**: October 1921 placed on disposal list. November 1921 sold. October 1922 left Rosyth in tow for Kiel and scrapped thereafter.

BATTLESHIP **CONQUEROR**
1909 programme. Beardmore, Glasgow. Laid down: 5 April 1910. Launched: 1 May 1911. Completed: November 1912. In service: 25 February 1913.

BATTLESHIP **MONARCH** (ex-King George V)
1909 programme. Armstrong-Whitworth, Elswick. Laid down: 1 April 1910. Launched: 30 March 1911. Completed: March 1912. In service: 6 April 1912.

BATTLESHIP **ORION**
1909 programme. Portsmouth naval yard. Laid down: 29 November 1909. Launched: 20 August 1910. Completed: 1 February 1912. In service: 2 January 1912.

BATTLESHIP **THUNDERER**
1909 programme. Thames Iron Works. Laid down: 13 April 1910. Launched: 2 February 1911. Completed: 15 June 1912. In service:

Dimensions
581-ft/177.68-m x 88.5-ft/27.06-m x 28.67-ft/8.77-m. Displacement: 22,500 tons (standard). 25,870 tons (full load). Armament: Ten 13.5-in/343-mm 45 calibre, sixteen 4-in/102-mm 50 calibre, four 3- pdr guns. Twenty 21-in/457-mm, six 14-in/356-mm torpedoes. Three torpedo tubes. Armour: 12-in/305-mm belt, 11-in/280-mm turret, 10-in/254-mm barbette, 11-in/

280-mm CT., 4-in/102-mm deck. Weight of armour: 6,460 tons. Machinery: Eighteen Babcock (**Monarch** Yarrow) boilers, four Parsons turbines, four shafts. 27,000 shp. Machinery weight: 2,420 tons. Speed: 21 knots. Fuel: 3,300 tons coal, 800 tons oil. Range: 6,730 n.m. at 10 knots, 4,110 n.m. at 19 knots.

Fate
Conqueror: June 1922 placed on disposal list. December 1922 sold. January 1923 arrived at Upnor and scrapped. **Monarch**: May 1922 paid off at Portsmouth. 20 January 1925 sunk as target ship. **Orion**: April 1922 paid off at Devonport. December 1922 sold for scrap. February 1923 arrived at Upnor and scrapped. **Thunderer**: November 1926 paid off and sold. January 1927 towed to Blyth and scrapped after April 1927.

BATTLECRUISER **LION**
1909 programme. Devonport naval yard. Laid down: 29 November 1909. Launched: 6 August 1910. Completed: May 1912.

BATTLECRUISER **PRINCESS ROYAL**
1909 programme. Vickers, Barrow. Laid down: 2 May 1910. Launched: 29 April 1911. Completed: 14 November 1912.

Dimensions
704-ft/215.29-m x 90.5-ft/27.68-m x 28.5-ft/8.72-m. Displacement: 28,500 tons (standard). 35,160 tons (full load). Armament: Eight 13.5-in/343-mm 45 calibre, sixteen 4-in/102-mm 50 calibre, two 3-in/76.2-mm AA, four 3-pdr guns. Twenty 21-in/533-mm torpedoes, two tubes. Armour: 9-in/229-mm belt, turret, barbette, 10-in/254-mm CT., 3-in/76.2-mm deck. Hull and armour weight: 1914 17,351 tons: 1924 18,234 tons. Machinery: Thirty-nine Babcock and Wilcox boilers, four Brown Curtis turbines, four shafts. 108,000 hp. Machinery weight: In 1914 5,407 tons, in 1924 5,775 tons. Speed: 29 knots. Fuel: 3,320 tons coal/450 tons oil or 3,480 tons oil/450 tons coal. Range: 2,800 n.m. at 25 knots, 4,900 n.m. at 18 knots and 5,200 n.m. at 12 knots.

Fate
Lion: May 1922 paid off into disposal list at Rosyth. January 1924 sold and scrapped at Jarrow thereafter. **Princess Royal**: March 1922 placed on disposal list. Scrapped at Rosyth after August 1923.

BATTLESHIP **AJAX**
1910 programme. Scotts, Greenock. Laid down: 27 February 1911. Launched: 21 March 1912. Completed: March 1913. In service: 31 October 1913.

BATTLESHIP **AUDACIOUS**
1910 programme. Cammell Lairds, Birkenhead. Laid down: 23 March 1911. Launched: 14 September 1912. Completed: 21 October 1913.

BATTLESHIP **CENTURION**
1910 programme. Devonport naval yard. Laid down: 16 January 1911. Launched: 18 November 1911. Completed: 22 May 1913.

BATTLESHIP **KING GEORGE V**
1910 programme. Portsmouth naval yard. Laid down: 16 January 1911. Launched: 9 October 1911. Completed: 16 November 1912.

Dimensions
597.5-ft/182.72-m x 89-ft/27.22-m x 28.7-ft/8.78-m. Displacement: 23,000 tons (standard). 25,700 tons (full load). Armament: Ten 13.5-in/343-mm 45 calibre, sixteen 4-in/102-mm 50 calibre, four 3-pdr guns. Three, later two, 21-in/533-mm torpedo tubes. Armour: 12-in/305-mm belt, 11-in/280-mm turret, 10-in/254-mm barbette, 11-in/280-mm CT., 4-in/102-mm deck. Machinery: Eighteen Babcock and Wilcox boilers (**Audacious** and **Centurion** Yarrow), Par-

sons turbines, four shafts. 31,000 hp. Speed: 21.7 knots. Fuel: 3,150 tons coal and 900 tons oil. Range: 4,060 n.m. at 18.2 knots.

Fate
Ajax: August 1926 in reserve at Devonport. October 1926 placed on disposal list. December 1926 sold and arrived at Rosyth to be scrapped. **Audacious**: Mined off Loch Swilly 27 October 1914. **Centurion**: In April 1937 recommissioned at Devonport as repair and maintenance ship. June 1944 sunk as blockship at Normandy. **King George V**: December 1926 placed on disposal list and sold. January 1927 arrived at Rosyth and scrapped.

BATTLECRUISER **QUEEN MARY**
1910 programme. Palmer, Newcastle. Laid down: 6 March 1911. Launched: 20 March 1912. Completed: 4 September 1913.

Dimensions
700-ft/214.07-m x 88.5-ft/27.06-m x 28-ft/8.56-m. Displacement: 26,350 tons (standard). 26,400 tons (normal September 1917). 29,680 tons (full load). Armament: Eight 13.5-in/343-mm 45 calibre, sixteen 4-in/102-mm 50 calibre, four 3-pdr guns. Fourteen 21-in/533-mm torpedoes, two tubes. Armour: 9-in/229-mm belt, turret, barbette, 10-in/254-mm CT., 2.5-in/63.50-mm. Armour weight: 5,140 tons. Machinery: Forty-two Yarrow boilers, four Parsons turbines, four shafts. 70,000 shp. Machinery weight: 5,190 tons. Speed: 27 knots. Fuel: 3,500 tons coal, 1,135 tons oil. Range: 5,610 n.m. at 10 knots, 2,420 n.m. at 23.9 knots.

Fate
Sunk on 31 May 1916 at Jutland.

BATTLESHIP **BENBOW**
1911 programme. Beardmore, Glasgow. Laid down: 30 May 1912. Launched: 12 November 1913. Completed: 7 October 1914.

BATTLESHIP **EMPEROR OF INDIA** (ex-Delhi)
1911 programme. Vickers, Barrow. Laid down: 31 May 1912. Launched: 27 November 1913. Completed: November 1914.

BATTLESHIP **IRON DUKE**
1911 programme. Portsmouth naval yard. Laid down: 12 January 1912. Launched: 12 October 1912. Completed: 10 March 1914.

BATTLESHIP **MARLBOROUGH**
1911 programme. Devonport naval yard. Laid down: 25 January 1912. Launched: 24 October 1912. Completed: 2 June 1914.

Dimensions
623-ft/190.52-m x 90-ft/27.52-m x 29.5-ft/9.02-m. Displacement: 25,820 tons (standard). 30,380 tons (full load). Armament: Ten 13.5-in/343-mm 45 calibre, twelve 6-in/152-mm 45 calibre, two 3-in/76.2-mm AA, four 3-pdr guns. Twenty 21-in/533-mm torpedoes, four tubes. Armour: 12-in/305-mm belt, 11-in/280-mm turret, 10-in/254-mm barbette, 11-in/280-mm CT., 2.5-in/63.50-mm deck. Machinery: Eighteen boilers, four shaft turbines with 29,000 hp. Speed: 21.25 knots. Fuel: 3,250 tons coal, 1,050 tons oil. Range: 7,780 n.m. at 10 knots, 4,840 n.m. at 19 knots.

Fate
Benbow: placed on disposal list September 1930 and sold March 1931. Scrapped at Rosyth after April 1931. **Emperor of India**: 22 January 1931 paid off and placed on disposal list. Ran aground 8 June 1931 when sailing from Portsmouth to be used as target ship. Used *in situ* 10–11 June, and then raised. Sold February 1932 and scrapped at Rosyth thereafter. **Iron Duke**: 30 May 1928 paid off at Devonport, and refitted: recommissioned as gunnery training ship 30 May 1929. Scapa Flow defence ship (AA/depot ship) September 1939 to March

1946. Sold for scrapping and 19 August 1946 towed to Faslane: towed to Clydebank for completion of scrapping September 1948. **Marlborough**: Paid off 5 June 1931. Placed on disposal list May 1932 and sold. 25 June 1932 arrived Rosyth for scrapping.

BATTLECRUISER **TIGER**

1911 programme. John Brown and Company, Clydebank. Laid down: 20 June 1912. Launched: 15 December 1913. Completed: 3 October 1914.

Dimensions
704-ft/215.29-m x 90.5-ft/27.68-m x 28.5-ft/8.72-m. Displacement: 28,500 tons (standard). 35,160 tons (full load). Armament: Eight 13.5-in/343-mm 45 calibre, twelve 6-in/152-mm 45 calibre, two 3-in/76.2-mm AA, four 3-pdr guns. Twenty 21-in/533-mm torpedoes, four tubes. Armour: 9-in/229-mm belt, turret, barbette, 10-in/254-mm CT., 3-in/76.2-mm deck. Hull and armour weight in 1914 17,351 tons, in 1924 18,234 tons. Machinery: Thirty-nine Babcock and Wilcox boilers, four Brown Curtis turbines, four shafts. 108,000 hp. Machinery weight: 5,407 tons (1914), 5,775 tons (1924). Speed: 29 knots. Fuel: 3,320 tons coal/450 tons oil or 3,480 tons oil/450 tons coal. Range: 2,800 n.m. at 25 knots, 4,000 n.m. at 22 knots, 4,900 n.m. at 18 knots.

Fate
July 1931 assigned disposal list. February 1932 sold. March 1932 stripped at Rosyth: towed to Inverkeithing and scrapped thereafter.

BATTLESHIP **BARHAM**

1912 programme. John Brown and Company, Clydebank.
Laid down: 24 February 1913. Launched: 31 October 1914. Completed: 19 October 1915.

BATTLESHIP **QUEEN ELIZABETH**

1912 programme. Portsmouth navy yard.
Laid down: 21 October 1912. Launched: 16 October 1913. Completed: January 1915.

BATTLESHIP **VALIANT**

1912 programme. Fairfield, Glasgow.
Laid down: 31 January 1913. Launched: 4 November 1914. Completed: 19 February 1916.

BATTLESHIP **WARSPITE**

1912 programme. Devonport navy yard.
Laid down: 31 October 1912. Launched: 26 November 1913. Completed: March 1915.

BATTLESHIP **MALAYA**

Armstrong, Clydebank.
Laid down: 20 October 1913. Launched: 18 March 1915. Completed: 19 February 1916.
The **Malaya** was the gift to Britain on the part of the Malay states, and supplemented the 1912 programme.

Dimensions
646-ft/197.55-m x 91.00-ft/27.83-m x 30.00-ft/9.17-m. Displacement: 27,500 tons (normal), 33,000 tons (full load). Armament: Eight 15-in/380-mm 42 calibre at 20 degrees, fourteen 6-in/152-mm, two 3-in/76.2-mm AA guns, four 3-pdr guns. Twenty 21-in/533-mm torpedoes and four torpedo tubes. Armour: 13-in/330-mm belt, turret, 10-in/254-mm barbette, 11-in/280-mm CT., 3-in/76.2-mm deck. Armour weight: 8,600 tons. Machinery: Twenty-four Babcock and Wilcox (**Barham/Warspite** Yarrow) boilers, four Parsons (**Barham/Valiant** Brown-Curtis) turbines, four shafts. 76,575 shp. Machinery weight: 3,765 tons. Speed: 24 knots. Fuel: 3,400 tons oil.

Fate
Barham: Lost on 25 November 1941 in 32°34'N 26°24'E in eastern Mediterranean to submarine attack. **Malaya**: Scrapped at Faslane after 12 April 1948. **Queen Elizabeth**: May 1948

sold. Scrapped at Dalmuir (superstructure) after 7 July 1948 and at Troon (hull) after 7 July 1948. **Valiant:** Sold in August 1948 and scrapped at Cairn Ryan (superstructure) after 12 November 1948 and at Troon (hull) thereafter. **Warspite**: Stricken in March 1946 and sold for scrap. Ran aground en route to breakers, 23 April 1946, and broken up *in situ* at Prussia Cove, Cornwall.

BATTLESHIP **RAMILLIES**

1913 programme. Beardmore, Glasgow. Laid down: 12 November 1913. Launched: 12 September 1916. Completed: September 1917.

BATTLESHIP **RESOLUTION**

1913 programme. Palmer, Newcastle. Laid down: 29 December 1913. Launched: 14 January 1915. Completed: December 1916.

BATTLESHIP **REVENGE**

1913 programme. Vickers. Laid down: 22 December 1913. Launched: 29 May 1915. Completed: March 1916.

BATTLESHIP **ROYAL OAK**

1913 programme. Devonport naval yard. Laid down: 15 January 1914. Launched: 17 November 1914. Completed: May 1916.

BATTLESHIP **ROYAL SOVEREIGN**

1913 programme. Portsmouth naval yard. Laid down: 15 January 1914. Launched: 29 April 1915. Completed: May 1916.

Dimensions
Designed as 624.25-ft/190.90-m x 88.50-ft/27.06-m x 30-ft/9.17-m. In March 1915 the **Ramillies**, then being built, was fitted with anti-torpedo bulges, increasing her beam to 102.5-ft/31.35-m: the **Royal Oak** was thus fitted in 1927. Other members of class were fitted after completion a shallower 101.42-ft/31.02-m bulges: **Revenge** October 1917/February 1918 refit, **Resolution** late 1917/May 1918 refit, **Royal Sovereign** in 1920. These were then refitted in full between 1926 and 1930. Weight of hull: 8,603 tons. Displacement: 27,500 tons (standard). 31,200 tons (full load). Armament: Eight 15-in/380-mm 42 calibre, fourteen 6-in/ 152-mm 45 calibre, two 3-in/76.2-mm AA, four 3-pdr guns. Twenty 21-in/ 533-mm torpedoes, four submerged tubes. Armour: 13-in/330-mm belt, turret, 10-in/ 254-mm barbette, 11-in/ 280-mm CT. 2.5-in/63.5-mm deck. Weight of armour: 8,250 tons. Machinery: Eighteen boilers, four Parsons turbines, four shafts. Designed for coal-burning with 31,000 shp and 21.5 knots: changed in 1915 to oil-burning with 40,000 shp and 23 knots: standard displacement rose to 28,000 tons. Machinery weight: 2,550 tons. Speed: 21.5 knots. Fuel: 3,400 tons oil.

Fate
Ramillies: Placed on disposal list December 1947. Sold 2 February 1948 and scrapped at Cairn Ryan (superstructure) after 23 April 1948 and at Troon (hull) after October 1948. **Resolution**: Placed on disposal list and sold February 1948. Scrapped at Faslane after 13 May 1948. **Revenge**: Placed on disposal list March 1948. Sold July 1948 and scrapped at Inverkeithing after 5 September 1948. **Royal Oak**: Sunk 14 October 1939 inside Scapa Flow as a result of being torpedoed by the German submarine U. 47. **Royal Sovereign**: Transferred to Soviet Union in 1944 and served as the **Archangelesk**, returned 4 February 1949 and placed on disposal list and sold. Scrapped at Inverkeithing after 18 May 1949.

BATTLESHIP **AGINCOURT**

Armstrong-Whitworth, Elswick. Laid down: 14 September 1911. Launched: 22 January 1913. Completed: 20 August 1914. Being completed as the **Sultan Osman I** for Turkey and requisitioned on the outbreak of war, but had been purchased by Turkey on 9 January 1914. She was to have been transferred to Turkish ownership on 2 August 1914.

Dimensions
671.5-ft/205.35-m x 89-ft/27.22-m x 27-ft/8.26-m. Displacement: 27,500 tons (standard). 30,250 tons (full load). Armament: Fourteen 12-in/305-mm 45 calibre, twenty 6-in/152-mm 50 calibre, ten 3-in/76.2-mm, two 3-in/76.2-mm AA. Ten 21-in/533-mm torpedoes with three tubes. Armour: 9-in/229-mm belt, 12-in/305-mm turret, 9-in/229-mm barbette, 12-in/305-mm CT., 2.5-in/63.5-mm deck. Machinery: Twenty-two Babcock and Wilcox boilers, four Parsons turbines, four shafts. 34,000 hp. Speed: 22.42 knots at 40,279 shp. Fuel: 3,200 tons coal, 620 tons oil.

Fate
Decommissioned 1919 and Brazil declined offer to purchase same year. In April 1921 work began to convert her to depot ship but halted December 1921: recommissioned for experimental trials. Sold on 19 December 1922 and scrapped in 1924.

BATTLESHIP **CABADA**
Armstrong-Whitworth, Elswick. Laid down: 27 November 1911. Launched: 27 November 1913. Completed: 30 September 1915. Being completed in Britain as the **Almirante Latorre** for Chile and requisitioned on the outbreak of war.

Dimensions
661-ft/202.14-m x 92-ft/29.13-m x 29-ft/8.87-m. Displacement: 28,000 tons (standard). 32,120 tons (full load). Armament: Ten 14-in/356-mm 45 calibre, sixteen 6-in/152-mm 50 calibre, two 3-in/76.2-mm AA, four 3-pdr guns. Twenty 21-in/533-mm torpedoes with four tubes. Armour: 9-in/229-mm belt, 10-in/254-mm turret, barbette, 11-in/280-mm CT., 4-in/102-mm deck. Weight of armour: c. 7,000 tons. Machinery: Twenty-one Yarrow boilers, four Brown-Curtis turbines, four shafts. 37,000 hp. Speed: 22.75 knots. Fuel: 3,300 tons coal, 520 tons oil. Range: 4,400 n.m. at 10 knots.

Fate
March 1919 reduced to reserve. Purchased by Chile April 1920 and transferred as the **Almirante Latorre** 20 August 1920: formal hand-over 27 November at Devonport.

BATTLESHIP **ERIN**
Vickers, Barrow. Laid down: 1 August 1911. Launched: 3 September 1913. Completed: 22 August 1914. Being completed in Britain as the **Reshadieh** for Turkey and requisitioned on the outbreak of war.

Dimensions
559.5-ft/171.10-m x 91.5-ft/27.98-m x 28-ft/8.56-m. Displacement: 22,780 tons (standard). 25,250 tons (full load). Armament: Ten 13.5-in/343-mm 45 calibre, sixteen 6-in 152-mm 50 calibre, six 6-pdr, two 3-in/76.2-mm AA guns. Ten 21-in/533-mm torpedoes with four tubes. Armour: 12-in/305-mm belt, 11-in/280-mm turret, 10-in/254-mm barbette, 12-in/305-mm CT., 3-in/76.2-mm deck. Weight of armour: 4,207 tons. Machinery: Fifteen Babcock boilers, four Parsons turbines, four shafts. 26,500 hp. Speed: 21 knots. Fuel: 2,120 tons coal, 710 tons oil. Range: 5,300 n.m. at 10 knots.

Fate
Paid into reserve at the Nore October 1919. Was to be retained as training ship but replaced by the **Thunderer**. May 1922 placed on disposal list and sold on 19 December 1922. Scrapped at Queensborough in 1923.

BATTLECRUISER **RENOWN**
Emergency programme. Fairfield, Glasgow. Laid down: 25 January 1915. Launched: 4 March 1916. Completed: 20 September 1916.

BATTLECRUISER **REPULSE**
Emergency programme. John Brown and Company, Clydebank. Laid down: 25 January 1915. Launched: 8 January 1916. Completed: 18 August 1916.

Dimensions
794-ft/242.81-m x 90-ft/27.52-m x 27-ft/8.26-m. Weight of hull: 10,800 tons. Displacement: 26,500 tons (standard), **Renown** 32,727 tons (full load), **Repulse** 32,074 tons (full load). Armament: Six 15-in/380-mm 42 calibre, seventeen 4-in/102-mm, two 3-in/76.2-mm AA, four 3-pdr guns. Ten 21-in/533-mm torpedoes with two submerged tubes. Armour: 6-in/152-mm belt, 11-in/280-mm turret, 7-in/178-mm barbette, 10-in/254-mm CT, 3.5-in/89-mm deck. Weight of armour: 4,770 tons. Machinery: Forty-two Babcock and Wilcox boilers, four Brown-Curtis turbines, four shafts. 126,000 shp. Machinery weight: 5,780 tons. Speed: **Renown** 32.68 knots at 126,300 shp on trials. **Repulse** 32.6 knots: 31.7 knots at 119,025 shp. Fuel: 4,243 tons oil. Range: 3,650 n.m. at 10 knots.

Fate
Renown: Placed on disposal list 1 June 1948 and sold in August for scrapping at Faslane.
Repulse: Lost 10 December 1941 in 3°45' North 104°24' East in the South China Sea to attack by Japanese land-based aircraft.

BATTLECRUISER **HOOD**
John Brown & Company, Clydebank. Laid down: 1 September 1916. Launched: 28 August 1918. Completed: 5 March 1920. The **Hood** was one of class of four ordered in April 1916. Construction of the **Anson, Howe** and the **Rodney** halted in 1918.

Dimensions
860-ft/263-m x 104-ft/31.80-m x 28.5-ft/8.72-m. Displacement: 41,200 tons (standard). 45,200 tons (full load). Armament: Eight 15-in/42 cal, twelve 5.5-in/50 cal, four 4-in AA, four 3-pdr guns. Six 21-in torpedo tubes. Armour: 12-in/305-mm belt, 15-in/380-mm turret, 12-in/305-mm barbette, 11-in/280-mm CT., 3-in/76.2-mm deck. Armour weight: 13,802 tons. Machinery: Twenty-four Yarrow small-tube boilers, four Brown-Curtis geared turbines, four shafts. 151,280 shp and 31 knots (as designed). Machinery weight: 5,356 tons. Speed: 151,280 shp and 32.07 knots. Fuel: 4,000 tons oil. Range: 4,000 n.m. at 10 knots.

Fate
Lost 24 May 1941 in 63°20' North 31°50' West in the Denmark Strait in surface action with German battleship **Bismarck** and heavy cruiser **Prinz Eugen**.

BATTLESHIP **NELSON**
1922 programme. Armstrong at Newcastle-on-Tyne.
Laid down: 28 December 1922. Launched: 3 September 1925. Commissioned: 10 September 1927.

BATTLESHIP **RODNEY**
1922 programme. Cammell Laird at Birkenhead. Laid down: 28 December 1922. Launched: 17 December 1925. Commissioned: 10 November 1927.

Dimensions
710-ft/217.13-m x 106-ft/32.42-m x 30-ft/9.17-m. Displacement: 33,950 tons (standard). 38,000 tons (full). Armament: Nine 16-in/406-mm 45 calibre, twelve 6-in/162-mm, six 4.7-in/120-mm AA and one (?) eight-barrel 2-pdr guns. Two 24-in/610-mm torpedo tubes. Final tertiary armament: six eight-barrel 2-pdr, sixteen 40-mm and sixty-one 20-mm guns. Armour: 14-in/356-mm belt, 16-in/406-mm turret, 15-in/380-mm barbette, 6.25-in/159-mm deck over magazines. Machinery: Eight Admiralty three-drum small-tube boilers, two sets of turbines and 45,000 shp (designed). Speed: 23.8 knots on standard displacement. Fuel: 4,000 tons oil.

Fate
Nelson: Stricken 19 May 1948 and used as target ship before being scrapped at Inverkeithing after 15 March 1949: hull scrapped at Troon. **Rodney**: Sold in February 1948 and scrapped at Inverkeithing after 26 March 1948.

BATTLESHIP **KING GEORGE V**

1936 programme. Vickers-Armstrong, Walker-on-Tyne. Ordered: 29 July 1936. Laid down: 1 January 1937. Launched: 21 February 1939. Commissioned: 30 September 1940. Operational: 19 January 1941.

BATTLESHIP **PRINCE OF WALES**

1936 programme. Cammell Laird, Birkenhead. Ordered: 29 July 1936. Laid down: 2 January 1937. Launched: 21 February 1939. Commissioned: 19 January 1941. Operational: 22 May 1941.

BATTLESHIP **DUKE OF YORK**

1936 programme. John Brown & Company, Clydebank. Ordered: 16 November 1936. Laid down: 5 May 1937. Launched: 28 February 1940. Commissioned: 20 August 1941. Operational: 22 December 1941.

BATTLESHIP **HOWE**

1936 programme. Fairfield Shipyard, Govan, Glasgow. Ordered: 16 November 1936. Laid down: 1 June 1937. Launched: 9 April 1940. Commissioned: 2 June 1942. Operational: December 1942.

BATTLESHIP **ANSON**

1936 programme. Swan Hunter, Wallsend, Newcastle. Ordered: 16 November 1936. Laid down: 22 July 1937. Launched: 24 February 1940. Commissioned: 14 April 1942. Operational: September 1942.

Dimensions

745-ft/227.83-m x 103-ft/31.50-m x 35.5-ft/10.86-m. Displacement: Design displacement of 35,490 tons (standard). 40,580 tons (full load). Maximum full load displacement: **Anson**: 45,360 tons (1945). Armament: Ten 14-in/356-mm 45 calibre, sixteen 5.25-in/133-mm 50 calibre guns. Four aircraft. Armour: 15-in/380-mm belt, 16-in/406-mm turret, barbette, 6-in/152-mm deck. Weight of armour approximately 12,000 tons. Machinery: Eight Admiralty three-drum small-tube boilers, four sets of geared turbines and 110,000 shp (designed). Single rudder. Speed: Between 27.5 and 28.3 knots. Fuel: maximum **Anson** 4,210 tons fuel oil: 183 tons diesel oil. Range: **Howe** and **Anson**: 6,100 n.m. at 10 knots, 2,600 n.m. at 27 knots. Final wartime tertiary armament: **King George V**. Mid-1945: eight eight-barrel Mk. VI 2-pdr, two four-barrel Mk. VII 2-pdr, two single 40-mm, six twin 20-mm and twenty-four single 20-mm guns. Fate: In reserve 1950. Stricken 30 April 1957. Scrapped at Dalmuir (superstructure) after 20 January 1958 and at Troon (hull) after May 1959. **Prince of Wales**. Late 1941: six eight-barrel Mk. VI 2-pdr, one single 40-mm and eight single 20-mm guns. Fate: Lost 10 December 1941 in 3°33'6" North 104°28'79" East in the South China Sea to attack by Japanese land-based aircraft. **Duke of York**. Laid down as the **Anson**: name changed in December 1938. April 1945: eight eight-barrel Mk. VI 2-pdr pompoms, six four-barrel Mk. VII 2-pdr, two four-barrel 40-mm, eight twin and thirty-eight single 20-mm guns. Fate: Stricken 30 April 1957. Scrapped at Faslane after February 1958. **Howe**. Laid down as the **Beatty**: name changed in February 1940. Mid-1944: eight eight-barrel Mk. VI 2-pdr pompoms, four twin 20-mm guns, thirty-four single 20-mm guns. Fate: Placed in reserve at Devonport in 1951. Stricken in April 1957. Towed to Inverkeithing after 27 May 1958 and scrapped after 4 June 1958. **Anson**. Laid down as the **Jellicoe:** name changed in February 1940. April 1945: eight eight-barrel Mk. VI 2-pdr pompoms, four four-barrel Mk. VII 2-pdr, two four-barrel 40-mm, six twin 20-mm and fifteen single 20-mm guns. Fate: Placed in reserve in November 1949. Towed to Gare Loch in 1951. Stricken 30 April 1957. Scrapped at Faslane after 17 December 1957.

BATTLESHIP **VANGUARD**

John Brown & Company, Clydebank. Laid down: 2 October 1941. Launched: 30 November 1944. Commissioned: 9 August 1946. Operational: 1 February 1947.

Dimensions
814.3 x 109 x 36-ft. Displacement: 44,500 tons (standard). 51,420 tons (full load). Armament: As finally designed: eight 15-in/380-mm 41 calibre at 30 degrees, sixteen 5.25-in/133-mm 50 calibre, eleven twin 40-mm/56 calibre, four 3-pdr AA as amended in 1942: nine eight-barrel Mk. VI 2-pdr pompoms, one four-barrel Mk. VII 2-pdr, and twelve twin 20-mm guns. AA as built: ten six-barrel Mk. VI 40-mm, eleven single 40-mm Mk. VII and one other AA gun. Armour: 14-in/356-mm belt, 13-in/330-mm turret, 16-in/406-mm barbette, 6-in/152-mm deck. Machinery: Eight boilers, four sets of geared turbines. 130,000 shp. Speed: 30.38 knots at 132,951 shp. Fuel: 3,800 tons. Range: 5,500 n.m. at 12 knots, 3,380 n.m. at 28 knots.

Fate
Placed in reserve in March 1956. Ceased to be flagship of reserve fleet at Portsmouth on 8 June 1960. Arrived at Faslane 9 August and scrapped thereafter.

THE UNITED STATES OF AMERICA

BATTLESHIP **SOUTH CAROLINA** (BB 26)
1905 programme. William Cramp and Sons, Philadelphia, Pennsylvania. Laid down: 18 December 1906. Launched: 11 July 1908. Completed: 1 March 1910.

BATTLESHIP **MICHIGAN** (BB 27)
1905 programme. New York Shipbuilding, Camden, New Jersey. Laid down: 17 December 1906. Launched: 26 May 1908. Completed: 4 January 1910.

Dimensions
451.25-ft/138.00-m x 75.9-ft/23.21-m x 24.5-ft/7.49-m. Displacement: 16,000 tons (normal), 17,900 tons (full load). Armament: Eight 12-in/305-mm 45 calibre, twenty-two (reduced to sixteen) 3-in/76.2-mm guns. Two 21-in/533 torpedo tubes. Weight of armament excluding turrets: 1,150 tons. Armour: 12-in/305-mm belt, turret, 10-in/254-mm barbette, 12-in/305-mm CT., 1.5-in/38-mm deck. Armour weight: c. 4,000 tons. Machinery: Twelve Babcock coal-burning boilers, two vertical four-cylinder triple expansion engines, two shafts. 16,500 ihp. Machinery weight: 1,854 tons. Speed: 18.8 knots. Fuel: 2,380 tons coal. Range: 5,000 n.m. at 10 knots.

Fate
South Carolina: Decommissioned at Philadelphia navy yard on 15 December 1921. Stricken 10 November 1923. Sold 24 April 1924. Scrapped thereafter. **Michigan**: Decommissioned on 11 February 1922. Stricken 24 August 1923. Sold 23 January 1924. Scrapped at Philadelphia navy yard thereafter.

BATTLESHIP **DELAWARE** (BB 28)
1906 programme. Newport News Shipbuilding, Newport News, Virginia. Laid down: 11 November 1907. Launched: 6 February 1909. Completed: 4 April 1910.

BATTLESHIP **NORTH DAKOTA** (BB 29)
1907 programme. Fore River Shipbuilding, Quincy, Massachusetts. Laid down: 16 December 1907. Launched: 10 November 1908. Completed: 11 April 1910.

Dimensions
517-ft/158.10-m x 85-ft/25.99-m x 27.1-ft/8.29-m. Displacement: **Delaware** 20,380 tons **North Dakota** 20,000 tons (normal), 22,400 tons (full load). Armament: Ten 12-in/305-mm 45 calibre, fourteen 5-in/127-mm 51 calibre guns. Two 21-in/533-mm submerged torpedo tubes. Armour: 11-in/280-mm belt, 12-in/305-mm turret, 10-in/254-mm barbette, 12-in/305-mm CT, 3-in/76-mm deck. Machinery: Fourteen Babcock boilers, **Delaware**: two four-cylinder triple expansion engines: 28,570 ihp. 21.44 knots. **North Dakota**: two Curtis turbines: 33,875 ihp.

Two shafts. Speed: 21.83 knots. Fuel: 1,930 tons coal, 380 tons oil, or 2,676 tons coal. Range: 9,000 n.m. at 12 knots.

Fate
Delaware: Taken out of service in August 1923 at Norfolk navy yard and crew transferred to the new battleship **Colorado**. Moved to Boston navy yard: decommissioned 10 November and stricken 27 November 1923. Sold 5 February 1924 and scrapped at Philadelphia navy yard thereafter. **North Dakota**: Decommissioned at the Norfolk navy yard on 22 November 1923 with the entry into service of the **West Virginia**. Thereafter served as target vessel. Sold 16 March 1931 and scrapped at Boston thereafter.

BATTLESHIP **FLORIDA** (BB 30)
1908 programme. New York Navy Yard, New York. Laid down: 9 March 1909. Launched: 12 May 1910. Completed: 15 September 1911.

BATTLESHIP **UTAH** (BB 31)
1908 programme. New York Shipbuilding, Camden, New Jersey. Laid down: 15 March 1909. Launched: 23 December 1909. Completed: 31 August 1911.

Dimensions
519.9-ft/158.99-m x 88-ft/26.91-m x 28.1-ft/8.59-m. Displacement: 23,400-ton (full load). Armament: Ten 12-in/305-mm 45 calibre, sixteen 5-in/127-mm 51 calibre guns. In 1917 also two 3-in/76.2-mm AA guns: after 1926 conversion eight 3-in/76.2-mm and two 1.5-in AA guns. Until this conversion two 21-in/533-mm torpedo tubes: after conversion three seaplanes and one catapult. Armour: 11-in/280-mm belt, 12-in/305-mm turret, 10-in/254-mm barbette, 12-in/305-mm CT, 5.83-in/148-mm deck. Machinery: Twelve Babcock boilers, four Parsons turbines, four shafts. 28,000 shp. Speed: 20.75 knots. Range: 5,810 n.m. at 10 knots.

Reconstruction
The **Florida** between 25 July 1924 and 24 June 1926 and the **Utah** between August 1926 and November 1928 at Boston navy yard: four White-Forster oil-burning boilers and four Curtis geared turbines, four shafts for 44,000 shp and 22 knots.

Fate
Florida: Decommissioned at Philadelphia on 16 February 1931 and stricken 6 April. Scrapping completed 30 September 1932. **Utah**: Converted at Norfolk navy yard to serve as target ship after 1 July 1931, and recommissioned 1 April 1932. After June 1935 also served as training ship. Sunk on 7 December 1941 at Pearl Harbor by Japanese carrier aircraft. Proved beyond salvage and wreck remains where it sank.

BATTLESHIP **WYOMING** (BB 32)
1909 programme. William Cramp and Sons, Philadelphia, Pennsylvania. Laid down: 14 October 1909. Launched: 9 February 1910. Completed: 25 May 1911.

BATTLESHIP **ARKANSAS** (BB 33)
1909 programme. New York Shipbuilding, Camden, New Jersey. Laid down: 25 January 1910. Launched: 14 January 1911. Completed: 17 September 1912.

Dimensions
562-ft/171.87-m x 93.2-ft/28.50-m x 28.6-ft/8.75-m. Displacement: 27,700 tons (full load). Armament: Twelve 12-in/305-mm 50 calibre, sixteen 5-in/127-mm 51 calibre, two 3-in/76.2-mm AA guns. Two 21-in/533-mm torpedo tubes. Throughout the inter-war period the **Arkansas** had three seaplanes. Armour: 11-in/280-mm belt, 12-in/305-mm turret, 11-in/280-mm barbette, 12-in/305-mm CT, 3-in/76.2-mm deck. Machinery: Twelve Babcock (mixed) boilers, four Parsons turbines, four shafts. Designed for 28,000 shp and 20.5 knots. Machinery weight: **Arkansas** 2,178 tons. Speed: *Wyoming* on trials 31,437 shp and 21.22

knots. Fuel: 1,990 tons coal and 400 tons oil or 2,641 tons of coal. After conversion 5,100 tons oil. Range: 8,000 n.m. at 10 knots.

Fate
Wyoming: Gunnery training ship. Decommissioned into reserve 1 August 1947. Stricken 16 September 1947 and sold on 30 October 1946 and scrapped at Newark after December 1947. **Arkansas**: October 1945 decommissioned and selected as target ship in Bikini tests. Survived Able test, 1 July 1946, but destroyed in Baker test 25 July 1946.

BATTLESHIP **NEW YORK** (BB 34)
1910 programme. New York navy yard, New York. Laid down: 11 September 1911. Launched: 30 October 1912. Completed: 15 April 1914.

BATTLESHIP **TEXAS** (BB 35)
1910 programme. Newport News Shipbuilding, Newport News, Virginia. Laid down: 17 April 1911. Launched: 18 May 1912. Completed: 12 March 1914.

Dimensions
573-ft/175.23-m x 95.5-ft/29.20-m x 28.5-ft/8.72-m. Displacement: 27,500 tons (normal) 28,367 tons (full load). Armament: Ten 14-in/356-mm 45 calibre, twenty-one 5-in/127-mm 51 calibre guns (reduced to sixteen in 1917–1918. Armour: 12-in/305-mm belt, 14-in/356-mm turrets, 12-in/305-mm barbette, 12-in/305-mm CT, 3-in/76-mm deck. Machinery: Fourteen Babcock (mixed) boilers, two four-cylinder expansion engines, two shafts: 28,100 ihp. Machinery weight: **New York** 2,048 tons, **Texas** 1,971 tons. Speed: 21 knots. Fuel: 2,850 tons coal. Range: 10,000 n.m. at 10 knots.

Fate
New York: 30 October 1945 decommissioned at Pearl Harbor. Survived atomic bomb tests of 1 and 25 July 1946. Towed to Kwajalein, decommissioned 29 August. Later towed to Pearl Harbor for examination. Sunk as a target 8 July 1948. **Texas**: 27 October 1945 decommissioned at Pearl Harbor. Transferred to Norfolk in January 1946 and laid up outside Baltimore after June 1946. Towed to San Jacinto national park in Texas, and on 21 April 1948 dedicated as a permanent memorial.

BATTLESHIP **NEVADA** (BB 36)
1911 programme. Fore River Shipbuilding, Quincy, Massachusetts: renamed Bethlehem Steel Company during 1913. Laid down: 4 November 1912. Launched: 11 July 1914. Completed: 11 March 1916.

BATTLESHIP **OKLAHOMA** (BB 37)
1911 programme. New York Shipbuilding, Camden, New Jersey. Laid down: 26 October 1912. Launched: 23 March 1914. Completed: 2 May 1916.

Dimensions
583-ft/178.29-m x 95.25-ft/29.13-m x 28.5-ft/8.72-m. Displacement: 27,500 tons (normal), 28,400 tons (full load). Armament: Ten 14-in/356-mm, twenty-one 5-in/127-mm 51 calibre guns, and two 21-in/533-mm torpedo tubes. Armour: 13.90-in/353-mm main belt, 18-in/457-mm turrets, 13.50-in/343-mm barbette, 15.98-in/406-mm CT, 3-in/76-mm deck. Machinery: Twelve **Nevada** Yarrow **Oklahoma** Babcock boilers, **Nevada** two Curtis turbines plus one cruising turbine, **Oklahoma** two four-cylinder triple expansion engines, two shafts. **Nevada** 26,500 shp. **Oklahoma** 24,800 shp. Speed: 20.5 knots. Fuel: 2,037 tons oil. Range: 10,000 n.m. at 10 knots.

Fate
Nevada: Survived Bikini tests in July 1946. Returned to Pearl Harbor and decommissioned 29 August. Sunk as a target ship on 31 July 1948. **Oklahoma**: Sunk at Pearl Harbor 7 December 1941. Operations to recover the ship began in March 1943 and she was raised

28 December 1943. Decommissioned 1 September 1944 and thereafter stripped, being sold for scrapping. While being towed to the west coast she parted her tow line in a storm and sank, some 540 miles from Pearl Harbor, 17 May 1947.

BATTLESHIP **PENNSYLVANIA** (BB 38)

1912 programme. Newport News Shipbuilding, Newport News, Virginia. Laid down: 27 October 1913. Launched: 16 March 1915. Completed: 12 June 1916.

BATTLESHIP **ARIZONA** (BB 39)

1913 programme. New York navy yard, New York. Laid down: 16 March 1914. Launched: 19 June 1915. Completed: 17 October 1916.

Dimensions

608-ft/185.93-m x 97.1-ft/29.69-m x 28.8-ft/8.81-m. Displacement: 32,567 tons (full). Armament: Twelve 14-in/356-mm, twenty-two 5-in/127-mm 51 calibre, four 3-in/76.2-mm AA guns. Armour: 14.02-in/356-mm belt, 18-in/457-mm turrets, 13.50-in/343-mm barbette, 16-in/406-mm CT, 3-in/76-mm deck. Machinery: Twelve Babcock boilers, four geared plus one cruising turbines, four shafts. **Pennsylvania** 31,500 shp. **Arizona** 34,000 shp. Machinery weight: **Pennsylvania** 2,396 tons, **Arizona** 2,462 tons. Speed: 21 knots. Fuel: 2,322 tons oil. Range: 8,000 n.m. at 10 knots.

Fate

Pennsylvania: Survived atomic bomb tests and towed to Kwajalein, decommissioned 29 August 1946. She remained there until sunk outside the atoll on 10 February 1948. **Arizona**: Sunk at Pearl Harbor on 7 December 1941. She was stricken 1 December 1942. Authorised as a memorial on 16 May 1958, she was thus dedicated on 30 June 1962.

BATTLESHIP **NEW MEXICO** (BB 40)

1914 programme. New York navy yard, New York. Laid down: 14 October 1915. Launched: 23 April 1917. Completed: 20 May 1918.

BATTLESHIP **MISSISSIPPI** (BB 41)

1914 programme. Newport News Shipbuilding, Newport News, Virginia. Laid down: 5 April 1915. Launched: 25 January 1917. Completed: 18 December 1919.

BATTLESHIP **IDAHO** (BB 42)

Addition to original 1914 programme. New York navy yard, New York. Laid down: 20 January 1915. Launched: 30 June 1917. Completed: 24 March 1919.

Dimensions

624-ft/190.83-m x 97.4-ft/29.79-m x 30-ft/9.17-m. Displacement: 33,000 tons (full load). Armament: Twelve 14-in/356-mm, twenty two 5-in/127-mm 51 calibre, four 3-in/76.2-mm guns. Two 21-in/533-mm torpedo tubes. Armour: 13.5-in/353-mm belt, 18-in/457-mm turrets, 13.5-in/343-mm barbette, 16-in/406-mm CT, 3-in/76-mm deck. Machinery: Nine Babcock boilers, **Mississippi** four Curtis turbines supplied by Newport News yard, **Idaho** four Parsons turbines from New York Shipbuilding, **New Mexico** two Curtis turbines supplied by General Electric. Four shafts 27,000 shp. Machinery weight: **New Mexico** 2,351 tons, **Mississippi** 2,298 tons, **Idaho** 2,285 tons. Speed: 21 knots. Range: 8,000 n.m. at 10 knots.

Fate

New Mexico: Stricken 25 February 1946. Sold on 13 October and scrapped at Newark after 24 November 1946. **Mississippi**: Between 27 November 1945 and 15 February 1947 subjected to conversion as a gunnery and experimental tender. Decommissioned on 17 September 1956. Sold on 28 November 1956. Towed from Norfolk for scrapping on 7 December 1956. **Idaho**: Decommissioned 3 July 1946 and stricken 16 September. Sold on 24 November 1947 and scrapped at Newark after 12 December 1947.

BATTLESHIP **TENNESSEE** (BB 43)
1915 programme. New York navy yard, New York. Laid down: 14 May 1917. Launched: 30 April 1919. Completed: 3 June 1920.

BATTLESHIP **CALIFORNIA** (BB 44)
1915 programme. Mare Island navy yard, Vallejo, California. Laid down: 25 October 1916. Launched: 20 November 1919. Completed: 10 August 1921.

Dimensions
624-ft/190.83-m x 97.4-ft/29.79-m x 30.2-ft/9.24-m. Displacement: 33,190 tons (full load). Armament: Twelve 14-in/356-mm, twenty two 5-in/127-mm 51 calibre, four 3-in/76.2-mm guns. Two 21-in/533-mm torpedo tubes. Armour: 14-in/356-mm belt, 18-in/457-mm turrets, 14-in/356-mm barbette, 16-in/406-mm CT, 2-in/51-mm deck. Machinery: eight boilers, two turbines, four shafts. 27,000 shp. Speed: 21 knots.

Fate
California: Sunk at Pearl Harbor on 7 December 1941. Refloated 25 March 1942 and on 7 June sailed for Puget Sound navy yard. Subjected to complete refit and modernisation programme which lasted until 31 January 1944. **Tennessee** and **California** placed in reserve at Philadelphia on 7 August 1946, decommissioned 14 February 1947. Both stricken 1 March 1959 and sold for scrap on 10 July 1959. Both were broken up at Baltimore thereafter.

BATTLESHIP **COLORADO** (BB 45)
1916 programme. New York Shipbuilding, Camden, New Jersey. Laid down: 29 May 1919. Launched: 22 March 1921. Completed: 30 August 1923.

BATTLESHIP **MARYLAND** (BB 46)
1916 programme. Newport News Shipbuilding, Newport News, Virginia. Laid down: 24 April 1917. Launched: 20 March 1920. Completed: 21 July 1921.

BATTLESHIP **WEST VIRGINIA** (BB 48)
1916 programme. Newport News Shipbuilding, Newport News, Virginia. Laid down: 12 April 1920. Launched: 19 November 1921. Completed: 1 December 1923.

BATTLESHIP **Washington** (BB 47).
1916 programme. New York Shipbuilding, Camden, New Jersey. Laid down: 30 June 1919. Launched on 1 September 1921. Cancelled 8 February 1922 when 75.9% complete: stricken under terms of Washington treaty. Used to test explosives and sunk 25 November 1924.

Dimensions
624-ft/190.83-m x 97.4-ft/29.79-m x 30.2-ft/9.24-m. Displacement: 33,590 tons (full load). Armament: Eight 16-in/406-mm, fourteen 5-in/127-mm 51 calibre, four 3-in/76.2-mm guns. Two 21-in/533-mm torpedo tubes. Armour: 16-in/406-mm belt, 18-in/457-mm turrets, 13.5-in/343-mm barbette, 16-in/406-mm CT, 3.50-in/89-mm deck. Machinery: Eight Babcock oil-burning boilers, two General Electric (**Colorado** Westinghouse) turbines coupled to two generators, four motors and four shafts. 28,900 shp. Machinery weight: 2,002 tons. Speed: 21 knots. Range: 8,000 n.m. at 10 knots.
Wartime tertiary armament. **Maryland:** 1945. Sixteen 5-in/127-mm 38 calibre in twin turrets, with forty 40-mm and eighteen 20-mm AA guns. **Colorado** ten 5-in/127-mm 51 calibre, eight 5-in/127-mm 38 calibre, forty 40-mm, and "up to thirty-two" 20-mm AA guns. **West Virginia** 1944 sixteen 5-in/127-mm 38 calibre in twin turrets, forty 40-mm, fifty 20-mm AA guns. The **Maryland** and **West Virginia** had three seaplanes, one catapult.

Fate
Maryland: Placed in reserve 15 July 1946. Decommissioned 3 April 1947 at Bremerton. Stricken 1 March 1959. Sold 8 July 1959. Scrapped San Pedro after August 1959. **Colorado**: Decommissioned into reserve at Bremerton 9 January 1947. Stricken 1 March 1959. Sold 22 June 1959. Scrapped at Seattle after July 1959. **West Virginia**: Sunk on 7 December 1941 at

Pearl Harbor by Japanese carrier aircraft. Salvaged in May 1942 and rebuilt at Puget Sound navy yard. Re-entered service July 1944. Decommissioned into reserve 9 January 1947. Stricken 1 March 1959. Sold 17 August 1959. Scrapped at Seattle after January 1961.

BATTLESHIP **NORTH CAROLINA** (BB 55)
Authorised 27 March 1934. New York navy yard. Laid down: 27 October 1937. Launched: 13 June 1940. Completed: 9 April 1941.

BATTLESHIP **WASHINGTON** (BB 56).
Authorised 27 March 1934. Philadelphia navy yard. Laid down: 14 June 1938. Launched: 1 June 1940. Completed: 15 May 1941.

Dimensions
728.75-ft/222.85-m x 108.33-ft/33.13-m x 32.96-ft/10.08-m. Displacement: 35,000 tons (standard displacement as stated), 38,000 tons (in reality): **Washington** 45,370 tons, **North Carolina** 46,770 tons (full load). Armament: Nine 16-in/406-mm 45 calibre, twenty 5-in/127-mm 38 calibre DP, four quadruple 1.1-in/28-mm and twelve 0.5-in machine guns. Three seaplanes. Armament weight: 8,120 tons. Armour: 12-in/305-mm belt, 16-in/406-mm turret, barbette, CT., 5.55-in/141-mm deck. Armour weight: 13,976 tons. Machinery: Eight Babcock boilers, four General Electric geared turbines, four shafts. 121,000 shp. Machinery weight: 1,881 tons. Speed: 28 knots designed: 28.5 knots recorded. Fuel: 6,580 tons oil. Range: 17,450 n.m. at 15 knots.

Fate
Both decommissioned into reserve at Bayonne, New Jersey, 27 June 1947, stricken 1 June 1960. The **Washington** sold on 24 May 1961. Scrapped at Kearney, New Jersey, between July and October 1961. The **North Carolina** purchased by the state of North Carolina and formally dedicated as a war memorial at Wilmington on 3 October 1961.

BATTLESHIP **SOUTH DAKOTA** (BB 57)
1936 programme. New York Shipbuilding, Camden, New Jersey. Laid down: 5 July 1939. Launched: 7 June 1941. Completed: 20 March 1942.

BATTLESHIP **INDIANA** (BB 58)
1936 programme. Newport News Shipbuilding, Newport News, Virginia. Laid down: 20 November 1939. Launched: 21 November 1941.
Completed: 30 April 1942.

BATTLESHIP **MASSACHUSETTS** (BB 59)
1939 programme. Bethlehem, Quincy, Massachusetts. Laid down: 20 July 1939. Launched: 23 September 1941. Completed: 15 May 1942.

BATTLESHIP **ALABAMA** (BB 60)
1939 programme. Norfolk navy yard, Norfolk, Virginia. Laid down: 1 February 1940. Launched: 16 February 1942. Completed: 16 August 1942.

Dimensions
680-ft/207.94-m x 108.17-ft/33.08-m x 35-ft/10.70-m. Displacement: 35,000 tons (standard displacement), 42,500 tons (full load). **Massachusetts** 45,216 tons, others 44,374 tons (full load) in reality. Armament: Nine 16-in/406-mm 45 calibre, twenty (**South Dakota** sixteen) 5-in/127-mm 38 calibre DP, and, as designed, three quadruple 1.1-in/28-mm and twelve 0.5-in machine guns. Three seaplanes, two catapults. Armour: 12.20-in/310-mm belt, 18-in/457-mm turret, 17.28-in/439-mm barbette, 16-in/406-mm CT., 5.79-in/147-mm deck. Armour weight: 14,200 tons (approximate). Machinery: Eight **Massachusetts/South Dakota** Babcock boilers and four General Electric, others Foster-Wheeler boilers and four Westinghouse, geared turbines, four shafts. 130,000 shp. Speed: 27 knots. Fuel: **South Dakota/Massachusetts** 6,950 tons, **Indiana/Alabama** 7,340 tons oil. Range: 15,000 n.m. at 15 knots.

Fate
South Dakota: In January 1947 placed in reserve at Philadelphia. Stricken 1 June 1962 and sold 25 October 1962 to Lipsett. Scrapped at New York after November 1962. Parts of the ship were purchased by the state after which she was named in order to serve at war memorial at Sioux Falls. **Indiana**: Placed in reserve at Bremerton, 11 September 1946. Stricken 1 June 1962 and sold 6 September 1963. Scrapped at Richmond, California, after November 1963. Parts of the ship were purchased by the state after which she was named. **Massachusetts**: Decommissioned at Norfolk 27 March 1947. Stricken 1 June 1962 and offered for scrap in 1964, but transferred to **Massachusetts** Memorial Committee 8 June 1965. Moored in the Fall River, Massachusetts, as war memorial since 14 August 1965. **Alabama**: Decommissioned at Bremerton 9 January 1947 and stricken 1 June 1962. Transferred to state of Alabama on 10 June 1964 and after September 1964 moored as a memorial in Mobile Bay.

BATTLESHIP **IOWA** (BB 61)
New York navy yard. Laid down: 27 June 1940. Launched: 27 August 1942. Completed: 22 February 1943.

BATTLESHIP **NEW JERSEY** (BB 62)
Philadelphia navy yard. Laid down: 16 September 1940. Launched: 7 December 1942. Completed: 23 May 1943.

BATTLESHIP **MISSOURI** (BB 63)
New York navy yard. Laid down: 6 January 1941. Launched: 29 January 1944. Completed: 11 June 1944.

BATTLESHIP **WISCONSIN** (BB 64)
Philadelphia navy yard. Laid down: 25 January 1941. Launched: 7 December 1943. Completed: 16 April 1944.

BATTLESHIP **Illinois** (BB 65).
Philadelphia navy yard. Laid down: 15 January 1945. Work halted: 18 August 1945, when 22% complete.

BATTLESHIP **Kentucky** (BB 66).
Philadelphia navy yard. Laid down: 6 December 1944. Construction suspended 17 February 1947 when 72.1% complete: launched 20 January 1950 to clear slip. Stricken 9 June 1958 and sold for scrap 31 October 1958 and scrapped at Baltimore thereafter.

Dimensions
887.25-ft/271.31-m x 108.17-ft/33.08-m x 36.17-ft/11.06-m. Displacement: 45,000 tons (declared standard displacement), 48,000 tons (in reality), **Iowa/New Jersey** 57,450 tons, **Missouri/Wisconsin** 57,216 tons. Armament: Nine 16-in/406-mm 50 calibre, twenty 5-in/127-mm 38 calibre, twenty quadruple and forty-nine other 20-mm AA guns. Three or four aircraft, two catapults. Armament weight: 10,800 tons. Armour: 12.20-in/310-mm belt, 17-in/432-mm turret, 17.28-in/439-mm barbette, 17.52-in/445-mm CT, 6.34-in/161-mm deck. Armour weight: 18,700 tons. Machinery: Eight Babcock boilers, four **Iowa/Missouri** General Electric, others Westinghouse, geared turbines, four shafts. 200,000 shp. Machinery weight: 2,500 tons. Speed: 33 knots. Fuel: 7,251 tons oil. Range: 15,000 n.m. at 12 knots.
Tertiary armament. **Iowa**: 1943–1945, fifteen quadruple 40-mm, reduced to fourteen. Sixty 20-mm, possibly reduced to fifty-two. **New Jersey**: 1943–1945, sixteen (possibly raised to twenty) quadruple 40-mm, reduced to fourteen. Sixty 20-mm, possibly reduced to eight twin and 41 single. **Missouri** and **Wisconsin**: 1944–1945, twenty quadruple 40-mm, reduced to fourteen. Forty-nine 20-mm, possibly two twin and forty-five single.

BATTLECRUISER **ALASKA**
New York Shipbuilding, Camden, New Jersey. Laid down: 17 December 1941. Launched: 15 August 1943. Completed: 17 June 1944.

BATTLECRUISER **GUAM**
New York Shipbuilding, Camden, New Jersey. Laid down: 2 February 1942. Launched: 21 November 1943. Completed: 17 September 1944.

BATTLECRUISER **HAWAII**
New York Shipbuilding, Camden, New Jersey. Laid down: 20 December 1943. Launched: 11 March 1945. Work halted 16 April 1947 when 84% complete. Various conversion plans abandoned by 1954. Stricken 9 June 1958. Scrapped at Baltimore after 6 January 1960.

The **Philippines**, **Puerto Rico** and the **Samoa** ordered 9 October 1940 and were to have been built by New York Shipbuilding Co. Cancelled 24 June 1943 without having been laid down.

Dimensions
808.50-ft/247.23-m x 91.08-ft/27.85-m x 31.83-ft/9.73-m. Displacement: 29,000 tons (standard displacement), 34,250 tons (full load). Armament: Nine 12-in/305-mm 45 calibre, twelve 5-in/127-mm 38 calibre DP, fourteen quadruple 40-mm, thirty to thirty-four 20-mm AA guns. Four seaplanes, two catapults. Armour: 9.02-in/229-mm belt, 12.79-in/325-mm turret, 10.98-in/279-mm barbette, 10.59-in/269-mm CT., 3.74-in/95-mm deck. Machinery: Eight Babcock boilers, four General Electric geared turbines, four shafts. 150,000 shp. Speed: 33 knots. Fuel: 3,710 tons oil. Range: 12,000 n.m. at 15 knots.

Fate
Alaska: Stricken 1 June 1960 and sold 30 June 1961. Scrapped at Kearney after July 1961.
Guam: Decommissioned at Bayonne on 17 February 1947. Stricken 1 June 1960 and sold 10 July 1961. Scrapped at Newark after August 1961.

Notes

CHAPTER 2

[1] The original introduction written by the author for the Naval Institute Press's reprint of Captain S. W. Roskill's *H. M. S. Warspite. The Story of a Famous Battleship.*

[2] Oscar Parkes, *British Battleships. Warrior to Vanguard, 1860–1950. A History of Design, Construction and Armament*, p. 356.

[3] The large cruisers were defined as the *König Wilhelm, Kaiser, Deutschland, Kaiserin Augusta,* the members of the five-strong *Viktoria-Luise* class which were the nameship, the *Freya, Hansa, Hertha* and *Vineta,* and the *Fürst Bismarck,* which was completed in 1900, and the *Prinz Heinrich* and *Prinz Adalbert,* then being built.

The *König Wilhelm, Kaiser* and *Deutschland* were built as armoured frigates on the Thames, and were the last major German warships built abroad. The *König Wilhelm* was launched in 1868 and was commissioned into service in 1869. She displaced 9,760 tons and carried 33 72-lb. cannon. In 1878 she sank the armoured ship *Grosser Kurfürst* in a collision off Folkestone. She was reclassified as an armoured cruiser in 1897 but was laid up in 1904 and used thereafter as an accommodation ship. The *Kaiser* was launched in 1872 and was commissioned in 1875. The *Deutschland* was launched in 1872 and commissioned in 1875. In their original state both had two funnels and three masts for a full rig. Originally they displaced 7,600 tons and carried eight 10.2-in/260-mm cannon. The *Kaiser* was rebuilt between 1891 and 1895 as a heavy cruiser. The *Deutschland* was recommissioned as a heavy cruiser on 25 January 1897.

The *Kaiserin Augusta* and the members of the *Viktoria-Luise* class were second-class cruisers. The *Kaiserin Augusta* displaced 6,056 tons and was the first triple-screw ship in the German Navy: she was launched in 1892 and was completed in 1896, and carried four 150-mm/5.9-in, eight 88-mm/3.46-in guns and five torpedo tubes. The *Freya, Hertha* and *Viktoria-Luise* all displaced 5,660 tons, the *Hansa* and *Vineta* 5,885 tons. The *Freya, Hertha* and *Viktoria-Luise* were launched in 1897 and were completed in 1898: the *Vineta* was launched in 1897 and the *Hansa* in 1898, and both were completed in 1899. All carried two 210-mm/8.3-in, eight 150-mm and ten 88-mm guns and three torpedo tubes.

The last three were armoured cruisers. The *Fürst Bismarck* was launched in 1897 and was completed in 1900. She displaced 10,570 tons and carried four 240-mm/9.45-in, twelve 150-mm and ten 88-mm guns, plus three torpedo tubes. The *Prinz Heinrich* was launched in 1900 and was completed in 1902. She displaced 8,759 tons and carried two 240-mm, ten 150-mm and ten 88-mm guns, plus four torpedo tubes. The *Prinz Adalbert* was slightly larger at 8,858 tons: she was launched in 1901 and was completed in 1903. She carried four 240-mm, ten 150-mm and twelve 88-mm guns, plus four torpedo tubes.

[4] For an examination of the contents of the 1908 German Navy law see pp. 43 ff and endnote 18.

[5] Parkes, Op. Cit., p. 435.

[6] And one, the Newfoundland fisheries dispute, dated from the Treaty of Utrecht in 1714.

[7] The locomotive torpedo was invented in 1866 and underwent a series of improvements that by the turn of the century meant battle lines would have to open. By about this time a torpedo would have a range of 1,000 yards at 35 knots or 4,000 yards at 20 knots, and it was not until 1907 that there was any major improvement on these figures. In that year the Hardcastle torpedo was developed. This used heated air to drive the motor with the result that the 4,000-yard range could be covered at 30 knots while the explosive charge carried an increase three or four times that of previous warheads.

[8] The first naval actions of the war had involved the Japanese surprise attack with torpedo-boats and block ships on Port Arthur and also the action at Chemulpo (Inchon), 8–9 February 1904: the declaration of war came on 10 February. The major events at sea prior to the battle in the Yellow Sea were the mining of the Russian flagship *Petropavlovsk* on 13 April and of the Japanese battleships *Hatsuse* and *Yashima* on 15 May.

[9] At the start of the war the Russians had the battleships (1901) *Peresviet,* (1897) *Petropavlovsk,* (1902) *Pobieda,* (1896) *Poltava,* (1902) *Retvizan,* (1898) *Sevastopol* and the (1903) *Tsarevich,* the armoured cruiser *Bayan,* the light cruisers *Boyarin*

and *Novik*, 25 destroyers, seventeen torpedo-boats and a dozen gunboats and assorted ships at Port Arthur. The decision to try to get the battle force to Vladivostok arose from the fact that at the beginning of August the Japanese forces besieging Port Arthur had closed to a distance that enabled them to fire into the harbour, thus ensuring that the destruction of the battle force was but a matter of time. In fact, it was not until December, when the Japanese finally secured good positions from which fire could be controlled, that the Russian warships in the base were finally destroyed either by direct fire or scuttling.

From the start of the Russo-Japanese war the Imperial Navy had its 1st Fleet, under Vice Admiral Togo Heihachiro, on the Port Arthur station. This formation consisted of the 1st Battle Squadron, the 3rd Cruiser Squadron, the 1st, 2nd and 3rd Destroyer Flotillas, the 1st and 14th Torpedo Boat Flotillas, and the 741-ton gunboat *Tatsuta*, which was employed as a reconnaissance ship (*tsuho-kan*).

The 1st Battle Squadron at the time of the battle in the Yellow Sea consisted of the (1902) *Mikasa*, (1900) *Asahi*, (1897) *Fuji* and the (1900) *Shikishima*, plus the armoured cruisers/second-class battleships (1903) *Kasuga* and (1904) *Nissin* which had replaced the (1901) *Hatsuse* and (1897) *Yashima* after these were lost to mines on 15 May. The 3rd Cruiser Squadron originally consisted of the second-class protected cruisers (1899) *Chitose*, (1898) *Kasagi*, (1898) *Takasago* and the (1893) *Yoshino*. The latter was lost on 15 May 1904 and her place in this formation was not filled: the *Takasago* was mined and lost in December. The 1st and 2nd Destroyer Flotilla each had four destroyers, the 3rd Destroyer Flotilla three. The 1st and 14th Torpedo Boat Flotilla each had four torpedo-boats. This is a definitive rendition provided by Dr. Tohmatsu Haruo of Tamagawa University in an e-mail to the author, 17 October 2001: source Nomura Minoru, editor, *Zusetsu Nippon Kaigun*, (Tokyo, Kawade Shobo Shinsha, 1997.)

It is somewhat curious but there seems to be no definitive statement of the ships that the *Kaigun* had with the 1st Fleet on 10 August 1904 at the battle of the Yellow Sea. According to the individual ship entries in Watts and Gordon, the Japanese employed the battleships *Mikasa*, *Asahi*, *Fuji* and the *Shikishima*, and the *Kasuga* and *Nisshin*: the armoured cruisers (1899) *Asama* and (1900) *Yakumo*: the second-class cruisers (1891) *Itsukashima*, (1891) *Matsushima* and the (1894) *Hashidate*, the second-class protected cruisers *Chitose*, *Kasagi* and the *Takasago*, and, in all probability, the third-class cruisers (1899) *Akashi*, (1904) *Niitika*, (1896) *Suma* and (1904) *Tsushima*.

These total four battleships with two armoured cruisers, two more armoured cruisers, and certainly nine and perhaps as many as ten other cruisers. Watts and Gordon do not give destroyer and torpedo-boat numbers.

J. N. Westwood, *Russia against Japan, 1904–05. A New Look at the Russo-Japanese War*, p. 81, states that the Japanese had the four first-class battleships and two armoured cruisers, that a third armoured cruiser joined the line, and that the Japanese had a fourth armoured cruiser and the old, ex-Chinese, battleship (1885) *Chin'en* on hand. Westwood also states that completing the Japanese order of battle were nine other cruisers, plus seventeen destroyers and 29 torpedo-boats. Richard Connaughton, *The War of the Rising Sun and Tumbling Bear. A Military History of the Russo-Japanese War, 1904–5*, p. 172, gives Japanese strength as the four battleships and two armoured cruisers, with eleven cruisers, and seventeen destroyers and 29 torpedo-boats. But for the *Chin'en* these totals could be deemed to be the same.

Dr. Tohmatsu Haruo in e-mails to the author, 19 and 22 October 2001, states that at the battle of the Yellow Sea the 1st Fleet had the 1st Battle Squadron with the battleships *Mikasa*, *Asahi*, *Fuji* and the *Shikishima*, plus the second-class battleships/armoured cruisers *Kasuga* and *Nisshin*. In addition there were two armoured cruisers, the *Asama* and *Yagumo*, along with the second-class protected cruisers *Chitose*, *Kasagi* and the *Takasago* from the 3rd Cruiser Squadron; plus the second-class protected cruisers *Hashidate* and *Matsushima*, the second-class battleship *Chin'en* and the reconnaissance ship (1892) *Yaetama* which, however improbably, together constituted the 5th Cruiser Squadron; and the third-class cruisers *Akashi*, *Akitsushima*, *Izumi* and the *Suma*, which together made up the 6th Cruiser Squadron.

The 1st Fleet had five destroyer flotillas in company on 10 August. These were the 1st, 2nd and 3rd Destroyer Flotillas each with three destroyers, and the 4th and 5th Destroyer Flotillas both with four destroyers. The 1st Destroyer Flotilla consisted of the *Asashio*, *Kasumi* and the *Shirakumo*. The 2nd Destroyer Flotilla consisted of the *Ikazuchi*, *Inazuma* and the *Oboro*. The 3rd Destroyer Flotilla consisted of the *Usugumo*, *Shinonome* and the *Sazanami*. The 4th Destroyer Flotilla consisted of the *Hayatori*, *Harusame*, *Asagiri* and the *Murasame*. The 5th Destroyer Flotilla consisted of the *Kagero*, *Yugiri*, *Shiranui* and the *Murakumo*.

The 1st Fleet also had no fewer than eight torpedo-boat flotillas in company on 10 August. These were the 1st Torpedo-Boat Flotilla with four torpedo-boats (*suirai-tei*), the TBs 69, 67, 68 and 70; the 2nd Torpedo-Boat Flotilla with three units, the TBs 38, 37 and 45; the 6th Torpedo-Boat Flotilla with four units, the TBs 56, 57, 58 and 59; the 10th Torpedo-Boat Flotilla with four units, the TBs 43, 40, 41 and 42; the 14th Torpedo-Boat Flotilla with four units, the (1901) *Chidori*, (n/d) *Nue*, (1899) *Hayabusa* and the (1900) *Manazuru*; the 16th Torpedo-Boat Flotilla with four units, the (1900) *Shirataka* and TBs 39, 66 and 71; the 20th Torpedo-Boat Flotilla with four units, the TBs 62, 63, 64 and 65; and the 21st Torpedo-Boat Flotilla with three units, the TBs 47, 44 and 49.

It would appear, therefore, that the battle and cruiser squadrons deployed four battleships, two second-class battleships/armoured cruisers, a separate second-class battleship, two armoured, five second-class and four third-class cruisers, plus one reconnaissance ship, while the destroyer and torpedo-boat flotillas numbered seventeen destroyers and 30 torpedo-boats.

[10] David C. Evans and Mark R. Peattie, *Kaigun. Strategy, Tactics and Technology in the Imperial Japanese Navy, 1887–1941*, pp. 102–107. See also Richard Connaughton, pp. 171–175, J. N. Westwood, pp. 81–87, and Peter Padfield, *Battleship*, pp. 168–171.

[11] The three Russian cruisers were caught by a Japanese 2nd Fleet under Vice Admiral Kamimura Hikonojo. This formation had under establishment the 2nd Cruiser Squadron, with the armoured cruisers (1900) *Izumo* (flagship), (1899) *Asama*, (1900) *Azuma*, (1901) *Iwate*, (1899) *Tokiwa* and the (1900) *Yagumo*, and the 4th Cruiser Squadron with the second-class cruisers (1885) *Naniwa* and (1886) *Takachiho*, and the third-class cruisers (1899) *Akashi* and (1904) *Niitaka*. It also had the 4th and 5th Destroyer Flotillas (each with four destroyers), and the 9th and 20th Torpedo Boat Flotillas (each with four torpedo boats) under command. In addition, it had the despatch vessel (1901) *Chihaya* on strength as a reconnaissance ship.

The Japanese warships involved in the action off Ulsan in August 1904 were the *Izumo*, *Azuma*, *Iwate* and the *Tokiwa*, which were joined during the action by the *Naniwa* and the *Takachiho*. In a hard-fought action in which the flagship *Izumo* was hit more than twenty times and the *Iwate* was badly damaged, the *Rurik* was disabled and sunk but the badly damaged *Gromoboi* and *Rossiya* escaped back to Vladivostok. This proved to be the Vladivostok squadron's last sortie.

[12] Ruddock F. Mackay, *Fisher of Kilverstone*, pp. 270, 322. One suspects the last. Mackay's book is by far the best biography of the many written about Fisher.

[13] Parkes, pp. 425–429 for details of the *King Edward VII*-class battleships, pp. 477–482 for details of the *Dreadnought*. Parkes, p. 482, states that on trials the *Dreadnought* made 26,350 hp and a top speed of 21.6 knots. Breyer, p. 115, gives figures of 24,700 shp and 22.4 knots.

[14] The persistence with the 4-in gun certainly marked British battleships as inferior to contemporary battleships abroad: the first German dreadnoughts had made the choice of 5.9-in/150-mm guns as secondary armament. Rather oddly, the first American dreadnoughts, the (1910) *Michigan* and (1910) *South Carolina*, were also equipped with the 3-in gun, but from the second class, the (1910) *Delaware* and (1910) *North Dakota*, the Americans adopted the 5-in gun as their standard secondary armament.

[15] For an examination of the position created for Japan by the *Dreadnought* see Chapter IV, pp. 104 ff.

[16] There was one exception to this basic definition. The light fleet carrier *Terrible*, laid down 19 April 1943 and launched 30 September 1944, was built at Devonport. She was the only carrier, whether fleet, light fleet or escort, built at Devonport and Portsmouth navy yards, and she is the exception that proves the rule.

[17] Review by Rear-Admiral P. W. Brock of Arthur J. Marder, *From the Dreadnought to Scapa Flow. The Royal Navy in the Fisher Era, 1904–1919. Volume I. The Road to War, 1904–1914*, that appeared *Mariner's Mirror*, 1962, Volume 48, pp. 156–159.

[18] The German navy law of 1908 seemingly had no provisions which formed the basis for major objection. Its main terms were that the life-span of battleships, hitherto fixed at 25 years, should be twenty years, and that the "large cruisers" which were to be built under the terms of the 1900 naval law should be battlecruisers. This meant that the 1900 arrangements, which allowed for the building of a Navy with 38 battleships and twenty large cruisers, would be superseded by a programme that allowed for the construction of 58 battleships and battlecruisers. Moreover, by lowering the life-span of battleships, the 1908 measure meant that a number of existing units needed immediate replacement. Thus in 1908 and in each of the next three years four capital ships would be laid down annually, and

thereafter, until 1917, two would be laid down. The significance of these arrangements lay in the fact that after the British government had reduced its own building programme in 1908 to just the *Neptune* and *Indefatigable* as part of its effort to advance the cause of The Hague conference of that year, the British had ten dreadnought battleships and battlecruisers built and building compared to the five in German yards – and this, by definition, would narrow to twelve and nine, with Germany committed to laying down twelve more in the next three years. The implications for Britain need no elaboration. See Parkes, p. 508.

[19] For the greater part of the material presented here, see the author's masters thesis, "*The Liberal Government and the Navy Estimates, 1906–1909*", University of Liverpool, 1971.

[20] For example, see Siegfried Breyer, *Battleships and Battlecruisers, 1905–1970*, pp. 263. Interestingly, on p. 269 Breyer notes: This first German battle cruiser (the *Von der Tann*) was the "reply" to the British *Invincible*. After the *Blücher*, it is somewhat difficult to believe that the new ship was anything but a response to the initial British move.

[21] And best provided in Jon Tetsuro Sumida, *In Defence of Naval Supremacy. Finance, Technology and British Naval Policy, 1889–1914*.

[22] R. A. Burt, *British Battleships of World War One*, pp. 133, 169–170.

[23] Robert Gardiner (editor), *The Eclipse of the Big Gun. The Warship, 1906–45*, p. 24.

[24] With sincere apologies, but it did seem appropriate: taken from the poem, "The Subject", by Lieutenant-Commander R. A. B. Mitchell, and presented as the preface in Captain S. W. Roskill, *H. M. S. Warspite. The Story of a Famous Battleship*.

CHAPTER 3

[1] With the *Australia* committed to operations in the Fiji-Samoa area, the task of escorting Australian forces which sailed for Colombo on 1 November 1914 was undertaken by the British armoured cruiser (1908) *Minotaur*, the Japanese armoured cruiser (1909) *Ibuki*, and the light cruisers (1913) *Melbourne* and (1913) *Sydney*. Also based on Singapore and searching for the German light cruiser (1909) *Emden* in the Indian Ocean were the Japanese light cruisers (1912) *Chikuma* and (1911) *Yahagi*. At this time the British pre-dreadnought (1904) *Triumph* and destroyer

(1903) *Usk* were off Tsingtao serving with one of three Japanese forces: the other two forces were committed to defence of the home islands and to covering the Formosa Strait as far south as Hong Kong.

[2] At Coronel the Germans had the armoured cruisers (1908) *Gneisenau* and (1908) *Scharnhorst* with the light cruisers (1908) *Dresden*, (1906) *Leipzig* and the (1908) *Nürnberg*. The British had various units gathering in South American waters at this time, including the armoured cruisers (1904) *Cornwall* and (1909) *Defence*, and the armed merchant cruisers *Edinburgh Castle* and *Macedonia* which at this time were searching for the light cruiser (1914) *Karlsruhe* off northern Brazil. There were also French warships in this area, but the French offer of the armoured cruiser (1904) *Condé* and the light cruiser (1896) *Descartes* for the force bound for Coronel and defeat was refused.

At this time too the North Pacific squadron, which consisted of the Japanese pre-dreadnought battleship (1902) *Hizen*, the armoured cruiser (1900) *Izumo* and the British light cruiser (1910) *Newcastle*, was supposed to move to the Galapagos Islands by 2 December, a deployment that was supposed to ensure that the German squadron was drawn onto the battleship (1899) *Canopus* and armoured cruiser (1902) *Cape of Good Hope*. (The *Hizen* was formerly the American-built Russian warship *Retvizan*: the *Izumo* had been on the Mexican west coast at the time of the outbreak of war in Europe.)

In the aftermath of Coronel and also the sinking of the (1909) *Emden* by the (1912) *Sydney* in the Cocos Islands on 9 November 1914, there was a recasting of formations with the intention of having the Japanese 1st Cruiser Squadron, with the armoured cruisers (1908) *Ikoma*, (1911) *Kurama*, (1907) *Tsukuba* and the (1901) *Iwate* and the light cruisers (1912) *Chikuma* and (1911) *Yahagi* under command, based at Suva in the Fijian Islands. At the same time the 2nd Cruiser Squadron, with the battleship (1910) *Satsuma*, light cruiser (1912) *Hirado* and the destroyers (1911) *Umikaze* and (1911) *Yamakaze* under command, was to take up station at Truk in the Carolines. The armoured cruiser (1909) *Ibuki* and (1904) *Nisshin* were to join the 2nd Cruiser Squadron once it was established at Truk, while the *Iwate* was to be transferred between squadrons, her place at Suva being taken by the armoured cruisers (1899) *Tokiwa* and (1900) *Yakumo*, previously on the Formosa Strait watch.

[3] On 7 August 1914 the Channel Fleet consisted of the flagship (1908) *Lord Nelson* with attached light

cruiser (1905) *Diamond*, with the 5th Battle Squadron with the (1904) *Prince of Wales*, (1904) *Queen*, (1902) *Venerable*, (1902) *Irresistible*, (1902) *Bulwark* (1901) *Formidable*, (1901) *Implacable* and the (1902) *London*, the 7th Battle Squadron with the (1896) *Prince George* and (1898) *Caesar*, plus the (1897) *Jupiter* and (1895) *Majestic* in dockyard hands, and the 8th Battle Squadron with the (1901) *Albion*, (1901) *Goliath*, (1899) *Canopus*, (1900) *Glory*, (1900) *Ocean* and the (1902) *Vengeance*, plus attendant cruisers and destroyers, under command. (The pre-dreadnoughts were distributed with the 5th Battle Squadron having the five *London*- and the three *Formidable*-class battleships, the 7th had *Majestic*-class battleships and the 8th had *Canopus*-class battleships.)

[4] In September 1914 the Grand Fleet had under command the fleet flagship (1914) *Iron Duke* and the light cruiser (1893?) *Sappho* and destroyer (1912) *Oak* attached, the 1st Battle Squadron with the (1914) *Marlborough*, (1910) *St. Vincent*, (1910) *Collingwood*, (1911) *Colossus*, (1911) *Hercules*, (1911) *Neptune*, (1909) *Superb* and the (1910) *Vanguard* and the light cruiser (1910) *Bellona*; the 2nd Battle Squadron with the (1912) *King George V*, (1912) *Orion*, (1913) *Ajax*, (1913) *Audacious*, (1913) *Centurion*, (1912) *Conqueror*, (1912) *Monarch* and the (1912) *Thunderer* and the light cruiser (1909) *Boadicea*; the 3rd Battle Squadron with the *King Edward VII*-class pre-dreadnought battleships (1905) *King Edward VII*, (1907) *Hibernia*, (1906) *Africa*, (1906) *Britannia*, (1905) *Commonwealth*, (1905) *Dominion*, (1905) *Hindustan* and the (1905) *Zealandia* and the light cruiser (1910) *Blanche*; the 4th Battle Squadron with the (1906) *Dreadnought*, (1909) *Bellerophon*, (1909) *Téméraire* and the (1914) *Agincourt* and the light cruiser (1911) *Blonde*; the 1st Battle Cruiser Squadron with the (1912) *Lion*, (1912) *Princess Royal*, (1913) *Queen Mary* and the (1912) *New Zealand*; the 2nd Cruiser Squadron with the armoured cruisers (1908) *Shannon*, (1907) *Achilles*, (1907) *Cochrane* and the (1907) *Natal*; the 3rd Cruiser Squadron with the (1905) *Antrim*, (1906) *Argyll*, (1905) *Devonshire* and the (1905) *Roxburgh*; the 1st Light Cruiser Squadron with the (1913) *Southampton*, (1914) *Birmingham*, (1914) *Nottingham*, (1910) *Liverpool*, (1911) *Falmouth* and the (1914) *Lowestoft*, plus destroyer formations.

Source: Sir Julian S. Corbett, *History of the Great War. Naval Operations. Volume I. To the Battle of the Falklands December 1914*, pp. 438–440. There is no date given for this order of battle, but since it includes the *Agincourt* it must be with effect on or after

7 September 1914, hence the first three words of this note.

[5] In addition, the Southern Force's remaining formation, the 7th Cruiser Squadron, was assigned a reserve role. It was based at the Nore with (after 8 August) the armoured cruisers (1902) *Bacchante* (flagship), (1902) *Hogue*, (1902) *Aboukir* and the (1901) *Cressy* under command. This formation was to take up station off Terschelling and await developments.

[6] The dreadnought battleships in service with the Grand Fleet throughout November 1914 were the (1909) *Bellerophon*, (1913) *Centurion*, (1910) *Collingwood*, (1911) *Colossus*, (1906) *Dreadnought*, (1911) *Hercules*, (1914) *Marlborough*, (1912) *Monarch* (which was damaged in a collision with the *Conqueror* in December 1914), (1911) *Neptune* (which began a refit on 11 December 1914), (1910) *St. Vincent*, (1909) *Superb*, (1909) *Téméraire*, (1912) *Thunderer* and the (1910) *Vanguard*, and the battlecruisers (1912) *Lion* and (1913) *Queen Mary*.

The following battleships were in dockyard hands during November 1914, in whole or in part: (1913) *Ajax* (with condenser tubes problems), the (1912) *Conqueror* (being refitted in November 1914 and badly damaged in a collision with the *Monarch* in December 1914), (1914) *Iron Duke* (with condenser tubes problems), (1912) *King George V* (undergoing refit between October 1914 and February 1915) and the (1912) *Orion* (with her perennial engine problems).

The battlecruisers (1909) *Invincible* and (1908) *Inflexible* left Cromarty on 5 November for service in the South Atlantic and did not rejoin until February 1915 and June 1915 respectively. The (1912) *Princess Royal* secretly sailed from Cromarty for Halifax on 12 November, arriving 21 November. The purpose of her sailing was to free cruisers for service in the Caribbean, just in case the (1908) *Scharnhorst et al* tried to elude British formations by using the Panama canal. In the event, however, after standing off New York, the *Princess Royal* herself sailed for the Caribbean. She sailed for home waters from Kingston, Jamaica, on 19 December. The (1912) *New Zealand*, it seems, was in dockyard hands throughout November 1914, apparently for routine refit.

The battlecruisers (1908) *Indomitable* and (1911) *Indefatigable* were at the Dardanelles and returned to home waters in November 1914 and February 1915 respectively: the (1913) *Australia* was in the southern oceans and did not join the Grand Fleet until February 1915.

The battleship (1913) *Audacious* had been lost on 27 October 1914. The battleships (1914) *Erin* and (1914) *Agincourt* had been commissioned and joined the Grand Fleet on 5 and 7 September 1914 respectively, but had not undergone full trials and working up, and could not be regarded as fully operational in November 1914: the battlecruiser (1914) *Tiger* joined the Grand Fleet on 6 November 1914, and was similarly placed. The battleships (1914) *Benbow* and (1914) *Emperor of India* both joined the Grand Fleet on 10 December 1914.

[7] The High Sea Fleet at the outbreak of war consisted of the fleet flagship (1912) *Friedrich der Grosse*; from the 1st Battle Squadron the battleships (1911) *Ostfriesland*, (1911) *Thüringen*, (1911) *Helgoland* and the (1912) *Oldenburg* from the 1st Battle Division and the (1910) *Posen*, (1910) *Rheinland*, (1909) *Nassau* and the (1909) *Westfalen* from the 2nd Battle Division; from the 2nd Battle Squadron the pre-dreadnought battleships (1905) *Preussen*, (1908) *Schlesien*, (1905) *Hessen* and the (1906) *Lothringen* of the 3rd Battle Division and the (1907) *Hannover*, (1908) *Schleswig-Holstein*, (1907) *Pommern* and the (1906) *Deutschland* from the 4th Battle Division; from the 3rd Battle Squadron the battleships (1912) Kaiser, (1913) *Kaiserin*, (1913) *König Albert* and the (1913) *Prinzregent Luitpold*; and from the Cruiser Squadron the battlecruisers (1913) *Seydlitz*, (1911) *Moltke*, (1910) *Von der Tann* and the (1914) *Derfflinger*, plus the light cruisers (1910) *Cöln*, (1910) *Kolberg*, (1910) *Mainz*, (1914) *Rostock*, (1912) *Straslund* and the (1912) *Strassburg*.

Source: Sir Julian S. Corbett, *History of the Great War. Naval Operations.* Volume I. *To the Battle of the Falklands December 1914*, pp. 437–438. Hans Jürgen Hansen, *The Ships of the German Fleets, 1848–1945*, p. 152, states that at the outbreak of war the German fleet consisted of fourteen "of the most modern dreadnoughts" and four battlecruisers, plus sixteen pre-dreadnoughts, thirteen heavy and 34 light cruisers, ninety torpedo-boats and 21 submarines.

[8] And this despite the efforts of Paul G. Halpern, *The Naval War in the Mediterranean, 1914–1918*.

[9] The Bolsheviks also scuttled nine destroyers and five transports on 30 June 1918, but on the previous day the battleship *Volya*, five destroyers and the seaplane carrier (1907) *Imperator Trayan* were surrendered to the Germans. By May 1918, however, the Germans had been able to secure Odessa, Nikolaiev and, crucially, Sevastopol. In the Ukrainian ports the Germans secured control of three light

cruisers, four destroyers, two gunboats and three submarines. At Sevastopol the Germans took over the pre-dreadnought battleships (1910) *Ioann Zlatoust* and (1911) *Sviatoi Evstafi* plus four older battleships, which seem to have been the (1902) *Panteleimon*, (1900) *Rostislav*, (1897) *Tri Sviatitelya* and the (1890) *Sinope*, three cruisers (including one ex-Turkish cruiser that had been sunk and then salved), twelve destroyers, one gunboat, one seaplane carrier, one armed yacht and fourteen submarines.

The scuttling – and exact numbers are disputed – ended all threats to Turkey in the Black Sea but also ended any chance of the Germans getting hold of good quality ships with which to menace the allies in the eastern Mediterranean. It seems that the Germans wanted to bring the *Volya* back into service, and also to re-commission the *Evstafi* and *Zlatoust* at the Dardanelles with Turkish crews "supplemented" by Germans. It also seems that the Germans had a chronic manpower shortage which meant that other than the *Volya* they could not man the surrendered ships, the result being that these other units were used as accommodation ships. When the British arrived on the scene, serviceable ships were taken over and those that were not serviceable had their engines demolished. See Paul G. Halpern, *The Naval War in the Mediterranean, 1914–1918*, pp. 544–547, and George Nekrasov, *North of Gallipoli. The Black Sea Fleet at War, 1914–1917*, pp. 136–137.

[10] Thus the Russian dreadnought battleship (1917) *Volya*, formerly the *Imperator Aleksandr III*, was surrendered at Sevastopol on 1 October 1918 to the Germans under the terms of the treaty of 16 August 1918 and was immediately sent for trials. At war's end, she was abandoned by the Germans and taken over by the British, who then transferred her to the White Russian forces with whom she served as the *General Alekseev* until 1920 when, with the collapse of the White cause throughout the Ukraine and Crimea she sailed for Bizerta, in French North Africa, where she was interned and subsequently scrapped (1936).

[11] Three other matters relating to the Dardanelles campaign need to be mentioned. The first relates to the fact that another Turkish battleship, the *Messudiya* (sometimes given as the *Messudiyeh* or *Messudieh*), was torpedoed and sunk inside the Sea of Marmara on 13 December 1914 by the British submarine B. 11 which had negotiated the outer minefields and the Narrows. Her loss was not recorded in the text because (a) it came before the 18 March 1915 undertaking, (b) having been launched in 1874 and despite a modernisation

programme, the *Messudiya* could not be counted as a battleship by 1914, rather a guardship that in any case had surrendered its main armament, and (c) least importantly, she sank in shallows and the guns from her secondary armament were recovered.

The second matter relates to the *Queen Elizabeth*, and to the fact that she was sent to the Dardanelles along with the seaplane carrier (1914) *Ark Royal*. With the aid of these seaplanes, the *Queen Elizabeth* became the first warship ever to fire her main armament with the aid of spotters, and by firing over the ridge of the Gallipoli peninsula she was also the first warship ever to engage a target beyond the horizon (5 March 1915).

The third matter was to note that after the loss of the *Majestic*, battleships were recalled from fire support duties, their place being taken by destroyers.

[12] Italy declared war on Austria-Hungary on 23 May 1915, Germany's response being to sever diplomatic relations with Italy the following day. Italy declared war on Turkey on 21 August and on Bulgaria on 19 October. Italy did not declare war on Germany until 28 August 1916, on which date Germany declared war on Roumania. San Marino declared war on Austria-Hungary on 3 June 1915.

[13] Perhaps worth more than an endnote, it must be noted that in the event the sortie resulted in the only sinking of a dreadnought in action during the entire war, and the sinking was full of irony: the (1915) *Szent Istvan* was sunk by a motor torpedo boat, by some margin the least of the battleship's enemies.

The *Szent Istvan* was in the company of the (1913) *Tegethoff*, which was attacked by a second motor torpedo boat, but its two torpedoes were very narrowly avoided. The *Szent Istvan* and *Tegethoff* formed the second echelon of the force assembled for this raid, the (1912) *Viribus Unitis* and (1914) *Prinz Eugen* having sailed the previous day.

[14] By way of comparison, the British fleet flagship (1914) *Iron Duke*, which had bunkers with 3,250 tons of coal and a range of 4,840 miles at 19 knots or 7,780 miles at 10 knots, steamed 14,184 miles and used 17,609 tons of coal during the war.

[15] There were two bombardment formations. The first consisted of the Italian armoured cruisers (1910) *San Giorgio*, (1910) *San Marco* and the (1909) *Pisa*. They were preceded by the British destroyers (1911) *Acheron*, (1910) *Acorn*, (1911) *Goshawk* and the (1911) *Lapwing* operating as minesweepers, and were escorted by the British destroyers (1910) *Nereide*, (1910) *Cameleon*, (1910) *Ruby* and the (1911)

Nymphe and eight Italian torpedo-boats. The second consisted of the British light cruisers (1914) *Lowestoft*, (1911) *Dartmouth* and the (1911) *Weymouth*, escorted by the British destroyers (1918) *Tribune*, (1911) *Badger*, (1911) *Fury* and the (1918) *Shark*. In addition, there were eleven American submarine chasers – there were to have been twelve but SC 244 fouled a net as she left Brindisi – to act as screen against submarines. These were the SC 215, 128 and 129 (Unit B), the 225 and 327 (Unit D less the absent 244), the 95, 179 and the 338 (Unit G), and the 337, 130 and the 324 (Unit H). There were also six Italian MAS boats on patrol.

The covering force consisted of the British light cruisers (1911) *Glasgow* and (1911) *Gloucester*, and the Italian minelaying-cruiser (1914) *Marsala*, the three Italian flotilla leaders (1916) *Aquila*, (1918) *Nibbio* and the (1917) *Sparviero*, all of which were fitted for minelaying, and the British destroyers (1911) *Jackal* and (1911) *Tigress* and Australian destroyers (1915) *Swan* and (1911) *Warrego*.

The support force consisted of the Italian dreadnought (1913) *Dante Alighieri* and the Italian destroyers, namely the (1915) *Ippolito Nievo* and (1915) *Simone Schiaffino*, and the flotilla leaders (1914) *Guglielmo Pepe*, (1914) *Alessandro Poerio*, (1916) *Carlo Alberto Racchia*, (1916) *Augusto Riboty* and the (1914) *Cesare Rossarol*.

Sources: Paul G. Halpern (editor), *The Royal Navy in the Mediterranean, 1915–1918*, pp. 557–567. Captain William Spencer Johnson IV (USN Rtd.) in e-mail of 23 January 2002 and letter of 24 January 2002 with copy of Chapter XV, "The Battle of Durazzo", and Appendix B, "An Account of the Operations of the U.S. Naval Forces which Assisted and Co-operated with British, French and Italian forces in the Bombardment of Durazzo, Albania, October 2, 1918", from Ray Millholland, *The Splinter Fleet of the Otranto Barrage*, pp. 220–240 and 302–307 respectively.

[16] "During her service with the 3rd Battle Squadron (the) *Dreadnought* spent practically her entire time alternating between No. 2 buoy at Sheerness and an anchorage in the Swin (in the Thames estuary) where she stayed for about two or three days at a time." (John Roberts, *The Battleship Dreadnought*, p. 22.) It may be noted that while her sea time was restricted, she nonetheless was in contact with the enemy seven times in 1917 and twice in 1918, on each occasion firing on German aircraft, and she did return to the Grand Fleet in 1918. The latter was not simply a case of an administrative arrangement following in the

wake of the 3rd Battle Squadron being wound up. From May 1918 the (1906) *Dreadnought* returned to the Grand Fleet's 4th Battle Squadron and undertook a series of exercises and sweeps, but after 5 August was undergoing refit at Rosyth and was paid off on 7 August. She was docked between 22 October and 6 November, and the end of the war ensured that she was not recommissioned. On 12 January 1919 she was reduced to a reserve commission at Rosyth, and, perhaps somewhat humiliatingly, was transferred on 25 February to the Reserve Fleet at Rosyth as tender to the (1911) *Hercules*.

[17] In this confused, and confusing, phase one German light cruiser formation mauled the British light cruiser *Chester* (c. 1740) before the *Invincible* and her sister ships intervened (c. 1755–1800), the *Wiesbaden* being crippled and the *Pillau* badly damaged. As the German cruisers tried to turn away, their escorting destroyers mounted two attacks on the British battlecruisers, the second becoming involved in a fight with British destroyers coming forward to attack the German light cruisers. The British destroyers from these two attacks were largely responsible for preventing a third attack materialising, just one torpedo being fired by the G. 104 at 1808. The clash between light formations then resulted in the *Shark* being disabled and the B. 98 being hit (1804–1815).

At the same time (immediately after 1805) the light cruiser formations from the British battlecruiser fleet moved forward to finish off the *Wiesbaden*, the destroyer *Onslow* having subjected the German light cruiser to withering fire at ranges that closed to 2,000 yards. As she did so, however, the *Onslow* found herself in the path of the advancing German battlecruisers, as was the *Acasta*. Both British destroyers fired torpedoes at the German battlecruisers but to no avail, and after torpedoing the *Wiesbaden*, the *Onslow* then attacked the head of the German battle line, but again without success (1825). Both British destroyers were heavily hit but managed to limp away to safety.

Again at this same time, about 1805, the units of the 1st Cruiser Squadron, the armoured cruisers *Defence*, *Warrior*, *Duke of Edinburgh* and the *Black Prince*, moved forward from their position alongside the battleships of the Grand Fleet to attack the *Wiesbaden*. This force was led by a commander, Rear Admiral Sir Robert Arbuthnot, an individual noted for such lack of cerebral capacity that even other British naval officers noticed. He led his formation at the *Wiesbaden*, failing to note that his course took him so close to the path of the *Lion* that she had to turn hard to port to avoid the *Defence* and *Warrior*: more unfortunately, this course took the *Defence* onto the few remaining guns of the German battlecruisers which very literally blasted her out the water (1820). The *Warrior* was badly damaged but staggered away in the direction of the *Warspite*, which had been badly damaged at the very time when the *Defence* was destroyed: inadvertently, the *Warspite* was able to afford the *Warrior* temporary respite. Badly damaged, the *Warrior* was taken in tow by the *Engadine*, but had to be abandoned on the morning of 1 June in rising seas some 160 miles east of Aberdeen.

[18] Room 40 deciphered the German signal giving course and speed for the return, and was able to plot the German course, which would have taken the German formations to Horn's Reef. From earlier signals Room 40 knew that the Horn's Reef had been specified as the route the German formations were to take. The Admiralty signal to Jellicoe gave just the signal with course and speed, and indicated no source. It never cited the other signals, and there was also another signal sent to Jellicoe that placed the German forces in so erroneous a position that Jellicoe, rightly, ignored it. The overall effect of these signals, coming on top of the earlier Admiralty signal informing him that the German battle force was in base, was to discredit the Admiralty in general, and intelligence and the Operations Division in particular, on this occasion when the information was correct: Jellicoe discounted the Horn's Reef option. No less importantly, there was what was not passed to Jellicoe: a request from Scheer for airship reconnaissance of Horn's Reef at dawn next day was not forwarded to Jellicoe from the Admiralty.

[19] Henry Newbolt, *History of the Great War. Naval Operations*. Volume V, pp. 432–433.

[20] The occasions when the German fleet, or sub-formations, mounted operations on the open sea after Jutland were as follows:
(A) THE SORTIE OF 18–19 AUGUST 1916. NORTH SEA Bombardment of Sunderland by scouting force consisting of two battlecruisers with three dreadnoughts, supported by the battle force. Overall eighteen battleships and two battlecruisers were involved in this operation: some sources state nineteen dreadnoughts were involved, but at this time the German Navy had eighteen, not nineteen, dreadnoughts in service. These were the (1909) *Nassau*, (1909) *Westfalen*, (1910) *Rheinland*, (1910) *Posen*, (1911) *Helgoland*, (1911) *Ostfriesland*, (1911) *Thüringen*, (1912) *Oldenburg*, (1912) *Kaiser*, (1912)

Friedrich der Grosse, (1913) *Kaiserin*, (1913) *Prinzregent Luitpold*, (1913) *König Albert*, (1914) *König*, (1914) *Grosser Kurfürst*, (1914) *Markgraf*, (1914) *Kronprinz* and the (1916) *Bayern*; and the (1910) *Von der Tann* and (1911) *Moltke*. In addition to cruisers and destroyers, the Germans committed 24 submarines and ten Zeppelins to reconnaissance. (German submarines torpedoed and sank the light cruisers *Falmouth* and *Nottingham*.) The British combined strength in their battle and battlecruiser fleets was 29 dreadnoughts and six battlecruisers, i.e. one dreadnought more and three battlecruisers less than at Jutland, which was exactly the same for the Germans. The *Westfalen* was torpedoed by the submarine E. 23 and was out of service until 4 October 1916.

(B) 18–20 OCTOBER 1916. NORTH SEA

Overall seventeen battleships and two battlecruisers were involved in this operation. These were the *Nassau, Westfalen, Rheinland, Posen, Helgoland, Ostfriesland, Thüringen, Oldenburg, Kaiser, Kaiserin, Prinzregent Luitpold, König Albert, König, Grosser Kurfürst, Markgraf, Kronprinz* and the *Bayern*; and the *Von der Tann* and *Moltke*.

(C) 4–5 NOVEMBER 1916. NORTH SEA

German capital ships employed on this operation were the *Kaiser, Kaiserin, Prinzregent Luitpold, König Albert, König, Grosser Kurfürst, Markgraf* and the *Kronprinz*; and the *Moltke* and (1913) *Seydlitz*.

(D) 5 MARCH 1917

A planned sortie was aborted after a collision in the Heligoland Bight between the *Grosser Kurfürst* and *Kronprinz*. The *Grosser Kurfürst* underwent repairs until 27 April 1917, the *Kronprinz* until 14 May 1917.

(E) 19 SEPTEMBER 1917. BALTIC

In the series of operations in support of the Riga offensive the Germans employed five battleships, the *Kaiser, Kaiserin, Prinzregent Luitpold, König Albert* and the *Bayern* and the battlecruiser *Moltke*. The *Bayern* was mined and seriously damaged in the Gulf of Riga on 12 October. Damaged forward, she drew 36 feet and it took nineteen days to get her to Kiel. The main German effort was made between 11 and 19 October 1917, the operation beginning on 12 October after a delay of thirteen days because of bad weather. The Germans employed four battleships for this specific operations. These were the *König, Grosser Kurfürst, Markgraf* and the *Kronprinz*. The *Grosser Kurfürst* was mined on 12 October.

(F) 17 NOVEMBER 1917. NORTH SEA

For this operation the Germans employed three battleships and two battlecruisers. These were the battleships *Kaiser, Kaiserin* and the *Prinzregent*

Luitpold, and the battlecruisers *Moltke* and the (1917) *Hindenburg*.

(G) 28 FEBRUARY 1918. GULF OF FINLAND

For operations in support of the Finns the Germans employed three battleships. These were the *Westfalen, Rheinland* and the *Posen*. The *Rheinland* ran aground on 11 April and suffered such damage that she was decommissioned when finally recovered.

(H) 23 APRIL 1918. STAVANGER

Overall seventeen battleships and two battlecruisers were involved in this operation. These were the battleships *Nassau, Westfalen, Posen, Helgoland, Ostfriesland, Thüringen, Oldenburg, Kaiser, Kaiserin, Prinzregent Luitpold, König Albert, König, Grosser Kurfürst, Markgraf, Kronprinz Wilhelm, Bayern* and the *Baden*; and the battlecruisers *Von der Tann, Moltke, Seydlitz, Derfflinger* and the *Hindenburg*.

The *Moltke* stripped one of her turbines and was heavily damaged. She was taken in tow by the *Oldenburg* but was hit by one of four torpedoed fired at her by the British submarine E. 42 on 25 April. Despite having some 2,100 tons of seawater in her, she safely returned to base. When she returned to service is not recorded.

When the Admiralty became aware that German formations were at sea, it ordered the Grand Fleet to sail, and it did with a strength of 31 dreadnoughts, four battlecruisers and two armoured cruisers, 24 light cruisers and 85 destroyers – a force inferior in capital ships but marginally superior in terms of cruisers and destroyers to the Grand and Battle Cruiser Fleets at Jutland. Four of the dreadnoughts were American.

It is worth noting that on this occasion the Germans were decidedly unfortunate in not falling upon one or other of Britain's convoys between Methil and Norway. German security was very tight, and the British picked up no indication of German moves until radio silence had to be broken following the breakdown of the *Moltke*. Had the German raid been conducted one day earlier or one day later, one convoy would have been destroyed. In the event, not a single ship was lost on either side.

[21] Some sources suggest that the Germans employed eight battleships and two battlecruisers, with one destroyer formation, in support of their salvage ships, but the total of four dreadnoughts and one battlecruiser is taken from Paul Kemp, *U-boats Destroyed. German Submarine Losses in the World Wars*, p. 21, and Arthur J. Marder, *From the Dreadnought to Scapa Flow. Volume III. Jutland and After, May 1916–December 1916*, p. 256.

CHAPTER 4

[1] These numbered eight destroyers from the 10th and 11th Destroyer Flotillas which arrived in the company of the protected cruiser (1899) *Akashi* in April 1917: in August the armoured cruiser (1900) *Izumo* and the destroyers (1917) *Hinoki*, (1917) *Kashi*, (1916) *Momo* and the (1917) *Yanagi* from the 15th Destroyer Flotilla arrived on station. The *Izumo* replaced the *Akashi* on station, and the Japanese also took possession of the British destroyers (1911) *Minstrel* and (1911) *Nemesis*, which were renamed *Sendan* and *Kanran* respectively. At peak strength, therefore, the Japanese Navy mustered one armoured cruiser and fourteen destroyers on station.

[2] The extent of Japanese financial weakness, and the limitations imposed on the defence budgets, were very considerable, and seldom properly appreciated. Some indication of both can be gauged by reference to various naval estimates immediately before the outbreak of the First World War. The British naval estimates for 1913–1914 were for £48,333,194 of which £27,406,890 was earmarked for new construction with another £3,481,500 set aside for works, buildings and repairs (home and abroad). The American navy estimates were for £31,123,740, which was trimmed by Congress to £28,932,630 by reducing new construction from three battleships to just one. The estimates for Germany were for £22,887,870. The estimates for France, Italy and Austria-Hungary were for £9,769,689, £7,269,056 and £5,985,715 respectively: these figures show how difficult it was for all these states, other than Germany, to finance their navies given their immediate commitment to their armies and their restricted industrial-financial base.

The estimates for Japan were for £9,860,912, which nonetheless placed her fourth in the spending order, but American spending on pay and new warships was about eight millions each, or not far short of the total Japanese outlay. It may be noted, moreover, that of the Japanese naval budget £5,549,298 was set aside for "extraordinary expenditure", most of which was work on bases and new construction though two items might be noted: production of charts was afforded the princely sum of £1,531 and £10,210 was set aside for "Investigation of Aeronautics".

[3] Wrigley, Chris (editor), *The First World War and the International Economy*. Chapter 5. "The impact of the First World War on Japan" by Kenneth D. Brown. Kennedy, Greg (editor), *The Merchant Marine in International Affairs, 1850–1950*. Chapter 3. "Opportunity versus Control: The Diplomacy of

Japanese Shipping in the First World War" by William Wray.

[4] Among the other warships ordered were ten cruisers, 50 destroyers and 67 submarines.

[5] The *Indiana*, *Montana*, *South Dakota*, *Iowa*, *Massachusetts* and the *North Carolina*, and the battlecruisers *Constellation*, *Constitution*, *Lexington*, *Ranger* and the *Saratoga*.

[6] These were the *South Carolina* and *Michigan*; the *Delaware* and *North Dakota*; the *Florida* and *Utah*; the *Wyoming* and *Arkansas*; the *New York* and *Texas*; the *Nevada*, *Oklahoma*, *Pennsylvania* and the *Arizona*; and the *New Mexico*, *Mississippi* and the *Idaho*.

[7] David C. Evans and Mark R. Peattie, *Kaigun. Strategy, Tactics and Technology in the Imperial Japanese Navy, 1887–1941*, p. 153.

[8] The battleships in reserve in 1919 were the *Dreadnought*, *Bellerophon*, *Superb*, *Collingwood*, *St. Vincent* and the *Neptune*, plus the *Agincourt* which awaited disposal: the battlecruisers in reserve in 1919 were the *Indomitable* and *Inflexible*. The *Colossus* (until 1920) and *Téméraire* (until 1922) served as training ships, and the *Hercules* was allocated general duties in 1919 but was discarded and sold in 1920. In addition , there were the battlecruisers *Australia* and *New Zealand*. All the 12-in-gunned battleships not already stricken and sold were placed on the disposal list in 1921.

[9] The cost of the *Hood*, launched in 1918 and completed in 1920, was £6,025,000: the cost of the *Nelson* and *Rodney*, built under the terms of the Washington naval treaty and laid down in December 1922 and completed in summer 1927, was £7,504,000 and £7,617,000 respectively.

[10] The Senate vote was 49 to 35 in favour of the Treaty of Versailles and the Covenant (and hence United States' membership) of the League of Nations. Ratification required a two-thirds majority, which meant the process failed by seven votes. There were twelve abstentions.

[11] A number of sources (e.g. Oscar Parkes, *British Battleships*, p. 654) give the total number of British capital ships discarded under the terms of the Washington naval treaty as 22, a total which would be correct if the *Thunderer* is included.

[12] Of the ten battleships and four battlecruisers with the 12-in main armament, only one, the *Australia*, survived 1922: she was ceremonially sunk

in home waters in 1924. The *Conqueror* and *Orion* were sold in 1922, the *Monarch* was sunk as a target ship in 1925. The *Lion* was sold in 1924, and the *Princess Royal* and *Thunderer* were sold in 1926.

[13] One assumes the missing three ships were pre-1905 cruisers of various description: the only other ships these could have been were German ships surrendered as reparation at the end of the First World War but these had already been sold and scrapped.

[14] It was a mark of the times that this treaty did not provide a definition of either a 'fortification' or a 'naval base': the terms were understood without any need for elaboration.

[15] The treaty was signed on 21 April 1930.

[16] The second London conference did result in agreement, but between Britain, France and the United States, and the Soviet Union and Turkey, plus Sweden, became parties to their agreement: in the context of the time, however, this agreement was next to worthless. The failure of this conference had been foreshadowed when Japan, needing to provide one year's advance notice of determination to end limitation, announced on 19 December 1934 her refusal to abide by this process. The second London conference opened, ironically, on 7 December 1935 and with a Japanese demand for naval equality with Britain: the Japanese delegation left proceedings on 15 January 1936. The conference formally ended on 25 March 1936.

[17] Oscar Parkes, *British Battleships*, p. 657.

[18] Captain S.W. Roskill, *H. M. S. Warspite. The Story of a Famous Battleship*, p. 161.

[19] France was entitled to build one battleship in 1927 and another in 1929 to replace pre-dreadnought *Danton*-class battleships: the loss of the *Courbet*-class dreadnought *France* in Quiberon Bay in August 1922 allowed her to build a third battleship. She chose, however, not avail herself of the opportunities thus presented, and therefore after the London conference was able to pick up commitments at two very different levels. The *Dunkerque*, ordered in the 1931 programme, was a replacement for the *France*: the *Strasbourg*, ordered in the 1934 programme, actually replaced the *Courbet*-class *Jean Bart*, which was renamed the *Océan* and relegated to training duties. Perhaps surprisingly, the *Dunkerque* and *Strasbourg* were defined as battleships (*bâtiments de ligne*) rather than battlecruisers (*croiseurs de bataille*).

[20] Siegfried Breyer, *Battleships and Battle Cruisers, 1905–1970*, p. 300.

[21] It should be noted that in the same period the Americans produced no fewer than 77 designs that ultimately gave rise to the *North Carolina* class. It may be noted that among these designs were ones for a battleship, with displacement of 35,000 tons, with three quadruple turrets with 14-in guns. William H. Garzke and Robert O. Dulin, *Battleships, United States Battleships, 1935–1992*, pp. 32–33.

[22] The (1915) *Barham* was sunk on 25 November 1941 and the (1916) *Repulse* and (1941) *Prince of Wales* on 10 December. If one takes the period between 13 November and 19 December 1941, basically a five-week period with the Japanese attack on Pearl Harbor slightly offset to the later part of this time, the British capital ships *Barham*, *Repulse* and the *Prince of Wales*, the fleet carrier (1938) *Ark Royal*, the escort carrier (1941) *Audacity*, the light cruisers (1935) (RAN) *Sydney*, (1919) *Dunedin*, (1935) *Galatea* and the (1934) *Neptune*, the destroyers (1920) *Thracian* and (1939) *Kandahar*, the escorts (1939) (RAN) *Parramatta* and (1940) (RCN) *Windflower* and the submarine *Perseus* were sunk, and on 19 December 1941 the battleships (1915) *Queen Elizabeth* and (1916) *Valiant* were badly damaged in Alexandria harbour as a result of Italian charioteer attack, and indeed were left resting on the bottom. These losses were heavier than those sustained by the Americans at Pearl Harbor, and apart from the *Queen Elizabeth* and *Valiant* could not be reversed by salvage. Of these losses, German submarines accounted for one battleship, one fleet carrier, one escort carrier, two light cruisers and one escort.

CHAPTER 5

[1] The only obvious examples are the destruction of the Vandal kingdom in North Africa, 533–534, the Norman conquest of England after 1066 and, uniquely in terms of continental scale, the Spanish destruction of the Aztec and Inca empires in Mexico and South America in the sixteenth century.

[2] The total of 81 capital ships with the great powers consisted of 27 American, twenty British, twelve Japanese, seven French, eight Italian, three Soviet, plus four German units, the latter total excluding the three *panzerschiffe*: in addition, Argentina and Brazil both had two battleships, and Chile and Turkey each had one.

[3] To be really perverse, the total could be amended to include the American battleships sunk at Pearl Harbor on 7 December 1941 since it could be argued that these were sunk after the decision of the war had been reached.

[4] These were the (1941) *Prince of Wales*; the (1937) *Dunkerque* and (1938) *Strasbourg*; the (1940) *Bismarck* and (1941) *Tirpitz*, the (1938) *Gneisenau* and (1939) *Scharnhorst*; the (1942) *Roma*; and the (1942) *Musashi* and (1941) *Yamato*.

[5] The pre-dreadnoughts were the (1905) *Hessen*, (1907) *Hannover*, (1908) *Schlesien* and the (1908) *Schleswig-Holstein* and the light cruisers the (1925) *Emden*, (1929) *Königsberg*, (1929) *Karlsruhe*, (1930) *Köln*, (1931) *Leipzig* and the (1935) *Nürnberg*.

[6] These were the heavy cruiser (1931) *Exeter* and light cruisers (1932) *Achilles* and (1934) *Ajax*: the *Exeter* was put of action, the *Ajax* was badly damaged.

[7] The British formations involved in this action were as follows: The heavy cruisers (1930) *Norfolk* and (1928) *Suffolk*; the (1920) *Hood* and (1941) *Prince of Wales* and the destroyers (1929) *Achates*, (1929) *Antelope*, (1929) *Anthony*, (1934) *Echo*, (1934) *Electra* and (1936) *Icarus*; the battleship (1940) *King George V*, the battlecruiser (1916) *Repulse*, the fleet carrier (1941) *Victorious*, the light cruisers (1937) *Aurora*, (1935) *Galatea*, (1941) *Hermione* and the (1940) *Kenya*, and six, seven or nine destroyers, depending on which page of the official history is examined; the battleship (1928) *Rodney* and the destroyers (1937) *Mashona*, (1937) *Somali* and the (1937) *Tartar*; the battlecruiser (1916) *Renown*, the fleet carrier (1938) *Ark Royal*, the light cruiser (1937) *Sheffield*, and the destroyers (1934) *Faulknor*, (1934) *Foresight*, (1934) *Forester*, (1934) *Foxhound*, (1934) *Fury* and the (1939) *Hesperus*; the destroyers (1937) *Cossack*, (1937) *Maori*, (1940) (Polish) *Piorun*, (1937) *Sikh* and the (1937) *Zulu*; the battleship (1927) *Nelson*, the fleet carrier (1924) *Eagle*, and, independently and separate from one another, the battleship (1917) *Ramillies*, the light cruiser (1939) *Edinburgh* and the heavy cruiser (1939) *Dorsetshire*.

[8] This little-known operation, beyond northern Nova Zemlya, saw the (1934) *Admiral Scheer* sink one ice-breaker off the Nordenskjoeld archipelago on 25 August: Dikson, and two ships, were subjected to attack on 27 August. Three days later the *Admiral Scheer* was back at Narvik.

[9] The (1929) *Königsberg*, which was sunk on 10 April at Bergen, was the first warship to be sunk by aircraft, which in this case were shore-based naval dive-bombers.

[10] The British ships were the (1915) *Warspite* and nine destroyers, the (1937) *Bedouin*, (1937) *Cossack*, (1937) *Eskimo*, (1934) *Forester*, (1934) *Foxhound*, (1936) *Hero*, (1936) *Icarus*, (1939) *Kimberley* and the (1937) *Punjabi*: the German destroyers sunk were the (1936) *Bernd von Arnim*, (1937) *Diether von Roeder*, (1937) *Erich Giese*, (1937) *Erich Köllner*, (1935) *Georg Thiele*, (1937) *Hans Lüdemann*, (1937) *Hermann Künne* and the (1936) *Wolfgang Zenker*, plus the submarine *U.64*.

[11] At Mers-el-Kebir the British employed the (1920) *Hood*, (1916) *Resolution* and the (1916) *Valiant*, the fleet carrier (1938) *Ark Royal*, the light cruisers (1935) *Arethusa* and (1926) *Enterprise*, and the destroyers (1929) *Active*, (1934) *Escort*, (1924) *Faulknor*, (1934) *Fearless*, (1934) *Foresight*, (1934) *Forester*, (1934) *Foxhound*, (1924) *Keppel*, (1918) *Vidette*, (1917) *Vortigern* and the (1918) *Wrestler*: the French squadron consisted of the (1913) *Bretagne*, (1937) *Dunkerque*, (1916) *Provence* and the (1938) *Strasbourg* with the destroyers (1931) *Kersaint*, (1933) *Le Terrible*, (1924) *Lynx*, (1937) *Mogador*, (1924) *Tigre* and the (1936) *Volta*. French warships in British ports were also seized on this day. These numbered three destroyers, six torpedo boats, twelve sloops, six submarines, three minelayers, sixteen submarine chasers, seven MTBs, 98 minesweepers and guard ships, 42 tugs and harbour craft, twenty trawlers and two small units, plus the battleships (1913) *Courbet* at Portsmouth and (1914) *Paris* at Plymouth. At Alexandria the battleship (1916) *Lorraine*, three heavy cruisers, one light cruiser, three destroyers and one submarine were interned and demilitarised by agreement by the removal of firing mechanisms.

At Dakar on 7 July the British attacked the resident French squadron, depth charges being dropped under the stern of the French battleship (1939) *Richelieu* by a motor launch which penetrated the harbour under cover of night: next day Swordfish from the light carrier (1923) *Hermes* hit the *Richelieu* with one torpedo. Though damaged, the French battleship was critically important in ensuring that the British attempt to seize Dakar (23–25 September) was a failure. The battleships (1915) *Barham* and (1916) *Resolution* were in the attack force along with the (1938) *Ark Royal*, three heavy cruisers, one light cruiser and ten destroyers. The *Resolution* was hit four times by coastal batteries on 24 September and on 25 September was torpedoed by the French submarine *Beveziers* while the *Barham* was hit once by fire from the *Richelieu*. After this time the attack was abandoned.

[12] The Italian order of battle consisted of the one convoy and six torpedo boats bound from Naples to Benghazi with cover provided by the heavy cruiser (1932) *Pola* with the destroyers (1938) *Ascari*, (1938) *Carabiniere*, (1938) *Corazziere* and the (1938) *Lanciere*; the heavy cruisers (1931) *Fiume*, (1932) *Gorizia* and the (1931) *Zara* with the destroyers (1936) *Alfredo Oriani*, (1936) *Giosue Carducci* and the (1936) *Vincenzo Gioberti*; the heavy cruisers (1933) *Bolzano* and (1929) *Trento*, and the destroyers (1937) *Artigliere*, (1938) *Aviere*, (1937) *Camicia Nera* and the (1938) *Geniere*; the light cruisers (1935) *Emanuele Filiberto Duca D'Aosta*, (1936) *Eugenio di Savoia*, (1935) *Muzio Attendolo* and the (1935) *Raimondo Montecuccoli* and the destroyers (1938) *Alpino*, (1938) *Bersagliere*, (1938) *Fuciliere* and the (1938) *Granatiere*; and the battleships (1915) *Conte di Cavour*, the (1914) *Giulio Cesare*, the light cruisers (1931) *Albercio da Barbiano*, (1931) *Amberto di Giussano*, (1933) *Armando Diaz* and the (1933) *Luigi Cadorna*, and sixteen destroyers drawn from five different divisions.

[13] The Italian order of battle consisted of the battleship (1940) *Vittorio Veneto* and the destroyers (1938) *Alpino*, (1938) *Bersagliere*, (1938) *Fuciliere* and the (1938) *Granatiere*; the heavy cruisers (1931) *Fiume*, (1932) *Pola* and the (1931) *Zara*, and the destroyers (1936) *Alfredo Oriani*, (1936) *Giosue Carducci*, (1936) *Vincenzo Gioberti* and the (1936) *Vittorio Alfieri*; the light cruisers (1937) *Luigi di Savoia Duca Degli Abruzzi* and (1937) *Giuseppe Garibaldi*, and the destroyers (1930) *Nicoloso da Recco* and the (1929) *Emanuele Pessagno*; and the heavy cruisers (1933) *Bolzano*, (1929) *Trento* and the (1928) *Trieste*, and the destroyers (1938) *Ascari*, (1938) *Carabiniere* and the (1938) *Corazziere*.

The British order of battle was the light cruisers (1934) *Ajax*, (1939) *Gloucester*, (1932) *Orion* and the (1933) (RAN) *Perth*, and the destroyers (1936) *Hasty*, (1936) *Hereward*, (1937) *Ilex* and the (1917) (RAN) *Vendetta*; the battleships (1915) *Barham*, (1916) *Valiant* and the (1915) *Warspite*, the fleet carrier (1940) *Formidable*, and the destroyers (1938) *Janus*, (1938) *Jervis*, (1937) *Mohawk* and the (1937) *Nubian*; and the destroyers (1936) *Greyhound*, (1936) *Griffin*, (1936) *Havock*, (1936) *Hotspur* and the (1918) (RAN) *Stuart*.

[14] The units lost off Crete were the heavy cruiser (1930) *York*, the light cruisers (1940) *Fiji*, (1939)

Gloucester and the (1919) *Calcutta*, and the destroyers (1938) *Juno*, (1935) *Greyhound*, (1939) *Kashmir*, (1938) *Kelly*, (1936) *Imperial* and the (1936) *Hereward*: the units lost off Norway were the carrier (1928) *Glorious*, the light cruisers (1925) *Effingham* and (1917) *Curlew* and the destroyers (1935) *Glowworm*, (1937) *Gurkha*, (1936) *Hardy*, (1936) *Hunter*, (1937) *Afridi*, (1929) *Acasta* and the (1929) *Ardent*.

[15] This view of events discounts the loss of the *Courageous*, on 17 October 1939 in the Western Approaches, when she was (mis)employed searching for submarines, and that of the *Glorious*, to which reference has been made. Also discounted from consideration is the battleship *Royal Oak*, sunk on 14 October 1939 inside Scapa Flow. These have not been included in this argument because of the exceptional circumstances that surrounded their loss.

[16] The four carriers employed in Operation Pedestal were the (1924) *Eagle*, (1925) *Furious*, (1941) *Indomitable* and the (1941) *Victorious*. The two not present were the (1940) *Formidable* and (1940) *Illustrious*. The old training carrier (1918) *Argus* was pressed into front-line service after the loss of the (1938) *Ark Royal* and did take part in Operation Torch before reverting to training duties, but is not considered "first-team" in this context.

[17] These were the monitors (1943) *Abercrombie*, (1916) *Erebus* and the (1941) *Roberts*, the British light cruisers (1918) *Carlisle*, (1919) *Colombo*, (1919) *Delhi*, (1941) *Mauritius*, (1943) *Newfoundland*, (1932) *Orion* and the (1943)*Uganda*, and the U.S. light cruisers (1943) *Birmingham*, (1939) *Boise*, (1938) *Brooklyn*, (1938) *Philadelphia* and the (1938) *Savannah*. The covering force consisted of the battleships (1927) *Nelson*, (1928) *Rodney*, (1916) *Valiant* and the (1915) *Warspite*, the fleet carriers (1940) *Formidable* and (1941) *Indomitable*, the light cruisers (1937) *Aurora*, (1941) *Cleopatra*, (1941) *Euryalus* and the (1936) *Penelope*; the reserve force consisted of the battleships (1942) *Howe* and (1940) *King George V* and the light cruisers (1940) *Dido* and (1942) *Sirius*.

[18] The units involved in covering the landings in southern Italy were the battleships (1942) *Howe*, (1940) *King George V*, (1927) *Nelson*, (1928) *Rodney*, (1916) *Valiant* and the (1915) *Warspite*; the fleet carriers (1940) *Formidable* and (1940) *Illustrious*, light carrier (1943) *Unicorn* and the escort carriers (1942) *Attacker*, (1942) *Battler*, (1943) *Hunter* and the (1942) *Stalker*; the monitors (1943) *Abercrombie*,

(1916) *Erebus* and the (1941) *Roberts*; and the British light cruisers (1937) *Aurora*, (1941) *Charybdis*, (1919) *Delhi*, (1940) *Dido*, (1941) *Euryalus*, (1941) *Mauritius*, (1932) *Orion*, (1936) *Penelope*, (1942) *Scylla*, (1942) *Sirius* and the (1943) *Uganda*, and the U.S. light cruisers (1938) *Brooklyn*, (1938) *Philadelphia* and the (1938) *Savannah*.

[19] The battleships detailed to Operation Neptune can be stated without fear of contradiction, but the detail of the naval forces committed to the Normandy landings seem never to command agreement between different sources: one notes the different totals given on pp. 18 and 32 of the British Navy's official history. Part of the problem lies in that the order of battle changed to meet varying requirements both on and after 6 June 1944, but it seems – from the unpublished naval staff history of Operation Neptune, pp. 55–56 – that allied naval forces were earmarked for bombardment duties at 0001 on 6 June 1944 thus:

The Western Naval Task Force [Rear-Admiral A.G. Kirk, USN, in the American heavy cruiser (1931) *Augusta*],

Bombardment Force "A" (committed to the support of Assault Force "U"), the American battleship (1916) *Nevada*, the British monitor (1916) *Erebus*, the American heavy cruiser (1934) *Tuscaloosa* [flagship of Rear-Admiral Deyo, USN] and (1936) *Quincy*, the British heavy cruiser (1919) *Hawkins*, the British light cruisers (1943) *Black Prince*, (1926) *Enterprise*, the Dutch gunboat (1926) *Soemba* and eight American destroyers,

Bombardment Force "C" (committed to the support of Assault Force "O"), the American battleships (1912) *Arkansas* and (1914) *Texas* [(Flagship of Rear-Admiral C.F. Bryant, USN], the British light cruisers (1937) *Glasgow*, and the French light cruisers (1937) *Georges Leygues* and (1937) *Montcalm* (flagship of Rear-Admiral Janjard, FFN; and nine American and three British *Hunt*-class destroyers,

Held in reserve were the American heavy cruiser (1931) *Augusta*, the British light cruiser (1943) *Bellona*, and seventeen American destroyers.

The Eastern Naval Task Force [Rear-Admiral P.L. Vian, RN, in the British light cruiser (1942) *Scylla*],

Bombardment Force "K" (committed to the support of Assault Force "G"), the British light cruisers (1934) *Orion*, (1935) *Ajax*, (1942) *Argonaut*, (1926) *Emerald*, the Dutch gunboat (n/d) *Flores*; and nine destroyers and four *Hunt*-class destroyers,

Bombardment Force "E" (committed to the support of Assault Force "J"), The British light cruisers (1939) *Belfast* [flagship of Rear-Admiral F.H. Dalrymple-Hamilton] and (1944) *Diadem*, and seven destroyers and four *Hunt*-class destroyers,

Bombardment Force "D" (committed to the support of Assault Force "S"), the British battleships (1917) *Ramillies* and (1915) *Warspite*, the British monitor (1916) *Roberts*, the British heavy cruiser (1924) *Frobisher*, the British light cruisers (1941) *Mauritius* [flagship of Rear-Admiral W.R. Patterson, RN], (1935) *Arethusa*, (1918) *Danae* and the Polish-manned (1918) *Dragon*, and thirteen destroyers and two *Hunt*-class destroyers,

Held in reserve were the British battleship (1928) *Rodney* and light cruiser (1942) *Sirius*.

The British battleship (1927) *Nelson*, held at Milford Haven, constituted the reserve held by the Allied Commander Naval Expeditionary Force for the support of the bombardment formations.

The commanders of the British bombardment formations were authorised to draw upon nine units earmarked for escort duties reference the assault forces with which to augment their commands should the need be demonstrated.

Bombardment Force "K" had no flagship because it was commanded by Captain E.W. Longley-Cook, presumably in the *Orion*.

It might be noted, as evidence of the difficulty of providing a definitive account of these proceedings, that the highly esteemed *Chronology of the War at Sea, 1939–1945*.

The Naval History of World War Two, by J. Rohwer and G. Hummelchen, states (p. 281) that the reserve for the western formation was a formation consisting of the *Nelson*, *Bellona*, three American destroyers and two French frigates: this same sources provides different listings for the destroyers and escorts for these various formations from the naval staff history.

[20] The extent to which the demands of the Normandy landings made inroads into British strength in the Mediterranean can be gauged by reference to the fact that on 6 June 1944 the British had two light cruisers, three AA light cruisers and ten destroyers on station in the Mediterranean, but to these totals have to be added submarines, minesweepers and escorts.

[21] For a full and detailed examination of this issue, see H.P. Willmott with Tohmatsu Haruo and W. Spencer Johnson, *Pearl Harbor*, pp. 142–157.

[22] In terms of June 1944 the Americans had the (1942) *Alabama*, (1942) *Indiana*, (1943) *Iowa*, (1943) *New Jersey*, (!941) *North Carolina*, (1942) *South Dakota*, and the (1941) *Washington* with their carrier task groups in the Pacific, plus the (1919) *Idaho*, (1918) *New Mexico* and the (1916) *Pennsylvania*, and the (1921) *California*, (1923) *Colorado*, (1921) *Maryland* and the (1920) *Tennessee* assigned to bombardment groups in the Pacific, the (1912) *Arkansas*, (1916) *Nevada* and the (1914) *Texas* to bombardment groups at Normandy. The (1914) *New York* was serving as gunnery training ship on the east coast, and three battleships, the (1942) *Massachusetts*, (1917) *Mississippi* and the (1923) *West Virginia* were in the hands of the Puget Sound navy yard. In June 1944 the battleships *Missouri* and *Wisconsin* and the battlecruisers *Alaska* and *Guam* had yet to be fully commissioned into service.

[23] Task Group 34.8 consisted of the battleships (1942) *Indiana*, (1942) *Massachusetts* and the (1942) *South Dakota*, the heavy cruisers (1943) *Boston*, (1931) *Chicago*, (1936) *Quincy* and the (1945) *St. Paul*, and nine destroyers, plus the British contingent which consisted of the (1940) *King George V* and the destroyers (1943) *Undine*, (1943) *Ulysses* and the (1943) *Urania*.

[24] In addition, the carriers (1943) *Bunker Hill* and (1943) *Wasp* and the heavy cruiser *Minneapolis* incurred minor damage as a result of near-misses. What is very interesting about the reports made at the time is that the total number of Japanese aircraft shot down by ships' gunfire was claimed to be 27, but the number claimed to have been shot down by American aircraft was 848, which was almost twice the number of aircraft embarked in the Japanese carriers.

[25] Two comments would seem to be in order at this point. First, it must be doubtful if any Japanese commander was aware of this development, not least because Japanese claims, at virtually every stage of the Pacific war, bordered on the grotesque in their exaggeration, for which there seemingly was no correction through a careful and deliberate briefing process. One hesitates to state how many times the entire U.S. Navy was sunk during the campaigns in the Solomons, with half a dozen carriers and the same number of battleships despatched by aircrew who seemed constitutionally incapable of admitting that some of their number, perhaps even themselves, did not actually hit a target. One would note that air claims are notorious for their exaggeration (see again the previous note) but the Japanese do seem to have taken the process and made it into an art form.

The second is more difficult to state. For many years one has firmly believed that the one critical advantage that the Japanese held over their various enemies was a willingness of the ordinary soldier, airman or naval personnel to die in order to fight. To this basic point, however, one has always added two caveats: that moral advantage cannot offset too great a material deficit, which was the Japanese problem, and that in resorting to *kamikaze* attacks Japanese airmen who died to fight found themselves outfought by Allied sailors who fought in order to live.

Yet writing the comment that the Japanese were prepared to die in order to fight in this text, however, prompted a thought which, one would admit, had never been previously considered: Japanese effectiveness in terms of sinking enemy warships when fighting in order to live. The problem of selecting the terms of reference for such a question was considerable, but as a rough rule of thumb the number of U.S. destroyers sunk in the course of hostilities seemed to provide the basis for an examination of this idea, and was adopted accordingly, E.& O.E. And the answer is interesting.

In the course of the Pacific war, the Americans lost 54 destroyers: these were units that were sunk. This total includes the (1937) *Cassin*, (1937) *Downes* and (1939) *Shaw*, which were technically not sunk but were left somewhat the worse for their experience by Japanese carrier aircraft on 7 December 1941 but which were later salved and returned to service. This total does not include the *Stewart*, which was scuttled at Soerabaja on 2 March 1945. This exception being noted, Japanese warships sank eighteen American destroyers, only three after 7 October 1943; Japanese submarines sank four American destroyers, the last on 26 October 1943; Japanese aircraft, whether shore-based or carrier-borne but excluding aircraft from *kamikaze* formations, accounted for ten American destroyers, the last on 26 December 1943; mines accounted for two American destroyers; natural causes accounted for six American destroyers. What is most notable is that apart from the one American destroyer mined off Okinawa, in 1945 Japanese action other than *kamikaze* attack failed to account for a single U.S. destroyer. Moreover, apart from the (1943) *Hoel* and (1943) *Johnston* sunk on 25 October 1945 and the (1943) *Halligan* mined off Okinawa in March 1945, all forms of Japanese action, excluding *kamikaze* attack, accounted for just one American destroyer after January 1944. In contrast, *kamikaze* attacks resulted in the destruction of fourteen U.S. destroyers and in another ten being written off, bringing the total wartime losses of U.S. destroyers in the Japanese war to 64. (For the desperate need-to-know, there were five destroyer escorts sunk and one written off, but they are not included in these totals.)

Therefore it would seem, *prima facie*, that it was not simply a case that the Japanese were prepared to die in order to fight but that the only way the Japanese could fight was to die. But there would seem to be a point here which one has never fully appreciated in the past. In other works, and in these pages, one has made the point that the Pacific war ended in November 1943, but there would seem to be a dimension to this perspective that has never attracted attention. After November 1943 Japanese effectiveness in terms of ability to sink American warships was all but no more in terms of conventional operations, i.e., *kamikaze* attacks excluded. For all their numbers, their warships and aircraft, in the Pacific after November 1943 the Japanese armed forces were responsible for the destruction of just one light carrier, four escort carriers (two in the actions off Samar on 25 October 1944), one heavy cruiser, fourteen destroyers with another ten *hors de combat*, five destroyer escorts and one more written off (with *kamikaze* attack having accounted for two of these), two minelayers, nine minesweepers (three by *kamikaze*s) with another five written off as a result of *kamikaze* attack, and seven high-speed transports (*kamikaze*s accounting for five of these losses). Submarines are more difficult to calculate but it seems that perhaps as many as 29 American submarines were lost after 30 November 1943, the majority to some form of Japanese action. Overall, it would seem that one could argue a case on the lines that by November 1943 the United States had grown into a strength that not merely ensured her victory both in individual campaigns and battles and in the war overall but which, in effect, denied the Japanese any means of effective response, even in such a matter as the sinking of warships of no very great individual worth. Put simply, and discounting U.S. submarines from consideration, apart from two destroyer-transports mined, between 26 December 1943 and 24 October 1944 Japanese warships and aircraft accounted for just one destroyer-transport mined and one destroyer escort torpedoed by a submarine.

Such were the conclusions prompted by a consideration of destroyer numbers, but when one considered all fleet units other than submarines, and the whole war, from December 1941 to August 1945, what was striking was how little the Japanese sank outside the first few months. Even if one includes the British and Dutch in south-east Asia in the account,

there are still very few sinkings registered by the Japanese even in the first six months of hostilities, while any consideration of Japanese action in terms of fleet units after 11 May 1942 really does point in the direction of a conclusion radically different from those given in standard accounts of the Pacific war. What is so noticeable about Allied losses are the peaks, or troughs, of August and November 1942 and outside those months there is so little that was sunk as a result of Japanese operations. The Japanese may have been unfortunate not to have exacted a higher toll of enemy numbers at Tassafaronga and Kolombangara, but even with these afforded some indulgence there is no altering the basic fact that between June 1942 and September 1944 Japanese action of every kind accounted for six heavy and two light cruisers, and sixteen destroyers, or less than one unit per month. The conclusion that this points to concerns Savo Island, and the fact that in standard accounts the Guadalcanal campaign is inevitably portrayed as the endurance course in which the U.S. Navy, learning from its victories and its defeats, came to prevail because of two matters – its strength in depth which meant that it, unlike its enemy, could take losses secure in the knowledge that, if balanced, the initiative would be fairly bought, and the improvement in night-fighting capability which meant that by the end of this campaign there was a basic equality of capability, i.e., that Japanese superiority in this battle was no more.

One would not dismiss this argument out of hand, but any very careful, detailed, consideration of Japanese operations prompts the thought that after May 1942 Savo Island was the exception because it resulted in a Japanese victory. There is a problem in the sense that consideration of Allied losses – simple numbers – can be misleading: for example, for much of 1942 the (1927) *Saratoga* was undergoing repairs after having been torpedoed, but she was never sunk: the only battle in which she fought in the whole of the war was the eastern Solomons. But this caveat being noted, the conclusion does seem to stand examination, and it may very well be that over nearly 60 years we have been considering the record from the wrong perspective.

[26] The other factor at work in determining the six-gun salvo, at least for the (1920) *Tennessee*, was the fact that the line of fire was forward of the beam and hence only the forward turrets could engage. The (1921) *California* used six-gun salvos to range, and once straddles were recorded (with the third salvo) by radar she went to nine-gun salvos. Spotting was

entirely by radar because neither the target nor the splashes were visible from the *California*.

[27] The change of course, ordered at 0401, involved a simultaneous turn of 150 degrees to starboard. The order was given by voice radio, and in the (1921) *California* was misheard as a fifteen degree turn, which she completed before she resumed fire. The (1920) *Tennessee* just managed to avoid the *California*, just passing under her stern after having reversed her engines, while the *California*, alerted to her error, completed a turn that placed her between first the *Tennessee* and the (1917) *Yamashiro* and then the (1917) *Mississippi* and the *Yamashiro*.

[28] The American battle line consisted of the (1924) *West Virginia* (twelve salvoes), (1921) *Maryland* (six salvoes), (1917) *Mississippi*, (1920) *Tennessee*, (1921) *California* (ten salvoes) and the (1916) *Pennsylvania*, and in that order.

[29] The (1917) *Yamashiro*'s sinking was tracked by radar from American battleships: for the (1920) *Tennessee* she disappeared at about 18,000 yards.

[30] This formation originally consisted of the heavy cruisers (1929) *Ashigara* and (1928) *Nachi*, the light cruiser (1925) *Abukuma* and the destroyers (1931) *Akebono*, (1939) *Kasumi*, (1939) *Shiranui* and the (1931) *Ushio*. (Plus the destroyers [1933] *Hatsuharu*, [1934] *Hatsushimo* and the [1934] *Wakaba*. The *Wakaba* was caught off Panay during the early morning of 24 October by aircraft from the *Franklin* [TG 38.4], which also sighted the first formation: in the afternoon of 24 October the *Fuso* was hit but not seriously damaged by American carrier aircraft.)

[31] The bow section of the (1915) *Fuso* sank at about 0420, within a minute or so of the sinking of the (1917) *Yamashiro*: the stern section sank within another hour.

[32] The identity of the single destroyer sunk by air attack would seem to be somewhat uncertain. It appears that the destroyer was the (1944) *Twiggs*, but most sources indicate that she was sunk by aerial torpedo and *kamikaze* attack.

The battleships damaged in the course of the Okinawa campaign were as follows: (1916) *Nevada*, 27 March, *kamikaze*, major damage: (1923) *West Virginia*, 1 April, *kamikaze*, minor damage: (1916) *Nevada*, 5 April, artillery, minor damage: (1941) *North Carolina*, 6 April, AA fire, minor damage: (1921) *Maryland*, 7 April, bomb, minor damage: (1919) *Idaho*, 12 April, *kamikaze*, major damage: (1920) *Tennessee*, 12 April, *kamikaze*, major damage:

(1914) *New York*, 14 April, *kamikaze*, minor damage: (1942) *South Dakota*, 6 May, ammunition explosion, minor damage: (1918) *New Mexico*, 12 May, bomb, minor damage: (1942) *Indiana*, 5 June, typhoon, minor damage: (1942) *Massachusetts*, 5 June, typhoon, minor damage: (1917) *Mississippi*, 5 June, *kamikaze*, minor damage.

Status is as officially designated. It would seem that the *Nevada*'s damage on 27 March was local, primarily to the deck and No. 3 turret, and was repaired in the immediate battle area. The *Idaho* had some blister compartments flooded as a result of a *kamikaze* near-miss, and had to be repaired at Guam: she returned to Okinawa on 22 May. The *New Mexico*, which seems to have drawn the short straw when it came to *kamikaze*s, was hit in Lingayen Gulf in January 1945 losing her captain and 29 killed and 90 wounded when her bridge was hit: in material terms she suffered very minor damage. The damage sustained on 12 May caused "serious fires," but the battleship remained on station until 28 May when she sailed for repairs at Leyte. The *Tennessee* was hit by a *kamikaze* which penetrated the main deck before exploding. While causing many fires and casualties, the damage does not appear to have been serious because the battleship remained on station until 1 May before sailing for repairs at Ulithi: by 9 June she had returned to Okinawa.

CHAPTER 6

[1] In fact, work on the design of the *Montana* class stopped in June 1942 and was never resumed: the decision of 21 July 1943 was merely a formality.

[2] The five battleships of the *Montana* class were the *Louisiana*, *Maine*, *Montana*, *New Hampshire* and the *Ohio*. Very strangely, Montana gave her name to the class that had been abandoned after the First World War, and was the only state in the Union never to have a battleship that bore her name.

[3] The design specification (August 1940) set out the requirement for 28 knots on 212,000 shp, the battleships having a standard displacement of 58,000 tons. A preliminary design specification indicated that 293,000 shp would be needed to give a battleship with a standard displacement of 66,500 tons a top speed of 33 knots. Such a requirement was wholly unrealistic because it would have necessitated either turbo-electric motors with reduced shaft length or six shafts, which in turn would have necessitated major redesign of the hull, and, apparently, a major increase

in length over existing (planned) 890-ft/271.27-m x 121.17-ft/36.93-m x 36-ft./10.97-m dimensions.

It is possible to argue that the acid test for the *Montana*-class battleships was the meeting of 25 July 1940 when President Franklin D. Roosevelt, having secured authorisation for four *Iowa*-class battleships, agreed to the construction of the *Illinois* and *Kentucky*. He refused, however, to approve contracts for the five *Montana*-class battleships on the grounds that their design had not been settled: he could have added that he refused to approve two of these because the New York navy yard that was earmarked to build them could not launch 58,000-ton ships. In fact, the *Montana* authorisation never represented itself, but even if Roosevelt had decided otherwise on 25 July 1940, one suspects that the order would have been lost at some stage, probably around mid-1943 when the orders for the remaining battlecruisers (namely the *Philippines*, *Puerto Rico* and the *Samoa*) were cancelled.

[4] Siegfried Breyer, *Battleships and Battle Cruisers, 1905–1970*, pp. 105–180. René Greger, *Battleships of the World*, pp. 84–131. Oscar Parkes, *British Battleships*. Ian Sturton (Ed.), *All the World's Battleships. 1906 to the Present*, pp. 50–92. M. J. Whitley, *Battleships of World War Two. An International Encyclopedia*, pp. 92–136.

[5] Breyer, pp. 433–441. Greger, pp. 72–81. Sturton, pp. 20–25. Whitley, pp.34–52.

[6] Breyer, pp. 374–387. Greger, pp. 142–149. Sturton, pp. 104–108. Whitley, pp 156–178.

[7] Breyer, pp. 319–321. Greger, p. 247. Sturton, pp. 14–16. Whitley, pp. 23–29.

[8] Breyer, pp. 404–406. Greger, pp. 244–246. Sturton, pp. 9–10. Whitley, pp. 18–22.

[9] Breyer, pp. 444–447. Greger, pp. 248–249. Sturton, pp. 17–19. Whitley, pp. 30–33.

[10] Breyer, pp. 323–325. Greger, pp. 251. Sturton, pp. 144–145.

[11] Breyer, pp. 442–443. Greger, p. 252. Sturton, pp. 146–147. Whitley, pp. 237–241.

[12] Kenneth J. Hagan, *In Peace and War. Interpretations of American Naval History, 1775–1984.* Dean C. Allard, Chapter 15. "An Era of Transition, 1945–1953", pp. 292–293, and Floyd D. Kennedy, Chapter 16. "The Creation of the Cold War Navy, 1953–1962," p. 305.

[13] Breyer, Op. Cit., pp. 188–255. Greger, Op. Cit., pp. 204–243. Sturton, Op. Cit., pp. 148–187. Whitley, Op. Cit., pp. 242–316.

[14] Breyer, pp. 180–187. Greger, pp. 132–135. Sturton, pp. 50–99. Whitley, pp. 92–136.

[15] Breyer, pp. 435–441. Greger, pp. 82–83. Sturton, pp. 26–27. Whitley, pp. 53–62.

[16] When the *Wisconsin* fired her main armament on 6 February 1991 it was the first time she had fired her guns since March 1952. William H. Garzke, Jr, and Robert O. Dulin, Jr, *Battleships. United States Battleships, 1935–1992*, p. 242.

[17] With apologies to John McCrae.

Selected Bibliography

Archibald, E.H.H., *The Metal Fighting Ship in the Royal Navy, 1870–1970* (London, Blandford Press, 1971).

Arnold, A.J., *Iron Shipbuilding on the Thames, 1832–1915. An Economic and Business History* (Aldershot, Hampshire, Ashgate Publishing, 2000).

Baer, George W., *One Hundred Years of Sea Power. The U.S. Navy, 1890–1990* (Stanford, Stanford University Press, 1994).

Bragadin, Marc Antonio, *The Italian Navy in World War II* (Annapolis, Maryland, Naval Institute Press, 1957).

Bennett, Geoffrey, *The Battle of Jutland* (London, Batsford, 1964).

Berezhnoy, S.S., *Battleships, Armoured Ships and Gunboats* (Moscow, Voyennoe Izdatelsvro/Military Publishing House, 1997).

Breyer, Siegfried, *Battleships and Battlecruisers, 1905–1970* (London, Macdonald, 1973).

Brown, David K., *The Eclipse of the Big Gun. The Warship, 1906–1945* (Annapolis, Maryland, Naval Institute Press, 1992).

Burt, R.A., *British Battleships of World War One* (London, Arms and Armour Press, 1986).

Campbell, N.J.M., *Battlecruisers. The Design and Development of British and German Battlecruisers of the First World War Era* (London, Conway Maritime Press, 1978).

Campbell, John, *Jutland: An Analysis of the Fighting* (London, Conway Maritime Press, 1986).

Careless, Ronald, *Battleship Nelson. The Story of H.M.S. Nelson* (London, Arms and Armour Press, 1985).

Chesneau, Roger, *Hood: Life and Death of a Battlecruiser* (London, Cassell, 2002).

Connaughton, Richard, *The War of the Rising Sun and Tumbling Bear. A Military History of the Russo-Japanese War, 1904–5* (London, Routledge, 1988).

Corbett, Sir Julian S., *History of the Great War. Naval Operations. Volume I. To the Battle of the Falklands December 1914* (London, Longman, Green, 1920).

Corbett, Sir Julian S., *History of the Great War. Naval Operations. Volume III* (London, Longman, Green, 1923).

Dulin, Robert O., Jr, and Garzke, William H., Jr, *Battleships. United States Battleships in World War II* (London, Macdonald and Jane's, 1976).

Dulin, Robert O., Jr, and Garzke, William H., Jr, *Battleships. United States Battleships, 1935–1992* (Annapolis, Maryland, Naval Institute Press, 1995).

Evans, David C., and Peattie, Mark R., *Kaigun. Strategy, Tactics and Technology in the Imperial Japanese Navy, 1887–1941* (Annapolis, Maryland, Naval Institute Press, 1997).

Fraccaroli, Aldo, *Italian Warships of World War I* (London, Ian Allan, 1970).

Fraccaroli, Aldo, *Italian Warships of World War II* (London, Ian Allen, 1968).

Friedman, Norman, *U.S. Battleships. An Illustrated Design History* (Annapolis, Maryland, Naval Institute Press, 1985).

Gardiner, Robert (editorial director), and Chesnau, Roger (editor), *Conway's All the World's Fighting Ships, 1922–1946* (London, Conway Maritime Press, 1980).

Gardiner, Robert (editor), *The Eclipse of the Big Gun. The Warship, 1906–45* (Annapolis, Maryland, Naval Institute Press, 1992).

Garzke, William H. Jr, and Dulin, Robert O. Jr, *Axis and Neutral Nations' Battleships* (Annapolis, Maryland, Naval Institute Press, 1990).

George, James L., *History of Warships. From Ancient Times to the Twenty-First Century* (Annapolis, Maryland, Naval Institute Press, 1998).

Greger, René, *Battleships of the World* (London, Greenhill, 1997).

Hagen, Kenneth J. (editor), *In Peace and War. Interpretations of American Naval History, 1775–1984* (Westport Connecticut, Greenwood, 1984).

Halpern, Paul G., (editor), *The Royal Navy in the Mediterranean, 1915–1918* (London, Navy Records Society, 1987).

Halpern, Paul G., *The Naval War in the Mediterranean, 1914–1918* (London, Allen and Unwin, 1987).

Halpern, Paul G., *A Naval History of World War I* (London, University College London Press, 1995).

Hansen, Hans J¸rgen, *The Ships of the German Fleets, 1848–1945* (London, Hamlyn, 1973).

Hough, Richard, *Dreadnought. A History of the Modern Battleship* (London, Michael Joseph, 1962).

Ireland, Bernard, *Warships. From Sail to the Nuclear Age* (London, Hamlyn, 1978).

Jentschura, Hansgeorg, Jung, Dieter, and Mickel, Peter, *Warships of the Imperial Japanese Navy, 1869–1945* (London, Arms and Armour Press, 1977).

Jones, Jerry W., *U.S. Battleship Operations in World War I* (Annapolis, Maryland, Naval Institute Press, 1998).

Jordan, John, *An Illustrated Guide to Battleships and Battlecruisers* (London, Salamander Books, 1985).

Kennedy, Greg (editor), *The Merchant Marine in International Affairs, 1850–1950* (London, Cass, 2000). Chapter 3. 'Opportunity versus Control: The Diplomacy of Japanese Shipping in the First World War' by William Wray.

Layman, R.D., *Before the Aircraft Carrier. The Development of Aviation Vessels, 1849–1922* (London, Conway Maritime Press, 1989).

Lenton, H.T., and Colledge, J.J., *Warships of World War II* (London, Ian Allan, 1964).

Mackay, Ruddock F., *Fisher of Kilverstone* (Oxford, Oxford University Press, 1973).

Macintyre, Donald, *The Battle of Jutland* (Evans, London, 1957).

Marder, Arthur J., *From the Dreadnought to Scapa Flow. The Royal Navy in the Fisher Era, 1904–1919. Volume I. The Road to War, 1904–1914* (London, Oxford University Press, 1961).

Marder, Arthur J., *From the Dreadnought to Scapa Flow. The Royal Navy in the Fisher Era, 1904–1919. Volume II. The War Years: To the Eve of Jutland, 1914–1916* (London, Oxford University Press, 1965).

Marder, Arthur J., *From the Dreadnought to Scapa Flow. Volume III. Jutland and After, May 1916–December 1916* (London, Oxford University Press, 1966).

Marshall, Ian, *Armoured Ships. The Ships, Their Settings and the Ascendancy that They Sustained for Eighty Years* (London, Conway Maritime Press, 1990).

Naval History Division, *Dictionary of American Naval Fighting Ships, Volumes I to VIII* (Washington DC, Government Printing Office, 1970–1981).

Massie, Robert K., *Dreadnought. Britain, Germany and the Coming of the Great War* (London, Pimlico, 1991).

Millholland, Ray, *The Splinter Fleet of the Otranto Barrage* (London, Cresset, 1939?).

Morison, Samuel Eliot, *History of United States Naval Operations in World War II. Volume VI. Breaking the Bismarcks Barrier. 22 July 1942–1 May 1944.* (Boston, Little, Brown, 1950).

Morison, Samuel Eliot, *History of United States Naval Operations in World War II. Volume VII. Aleutians, Gilberts and Marshalls. June 1942–April 1944* (Boston, Little, Brown, 1952).

Morison, Samuel Eliot, *History of United States Naval Operations in World War II. Volume VIII. New Guinea and the Marianas. March 1943–August 1944* (Boston, Little, Brown, 1953).

Morison, Samuel Eliot, *History of United States Naval Operations in World War II. Volume XII. Leyte. June 1944–January 1945* (Boston, Little, Brown, 1958).

George Nekrasov, *North of Gallipoli: The Black Sea Fleet at War, 1914–1917* (Boulder, Colorado, East European Monographs, 1992).

Newbolt, Henry, *History of the Great War. Naval Operations. Volume V* (Longman, Green, 1931)

Nomura, Minoru (editor), *Zusetsu Nippon Kaigun* (Tokyo, Kawade Shobo Shinsha, 1997).

Padfield, Peter, *Aim Straight. A Biography of Admiral Sir Percy Scott* (London, Hodder and Stoughton, 1966).

Padfield, Peter, *Battleship* (Edinburgh, Birlinn, 2000).

Parkes, Oscar, *British Battleships. Warrior to Vanguard, 1860–1950. A History of Design, Construction and Armament* (London, Seeley Service, 1966).

Patterson, A. Temple (editor), *The Jellicoe Papers. Selections from the Private and Official Correspondence of Admiral of the Fleet Earl Jellicoe of Scapa* (London, Navy Records Society, two volumes 1966 and 1968).

Patterson, A. Temple, *Jellicoe. A Biography* (London, Macmillan, 1969).

Pears, Randolph, *British Battleships, 1892–1957. The Great Days of the Fleets* (London, Putnam, 1967).

Polmar, Norman, and Friedman, Norman, *Warships. From Early Steam to Nuclear Power* (London, Octopus Books, 1981).

Preston, Antony, *Battleships of World War I* (London, Arms and Armour Press, 1972).

Preston, Antony, *Battleships* (London, Bison Books, 1981).

Raven, A., and Roberts, J., *British Battleships of World War II. The Development and Technical History of the Royal Navy's Battleships and Battlecruisers, 1911–1946* (Annapolis, Maryland, Naval Institute Press, 1976).

Reynolds, Clark G., *Command of the Sea. The History and Strategy of Maritime Empires* (New York, William Murrow, 1974).

Reynolds, Clark G., *Navies in History* (Annapolis, Maryland, Naval Institute Press, 1998).

Roberts, John, *The battlecruiser Hood* (London, Conway Maritime Press, 1982).

Roberts, John, *The battleship Dreadnought* (London, Conway Maritime Press, 1992).

Rohwer, J¸rgen, and Hummelchen, Gerhard, *Chronology of the War at Sea, 1939–1945. The Naval History of World War II* (Annapolis, Maryland, Naval Institute Press, 1992).

Roskill, S.W., *The History of the Second World War. The War at Sea. Volume I. The Defence* (London, Her Majesty's Stationary Office, 1954).

Roskill, S.W., *The History of the Second World War. The War at Sea. Volume II. The Period of Balance* (London, Her Majesty's Stationary Office, 1957).

Roskill, S.W., *The History of the Second World War. The War at Sea. Volume III. The Offensive. Part I. 1st June 1943–31st May 1944* (London, Her Majesty's Stationary Office, 1960).

Roskill, S.W., *The History of the Second World War. The War at Sea. Volume III. The Offensive. Part II. 1st June 1944–14th August 1945* (London, Her Majesty's Stationary Office, 1961).

Roskill, S.W,, *H.M.S. Warspite. The Story of a Famous Battleship* (Annapolis, Maryland, Naval Institute Press, 1997).

Roskill, S.W., *The Strategy of Sea Power. Its Development and Application* (London, William Collins and Sons, 1962).

Roskill, S.W., *Naval Policy between the Wars. Volume 1. The period of Anglo-American Antagonism, 1919–1930* (London, William Collins and Son, 1968) and *Volume 2. The Period of Reluctant Re-armament, 1930–1939* (London, William Collins and Son, 1976).

Steinberg, Jonathan, *Yesterday's Deterrent. Tirpitz and the Birth of the German Battle Fleet* (London, Macdonald, 1965).

Showell, Jak P. Mallmann, *The German Navy in World War II. A Reference Guide to the Kriegsmarine, 1935–1945* (London, Arms and Armour Press, 1979).

Silverstone, Paul H., *U.S. Warships of World War II* (London, Ian Allan, 1968).

Skulski, Janusz, *The Battleship Yamato* (London, Conway Maritime Press, 1988).

Skulski, Janusz, *The Battleship Fuso* (London, Conway Maritime Press, 1998).

Stillwell, Paul, *Battleship New Jersey. An Illustrated History* (Annapolis, Maryland, Naval Institute Press, 1986).

Stillwell, Paul, *Battleships* (New York, MetroBooks, 2001).

Sturton, Ian (editor), *All the World's Battleships, 1906 to the Present* (London, Conway Maritime Press, 1987).

Sumida, Jon Tetsuro, *In Defence of Naval Supremacy. Finance, Technology and British Naval Policy, 1889–1914* (Boston, Unwin Hyman, 1989).

Sumrall, Robert F., *Iowa class Battleships* (Annapolis, Maryland, Naval Institute Press, 1988).

Sweetman, Jack, *American Naval History. An Illustrated Chronology of the U.S. Navy and Marine Corps, 1775–Present* (Annapolis, Maryland, Naval Institute Press, 1991).

Tarrant, V.E., *Battlecruiser Invincible, The History of the First Battlecruiser, 1909–16* (London, Arms and Armour Press, 1986).

Tarrant, V.E., *Battleship Warspite* (London, Arms and Armour Press, 1990).

Tarrant, V.E., *Jutland. The German Perspective. A New View of the Great Battle, 31 May 1916* (London, Arms and Armour Press, 1995).

Uhlig, Frank Jr, *How Navies Fight: The U.S. Navy and its Allies* (Annapolis, Maryland, Naval Institute Press, 1994).

Watts, Anthony J., and Gordon, Brian G., *The Imperial Japanese Navy* (London, Macdonald, 1971).

Weir, Gary E., *Building the Kaiser's Navy. The Imperial Navy Office and German Industry in the Tirpitz Era, 1890–1919* (Annapolis, Maryland, Naval Institute Press, 1992).

Westwood, J.N., *Russia against Japan, 1904–05. A New Look at the Russo-Japanese War* (London, Macmillan, 1986).

Whitley, M.J., *Battleships of World War II. An International Encyclopedia* (London, Arms and Armour, 1998).

Willmott, H.P., *Grave of a Dozen Schemes. British Naval Planning and the War against Japan, 1943–1945* (Annapolis, Maryland, Naval Institute Press, 1996).

Willmott, H.P., with Tohmatsu, Haruo, and Johnson, W. Spencer, *Pearl Harbor* (London, Cassell, 2001).

Woodward, E.L., *Great Britain and the German Navy* (London, Cass, 1964).

Wrigley, Chris, (editor), *The First World War and the International Economy* (Cheltenham, Edward Elgar, 2000). Chapter 5. 'The impact of the First World War on Japan' by Kenneth D. Brown.

Yoshimura, Akira, *Battleship Musashi. The Making and Sinking of the World's Biggest Battleship* (London, Kodansha International, 1999).

Index

Classification and spelling, and indeed even the names, of certain ships, specifically Russian ships of the Russo-Japanese war, present particular problems; e.g. there was a Russian battleship generally known as the *Admiral Apraxin*, but its correct name, when allied with contemporaneous spelling in English, appears to have been the *General-Admiral Graf Apraksin*. No less interestingly, in seeking the classification of Russian ships, one was more than somewhat surprised to find certain units defined as 'intermediates,' a definition never previously encountered, and a fleet named the Euxine Fleet, Euxine being the name used in Tsarist Russia for the Black Sea and which derived from Greek times.

The list has been compiled on the basis of what seems reasonable, and one asks the reader's indulgence in these and related matters, perhaps the most obvious being that a number of Russian ships merited the definition of coastal defence battleship, or what was in effect a short-range second-class, even third-class, battleship. These have been entered under the label 'cdb', protected cruisers under the label 'ptc'.

Acknowledgements

n the preparation of this book acknowledgement is due to those who, over many years, provided me with the basis of knowledge and critical facility that made this work possible. To attempt to list them all is impossible, but they have the satisfaction of knowing that without them this book could never have been written and also that they are not responsible for the various errors that may be within its pages.

Nonetheless there are two individuals whose unwavering personal support and loyalty command acknowledgement. They are Michael Coles and Steven Weingartner, and invidious though it might be to name names within this category I do so with the simple statement that the book could not have been attempted, still less completed, without their quiet contribution and benefaction.

Second, I acknowledge my debt to those at Cassell without whose patience, tact and ability this book would probably have gone the way of the ships cited in these pages. Specifically, I thank Angus MacKinnon, who commissioned the book and then spent much time and effort in seeking to ensure its success. I acknowledge, too, my debt to Harry Green and David Hoxley, and I apologise for the various problems I rolled into their respective paths during the preparation of this book. I likewise acknowledge two very quiet contributions, on the part of Elaine Willis and Barry Holmes: for the latter's unfailing humour in the face of great adversity, and yet another set of corrections, I am truly most grateful. I trust all will accept this short and poor acknowledgement of their support, good judgement and unstinting endeavour.

Third, I acknowledge my debt to certain persons who provided professional help and guidance that contributed much to the making of this book. I sincerely thank Tony Clayton, Spencer Johnson, Michael Orr, Sarah Palmer and Tohmatsu Haruo for providing me with material from the area of their specialist knowledge and expertise, and I thank librarians Jennie Wraight, Iain MacKenzie, Andrew Orgill and Ken Franklin who ensured my access to their libraries, collections and personal knowledge, and who were untiring in their attempts to provide answers to the most impossible of questions.

A special acknowledgement has to be made to those professional colleagues and friends who provided me with support at a time of very great professional difficulty. Among those are Tim Bean, Patrick Burke, Nigel de Lee, Christopher Duffy and Paul Harris, and John Andreas Olsen and Jack Sweetman. To these especially, but to all who so aided me, I owe a special debt which I will discharge in due course.

H.P. Willmott *Englefield Green, Egham, Surrey 28 July 2002*

There remains one group that always appears in my acknowledgements and for one reason: they have always been the means of ensuring sanity. I acknowledge my debts to and my love for my dogs, Everton, Sherry, Kondor, Jamie and Suki: I trust they are at peace. I acknowledge my present debt to and love for Lancaster, Mishka and Cassie, and Junior and Yanya. I trust that much time will pass before they join their predecessors and chase together across the celestial fields.